RULIN

Conquest to Liberal Governmentality –
A Historical Sociology

Ruling by Schooling Quebec provides a rich and detailed account of colonial politics from 1760 to 1841 by following repeated attempts to school the people. This first book since the 1950s to investigate an unusually complex period in Quebec's educational history extends the sophisticated method used in author Bruce Curtis's double-award-winning *Politics of Population.*

Drawing on a mass of archival material, the study shows that although attempts to govern Quebec by educating its population consumed huge amounts of public money, they had little impact on rural ignorance: while near-universal literacy reigned in New England by the 1820s, at best one in three French-speaking peasant men in Quebec could sign his name in the insurrectionary decade of the 1830s. Curtis documents educational conditions on the ground, but also shows how imperial attempts to govern a tumultuous colony propelled the early development of Canadian social science. He provides a revisionist account of the pioneering investigations of Lord Gosford and Lord Durham.

BRUCE CURTIS is a professor of Sociology and of History at Carleton University.

Ruling by Schooling Quebec

*Conquest to Liberal Governmentality –
A Historical Sociology*

BRUCE CURTIS

UNIVERSITY OF TORONTO PRESS
Toronto   Buffalo   London

© University of Toronto Press 2012
Toronto Buffalo London
www.utppublishing.com
Printed in Canada

ISBN 978-1-4426-4118-1 (cloth)
ISBN 978-1-4426-1049-1 (paper)

Printed on acid-free paper

Library and Archives Canada Cataloguing in Publication

Curtis, Bruce, 1950–
Ruling by schooling Québec: conquest to liberal
governmentality: a historical sociology / Bruce Curtis.

Includes bibliographical references and index.
ISBN 978-1-4426-4118-1 (bound)   ISBN 978-1-4426-1049-1 (pbk.)

1. Education – Québec (Province) – History – 19th century.
2. Education – Quebec (Province) – History – 18th century.
3. Education – Political aspects – Québec (Province) – History –
19th century. 4. Education – Political aspects – Quebec (Province) –
History – 18th century. 5. Québec (Province) – Politics and
government – 1791-1841. 6. Canada – Politics and government –
1763-1791. 7. Québec (Province) – History–1791-1841.
8. Canada – History – 1763-1791. I. Title.

LA418.Q8C87 2012   370.9714'09033   C2012-902655-7

University of Toronto Press acknowledges the financial assistance
to its publishing program of the Canada Council for the Arts
and the Ontario Arts Council.

   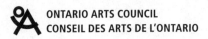

University of Toronto Press acknowledges the financial support
of the Government of Canada through the Canada Book
Fund for its publishing activities.

This book has been published with the help of a grant from
the Canadian Federation for the Humanities and Social Sciences,
through the Awards to Scholarly Publications Program, using funds provided
by the Social Sciences and Humanities Research Council of Canada.

'Take your time, man, take your time.'
– Fred McDowell, *I do not play no rock'n'roll.*

Contents

Acknowledgments

Another decade of research, another eighteen months passed as a semi-hermit, digging in another mound of material and piling up another mountain of debts: to the Social Sciences and Humanities Research Council, Carleton University, archivists (even the surly ones in Belfast), ski maven, theory reading group, a generous gang of students and colleagues, readers, editors, publisher, ma chère Michèle. My sincere thanks to all.

I wish winters still had the bite they had when I was a kid. I got ready to write in the deep cold back of beyond. Stocked up. Got my skis repaired and a sleigh to haul my stuff. More panels. Bigger battery bank. Cordwood. But spring was early in 2009 and winter 2009–10 was the warmest in sixty years. My distant neighbours in creeping Ruburbia to the east still grumbled. Ah, Ruburbia! City comfort and country bliss! But warmer meant icier roads, so for them it was even more like the suburbs with even less to do. They get fat and scratch their heads at me humping supplies in three kilometres.

Back here the lake finally froze smooth and transparent, which made for some crackly, spooky skating. A deeper late February freeze had the lake gods garrumphing night and day. The ice got so cold it clambered up on shore, shoving rocks and docks out of its way before collapsing with fatigue. One crisp blue afternoon, Doug and I felled three dead forest giants onto the pond ice – KABLOOM! – and sawed them up. Splitting wood is a relief from splitting hairs in a manuscript.

Lots of tooth and claw. A merlin picked a woodpecker off the feeder and ate it alive, which only one of them seemed to enjoy. On a warm March day I watched a lone coyote chase on the ice, fight with twice, wound, and finally, as it got dark, kill a buck. It took about three hours. Very exciting. At dawn there were hooves, hide, head, spine, and guts left over, but everyone in the neighbourhood heard the dinner gong and came to feed. It did look fresh, but I substituted pasta with tomato sauce. After a few days of fox, eagles, ravens, and smaller things, there were just patches of fur. When the pond thawed, it was covered with deer hair. The spring birds plucked it up for nesting material. Then the black snake slithered up the power cable to swallow the flycatcher's brood under the eaves. It coiled its way up my walking stick and peered quizzically at me through the window as I wrote. Tongue, flick, flick, flick, why doessss he never get up and have fun? Now maybe I can.

Lady Aylmer liked Quebec in winter. She wrote to an English correspondent in 1831 that her rooms were kept at 64°F (17°C) 'at which degree it is very agreeable and healthy and I assure you that I have never felt a sensation of Cold, since the Winter began.' On the other hand, 'the Canadian[s] keep their houses warmed by stove heat up to a degree that few Europeans could support.' 73°F (22°C). I was hot for the Canadians while writing this, but I thought English proto-sociology was pretty cool.

Clear Lake, February 2009–June 2011

RULING BY SCHOOLING QUEBEC

Conquest to Liberal Governmentality –
A Historical Sociology

Introduction

This book presents a historical sociology of rule and government in the British North American colonies of Quebec and Lower Canada from the Conquest of New France in 1759 to the Union of the colonies of Upper and Lower Canada in 1841.[1] It uses the problem and the practice of schooling the people to follow the course of a broad shift in the logic of colonial government, from one based on the ignorance and pastoral simplicity of political subjects, to one predicated on their cultivated intelligence and active engagement in their own self-government. By the end of the period, the semi-feudal relations which prevailed in 1759 were in retreat; the conception of mixed monarchical government that had presided over the colony's 1791 constitution had been thoroughly discredited; and imperial officials with some colonial allies worked to create a state system that embodied a liberal mode of government.

The proponents of the latter held that people should govern themselves responsibly in representative institutions. To be able to do so freely, they had to be trained in public schools: schooling the people, in the view from the centre, entailed the administration of population. Liberals thought schooling was a sort of machine that could create solidarity across differences of language, ethnicity, class, and religion by fostering interpersonal familiarity and by promoting a generic Christian morality. It was meant to ensure respect for, and perhaps rational appreciation of, a liberal political order and a new nationality. Rough anticipations of this educational scheme were elaborated already in the 1780s, but complex political struggles blocked it for half a century.

This book has four overlapping objectives in whose pursuit it cuts across disciplinary boundaries. One is primarily documentary. The historical literature on Quebec elementary or common schooling in the period before 1841 is sparse. The details of debate, conflict, law, legislation, administration, and educational conditions are largely unknown, even as the educational past is rewritten to promote current political projects. In such a context, documentation is in part a work of correction. A second and related objective is to read colonial political struggle through the lens of schooling. I seek to restore schooling to its rightful place as an engine of solidarity and difference, liberty and domination. My third objective is to trace the mutual relations between projects for ruling by schooling and the emergence of the new forms and techniques of knowledge involved in 'the social science.' Finally, the book aims to advance the literature on liberal governmentality by treating seriously Michel Foucault's injunction to triangulate the study of state formation around the axes of sovereignty, disciplinary practices, and government.

Reflexive Historical Sociology

Embedded in the narratives I write is a reflexive historical sociology. Reflexive sociology scrutinizes analytic categories in an effort to grasp their effects on objects of knowledge and on the logic of explanation. A reflexive historical sociology additionally investigates the appearance and development of the forms and categories of social life. Work using this approach may employ many of the research strategies of, and share sources with, other varieties of historical work – this book certainly does. Yet in keeping with post-Kantian strands in social theory, reflexive historical sociology attends to the shifting constitution or configuration of human subjectivity. In contrast to the universal Kantian subject engaged primarily in rational reflection on a world constituted through its own categories of thought, such sociology stresses the practical and transforming engagement of subjects with material and social conditions. It approaches human knowledge not in a quest for universal criteria of certainty or truth. Instead, it tracks what passes for knowledge at any given moment, attends to its characteristic forms and to the ways in which it is made stable, self-evident. It examines practices of knowledge production and attends to the deployment of knowledge in social relations. In place of Kantian notions that fixed and eternal (Newtonian) categories of time and space subtend human experience, reflexive historical sociology treats temporality and spatiality as variable products of social practice.[2]

These preoccupations do not displace sociology's long-standing interests in inequality, power, and domination: quite the contrary. It was precisely the genius of one of the pioneers of reflexive historical sociology – Norbert Elias – to demonstrate that one could explain wide-ranging changes in the form of the self – in the relation of self to self, self to others, and body and soul – in terms of state formation and class struggles for dominance and prestige. Elias showed that seemingly trivial matters, such as changing manners at table or shifts in the management of bodily excretions, are inextricably bound up with large-scale structures and practices of power. One obvious gain from such a stance for historians of politics and rule is a broadening of the field of inquiry and of the definition of the political.[3]

Thus politics, following the lead of people such as Elias, is restricted neither to the clash of ideas and doctrines, nor to heroic events of blood and steel. Politics, like other forms of social practice, is to be approached in terms of the tactics and strategies available to individuals and groups in the struggle for power by virtue of their structural locations in relation to a historical distribution of resources. Such a distribution provides instruments for practice, while being itself an object of practice, one of the stakes at issue. Political resources are whatever those engaged in politics use for advantage in the field of power; their efficacy is itself contingent and, for the analyst, a matter of empirical investigation. The methods of reflexive historical sociology thus provide opportunities and liabilities: opportunities to broaden the domain of inquiry; liabilities that stem from the interconnectedness of all social phenomena. I have foreclosed many possible lines of investigation in relation to political government from the need to describe and to analyse attempts to rule by schooling. Some traces of a more detailed game-theoretic analysis remain in my interest in such things as the 'charm offensives' launched at times by colonial governors. I offer biographical information about key actors, where possible.[4]

The four preoccupations of reflexive historical sociology – subjectivity, knowledge, time, and space – provide so many axes of analysis for an engagement with projects to rule through schooling and to govern through education. While following closely the unfolding of struggles over colonial rule and government in this book, I focus especially on subjectivity and knowledge. Certainly the dynamics of educational government had implications for the spatial and temporal dimensions of social relations. The urban monitorial schools affected the rhythms of life, for instance, as large groups of school boys and girls came and went at more or less regular hours. Inside these institutions, learning activities and the evolutions of bodies were meant to be disciplined by the clock, not by the task or the season. The spatial dimensions of life were no less affected, not simply by the material presence of schools, but also by the creation of new kinds of segmentation of activity and by the creation of novel – and controversial – zones of association for young people. When invested in statistical forms, activity in such spaces helped to figure a domain of regularities that formed part of 'the social,' the object of the social science.[5] As we shall see, projects for ruling and for schooling the colony in the 1830s both involved schemes for dividing and re-dividing territory – to create new units of political government and to establish school sections so as to 'catch' the school-age population.

Documentation

The educational history of Quebec and Lower Canada is both fascinating and dauntingly convoluted. I unpack it in richly documented narratives based on a wide variety of sources.[6] This case has features of general interest to historians and sociologists of colonialism and education. Lower Canada was a semi-feudal peasant society, the only one of its kind in North America. Literacy rates for French-speaking peasants were exceptionally low and engagement with print culture was quite limited. There was no printing press in the colony until 1764. While newspapers multiplied rapidly in Britain and America in the eighteenth century and, in the latter especially, enjoyed wide freedom to publish on political matters, the French regime had attempted to centralize printing and to regulate printed material closely. The colonial book trade was quite restricted.[7] The French Crown had equipped its colony with versions of imperial educational institutions, including an important college run by the Jesuits in Quebec and several women's religious houses. These made it possible for the tiny colonial nobility and bourgeoisie to school their sons and daughters, but there were almost no schools for the peasantry. Across the French regime, one historian has found traces of only twenty-nine schools, most of them ephemeral, for a population which amounted to about 60,000 by 1760. The Jesuit College was closed after 1759, as the British continued an earlier French ban on the Jesuits, and from the American invasion of 1775 it served as a military barracks. The Jesuits' Estates, meant to support education, were diverted to other ends until 1831. The ban on the Jesuits removed the colony's main male teaching order, and, until the French Revolution, the British prohibited the immigration of priests.

The eighteenth-century 'reading revolution,' which was propelled by increasing volumes of cheap print, non-Conformist Protestant reading practices, and the growth of commodity production and exchange, bypassed New France. The Catholic clergy had an obligation to teach its flock, but there were few priests and fewer still who were well educated. In sharp contrast to the situation in the adjacent American states, where near universal literacy had been achieved by 1820, perhaps one in ten French-speaking men and women in Lower Canada could sign his or her name in 1800, while an optimistic estimate put the number at about one in three in 1830. In the Eastern Townships border region of the colony, largely populated by American and British immigrants, by contrast, the great majority of men could sign their names.[8]

There was no literacy test for the exercise of the franchise, and its modest property qualification meant that most landholders could vote. The shifting tactics and strategies of government in this context are especially interesting. By the early 1800s, all political factions insisted on the necessity of educating the people, but intensifying antagonism over the means and ends of rule precluded agreement over how to do so. A section of the peasantry was led by a professional petty bourgeoisie in two waves of armed insurrection against the colonial executive in 1837–8, both suppressed by bloody force of arms. Many contemporary commentators attributed insurrection to a lack of education, caused by the absence of schools, but also by archaic social institutions.

Surprisingly, lagging literacy rates in Lower Canada coexisted with innovation in educational practice and with very large government expenditure on rural schooling. The latest European innovations in pedagogy and curriculum were in place in the colonial cities by the late 1810s, and colonial activists toured Europe and America in search of best practice. The international movement for monitorial schooling found energetic colonial partisans. By the mid-1830s, urban school societies provided more school spaces than they could fill. There were infant school societies on Samuel Wilderspin's plan, and even J.-J. Jacotot's 'universal pedagogy' had its active partisans. In several years of the 1830s, expenditure on schooling was the largest item in the colony's budget. Subsidies for rural elementary schools were as much as £23,000 a year, a staggering sum when one appreciates that to school Ireland in the same decade and to support English school societies, English governments were spending in each case about £33,000. Lower Canada's population in 1831 was about 511,000; Ireland's over 5,000,000. I examine the forces that caused lavish colonial expenditure to have little impact on rural ignorance.

Through its work of documentation, the book makes a contribution to literatures concerned with the development of liberal modes of government in the transatlantic world and in the European empires. Students of Lower Canadian development have long been interested in the debate around neo-republican political theory in the British Atlantic sponsored by J.G.A. Pocock and Quentin Skinner.[9] Yet while schooling and political subject formation, the global circulation of innovative pedagogical practices, and the effects of colonial educational experiments on imperial social organization figure centrally in the international literature, they have remained peripheral to Lower Canadian debate. Elsewhere, scholars have been particularly fascinated with the phenomenon of monitorial schooling – the application of factory division of labour, military discipline, and rational accounting practice to large-scale instruction – and I align the Canadian literature in relation to that fascination.[10]

Monitorial schooling figured centrally in political conflicts over education, beginning with an attempt by a broad alliance of laymen in the mid-1810s to launch a Lancasterian Free School Society, which I discuss in chapter 2. I follow the political battles over monitorial schooling and, in chapter 3, examine the various urban monitorial school societies. The book investigates the conditions under which monitorial pedagogy fell out of favour in the later 1830s. I flesh out in passing the Canadian career of the ebullient scoundrel Joseph Lancaster, claimant to the title of 'inventor' of monitorial schooling, whose blandishments seduced colonial politicians between 1828 and 1833.

Monitorial schooling is important for the study of liberal government and colonial state formation because it aimed at the rapid, serial manufacture of political subjects. It stands between the governmental strategy of governing through ignorance, on the one hand, and that of anchoring rule in an enriched interiority on the other. It was a pioneering form of population government. In a riff on Pocock's 'Machiavellian moment,' I show that there was a moment, a period, in the unfolding of political conflict in Lower Canada where politicians and intellectuals thought that the rough machining of political subjectivities was a pressing necessity, a technical possibility, and a solution to entrenched political antagonisms. The attempts by English liberals in 1836–41 to eliminate the grounds of colonial political struggle by making colonists govern themselves in representative-democratic institutions coincided with the abandonment of the mechanical production of political subjects.[11]

Schooling and Politics

More than sixty years have passed since L.-P. Audet published the first of six volumes of *Le système scolaire de la province de Québec*, the only other extensive work to cover schooling across the entire period studied here.[12] Audet's work has remained useful for its broad narrative outline of the development of elementary schooling and for its reproduction of school legislation. In his wake, scholars examined and debated a number of issues he raised, especially concerning the role of the Episcopal churches in school provision.[13] I revisit and revise several of his widely accepted claims in this and other areas. Yet Audet left a great deal of the historical record untouched, and most subsequent scholarly attention has been devoted to a later period, when something resembling a public school system was launched. A number of studies on which I draw have taken up particular dimensions of the earlier history of schooling, and one recent contribution examines English-language schooling across a long historical period. There is no other detailed investigation of schooling and politics for the period.[14]

Audet's research was conducted before Bernard Bailyn's 1960 *Education in the Forming of American Society* launched the revisionist wave in North American educational historiography.[15] Before the revisionists wrote them back into the mainstream, questions of education had been the preserve of professional educators (Audet was one) who wrote heroic narratives of middle-class reformers bringing enlightenment to the ignorant masses. Audet's view of education was similar, although the absence in Lower Canada of the 'common school revolution' that brought universal, tax-supported public schooling to other jurisdictions generated an uneasy analysis.

Pre-revisionist historiography did not distinguish between education and schooling. Doing so enabled revisionists to treat seriously the oft-repeated mantra of late eighteenth- and nineteenth-century activists: 'all the world's a school.' On the one hand, the distinction led to the insight that social relations, structures, and practices of all sorts exert formative influence on subjectivity. On the other hand, varieties of schooling could then be analysed as technologies of subjectification and as political projects aimed not simply at 'enlightenment.' Revisionists were divided among themselves as to how to characterize the nineteenth-century common school movement. Yet, especially as social theory began to engage more systematically with subject formation, revisionist themes broadened and deepened the field of investigation.

The Quebec literature largely escaped the wave of revisionist thinking, something that is odd from the point of view of international educational historiography. The wave coincided with the striking liberalization and secularization of Quebec society known as the 'Quiet Revolution.'

Perhaps at that time Quebec historians and sociologists had their own accounts to settle with a cultural and intellectual tradition in which the Catholic Church's illiberalism stood out most markedly. The educational history and historical sociology that appeared in monograph form in Quebec as English-Canadian, American, and some other historiographies engaged with social control, social reproduction, and resistance – Chabot's *Curé de campagne* (1975), Fahmy-Eid's *Le clergé et le pouvoir politique au Québec* (1978), Jolois's *Joseph-François Perrault* (1969) and Labarèrre-Paulé's *Les instituteurs laïque* (1969) – more or less called the Church to account.[16]

Feminist engagement with educational history and patriarchal domination in Quebec, by contrast, took place at the moment in which attempts to rehabilitate religious vocations as forms of self-affirmation for women were particularly strong. Many participants in this literature were themselves professing Catholics. While the internal stratification of women's religious orders was noted in feminist work, little connection remained between religion and large-scale social and political-economic domination. Questions of tithing, taxing, and pro-natalist policy, for instance, received little attention. That the context of self-affirmation for some women involved self-sacrifice and dedication to a conception of community was stressed at the expense of the repressive dimensions of the Church's hegemony. It is also striking that the most recent work on political liberty in Quebec and Lower Canada ignores matters of religion.[17]

Not to distinguish education from schooling and not to deal with the political economy of religion is to be unable to engage with the key Lower Canadian debate of the period from 1815 onwards. This debate – and political struggle – centred on the Catholic Church's claim to be educating 'the people' by teaching young people to read the catechism and to learn their religious obligations, while providing a collegiate education to the elite. The Church could claim to 'educate' the people until the 1830s without schooling it – without providing schools, schoolbooks, trained teachers, and so on. The Anglican Church insisted that schooling could not be divorced from doctrinal instruction. Both churches opposed lay reading of sacred texts. For most other Protestants and many Catholic laypeople, education in schools was something quite different from mere religious knowledge and piety in conduct, even if many Protestants demanded the use of the Bible as a school book. For political liberals, schooling was primarily a secular phenomenon.

The relative disinterest of Quebec scholars in the early history of elementary schooling contrasts with extensive and vibrant literatures on intellectual history, including history of the book.[18] Much of this work has involved inventory making, yet one leading scholar, Yvan Lamonde, has urged contributors to treat reading as a physical, as well as an intellectual, encounter between the book and the individual reader.[19] I extend Lamonde's focus on individual readers and the book market by treating reading and writing as distributed phenomena and by attending to how, as well as to what, people learned to read, using an approach inspired by the so-called 'new studies in literacy.'[20] This approach does not focus on literacy as a technical capacity of individuals and does not limit itself to individual reading practices. Instead it focuses on the relations between 'literacy events' and 'literacy practices.' Literacy events are occasions of whatever sort on which individuals or groups encounter print culture. Literacy practices include all the ways in which they deal with print culture, and these ways may include not reading or writing. The key question posed is then not 'who can read and write?' Reading and writing are not unitary practices. People may be technically able to read and write and yet not care, or not be allowed to do so; they may be able to read or write well or ill. The key questions instead are, what are the occasions on which people must engage with print culture, and how do they do so?

Communities may meet the demands of print culture by delegating reading and writing to some of their members; conversely, some community members may arrogate reading and writing as such, or some forms of them, to themselves to the exclusion of others. The distribution of literacy practices in a community or society is both a means and index of power. While all literate societies delegate some forms of reading and writing to specialists, the delegation of reading and writing by Lower Canadian peasants to priests, professionals, and to members of the provincial parliament (MPPs) was contentious from the early nineteenth century and was bitterly debated before and after the Rebellions of 1837–8.

I attend to methods of reading instruction. Both what is read and how it is meant to be read involve techniques of subjectification. In the case I investigate, there was a contested transformation underway in which reading instruction was first closely tied to oral culture. In Catholic Quebec and Lower Canada, as well as in early Protestant New England, students learned to read first in order to recite, and recitation of precepts under supervision was seen by educational authorities to be essential to moral training. In contrast to New England's students, however, young Catholic Lower Canadians commonly learned to read first in Latin and only later in the vernacular, chiefly in books of piety. Monitorial pedagogy changed matters by loosening the bonds of teachers' authority, as students in large groups taught one another to read and cypher. At first, monitorial students did not have access to books. They too read aloud and recited precepts collectively, but to its critics this pedagogy of learning by doing seemed to produce unregulated and hence potentially dangerous reading practices. The pedagogy also encouraged interpersonal competition and individual mobility.

By the middle 1830s, liberal school reformers rejected reading to recite and the repetition of precepts as the substance of moral training. In liberal governmentality a deeper and more rational interiority was demanded of a reader trained to be self-governing. Such interiority was to be produced by silent reading and by careful examination by teachers of the understanding of what was read. Constant interrogation would ensure that students learned to read for proper sense, not for sound. Liberal reformers launched serious attacks on rhetoric, but more so on the spelling book – the ubiquitous vehicle of phonics. The Irish school curriculum, which imperial officials sought to install in the colony from the middle 1830s, did away with spelling books and taught to read using a sight method coupled with interrogation. The Irish system also embodied a serious assault on the imagination, which it regarded as dangerously misleading, and replaced fiction in almost all of its forms with lessons of 'useful knowledge.' Writing did not involve composition but most often the copying of set pieces, including letters in standard forms. It would be much later in the nineteenth century before educators concluded that the people might have something of its own worth expressing.[21]

Debates over reading and speaking were thus not arcane pedagogical debates in Lower Canada. They were at the centre of politics and political struggle. The matter is the more interesting since the conditions of the franchise enabled most peasant proprietors to vote, and a handful at least of MPPs were themselves unable to sign their names. The rural school trustees elected under the various elementary school acts in place from 1829 were not themselves required to be literate. As Signorini has argued, illiterates in office can often impress their illiterate constituents, but where printed text is a modality of politics, they cannot lead but must be led. The political hegemony of the rural petty bourgeoisie and the clergy was anchored in part in command of print culture.[22]

The People, Population, and the Social Science

In an essay on the concept of 'the people' in Lower Canadian political discourse after the French Revolution, Maurice Lemire argued that, 'of all the questions asked in relation to the people, the most important concerned its education: should it be educated just enough to keep it in a state of subordination, or to enable it to improve its condition?'[23] 'The people' is a discursive political entity which was present throughout the period with which I am concerned. Yet the concept gave way increasingly to a second construct: 'the population,' located in territory. Practical attempts to rule, to administer, and to school the colony came to work through this concept. Lower Canada played an important role in the elaboration of 'population thinking,' in the development of its analytic companion, the 'social science,' and in the implication of both in political administration. Attempts to school to rule the colony, especially from the end of the 1820s, involved English state servants and their colonial allies in novel efforts at social investigation and analysis.

The 'discovery' of population for Michel Foucault was the axis on which the transition to liberal government turned. He argued that it made it possible to govern through the individualizing and totalizing initiatives that he thought were characteristic of pastoral power. By contrast, Jacques Rancière argued that the concepts 'the people' and 'population' embody the central tensions of inequality and domination in modern politics. The people, he suggests, is the unruly whole whose parts refuse to be incorporated in the body politic because the formal promise of a unitary social body cannot nullify the reality of substantive inequality, domination, and exclusion. Population, by contrast, he argues is a 'police' (i.e., a policy) concept.[24] In other words, population is an administrative concept contained in the practices through which authoritative bodies, state agencies especially, attempt to order and organize the people. To put it formulaically, the people is the unruly; the population is the ruled. A central claim of this book is that social science is inextricably bound up with the conceptual and the administrative move from 'the people' to 'population,' and hence with the development of a liberal mode of government.

Population is a political abstraction, and abstractions emerge most fully out of rich contexts of empirical determinations.[25] Population acquired density and substance through the cumulative efforts of observers and administrators to know social conditions and relations and to intervene in them. Some of the desire to know was based on the pleasure individuals and groups found in making inventories. The techniques and practices of proto-social scientific knowledge production were continuous with such amateur efforts. This knowledge of population was also propelled by the practical engagement of politicians, intellectuals, or administrators with concrete problems. Without accepting that population is 'discovered,' I take the rise of population thinking and planning, and emergent attempts at knowing and administering population, to be indices of the development of liberal government.

Attending to the increasingly systematic attempts to generate knowledge of population and to configure it in politically congenial ways provides a genealogy of the social science. The latter contained speculative elements, but it was eminently practical and experimental. In the first decades of the nineteenth century its now taken-for-granted techniques for shaping and forming knowledge were in an early stage of construction, and its practice involved lots of blind alleys and false starts. For a reflexive historical sociology, open to contingency, the latter can be as informative as the 'successes' of social science. The ambition to know and to cast knowledge in particular forms may certify the ambition to rule and govern in particular ways, even if that ambition is frustrated. Later chapters of the book follow attempts to know educational conditions and to plan educational futures.

The earliest colonial debates over the educational condition of the people focused on the purported numbers of men and women able to read and to write in each parish or seigneury (the semi-feudal estate). In the eighteenth and first decade of the nineteenth centuries, there was little or no attempt to present them in population terms. Rather, commentators assumed that parishes needed a critical mass of readers and writers in order to deal with print culture, not that all residents needed to read and write to any serious degree.

Debate over the education of the people shifted markedly after the 1791 organization of constitutional government enfranchised rural land owners and after the immigration of considerable numbers of American and British Protestants in the wake of the American war. The new conditions of political subjection involved in representative government, combined with political disaffection during war with the United States, led all secular political factions to demand insistently that the people be schooled. New forms of political subjection correlated with demands for new forms of political subjectification and new forms of knowledge.

While the educational condition of the people was a staple of colonial political discourse, in the first four decades of the nineteenth century politicians and social observers came to invoke population concepts to estimate educational conditions. They tended now to assume that all residents ought ideally to be able to read and write and calculate, and they tied political stability, economic progress, health, and morality to a schooled population. Jean-Guy Prévost and Jean-Pierre Beaud have offered a number of insights into the logic of this shift in ways of knowing. Prévost's exemplary account of the incendiary text by the Scot Robert Gourlay, *A Statistical Account of Upper Canada,* placed his work in a developing genre of investigation, in which Gourlay had had earlier experience, situated it in comparative international perspective and pointed to its adoption of novel ways of representing its findings.[26]

The *Statistical Account* was one of two internationally influential colonial statistical productions of the 1810s – a period in which 'statistics' retained its omnibus character of social description. Jean-Pierre Beaud has examined the other: Joseph Bouchette's *Topographical Description of the Province of Lower Canada* (1815; 2nd ed. 1833). His comparison of the two editions of the work, and of a subsequent publication by Bouchette on the same subject, *The British Dominions of North America* (1831), provides a striking demonstration of the shift in conceptions of the world produced by population thinking. These works were published on either side of the 1825 census and were very highly regarded in European statistical circles. One striking difference between them, Beaud points out, is that in 1815 Bouchette made no use of that (to us) most banal of statistical concepts, 'the percentage,' while it was a key element in the conceptual structure of his 1831 work.

The 1815 *Topographical Description* took the seigneury as its unit of analysis, describing its initial concession and tracing ownership to the present. Bouchette described the physical terrain and settlement features of individual seigneuries, giving an account of churches, bridges, roads, and local production, before following the road on to the next seigneury. There was little or no attempt at aggregation or comparison: objects existed in their singularity. A key concern of *The British Dominions* by contrast, was the calculation of rates of past and future population growth at the level of the colony as a whole, a shift in the object and in the logic of analysis. Here the percentage was at the heart of the analysis.[27] It is no coincidence that the second edition of the *Topographical Description* made use of 1831 census results to re-situate the seigneury in the new register of population – aggregating information about population and production at the level of the county (the census commission district) and ranking counties. In contrast to the singularities frozen in lineages described in the first account of seigneuries, rates of population growth pointed to a dynamic process located in a new domain whose tendencies were susceptible to analysis and, perhaps, to mastery.

The point is that across the period studied here, new ways of questioning means and ends of government, and new ways of articulating and justifying

answers to problems of government emerged. The state reformers of the
1830s took their distance from schooling as an organic dimension of local
social life and addressed it as a sort of machine or engine that could work
on the raw material of population at the level of colonial territory. Such
work is characteristic of a liberal governmentality.

Liberal Governmentality

I engage with Michel Foucault's analysis of the liberal mode of government, analysis which I see as compatible with a reflexive historical sociology. The concept 'governmentality' reappeared suddenly in Foucault's
1977–8 lectures, *Security, Territory, Population*. Foucault analysed the emergence in European political thought after about 1750 of new ways of
asking and answering questions concerning the means and ends of political rule and state government. In contrast to a well-developed science
of police, whose utopia was the detailed regulation of all aspects of social
life, in the new mentality the world to be governed was seen to contain
independent, intractable regularities. The existence of such regularities
had been revealed by the investigations of police science, especially early
statistics. In particular, Foucault argued, such investigations uncovered
patterns in vital events and thus subtended the emergence of the novel
concept: 'population.'[28]

In a liberal mode, government works on population in territory and
seeks to create systems of security. One of its leading instruments was the
new science of political economy, which held that society or the nation
could be protected from scarcity and want and could enjoy the benefits of
'civilization' – could be in a condition of 'security' – by the free operation
of the market. With moral philosophy, political economy was a progenitor
of moral science and moral economy, and, through them, of social science.[29] In contrast to the regulatory practices that Foucault characterized
as 'mercantilist' and that attempted to control production, exports, imports, and consumption, liberal governmentality embraced principles of
laisser aller, laisser faire. That is, the role of government was to put in place
and to ensure the operation of the structures and regulations that made
such free action possible.

Ongoing debate in Canadian historiography over liberalism has often
cast it in terms of Thatcherite conceptions of a political ideology meant to
destroy 'society' in the interests of the 'individual' and of capitalist accumulation. Some contributors contrast such liberalism to neo-Roman republicanism, which is seen to privilege the collective over the individual, and to

empower the individual through the collective. Foucault's conception of a liberal mode of government is rather different. Liberalism is not seen first and foremost as an ideology, but as a shifting set of responses to a common set of problems of government: how to organize a self-replicating system of rule, given the existence of intractable regularities in the world and given the existence of human freedom (as 'freedom'). Government itself is broadened in this conception to include all actions that seek to structure the actions of others (the 'conduct of conduct'). As Foucault argued in *The Birth of Biopolitics*, liberal solutions can involve widely different degrees of social planning and regulation in response to the common problem. Given the proposition that the role of governments is to structure the conditions ensuring the exercise of freedom, any limitation on freedom is potentially an object of regulation. One must include the inability or refusal of people to embrace their freedom as one potential limitation.[30]

In his last renditions of 'governmentality,' Foucault spoke of it in keeping with his technological conception of power. He identified four technologies: of signs and symbols, of production, 'technologies of power, which determine the conduct of individuals and submit them to certain ends or domination, an objectivizing of the subject' and 'technologies of the self, which permit individuals to effect by their own means or with the help of others a certain number of operations on their own bodies and souls, thoughts, conduct, and way of being, so as to transform themselves in order to attain a certain state of happiness, purity, wisdom, perfection, or immortality.' He then commented, 'this contact between the technologies of domination of others and those of the self I call governmentality.' I also take up this conception.[31]

'Governmentality' largely disappeared as a concept in Foucault's work after the 1977–8 lectures. Stephen Collier has argued that, partly under the influence of emerging actor-network studies in sociology of science, Foucault began to analyse power relations in terms of series of techniques and tactics, and to relate shifts and changes in such relations to recombinations and to reconfigurations of existing elements.[32] Yet the propositions that liberal government can be understood as based on investigation to discover the regularities of an intractable world; that it involves techniques and tactics to govern through the freedom of political subjects; and that liberal governmentality articulates projects of domination with projects of subjectification have proved quite fruitful for sociological analysis. They have sponsored a genre of research: 'governing through.'[33] I pick up this dimension of post-Foucauldian work by analysing attempts to govern through education, to rule by schooling.

It is more appropriate to engage with Foucault's analysis of liberalism here because leading members of English Whig and Radical factions attempted to sort out governmental problems in Lower Canada in the insurrectional decade of the 1830s. These people were coming to be known as 'liberals,' as the adjective 'liberal,' meaning generous or open-minded, came to be used as a noun describing a political analysis and program. Most of them were convinced that colonial political independence was inevitable. Imperial rule in this situation aimed not at what Sir George Gipps called the preservation of a 'bare empire,' but rather the extension to the colony of the 'civilizing' institutions of British government. With its obvious chauvinism, this analysis held that state sovereignty was to be used to fit the people for the exercise of liberal freedom. A variety of plans were elaborated to render the colony governable by separating specific population segments into new territorial units and subjecting them to representative government. Similar attempts were made to identify and to 'catch' on the ground that population segment thought to be in need of direct schooling. The most outrageous (if not the most often studied) of such plans was proposed in Lord Durham's 1839 *Report on the Affairs of British North America.* It recommended the elimination of the 'barbaric' feudal institutions that were held to stupefy the French-Canadian peasantry and proposed to put representative local government bodies in their place. Schooling was described by one of Durham's aides as 'the most powerful instrument' of nationalization. I flesh out Durham's work in the later chapters of the book and give a revisionist account of his sociology in my Conclusion.[34]

Liberal freedom had substance. Projects for the creation of autonomous rational political subjects enjoying freedom of movement, of assembly, of speech, and of property, subjects freed also from ignorance and religious superstition, constituted a progressive movement in colonial political development. The liberal mode of government had a universalizing moment which provided grounds for pushing against existing forms of domination, and against its own inherent limitations. At the same time, liberal freedom was cast as freely given obedience to the rule of white, adult men of property. For 1830s liberals, it was perfectly legitimate to deprive those who, because of their age, ignorance, sex, or 'race,' were not willing or not able to be rationally free, of their freedom. It was equally legitimate to coerce people into freedom despite their resistance to it. Thus, liberalism as a program of government contained a logic of exclusion that worked against its universalizing moment, and a logic of domination that worked against its support for freedom. The tension between these two moments was one element that propelled political conflicts around colonial government.[35]

Mercantilism and Liberalism

Finally, for heuristic purposes and with an awareness of the dangers of over-simplification, I contrast two broad strategies of political subjectification in relation to education: mercantilism and liberalism. The first I treat as predicated on government through illiteracy, ignorance, and, often, personal dependence; the second on government through literacy, a disciplined intelligence, and practices of self-regulation.

Mercantilism was primarily an economic doctrine that flourished from the sixteenth to the mid-eighteenth centuries, and its exact substance and impact remain matters of debate. Most commentators agree that mercantilism was preoccupied with increasing the wealth and might of the state by ensuring a favourable balance of trade. It supported protectionist initiatives and the careful regulation of foreign commerce, commonly through the granting of state monopolies. It promoted colonies as sources of raw materials and outlets for domestic production. The measures of national wealth were the accumulation of bullion and populousness.

A flourishing body of the poor was essential for the production of export surplus, and mercantilist doctrine urged policies for ensuring that all the poor were kept hard at work. The favourable balance of trade also depended on restricting the needs and thus the consumption patterns of the poor. Anything that created an aversion to rude labour and anything that stimulated a taste for luxuries, especially foreign luxuries, could reduce the export surplus. Hence, noted John Middendorf, 'the mercantilist dislike of any measures to educate the workers. Literacy, by raising the worker's pretensions for better things, would keep him from his duties [and] the doctrine deliberately set forth the view that national wealth absolutely depended upon the poverty and ignorance of the nation's workers.' This 'doctrine of the utility of poverty' found its English apotheosis in Bernard de Mandeville's 1723 caricature, 'An Essay on Charity, and Charity-Schools,' in which the English charity school movement was denounced as a form of false benevolence, certain to give the poor a taste for finery and a desire to get above themselves.[36]

In France, the 1750 Academy of Dijon essay prize went to Jean-Jacques Rousseau's 'A Discourse on the Moral Effects of the Arts and Sciences.' Rousseau repeated a set of commonplaces about the dangers posed to republican government by excessive learning. The development of arts

and sciences led to luxury and profligacy, to a decline in the strength
and hardiness of the physical body, to an 'effeminacy of manners' that
undercut the martial spirit necessary for the defence of the republic. All
great civilizations could be shown to decline under the deformations
worked by the growth of refined learning on the social body and spirit.
Learning, he wrote, 'tends rather to make men effeminate and cowardly
than resolute and vigorous.' Children were in need of teaching, he
agreed, lest they fall prey to idleness, but they needed to be taught practically to behave, not to speak dead languages or to master useless arts.[37]

Mercantilist denunciations of luxury and excessive instruction were
similar to those of the Catholic Church. It is not the case that the Church
opposed popular education. In the wake of the Council of Trent, it had
endorsed the obligation of its pastors to teach the faithful to read in the
catechism, to know elements of liturgy, and to write in order to be able
to sign the marriage register. Yet it defined those things as sufficient for
the people's education and it too warned of the dangers to state and nation of an overly instructed populace. As Cardinal Richelieu had put it in
an emblematic text of 1688, which already contained all of Rousseau,

> Just as a body which had eyes in all its parts would be monstrous, so too would
> a State be if all its subjects were learned; there would be little obedience, so
> commonplace would pride and presumption be. The trade in Letters would
> completely drive out that in commodities, would ruin Agriculture, the true
> wet nurse of the people; and shortly would dismantle the Nursery of soldiers,
> who are better brought up in severity and ignorance than in the politeness of
> the sciences: Finally, it would fill France with troublemakers better fitted to
> destroy individual families, and to disturb the public peace, than to procure
> any benefit to the estates.[38]

Most of the Lower Canadian Catholic clergy sought to keep the colonial peasantry safe from the temptations of luxury and dissipation. In
clerical eyes, the good life for the *habitants*, as Lower Canadian tenant
farmers preferred to be called, was one spent in cultivating the soil,
multiplying God's flock, supporting His clergy, and worshipping His
name in splendid temples.[39] The emergence of liberal and republican
movements in Lower Canada challenged the hegemony of the Catholic
Church, yet as I show, its pastoral model of pious peasant ignorance
ultimately triumphed.

Mercantilist doctrine did not prevent the organization of parish schools
in European countries, nor did it prevent the spread of urban schooling,
print culture, and literacy. Most post-Reformation states delegated the

moral education of the people to a state church and left people to their
own devices for any other form of instruction. Nor was it the case that a
mercantilist doctrine of the utility of poverty and ignorance for the mass of
the people was simply replaced by a discourse promoting popular intelligence through schooling. The two discourses coexisted. Within a very few
years of his Dijon prize-winning essay, for instance, Rousseau's 'A Discourse
on Political Economy' argued that republican government depended
upon the support of a general will that it needed itself to instruct. Now he
argued such government faced an unavoidable paradox: it needed to rule,
but it needed to rule through the liberty of the ruled. Rousseau noted that
'government which confines itself to mere obedience will find difficulty in
getting itself obeyed.' By contrast 'the most absolute authority is that which
penetrates into a man's inmost being, and concerns itself no less with his
will than with his actions.' 'Make men,' he concluded, 'if you would command men.' To make citizens, argued Rousseau, it was necessary to begin
with children, and these should be habituated to understand themselves
and their individuality in relation to the state. 'Public education, therefore,
under regulations prescribed by the government, and under magistrates
established by the Sovereign, is one of the fundamental rules of popular
or legitimate government.' Given sometimes romantic notions of republicanism in the literature on Lower Canada, it is important to stress that
coercion and state administration of schooling were not at all alien to republican political theory.[40]

Rousseau's contemporaries in Scotland supported popular schooling
as well, although on different grounds. The tendency of detail work in
new manufactories to degrade workers intellectually led writers such as
Adam Smith to call for state-sponsored education in public schools. His
articulation of a 'compensatory' model of schooling was developed and
promulgated in English Utilitarian circles in the first decades of the
nineteenth century by James Mill. Mill argued that society depended
indeed on the labour of the vast majority of the people and that nothing should be allowed to undermine the motive to labour. Nonetheless,
workers must share in the increased civilization that resulted from their
lives of drudgery. Education was their best reward, and the best guarantee of political order. Mill's mentor Jeremy Bentham went one further,
designing his Chrestomathic school in which instruction for the 'middling orders' would be based on monitorial pedagogy and would proceed systematically through all the significant branches of human
knowledge.[41] The tension between the preservation of the subject in a
necessary state of ignorance, and the development of its intelligence so
as to make it fit to be ruled or to rule itself, helps frame my analysis.

Chapter Outline

Chapter 1 begins with the Conquest of Quebec in 1759 and outlines initial imperial plans to eliminate French institutions and to organize an elected Assembly. These plans were rejected by the first two colonial governors, who sought to rule indirectly through the existing French authorities. Indirect rule was made official in the 1774 Quebec Act, which recognized the rights of the Catholic Church and the seigneurial regime. Following the American invasion of 1775–6 and the later defeat of the British in the American War, new attempts were made to anglicize the Quebec territory, in part through the creation of a non-sectarian university. Their failure is detailed in chapter 1, which also considers the Enlightenment and anti-Enlightenment discourses present in the colonial press. The loyalty scare of the 1790s is examined, and early attempts to win peasant 'hearts and minds' through the medium of printed text are outlined. The chapter ends with a description of the kinds of schools that existed in the two main colonial towns to 1800.

Chapter 2 traces the complex course of school politics from the creation of the Royal Institution for the Advancement of Learning in 1801 to the passage of the 1829 Trustees School Act. I follow the conflict between the two Episcopal churches over the schooling of the people and point to the temporary truce between them which made it possible for them to defeat an attempt at urban lay school organization. Repeated attempts by the Assembly to organize parish schools were defeated by executive government in the colony or in England; the best attempt was side-swiped by imperial intervention. I detail the scheme eventually worked out by the Episcopal churches to divide control over schooling between themselves and explain its surprising defeat by the Assembly, in the wake of the liberal Canada Committee report of 1828.

Chapter 3 focuses on monitorial schooling. It details the substance of this pedagogy and points to the debate that surrounded it in England and Canada. The chapter describes the urban market in schooling on the eve of the 'monitorial moment' and then offers detailed accounts of the various monitorial school societies at work in the colony in the period before 1841.

Chapters 4 and 5 examine attempts by executive and legislature to school the countryside, from the passage of the Assembly's 1829 School Act to the refusal of its 1836 School Bill by the Legislative Council. Some attention is paid in chapter 4 to the practical workings of the schools in order to demonstrate that the Assembly's Permanent Committee on

Education grappled actively with emerging problems of school management. The bulk of this chapter is concerned with the workings of the 1829 act and the revisions to it, both those that made it into law and those that were refused or blocked in the context of heightened political antagonism between branches of the colonial state. This chapter ends with the failure of the 1836 School Bill and the closure of the colony's rural schools. Chapter 5 presents a detailed portrait of rural school conditions in the same period.

Chapter 6 focuses on the working of the 1836 Normal School Act, which was intended to supplement the 1836 School Bill and to provide trained teachers for the colonial schools. The chapter details Jean Holmes's investigations of educational institutions in the United States and western Europe before describing the fiasco of the Montreal Normal School, British North America's first dedicated teacher training institution.

Chapter 7 takes up the theme of liberal governmentality and social science, first through an examination of the neglected work and political significance of the Gosford Commission on Lower Canadian grievances. The chapter draws attention to the importance of this body for colonial political history, while for the historical sociology of schooling it stresses the importance of approaching schooling through the lens of population government. The Commissioners proposed for Lower Canada the means of ruling by schooling which they believed had worked in contemporary Ireland, and the link between the two colonies in this regard is examined.

The bulk of chapter 7 is an account of the operations of the 1838–9 Buller Education Commission established by Lord Durham and charged with producing 'complete statistics' of Lower Canadian educational conditions. The Commission's inquiry was the most ambitious social investigation in the colony's history (with only the 1831 census being as extensive) and it pioneered investigative techniques and practices. While the inquiry failed in its broad objectives, nonetheless it embodied and extended a way of thinking through problems of political government, which it proposed to solve by reconfiguring the relations between population and territory.

The book's last chapter examines the primitive sociology of 'national character' that underlay attempts to reconstruct colonial government in the wake of the Rebellions. Schooling was seen explicitly as a 'mighty engine' for the production of 'character,' while imperial and colonial politicians who championed liberal representative government invoked educational criteria to justify an anglicizing social policy known to be against the expressed interests of the majority. The attempts by members of the Durham mission to enlist the Catholic bishops in the anglicizing project are detailed, and the chapter shows the ideological work undertaken by the Durhamites to claim that nothing done by the colonial Assembly in the field of education was worth saving. This ideological work was the more necessary because competing plans for school reform based on the Assembly's legislative platform were also being elaborated.

Rebellion and the hostility of the Bishop of Montreal had prevented the Education Commission from generating school statistics for the Montreal district. The chapter examines the attempt sponsored by the dictatorial Special Council to do so by sending an inspector to tour the district in person. The tour of inspection was a still novel method of social scientific investigation, and this one revealed a number of interesting anomalies in the operations of the Assembly's school legislation.

The chapter then considers the complex, authoritarian, but brilliant blueprint for a comprehensive colonial educational system designed by Christopher Dunkin at the instigation of governor Thomson and the latter's attempt to bully the Catholic bishops into some measure of acceptance of school reform. However, the grand schemes to anglicize Canada by joining the colonies of Upper and Lower Canada through the 1840 Act of Union and thereby ensuring an English-speaking majority in parliament came to naught, and grandiose school reform sputtered out at the same time. The chapter concludes by showing that the School Act of 1841, meant finally to overcome the political and administrative barriers to schooling the rural population in what was now Canada East, in fact retreated even from most of the progressive measures of the Lower Canadian Assembly.

The Conclusion offers a brief sketch of what happened in the field of schooling in Quebec in the 1840s. I point to some of the ways in which my analysis and my work of documentation trouble versions of the literature on the Rebellions of 1837–8. I point to the work that remains to be done on Lower Canada's royal commissions and I offer a revisionist account of Lord Durham's sociology of 'race' and national character.

1

The Battle between
the Sword and the Mouth

Political ferment around education was intense in the period from the Conquest of Quebec in 1759 to the creation of the Royal Institution for the Advancement of Learning in 1801. The imperial government's intention to anglicize the newly conquered colony was undermined by its first two governors, who preferred to preserve existing conditions of indirect rule and to maintain peasant ignorance as a bulwark against American republicanism. However, the American war and the French Revolution forced colonial rulers to struggle for the 'hearts and minds' of the *habitants*, as Enlightenment discourse flourished in the colony and as political disaffection grew. In the late 1780s and early 1790s, the colonial executive narrowly failed to create a non-sectarian, tax-supported system of schools, crowned by a university. That attempt would have equipped Quebec and Lower Canada with something resembling the school system of New York State and would likely have changed the course of colonial history dramatically.

Such a school system was entirely possible at this moment because of weakness and internal division in the Catholic Church, the absence of an Anglican Church establishment, and broad support for state schooling by urban elites, by the governor, Lord Dorchester, and by his Executive Council led by William Smith. But the advent of assembly government in 1791, the radicalization of the revolution in France, war between France and England, and an increased assertiveness on the part of the Episcopal churches made the English Colonial Office back away from the prospect of ruling Quebec through non-denominational public schooling, even as a tighter relation between print culture and political rule emerged in colonial society. The failure of the plan for a Quebec university helped to paralyse initiatives for popular schooling for forty years. The failure to create non-denominational schools lasted for two hundred. These matters are the focus of the present chapter.

It seemed after the Conquest that the English Crown would proceed to a rapid anglicization of its new colony. Such was established policy, and there was the local precedent of Acadia, which had been subjected to wholesale population displacement in 1755. During the military occupation of 1759–63, the governors in Quebec, Three Rivers, and Montreal intervened in local and transatlantic trade to insist on the use of standard English weights and measures, the English language, and other 'customs' and 'usages.' The French card money in circulation was banned as being 'of no real value, and a manifest Imposition on the Publick,'[1] and the English seemed set to abolish the Catholic Church. Most churches and their religious relics had been protected from the depredations of war, but considerable numbers of priests fled the colony, and when Bishop Pontbriand, who had been nothing but conciliatory towards the conquering English, died in June 1760, Governor Murray refused to accept the Church chapter's candidate as his successor, the abbé Montgolfier, a Montreal Sulpicien. Murray hoped the conquered people would freely adopt the Church of England, but that Church sought a more aggressive policy.

The Catholic Church was in a relatively weak position, although it carried out important ideological and administrative activities and owned substantial seigneurial property. According to Marcel Trudel, its male personnel amounted to 196 secular and regular priests at the beginning of 1759. At the end of 1760, 163 remained and the number continued to decline, even as population grew rapidly from English immigration and from natural increase.[2] Serge Gagnon numbered the priests having a pastoral charge at 112 at the creation of Lower Canada in 1792, rising to 142 in 1801, while Yvan Lamonde put the entire clerical corps at 148 in 1791, 168 in 1805, and 182 in 1812. There was considerable population growth across this period with at least 60,000 inhabitants in 1763 and perhaps 160,000 in 1801. Gagnon argues that the clerical corps as a whole was increasingly undertrained and overworked.[3] Its global effectiveness at intensive parish management, including extracting the tithe, demands closer scrutiny than can be offered here, but the Church did not command the necessary personnel to undertake any ambitious incursions into social policy.

Under French rule, the Church had been unambiguously a state church subordinate to, if at times in some tension with, the Crown. The Church governed the known and the unknown, attempting to specify the legitimate contours of the former and the appropriate means of containing the terror potentially provoked by the latter. Such was the natural sphere of education before there was any substantial conception of universal schooling. In keeping with general Catholic Counter-Reformation strategies, the Church sought to generalize knowledge of the catechism and of liturgical practices, as well as the ability to sign the marriage register, while working to contain or repress Protestant tendencies, cartomancy, faith-healing, and other forms of unauthorized superstition.

An earlier educational historiography held that there was a substantial decline in literacy and intellectual culture after the Conquest, due to the emigration of large numbers of literate officials. Yet, as Pierre Tousignant has argued, the emigration was of about 300 people.[4] In any case, it was countered by immigration of literate anglophones and of English teachers willing to teach in French. The proof that the peasantry of New France was overwhelmingly illiterate is to be found not so much in signing rates – about 10 per cent for marrying male peasants before 1800 – as in the enduring absence of popular participation in print culture and in the culture of the book. There was no press in New France, trade in books was small, and books did not make it into peasant estate inventories. There were occasional mentions of rural itinerant teachers, but they remained marginal figures who did nothing effective to counter a peasant culture in which, as J.-É. Roy put it, 'people even seemed to take some pride in declaring their ignorance, just like the great medieval lords ... In truth, no one read, no one wished to read, people had a holy terror of books and mistrusted those who, by some chance, had got a bit of learning.' Roy claimed that five or six residents in the seigneury of Lauzon, with a population of over a thousand adults, could read and write in 1800, perhaps a low estimate.[5]

Following the 1763 Treaty of Paris, Governor Murray's official instructions called for the creation of an elected assembly. The imposition of oaths of Protestant supremacy for all public officials would have debarred Catholics both from the assembly and from state administration. With notorious ambiguity, the colonial Catholic Church was to enjoy the privileges it had in England – officially, none. Anglicization was to proceed by the adoption of English law and language, the surveying and granting of lands to British settlers, and the setting out of parishes with provisions for the encouragement of schools and the promotion of Protestant ministers and schoolmasters.

In 1764, the Archbishop of York submitted a detailed plan to the English ministry for the religious government of Quebec, one which was

amended and re-submitted in 1767 as the 'Heads of a Plan for the establishment of ecclesiastical affairs in the Province of Quebec.' Under the
plan, the 'Superintendent of the Romish Church' was to take the oath of
allegiance to the governor and was to serve at his pleasure. The Jesuits'
Estates were to be given to the Society for the Propagation of the Gospel
(SPG), the missionary arm of the Church of England, which was especially
active in colonial British North America.[6] The dissolution of the Jesuit
order was to be enforced, with its missionaries replaced by Anglicans. The
Chapter would be dissolved, and while the Recollets and the female religious orders were to continue, they were not to recruit new members. On
their eventual extinction, their properties would also revert to the SPG.
Similarly the seminaries in Quebec and Montreal would be allowed to
train a few priests to satisfy current demands, but their surplus income
would also go to the SPG. The Bishop of London and the SPG would wean
the Canadians away from the Catholic Church through the creation of
schools and the provision of Protestant teachers.[7]

In Quebec, however, Governor Murray had moved towards a more
pragmatic policy and frequently found himself in conflict with much of
the colonial English merchant group over trade and tax policy and over
the preservation of French law in local practice. The merchant group denounced French institutions as slavish and stupefying and argued that the
French dissipated in idleness and luxury income that could be used for
trade. However, as with many of his successors, Murray's class-cultural
prejudices were more powerful than his ethnic and religious prejudices.
Class prejudice led him to prefer landed property, aristocratic manners,
and military prowess to capital in trade. The former represented the hierarchical social organization characteristic of the first half of the English
eighteenth century at least, which the Crown was interested in preserving
in much of its growing empire. The growing 'excesses' of popular democracy in the Thirteen Colonies sharpened that interest.

Murray was disgusted by what he considered the rapacious ignorance of
the English and American merchant speculators who flooded into the colony, snapping up seigneurial properties at fire sale prices and trying to
monopolize all branches of foreign and domestic trade. If he followed his
instructions to establish an assembly and limited the franchise through
tests of religious allegiance, 200 or so Protestant households would elect a
government to rule over 60,000 French residents. On the other hand, the
Catholic clergy and the old seigneurs were of a piece with hierarchical social organization based on landed property, and both they and the militia
system were practically useful as elements of governmental infrastructure.

Murray became increasingly sympathetic to the Catholic clergy and supported the appointment of the Vicar General J.-O. Briand as Superintendent of the Romish Church in 1766. Briand reciprocated by submitting pastoral letters, *mandements*, and appointments of priests for Murray's approval.[8]

In fact, the Church enjoined loyalty to British authority and offered administrative cooperation from the earliest period of conquest. In January 1761, for instance, the clergy replied to a circular from Governor Murray seeking to identify needy families, and, in the following year, the Vicar General Montgolfier declared that prayers for King George were to be included in the Catholic liturgy.[9] Perhaps at Murray's instigation as well, sometime in 1763 J.-O. Briand drew up a memorandum in which he discussed possible lines of policy in relation to the colony's premier educational institution, the Jesuits' College at Quebec, whose extensive estates were subject to a claim of right of conquest by the British commander, Lord Amherst. The government could simply abolish the college, Briand suggested, or it could 'require the seminaries to keep their schools open to people of whatever religion and for whatever vocation they might wish to pursue.' This line of policy would have all sorts of 'inconveniences' and Briand preferred a third line, which was to preserve the College and the Jesuit order, because the latter had a particular calling to teach and because its continued existence would encourage emulation and educational improvement more generally.[10]

Murray's successor as governor, Sir Guy Carleton, was in turn quickly convinced that Quebec was best ruled indirectly by enlisting the allegiances of its 'natural' leaders, the seigneurs and the clergy. Carleton thought the English merchant traders were a transient group and that the colony was bound to remain overwhelmingly Canadian, while even in the late 1760s he was concerned about military security, given the increasingly rebellious situation in the Thirteen Colonies and the small force of regular troops at his command. Carleton appointed a number of leading Canadians to civilian and military office and worked to extend the arrangements that Murray had made with Bishop Briand. He rejected that part of his instructions which called for the convening of a representative assembly, preserved much of French law, and convinced the imperial authorities as early as 1771 to make new grants of land under seigneurial tenure.

In testimony before the Commons committee on colonial government in 1774, Carleton, his attorney general, Francis Maseres, and his chief justice, William Hey, all claimed that there was no interest in an elected assembly on the part of the Canadians. What they had seen of English

law under military government had given the lie to claims about its superiority and they saw assemblies as riotous institutions designed to impede the good work of civil servants. When asked had 'any pains been
taken to explain to such persons the excellence of [an English] constitution, and the advantages that would arise from it, or have they been
left to conjecture?' Carleton replied, 'It is a difficult matter to instruct
a whole people in lessons of politics, and I have never attempted it.'
According to Hey, the Canadians were 'in general, a very ignorant people – a very prejudiced people' who knew nothing about English law and
were best off with council government.[11] The preservation of the ignorance of the Canadians should continue on the model of the ancien régime. No immediate attempt was made to administer population by central government or to remake political subjectivities.

Despite opposition in the English Commons, the Quebec Act of 1774
(14 Geo. III, c.83) effectively reversed the earlier policy of anglicization,
explicitly guaranteed to Canadians their law of property and other civil
rights, affirmed the right of the Catholic Church to the tithe, and made
Roman Catholics eligible for government office. While later instructions
to Carleton enjoined him to encourage the establishment of the Anglican
Church in the colony, he effectively ignored them until the 1790s and
allowed the Catholic Bishop wide latitude in the practical management
of religious affairs.[12]

Republican Wrath

The support of British government for feudalism and the imposition of
a state church, a Catholic one at that, was politically outrageous to
American republicans. It seemed to confirm fears that the imperial authorities were planning to impose the Church of England as a state
church to the south.[13] The Continental Congress was not mistaken in its
expectation of widespread support among the Quebec peasantry for the
invasion it undertook in the summer of 1775. Despite Bishop Briand's
distribution of a circular instructing priests to consider heretical all those
who supported the cause of the 'Bostonnais,' and despite the attempts of
seigneurs acting as militia commanders to raise the *habitants* against the
invaders, the Americans were generally welcomed. Peasants became less
enthusiastic after being paid in military scrip of doubtful value, but priests
who tried to organize resistance were sometimes handed over to the
American forces and some churches were seized. On the Île d'Orléans, a
militia recruiting drive led by the chief justices met with armed opposition,

and similar actions occurred in other parts of the colony. In both Berthier and St Cuthbert parishes the militia refused to muster. In the Beauce, the seigneur Gabriel-Elzéar Taschereau, who was commissioned as a militia captain, failed to discipline his disaffected troop and the Bostonnais rewarded his attempt to do so by auctioning off his possessions at knock-down prices to his tenants.[14]

In May 1775 in Montreal, a newly inaugurated bust of George III was 'daubed black and decorated with a necklace of potatoes, a cross and placard bearing the inscription, "*Voilà le Pape du Canada et le sot Anglais.*"' The invasion gave colonial political and military authorities their first practical demonstration that the strategy of indirect rule was flawed and that it might be necessary to struggle actively to win peasant 'hearts and minds.'[15]

Reading, printing, writing, and speaking were media of and instruments in the battle for colonial hegemony. The Continental Congress published a letter calling on the inhabitants of Quebec to join in the fight against British rule, promising the abolition of the tithe and feudal rents, freedom of the press, and other civil liberties. There were demonstrations organized by a group called les Fils de Liberté in favour of the American forces before the occupation of Montreal, and Congress's letter was translated by a Montreal lawyer, the French-born Valentin Jautard (1736–87). With another Frenchman, Fleury Mesplet (1734–94), who came to Montreal as the printer for the American forces (via Boston, where he had had some association with Benjamin Franklin), Jautard organized the printing and distribution of the letter and several other propaganda pamphlets in the countryside. While Quebec was under siege during the winter of 1775-6, the Americans fired arrows with propaganda pamphlets attached over the city walls. According to the Executive Councillor François Baby, Congress's letter was widely distributed and read aloud.[16]

After the Americans had been driven out, a loyalty commission sent to tour the parishes around Quebec City in the spring of 1776 found evidence of widespread disloyalty to the Crown by militia officers and by the *habitants* more generally. Militia officers in thirty-seven of fifty parishes were removed from command and barred ever again from holding government office. Many *habitants* were found to have provided comfort to the occupying army. In each parish, the loyalty commissioners conducted a sort of public purgative ceremony in which they displayed their command of the power of texts. They assembled the militia and local notables in front of the church, read their commission aloud, and delivered a speech about loyalty which the assembled company was required to applaud. They then interrogated those present about their conduct during the occupation. On the Île d'Orléans, the commissioners found that militia officers still had their American commissions in hand. They forced one of them, a man named Bauché, to hand over his commission, 'which was read aloud ironically,' and then made him set fire to it himself, a proceeding which seemed 'much to impress the entire assembly.' Many of the acts punished involved reading and speaking. At St Féréol, for instance, Chretien Giguere was punished for having spoken several times at the church door, boasting of the power of the rebels. 'Caron du Plaquet dit Chevalier innkeeper in the city carried on his trade during the winter at Ste Anne he was the one who read out all the congress' orders at the church door. He wrote answers to the congress for the parish captain.' And there was the notorious wife of Augustin Chabot, known as the gossiping Queen of Hungary, who went from door to door twisting the minds of her credulous neighbours against the king.[17]

An Opposition Press

Fleury Mesplet and Valentin Jautard remained in Montreal after the American forces were driven out and launched a newspaper in June 1778, modelled on Addison's English *Spectator*, called the *Gazette du Commerce et Litteraire, Pour la Ville & District de Montreal*. It ran for a year before both were imprisoned under the campaign of political repression launched by Governor Haldimand. Jautard would die a few years after his release in 1783. The *Gazette* had a circulation of 300 copies at most and its editor and publisher were discreet in their language, but it was an Enlightenment voice in a context where such voices were politically charged.

The paper printed letters in which correspondents debated cultural and educational questions and it mounted a direct assault on mercantilist cultural policies. It articulated some of the themes concerning the peasantry that would echo through political debate in French Canada for many decades. In the paper's second number, for instance, one of its most prolific correspondents, 'Le Spectateur tranquille,' complained of the refusal of rural parents to allow their children to go to school, or, if they were sent to school, to forbid the master to correct them, which allowed them to grow up ignorant and vicious. The absence of a good education led to poor agricultural practices: the peasants did not manure their fields and they clear cut their lands, with the result that they had no materials with which to fence and nothing with which to heat their houses.[18] 'Lui Seul' complained again in the third issue about the failure of parents to attend to their children's early schooling and, worse, that the prevailing pedagogical practice meant that 'no one knows how to read … they are taught to read the Latin Language as much as the French. – Here the Latin Language, it might be said, is the only one they read.'[19] In fact, some rural schools taught beginners in Latin at least until the 1830s, a practice meant to provide cantors and to ensure the other-worldly orientation of reading and schooling.

The Shepherd and the Fox

A debate, supposedly involving six different correspondents promoting and attacking mercantilist conceptions of popular schooling began in the *Gazette* in July and continued until October 1778. 'Ignorance is the wet nurse of simplicity, it will be hard to find a simple man who is vicious; how many people would never had done evil, if only they had not become familiar with it,' began 'Moi Un,' in a response to 'Spectateur tranquille's' complaints about the absence of schooling. For Moi Un, the city was the theatre of vice, the village that of virtue, and the introduction of a bit of learning into the villages would produce people who were pretentious, arrogant, and prone to disputes. There was no necessity for the people to learn to speak Greek or Latin, and if once they learned to read French, there would be no telling where they would stop reading. They might start with Fénélon and Labruyère, but they would go from there to Rousseau's *La Nouvelle Heloïse* and Voltaire, destructive both of religion and the state. As Moi Un put it, 'The least able pastor will govern a flock of sheep & will never be able to govern a fox.'

This defence of pastoral government of the ignorant generated the predictable response from 'L'Observateur' that education was necessary for members of all occupations to know how to go about their business effectively. Moreover, instruction was necessary both for the governed and for their governors, for 'every Citizen whatever his profession has duties to fulfil. How can he fulfil them if he does not know them? Without a knowledge of History, of Politics, of Religion; how could those who are put in charge of the government of States know how to sustain order, subordination, security & abundance?' To this, 'le nouv[eau] Agrippa' responded that extensive education in France had led to the decline of martial prowess, and those in other occupations who spent their time in study did not learn how best to master their business. 'Votre Serviteur' responded that it was clear that exposure to science and learning among new peoples gave them 'gentler passions and manners, a better ordered police, more humane laws, [and] brought them out of the darkness in which they had languished for so long.'[20]

After this debate over mercantilist cultural policy the *Gazette* announced the formation of a Voltairian Academy in Montreal for the pursuit of truth and science. Perhaps Fleury and Jautard were themselves most, if not all, of the paper's pseudonymous correspondents, and the Academy may have been an imaginary device.[21] The denomination 'academy' was a claim to the legitimacy of the authoritative forms of scientific knowledge produced in contemporary France. Indeed, the announcement of its formation was presented as a response to an earlier advertisement carried in the *Gazette* for an 'Anti-Dictionnaire Philosophique' meant to discredit the ideas of Voltaire. The putative president of the Academy, who signed himself 'L.S.P.L.R.T.,' declared that the institution's purpose was to subject all ideas of whatever tendency or origin to critical scrutiny. There followed some debate – whether manufactured by Mesplet and Jautard or not – for and against critical thought, and Mesplet both refused to reveal the identities of correspondents and defended himself against charges that his ideas were insulting to Montrealers, 'having attended carefully to insert nothing against Religion, Morals, the State or the Government.'[22]

The ideas expressed in the *Gazette* echoed debate and discussion in Europe and America, and the paper's circulation was small. Still, in the midst of the ongoing conflict between England and its American colonies, it had some subversive potential, if only by exposing readers in Montreal to criticism of existing cultural and economic conditions. Its denunciations of the ignorance of colonists dovetailed with practical demonstrations of their shaky loyalties in some parts of the colony and with the limited influence that the Catholic Church showed itself able to exercise over a peasantry that was promised the abolition of tithe and seigneury by the American invader. In effect the *Gazette* attacked the reigning policy for popular ignorance, and, despite Mesplet's claim that the paper was not political, the government closed it in June 1779.

Towards Ruling by Schooling

Under General Haldimand and his two lieutenant governors, the Quebec administration's educational policy was limited to the appointment of English schoolmasters at Quebec, Montreal, St John's, and at Baie des chaleurs, but it took steps to anglicize the law, establishing habeas corpus and trial by jury for civil suits. After his return from England in October 1786, Carleton, now Lord Dorchester, aimed to pursue a more energetic policy of anglicization. Dorchester was charged with conducting a fact-finding mission in Quebec on colonial social and governmental conditions, but the success of the Bostonnais in 1775–6 had disenchanted him with his earlier project of ruling Quebec indirectly through its French leaders, and he now sought to manage ecclesiastical affairs more actively. He made the controversial appointment of Charles-François Bailley de Messein, a priest of aristocratic background and elite education who had tutored Dorchester's children and had accompanied him to England in 1778, as co-adjutor to Bishop Hubert of Quebec. In a shift of imperial policy as revolution in France unfolded, after 1793 Dorchester strengthened conservatism in the Catholic Church by permitting the immigration of some French Royalist priests. These men preached in the countryside against the 'French principles.' On the other hand, he supported the manoeuvring of Charles Inglis to be appointed Bishop of Nova Scotia (which included Quebec) in 1787, the first Church of England bishop in North America, and an appointment that had been impossible before American independence.[23] Inglis had been in New York as Carleton organized its evacuation in 1783, and his Tory, anti-democratic views made him anathema to American patriots. Inglis's appointment would be followed in 1793 by the creation of a new diocese of Quebec and the appointment of Jacob Mountain as bishop.

Yet Dorchester was not intent on ruling only through religion. The development of an English, or at least of an anglicized, civil society also figured in his projects; with him as his chief justice he brought the American William Smith, former chief justice of New York. A man of considerable intellectual stature, Smith was Presbyterian in religion, Whiggish in his politics, and intent on a project for the union of the British North American colonies, the anglicization of Quebec, and massive immigration from Britain. Dorchester divided his Executive Council into separate investigative committees and appointed Smith to chair those on justice and on education. The only subject on which the governing Council as a whole managed to agree in this period was a plan elaborated by Smith on the New York model for a Quebec school system presided over by a university.

The education committee was appointed in the wake of a formal request from Dorchester of 31 May 1787 for the Executive Council to consider colonial educational conditions, to identify the means of overcoming existing defects and to determine the likely expense and sources of revenue for so doing. The Councillor and lawyer Pierre-Louis Panet was charged with distributing a circular, ostensibly to gather information on the state of education in the districts of Quebec and Montreal, but also to stimulate discussion. Under the heading, 'The condition or present state of education,' the circular sought a list of parishes, the names of clergy with the numbers of their parishioners and the amount of church revenues, and the numbers of schools with their level of support. 'Can it be true, that there are not more than half a dozen in a parish, that are able to write or read?' it asked.

The second heading asked for 'the cause of the imperfect state of instruction' and again called for details about schools, while the third concerned remedial measures and posed the provocative questions: 'Suppose a union for this purpose safe to the Catholic as well as to the Protestant persuasions, and encouraged by all enlightened and patriotic characters, whatever the diversity of their religious tenets, is it possible to hope, to take a step towards establishing a University in the province? or to find schools introductive of a University? How may instructors be acquired? By what means can a taste or desire for instruction be excited in the parishes?' A rather disjointed set of possible answers was provided to these last questions.[24] As the third heading suggests, Dorchester and Smith had already formulated a project for a non-sectarian public university, and the promotion of education was to involve the creation of a desire for it on the part of its potential subjects.

It is not clear that the circular was distributed; in any case, Smith and Dorchester already thought they knew what was important to know about colonial educational conditions and Dorchester organized a petition to support their reform plan. Smith wrote in August 1787 to his English friend John Collet Ryland that 'nothing has been done to dispel that ignorance which it suited the old Despotism of France and of Rome to support among 120 thousand Inhabitants settled on the Banks of a fine River' and 'except the Priests and a few women not five persons in a parish are able to write or read.' He described the Education Committee but told Ryland he had been too busy with other political matters to convoke it. Nonetheless, he added, when the committee did meet he would 'forward the design of beginning with an University that the Country may from that Reservoir be water'd thro' all its villages. The Catholics must be brought into the scheme and the Plan for that purpose imbraces only the Sciences.'[25]

Smith was not simply repeating his own prejudices or impressions of educational conditions. The government's own intelligence-gathering efforts demonstrated the dearth of colonial schools, and peasant ignorance was beginning to appear as an obstacle to economic development and state administration. Such ignorance became more alarming to sections of the ruling clique as the revolution in France unfolded. Already the 1784 census had revealed that 'for the entire population there was only a single school for writing and reading, and that at Vaudreuil.'[26] The peasantry was overwhelmingly illiterate, as documents reaching central government revealed. It was seen as an inert body, but one susceptible to leadership by local 'agitators,' some of them, perhaps, the curés. A 1788 report describing the general condition of the colony stressed peasant illiteracy and demoralization. 'Out of the towns of Quebec and Montreal,' it was claimed, 'there are not upon an average, three men in a parish who can read and write.' The situation had several causes, but the most important was the desire of the clergy to 'preserve their dominion over the peasantry.' While 'it might have been good policy, under the French government, to keep the inhabitants in this wretched state of ignorance,' the report continued, 'it is a question, whether it is good policy under the present government.' The *habitants* remained attached to the French government, as they had shown in the war, but 'nothing will have a greater tendency to anglify them than illuminating their understandings, when they will discern the advantages resulting from the mildness of a British government. To effect this, public free schools ought to be established in different parts of the province, to teach the inhabitants the English language.'[27]

The 1788 report expressed a position shared by most English members of the governing circle, now including Lord Dorchester. With a chauvinistic cultural and religious self-confidence, its proponents were convinced of the superiority of English Protestantism, freehold property, market exchange, and parliamentary government over the mummery and mystifications of French Catholicism and over the degrading and deadening exactions of the feudal system. Teach the mass of the peasantry the English language and they would understand the beauties of English government. Reading English would make people rational and lead them to Protestantism, the rational religion. Schooling would undermine feudal dependencies and stimulate the spirit of industry. Just this line of argument would be made repeatedly over the course of the following sixty years.

While not all members of governing circles saw schooling as the necessary medicine, the malady of peasant ignorance and clerical power was increasingly obvious as an obstacle to state administration. Attempts to introduce a court system and local territorial units for the administration of justice underlined the popular lack of appreciation for English government. Members of local elites insisted on the necessity of bringing petty claims courts to the local level, to encourage commerce by allowing merchants to recover debts, and to encourage agriculture by resolving the endless petty disputes over fences and livestock that distracted *habitants*. A group of petitioners from Laprairie argued in 1790 that a healthy fear of justice was the only means to govern the ignorant:

> there is nothing other than Fear which keeps one part of men to their duty (Especially People without Education) So the Neglectful, the Slothful &c Seeing the Sword of Justice Suspended above their Heads ready to Strike them & with no Hope of delay, will comply with the Just Demands of their Neighbours, Without it Being necessary to Force them to it by the Law.[28]

Petitions showed central government that the great majority of peasant men did not sign their names, and there were endless claims about peasants being duped into signing documents they could not possibly understand. Since curés often authenticated the 'Xs' of *habitants*, members of government could also see that they were active in rural politics.

Letters in the press also complained that the curés were impeding trade by proscribing the lending of money at interest (something that Catholic doctrine accommodated formally only in the later 1820s) and were opposing the organization of local court circuits in order to maintain their influence over dispute resolution. Since the Executive Council had proclaimed acceptable rates of interest, opposition to usury was opposition to English government. Its moral effects were obnoxious. It tended to 'increase laziness and indolence on the part of the Canadian habitant, and kills the spirit of enterprise.' The Bishop should be called upon to instruct his curés to confine themselves to spiritual matters.[29]

Important colonial figures promoted popular schooling as a necessary means to sound police and social order. The seigneurs and merchants in Trois-Rivières petitioned the Executive Council for town government and district courts early in 1789. William Grant wrote to the Executive Councillor Charles Deléry to emphasize as well 'the utility and the necessity of The Establishment of a public School In this city ... We Regard Ignorance, as the Source of Many Evils, And Nothing would Contribute more to Extend And Facilitate the maintenance of Good order & Police, than to have educated people to govern.' The government should grant the town a salaried schoolmaster, on condition that he teach a fixed number of students free of charge.[30]

The press continued the debate around the necessity of education. Fleury Mesplet's relaunched *Montreal Gazette*'s first article argued that 'it is necessary now a days that every Person understand to read, write and keep Accounts, to be able to keep an Intercourse with the Age; he that cannot read is unfit for the present Generation, he will become wretched, and will be dangerous.'[31] James Tanswell and William Moore's *Quebec Herald* followed a similar line, but also denounced the pretensions of the lower orders to independent learning and warned of the political dangers of Sunday schools with their Methodist enthusiasts. Staunch advocates of liberty of the press, Tanswell and Moore argued that 'the strength of empire consists in the spirit of its members, and not altogether in its possessions and pecuniary resources,' and then asked 'how is that spirit to be roused or properly directed? The understanding must be enlightened, the ideas elevated, the heart enlarged, ignorance, avarice, and luxury render men indifferent under what form of government they live ... Liberty ... cannot be understood or valued, and consequently will not be duly supported, without a competent share of improvement moral and intellectual.'[32]

The University of Quebec

Despite his own diagnosis of the educational malady, and despite pressures for government intervention, William Smith was preoccupied in 1787 by the work of drafting a report on the administration of justice in the colony, an intensely controversial subject that divided the ruling group itself. As well, both he and Dorchester understood that the success of their university plan depended upon countering Lord Amherst's claim by right of Conquest to the Jesuits' Estates and upon gaining control over the Jesuits' College in Quebec, which had been turned into a military barracks in 1776. Thus, in a dispatch of December 1787, Dorchester sent the Colonial Office a petition bearing 195 signatures from members of the colony's elite in favour of the return of the estates and the restoration of the college for public education. The dispatch included a thirty-three-page '*Case. Stating the Rights which the Canadians have to be educated in the College at Quebec out of the Estates belonging to it, in support of their Petition to the Right Honble Lord Dorchester.*'

Although the petitioners were agitating first and foremost for a university, it is striking that they insisted that the safety of the state and the security and prosperity of the people depended upon the education of 'men' without distinction in state institutions. The language of the *Case* and the propositions it supported contrasted starkly with the disinterest in 'the political education of a whole people' expressed by Carleton before the Commons committee in 1774. 'A public and free Education is essentially necessary and advantageous in every good Government,' the *Case* read, and so colonists 'should receive Instruction early in life.' If they did, they would become 'members of the State, they support it, contribute to its prosperity, and love it, with those exquisite Sentiments which, for want of Education, the unimproved and ignorant man, has for himself only.'

Again, in language that anticipated the common school gospel of the 1820s and 1830s, the petitioners stressed that 'children brought up in common, upon the footing of Equality, instructed in the Laws of God and man,' would 'learn first by Education, and afterwards by Sentiment, to Substitute manly actions for that dangerous Slothfulness and poverty in which a state of Ignorance, and of Indifference to great things, absorbs them.' The 'in common' meant first and foremost that French Catholic children would be exposed to the culture of their English counterparts, but it also implied education for the whole people. Were Canadians subject to such an education, government need 'harbour no fear of any attack or invasion from a neighbouring Enemy.' The remedy for popular ignorance involved local electoral management of instruction in secular state institutions. As the petitioners put it, 'the College is for education that which the parochial Church is to Christians; The one makes them Children of God, the other Children of the State.' That reference to the parish did not imply parochial clerical control of schooling, because 'a College for Education, or any other thing concerning the common Interest of the Settlers, can never be better preserved and managed, than by the Deliberations of the Proprietors of Lands and real Fathers of Families, having an essential interest therein.'[33] Already then, in the late 1780s with official sanction, an important section of the colonial elite called for the local electoral management of a more or less universal, non-sectarian educational system. In fact, the argument was for the kinds of local school corporations initiated in New York State.

The petition with its *Case* languished in the Colonial Office in London, and Lord Amherst's claims were far from being settled. It is unlikely that officials in London paid much attention to the educational dispatch, given how incensed they were at Dorchester's forwarding of Smith's undigested report on the administration of justice. Smith had been pressed for time, and bitter divisions in his justice committee made it impossible to abstract a clear line of policy from his investigations. Officials in London had not the patience to wade through a mass of arcane and disorganized legal documents.[34]

The university plan might have gone no further had the new Anglican Bishop of Nova Scotia, Charles Inglis, not begun to correspond with

Dorchester about educational matters at length, and had he not offered advice as to the internal organization and government of a university for Quebec. He visited Quebec in the summer of 1789, saw conditions on the ground, and discussed educational reform. He thought pejoratively that Dorchester's proposed university was a 'novelty': it was to have a professor of agriculture, and, more strikingly, it was to be non-denominational, open to Catholics and Protestants alike, not presided over by a clergyman, and without either a professor of theology or theological instruction. Inglis was opposed to such a radical redistribution of the relations between church and state, although he recognized that, given the predominance of Catholicism in the colony, some concessions would be necessary for an anglicizing educational project to proceed.[35] Nonetheless, Inglis himself was agitating for a university charter for a King's College in Halifax which would train Anglican clergymen and at which only those subscribing to the 39 Articles would be admitted. King's was chartered as a grammar school in 1788, but to Inglis's disgust when it gained university status in 1802 it was placed under lay direction.[36]

It was Inglis's initiative that pushed William Smith to pursue his educational project more energetically. The two had a controversial history in which another King's College – what would become New York's Columbia University – figured centrally. Anglicans in New York State had been agitating in the 1750s for the creation of a denominational university, located on lands belonging to their Trinity Church, and Smith had been a leading opponent of the plan, which he and other Presbyterians saw as a step towards the establishment of an American episcopate. Inglis at the time was a schoolmaster in Pennsylvania, but after his ordination in 1758, he worked as a missionary and then as one of the curates of Trinity Church. A Tory and tireless advocate for a colonial episcopate, Inglis, like Smith, had been evacuated from New York in 1783 and also like Smith had vied for Carleton/Dorchester's patronage in London. The competing plans of the two men for a Quebec university replicated the terms of their earlier conflict.[37]

On 23 August 1789, William Smith wrote directly to Bishop Hubert and to his co-adjutor, Bailly de Messein, seeking answers to his questionnaire and inviting their opinions on his educational proposal. Hubert, whose response was widely publicized, declined to provide a list of parishes and curés, and claimed that the tithe was too small and irregular to calculate in a useful manner. In any case, he argued, the Council did not need such information, since the plan for a university was simply impractical. History showed that universities came into existence only when agriculture was sufficiently advanced to allow for the development of large towns, and that certainly wasn't the case in the colony. There were only four towns of any sort, but William Henry (Sorel) was effectively empty, and Trois-Rivières was extremely small. Montreal could only furnish ten or twelve students every two years for the Quebec seminary, and most of those quit before going beyond the rhetoric class, even though philosophy was free. A university was a body composed of colleges, but the colony at best was capable of supporting only two very small ones. Until agriculture was further advanced and more waste land cultivated, it was idle to think of a university.

It was the prospect of a union of 'enlightened' members of different religious denominations that particularly exercised Msgr Hubert. It made no sense to propose that a university should be directed by such people, because by definition they would have no strong prepossession for education, religion, or country. As Hubert put it, 'in the stile of modern writers, *a person unprejudiced in his opinions,* is one who opposes every principle of Religion, who, pretending to conduct himself by the law of nature alone, soon becomes immoral and not subordinate to the Laws, so necessary to be inculcated upon youth, if it be intended that they should conduct themselves uprightly. Men of this character (and this age abounds with them, to the misfortune and Revolution of Nations) would by no means suit the establishment proposed.'[38] This claim would be reiterated repeatedly by the opponents of secular schooling in the following half-century.

For the rest, Hubert claimed that descriptions of the illiteracy of people in the countryside were being grossly exaggerated to discredit the clergy; in fact, there were between twenty-four and thirty literates in each parish, more women than men. There were no existing defects in the colleges in Quebec and Montreal, and English students were admitted freely and treated fairly. If there was discouragement to instruction, perhaps the cause was 'the preferences given to old subjects, and even to strangers, over the Canadians, in appointments to public offices and places of trust, but,' Hubert added, 'this is not within my sphere.' The government should enlist the curés and the magistrates to promote education and should establish a third college by restoring the Jesuits' Estates and college to their original purpose.[39]

Despite Bishop Hubert's evident opposition, the Executive Council Committee formulated and published a plan for a system of public education. The lack of schooling in Quebec had produced 'a people in a state of *base barbarism,*' and to remedy this condition there needed to be, first, '*Parish* free-schools, or a school in every village, for reading, writing, and the four common rules of Arithmetic,' and, second, 'a *County* free-school, one at least, for further progress in Arithmetic, the Languages, Grammar, Book-keeping, Gauging, Navigation, Surveying, and the practical Branches of the Mathematics.' Council agreed with the Catholic Bishop that the establishment of a university on a grand scale was too ambitious, but a modest college with a rector and four professors would suffice for British North America. Given that the project could not be executed without the union of all denominations, Council resolved that 'Christian Theology be no branch of instruction in this College' and that powers of inspection be vested in the Crown. There should be a governing board composed of equal numbers of Protestant and Catholic clergy and laymen, and the university charter should contain clauses 'to repel every appropriation and by law, touching the funds or government of the College, to any other than the promotion of science *at large*, as afore-mentioned; in exclusion of all biasses, ceremonies, creeds and discriminations, either of the Protestant or Catholic communion.' Council saw the university both as a stand-alone institution, able to receive support from a variety of sources, and as the oversight body for the inferior schools. It would train teachers and members of the liberal professions and would probably draw students from throughout British North America and beyond.

While the university might be supported out of the Jesuits' Estates and private donations, the local schools would need local support. Council presented another radical idea: 'the erection of the village and county schools would require an act of the legislature; rating each parish in assessments, for the free-schools of its *own* district.' The tax would mean that people unable to pay school fees would be schooled for free, a startling idea in its own right in 1790. But the implications of a parish property tax were more radical still: the execution of such a tax would have entailed the appointment of assessors and some form of property registration – things completely alien to the seigneurial system and a challenge to the Catholic clergy's draining of surplus peasant production in the form of the tithe. This innovative plan was endorsed unanimously by the Executive Council, including its French Catholic members, and published, with Bishop Hubert's objections, in pamphlet form in 1790.[40]

Catholic Division

Bishop Hubert's position in response to the committee was publicly opposed by his co-adjutor Bailly de Messein, a man of aristocratic manners and background who had been trained in the rhetorical style current in Paris's Louis-le-Grand college and who was concerned earlier in his course at the Séminaire de Québec with forming young people able to influence public affairs by their command of speech.[41] In his answer to the committee's queries, dated 5 April 1790 and subsequently printed as a pamphlet, de Messein denounced Hubert's position on the university and on educational conditions, intimating repeatedly that they were not, and could not in fact be, the opinions of someone as generous as Hubert. It was absurd to propose that colonists needed to wait until 'we have cleared the land up to the Arctic circle,' and it was absurd to suppose 'that without instructors and teachers young people will prepare themselves for a University.'[42] It was high time to establish such an institution, and, with respect to the question of who should direct it, the answer was also clear: the government. Bailly de Messein's position was the first – and the last – time that a Catholic Bishop in Quebec would energetically advocate mixed religious instruction under the guidance of the civil power.

Hubert's response to the Committee of Council and Bailly de Messein's criticism of it produced a wave of controversy in the press and in government circles. Hubert defended himself at length to Dorchester against de Messein's attack in the spring of 1790, arguing that it was prompted by the latter's jealousy at not having been named Bishop himself.[43] In a long piece entitled *Réflexions sur les établissements à faire pour des Ecoles dans les Campagnes & des Collèges dans les villes*, Hubert (or one of his fellow clerics) argued that, while everyone could see advantages in the institutions proposed, there was no means possible to create them under the existing system of government. All citizens who understood their interests would oppose the levying of a tax for schools by the Quarter Sessions. If government wanted an educational tax, Council could authorize the *habitants* to tax themselves and could work to convince them through the curés and educated people in the countryside that they should do so. The dangers of a secular university education were clear; it was to be feared that 'those who would attend these colleges might be godless, & that unprejudiced masters might produce unprejudiced disciples, that is to say, people who will not be predisposed in favour of any particular religion, if not simply biassed against all.' Associating bishops with laymen in educational matters would revive the old religious disputes of Europe, and it was unfair to use the Jesuits' Estates, intended for Catholic education, to support secular instruction.[44] Hubert repeated his defence to Lieutenant Governor Alured Clarke in November 1790 and complained of Bailly de Messein to the Congrégation de la Propagande the same month. Bailly de Messein was threatened by Rome with removal if he did not conduct himself more calmly, and Hubert was roundly praised for beating back what was seen as a Protestant incursion.[45]

Hubert fared less well in the press, English and French, although an author calling himself 'Le Bon Sens/Good Sense' did denounce Bailly de Messein in a paid advertisement in Quebec and Montreal newspapers.[46] In May, June, and July 1790 the *Montreal Gazette* published letters, and responses to letters, from a 'Curé de campagne,' thought to be de Messein, attacking Hubert's position.[47] A petition of October 1790, signed by a very large number of members of the male colonial elite, French and English, including one of the professors in the Séminaire de Québec and a Récollet from Montreal, again called on Dorchester to establish the university and to support it out of the legacy offered by Simon Sanguenet of the seigneury of La Salle.[48] News of the petition produced a new wave of criticism of the Church's opposition to the education of the people.

In a city called 'Malronet,' the people were victims of an 'Infamous Fraud,' according to 'Le Philanthrope,' writing in the *Montreal Gazette.* There were three orders of people living here – the nobility, the clergy, and the common sort, who were despised by the first two orders. But then a benevolent goddess shone the light of liberty on the city, and as soon as the common people began to think for themselves, no nobility other than that of talent and virtue was recognized and intolerant clerics lost all influence. Enlightened people went so far as to propose the creation of a university: the two great orders trembled! They joined together to beat back the threat, and the clergy, 'which always had a marvellous ease in inventing sleights of hand,' took charge of the defence. Not a university, but another college was needed, provided the clergy could direct it. Said the clergy to itself, 'while others will be taught discoveries that they could use against us, our young people who will have toiled away at our principles, accustomed from childhood to think only by us and for us, will support us & will plead our cause, convinced that it must be their own.'[49]

'Un Citoyen' was rather less lyrical than Philanthrope, but no less pointed. Hubert's response to the Committee of Council was a scandalous neglect of his pastoral obligations, and Bailly de Messein's attack on him was thoroughly justified. The country had no greater or more urgent need than that of popular instruction, and Council's plan was liberal and benevolent. Hubert's opposition lent tacit approval to 'the sophisms of the critics, who affirm that religion can only survive if favoured by obscurity & the shadows of ignorance.' The time was past when a false politics could find 'under the cloak of religion a dangerous mask to veil its iniquitous plots.' Hubert was weakening the church by allowing opposition to subsist between himself and his co-adjutor.[50]

'Civis' simply urged Montrealers to imitate their fellow citizens from Quebec and to agitate for a university of their own, for with the coming of the new constitution, the result would be 'the establishment of Schools throughout this extensive Province where the useful parts of a common education may be taught to the peasantry.'[51] 'L'Homme Mûr' also urged his fellow French citizens to support the university project enthusiastically. They must be impressed with 'the necessity & the advantages of an educational project as well executed as it is generously conceived in a Province which has always been prey to ignorance & to its daughter, superstition; in which the *habitants* were so much the playthings of fanatical and absurd Pastors before the Conquest, & of whom two-thirds still endure in slavery.'[52] In late December, 'Citoyen' called the Montreal Catholic churchwardens to task for their mismanagement of the vestry's funds, in part through allowing the Sulpiciens to appropriate some of it for the embarrassingly inferior education offered in their college. Over twenty years, he claimed, the churchwardens had wasted more than £150,000 on all kinds of junk, 'Fruits of luxury & bizarre taste,' in church decoration, when they could have been instructing young people.[53] Even the Montreal Debating Society took as its subject in March 1792, 'What plan of Education may be most for the advantage of the rising generation in this Country?' The clear winner was the position '"*that there be Parochial Schools established throughout the Country and that a Grammar School be instituted in each of the Towns.*"' As Samuel Neilson put it in the prospectus for his *Quebec Magazine*, the political world was atremble from the spread of new ideas: 'the sword of the mouth is opposed to the sword of steel, and the world waits the result of the Contest.'[54]

The Failure of the University Plan

William Smith and Lord Dorchester opposed the Constitutional Act of 1791 that created the new colony of Lower Canada because it established an elective assembly without the educational system that was its necessary precondition. As Smith put it, 'as to the main Body of the Canadian Peasantry, their Want of Education, even of the very lowest Kinds, has left them in such a State of extreme Ignorance as to disqualify them for the smallest Attention to any Measures of political Speculation.' Under the administration of Sir Alured Clarke, the new Legislative Council was enjoined in 1793 'to make due provision for erecting and maintaining of Schools, where Youth may be educated in competent learning and in the knowledge of the principles of the Christian Religion,' and Smith again prepared a report on the subject. Nothing had been done, he repeated, to remedy the state of popular ignorance, and 'if a Tyranny draws security from the Ignorance of its Slaves, all the Motives of Policy under the Constitution now given to the Province must be on the Side of its general Illumination.' In late winter or early spring of 1793, the Assembly gave first reading to 'An Act for the instruction of youth in useful learning by the establishing of schools in the different parishes of this province, and to enable the children of the poor and necessitous to share the common benefits arising therefrom.' It also considered a petition from the Quebec district on parochial schools and the Jesuits' Estates. A nine-member committee was named to petition the Crown on the latter. The details of the 1793 School Bill remain unknown, but it is clear that the MPPs planned to support the schools out of a tax on wine and spirits. However, the tax bill was rejected 'as premature and contrary to Parliamentary Custom.' The Assembly's petition on the Estates was sent to Council on 11 April, and Governor Clarke attempted to pressure the Colonial Office to act on the matter of education. He received the official reply that any university would have to await the firm establishment of a Protestant clergy in the colony.[55]

Although the existing literature has ignored it more or less completely, this moment was the turning point for colonial political and educational history. Conditions were entirely ripe for an embrace of the governmental trajectory put in place in the American states, which Nancy Beadie has argued convincingly led to universal literacy, but the opportunity was lost. There was no established Protestant clergy and there never would be; hence the university project, with its tax-supported, secular elementary schools, was never realized. Without Catholic cooperation it was not feasible in any case. Besides, the will of Simon Sanguenet that bequeathed the seigneury of La Salle to a future university was successfully contested by his heirs, and the fate of the Jesuits' Estates remained unresolved. With revolution in France followed by war, the hand of the Catholic Church as the guarantor of peasant loyalty was strengthened, even as its opposition to secular education was underlined.[56] The appointment of Jacob Mountain as Anglican Bishop of Quebec in 1793 further undermined the possibilities for non-denominational educational institutions.

The period from the defeat of the Americans in Quebec in 1776 to the refusal of the university plan in 1793 was one in which Enlightenment educational discourses and projects flourished. Despite its cultural and religious chauvinism, Smith's university plan had the potential to change social, political, economic, and religious relations in Quebec dramatically

by undermining seigneurial and clerical power – economically through
local taxation, property registration, and assessment; politically through
the introduction of elected assemblies and the creation of a secular sphere
of association; and culturally through work on the *habitants* to create a
'taste,' a 'desire' for instruction and familiarity with print culture.

In this last dimension, the plan's ambition to shift the grounds of rule
in the colony is particularly evident; to shift it away from the authoritative word spoken by religious or military officials towards some kind of
individual rational appreciation of political questions. One need not assume that a peasantry incited to read would have been content to read
what its rulers wanted it to read. What is germane to the analysis is that
the remedy for peasant credulity was to teach peasants to read and to
judge for themselves: an active project of subjectification. However,
with the execution of Louis XVI, war, the loyalty panics of the later
1790s, the reinforcement of the personnel of the Catholic Church after
1793, and the successful agitations of the Church of England for a
Quebec diocese, the window of opportunity for a secular educational
transformation in the colony closed.

Suspicions

English authorities needed but were suspicious of the Catholic clergy.
The ferocity with which some curés were prepared to oppose what they
saw as democratizing Protestant educational initiatives was underlined
by a conflict which attracted a good deal of attention in 1792–3 between
the schoolmaster Louis Labadie and curé Jean-Baptiste-Noël Pouget of
Berthier. Berthier would continue to be a hotspot in school politics
through the 1830s. Labadie was a much-sought-after teacher who had
attended the Petit Séminaire de Québec for two years starting at age
twelve and who, by age seventeen, was teaching a popular school in
Beauport. He was invited by Pouget to teach the vestry school in Berthier-
en-haut for five years. After his arrival, his school attracted the attention
and support of members of the colonial elite both in Montreal and
Quebec. One visitor marvelled at the tranquillity and politeness of
Labadie's students and argued that every parish should be so lucky as to
have such a teacher.[57]

Curé Pouget had a reputation as a violent man, having been accused of
roughing up one of his parishioners after mass in an effort to get him to
inform on militia officers whom Pouget thought had slandered him.[58]
Labadie, supported by a number of notables from Berthier and from

Quebec and Montreal, sued Pouget on the grounds that the latter had seized his possessions and locked him out of his school, supposedly because Labadie offered to instruct pauper children in the parish at his own expense. Labadie claimed that Pouget mobilized the *habitants* against him. Pouget was denounced in the Montreal press as an 'ENEMY OF EDUCATION, for opposing the establishment of a School for the poor in his Parish.' Yet one account of Labadie's school revealed that the Bible occupied a central place on a raised dais and that the students read aloud from it daily, enough to alarm any curé who wanted exclusive control of the sacred book. Labadie wrote that Pouget had come into the school and had attacked him in front of his scholars, *'threatening me with his fist & his stick, callling me a rogue, &c. He told me, that I was his servant, his slave; that he was my master, & he would do with me as he wished.* Then he added, *I order you to drive away anyone who meddles by visiting your school in the future by booting them in the ass. Here I'm King, Pope, Bishop, &c.'* Labadie, supported by the seigneur, regained control of his school and it appeared to flourish, but he moved to Verchères later in 1792, encouraged by a Montreal Constitutional Club. There he organized demonstrations of loyalty to the king as war with France broke out.[59] To laymen who had supported a secular educational system, the incident underlined the violence with which the curés seemed willing to defend popular ignorance.

The Loyalty Scare

A paranoid frenzy broke out in ruling circles about the loyalty and intelligence of the clergy and the *habitants* as war with France began. Lieutenant Governor Clarke issued a proclamation early in 1793 urging enforcement of the laws that 'discourage and suppress all Vice, Profaneness and Immorality,' for such things unchecked 'may justly draw down the Divine Vengeance upon us and our Country' in such dangerous times.[60] A second proclamation in November called for the arrest and seizure of all persons engaged in spreading sedition, and, as invasion fears were fuelled by reports of French spies distributing the pamphlet *Les Français libres à leurs frères les Canadiens* in the countryside, the ruling groups organized vigilance associations to root out troublemakers and to make people sign declarations of loyalty.

The lead was taken by an Association Loyale de Montréal, whose organizing committee of twelve included the notary Joseph Papineau. The association met frequently between May and November 1794 to oppose 'the seditious attempts lately made by wicked and designing men, in circulating false and inflammatory writings, in exciting by false news, the dread of our fellow subjects against the powers of our Government and the laws.' A loyalty declaration was printed with the signatures of the Montreal members on one side and with the obverse left blank for the reception of more signatures. Five hundred copies were printed and distributed to local militia officers and curés with the aim to 'undeceive the ignorant.'[61] The exercise was explicitly coercive in some places: in William Henry, for instance, loyalists declared their determination 'to be vigilant in their inquiries to discover and point out ... every person that has not signed the Association with their reasons (if any they have).'[62]

Councillor George Allsopp was alarmed by the refusal of *habitants* around Quebec City to declare their loyalty. 'There is a probability of obtaining some signatures in Cap Santé,' he wrote to the governor's secretary, 'but the people of Ecureuils are totally averse[,] not even the Captn of Militia is disposed to sign consequently the others will not, they have various idle pretences, I have talked to the principals to no purpose nor has the Priest any success.' None of the people had been willing to vote at the last election, and Allsopp thought perhaps those who refused freely to sign the declaration should be forced to take the Oath of Allegiance. He admitted that if the declaration was in fact voluntary, 'any Compulsion would be improper' but at least 'the oath would bind their fidelity.' In response to a circular to the associations, the government heard of more recalcitrance: no signatures from St Charles, St Joachim, or Lotbinière, only a few from Rivière Ouelle and L'Islet. The 'Association du Comté de Leinster' attributed peasant receptiveness to sedition to 'the prejudices of a neglected Education.'[63]

Some observers noted that the refusal of peasants to sign had more to do with their suspicions about what they were committing themselves to in putting their marks to documents they could not read or understand than with political disaffection. Others claimed that people thought one signature from a community to be sufficient: an instance of delegated writing. Nonetheless, through the declaration, print became more directly implicated in attempts to rule the people.

The executive also undertook to counter French propaganda with a didactic pamphlet of 1794, *Le Canadien et sa femme*, by the Legislative Councillor François Baby. Baby adapted the form of the catechism – the most common text in Lower Canadian peasant culture – for political purposes. He used a series of answers by the *habitant* André to the questions of his wife Brigitte (perhaps a latter-day Queen of Hungary), who gave voice to all the political rumours and fears of their parish. Much of the eighteen-page pamphlet defended the recently revised militia laws as just and necessary, but André also corrected Brigitte's mistaken notions about liberty and about the conduct of the *Bostonnais* in 1775. In fact, he explained, invaders threatened to come to the colony because they were miserable in their homeland and did not enjoy British liberty. Son Joseph, who eavesdropped on his parents' discussion, declared 'I wish to obey and to serve God, my King and my Country.'[64] Print was meant to correct the gossip from which the *habitants* derived their distorted political information.

Executive government saw evidence that it was losing the struggle for hearts and minds. Matters were exacerbated by the passage of the new militia law, changing the conditions of muster, and a new road law which imposed new levies in the countryside. At the fall 1796 Quarter Sessions in Montreal, the justices called on the government to suspend the road law in the district, for it was causing disturbances 'in a moment of effervescence in the minds of the multitude.' Lieutenant Governor Prescott called on his attorney general, Jonathan Sewell, to investigate, and Sewell warned that 'the district of Montreal particularly the Island was greatly disaffected to his Majesty's Government.' Writs under the provisions of the road law could not be executed; on one occasion the sheriff's officer had been 'violently & dangerously beaten,' and on another he had been opposed 'by Men to the number of Ten and upwards in Arms.' At the root of this trouble, claimed Sewell, was

> that a Pamphlet of a most seditious tendency signed by Adet the Ambassador from the French Republick to the United States was now in circulation in the District – that this Pamphlet bore the Arms of the French Republick and was addressed to the Canadians assuring them that France having now Conquered Spain, Austria and Italy had determined to subdue Great Britain – and meant to begin with her Colonies – That she thought it her duty in the first Instance to turn her attention to the Canadians to relieve them from the Slavery under which they groaned – and was taking steps for that purpose – That it pointed out the supposed advantages which the Republican form of Government possessed over the British and concluded that in a short Time there would be heard only the Cry of Vive La Republique from Canada to Paris.

Prescott set out to locate the priests who had immigrated to the colony after 1793 and issued a proclamation calling on all French nationals, except the immigrant priests and the Sulpiciens, to quit the colony immediately.[65]

Sewell nicely summed up the belief of most of the colony's governing clique in 1797: 'Ignorance, profound Ignorance, is too surely the Characteristick of the Canadians, and certainly renders them liable to be imposed upon by the grossest assertions.'[66] It was not only members of government or English observers who were alarmed, as one can see from the 1798 pamphlet, *Avis au Canada*, written by a twenty-four-year-old Denis-Benjamin Viger. Viger devoted about fifty pages to the unspeakable atrocities committed in France and in neighbouring regions by the revolutionary government and its armies, in an effort to 'give the *habitants* in this fortunate country striking and scientific proof of the horrible effects of anarchy and impiety.'[67]

The creation of a colonial school system under the direction of the Church of England was one solution soon accepted in ruling circles as a way of enlightening and assimilating the *habitants*. The countryside contained almost no schools. In the cities of Quebec and Montreal, those parents who could not gain access to the seminaries, where admission was selective and enrolments were small, were left to vagaries of the market, which I now describe briefly.

Schools and Teachers to 1801

Only crude estimates of the kind and quantity of schooling available in Quebec in the wake of the Conquest exist, and measures of its impact are equally imprecise. The peasantry had occasional exposure to petty schools in the seventeenth and eighteenth centuries. Louis-Phillipe Audet presented traces of twenty-nine petty schools as proof of a serious attempt at popular schooling under French rule, yet these usually ephemeral institutions can have had little impact on popular learning or culture.[68] The petty schools were supplemented by the efforts of women religious, the Ursulines and the Soeurs de la Congrégation de Notre Dame, who established convent schools in Quebec, Montreal, and Trois-Rivières in the second half of the seventeenth century. The numbers taught as convent boarders were quite modest, but a few women religious also taught in the countryside. An occasional school taught Latin, but beyond the parishes neighbouring the towns, there is little evidence of the existence of schools. The Jesuits in Quebec, the Recollets in Trois-Rivières, and the Sulpiciens in Montreal all conducted boys' schools in the eighteenth century. Audet suggests one hundred elementary school students in 1733 were in the Jesuits' institution, and the progress of students through the elementary branches led to higher instruction and eventually to the offering of the entire classical course in a large complex of college buildings. But the college closed in 1759. The Séminaire de Québec also began sponsoring elementary schools in 1699, and, before the Conquest, seminarians in Quebec attended the Jesuit college. Ephemeral organizations of male teaching brothers occasionally swelled the numbers of schools somewhat, and there was also a very modest market for urban lay teachers.

No exhaustive inventory of urban and village schools is possible for Quebec/Lower Canada before Jacques Viger's Montreal school censuses of 1825 and 1835 (which are discussed in a later chapter). Audet estimated that the three towns of Quebec, Trois-Rivières, and Montreal, with a combined population of about 33,000 had twenty schools altogether in 1790, but his population estimate is exaggerated and he tells us nothing about what qualified as a 'school.'[69] The question of definition is important because some of the urban private institutions run by better-educated men and women taught individuals or a handful of students. Others taught children in the day, adults at night, and some of the Protestants taught Sunday school as well. They might advertise these schools as separate institutions. Most teachers scrambled to make a living, and many did a variety of print-related tasks for pay, such as composing letters and drawing up contracts, keeping accounts, translating, and acting as booksellers and stationers. In Berthier in 1793, Louis Labadie sold school texts, religious books, and salted fish.[70]

In his first pastoral visit and enumeration of Quebec in 1792, curé J.-O. Plessis noted only six school teachers, five of them in the Upper Town, but he tended not to enumerate Protestants in this exercise. In his enumeration of 1795, he found thirteen teachers, but he called the government schoolmaster James Tanswell 'language teacher,' not 'schoolmaster.' Other sources suggest Tanswell's school had at least one assistant master. Plessis recorded the second government-funded schoolmaster, John Fraser, only as ' … Fraser,' in his house in rue des Jardins. In 1798, Plessis listed sixteen teachers in Quebec, fourteen in 1805, and in that year gave Quebec's population, including its suburbs, as 7,397 Catholics and 1,465 Protestants, for a total of 8,862. Of the fourteen teachers he identified that year, only two advertised in the press.[71]

The schools for elite and well-to-do households rarely advertised their existence. Most urban Protestant clergymen supplemented their incomes by boarding a few students and teaching classical subjects in their own homes. Fees were high and parents would have known about such educational opportunities through their social networks. Alexander Spark was one who taught. He had come to Quebec about 1780 to assist in an academy run by a Mr Reid (of which no trace survives). After ordination in Scotland, he returned to tutor the young John Caldwell, the future defaulting Receiver General and seigneur of Lauzon. As minister to St Andrews Church from 1795, Spark regularly tutored young men in the classics and mathematics. For a time he also edited the *Quebec Magazine/Le Magasin de Québec* and was managing editor of the *Quebec Gazette/Gazette de Québec* between 1793 and 1796. He had no need to advertise his willingness to tutor young men. In his 1805 enumeration of Quebec, curé Plessis identified Spark's close friend Daniel Wilkie as a 'schoolmaster' (calling him 'Mr. Wilky'), but not Spark.[72] An equally prominent teacher named Alexander Skakel did advertise his classical school when it first opened in Montreal in 1799, but apparently not thereafter, although he regularly advertised a course of winter evening lectures in natural philosophy from at least 1813 until the lectures ceased to draw an audience about 1840.[73] The main exception to the silence of the elite schools was the English day school of the Collège de Montréal, which repeatedly announced that it accepted English-speaking elementary students at the extremely modest sum of one guinea a year, payable quarterly.[74]

Newspaper advertisements are a rough measure of the availability of schooling, for some people advertised as a speculation. Many newcomers to the colony tried their hand at teaching for a time and many of them advertised their wares in the public prints, announcing they had recently started a school, or would do so if given sufficient encouragement. The Loyalist immigration flooded the urban market with would-be teachers, and as early as 1782 John Pullman, who had been licensed by government to teach in Montreal, complained to Governor Haldimand that there were so many of them in the field that he could not make a living.[75] Perhaps one loyalist was W. Sarjeant, whose single advertisement read:

> W. Sarjeant, informs his Friends and the Public, that he has taken and fitted up Appartments in Mr. Lemoine's House on the Hill for the reception of a few young Gentlemen, the number will not exceed six, these may be instructed in the Public School, and have the Advantage of private Tuition, as after hours will be devoted to the more particular and interesting branches of Education. Gentlemen that have omitted in their early part of Life, those requisites so essential to a Man of Business, have now an opportunity of improving themselves.[76]

Five years later, L. Dulongpré announced that he planned to open a 'Boarding School for Young Ladies, in which they will be taught Reading

Writing and Arithmetic, the French and English Languages, Musick, Dancing, Drawing and Needle Work.' He wrote that he would limit himself to eight students to begin with and would take no more than sixteen altogether, none older than fourteen nor younger than seven, at a cost of 26 guineas each annually, to be paid quarterly and to include washing. Dulongpré taught for a few years, but could not make a living at it.[77]

Despite the existence of many transients, a few male and female teachers stayed in business for considerable periods of time. The government schoolmasters, Finlay Fisher in Montreal and James Tanswell in Quebec, both kept school from at least 1778 and taught for the whole of their working lives, both dying in harness in 1819, Fisher aged about sixty-two and Tanswell seventy-four. Both men advertised their schools, but they were able to rely on the government grant for much of their careers, with Fisher taking the position of Royal Institution schoolmaster in 1818. Single and childless, with brothers active in trade, Fisher amassed a respectably comfortable estate, while Tanswell's heavy domestic expenses seem to have kept him scrambling to make a living. On the other hand, Tanswell was able to take in boarders for whom his successive wives 'found' and he sometimes taught with one of his sons and one of his grandsons. For his part, Fisher met the demand for respectable schooling for girls by renting out part of his house to female teachers. One of them, a Mrs Allen, assured potential clients in 1790 that 'Her School Room is intirely separate from the apartement in which the Young Gentlemen are instructed.'[78]

A few private teachers survived for some years, and the school market offered a degree of choice for those able to pay substantial fees. The successful women teachers offered the range of subjects thought necessary to make accomplished young ladies, hired specialists to teach some of them, and provided room, board, washing, and moral supervision. One of them was Mrs Brooks, who was first recorded by J.-O. Plessis as a schoolmistress at no. 1 rue du Sault au Matelot in Quebec in 1795 and at no. 2 rue du Buade in 1805. She moved to Montreal about 1808 and by 1815 was offering to board young ladies and to teach them reading, writing, arithmetic, grammar, history, geography with the use of globes, French grammar, music, drawing, dancing, bookkeeping by double or single entry, and all kinds of needlework, with 'Filligree' and other ornamental works. She was still advertising in Montreal in 1830.[79]

One of Brooks's competitors in both towns was a Mrs Sketchley, who started her young ladies' boarding school in Quebec some time around 1789, moved it to Beauport in the spring of 1790, and then taught with her husband for a number of years in Montreal. At Quebec, she offered instruction in reading, writing, drawing, and all kinds of needlework, for an annual fee of £25, which included washing and books, but not drawing books, pencils, or colours. If 'parents wash them at home,' she would take the girls at £20, 'music and dancing to be paid for apart. Each young lady finds her own bed, table, spoon, knife, fork, and towels.' Brooks claimed she had fifteen students and would accept no more than twenty. She moved to Montreal about 1794, and the following year her husband or brother was offering to teach basic subjects as well as bookkeeping, surveying, and navigation to male day students. Parents could be assured of the quality of his teaching 'as he received his Education in a Capital Boarding School in England.' Mr Sketchley also offered evening lectures on 'Geography and the Solar System' for 2s./6d.[80]

One could save a penny on Sketchley's lecture fee by going instead to hear Robert Tait's 'Course of Original Lectures on Education.' Tait kept a Montreal day school from about 1796 to at least 1817, claiming in the earlier year that he had twenty years' experience in Edinburgh. Tait offered to teach English grammar, with elocution, writing, arithmetic, bookkeeping, and on demand the learned languages, 'Geography, with use of Adam's new furniture Globes,' practical mathematics, and, for his advanced students, rhetoric with composition, logic, ethics, and natural philosophy.[81] In addition to single men, widowed women, and husband and wife teams, even before 1800 there were schools kept by fathers and daughters, mothers and daughters, sisters, and men in association with other men. There were day schools as well as boarding schools and a few specialist instructors, such as the painting and drawing teacher veuve Rivière, or the teacher of instrumental and vocal music, Charles Watts.[82]

Fees for the boarding schools were beyond the reach of the vast majority of residents. Dulongpré's 26 guineas (£27.6s) for a year's boarding was close to the standard. The Misses Laing in 1800 wanted £25 for girls under ten and £28 for older girls, with an extra charge for French, drawing, or dancing. Mrs Chillies in Beauport wanted 15 guineas in 1788 for a year's instruction in her 'genteel Boarding School,' but the price was deceptive because she demanded an extra $16 a year for teaching writing and arithmetic and then an extra $12 for French, for a total of over £20. The Washington Academy in Albany, New York, in 1787 advertised the 'common' branches at £5 a year, or £8 for an English education, plus a load of firewood, the students presumably boarding themselves. Most day school teachers did not publish their terms. Two exceptions were Joseph Westley of Montreal, who offered to teach reading, writing, and arithmetic in 1789 for 3s.6d. a month, and Jeremy McCarthy in Quebec, who advertised arithmetic and bookkeeping for 10s.6d. a month, any of the practical branches of mathematics for £5.5s. a month, and practical and theoretical instruction in the art of surveying for £10.10s.[83] Instead of publishing their fees, most day teachers advertised 'reasonable' or 'moderate' rates and invited those interested to come and consult with them personally. Enrolment of a student typically also required the payment of an entry fee, and usually the first quarter's fee in advance, a practice meant to ensure that fish were well hooked.

Apart from reports of Louis Labadie's school at Berthier, the press did not describe what went on in day or boarding schools. Labadie's school was said to contain four 'orders' of students, and in late 1792 he had '44 Scholars, 14 poor, and five Savages' in attendance, a very large number. Those in the first 'order' were learning to write; in the second they were reading about agriculture and using other books; in the third, they read the Psaulter in French; and in the fourth, they were learning the alphabet and how to spell. Labadie used Fleury Mesplet's *Gazette de Montréal* as additional reading material. He offered to sell, and thus probably used himself, the 'Alphabet Latin – Ditto Français – Pseautier Latin – Ditto Français – Livre pour l'Orthographe – Dictionaire de Boyer – Neuvaine de St François-Xavier – Dévotion de St Antoine de Padou – L'Ami des petits Enfans – Papier à écrire – Le petit St Suaire – Cahéchisme de Quebec, petit & grand, &c.'[84]

Including the Collège de Montréal and the government schoolmasters, at least fifteen schools advertised in the Montreal press between 1788 and 1800. In Quebec, eight schools were advertised in the same period. There were also occasional advertisements in the Quebec and Montreal papers for schools at Berthier, Verchères, and L'Assomption, and government schoolmasters were appointed at St John's (St Jean sur Richelieu) in 1783 and somewhere on the Baie des chaleurs in 1786. Yet almost all of these schools were very small, rarely taking more than a dozen students and catering to well-to-do households. They can have had little or no impact on popular learning, and in the countryside, especially before the early nineteenth-century expansion of village clusters, access to any kind of basic instruction was almost entirely lacking.

Conclusion

While the English conqueror had first thought to continue to rule Quebec through its French institutions and had relaxed prohibitions against the holding of office by Catholics to do so, an increasingly unruly

people made the strategy of governing through popular ignorance un-
appealing, especially in the wake of the American war and the French
Revolution. Yet the best chance of disciplining the people in secular
schools – and of assessing property and levying taxes to do so – was abandoned by the imperial government, even as the franchise was extended
to illiterates. British North America did not usually receive sustained
attention from imperial governments. In the 1790s, imperial Tories had
a vague idea that the Church of England should be established in the
colony and that it should organize parish schools. As the following chapter shows, such a project proved chimerical. Yet the sporadic pursuit of it
helped reproduce popular ignorance for several decades more.

2

The Eunuch in the Harem:
School Politics, 1793–1829

Having abandoned William Smith's project for a secular public school system, the imperial government and its colonial executive undertook a half-hearted and incoherent attempt to confide the schooling of the people to the Church of England. Legislation to that effect was passed in 1801, but the administrative body needed to put it into effect was not created for almost twenty years. In the intervening period, the executive adopted the legally dubious practice of funding select Anglican schools out of general revenue. Intense opposition from the Catholic Church and from much of the laity, combined with a lack of resources, ensured that this attempt faltered and was abandoned. The Catholic Church opposed what it saw as a Protestant incursion into its domain but itself had no interest in offering substantial schooling to the people.

Repeated attempts in the 1810s and 1820s by an increasingly assertive Legislative Assembly to put in place some sort of parish school system were consistently blocked. Most commonly the Legislative and Executive Councils, dominated by merchant capital and seigneurial property, opposed incorporating local government bodies to manage schooling and to impose school taxes. Some schemes failed in the Assembly, as the seigneurial faction there opposed property taxation; as the majority refused to grant administrative powers to executive government; or as members were seduced by promises of the Catholic Church to educate the people. Perhaps the most promising plan for a parish school system in 1821–2 was sideswiped by the Colonial Office's attempt to resolve struggles between the Assembly and the executive over the expenses of government (the Civil List), which the Assembly refused to vote without rights of oversight.

The Episcopal churches blocked each other's educational initiatives wherever they could before about 1820, but they also cooperated to impede lay efforts to school the towns and the countryside. Their most significant success was in destroying the efforts of a broad urban alliance to organize monitorial schooling through a Montreal and Quebec Free School Society. Yet by the 1820s, it was obvious to Anglican educational activists that they could not achieve an educational monopoly. Their dreams of schooling Catholics faded as they faced growing competition for Protestant loyalties from Methodists, Baptists, and other sects.[1] At the same time, the Catholic Church received legislative authorization to use vestry funds to subsidize rural schools, but its clergy did little. With the encouragement of the colonial executive, the Episcopal churches then tried to work out a scheme to share responsibility for schooling the people. Convoluted negotiations resulted in draft legislation to that effect in 1829.

Lay exasperation with the two churches intensified. The Anglicans were seen as bloated sinecurists, sucking up public resources while offering an expensive education to a select few. The Catholic clergy argued that it was forced to keep the peasantry ignorant to protect it from Protestantism, but given the means to organize its own rural schools, it made no serious effort to do so. One political commentator compared the Catholic Church to a eunuch in a harem. At the same time, political antagonism between legislature and executive increased under the maladroit administration of Lord Dalhousie. His eight-year reign, which ended in 1828, was marked by a failed attempt to reunite Upper and Lower Canada in 1822, by a botched effort to encourage the transformation of seigneurial into socage tenures – which would have made the seigneurs sole proprietors of ungranted lands – and by repeated battles over state finance with the Assembly. Other liberalizing initiatives, such as the making of a detailed census, were blocked or eviscerated by the executive, while the Assembly became intransigently opposed to the extension of administrative organization.

By the end of his regime, Dalhousie was effectively incapable of governing with parliament. His colonial opponents, organized in a new *parti patriote*, launched a monster petition against his rule in the winter of 1827–8. An imperial parliamentary Canada Committee, in which the rising Radical faction of the opposition Whig party played an important role, rehearsed colonial grievances. While it had some harsh words for the tactics of the Assembly, it thoroughly condemned the Dalhousie policy. The Committee resolved that the imperial government should not intervene in local colonial politics in matters not affecting the trade or foreign policy of Great Britain, but rather should respect the wishes of the colonial legislature. It urged modifications to the colonial Councils to make them more popular, encouraged attention to education and land reform, and recommended that all sources of colonial revenue be ceded to the legislature in exchange for a permanent Civil List.

As a new governor, Sir James Kempt, began to act in keeping with the Committee's recommendations, the plan of the Episcopal churches to monopolize schooling came before the legislature. In a move which has puzzled historians, but which this chapter explains, the Legislative Assembly rejected the plan and substituted its own secular Trustees School Act in 1829.

Jacob Mountain and the Royal Institution

On the eve of the wartime loyalty scare of the 1790s, the Church of England's newly created See of Quebec received its first bishop, Jacob Mountain, former secretary to the Bishop of London and associate of William Pitt. Mountain arrived in the colony in November 1793 with a large entourage. To his enormous indignation, there was little that could be called a Church of England in the colony. Although the new bishop liked to think of his institution as 'the established church,' there was no establishment: no cathedral, no bishop's palace, no legally erected parishes, no tithe, no schools, no poor law, and, besides himself and his brother, nine clergymen, five only of these in Lower Canada, and three of them French-speaking.[2]

Eighteenth-century English imperial policy had prevented the installation of the state church in the American colonies. Only after the American war did the Church create North American dioceses, and then efforts on the part of the imperial government to replicate the Church's English position in the colonies were haphazard and inconsistent. Even strong Canadian proponents of the Church of England argued that it should have 'as much *splendour* and as little *power* as possible.'[3] By contrast, although it was understaffed and under stress, the colonial Catholic Church had its own network of priests, parishes, women religious, and seminaries, and the right to tithe. Criminal sanctions were imposed on anyone guilty of disturbing church services. Shortly after Mountain's arrival, the Catholics received a boost in manpower from a contingent of ideologically committed French Royalist priests.

Nonetheless, Jacob Mountain used a seat on the Lower Canadian Executive Council to agitate for the extension of the rights and privileges of his church and to promote its claims to a monopoly of state-supported education in the colony.[4] Rebuffed initially, he declaimed repeatedly about the necessity of establishing parish and grammar schools under Anglican control. 'At present,' he wrote formally to Lord Dorchester in the summer of 1795, 'it is a matter of sufficient notoriety that either from incapacity or inattention in the Parties employed there is not a Gramr School in the Province that is worthy of the name, – that of inferior Schools there are none wch proceed upon the [Anglican] principles stated above. The abuse is of great public moment.' There was a pressing necessity to lead 'the inhabitants to embrace by degrees the Protestant Religion, & to bring up their Children in it.' If that could be done, 'in a few years it would form a new race of subjects & of Christians in this Country' and the 'gradual introduction of English acquirements, English habits & English sentiments ... would dispel the thick cloud of bigotry & prejudice which rests upon the country, & break down the partition wall which divides the *English* from the *Canadian* inhabitants.'[5]

In reality, a successful strategy of assimilation under the direction of a Protestant state church in Lower Canada was extremely unlikely from the outset. Mountain had few of the powers of the Church of England in the imperial country. The government lawyers ruled that there was no tithe for his church; that the bishop had no power to erect parishes, to establish a Church court, or to issue marriage licences; and that the churchwardens in existence in Quebec, Sorel, Trois-Rivières, and Montreal were not corporations and had no power to convoke their parishioners or to assess them for church purposes. Worse, the attorney general ruled in 1795 that the French law was in effect in the colony and 'it recognizes the Church of Rome only.'[6]

Still, Mountain hatched a scheme for the establishment of an Anglican-dominated corporation which he hoped would take control over the Jesuits' Estates and over colonial schooling. He was aided by Attorney General John Sewell, Civil Secretary Herman Ryland, several other Executive Councillors, and by a receptive governor, Robert Shore Milnes, who took office in July 1799. Mountain first secured the Colonial Office's approval for government salaries for schoolmasters in the main towns, and then produced a report outlining a more general plan for parish schools. To Milnes, Mountain wrote of the absence of schools, except for girls, outside the towns, and of the dangerous divide which existed because the mass of the population did not understand English. He urged the government to appoint schoolmasters in all places with a considerable population and to appoint commissioners to oversee them. The American border region especially needed resident clergymen, for without them the English inhabitants would either have no religious teaching or, worse, be subjected to American 'Enthusiasts,' well-known advocates of democracy. 'It appears to be extremely desirable in a Political, no less than in a Religious point of view,' he wrote, 'to prevent Teachers of this description from obtaining a permanent establishment among them.' At the same time, Mountain called Milnes's attention to the pitiable condition of his co-religionists owing to 'the insufficiency of the present Place of Worship' in Quebec 'of which by sufferance we have the use, – of the indecorum of mixing our purer service with the offensive Emblems of Popish Superstition, – of the degradation to which our Church is thus subjected, – & of the manifest injury to our Holy Religion which results therefrom.'[7]

Mountain's school plan was considered in the Legislative Council, embodied in a bill and presented to the Legislative Assembly, where it produced one of the first major political conflicts in this still new branch of government.[8] The bill proposed to place the management of colonial schools under the direction of a corporation to be appointed by the governor and to be presided over by the Anglican bishop. A majority of residents in a parish, township, or seigneury who provided a lot of ground and built and furnished a schoolhouse could petition the corporation for aid. Investigating commissioners would be appointed, and, if approved, the school was to be recognized and its master's salary subsidized. The corporation would frame rules and regulations for school management, and teachers were to be appointed by the governor, to serve during pleasure.

The bill was strenuously opposed in the Assembly in May 1801 by a group of French-Canadian members led by the staunchly pro-British Clerk of the Court of King's Bench, Joseph-François Perrault. The group attempted to substitute an entirely different bill at second reading, which so outraged the conservative majority that an attempt was made to censure Perrault. He failed to have the bill referred for further study. In fact, the French-Canadian members could have commanded a majority against the bill in the Assembly, but, in an often repeated pattern, several of them were absent and some voted to support the bill. 'An Act for the Establishment of Free Schools and the Advancement of Learning in this Province' (41 Geo. III, cap. 17) was passed in 1801 and received royal sanction in 1802.[9] The corporation was to be known as the Royal Institution for the Advancement of Learning (RI), and schools created under the act were to be 'schools of royal foundation.'

Despite the explicit agenda of anglicization pursued by Governor Milnes during his administration (1799–1805) and despite a similar agenda pursued with more force and less subtlety by his successor, Sir James Craig (1807–11), it was 1818 before the corporation planned under the act of 1801 was named, and the Jesuits' Estates remained under the control of appointed commissioners until much later. The 1801 bill had been followed by a proposal from the governor to appropriate a large block of public lands for school support (as was the case in New York), but no lands were ever granted.

The failure of government to act in these matters remains mysterious, and the existing literature has not dealt with it. Perhaps, as was the case in Upper Canada, the executive opposed an administratively strong Church of England to avoid bringing the Poor Law to the colony. Perhaps it hesitated to empower local officials to tax property, given the belief that the New England town meetings had helped foment American democracy. Or perhaps Milnes and Craig were concerned not to alienate further the Catholic Church as war with France unfolded and fears of American invasion grew. Yet Craig was an especially enthusiastic participant in abortive efforts to subordinate the Church completely to Crown authority – at least until his attempt to suppress the new *parti canadien* underlined the useful influence of the clergy. In any case, the refusal of the Catholic bishops to sit on the board of the RI, as well as Bishop Plessis's later refusal to sit on the board of McGill College,[10] undermined this kind of educational project. By the 1820s, Catholic Bishop Lartigue was refusing categorically to associate with Protestants in public functions.

The practical weakness of the Church of England made symbolic politics especially important to Jacob Mountain and his successors. They agitated in the Executive Council and in correspondence with the governors against the Catholic Church's superior position. Mountain complained of the shabby material conditions of his clergy and about the arrogance of his Catholic counterpart in having himself styled 'Monseigneur – Sa Grandeur – le reverendissme, et illustrissime.' References to him as 'the Bishop of Quebec' in the public prints were illegal and should be stopped, Mountain protested, because they placed 'the Pope's Bishop (for such he is) above the King's.' 'The superior advantages which the Church of Rome is known to possess in this Province' hindered settlement and it was 'fatally injurious to the interests of the Government, to leave to the Romish Bishop, the entire Patronage of that Church; – to permit him to erect Parishes; & to do other acts of authority.' It was disgusting to see the Catholic clergy parade 'in pomp and ceremony' in the streets of Quebec.[11]

There were more direct skirmishes in the following decade. If it was not bad enough that the Catholic bishop appeared in the public prints with the ludicrous titles 'Le Lord Evêque de Quebec. Monseigneur L'Evêque de Quebec,' Mountain complained in 1813 that an English-speaking priest, aptly named French, had been trying to convert Protestants. Already two men in Quebec had 'fallen.' Mountain's nephew Satter attempted to reason with them and gave them some helpful tracts from the Society for Promoting Christian Knowledge (SPCK), which French seized angrily, claiming they 'grossly not to say impiously misrepresented the doctrine of the One holy, Catholic & Apostolic Church.' These actions amounted to 'TREASON' according to Mountain, and he warned that if the government did not act against them under the law, 'we shall be compelled to defend our Faith, by openly exposing the errors, the superstitions, & the idolatries, of the Church of Rome.'[12] Satter and Jacob Mountain complained again of the 'Case of E. Burnup,' a woman converted by the sisters on her deathbed in the Hôtel Dieu, brought back to the true faith by the Mountains and then horribly mistreated by the nuns. Hannah Radden was converted in the same place. Satter Mountain had worked 'to point out to her the principal errors into which the Roman Catholics have fallen' and 'remonstrated with her upon the guilt & danger of deserting the true in favour of a corrupt & superstitious Faith,' but to no avail.[13]

The Church of England was fighting a losing battle. Practically, administration and rule in the colony were already tightly bound up with the infrastructures of the Catholic Church. It was that Church, for instance, at the request of the executive, which warned Catholics of the political dangers of *Le Canadien* newspaper in 1810 and it was the Church that conducted a census in 1813. It was the Church which investigated the conditions of peasant households in the famine years of 1816 and 1817, again at the request of an executive concerned with famine relief. Without much hesitation, successive bishops had government proclamations read out after mass, held prayers of thanksgiving for the victories of British arms, preached obedience to the militia laws, and so on. Indeed, the relation was so intimate between the Church and executive government that Governor Sir George Prevost could write casually to Bishop Plessis in 1815, 'Your Grace, Have the goodness to put into French the speech with which I intend to prorogue the Legislature,' and see his request granted at once, apparently unconcerned that his political pronouncements would be filtered through the Church.[14]

Bishop Plessis was invited to present his thoughts on improving the state of the Catholic Church in the colony in 1812, and most of the suggestions in his *mémoire* of 15 May on the subject were enacted within five years. For instance, Plessis reported that the bishops of Quebec had always been respectfully recognized as such in the public prints, until threats were made recently of lawsuits; he wished this title to be formally recognized. By

September of 1813, he learned that his salary would be raised to £1,000 and that he would be now officially styled 'the Catholic Bishop of Quebec.' In the *mémoire* he said he also thought it strange that, as representative of 19/20ths of the colonial population, no Catholic bishop sat in the government councils; in 1818 he was sworn into the Legislative Council 'by the Style and title of "the Bishop of the Roman Catholic Church of Quebec."'[15]

The point is that colonial government could not delegate schooling to an official Anglican state church, and neither of the Episcopal churches was willing to cooperate with the other to school the people. That government should itself school population was not yet on the political horizon. Looking back on the period from 1824, the colonial secretary, Lord Bathurst, described the attempt to incorporate a Church of England body through the School Act of 1801 as a mistake.[16]

Schools of Royal Foundation

While the board which was meant to organize, supervise, and finance the 'schools of royal foundation' did not come into existence legally until 1818, and practically until 1820, successive administrations approved the creation of schools and funded them out of general government revenues, despite the dubious legality of such proceedings. The fiscal crisis following the peace of 1815 led the Colonial Office to look more closely at colonial finance.

Under the provisions of the act of 1801, steps towards the organization of a school were to be taken first by a majority of local residents, or by a number of residents sufficient to bear the cost, petitioning the governor for the appointment of commissioners. These commissioners would select a site and would draw up a plan for a schoolhouse, which was not to be larger than 80 feet by 40 feet, including accommodation for the schoolmaster. They would then name a number of local trustees – who might be the churchwardens – to estimate the cost of purchasing the lot and building the house, and to impose a rate on local residents to raise the necessary money, in the same manner as was done for the construction of a church or presbytery. These trustees or 'sindics' were granted the power to distrain and sell the goods of anyone who refused to pay the assessment. Once purchased, title to the house and grounds was to be made over to the corporation of the Royal Institution, and then the governor would appoint a schoolmaster and make provision for his salary out of the funds at the corporation's disposal. The schoolhouses were also to serve as venues for circuit court sittings and as polling places for provincial elections.

There was a legal problem, however, as Attorney General Sewell explained in response to one of the first applications for government support for a school. Under the 1801 act, the lot of land and the schoolhouse constructed on it 'must be conveyed to "The Royal Institution." But as that Body is not yet created' Sewell could 'not see how that can be done.' The appointment of the commissioners was 'a preliminary Step and therefore may be taken without any impropriety,' although 'in strict regularity' no teacher could 'be named before the School is ready' and the school couldn't be 'ready' until title had been conveyed.[17]

Nonetheless, by 1818, thirty-seven schools of royal foundation were funded, most of them in the Eastern Townships and the western part of the province, as well as in Gaspésie and in a few of the seigneuries. The schools reported 1,048 students in attendance at a cost of £1,883.10 stg.[18] It was rare to find a curé actively involved in the establishment or supervision of such schools. To the curé of les Éboulements, who asked in 1810 if he should agree to supervise a government school, Bishop Plessis replied that indeed he should 'if the government wishes to place under your supervision as curé, a school for which it will undertake to pay the master.' But if government reserved the right of inspection and the right to appoint the teacher ('and it cannot do otherwise according to the present law'), it would unwise to accept.[19] In several areas where foundation schools were established, skirmishes broke out over the management of the school, the content of the curriculum, and the language of instruction.

The parish of St-Joseph-de-Lévy, part of the Caldwell seigneury, was a rare Catholic parish to petition for the establishment of a royal foundation school, in this case as a result of lay/clerical conflict. Here, the prospective teacher was François Malherbe, who had been teaching in the region since his marriage in 1793. In 1802, when he was teaching at Rivière Ouelle, his students produced a loyal address to the government. Some parish residents invited him to come to St-Joseph, where he first taught a mixed school of fifteen students in a rented house, before his supporters installed him and his family in part of the presbytery over the curé's objections. To remove Malherbe, the curé reluctantly joined in a petition to the government in 1805 for a royal foundation school, which was granted.[20]

Terrebonne

There were two competing schools of royal foundation from 1811 to 1823 in Terrebonne, the parish and seigneury north of Montreal which had an ethnically mixed population and English-speaking seigneurs. One school had an English and the other a French schoolmaster. Terrebonne's schools have been invoked as proof that the Royal Institution was benign in its relations with French Catholics, since that body decided in 1823 to support only the French school,[21] but the case better shows in microcosm some of the struggles over popular culture and education that characterized contemporary colonial rule. Two visions of education clashed here: English grammar schooling, promoted by the Scotch and English seigneurs and wealthy merchants, and the mercantilist model of the ancien régime, with rudimentary instruction in Latin and French, promoted by most French residents, including the curé, a magistrate, merchants, and a number of illiterate men and women.

People around Terrebonne seemed particularly unruly to executive government and political activities in this parish had been a source of concern since the 1790s at least. Official ears were filled with rumours and reports of American agitators, French pamphleteers, Irish Secret Societies, and treasonous conspiracies at work. Much of the authorities' initial concern centred on the landowner and merchant Charles-Jean-Baptiste Bouc, who was elected to the Assembly first in 1796 and whom the executive disdained as leader of the political opposition in the Montreal district. Bouc was a man not to be trifled with, a rougher specimen of those upwardly mobile peasants, artisans, and professionals whose rise to prominence in the Assembly so disturbed those with aristocratic pretensions in the ruling group. Between 1796 and 1804, Bouc was expelled four times from the Assembly on the grounds of fraudulent trading and was re-elected four times, until a law was passed formally preventing him from sitting. An attempt was made in 1801 to have him tried for incitement for riot and, in that year of invasion fears, he was responsible for convincing the executive that in Terrebonne one Beauchamp (or Deschamps) had been meeting in the night with agents of the French government and had sought Bouc's help to organize an uprising. In a piece of amateur cloak-and-dagger work, the Executive Councillor Pierre Panet went after dark to Beauchamp's house, wrapped in a cloak with his hat pulled low, pretending to be the French agent in question. A stunned and frightened Beauchamp denied any knowledge of agents or conspiracies, and when Panet revealed himself and called on Beauchamp in the king's name to tell the truth, Beauchamp fell to his knees pleading his innocence. Panet brought Bouc and Beauchamp face to face the following day and concluded it was Beauchamp who was truthful. Bouc, 'this man at once ignorant, stupid, impudent and sly,' wrote Panet to Secretary Ryland, had been fooling the authorities in an effort to make himself important. Panet suggested his militia commission be revoked, but Bouc was at it again, stoking invasion fears in 1807.[22] Presenting the peasantry as ignorant and easily duped from its lack of education was a commonplace in elite discourse, yet the executive's profound ignorance of and remarkable credulity about local conditions were also evident.

The Terrebonne royal foundation school was organized in the midst of heightened political agitation between executive government and the new *parti canadien* in the Assembly, which had organized its own press organ, *Le Canadien*. School commissioners were appointed, named the Catholic churchwardens to be 'sindics,' and called on them to assess the inhabitants to pay for school property. The churchwardens refused to act. When one of the commissioners applied to the courts in Montreal for a writ to compel them to comply, the churchwardens argued there was no corporation of the Royal Institution in existence to hold title to a school. Attorney General Ogden agreed and urged the commissioners to call on Governor Craig to appoint school trustees directly. 'The Lot of ground may be then conveyed to them,' he wrote, 'and you may be enabled to proceed,' which seemed to solve the commissioners' problems, except that he immediately presented them with another. They had wondered where the money to buy the lot would come from if the sindics did not assess the inhabitants, and Ogden replied, 'I have only to refer you to the Preamble of the above mentioned act, to remove all doubts on that subject, the money must be taken from the funds there mentioned– "viz the revenues arising from the Lands of the Crown set apart for this purpose.["]' There were no such lands.[23] Somehow the trustees were convinced to assess property and to build a school.

The Terrebonne school commissioners, with other magistrates, were frightened by accounts of political disloyalty and popular disorder in reaction to Governor Craig's suppression of *Le Canadien* and his imprisonment of its owners and publisher on the grounds of an apprehended insurrection. They attempted to control popular reading, speech, and display. In late March 1810, they took depositions from a number of residents concerning seditious and treasonable practices in the parish and arrested a certain Laforce, who was imprisoned after an examination before the Executive Council. His crime was to have read out passages of *Le Canadien* to a crowd of parish residents and to have distributed the election song:

Canadians, your Representatives / Have caused to fall / The Judge who through stubbornness / Chased after it all. Rascals, to abuse you, / Make

frivolous speeches / Do not be misled / By such dull beseeches. When will
you dare to expel, / People, this scum / Which the Government would pay /
With the skin of your bum? / Vote for the Representatives / That the nobles
disdain / Lead them triumphant / All elect them again.[24]

Unrest continued. Roderick Mackenzie and Thomas Porteous, magistrates, wealthy merchants, both at one time or another seigneur of
Terrebonne and both involved in the promotion of the town's school,
were walking peacefully in the streets late one fall evening in 1810 when
they came upon 'several persons in disguise making much noise and
outcry to the disturbance and terror of His Majesty's subjects *Battant*, as
it is vulgarly called, *Le Charivari*,' in front of the house of the recently
married Pierre Lamoureux. The justice of the peace Jacques Oldham
demanded those in disguise uncover themselves, and when he tried to
seize one of them, he was hit with a club. Another of the demonstrators,
who 'was disguised in Petty Coats and on his head a Straw Bonnet and
armed with a large square stick,' was seized, uncovered, and revealed to
be none other than Jean-Baptiste Bouc. He was carried to the manor
house to appear before the magistrates, where in a rage he smashed the
mahogany table on which they were writing. They committed him to jail
in Montreal but he was bailed even before he reached it by Jean-Marie
Mondelet and came back to the parish to insult them again. They complained the authority of the law was thrown into question. If it had merely
been a question of drink and impulsiveness, it would not be so serious,
but Bouc was supported by many people in Montreal: 'Witness Young
Mr Papineau who countenanced his behaviour by obtaining his liberty
from the Master of the Police.'[25]
   Such political and cultural conflicts between the Scottish and English
merchants and French-Canadian residents over reading, singing, and
popular justice also played out in the domain of schooling. The English
school commissioners petitioned the governor directly for support of their
school, and in 1812 they were awarded a salary of £60 for their schoolmaster, Paul Joseph Gill, and possession of the schoolhouse built at the
parish's expense. Gill had been advertising his school in both the Montreal
and Quebec newspapers since the summer of 1811. It was an English grammar school in which he taught Latin, Greek, mathematics, astronomy, and
geography, in addition to the basics. Gill offered to find accommodation
for out-of-town students, and while he did not name his fees, his successor
wanted £30 for those under and £35 for those over thirteen years of
age.[26] The school was for well-to-do students and instruction was offered

in English, but the English Protestant commissioners were opposed by the French Catholic trustees: Gill's appointment was a coup which resembled their ongoing attacks on opposition politicians.

Early in 1811 and again the following year, Bishop Plessis urged the curé of Terrebonne, Jacques Varin, to open a school under his own control to take Catholics away from that of royal foundation.[27] Varin boarded a former seminarist named Augustin Vervais in his presbytery and placed him, with the support of the trustees, in Gill's school as an assistant to teach the French children. Sometime afterwards, Vervais moved into a rented house and the trustees complained to the governor that Gill's school, which they had built at their own expense, was of no benefit to them. Gill's exorbitant fees meant that only six or eight of his students were parish residents. Had the trustees been charged with supervision of the school, as the act of 1801 intended, they said they would have made it a parish free school. Seventy or so parish residents now joined them to petition for a second school in the parish, arguing that the large population made this necessary. They wanted not a grammar schoolmaster like Gill, but 'a French and Latin school master,' and since Augustin Vervais was now teaching in this way in a rented house under the supervision of the curé and the churchwardens, they wanted him to be appointed as their government schoolmaster.

Getting wind of these proceedings before the petition was delivered to government, Roderick Mackenzie warned against naming Vervais as anything other than Gill's assistant. 'Everything that Catholics could do was done by them in opposition to the establishment of this School,' he claimed, and if Vervais got his own school, Gill's 'excellent School could not long survive,' for two such different schools under one roof was an impossibility. In fact, 'during the time Mr.Gill employed him as an assistant,' Vervais 'used to take his hat and leave the School while Mr. Gill taught the English and Scotch Catechisms. A worse example than this Mr Vervais could not shew.' Still they wanted both masters to teach in the parish schoolhouse, which was large enough to accommodate all parish children. The response of government – a gesture to Mackenzie or a discouragement to the trustees, or both – was that the appointment of a second master was possible if the trustees would provide a second schoolhouse with accommodation for him. 'Will it not tend to perpetuate that Distinction – of Nation, English & Canadian, which it were so desirable should be forgotten for ever,' if a second house were built, asked the trustees? And if they did build, would they be compensated for the first building they paid for, which was of no use to them? They were told a second building was required and they would not be compensated for the first one.

Nonetheless, the trustees responded within six months that their new school was ready, 'situate upon the main Street, in the Centre of the Village, and consists of a School-Room 24 feet long, by 15 feet wide, with a Hall, Bed-Chamber & Kitchen for the accommodation of the Master.' They called for the appointment of Vervais as their schoolmaster and, after taking the oath of allegiance and paying the requisite fee, Vervais took up his commission on 31 December 1814. The following month he advertised that in his 'capacity as Preceptor established by the Government' he would willingly teach French to a few English boarding students. In the summer of 1816 he petitioned unsuccessfully for an increase in his £50 annual salary, claiming he was teaching sixty-seven students.[28]

Thus far, the Terrebonne case demonstrates not the tolerance of the Royal Institution, but the failure of the English-speaking elite to control the schooling of the majority, even with the backing of the executive. It also vindicates the claims of the Catholic clergy that the Royal Institution was an anglicizing, proselytizing body. Gill was not only teaching in English, but he was teaching Protestant catechisms when the Catholic students were present.

In 1823, faced with pressure from the Assembly to trim its expenditure and unable to justify two schools in a single village, the board of the Royal Institution ordered Augustin Vervais to take the vacant school in St-Joseph-de-Lévy and instructed James Walker, now the English teacher, to teach in French or to hire an assistant who could do so. This decision produced such an outcry that less than a month later Vervais was re-appointed for Terrebonne, given a salary increase, and told to hire an English-language assistant, while Walker was ordered to St-Joseph. Walker was particularly incensed at such treatment, claiming it was the French residents who opposed the Royal Institution and it was they who made it a notorious failure. After twenty years in operation, what was supposedly a parish school system had schoolmasters in only 37 of the colony's 200 parishes. From Trois-Rivières to Hull there were only four schoolmasters, and in his own county, which had a population of over 1,400, the board was now willing to support only one school! Moreover, more than half of those supposed to be in attendance as free scholars in the French schools 'do not attend regularly, and the greater part there are grounds to suspect are seldom there, nor does the Master trouble himself much about them.' In his own case, 'the other day, a boy of twelve years of age entered my school, who had been a year in the French School. I was surprized to find that he scarcely knew a letter of the Alphabet, the more so as he appeared to be a boy of whose abilities I at first sight formed a favorable opinion, and asked how this happened, "Le maitre," said he, "ne montre jamais a nous autres – cet les autres enfans qui nous montrent a lire."'[29]

The Royal Institution board was unmoved, perhaps because it supported mutual instruction, and Walker's protests came to naught. Vervais hung on to the school in Terrebonne for another three years, until he was dismissed 'on the grounds of gross incompetence & dereliction of duty.' The dismissal produced another tide of texts, with Vervais claiming that he had been systematically undermined by 'three or four individuals' who had been 'supported by some people dependent on them, some by lack of fortune, some by self-interest and others as a favour.' This was the by-then-standard language of corrupt officialdom working against the people invoked by the Assembly's *parti canadien,* and Vervais claimed that he had support in high places: L.-J. Papineau, Speaker of the Assembly, and D.-B. Viger were both on his side. Nonetheless, the dismissal stood. Bishop Lartigue found him a place in the parish school in St Jacques, at which he could not make a living. Later he taught under the act of 1829.[30]

The Terrebonne school continued to figure in colonial politics, especially in the 1830s when it was taught by the *patriote* activist F.-X. Valade. As a school of royal foundation it demonstrated the failure of the ruling groups to gain control of popular schooling. It also showed that here the Royal Institution was indeed a Protestant proselytizing initiative and that its appointed commissioners overruled local trustees.

Administration

The policy of funding schools in the absence of an RI board left administrative matters by default to the various civil secretaries in office between 1802 and 1819.[31] There was no regular inspection of the schools, no rules and regulations for school management, nor provisions for the removal of lazy or incompetent or brutal teachers. Several teachers apparently never taught anyone anything, and there were numerous and often serious complaints to be addressed.

For instance, twenty residents of the parish of St-Roch petitioned in April 1816 against their RI teacher's 'almost Daily habit of getting drunk' and against his frequent absences from the schoolhouse. The teacher, J.-B. L'Hereux, responded a month later that the claims about him were 'false and maliciously reported … from a spirit of hatred and revenge' and a month after that sent another letter to the civil secretary with a note from the curé confirming his good character, a statement of support from the current and past churchwardens, and a petition in his favour signed by thirty-six local residents. Secretary Cochran then wrote to one of the local notables for his views and this person supported the original petition. L'Hereux was dismissed seven months after the initial complaints.[32]

From the Township of Easton, residents claimed that Robert Chambers was so disgusting in his treatment of his scholars that parents would not send to him; they said he had drawn his government grant but had taught no one for three years. Chambers managed to hold on to his post for another four years, until the Royal Institution dismissed him for negligence and incompetence. There was the relatively straightforward case of Mr Green in Drummondville, who was 'perfectly insane' and needed to be replaced, but a more complicated correspondence, from Douglastown in Gaspésie, held that Jeremiah Shea was either 'an uncouth, overbearing, tyranical, brutal man, totally unfit for training up, Youth, in the path of education & virtue,' or 'a fit and proper person to educate our children [who] has exerted himself faithfully in the discharge of his duty as a Schoolmaster.' No one on the spot could adjudicate. There were many other more or less mundane administrative matters for the central government to attend to, such as the claim from a person in L'Ancienne Lorette that the trustees had not built a school; or the wave of petitions from teachers for higher pay as the famine years of 1816 and 1817 cost them their paying students and raised the price of provisions; or the attempt by one group to have a priest as their schoolmaster.[33]

Central government could not even keep track of its own schoolmasters. A survey of officers paid by government in 1817 revealed that John Sullivan Hutchins of Lachute received the government school money but subcontracted the teaching to others. In his parish, he wrote, 'we have been under the necessity of employing various teachers; and have almost constantly kept two other schools in temporary houses in convenient parts of the Parish for the purpose of instructing the youth in the Rudiments of Education, it being impossiable that one teacher would instruct the one half of the Youth of the Parish.' As well, given that there was no law to regulate the parish schools, 'we had recourse to bye Laws, Rules and Regulations, formed by a select Committee chosen by the Parishioners.'[34] Again, a convoluted set of struggles in Kamouraska began when the school commissioners sought to have Thomas Costin removed as teacher on the grounds that he spent 'in debauchery the precious time he ought to have devoted to the education of the children committed to his care.' Costin steadfastly refused to give up the schoolhouse, and there was no practical means to remove him. This situation also led to a petition protesting the lack of regular supervision of the schools and calling for government to produce rules and regulations and to appoint local boards of trustees to enforce them. In an example of fledgling teacher organization, Messrs Bingham, Laflin, and Baker, who were in conflict with their local commissioners over working conditions, petitioned the governor 'for directions relative to the Conduct of the School Masters in the Management of these Free Schools.' A 'monstrous doctrine!' declaimed the commissioners.[35]

The Challenge from Abroad

The Catholic Church did not effectively organize its own schools as a means to oppose those of royal foundation. It preferred to block attempts to organize them and to allow its clergy to open vestry schools. Very few did so. The two Episcopal churches were driven out of their lethargy in the 1810s by a threat from an alliance of urban laymen and members of dissenting religious groups, including some leading merchant capitalists and members of government. The group aimed to school the urban working class and the peasantry using the monitorial methods of the English Quaker schoolmaster Joseph Lancaster.

The catalyst for the group's formation was the visit of Thaddeus Osgood, an American college-educated Congregationalist missionary, who came to Lower Canada in 1807 and toured some of the rural settlements distributing Protestant religious tracts and elementary books for children. He claimed initially to have the support of the Anglican bishop, but the latter, his Catholic counterpart, and some members of the elite saw Osgood as a dangerous Methodist bent on spreading democratic and enthusiastic doctrines among the unwary. At least from the 1790s, the press had been denouncing such men as 'the lowest class of the people, whom a little learning has made mad or cunning, and who prefer the indolent labour of their heads, to the more irksome employment of their hands.' 'O.E.D.' ranted in the *Quebec Mercury* in 1808 against these vulgar, uncouth, and aggressive Americans who were not even 'ashamed to go, with the effrontery of Satan, from family to family, and tavern to tavern, preaching Allen's Bible and Paines' age of Reason.' They were introducing corruption to the French Canadians, of whom O.E.D wrote, 'no civilized people are so illiterate and ignorant, in a body, as they, yet as liberty and equality have not got a footing in their minds (excepting such as frequent the States) they continue, to this day, a polite and mannerly people, in the midst of ignorance.' Thaddeus

Osgood's activities earned him a stinging denunciation in the Montreal press. The *Gazette* warned that he had come to the colony with the support of a society in Massachusetts to subject 'Canada to the spiritual authority of the United States' and to introduce 'enemies of all order and subordination cradled in the lap of republicanism.' He was compelled to meet government authorities to allay fears that he was a political subversive.[36]

Osgood solicited funds from the public and from government for the production and distribution of children's books and elementary reading cards. He lectured in Quebec (in the Methodist chapel) and in Montreal on the importance of non-sectarian elementary education for the poor and he contracted with the Quebec printer and politician John Neilson to print material for him and to act as his retail agent. His books were on display in Neilson's shop so that people could see that there was nothing in them harmful to religion or society, and Osgood claimed they could not fail 'in correcting the morals and improving the minds of such as are destitute of the means of improvement.' His project attracted the interest of a number of leading Quebec merchant capitalists, Executive Councillors, MPPs, and moderate clergymen, such as Alexander Spark and David Wilkie, all of whom were alive to the social challenges resulting from the wartime economic boom, including the increase in urban pauperism and proletarianization. Osgood elaborated a plan for the establishment of a book society in Quebec and late in 1812 left the colony for England on a fund-raising tour.[37]

In a precocious example of 'learning from abroad,' Osgood used part of his time 'to travel & view all the most distinguished schools & newest improvements,' including those in 'Scotland, Ireland, and all the most populous towns in England.' He collected the enormous sum of £1700 stg. by aligning his Society for Promoting the Education of the Poor with the non-sectarian British and Foreign School Society (BFSS). By 1814, the latter was fighting a losing battle in England against the Church of England's educational arm, the National Society, in the struggle for working-class education, but it had begun to interest itself actively in colonial education. Leading members of the Society met in London in May 1814 and resolved that money be raised and spent on schools and teacher training in Canada 'on such liberal principles as shall embrace the whole community.' The schools should adopt Joseph Lancaster's 'British system' of instruction, and a Canadian committee of representatives of all religious denominations should be appointed to oversee them. As it would do on other occasions, the London meeting then named without prior consultation the governor, the Anglican and Catholic bishops, and some of their clergy, as well as the Presbyterian Alexander

Spark, as a Canadian Committee. If any refused to accept (all but Spark did so), Osgood was authorized to enlist other committee members 'of known respectability' to prevent delay in starting schools. What was to be the Canadian Free School Society should then add a ladies' committee and should organize two boys' and girls' schools, one of each in Montreal and Quebec. Robert Johnston, a twenty-year-old who had 'been for some Time engaged in the Schools in the Borough Road and at Bristol,' was to accompany Osgood at an annual salary of £120. Osgood himself was recommended to the care of Governor Prevost by Joseph Fox, the wealthy Baptist president of the BFSS, who also explained that Robert Johnston had been 'trained by the Society in the practice of the British System of Education; which possesses the essential advantage of uniting persons of all religious persuasions.' Prevost was urged to aid Osgood's goal of realizing King George III's wish '"That every poor child in his Dominions, should be taught to read his Bible."'[38]

In Quebec in June 1814, a meeting at the Union Hotel with Claude Dénéchau in the chair appointed a temporary management committee for Canadian schools, consisting of Osgood, Spark, Neilson, François Blanchet, and Col. Têtu. A permanent committee including these men, with the addition of John Caldwell, Ross Cuthbert, and William Coltman, with John Mure as president, was formed the following year. The School Society's membership overlapped that of the Book Society organized at the same time, and the latter included two of Quebec's leading (and competing) private schoolmasters, Daniel Wilkie and Robert Collier. John Mure was centrally involved in both projects. By early October 1814, the School Society announced the imminent commencement of a boys' school in Quebec 'on the improved plan of Education, which has been found extensively useful in England and Scotland' and urged those interested to contact Spark or Osgood. A building formerly occupied as a theatre was fitted up for the reception of 300 boys, and people were told that instruction in the elementary subjects would be offered for free from November 1814 until May 1815. Candidates for teaching positions in the school applied to the committee.[39]

The Quebec Society had some initial success. It attracted about 200 students to the boys' school, but by December 1814 the girls' school had yet to open, and in February 1815 the school moved to smaller accommodations in the Lock House. The Society invited its subscribers to refer more students to it, and Osgood lamented the lack of good school accommodation in the town. 'It is a very extraordinary circumstance, that in this City, [there] are nearly 22,000 inhabitants' – a more than generous estimate – 'no building has ever been erected for a public School, for elementary instruction, accessible to children of all denominations.' He claimed the lack was costing the town £3,000 annually in poor relief and foregone wages. In April, he made another plea for public support in an article entitled 'Education. *For all classes of the Community*,' and John Mure solicited the governor's support for the Society's efforts. Shortly thereafter, Mure and William Coltman, another Executive Councillor actively involved in the Society, were appointed commissioners to the Jesuits' Estates, which might suggest some thought on the part of government to direct revenue towards the Free School.[40]

However, the Society failed to receive the public funding necessary to run charity schools on a large scale, and the bishops convinced Governor Prevost to abandon it in 1815. Its efforts at fund-raising failed and its initial funds were soon exhausted. Osgood himself was forced to take the post of government schoolmaster in Stanstead Township, where he worked for three years. In April 1817, the school's assistant master, Clément Cazeau, who had been appointed in mid-1815 to teach in French, was let go. An appeal to the legislature did not result in a grant, and while Johnston continued to advertise the 'Free School on the British System of Education' until May 1817, he soon moved to Kingston, Upper Canada, to teach for the Midland District School Society. In August, the Quebec Free School closed for good.[41]

Less information has survived about the Montreal Free School. We know that several months before the Quebec school was started a teacher named James Edwards advertised a school in St Eloi Street taught on the 'LANCASTRIAN System' and invited people to visit it. As the Quebec school opened its doors, the press announced that Mr Gibb or Mr McGinnis would furnish tickets of admission to a school for 300 students that was opening in Montreal. Tuition was set at $1 a quarter for elementary subjects; boys and girls would be accommodated in separate rooms and a night school was also planned. The Gibb in question was probably the wealthy Scottish merchant trader James Gibb, the same sort of person attracted to the Quebec project. In January 1815, 'a Friend to the Destitute' published a prospectus 'For Erecting a School House in Montreal. For the accommodation of all the Children of both Sexes, unprovided with the means of Education.' In the contemporary code for a Lancasterian school, the author stated that the plan of instruction was to be one 'which has been found most successful in Great Britain and Ireland,' and while moral education would be offered, 'no interference shall ever take place in the School, respecting catechisms and religious creeds.' No further trace of this project has survived, and Edwards did not again advertise his school.[42]

Consequences

These initiatives have largely been ignored in the literature, but they had three lasting consequences. They joined important members of the French- and English-speaking merchant and government elite with professionals, both Catholic and Protestant, dissenting clergy, and members of the *canadien* faction in the Assembly in the pursuit of a common project for secular schooling. Men of the highest social standing in Quebec society, such as William Coltman and John Mure, and their political opponents, John Neilson and François Blanchet, shared the conviction that colonial society would be improved through the free collective education of the poor and the working class. Such positing of a sphere of universal social practice beyond religion and politics and such mass discipline of population are constitutive elements in liberal-democratic state formation.

The initiatives also marked the beginning of the colony's 'monitorial moment,' which is discussed in more detail in the following chapter. The project gave leading members of Quebec society their first exposure to Lancasterian pedagogy. Three of the supporters of the Free School Society – J.-F. Perrault, John Neilson and François Blanchet (who may have been familiar with the New York Free School Society established in 1805) – became leading proponents of colony-wide monitorial schooling. Finally, the Free School shook the two Episcopal churches out of their lethargy. Anglican and Catholic bishops mobilized to kill the Quebec Society, attacked Lancasterian schools when they appeared elsewhere, and took some steps to organize their own alternatives in an attempt to monopolize the field of popular education. They both used the spurious – but effective – charge that non-denominational religion was godless, and that children not exposed to denominational religious principles would be incapable of acquiring any sort of firm moral, religious, or political principles.

In a letter to Governor Prevost in December 1814, Bishop Mountain spoke for his Catholic counterpart that 'after mature consideration' he thought Osgood's plan for educating the poor could not work. He noted that 'the Roman Catholic Bishop has, with great openness & fairness, declared his determination, not only not to accede to it, but to oppose [it] to the utmost of his power,' enough to kill a plan meant to embrace the entire community. Mountain proclaimed that 'Religion should be the basis of all Education; & more especially the Education of the Poor' and 'the plan of bringing up children without an attachment to the principles of any particular Church, will almost invariably issue, in their having no principles at all.' There was also the question of his associating himself with a lowlife of Osgood's sort. Without going into Osgood's character in detail, '& considering him solely as an itinerant Methodist Preacher,' Mountain thought 'it would be evidently improper, that the Bishop of the Church of England in this Country, should become his associate.'[43]

Bishop Plessis had written earlier to an agent in London with an urgent plea for an English-speaking Catholic teacher trained in the Lancasterian method. The teacher should be sent to Canada in the spring of 1815 so that the charity school planned by Plessis's co-adjutor could draw English-speaking Catholic children away from a school 'which has just been established at Quebec under a vast and dangerous plan.'[44] Both Churches would later respond with their own urban monitorial charity schools to counter continuing lay efforts, but such was not their initial response.

Schools for the Elite

In keeping with their shared vision of popular education as moral training for the people with sponsored mobility for a select few (usually boys), both churches sought first to promote elite secondary schools. The Anglicans organized 'Free Grammar Schools' (after 1819, 'Royal Grammar Schools') in Quebec and in Montreal, institutions which offered a classical education under a university-educated clergyman to fee-paying boys. A few students – typically respectable middle- or upper-class boys whose families had fallen on hard times – were accepted free of charge on the recommendation of some reputable gentlemen. The Cambridge-educated R.R. Burrage in Quebec offered 'A Classical and Mathematical Education, according to the system used in the Free Grammar Schools and Universities in England' from late 1816, with an assistant to teach elementary classes. Alexander Skakel offered a similar course in Montreal. He received £200 from government and was expected to take twenty students free of charge. His assistant was paid between £60 and £80 out of his own funds.[45] Later, both Burrage and Skakel would be involved in the management of the monitorial National Schools.

While Bishop Plessis had written to England in search of a Lancasterian teacher, and while Bishop Panet was supposedly organizing a school, no Catholic school for the urban poor appeared until 1821. Plessis was much more concerned in 1817 with the status of the College at Nicolet for which he sought letters patent. He did not mention that the College offered elementary instruction to some of its sixty students, preferring to stress that the classical course followed there, as well as in the Seminaries in Quebec and Montreal, prepared students 'practice to their advantage whatever profession might please them, either the holy orders, or the law, either medicine, navigation, surveying, trade &c.'[46]

Parliamentary Activity

While the Free School Society exhausted its English funds, its supporters promoted monitorial schooling in the Assembly. The American-educated medical doctor and scientific intellectual François Blanchet led the charge. An 1814 attempt by Blanchet and J.-T. Taschereau for a school act that would have provided £60 to any parish seeking a teacher had failed, but in 1815 the Assembly debated and lent its support to Joseph Lancaster's monitorial pedagogy. Some 1,500 copies of his work were printed and distributed to draw attention to his system. In January 1816, Blanchet proposed to revive William Smith's 1789 educational plan. The House passed a resolution calling for the establishment of a college and prepared an address to the Prince Regent on the colony's claim to the Jesuits' Estates. After a discussion of the costs of establishing a college, Blanchet proposed the creation of a £10,000 fund for this purpose, and, while defeated on that matter, he carried a motion to demand a copy of the will of James McGill, which had donated £10,000 for the creation of a college under certain conditions. Blanchet's aim was to ensure any such college would be non-denominational.

Blanchet's 1816 'Bill for encouraging and facilitating the establishment of Schools throughout the Province' was a rough copy of the school system in place in Scotland. It made churchwardens corporate bodies able to hold property for school purposes and placed the schools under their supervision and that of the parish curé or minister. In places without parish organization, the militia officers and justices of the peace could act in their place. Fees were to supplement a modest schoolmaster's salary raised by property assessment, as was done in church matters. After heated debate on the questions of taxation and of clerical supervision and inspection of the schools, the bill died on the order paper. There were complaints that Blanchet advocated a secular college but placed the parish schools under the direction of the clergy and the churchwardens. The notary Thomas Lee was one member who opposed clerical supervision, saying that it was unnecessary and that he, as a parent, was best qualified to supervise his children's education. He complained that he was slandered as irreligious by other members.[47] Blanchet also attempted to secure funding for Lancasterian schools in Quebec

and Montreal with the support of J.-T. Taschereau, but the measure was
denounced by others as a kind of state absolutism for removing parental
choice in schooling and for forcing cities to adopt a method the Assembly
meant only to publicize.[48]

Blanchet's educational activities cost him his seat in the spring 1816
elections after his opponents claimed his Scottish-style system would force
the *habitants* to learn English, while taxing them heavily in a famine year.[49]
He regained his seat in an April 1818 by-election and promoted another
version of his school bill. Blanchet acknowledged that he had earlier supported a secular college, but he saw no reason to fear the involvement of
the clergy in the schools. Yet other voices opposed any religious control
over schooling. The editor of *Le Canadien* thought that religion had no
place in a debate that concerned the creation of 'Parish schools to show
the youth of the country how to read and write ... to speak of religion
when it's a matter of education, is to set sail on a sea of uncertainty and to
run the risk of never making it safely to port.'[50] This lay position was a
decade away from success.

The School Acts of 1818 and 1819

The Assembly passed an act for the creation of parish schools in 1818
and a close copy of it again in 1819, after the 1818 act was rejected in
England. The 1819 act was then refused by the governor, the Duke of
Richmond. Both acts copied much of the bill which had cost Blanchet his
seat in 1816: the change in the Assembly's position remains to be explained, but it signalled a growing gap in educational policy between the
Assembly and the Councils. The acts made the churchwardens trustees,
empowered with the curé or minister to levy a school rate, to purchase
a lot, construct a schoolhouse, and to hire a teacher to teach reading,
writing, and arithmetic to all parish children without distinction. *Le
Canadien* commented that there could be no objection to the plan, for it
merely extended the power of existing corporations; it was perfectly reasonable that peasants should pay for their own schooling; and the public
would be able to supervise the clergy in this matter as it would any public
officials. To the claims of 'un Citoyen' writing in Michel Bibaud's *L'Aurore*
that no new law was needed because the act of 1801 was a good one and
the power of appointment of schoolmasters by the government had been
used modestly, *Le Canadien* objected that that act took away the historic
rights of the clergy and gave control of education to 'people who know
nothing of the country or its customs' (read, the English). The *habitants*

and the clergy undoubtedly wanted schooling, but they wanted it to be under their own control, 'and not under the direction and control of people with whom they are not acquainted.' *Le Canadien* argued the Assembly should petition the Crown to repeal the 1801 act, especially since the teachers appointed under it were 'people without morals or without ability, such that the schools remained deserted.' It looked to *Le Canadien* as if the colonial executive wished to make the colony immoral while keeping it ignorant.[51]

On the other hand, Attorney General George Pyke reported to the Executive Council that the 1818 act offered nothing to colonial subjects 'which they cannot more safely and fully obtain under the operation' of the School Act of 1801. The danger of the 1818 act was that it created a very large number of perfectly independent corporate bodies which were to have control over all aspects of local schooling. 'The correct Education and proper Instruction of Youth are objects of the first importance in every Country,' Pyke observed, 'and it is that importance which renders it necessary that they should be under the immediate guidance and controul of the Crown so as that the united interests of the Sovereign and the people should be attended to and preserved.' The School Act of 1801 had been reserved for royal assent even though it created only one corporation; Pyke recommended the 1818 act be reserved as well, and it was subsequently disallowed.[52]

As for the act of 1819, Attorney General George Uniacke noted that official instructions to governors stated clearly that assent was not to be given to bills containing provisions disallowed in the past; the 1819 act also created new corporations.[53] Uniacke thought an act like that of 1801 'would in Colonies where Knowledge is more generally diffused, be the most advisable course: in this Country it has not in practice answered the object, arising in some degree from the difference of Religion, and from the people not participating in any way in the selection of the person to Educate their Children.' It was for those reasons the Assembly sought to give local elites control over schooling, but its legislation 'does not leave to the Executive, that ultimate controul necessary probably in this colony to the security of the Government,' despite revisions made in Council, and accepted by the Assembly, to allow the governor to remove teachers on the recommendation of trustees. Uniacke, who was quite popular with the *parti canadien* leadership, thought the 1819 law could be made acceptable by giving the executive sole power to appoint and remove schoolmasters and to inspect the schools. In his opinion, such would be 'the best practical mode of Educating the people of this

Country.'[54] The majority in the executive preferred Pyke's position on the act of 1801 but took no effective action to organize schools.

The Incorporation of the Royal Institution

The Executive Council did act finally to incorporate the Royal Institution. The catalyst for this action by Sir John Sherbrooke and the Duke of Richmond in 1818–19 was not pressure from the people or from the Assembly for schools, but rather pressure from the colonial elite to give effect to the provisions of the will of James McGill. This exceptionally wealthy merchant and politician had died in 1813, leaving £10,000 and the forty-six-acre estate known as 'Burnside' on the edge of the Mountain in Montreal for the creation of a university or college bearing his name. There was a proviso to the effect that the corporation of the Royal Institution was to charter the college within ten years of McGill's death.[55] Early in 1814, McGill's executors petitioned the executive to create the corporation anticipated by the School Act of 1801 and in March the Executive Council recommended that a draft instrument for that purpose be created by the law officers of the Crown.[56] However, another four years elapsed before Sir John Sherbrooke's administration drew up the relevant instrument, another year passed before it was executed and appointments were made, and it was early 1820 before the new board of the Royal Institution for the Advancement of Learning actually convened and set to work.[57] In an earlier and parallel development, Bishop Mountain and the Anglican clergy were incorporated as the management body of the Clergy Reserves.[58]

The incorporation of the Royal Institution (RI) temporally reinvigorated Anglicans and led them again to fantasize about schooling all the people. The RI board was stacked with High Church Anglicans, presided over by Bishop Mountain, and effectively dominated by members of the Anglican Diocesan Committee of the Society for the Promotion of Christian Knowledge (SPCK) in Quebec. Joseph Langley Mills, an Anglican missionary, was secretary of both bodies, and one member of the RI board, John Richardson, was vice-president of the Diocesan Committee soon established in Montreal. The Quebec Diocesan Committee had been formed in 1818 by G.S. Mountain, and it moved to combine the SPCK's work of distributing Bibles, testaments, and religious tracts, of establishing libraries and encouraging parish schools, with the work of the other Anglican educational body, the National Society for the Promotion of the Education of the Poor, by organizing urban monitorial schools in Montreal and Quebec.

Once in place, the RI board moved quickly to inform itself about conditions in the thirty-seven schools it was funding. It circulated a questionnaire to its teachers seeking information about when they were appointed, what their salary was, where and what they taught to how many fee-paying or free students, who built their school, and if it was subject to regular 'visitation.' As a result, several aged or incompetent teachers were forcibly retired and others were fired or reassigned. The board distributed a formal statement of the conditions in law for the support of an RI school and warned that non-conforming schools would no longer be funded. It received petitions for the creation of new schools and considered the fitness of prospective teachers (ruling in the case of Miss Dalrymple that women were not eligible). The board formulated rules for school management and arranged to inspect its schools, where possible by a missionary of the Society for the Propagation of the Gospel (SPG).

The appointment of visitors allowed the new RI board to adjudicate local disputes relatively quickly. For instance, a number of Catholic residents at St John's (St Jean sur Richelieu) complained that schoolmaster Archibald Campbell refused to teach children free of charge and had only twelve students, while their teacher taught thirty and was likely soon to have some of Campbell's twelve; they wanted their teacher as government schoolmaster. Rev. W.D. Baldwyn was sent to investigate and reported that 'many of the charges originated in "private pique & resentment," & that no case has been made,' while the petition accompanying the complaint '"contains the names of several persons, who have no children to send to school, & that several of the names are forged."'[59]

The board's initial rules for schools seemed anodyne. Schools were to adopt a 'uniform system' of instruction and to use books from a list to be drawn up by members of the board's various religious denominations (there were only Anglicans). Local clergy were to visit the schools and the board would name a group to superintend each school more directly. Local visitors would report on the condition of the school and the conduct of the master every six months, before his pay came due. They were to examine the school publicly once a year and, initially, they were to specify rules and regulations for school management. They could regulate school fees and specify which students should be admitted free of charge. Finally, the schoolmasters were to enforce Sunday church attendance for the Protestant children. Attendance was to be at the Church of England, and the books to be used in English-language schools were to be those of the English National Society. These rules were soon supplemented with others that specified maximum school fees and required teachers to teach one-third of their students free of charge. Hours of instruction and attendance as well as the nature of the attendance register were defined.[60]

The board of the Royal Institution would insist repeatedly that it had no interest whatsoever in proselytism and that Catholic parents and clergy could manage their own schools independently and teach out of their own approved books. Helen Kominek, who has shown that the 'uniform system' of instruction to be adopted was meant to be the Madras System of the English National Society, which used the Church of England catechism and insisted on Sunday attendance at Church, suggests that the board was most interested in acting against the perceived threat of dissenting Protestant sects, rather than in confronting the Catholic Church at the local level.[61] Yet, however broadly or narrowly the Royal Institution leadership envisioned its educational project, it proved unable effectively to organize local elementary schooling; by 1824 it supervised forty-one schools, and at its height in 1829, eighty-four schools – a minor contribution to the schooling of a rapidly expanding rural population.

Opposition to the Royal Institution

The Institution was attacked more or less ferociously from all quarters. The colonial and imperial governments offered little or no substantive support, despite the former's vote of confidence in the 1801 School Act. The RI's attempts to secure permanent funding were rebuffed: it did not gain control over the Jesuits' Estates, and the school lands promised in the early 1800s never materialized. Government refused to pay its secretary's salary. Such treatment seems to embody the position of men such as Herman Ryland, that the church should have splendour rather than power.

The Assembly's majority *parti canadien* saw the incorporation of the RI as a move to circumvent the legislature's efforts to organize locally controlled, tax-supported elementary schooling and non-denominational higher education. It reeked of another attempt at anglicization, of an attempt to despoil the Jesuits' Estates granted for Catholic education and to keep the *habitants* ignorant of their political rights. The fat salaries apparently paid to under-worked Anglican clergymen-cum-schoolmasters were another instance of venality on the part of the executives' 'creatures,' and for some MPPs, the RI was even more obnoxious because it provided the Catholic clergy with an alibi for its own dissembling opposition to schooling the people. Already in a deepening conflict with the executive over the Civil List and over the executive's refusal to offer a systematic accounting of its expenditures, the *parti canadien* worked to reduce the RI's outlays on individual schools, from an average of about £1.10s. per student to 10s., while continuing to push for official sanction of its own school legislation.

The Catholic bishops undermined the Institution. Bishop Plessis refused a seat on the RI board, and both he and his suffragan Bishop Lartigue instructed their priests not to act as RI school visitors but to organize their own vestry schools. Priests who had quibbles were told what to write in response to invitations from the RI board, and it was made clear to them that to act as visitors was to make themselves into Bishop Mountain's lackeys. Some Catholic parents who sent their children to Protestant schools, or to mixed boys' and girls' schools, and the teachers who taught in them were refused the sacraments. While very few priests responded to the injunction to organize their own schools, fewer still agreed to have an RI school in their parishes; those who did saw the RI as a way of financing schooling without detracting from their interest in having a grandiose church and luxurious presbytery.[62]

The Catholic bishops were under pressure themselves from Rome to preserve denominational segregation in schooling and of their own accord saw the segregation of the sexes as a fundamental tenet of moral education. A papal Bull of 1817 had denounced the growth of Bible societies and had warned against the threat to Catholicism from Bible distribution. Both the Royal Institution, which mandated the use of the Testament at school, and the Lancasterian societies, which used scripture extracts 'without note or comment' for reading lessons, were seen as threats; already in 1817 one priest expelled a Lancasterian teacher from his parish by buying up the lot of ground on which his schoolhouse was located. Correspondence from Rome tended to mention 'Methodists' as a particular danger.

In 1820, Cardinal Fontana from the Propaganda in Rome wrote to J.-J. Lartigue that the Holy See had heard of the spread of Bible societies promoting mixed denominational schools in Ireland. If such were the case in Lower Canada, Lartigue was told to organize schools where the peasants and the poor would be taught free from exposure to such heretics. Also in the 1820s, Plessis tried to get Lartigue to produce a new Catholic version of the Testament for popular consumption. Lartigue delayed the project indefinitely, however, in keeping with his more rigid insistence that laymen should not have any unmediated access to sacred texts.[63]

In Defence of Peasant Ignorance

In this political climate, Catholic ideologues felt compelled to defend their stance on educational matters in the public prints, especially with respect to Lancaster's monitorial pedagogy. Their defence provoked a diverse lay reaction. One participant in the debate around ignorance, the flamboyant French aristocrat Chevalier Robert-Anne d'Estimauville, recycled the eighteenth-century criticism of public schools as breeding grounds for vice and promoted an estate-based craft education for the peasantry in the style of the ancien régime, whose relic he was. His position was easily dismissed as quaint.[64] However, the abbé J.-L.-J. de Calonne launched a virulent attack on the jointly obnoxious influence of the London Bible societies and the Quebec Free School. De Calonne was an aging French Royalist, confessor to the Ursulines in Trois-Rivières and curé of La Visitation. He denounced the Free School for removing religious instruction from the schoolroom and quoted approvingly Bossuet's *De l'indifférence en matière de religion:* 'Let us never forget, religion is the people's only education.' Moreover the monitorial pedagogy, 'by substituting drill for instruction, and by putting' in people's hands 'a silent stone [a denunciation of writing on slates], in place of the book from which they imbibed such lofty and important lessons,' was really 'worthy of a materialist philosophy.' In de Calonne's widely reprinted work, what the people needed to know, and all it needed to know, were the precepts contained in its catechism. The Lancasterian discipline of the body was no substitute for the consideration of higher things. Because it was the clergy's right and duty to teach the catechism, public schools were unnecessary.[65]

De Calonne's position was endorsed in *La Gazette des Trois Rivières* by 'Philateles,' who warned that the 'societies devoted to spreading the holy Bible among all classes of society' tried to improve minds without attending to morals! Philateles claimed de Calonne was not against education, and those who accused the clergy of wishing to 'keep the people in a state of ignorance' had only to look to the schools they created out of their own pockets in the countryside. Philateles did not number them.[66]

From within the clergy, a response to de Calonne came from 'le Campagnard,' the curé of Ste-Anne-de-la-Pocatière, Charles-François-Painchaud, who would successfully sponsor a college in the later 1820s. Painchaud was especially concerned to debate the lay critics 'A.B.C.' and John Neilson.[67] What started as a relatively straightforward defence of teaching peasants to read the catechism and to write and calculate, which Painchaud said he supported, soon sprawled over the relationships among

education and religion, social class, industry and morality, comparative social structure, colonial history, imperial and ethnic domination, and the political interests of the Lower Canadian clergy, before ending with Painchaud
insisting that peasants were better ignorant than Protestant.

Painchaud tried to argue that since religious and moral instruction were
necessary prerequisites to literary instruction, education had to be under
clerical control, but his opponents countered that 'any man of good morals
could be quite fit to teach reading, writing, and counting, without being fit
to teach religion.' They claimed that there was no more relationship between 'religious instruction and the art of reading, writing, and counting'
than there was between 'religious instruction and tillage, shipbuilding,
navigation, military drill, or the most frivolous arts.' Indeed the editor of *Le
Canadien* commented that if recent improvements in pedagogy were dangerous, one might as well say 'we should burn all the water or steam mills
and go back to grinding grain by hand.' To another commentator, de
Calonne was harkening back to those halcyon days where 'the people was
bought and sold with the land; where it could be taxed and toiled until it
cried for mercy, as much a serf in mind as in body.'[68]

Painchaud countered his critics by invoking the horrors of the French
Revolution. It demonstrated the results of a philosophical in the absence
of a moral education. Morality was worse in proportion as European
countries lacked religion; for that reason in France the government had
banned Lancaster's schools in favour of those of the Christian Brothers.
Painchaud quoted from a speech in which Sir Robert Peel claimed that
English artisans were far more dangerous politically from their education than they had been from their ignorance and cited moral statistics
in support. Painchaud said his opponents – 'Liberals' and 'Philanthropists'
– threatened the safety of the political order with their plans, and he
concluded: 'A good catholic will never be a rebel, but one of your
Philanthropists will often be.' But if workers in England were more rebellious, replied A.B.C., who called himself 'a liberal – a friend to education,' it was not because they were more educated, but because their
condition had worsened; he made sport with Painchaud's statistics.[69]

In its final stages, the debate turned to Lower Canadian educational
policy. Painchaud conceded to his opponents that the *canadiens* were being injured by their inability to compete in the face of immigration and
the growth of commerce. They risked cultural and economic subordination, and a ruined people would not be able to defend its religion.
Schools were urgently needed in town and country, and if government
and people shared the same religion it might be acceptable to organize

government schools. The clergy did not oppose education; the truth of its support was evident in the schools and colleges it sustained. It did oppose the schools promoted by the act of 1801. They were controlled by the Anglican bishop and, had the clergy participated in the act, 'these schools would thus today generally be conducted by Protestants, and even by ministers, who would not have failed to drown them in Bibles.' He knew himself of two students who attended such a school, and while they were Catholics when they entered it, they were soon as Protestant as made no difference. His conclusion was clear: 'no doubt, it is quite unfortunate that the people should be so ignorant still,' but of two evils did not prudence counsel the lesser? After the failure of the 1821 School Act, Painchaud put the clergy's attitude towards the education of the people more succinctly: 'We are thus forced to keep them in an ignominious ignorance, or to endanger them at the hands of ministers or schoolmasters of a foreign Religion.' It was far preferable for the clergy to keep the bulk of the rural population ignorant for the sake of their souls and their cultural heritage.[70] De Calonne and Painchaud paid lip service to schooling the people, but defined education as the absorption of moral precepts under clerical supervision.

To a young Ludger Duvernay, editor of the *Gazette des Trois Rivières*, what de Calonne and Painchaud had delivered was a funeral oration for the working-class education that the Quebec Free School promised. 'Gentlemen as much of the Catholic as of the Anglican clergy have discouraged the only Lancasterian school established in Lower Canada.' It was a painful defeat for political improvement.[71]

Educational Conditions

For a time, newspapers editors such as Flavien Vallerand of *Le Canadien* were prepared to believe that the Catholic clergy was eager to organize schools but had been prevented from doing so by government or by the Protestant Scottish and English elite. Of course, as Richard Chabot has demonstrated, such was not the case. The typical rural curé believed that 'putting in place a system of teaching accessible to all' would have 'disastrous consequences for religion' and was apathetic about promoting schooling even when faced with his bishop's injunctions to do so. A curé's status in the Church and in the eyes of his fellows, Chabot remarked, depended on the splendour of his buildings and ornaments, and he related his own chances for salvation to the apparent blessing of a grand establishment. There was ample wealth even in poor parishes without schools to support lavishly decorated churches and chapels, and the curés themselves lived far more comfortably than did schoolmasters, even if church and presbytery construction were typically supported by the majority of parish landowners.[72]

For his part, Bishop Lartigue reassured an anxious Office of the Propaganda in Rome in 1821 that there was little danger from Methodist teachers in his district and that he was working with the Bishop of Quebec to counter the threat presented by heretical academies. He claimed that schools organized by the curés far outnumbered government schools, that Catholics were proposing new laws to counter Anglican zeal, and, if he got the support of his clergy, he would spare no effort in establishing more schools. Indeed, he said, more schools had been organized in town and country in the past ten years than in the previous forty, and were it not for obstructionist government, schooling would be ubiquitous.

Rome responded to this reassurance by sending Lartigue a questionnaire on educational conditions, which he was to distribute to his clergy. At least some of the results alarmed him, for there were many co-educational schools and there were many men teaching girls. He put a happy face on the results: there were 118 schools in his district, with a total of 168 teachers and with 3,712 students. Better still he wrote, of that number, 510 were boys attending one of his three colleges and a further 465 girls were taught in the schools of the Congrégation de Notre Dame. By contrast, there were only 26 Protestant schools and 12 schools under government authority. To a bishop whose conception of popular schooling was primarily one of moral discipline with selective recruitment to religious vocations, these numbers may have seemed cause for celebration: there were petty schools for the peasantry, and young men in the colleges could replenish the clergy. But to anyone interested in common schooling they were dismal: 2,837 elementary students was a tiny proportion of a Catholic population estimated at 200,000.[73]

Much of the press tried to define the contours of that dismal reality. A piece in both the *Montreal Gazette* and *Le Canadien* pointed out that while everyone in the colony knew from daily experience that education was seriously lacking, the malady stood out more clearly if one compared the numbers of schools and colleges with the size of the population in need of schooling. A generous estimate would find the colony had thirty-seven Royal Institution schools, thirty-two Catholic parish schools, eleven girls' schools run by women religious, twenty-five urban private schools, and three Catholic colleges. A similarly generous estimate would give the number of students in attendance as about 4,000. Since there was no population census for Lower Canada, one had to estimate population size, but the militia records suggested it might be 500,000, and given that in the New England states about one-quarter of the population was fit to attend school, there must be about 125,000 potential students in Lower Canada. Even if the colony had only half the school-age population of rural New York State there would still be 70,053 of school age. With 4,000 in school, there must be 66,053 not in school. 'We almost blush to publish it,' the editor concluded.[74] Again and again much of the press stressed the demonstrable uselessness of the Royal Institution.

The School Act of 1821

A remarkably tenacious Legislative Assembly again tried to craft an acceptable parish school act in 1821, sponsored this time by John Neilson, Reform MPP, printer, editor of the *Quebec Gazette,* and friend to the Catholic clergy. Rumour had it that this bill would be acceptable to Governor Dalhousie if it passed both houses of parliament. The Assembly's bill again created parish school corporations, empowered to hold property to the amount of £200, to solicit donations, and to manage local schools, but it modified the membership of the corporations so that they would include locally elected representatives in addition to the curé and the churchwardens. The bill was amended in the Legislative Council such that the corporation could hold only £100, and its membership was specified as the curé, the seigneur, the senior churchwarden, and the two senior militia officers, which reduced the number of elected members to one (and on a very restricted franchise at that). Further amendments obliged the school corporation to report to the governor, gave him the power to negate any claims the seigneur might have to the land on which the schoolhouse was built, and allowed him to remove schoolmasters at pleasure. An attempt in Council to specify that only Church of England clergymen could be school visitors failed, and Council accepted a provision for matching grants for schoolhouse construction. The Assembly accepted these amendments, which constituted a major compromise on its part, although the grant for schoolhouse construction was seen to be generous. As *Le Canadien* commented, the Assembly had no choice but to accept: 'By refusing these amendments, we would have had to stick with ignorance,' and the bill passed on 4 March 1821. Because it created new corporations, Dalhousie reserved the act.[75]

Both the Speaker of the Assembly Louis-Joseph Papineau and Quebec Bishop Plessis attempted to secure the act's sanction by writing to the

Colonial Office. In London in 1822 to oppose the projected Union of the Canadas, Papineau stressed the urgent need for colonial schools, while Plessis wrote to the colonial secretary underlining the Canadian clergy's support for the bill. Despite the fact – or perhaps because of the fact – that the act offered a real resolution to conflict between the Episcopal churches over schooling, the Colonial Office attempted to use it to leverage a solution to colonial struggles around state finance. Lord Bathurst wrote cordially to Plessis (in French): 'His Majesty believes it to be necessary for the general interests of the Colony to defer the consideration of this bill until such time as the Legislature shall have come to a conclusion on the other measures which have long been under discussion.'[76] The 'other measures' referred to the ongoing struggle over the Civil List, with the Assembly refusing to make a permanent vote of the expenses of government, and Council refusing to submit to the Assembly's fiscal scrutiny. Again in this parliamentary session, no agreement was possible. Dalhousie himself thought that there should be two separate lists of necessary government expenditures, one covering the bare minimum of offices necessary for civil administration to be permanent, or for the life of the king, and a second accorded periodically for fluctuating contingent expenses. London, however, seems to have joined the two lists and to have instructed him that no other public business was to advance until the matter was settled. Dalhousie was still able to cover administrative salaries out of the Crown revenue, but doing so left no funds for public improvements.[77]

Two immediate consequences of the reservation of the 1821 School Act were the organization of the Société d'Éducation du District de Québec, which is discussed at length in a later chapter, and the formation of the 'Association pour faciliter les moyens d'Education dans la classe des citoyens qui n'existe que du produit de ses mains, dans la Rivière Chambly.' The latter was an initiative of the legislative councillor and wealthy seigneur Charles de St Ours, supported by a number of clergymen and merchants, at a meeting held in the presbytery in St-Charles on 1 April 1821. The meeting lamented the deplorable state of public education and formed a committee of seven to solicit subscriptions for curé Girouard's new College at St-Hyacinthe. Select boys from the *habitant* and artisan populations would be chosen by the curés for a subsidized education, with the expectation that those able would move on to classical study at the Collège de Nicolet. A second association of the same sort was formed to support a new college in Varennes. Although the *Montreal Gazette* declared that the Chambly Association opened 'a new

era in the history of education in this country,' in effect the plan formalized and extended somewhat the model of elite-sponsored mobility for
promising peasant boys characteristic of the ancien régime. This was
called 'public education,' but it was not the education of any sizeable
public and it offered nothing to girls. St Ours and others of his class were
not envisioning common schooling.[78]

The Vestry School Act and Its Rivals

The 1821 School Act was never sanctioned, and the Assembly was left to
look for other solutions for the lack of schooling in the countryside.
Elementary school bills were re-introduced repeatedly in the years which
followed, all of them dying in one way or another: being left on the order
paper when parliament was prorogued, not making it onto the order
paper; failing in Council, or, in the case of Joseph-François Perrault's bill
of 1824–5, dying in committee from the opposition of educational activists in the Assembly. School money bills were accepted, by contrast, and
the Assembly began subsidizing a large number of urban school societies, colleges, and convents, as well as several academies and literary
and scientific associations. A more marked divide in educational conditions developed between town and country.

The exception to the string of refusals and failures was the Vestry
School Act of 1824 (La loi des fabriques), a weak compromise which was
accepted by some educational activists only as better than nothing at all.
The 1824 act followed the Colonial Office's refusal of Lord Dalhousie's
suggestion for the creation of a second Royal Institution to organize
Catholic schools and also followed the work of an Assembly special committee on the state of education, chaired by Louis Lagueux, the recently
named president of the Société d'Éducation de Québec.[79]

The Assembly committee examined the state of education and suggested improvements. It urged the Assembly to redouble its efforts in
regard to the Jesuits' Estates, whose revenue it thought could sustain
schooling. Its main report reproduced the testimony of a few Quebec
City educators and educational activists: Antoine Parant, the superior of
the Petit Séminaire; J.L. Mills, Secretary to the Royal Institution; J.-F.
Perrault of both the Société d'Éducation du District de Québec and the
Quebec British and Canadian School; and the teachers Daniel Wilkie,
R.R. Burrage of the Quebec Royal Grammar School, and the retired
petty schoolmaster Jean-Baptiste Corbin. While the three schoolmasters
spoke about their conditions of work – or, in the case of Corbin, about

his inability to make a living from French-Canadian families in Quebec – the action centred on Parant, Mills, and Perrault. They offered a rehearsal of the debilitating denominational antagonism that blocked popular schooling, and Perrault pointed to a lay solution.

Each spoke in support of a particular educational project – Parant in support of what became the Vestry School Act, Mills in defence of the Royal Institution, and Perrault in favour of a much more ambitious and interesting project for lay schooling of the colony as a whole derived from the Quebec Free School Society experiment. Both Parant and Perrault attacked the RI, and we recall that Perrault had opposed the act of 1801 when it was originally presented to the Assembly.

The witnesses agreed on the lamentable state of education, although Mills claimed that the RI was making good progress in the Townships. Perrault declared that there was less rural schooling than there had been five years earlier because the RI had fired about half its teachers: no loss in any case, since they were mostly miserable, immoral men. By Parant's estimate, perhaps a quarter of the rural French-Canadian population could read more or less well, but a tenth at best was able to write, and pretty miserably at that. Even such modest literary capacity in the countryside was due to the efforts of the curés, and it was important that nothing be done to limit their powers. The lack of progress was caused by the Royal Institution because rural people had no control over teachers under the act of 1801 and, since the curés could not supervise the schools, people would not send their children to them. For Parant, the remedy was clear: parish schools should be established under the control of the curés and churchwardens and they should be funded by the vestries. If a law to that effect existed, 'soon there would be an upsurge of permanent Schools in all the Parishes,' which would then be generously endowed by various curés and by rich citizens. According to Parant, such people were constantly complaining that existing conditions prevented them from funding education.

For his part, J.L. Mills furnished the committee with a complete account of the Royal Institution's existing schools, its teachers, rules for school management, and its textbook list. In his version, educational backwardness was caused by the systematic opposition of the Catholic bishop to the RI. He refused to sit on the RI board, the curés refused to participate and replied vaguely or evasively when asked to explain themselves. As a result, there was only one curé on the list of RI visitors. Mills would have been able to point to the RI's rules to refute claims that the curés could have no control over RI schools, and one can imagine his irritation at Parant and Perrault's claims to the contrary. Still, the main problem in his opinion was denominational antagonism, and, while he did not expect cooperation soon, he thought the ultimate remedy lay there. In its absence, the best solution was to create separate Catholic and Protestant Royal Institutions. Such a policy would leave control over education in the hands of government where it belonged but would ensure appropriate clerical supervision of the schools.

By contrast, J.-F. Perrault sketched the legislation he was attempting to have introduced to the Assembly. The best means to improve educational conditions in this account was to establish a central board of elementary education in each colonial district charged with establishing schools in both town and country. Anglicans, Catholics, and Presbyterians would determine the course of study in their respective schools and all others would follow the plan adopted by the British and Canadian school at Quebec. Perrault put his plan's cost at about £3,000 per district.[80]

As the Education Committee was still sitting, D.-B. Viger, Bishop J.-J. Lartigue's cousin and a man friendly to the Church, introduced an act to allow for the creation of vestry schools. It was sanctioned on 9 March 1824. As amended by the Legislative Council, the legislation empowered church vestries on their own authority to acquire and hold property and to support one or more elementary schools in their parishes. A vestry could receive donations for educational purposes, but within ten years donations of land, with the exception of an arpent for a schoolhouse, were to be sold or otherwise disposed of. The vestry's educational holdings were to be limited to £100 for the purpose of building each school and to £50 for its annual support, with a school permitted for every 100 families. Until they could accumulate enough to establish a school, the vestries were allowed to divert a maximum of 25 per cent of their revenues to a school fund, subject to the usual regulations of vestry finances. On the third Sunday after Easter each year the vestry was to report on its school finances, the numbers of students in attendance, and the names of teachers. This was the act's only reporting provision, and the report went not to government, but to the district prothonotary's office, where any resident landowner was to be able to consult it. The act did not mention that in practice vestry expenditure was subject to the bishop's approval.[81]

The new law effectively removed the grounds on which the Catholic clergy had argued in support of peasant ignorance. Given Parant's claims, there were high hopes for it. Bishop Lartigue thought that it provided the basis for a new school system directly under clerical control. *Le Canadien* believed the 1824 act could lead to a rapid multiplication of schools if the vestries were zealous, although by June 1824 the editor had yet to hear of any new schools. Competition from new immigrants made it 'imperatively necessary for the native-born to enlighten themselves.' One could see from John Neilson's Val Cartier settlement that educated farmers could draw profit even from poor land, but 'if instruction does not soon shake Canadian farmers out of their old routines, they won't keep up long' with immigrants.[82]

Nonetheless, despite repeated exhortations from the bishops, the curés and churchwardens did little and very few schools were organized. It was impossible for the Assembly to discover just how few because when asked to report on the matter to an education committee investigating the workings of the act in 1826, Bishop Panet pretended that he had no control over the curés and no power to make them report. His successors would use this idle excuse when faced with later government inquiries. The 1826 House committee investigation resulted in a declarative act (7 Geo. IV cap. 20) increasing the amount of property the vestry could hold for school purposes. Two additional recommendations were not acted upon but signalled a growing lay dissatisfaction with the moribund, elite-dominated vestries. The first was to amend the 1824 act to give to 'give Parishioners in general Assemblies' the right to decide to establish schools, instead of making them depend on the churchwardens and the curé, and to order that a quarter of vestry funds be directed to their support. Second, if that right was accorded, 'it would be necessary to declare by law which Persons would have a deliberative voice and vote in said Assemblies.' The suggestion was that those persons be all landowners with property of a certain minimum value, and it foreshadowed attempts to democratize the vestries in the early 1830s.[83]

Joseph-François Perrault's 1825 School Bill

Before his attendance at the Assembly's education committee, J.-F. Perrault had drafted a school bill but could not find a sponsor for it before the 1824 elections. As 'Un Ami de l'Education,' he detailed it in a February 1824 issue of Le Canadien. The bill improved on denominational schooling because it provided for better rural teachers and for schools in areas where the religious denominations were mixed. Everyone knew about 'these wandering village Schoolmasters who run around the back country teaching how to learn nothing,' and Ami feared the vestries would be fooled by them, because in the parishes 'it is now quite difficult to find a committee capable of judging literary abilities.'

Perrault was not romantic about the self-educating people. His bill proposed urban district boards of education composed of well-to-do citizens
to organize schools and to train teachers. The boards would establish
schools in both town and country, and make all rules and regulations for
them, beyond some basic guidelines specified in the bill itself. Care
would be taken not to interfere with religious principles. All Catholic,
Anglican, and Presbyterian clergy and members of the two houses of
parliament would be honorary members of the boards, but without voting rights. The voting members would be chosen from subscribers who
paid 40s. annually and the boards would be very large: forty members,
divided into six separate committees, to deal with finance, correspondence, general superintendence, and Catholic, Anglican, and Presbyterian
education. The committees would meet weekly, the boards monthly, and
the latter would report every six months to their members, providing
statistical information. The boards would be incorporated so that they
could hold and acquire land and build schools, and the provincial treas-
ury would support them with a grant. The general superintendence committee would deal with applications for the creation of schools in parishes
with a mixed population, would regularly inspect schools and investigate
complaints. The schools would use the pedagogy of the Quebec British
and Canadian School.[84]

The scheme was supported in the press before it was presented to the
Assembly, in the context of a discussion of Michel Bibaud's projected literary magazine, the *Bibliothèque Canadienne*. 'Ami de son pays' wrote that the
success of such a magazine depended upon an educated public and again
described the plan for district boards of education. The state of New York
easily raised £70,000 from land taxes and it was ridiculous to think that
Lower Canada could not raise at least £10,000. Ami said it was shameful
that his countrymen could not attend school in their native tongue.[85]

Perrault's bill was introduced to the Assembly by Joseph Le Vasseur
Borgia at the start of the January 1825 session, shortly after Louis-Joseph
Papineau had won a contested election for Speaker. Borgia was one of
Perrault's long-standing professional and political enemies, but he was
moving away from the dominant *parti canadien* in the Assembly. He stressed
that the bill aimed at lay control of schools. The clergy had arrogated education to itself and 'he thought that had not been to the people's advantage.' While Borgia did not think the bill could pass as drafted, he thought
it deserved serious debate, and others echoed his position. Amable
Berthelot especially spoke in favour of the bill's encouragement of
Lancaster's monitorial pedagogy, describing it as important an innovation

in the field of education as was Newton's work in physics, while François Blanchet argued that the legislature should give every possible encouragement to the spread of Lancasterian schools.

But the *canadien* party leadership was against the bill, first because it empowered the towns at the expense of the countryside, and second because party conservatives thought the Vestry School Act was sufficient for rural schooling. John Neilson argued that the towns alone should not have the power to organize schools, that education should be left to the interests of individuals and to those who could pay for it, but that the colony should imitate the excellent system in the State of New York, where no educated child was a criminal. He spoke against denominational segregation in education. Despite voicing support for a New York–style system, which had a central board of education, he did not now propose that system: rather, the Assembly had passed the Vestry School Act in 1824; for the moment that was sufficient. Other leading party members took the same position, with Jules Quesnel arguing that the noble efforts of the clergy had given the colony all its educational institutions, and with D.-B. Viger declaring that the 1824 act 'appeared to him to be sufficient for the moment'; there had already been 'five or six schools established under this law over the past year.' Perrault's bill died in committee.[86]

Most of the education work of this session of parliament was devoted to investigations of the Jesuits' Estates and to the granting of subsidies to particular institutions, but the education committee also called for an account of the Royal Institution from J.L. Mills, apparently as a reaction to J.-F. Perrault's earlier charges against it. Mills reported that the RI now had fifty-four schools under its supervision with applications for more under consideration. All the masters save one were appointed according to the 1801 act, and their salaries ranged from a high of £100 stg. per annum in Montreal and Quebec, where each master also supported a schoolmistress, to a low of £11.5s. stg. in Stanstead, where the payment was only an encouragement. Mills refuted Perrault's claim that the RI had rid itself of half its teachers. Some had been found incompetent and dismissed when the board was first organized, but it was now impossible for any RI teacher to be paid without keeping school because a visitor's report was required before payment. Mills was especially incensed at claims that the Catholic clergy had no right to supervise RI schools. 'The facts are notoriously the reverse,' he wrote. 'The Roman Catholic Clergy in every instance were requested to superintend these Schools in their respective Parishes & in every instance but one they declined doing so; & so far from the Inhabitants themselves having no voice in the nomination of their Schoolmasters, it is the invariable rule of the Board to consult their wishes & to solicit their recommendation, before any appointment can take place.'[87]

More Vocal Support for Secular Schools

Perhaps Mills's replies to the Assembly reassured members that the Royal Institution would provide education for Protestants, while the Vestry Act would furnish Catholic schools. Yet Perrault's initiative for lay district school boards had considerable support among urban intellectuals and sections of the press, which worried the Catholic bishops. The latter, although pleased with the Vestry School Act, were facing a number of internal as well as external tensions beyond the lay challenge in educational matters. Jean-Jacques Lartigue's authority as suffragan bishop of the Montreal District was contested, both by the Sulpiciens in Montreal and by members of his own clergy, especially with regard to his discretion to move priests from one parish to another. The contest was made public by the curé of Longueuil, Augustin Chaboillez, in a pamphlet of 1823 entitled *Questions sur le gouvernement ecclésiastique du district de Montréal*, and while members of the lay elite came to Lartigue's defence, Governor Dalhousie, for whom Chaboillez was 'one of the few Canadian Clergy well educated, well informed & of affable well-bred manners,' saw an opening in this apparent discord for a reassertion of the Crown's authority over the Church. Dalhousie urged the Colonial Office to have the Crown license all Catholic clergy and to have all assignments of the clergy subject to direct government approval. The Colonial Office was already actively supporting the efforts of the Society for the Propagation of the Gospel to distribute Bibles and Testaments in the colony. Moreover, Dalhousie saw both Bishops Plessis and Lartigue as lying political schemers, as shown by their intervention against the Union Bill of 1822. Lartigue seemed particularly obnoxious because of his extensive family connections in the *parti canadien*.[88]

The Catholic bishops also faced a renewed challenge from the seemingly irrepressible Thaddeus Osgood. This time, Osgood raised funds in England for a new educational association 'For the Promotion of Education and Industry among the Indians and Destitute Settlers in Canada,' once again affiliated with the British and Foreign School Society, and he secured the support of such highly placed imperial officials as Wilmot Horton in the Colonial Office. Subscriptions raised on both sides of the Atlantic enabled him to import two BFSS-trained teachers to Canada, along with a large number of tracts and elementary schoolbooks. Bishop Lartigue faced what he considered to be outrageous Protestant poaching on the Church's Indian missions. At Caughnawaga, for instance, Osgood's school, which had been encouraged by Sir John Johnston, had an enrolment of over one hundred in 1827 before the Catholic missionary told Indian leaders that those who attended would be refused the sacraments. Osgood would continue his efforts at Lorette and in the cities.[89]

In the midst of these pressures J.-F. Perrault was stirring up lay opposition to clerical control over schooling and presiding over a Lancasterian school in Quebec. He had press support. As his 1825 bill was being considered, Nahum Mower's *Canadian Courant* reprinted a speech by Governor Clinton of New York in which he tied the safety of republican liberty to 'the great bulwark' of education as 'the culture of the head and the heart.' Clinton pointed to his state's impressive educational statistics and claimed that no child schooled in the New York city free schools (which used Lancaster's pedagogy) have ever been convicted of a crime. After Perrault's bill was sent to committee, Flavien Vallerand in *Le Canadien* reminded readers of Blanchet's failed 1816 School Bill and asked rhetorically, 'Will Lancaster's name be frightening only in Canada?' People had been talking about education for forty years and still there was barely one good country school. Canadians were surrounded by people making great efforts to spread education, but it seemed that there were still 'people to believe that the light of learning shall not shine on us.' It was past time that 'Canadians finally think for themselves and not through charlatans who aim to manage all their secular affairs.'[90]

Vallerand printed material from an aptly named 'Franc Parleur' [plain speaker], who complained that the Vestry Act was being used in the Assembly to claim that the problem of rural education had been addressed, but while Parleur had heard endless accounts of the good the clergy had done for education, it was surprising how little had resulted concretely. How was it possible, he asked, that the clergy managed almost everywhere 'to gild the Churches magnificently, to have superb Chandeliers and Turkish carpets in the nave, to have the churches and presbyteries renovated thousands of times and to add another thousand luxurious ornaments to them, and these same men have not been able to establish a respectable school in their locales?' He was not insisting that the clergy organize the schools themselves, 'but at least let them not act like the Eunuch in the harem, who can do nothing himself, and who stands in the way of anyone who does want to do something.'

Parleur also argued that it was necessary to give the towns control over country schooling because most areas of the countryside were unable to form competent school boards. His was a rare French-speaking voice (Perrault's was another) at this moment to point out that the growing reform belief in the self-educating people assumed that real people were actually capable of educating themselves, but such was not the case in the countryside. The people needed to be schooled, but it could not be left to school itself. Country places could have day-to-day supervision of their schools but should not control them, and especially should not control hiring decisions. He concluded by pointing out that Perrault was the president of an Education Society which had resisted clerical influence since its formation and also, 'mirable monstrum,' had been president of another society 'strongly supported by the altar.' Both societies used Lancaster's method, but the secular school had more success than anyone thought possible. In consequence, Perrault was removed from the confessional society and the clergy substituted 'a person who knew enough plainchant to dance to the Cathedral's tune.' Whatever the case, Parleur concluded, the Vestry Act was insufficient to provide rural schooling.[91]

The Catholic bishops worked to oppose Perrault's plan from the outset. Lartigue wrote to Plessis in January 1825 to warn him that the 'Quebec Philosophers' in the Assembly were determined to destroy the principles of the Vestry Act in order to substitute 'the bible system, veiled under the name of Lancaster.' He claimed that Perrault had become a maniac for the system and wasn't clever enough to notice that Borgia Le Vasseur and his pals wanted to use it to destroy the influence of the clergy. The latter, he warned Plessis, had not been sufficiently diligent in organizing schools. 'We must abort this new impious scheme,' he concluded. A month later Lartigue warned that the bill had obviously been written by a Scottish or Anglo-American hand; it had to be stopped and the curés had to be spurred to action. Friends of the clergy in the Assembly, Neilson, Quesnel, Viger and others, did stifle Perrault's bill; the Church's influence led to Perrault being removed from the Société d'Éducation; and Plessis assured Lartigue that his own clergy was busily organizing schools.

But then up popped Thaddeus Osgood again. His work made Lartigue complain to Bishop Panet in November 1826 about the dangerous laxity of the clergy in matters of popular schooling: 'I am indignant at the carelessness of most of the curés in my district on this point: why won't they take advantage of the 1824 parish school Bill?' Lartigue was exercising the Sulpiciens to sponsor the Christian Brothers' teaching order to come to Canada, given the wealth of the former and the success of the latter in Ireland, and he stressed again that 'the moment is critical; if these protestant schools seize our young people, there may be no remedy left.'[92]

For a Second Royal Institution

As with *parti canadien* conservatives, the colonial executive opposed lay schooling of the countryside. Instead, before the passage of the Vestry Act, Lord Dalhousie's administration proposed to sponsor a Catholic counterpart to the Royal Institution. Some eighteen months after the RI board set to work, Lord Dalhousie reported Catholic dissatisfaction with it to the Colonial Office and floated the idea of a Catholic board. After the failure of the 1821 School Act, Jean-Thomas Taschereau drafted a bill to that effect and shared it with Bishop Plessis, inviting Plessis to communicate his thoughts to Dalhousie. Taschereau was a commissioner for the creation of an RI school in 1815 and was appointed to the RI board in 1822. The scheme for a second RI had the support of the Church of England majority on the institution's board. The board had concluded that engagement with Catholic education was more trouble than it was worth. Leaving the Catholics to their own devices would free the Anglicans to concentrate on solidifying their position against potential challenges from Presbyterians and dissenting Protestant groups.[93]

Plessis was interested in pursuing the project, and Dalhousie presented it to the Colonial Office in June 1823, enclosing Taschereau's "Bill for establishing free schools and more effectually to encourage the advancement of learning in this province than heretofore," and asking if he was to sanction the bill if it passed the Assembly. In London, however, the Crown lawyer stressed that conflict was likely to arise from the existence of two independent bodies and advised against accepting the bill. In late spring 1824, having heard nothing of its fate, Plessis urged Dalhousie to push for the project while he was in London, and, while Dalhousie complied, imperial authorities also had in hand a memorandum from James Stuart, soon to be named attorney general in Lower Canada, opposing the proposal because it would strengthen the Catholic Church. Sir James Stephen's position in the Colonial Office was that work should be done in the colony to overcome the objections of Catholics to the existing Royal Institution. Lord Bathurst delivered the official response to Dalhousie in mid-December 1824, accepting the reasons Catholics might have for not sending their children to schools organized by the existing RI, and expressing a willingness to approve a proposition for their education, but stressing that he could not 'consent to its being in the shape of a corporation vested with the same rights as those enjoyed under the existing act.' Bathurst said he would never have supported the original legislation creating the Royal Institution and certainly was not prepared to support another of the same sort. In sharp contrast to policy in relation the rest of the empire, however, Bathurst was 'very ready to agree to a Bill for the establishment of Roman Catholic Schools.' The Schoolmasters could be Catholic and could be paid with public money, but 'these Schoolmasters must not be appointed without the consent of the Crown, and in case of misconduct must be removable by the Crown.' Dalhousie replied that he would pursue the project no further and shared the Colonial Office's rejection of the plan with the dying Bishop Plessis.[94]

However, the board of the Royal Institution was not content with the failure of the scheme. Nor, it seems, were Bishop Plessis or his successor, Bishop Panet – for all their assurances to their suffragan Bishop Lartigue about the enthusiasm of the Quebec clergy for the Vestry Act. The RI board petitioned the Crown in March 1825 for financial aid to defray the salary of Secretary J.L. Mills and to relieve it of the responsibility of providing schools for Catholics in Canada. The following year, Mills proposed that the way to allow Catholics to organize schools and the way for the Church of England to focus its efforts on its own flock was to create two autonomous denominational school boards within the RI.[95] There followed three years of convoluted negotiations, marked by caution and suspicion on the part of Bishop Panet as to the government's intentions, attempts to limit or circumvent the project on the part of a number of Executive Councillors, and outright opposition to the plan from Bishop Lartigue and from dissenting Protestant sects. In one of the ironic twists of Lower Canadian educational development, when offered a completed and workable plan for a Catholic committee in the RI in 1828, Bishop Panet insisted that the matter be submitted to the legislature, which then buried the proposed Royal Institution Bill of 1829.

Historians have been puzzled by the failure of this project, but to date no one has traced the course of events. Given that the province of Quebec ended up with denominational school boards, it is worth following the machinations that prevented their organization at a moment when the ruling groups actively supported religious control of schools.

Two Denominational Committees in the RI

In March 1826, Lord Dalhousie forwarded to Bishop Panet a set of propositions from J.L. Mills of the Royal Institution for the creation of two separate denominational committees. Dalhousie enclosed Taschereau's 1822 School Bill and Lord Bathurst's declaration that the bill was unacceptable and invited a response to the RI's proposition. Panet copied the material to

Bishop Lartigue for comment and then posed a set of detailed questions about the proposal to Dalhousie. He commented to Lartigue that he would not be surprised if Dalhousie simply did not respond.

The plan looked interesting, wrote Panet to Dalhousie, and it might well succeed while Dalhousie remained in office, but a future governor might not be as good as he. Panet then posed six questions and sought permission to discuss the plan with other members of his clergy. Would there be as many Catholic members of the board as there were of all other denominations? What would be the relation between the new Catholic body and the existing institution? Would the committees each make their own rules and regulations for schools, or would they be made by the whole board? Would the Catholic committee or the board as a whole recommend teachers to the governor? Would donations and legacies belong to the whole board or to the separate committees? Would it not be necessary to amend the act of 1801 to give effect to the scheme? Dalhousie passed the queries on to J.L. Mills and sent Mills's replies to Panet on 9 June 1826: the board's intention was to name an equal number of Catholic and Protestant members, although this depended upon the agreement of the government. Each committee would depend on the corporation but would be autonomous in relation to its own schools, for which it would make all rules and regulations, nominate teachers, and specify salaries. No property donated for Catholic schools could be diverted to any other purpose. Finally, Mills declared, it would not be necessary to amend the 1801 act if the proposal was agreeable to all concerned. Seeing all his possible objections answered, Panet stalled for time on the pretext that he was about to leave on his annual pastoral visit. He then sent copies of Mills's replies to Lartigue.[96]

Despite Lartigue's serious opposition to the plan, Panet wrote to Dalhousie in November 1826 that, 'convinced of the inestimable advantages of a good education, and filled with desire to procure it, insofar as it depends on me, for the people of my Diocese, I can assure Your Excellency that I enjoy a most lively satisfaction in the belief that the views of the Trustees of the Royal Institution agree with my own.' Nothing could be better in itself or truer to the original spirit of the act of 1801 than to have two separate committees, he declared, and he would support rules and regulations formulated by the board so long as they did not run counter to his religious principles or injure his flock. He hoped for a speedy consolidation of the project under Dalhousie's leadership. But then came the important question: who should be on the Catholic committee? In Panet's opinion, it ought to include the Bishop of Quebec and his co-adjutor, the vicar general of each district, the directors of existing educational institutions, and the curé of Quebec: at least nine Catholic clergymen, in other words, or more if one included all college directors. The governor might also name lay Catholics as he pleased.[97]

Three weeks later, Panet wrote triumphantly to Lartigue that the arrangements for the two committees were almost complete and that Panet's long-time adviser, J.-R. Vallières de Saint-Réal, a member of the RI board and of the Société d'Éducation de Québec, was arranging matters. 'When everything is settled,' he crowed, 'we will establish, as far as possible, schools in the country parishes and in that way we will paralyse the protestant schools.' There was no discussion between the two men of the benefits of education for the Catholic population; they shared the same ancien régime model of schooling. When Lartigue expressed doubts about the propriety of Panet agreeing to preside over the Catholic committee, Panet insisted that it was quite appropriate for him to do so and that Bishop Plessis would have done the same.[98]

Some of the press welcomed the initiative, seeing it as an encouraging demonstration of the growing possibilities for religious cooperation in the colony,[99] but new obstacles immediately appeared. Dalhousie wrote to Panet in December 1826 that he agreed entirely with Panet's position and that there would be two independent committees. He agreed to make new appointments and proposed to invite a number of current members of the RI to resign to make room for new members. Each committee would require its own secretary, who should receive a salary. An enclosed communication from the RI board reaffirmed the plan for separate committees but now proposed that the Catholic bishop be one of five ex officio members appointed, instead of the nine proposed by Panet. Moreover, since three Protestant members of the RI resided in Upper Canada, the board wanted to have three Catholics from the upper province on the Catholic committee. It suggested Bishop McDonnell, his vicar general, and Jacques Baby. If Panet preferred, however, the resignations of the Upper Canadian members could be secured and additional Catholic members from Lower Canada appointed, to ensure equal numbers on both committees. Altogether, they suggested a combined board membership of twenty-two, accepting Panet's suggestion that vacancies be filled by the governor when they arose.

Panet responded at once with enthusiasm, stating he had not meant to exclude laymen from the board in suggesting clerical members; rather he had expected the combined board to be larger than the current one. To give the new Royal Institution the status it needed in the eyes of the *habitants*, he had planned to name clergy from each district to it, but he was willing to accept a smaller board. If the number of lay members was to be at least equal to the clergy, however, it would be best to name people resident in Quebec who could actually attend meetings: the idea of appointees from Upper Canada was not interesting. Then there was the matter of who was to preside over the institution. It was reasonable, Panet agreed, for the bishops to preside over the respective committees, for in Christian countries the education of youth should be in Christian hands. But no single bishop could preside over the institution as a whole without giving offence to the other denomination. Moreover, since the corporation as a whole would be involved in temporal matters such as the administration of funds, 'the President or Principal of the reorganized Royal Institution ought to be a layman.' Still, if a lay president was not acceptable to Dalhousie, Panet was willing to accept that the presidency could alternate between the Catholic and Protestant bishops, so long as the principle of complete equality was fully respected.

Dalhousie pointed out in January 1827 that he thought a lay president a bad idea; in any case, Lord Bathurst had ruled in 1818 that the principal would be the Lord Bishop of Quebec. In his absence, the Catholic bishop of Quebec would preside. Panet agreed even to this arrangement, saying he hadn't realized there were official instructions on the matter. However, he trusted that the Catholic bishop would be an ex officio member and president of the Catholic committee. He agreed to a suggestion from Dalhousie that the Speaker of the Assembly, when a Catholic, should also be a member ex officio. Such an arrangement would impress the people by showing the cooperation of its principal leaders in support of the schools. Now Panet sent a list of his choices for members of the Catholic committee, five clergy, to include himself and his co-adjutor and six laymen. The people needed to see leading clergy in the organization if it was to succeed, he noted. For the lay members, in addition to the Speaker, he suggested Charles-Étienne Chaussegros De Léry, James Cuthbert, J.-T. Taschereau, Louis Montizambert, and Joseph-Rémi Vallières de Saint-Réal. Taschereau and Saint-Réal we have encountered already. Chaussegros De Léry and Cuthbert were both well established, wealthy Catholic seigneurs, the latter a Legislative Councillor, and the former recently appointed to the Executive Council. Montizambert was a long-serving Provincial Secretary and assistant Secretary. Together, Panet's lay members had wealth, prestige, and intimate knowledge of and direct involvement in the inner workings of government. Panet concluded the letter containing his list with the remark, 'I beg Your Lordship to have the goodness to place the final seal of approval on the arrangement as proposed.'[100]

Matters now seemed set between the churches and the administration. *La Minerve*, the mouthpiece of the Assembly's new reform *parti patriote*, welcomed Dalhousie's message to the Assembly of 13 February 1827 in which he announced the project for the two committees and called for the Assembly to grant £3,000 for it with an additional £100 for school-books. Ludger Duvernay wrote that the plan should indeed increase the numbers of schools and scholars markedly, and the resulting competition for new schools would increase the mass of knowledge in the colony. He did oppose Dalhousie's announcement that he planned to pay Secretary Mills's salary: this should have been submitted to the Assembly. The Assembly, on a motion by Vallières de Saint-Réal, voted an address to Dalhousie on 21 February calling for detailed information about the progress of the plan.[101]

Lay Reaction and the School Bill of 1827

A growing number of MPPs were opposed to the extension of denominational religious control. To counter the RI plan, François Blanchet, who had been absent from educational debate since the passage of the Vestry Act of 1824,[102] sponsored a bill for a £10,000 fund to encourage the creation of lay schools in the Quebec District. Schooling was going nowhere, Blanchet claimed, because monarchical government had habituated the people to apathy. That type of government had appointed 'a particular class of men' to oversee education, but that class – the clergy – could not have the same interest in this matter as the people itself. His bill would charge the people more directly with the educational mission and would give it the means to establish its own schools. Where such was the case already, schools multiplied rapidly: 'He saw in the new Townships as many as four or five schools, while at Kamouraska, for instance, such a rich and populous parish, there was only one,' a demonstration of 'the superiority of one method over the other.' Indeed, his Kamouraska example was well chosen: there the seigneur, the curé, and notables were agitating for the creation of a college in a parish which had almost no elementary schools.

Blanchet's bill empowered male household heads to assemble and to apply to the executive for the establishment of a school. His school fund would offer them £100 in matching funds for construction costs and would place the management of the schools 'entirely under the people's control.' Such was 'assuredly the most liberal system.' Blanchet stressed that his bill did not prevent the operation of vestry schools or RI schools; it would add another ingredient to the mix. But he was clear that clerical control over schooling was a failure. In the ensuing debate, there was broad agreement on the principle of the bill and concern that strict accounting measures be put in place for any grant. D.-B. Viger did urge members not to forget the good work being done under the Vestry Act; one member claimed that rural farmhouses were so far apart that it would be best to fund itinerant teachers; and MPP Davidson urged the House not to proceed with the bill, but instead to wait for the formation of denominational committees in the RI. But Blanchet drew on the majority's growing impatience to forestall the extension of a manifestly inadequate clerical investment of the field of education. The incipient local democracy of the new Townships provided a better alternative, and Blanchet's 1827 School Act sailed through the Assembly – only to die in Council when parliament was prorogued.[103] However, it was a short step from voting £10,000 for one colonial district to supporting local demand for schooling throughout the colony.

Two Committees and the Catholic Bishops

Dalhousie moved forward with the plan for denominational committees in the RI after the prorogation of the Assembly, but new sources of delay occurred: first, the RI member and lieutenant governor of Upper Canada, Sir Peregrine Maitland, refused to resign his seat until Lord Bathurst had ruled on the matter. Dalhousie wrote to the Colonial Office seeking permission to remove two members of the RI board. Then the Chief Justice ruled that under the 1801 act it was not possible for the Catholic bishop to act as principal of the Institution in the absence of the Lord Bishop of Quebec, and since the act specified the number of members of the corporation, it could not be increased without amending the law. More astute in its manoeuvring than Bishop Panet proved to be, the board of the RI proposed to reduce the number of new appointments rather than to involve the Assembly. Secretary Mills reported the new proposition to the executive in mid-December 1827, suggesting a new and smaller Catholic committee to consist of Bishop Panet and the principal of the Séminaire at Quebec, both to be ex officio, with the active members to be the co-adjutor Joseph Signäy, and de Léry and Cuthbert. The board proposed to remove its inactive members, most of whom lived in Montreal (one, Ross Cuthbert, had lost his mind), to balance the membership.[104]

Panet learned that the administration would proceed with the plan for two committees in December 1827, but it was March 1828 before Dalhousie copied him the board's recommendations and May before he reacted to them with shock and suspicion. Throughout this process, Bishop Lartigue was constantly barking at Panet not to participate in the Royal Institution or in any government educational project. Early in 1825 Lartigue had opposed the notion of separate committees because the Speaker of the Assembly was to be a member of the Catholic committee, and that person someday might be a Protestant. In 1826 he denounced the entire scheme as a ploy on the part of the Protestants to enlist a few Catholic priests and laymen as window dressing in order to hide their attacks on the Church, to force Catholics to read the Bible at school, and to interpret it in the heretical Protestant manner. The sinister intentions of the Crown were evident in the very name of the organization, 'Royal Institution,' and in its refusal at once to create a separate Catholic RI. In any case Catholics had no need of the venture. 'We can do without it,' Lartigue declared, 'because our four colleges are already enough for literary education and our parish schools, as established by the last bill, are enough for primary education.' Let the curés get busy![105]

Lartigue retailed gossip from Councillor James Cuthbert that the Colonial Office had agreed to a separate Catholic Institution and that the RI and Dalhousie were hiding the fact. When he saw the answers of the RI board to Panet's queries, he warned him that they were vague, insidious, and suspicious. He urged Panet to have nothing to do with the project unless he got a full, detailed specification of every aspect of it, warning that the RI was already thinking about mixed denominational schools. In March 1827, Lartigue hammered away again at the same point: if the project went forward, the government would have 'two important means little by little to tyrannize and to overthrow religion in this country.' And when the project for the two committees ran into difficulties later that year, Lartigue urged Panet to take advantage of the situation to walk away from the whole wretched trap.[106]

Dalhousie and Lartigue shared a personal antipathy and felt mutual distaste that made the latter even more deeply suspicious of any plan of the former that might affect the Church. Lartigue warned Panet after the 1827 elections that Dalhousie had not done nearly enough to encourage the Catholic clergy, that he had voted against Catholic emancipation in the Lords, and that he was scheming to import Scottish ministers into the colony. He was not to be trusted. We have seen that Dalhousie supported Lartigue's clerical opponents, and he also opposed

Lartigue's appointment as co-adjutor on the death of Bishop Plessis. Lartigue complained that Dalhousie blamed him for political unrest in the colony because he was cousin to D.-B. Viger and L.-J. Papineau, and in this Lartigue was correct; but Lartigue did not hesitate to use Viger to promote his political views. Dalhousie believed his candidates fared poorly in the 1827 elections because the clergy was directly involved in opposing them; there was some evidence that a priest named Kelly campaigned against Attorney General Stuart. Dalhousie explained as much to the Colonial Office, claiming that while Bishop Panet was well-disposed towards government, Lartigue was actively promoting the popular cause. Dalhousie placed Lartigue in 'The Clique' headed by Papineau, ignoring the increasingly large political differences that separated them.[107]

Nonetheless, as with cousin Papineau, Lartigue's political principles were rigid and not subject to compromise: in this case, a Protestant government and a Catholic Church should have nothing whatsoever to do with each other in educational matters. The differing positions of Lartigue and Panet on schooling also mirrored the broader-based regional competition and antagonism that pitted Quebec against Montreal. Speaker Louis-Joseph Papineau participated in these oppositions as well, declaiming frequently in private against the Quebec members of the Assembly, whom he saw as spineless at key moments and overly keen to bask in the personal attentions of the executive.[108] While Lartigue railed against accusations that he opposed education and pointed to his colleges and to his curés' efforts in the cause, at no time in this period did he entertain the notion of any dedicated educational administrative body able to supply schools with teachers, books, supplies, or programs of study, or to ensure the quality of existing schools. He did indeed believe that 'religion was the education of the people'; if his priests ministered and the people was pious, it got what it needed.

After considering the proposal from the RI board for a new and much smaller Catholic committee, after all this prodding from Lartigue, and despite a long communication from Vallières de Saint-Réal encouraging him to accept it, Panet informed Dalhousie on 3 May 1828 that he was not willing to move from the proposition he had accepted earlier. As he had explained then, if the project was to succeed it was necessary to have the leading members of the Catholic clergy permanently in office at the head of the committee. He had carefully considered the matter and had consulted widely in December 1826 before he suggested his list of five clergy and six laymen. If the existing board of the RI thought these were too many Catholic members, it had only to increase its own numbers. 'It is certain,' he concluded, that the proposed change 'will not at all be approved by the Clergy and the Catholic population of this Province.'[109]

When Panet's opposition was presented to the board of the RI, the latter argued that there was a misunderstanding and that it was not calling for any change in what had been agreed to. The board maintained that Panet's 1826 list had been described by him not as 'Definitive,' but rather as a 'mere *project.*' The board's position then was that the number of members would continue to be eleven, as formerly, but that five of them would be Catholic and five Protestant. It made no practical sense to increase the number of members ex officio because such members rarely attended board meetings, and if there were eleven Catholic members, to find enough Protestant clergymen to serve ex officio, the Board would have to appoint people who did not reside in Lower Canada. Nonetheless, in order not to sacrifice the entire project, 'the Board accede[d] to the wishes of the R: C: B; in both the particulars mentioned in his last letter.' Dalhousie's marginal notation on the RI board's response read, 'Let the arrangement be proceeded in.'[110]

There the matter rested for five months during which Lord Dalhousie left the colony and was replaced by Sir James Kempt. To acquaint himself with current conditions of administration, Kempt sought reports from his attorney general on a number of pending matters. On the Royal Institution, which Kempt learned was now managing 82 schools attended by 3,439 students at a yearly cost of £2,000, James Stuart delivered the alarming opinion 'that none of the Letters Patent appointing additional Trustees' to the board 'since the Letters Patent issued on 8:th Oct:r, 1818, are valid' and as a result serious legal doubts existed 'as to the present competency of the Board for ordinary Business.' In response to this opinion, Secretary Mills wrote that it was urgently necessary for Governor Kempt to do what he could to complete the arrangement worked out with Panet by naming new members to the RI by letters patent and to allow time for the introduction of new legislation if Panet insisted on increasing the size of the board.[111]

The Catholic laymen involved then attempted to revive the project for a ten-member board with a principal. J.-T. Taschereau submitted the RI board's proposal to the principal of the Séminaire de Québec, Jérôme Demers, and asked that it be presented for Panet's consideration. Taschereau explained that it was not possible to have more than ten members on the RI board, and so he proposed to name Bishop Panet ex officio, Bishop Signäy, Speaker Papineau, Vallières de Saint-Réal, and himself. Panet, weary and wary and privy to James Stuart's judgment, now remarked 'I am even more of the opinion that the Legislature should intervene in the proposed arrangements to resolve matters in such a way as to remove all difficulties, as much with respect to the number of members who will compose the Royal Institution, as with respect to any other item which might appear unacceptable and not authorized by the 1801 act.' To Sir James Kempt, Panet wrote that he was still prepared to accept the plan of 1826, but, 'as we are given to understand that doubts exist as to the competence of the members of the present corporation, it will be necessary, in my view, to refer all our arrangements to the Legislature, so that in its wisdom it may take steps to remove all obstacles.'[112]

The Rejection of Denominational Schooling

And so a new Royal Institution bill was drafted, passed in the Legislative Council, and sent early in March 1829 to the Assembly for confirmation. The Assembly had resolved in response to an earlier message from Governor Kempt that the act of 1801 should be amended and that £2,000 should be voted for the support of the RI. 'An Act to authorize the formation of two separate and distinct boards of trustees in the Royal Institution for the Promotion of Learning' contained Panet's demand for an RI board of twenty-two members, eleven of whom would be Catholics, presided over by their bishop and charged with organizing and managing Catholic schools. The Anglican board was now to include the minister of St Andrews Church at Quebec. The act also clarified that current members of the board such as the lieutenant governor of Upper Canada could resign and their functions could pass intact to new appointees. The new act passed second reading and 400 copies were ordered printed, but then, in what seemed a surprise move, Vallières de Saint-Réal, one of its sponsors, and the Irish-Catholic MPP John Cannon carried a resolution that amendments to the 1801 act be considered later in the session. The bill was sunk. Some machinations followed in which Lartigue and Plessis considered further amendments to the 1801 and 1824 acts, but effectively the plan for separate denominational school boards died in March 1829.[113] In its place the Assembly passed 9. Geo.IV cap. 46, 'An Act for the encouragement of elementary education,' or more popularly, the Trustees School Act.

These moves have surprised some observers, but in fact the Assembly had shown little or no sympathy for the Royal Institution from at least 1815. As we have seen, it had tried again and again to enact alternative school legislation. The promises of the Catholic clergy to school the people if allowed to do so were given the lie by its inaction under the Vestry School Act. Since the prorogation of 1827 momentum had been building for a renewal of Blanchet's proposed school act among the MPPs; the 1829 Trustees' School Act was an elaboration of it.

The 1828–9 legislative session followed the report of the imperial Canada Committee on colonial grievances and the recall of Lord Dalhousie, who left office in September 1828, days before the Committee report arrived in the colony. The Committee itself was formed after Dalhousie's desperate final attempts to master the Assembly and to resolve the endless struggle over the Civil List, by proroguing parliament in 1827, suspending habeas corpus, removing opposition militia officers from office, and using his powers of patronage in a new round of elections. Despite a number of outrageous practices, including Attorney General James Stuart's arrest and trial of people who voted against him at Sorel, a radicalized opposition party was returned in force. At the opening session of the Assembly in November 1827, Louis-Joseph Papineau was elected speaker by a large majority, Dalhousie refused to accept his election, and parliament was prorogued again without any business being conducted. Dalhousie continued to spend public money without the authorization of the Assembly in violation of the constitution.

While Dalhousie had some support and while a large petition from the Eastern Townships was critical of some of the Assembly's stances, what was now the *parti patriote* organized 'Constitutional Associations' in much of the colony and coordinated a massive petition in support of a statement of grievances in late 1827 and early 1828. The document, bearing some 87,000 names (a large percentage of the adult population), but only 9,000 signatures, castigated virtually every aspect of Dalhousie's administration, and was carried to England early in 1828 by a delegation of three, including the MPP and educational activist John Neilson. Dalhousie continued to attempt to discipline the opposition, removing a number of magistrates active in promoting the petition and bringing charges of seditious libel against the *Quebec Gazette*, Montreal's *Canadian Spectator*, and the activist Dominique Mondelet.

The arrival of the delegation, news of political events in Canada, and the Eastern Townships' petition stimulated a passing burst of imperial interest in the colony, in large part because the Canadian question intersected with Whig and radical Whig muscle flexing against the Tory ministry in power. In England, of course, the conjuncture was one of intense agitation for political-economic and administrative change, spearheaded by the struggles for Catholic emancipation, electoral and welfare reform, and for the end of the patronage politics known as 'Old Corruption.' The Canada Committee report chastised the Canadian Assembly for exceeding its constitutional powers by demanding the right to decide annually which administrative and executive officers would receive what salary. It stressed that state administration needed to be free from political interference. It supported demands of English-speaking settlers in the Townships for political representation, registry offices, land reform, and English property law. Yet the substance of the report was a comprehensive denunciation of Lord Dalhousie's administration. Two recommendations in the Canada Committee report were particularly portentous: that the Crown should renounce its claims to the greatest part of colonial revenue in exchange for a limited permanent Civil List for judicial and executive salaries; and that the imperial government should not intervene in colonial affairs except in matters directly affecting imperial interests. In response to a conciliatory speech from Dalhousie's replacement, Sir James Kempt, which expressed the substance of the Committee report, in December 1828 the Lower Canadian Assembly resolved to vote a permanent list for judges, the governor, and the Executive Council on certain limited conditions, and affirmed the principle of imperial non-interference in colonial affairs.[114]

Peter Burroughs remarked that 'the committee's report might have provided the basis for the restoration of Anglo-Canadian understanding had the British [Tory] government acted at once to capitalize on the good will that had been temporarily generated in Lower Canada,' but it did not do so.[115] No imperial legislation was passed to change the nature of colonial political representation; Governor Kempt reserved the colony's own 1829 Representation Act. No legislation granted control over revenue to the Assembly in an exchange for a Civil List; when the 1831 Howick Act did grant the Assembly control over the revenue, it did not demand a permanent list in return, and the Assembly renounced its resolution of 1828, ensuring that the struggle over finance would continue to escalate. The imperial government adopted a non-interventionist colonial policy in most local matters; yet bitter antagonism between the majorities in the Assembly and the Legislative and Executive Councils after 1832 could only be resolved by imperial intervention – or by revolution. Educational policy in the 1830s would be inseparably bound up with these struggles.

The successful passage of the 1829 School Act and its proclamation by Sir James Kempt were due in large measure to the Canada Committee's promises of non-interference and to a 'charm offensive' launched by Kempt, but it was a very near thing, with the act making it through Council only on the deciding vote of the speaker. Still, the Canada Committee report seemed to signal a dramatic shift in the balance of power in the colony, with the abandonment of the French-baiting tendencies of imperial Tories; a denunciation of the secrecy, autocracy, and fiscal laxity of the Dalhousie years; and a move towards a more democratic management of a more inclusive civil society. There were directly legal moves in that direction, actions against the defaulting receiver general and the abusive attorney general, the dropping of libel charges against Dalhousie's political opponents, for instance, which cowed some Council members and encouraged division among the rest. Robert Armour Sr of the Tory *Montreal Gazette* was told to tone down his political rhetoric. The Assembly passed a raft of legislation, much of it presented and lost during the Dalhousie regime, whose global tendency was towards the creation of a secular-rational polity with local representative administration. New legislation aimed to remove the civil disabilities of Jews and to eliminate the monopoly of the Episcopal churches over the legitimation of vital events, to identify and specify the limits of parishes civilly, and to incorporate the towns of Quebec and Montreal. A great many of these acts were in fact lost by small majorities in the Council, but they speak to a democratizing and liberal state-forming moment in the colony, one in which the grounds of government itself were in play.

Speaker Louis-Joseph Papineau made an impassioned speech in the Assembly early in 1829 insisting that all religious denominations in the colony should enjoy equal rights and equal encouragement. The question of civil equality was at the centre of the debate over political representation that followed. French-speaking members insisted that representation by population was the only equitable form, while English-speaking Tories and some Eastern Townships reformers insisted that population and territory together should be the basis of representation – as indeed the Canada Committee had recommended. The latter position was justified on the grounds that future population growth from immigration would be in the Townships; the Assembly should anticipate this development by according them more seats now. Some Tories suggested that wealth also be a criterion for the distribution of seats. Both suggestions were rejected as ploys to multiply the number of English-speaking MPPs, and Denis-Benjamin Viger spoke for the majority in stating 'the Canadien people as the most numerous must be preponderant.'[116] The increasing invocation of population arguments in political debate also points to a shift towards civic equality as a ground of legitimation. Kempt himself offered some real, if limited, legislative encouragement in these matters.

At least as effective was his 'charm offensive,' which was intended to open some common ground for political discourse among the competing factions. L.-J. Papineau noted that Kempt's pointed courting of all factions at public as well as at more intimate events meant that members of Council and of the Assembly were no longer actively shouting insults at one another in the parliamentary lobby in public hearing. The high Tories in the Councils were shocked when Kempt invited large numbers of Dalhousie's *canadien* opponents to his winter ball, where he chatted amicably with Dominique Mondelet, so recently imprisoned for seditious libel. Papineau himself, a political pariah in the eyes of the executive for at least a decade, was fawning in his adoration of Kempt, convinced of his good intentions, and eager to show him personally the beauties of the Chambly river region.[117]

The Assembly Committee

If the conjuncture was momentarily favourable for the passage of a secular rural school act, an education committee of the Assembly, which had been sitting for a number of months, had become ever more convinced of its necessity. The new *patriote* party press bolstered its conviction. In the first place, the committee had undertaken to gather all available information about the effects of the existing provisions for schooling along denominational lines. The Assembly clerk Edward Glackemeyer forwarded a printed questionnaire to J.L. Mills of the Royal Institution and to Bishop Panet of Quebec in December 1828 seeking a detailed account of numbers of schools directed by them in each county, with entries for teachers; average attendance and school fees; curriculum; pedagogy and arrangements for school inspection; and for supplementary remarks. Some college directors were also contacted and sent their responses. Mills's reply has not survived, but the education committee saw from it that the RI was funding 82 schools with some 3,600 students. Bishop Panet's secretary, on the other hand, declared that he could not provide any exact or comprehensive information, 'because the gentlemen Curés who generally manage schools in the Country parishes, are not in the habit of accounting for them' to the bishop. The latter could only learn of the existence of schools 'usually verbally.'[118] Barring some inordinate level of credulity on the part of the education committee, such a reply must at least have underlined the Church's failure to make any systematic use of the Vestry School Act, if not its continuing hostility to any government involvement in schooling. The response hardly seems astute from a cleric seeking parliamentary support for a Catholic committee in the RI.

That existing denominational arrangements produced little in the way of schooling was an argument in itself against solidifying or extending them, and the 'Papineau clique' at least knew that Bishop Lartigue opposed any such extension. Lartigue urged his cousin D.-B. Viger simply to repeal the 1801 act and to create completely independent denominational school boards.[119] At the same time, religious denominations excluded from the RI protested vociferously against the plan for a new board. The Wesleyan Methodists' spokesman in the Eastern Townships, Richard Pope, was especially offended by the efforts of the Anglicans to use the RI to dominate all Protestant education. The Methodists had about 25 Sunday schools in May 1827 with 1,734 students, who were forced to attend the nearest day schools during the week. Pope wrote that 'the very oppressive manner in which these schools is conducted by many of the agents of the Royal Institution, has been, and still is painfully felt by all denominations of Dissenters, and by the Wesleyan Methodists in particular, they having large Congregations & Societies in the Townships.' The Anglicans made matters worse by doing everything they could to control the schools even in Stanstead where there was no resident Anglican minister. There, the Rev. Hartley Johnston used the government money to get support for an RI school, which he refused to allow any other denomination to use for Sunday service, and there were like abuses elsewhere. As well, Pope complained, government money went only to wealthy places instead of those most in need. He commented that 'the more effectual way to realize the end the Legislature has in view, – the general spread of Education, – would be to appoint a board of Directors in every Township, selected from every neighborhood & from every denomination, who should be required, after investigating the case, to send every poor child to the nearest school, and pay for its education either in whole or in part as the circumstance might require.' People in the Townships did not want denominational control over the schools.[120]

The Methodist Pope was a relative unknown, but the Presbyterian ministers James Harkness of Quebec and Henry Esson of Montreal were familiar to the urban educational activists in the Assembly. Esson especially had high standing as a scholar, co-founder of the Montreal Academical Institution, and vocal opponent of the claims of the Church of England to the Clergy Reserves. As a faction of the *parti patriote* later attempted to democratize the Catholic vestries, Esson supported male democratic management of Presbyterian churches. Esson

and Harkness were scathingly critical of the plan for two denominational boards in the Royal Institution.

'The Presbyterian population are in general dissatisfied with the manner in which the Institution is composed,' they wrote in a memorial, 'as
well as with the partial and proselytizing spirit in which its administration
appears to them to have been hitherto conducted.' It was particularly offensive that Presbyterians, who they claimed were more numerous than
Anglicans, had no share in educational government. If there was to be
denominational control of education, they wanted their fair share and the
act of 1801 should be amended to that end. Their inclusion in the Royal
Institution could be justified in precisely the same terms as that of the
Catholics. But their preferred solution was for a system in which education could not 'be made subservient to the views of a sect or party.' In the
current context, where the rights of different religious groups in the colony were uncertain, 'religious jealousies must needs prevail and can only
be effectually allayed by an equal and impartial distribution of power and
influence in all matters connected with Religion and Education.'[121]

The Assembly's education committee, after considering such petitions,
denounced the policy of funding the Royal Institution as the granting of
a monopoly to one religious sect. The proposal for denominational boards
in the RI only extended the monopoly to two or three sects. The committee declared that there was no need for elementary schooling to be controlled by the clergy. It could have influence over morality by visiting the
schools. In the committee's thinking, population distribution, not civil or
religious distinctions, should guide educational policy: 'The people of this
province ought to receive, under a strict management of public funds, aid
in proportion to its numbers, without any distinction in relation to religious belief.'[122] Thus the 1829 School Act was conceived quite explicitly as
a means to provide secular, locally controlled elementary schooling in
keeping with population distribution. Not language, not national origin,
not sex, not religious belief, and not political allegiance defined 'the
people's' right to schooling; rather, that right was defined by the people's
relation to territory and state authority. In conception, at least, the 1829
act embodied a liberal governmentality. But the government was not yet
prepared to school population; the autonomous people was to school itself. Here again it would prove itself unruly.

The practical workings of the 1829 act are examined below. First, however, it is important to address the condition of urban education and
schooling. The reality of schooling the urban poor in purpose-built institutions also shaped common understandings of educational government.

3

The Colonial 'Monitorial Moment'

The defeat of the Quebec and Montreal Free School Society in 1817 was a temporary setback to efforts by dissenting clergy, lay bourgeois and petty bourgeois activists, in and outside parliament, to school the urban working class and the poor and to provide affordable schooling for some of their own children. Their continuing activities pushed the Evangelical churches to open charity schools in 1819–21 in an attempt to pre-empt lay efforts, but lay schools followed in 1822–3.

Pressure for large-scale schooling came from a variety of quarters. Some members of the dominant groups were alarmed by an increase in urban pauperism, unemployment, and household decomposition provoked by the colony's changing political economy and the wartime boom. These people included philanthropists preoccupied by human misery, poverty, and ill health, and others concerned first with disorder, immorality, intemperance, and prostitution. The wartime boom increased the numbers of unruly children roaming city streets – or at least drew attention to them. In Quebec the military garrison worked to augment the city's supply of foundlings. Well-governed city populations were seen to be schooled populations.

Another source of pressure was from the fairly broad urban strata ranging from artisans to reasonably well-to-do small merchants and manufacturers (called 'mechanics'). These strata were growing in size as the timber trade replaced the fur trade as the colony's most important economic activity after 1800, and as agricultural exports increased alongside investment in transportation infrastructure. Logging, canal- and shipbuilding, the growth of petty manufacturing, retail and wholesale trade, and a general extension of print culture together made literacy and numeracy increasingly important for 'middling' strata. The cities supported robust private markets in schooling, but physical educational infrastructure was primitive. Small private schools in house rooms could not meet the growing demand for schooling, either at all or at a price people could afford, and matters were made worse by a dramatic postwar inflation. The existing Catholic seminaries and convents were selective in their admission procedures and offered a classical curriculum to a limited number of students drawn from throughout the colony.

Urban population growth was significant. Between 1800 and 1830 the large towns of Montreal and Quebec became small cities, Trois-Rivières became a small town, and the number of village clusters with populations ranging between 300 and 1,500 increased markedly. Montreal, said to have about 9,450 inhabitants in 1806, grew to 18,767 in 1821, to 26,154 in 1825, and, with the surrounding county, to 43,773 by 1831. Quebec's population was reported as about 8,850 in 1805, 18,191 in 1818, 22,101 in 1825, and, with the surrounding county, 36,179 in 1831. After a brief decline in the wake of the 1832 cholera, population growth continued apace until the Rebellion of 1837.[1]

A common international solution to the rise of urban pauper and proletarian populations and to the demand from middling strata for cheap education was the organization of large-scale 'monitorial' schools. That solution was adopted in Lower Canada as well, and this chapter concerns the colony's 'monitorial moment,' that is, the period in which an earlier mercantilist opposition to the schooling of the 'lower orders' was effectively displaced by moves to train and discipline young people collectively in schools, in the name of morality, social order, economic prosperity, and, to a lesser extent, social mobility. From above, monitorial or mutual systems of instruction were trumpeted in language redolent of factory production as 'powerful moral engines.' The large-scale manufacture of social subjectivities involved the application of practices common in the military, the factory workshop, and the counting house to large numbers of young people grouped together for this purpose. Early nineteenth-century observers were frequently astonished at the seeming ability of the method to transform masses of ignorant young people into orderly and cheerful readers and writers within the space of a few weeks. More subtly, they came also to think increasingly of children as an undifferentiated social category in need of discipline in purpose-built institutions. An earlier debate over the relative merits of domestic and school education ceased. Monitorialism was thus implicated both in new practices of subjectification and in the emergence of a new domain of knowledge, practice, and government, part of what came later to be configured as 'the social,' the realm whose study was the object of the emerging 'social science' and of social statistics.

Working classes were often less than enthusiastic about the moralizing militarization of their children by the dominant classes; local child-minding services or 'dame schools' remained popular in Europe as they did in urban Lower Canada. European cities often offered working-class parents a variety of alternative institutions. In England, for instance, Owenite and Chartist educators offered schooling on models that extended and deepened the forces of the student well beyond those stressed in the monitorial school, without its strict regimentation. Such alternatives did not exist in Canada.

Educational practice in Lower Canada was transformed by monitorialism most immediately by a dramatic increase in the numbers of people having access to schooling. After 1819, religious and lay organizations competed to school the poor, the working class and the lower middle class. Taken together, these organizations – the National Society (Church of England) from 1819, the Société d'Éducation du district de Québec (Catholic) from 1821, the British and Canadian School Society (lay) from 1822–3, the Montreal Orphan Asylum (lay) from 1822, the Montreal Recollet School (Catholic), the Quebec and Montreal Infant School Society (lay) from 1829, and later the Trois-Rivières education society – came to dominate the urban educational field.

I begin with an account of the development and substance of monitorial pedagogy and then present a brief version of the English debate between the evangelical Anglican Sarah Trimmer and the liberal reformer Henry Brougham over schooling the poor in this way. The debate nicely encapsulates the shift in educational governmentality from a strategy of promoting pious ignorance to one of disciplining a growing popular intelligence.

I then give an overview of the private market in schooling in Quebec from 1800 to 1820, drawn from newspaper advertisements and from some other sources, to show the kind and cost of schooling on offer in the city before the 'monitorial moment.' For Montreal, where the market was quite similar, I examine the remarkable school inventories compiled for 1825 and 1835 by Jacques Viger. These contain an early amateur attempt to appropriate school conditions in statistical forms and to relate the schooled population to population as a whole. Having established conditions before the monitorial moment, the chapter then documents the organization, development, and conduct of the monitorial schools in Quebec and Montreal to 1841, with some attention to the projects spun off from them.

What Was Monitorial Schooling?

Joseph Lancaster was the master of a charity school in Southwark, London, in the late 1790s when he came across the printed description of a school for orphaned and abandoned Eurasian children of British soldiers run by the Anglican clergyman Andrew Bell in the Madras Asylum. Bell employed some of his own students as assistants, taught beginning writers to trace out their letters in sand, as local teachers did, and adopted what was seen as a very innovative phonic method of teaching to read. The students were grouped in achievement classes, where taking places was encouraged; regular records were kept of individual comportment; and misconduct was dealt with weekly by a jury composed of the school as a whole. Bell eliminated corporal punishment. He suggested that his method could be applied to school the English poor, although he stated in passing that they need not be taught to write.

Lancaster and Bell had a friendly interview at Christmas 1804, and Lancaster set about extending and developing Bell's scheme, adding a large number of refinements. He published an expanded description of his system in 1805 as *Improvements in Education, as It Respects the Industrious Classes,* and his work early attracted broad support in England from Non-Conformists in the manufacturing bourgeoisie and from the circle around Jeremy Bentham and James Mill. Already in 1807 the Whig MP Samuel Whitbread was proposing a national Lancasterian school system. Lancaster attracted royal patronage for the Royal Lancasterian Association, and on that basis and through his own tireless efforts at promotion, the method spread rapidly in England, across the Irish Sea, onto the Continent, and very quickly across the Atlantic as well. It was soon adopted in several American states and taken up in Latin and South America.

Lancaster proposed that one master could teach up to a thousand students by dividing them into achievement classes under the supervision of student monitors. He reduced the necessary material supplies for the schoolroom dramatically and displaced most administrative labour onto monitors as well. Lancaster adopted, invented, or extended methods for teaching reading, writing, and arithmetic cheaply and efficiently. Books, paper, pens, and ink were eliminated for all but the most advanced students. Beginners learned to write their letters in sand, later moving on to writing on slates. Lancaster adopted Bell's phonic method of teaching to read but also based instruction in arithmetic on the reading and copying of problems and solutions, in contrast to the prevailing method of teaching by rules. Any student able to read, it was claimed, could teach arithmetic without knowing anything about it and could learn arithmetic by teaching it. Moreover, students learned to write as soon as – if not before – they learned to read, and they learned to read in the vernacular. Writing was by dictation; there was no place for composition, at least for the great majority of students.

Although there was to be a school library in Lancaster's plan, all but the most advanced classes used reading lessons printed on large cards posted along the walls of the schoolroom. Classes of ten under the supervision of a monitor regularly and frequently moved from their seats in rows facing the front of the schoolroom, where collective work was done, to teaching circles arranged facing the walls. Elaborate systems of signalling and signage by 'telegraphs' were used to coordinate movement. Lancaster promoted individual achievement by encouraging 'emulation' through the taking of places in the monitorial groups, each student wearing a number attesting to its standing. An elaborate system of accounting, worked by specialized monitors who distributed tickets and emblems and kept records, made frequent individual promotion and demotion possible. Lancaster encouraged students individually to accumulate tokens, which could be exchanged for prizes, and to compete for achievement medals. Achieving students wore tickets in the schoolroom, inscribed with such messages as 'Merit in Spelling' or 'Merit in Reading' and pasteboard prints were also worn. The best students were distinguished by different grades of medals. Classes in the school were encouraged to compete among themselves for pride of place, and misbehaviour was dealt with by the distribution and recording of demerit tickets, as well as by a school jury. Lancaster's punishments included practices regarded as controversial, ranging from the attaching of weights and shackles to the bodies of delinquents, punishment parades before the whole school, in which offenders wore demeaning costumes, and cross-gender public humiliations. Students were not beaten.

Well-run monitorial schools were busy places which may have been enjoyable for students, at least on short acquaintance. The individual elements in their novel combination of military drill, the manufacturing division of labour, rational accounting, interpersonal competition for scarce resources, and systems of signage and symbolism had their own autonomous histories; Lancaster's particular genius lay in articulating them. Students and monitors acted in unison on command from a central authority. The learning process was decomposed into simple elements through which students could cycle rapidly, and there was a clear distinction among various teaching and learning tasks in time and space. The student body was both broken down into its individual atoms, as students competed with one another, and periodically reconfigured as groups and classes, or as the school jury. Interpersonal competition for prizes was both immediate, in the taking of places, and prospective through the keeping of daily records of merit and demerit, which were periodically totted up. Such accounting was meant consciously to instil in students a sense that moral credit could be accumulated through good conduct and that it would be rewarded both materially and through increased status. The practice may have operated to encourage foresight or to delay gratification.

Especially significant were Lancaster's severing of technical from doctrinal religious instruction and his encouragement of social mobility. As he put it in his *Improvements*, 'above all things, education ought not to be subservient to the propagation of the peculiar tenets of any sect,' a position congenial to his Quaker loyalties, but one which supposed the existence of a common civil society, based on a generic Christian morality. As he described it, this morality involved 'a reverence for the sacred name of God and the Scriptures of Truth; a detestation of vice; a love of veracity; a due attention to duties to parents, relations, and to society; carefulness to avoid bad company; civility without flattery; and a peaceable demeanor.' These were things all Christians supposedly could agree upon, and Lancaster used the New Testament as his source for basic reading lessons. As well, in contrast to the reigning pattern in England and in many other countries of what R.H. Turner called 'sponsored mobility' – whereby elites selected individual poor, peasant, or working-class children for promotion to an educated future – Lancaster encouraged 'contest mobility,' whereby the best-performing students could receive material rewards and prestige (limited as they were) on their own merits. For conservative observers, this shift was particularly menacing.[2]

The monitorial system was trumpeted as capable of manufacturing readers, writers, and calculators quickly and cheaply according to a plan that limited their autonomy. In many countries, it seemed like a quick and easy fix for the problem of unruly urban pauper children. In the United States, its generic Christianity had an especially broad appeal, and by the 1820s it was in use in cities from Georgia to Maine and from Massachusetts to Ohio. Yet the system's limitations were also clear to observers from the outset, and it did not make progress in places such as Scotland that had established traditions of parish schooling. Monitorial schooling allowed no room for individual variation or autonomy either in teaching or in learning strategies and was not fit for any subject that could not be learned by rote.[3] It eventually went out of fashion as schooling was tied to the production of more complex interiorities.

Sectarianism, Ignorance, and Monitorialism

Lancaster's version of monitorial schooling was violently attacked in England by evangelical Anglicans. They succeeded in removing the royal patronage, and Lancaster's own increasingly erratic conduct led his erst-while supporters to remove him in 1814 from what was by then called the British and Foreign School Society (BFSS). He led a peripatetic life, including a stint in Lower Canada from 1828 to 1833, until his death in New York City in 1838. The Anglicans, who had organized their own mon-itorial society in 1811, the National Society for Promoting the Education of the Poor, based on Andrew Bell's method, used their superior resour-ces to counter the Lancasterian organization's efforts in England and by 1820 had effectively dominated their opposition. However, the BFSS was more successful in exporting its version. The two systems were essentially the same in their pedagogical methods, but the Anglican version refused the notion of a generic Christianity, insisted on the teaching of the Church of England catechism, on student attendance on Sundays at its church, and on the use of its schoolbooks for advanced students. It was less sympathetic to social mobility.

The competing strategies of educational government that distinguished Anglican and lay versions of schooling were well exemplified in the English debate between the evangelical charity-school author Sarah Trimmer – who was influential in breaking the personal connection between Andrew Bell and Joseph Lancaster – and the liberal Henry Brougham.

Written in 1805 at the height of wartime panic around revolution, democracy, and republicanism, Trimmer's attack on Lancaster's schools assumed an immanent relation between school government and the gov-ernment of the state. For her, school-based pedagogical practices produced political subjects. The internal organization of schools and the substance of schooling could bolster or undermine political government by establish-ing desires and habits of mind and body necessary for it or inimical to it. Trimmer attacked Non-Conformists or Dissenters for undermining the co-herence of church and state that she held to be essential for national unity and for substituting a generic morality for orthodox Christianity. She equated generic morality with the absence of robust beliefs of any sort. At least as serious were the monitorial school's collective discipline of the poor, its supposed encouragement of unregulated reading and writing, and its practice of distinguishing the most promising students by awarding them prizes and by promoting them to be the monitors of their fellows. The critique sounds quaint to modern ears, given that Trimmer lost this battle, but she was debating schooling in relation to subjectification, polit-ical order, freedom of belief, and social mobility.

The distribution of honours was improper in principle, she argued, be-cause people should learn to do what was right for its own sake. For the poor, especially, distinction at school could lead to a dangerous love of distinction in life. 'The great object of the labouring part of the community is rather to earn money by honest industry sufficient to maintain themselves and their families, than to gain distinction by their talents,' wrote Trimmer. The pursuit of idle honours would undermine the need to labour, and, worse, it could lead to revolutionary interests, 'especially in times which furnish recent instances of the extention of a race of antient nobility in a neighbouring nation, and the elevation of some of the lowest of the people to the highest stations. Boys,' Trimmer continued, 'accustomed to consider themselves as the nobles of a school, may in their future lives, from a conceit of their own trivial merits … aspire to be nobles of the land, and to take the place of the hereditary nobility.' The best student at school was entitled to some mark of distinction, but it should not be 'such as may kindle in his heart ambitious desires, unsuitable to [his] station.'

The structure of the monitorial school created a distinction between leaders – monitors – and the rest of the student body and encouraged the mass to follow the ambitious. This tendency was evil in its own right, but it was dangerous given that the school used collective instruction and physical and mental drill. For Trimmer there was a real question, 'whether it is consistent with sound policy to train all the youths of the lower orders in these evolutions, lest hereafter they should be drawn in, by ill-disposed persons, to employ their knowledge of them to bad purposes?' The monitorial school risked creating revolutionary armies open to command by designing leaders.

Finally, Trimmer warned against the monitorial school's ambition to turn poor boys and girls into readers and writers. Of course she knew that she might be seen as 'illiberal and narrow minded' for objecting to having the poor read the same sorts of books as the higher classes. Yet both observation and theory had taught her 'that the happiness of the labouring part of the community is promoted far more by teaching them things that are likely to be useful to them in their proper station, than by the study of the sciences.' An exceptionally talented boy might move to advanced study, but such sponsored mobility was to be rare. It was all very well to teach poor boys to read and to write, and it was quite proper to teach people to have a sufficient share of reading 'in this day of general literature' so that they could read their Bible at home, 'but this indulgence is certainly carried too far when a taste is excited in them for studies which might tend to render them discontented in their proper station, and to alienate their minds from those employments which must be performed by the bulk of the people in every nation.'[4]

Other Tory evangelicals – and such important Romantics as William Coleridge and Robert Southey – echoed Trimmer's position. It was contested in turn by Dissenters and by reforming Whigs, especially Henry (later Lord) Brougham, the leading parliamentary proponent of an English national working-class school system. Writing in the *Edinburgh Review*, Brougham emphasized that all the objections to teaching the poor to read and write had been anticipated by Bernard de Mandeville in his 1720s *Fable of the Bees,* 'excepting the common addition of the French Revolution, which is now-a-days added to every argument against improvement.' Unless the poor learned to eat books and ink, reading and writing would not remove the necessity of labour. Keeping the poor contented in their station, on the other hand, did undermine the motive to labour, because contentment created laziness, while the promotion of new needs and desires stimulated effort. As Brougham lucidly summarized the strategic problem,

> Immoral or seditious books may, it is very true, be read by the people, if you teach them to read; but, then, so may improper discourses be heard, and improper pictures gazed at. And unless every one of them is kept equally ignorant, it signifies nothing to restrain a few, or even the greater number; for one man may read and tell; and they who repeat may make it worse; and, unless every book containing free discussion is prohibited, it is of no use to keep the multitude on short allowance of reading; because the few they do read, may do all the mischief: nay, the less a man reads, the more likely he is to be mislead by plausible errors, or injured by unsound morality; so that what is so safe to the well informed, that no legislature could think of suppressing it, may to the ignorant be dangerous in the extreme. And, accordingly, the evils which are now not unfrequently occasioned by the daily press, are owing entirely to the ignorance of the community.

In Brougham's view, existing social conditions inevitably entailed the general spread of reading and writing and the development of social mobility. The question was no longer how to prevent such things, but rather what class in society was to direct them.[5]

The Colonial Twist

Members of the established and rising ruling groups in the imperial country faced a strategic problem in the politics of literacy and learning quite different from that existing in the colony. In the imperial country, they confronted a rapidly expanding working class, in which a large stratum of artisans was already largely literate, and which by 1815 was developing its own network of schools and elaborating its own critique of rote learning. Tory governments attempted to repress critical newspapers and to censure other elements of print culture, but it was again increasingly obvious that working-class political and intellectual culture had to be confronted on its own grounds and channelled in agreeable directions if landed property or the new industrial bourgeoisie was to win the battle for political hegemony. As well, the demoralization and degradation of a new manufacturing proletariat by barbaric capital concentrated large groups of workers, rendered ignorant by conditions of life and work, in cities where they were beyond the direct personal supervision of the ruling groups. Attempts to school workers directly were supplemented by ideological campaigns, such as the popular didactic tracts and tales written by Harriet Martineau, that were meant to convince that capital and labour shared common interests.[6]

By contrast, in Quebec/Lower Canada the great majority of people did not read and write. Petty bourgeois intellectuals and professionals constituted the main opposition to existing colonial rule. It was their hegemony of the peasant population that was especially contentious, but neither Church nor state confronted a self-educating working class, nor was there an indigenous popular literary culture, as was the case in peasant Ireland, whose educational history, as we shall see, was intertwined with that of Lower Canada. Keeping the people ignorant was a real strategic possibility in Lower Canada, in the countryside especially.

Schooling in Quebec, 1800–1820

The private market in schooling in Quebec centred on boarding, preparatory, and day schools offering more or less advanced instruction in English for those able to pay fees, with some teachers targeting young working men by teaching commercial subjects at night. An unknown number of ephemeral petty or 'dame' schools offered child-minding services and rudimentary instruction in working-class neighbourhoods. Most schools were very small, ranging from a handful of students to twenty or thirty at the most. Teachers who advertised in the press described their institutions as 'day and boarding' schools, 'ladies' boarding schools,' 'English' schools, 'academies and day schools,' 'English and commercial academies,' and so on, and they all chased after a restricted supply of middle- and upper-class young people from the city and its environs. Many supplemented their teaching with other cultural or print-related services.

In his 1805 pastoral visit to Quebec City and suburbs, curé J.-O. Plessis identified 11 Catholic and 3 Protestant schoolteachers for a Catholic population of 7,397 (1 teacher for 673 residents) and a Protestant population of 1,465 (1 teacher for 488 residents). In 1818, curé Joseph Signäy identified 15 Catholic and 17 Protestant schoolteachers, excluding the teachers at the Seminary and women religious, for a Catholic population of 12,565 (1 teacher for 838 residents) and a Protestant population of 3,503 (1 teacher for 206 residents).[7] Five of his Catholic schoolteachers were English-speaking Irishmen. Both Plessis and Signäy were selective in their identifications of 'teachers.' While no teachers advertised their services in *Le Canadien* between these two enumerations, to the end of 1820 at least 64 different English-speaking teachers – and one French-speaking teacher – 43 men and 22 women, advertised their services in the pages of the *Quebec Mercury*.[8]

The city's leading private schoolmaster, Daniel Wilkie (1777–1851), played an important role in social and cultural life and intervened in colonial politics. A Scottish farmer's son with a master's degree from the University of Glasgow, which he earned on the basis of a prize-winning essay in defence of Socinianism, Wilkie came to Quebec in 1803 and opened an academy in place of James Fraser, the recently deceased, government-subsidized schoolmaster.[9] As with his Upper Canadian counterpart, John Strachan in Cornwall (whose educational trajectory but not whose religious politics he shared), Wilkie's school was soon a favoured destination for the sons of the political and merchant elite, English and French, Protestant and Catholic. He taught a complete course, from elementary instruction through the classics to bookkeeping, philosophy, geography, mensuration, trigonometry, and so forth. Evening classes in practical subjects were offered for young working adults, a Scottish innovation. Wilkie held open examinations to publicize the school, and by 1811 he was teaching according to a 'representative system,' an adaptation of the monitorial pedagogy he promoted for Quebec's working class.[10] His exams often drew the governor general and his suite, while the list of student prize-winners read like a ruling-class 'Who's Who': in 1811 there was a Young, Macaulay, Buchanan, Cuthbert, Fraser, Black, Sewell, Desbarats, Craigie, Stuart, Neilson, Freer, von Iffland, and a Huot. Chief Justice Jonathan Sewell's son gave the public address at the 1809 examination, and the children of Legislative Councillors and wealthy merchants were still much in evidence in 1820.[11]

In the 1810s and 1820s, Wilkie was charging very high fees – £32 annually for boarders, with extra charges for lessons, and for day students, £3 a quarter – but he was in financial distress nonetheless. He attempted repeatedly to find some secure pulpit and tried unsuccessfully to get the government salary paid to James Tanswell on the latter's death. One reason for his difficulties was that his upper-class students were lazy and Wilkie got little support from their parents. As the 1810s wore on, he was subject to intense competition for students, exacerbated by the opening of the Royal Grammar School in 1816, and was under pressure to lower his fees. Still, Wilkie's school was a venue for the formation of personal relations among children of the colonial political and merchant elite, and a quarter of his students were French-Canadian.

Two of his political interventions were important: a clever early pamphlet on the need for schooling, and testimony before the Assembly's 1824 Education Committee. The pamphlet of June 1810 was Wilkie's intervention into the political crisis surrounding Governor Craig's closing of *Le Canadien*, the mouthpiece of the new *parti canadien* in the Assembly, and the arrest and imprisonment of its proprietors on grounds of seditious libel. Wilkie's pamphlet addressed the Catholic clergy and the seigneurs, called for solidarity among all classes of colonial subjects, and attacked the prejudices 'which have prevailed in this age against the instruction of the lower orders, and particularly those which have hitherto prevailed against the instruction of the Canadians.' He refuted the conventional mercantilist arguments against teaching the 'lower orders' to read and invoked a comparative sociology to demonstrate the beneficent political, moral, aesthetic, and economic consequences of general instruction. 'It is ignorance alone,' he insisted, 'that perpetuates the dissensions that disturb this Province.'

The dangers of popular ignorance were obvious. Ignorant people could not recognize their own interests, were not open to rational argument, and could not learn from history or the experience of nations. 'It is on ignorance and credulity,' wrote Wilkie,' 'that the ascendancy of demagogues and revolutionists has always been founded.' In making such a claim he was by no means parroting the line articulated by Governor Craig and his Tory councillors. In fact, Wilkie attacked and refuted the position of Judge de Bonne's reactionary *Le Vrai Canadien*, a newspaper begun explicitly to counter the liberal influence and arguments of *Le Canadien*. De Bonne's paper maintained that while 'it has been claimed that the least educated class is not at all equipped either to be improved or to be spoiled by the public prints,' that opinion was 'an

error from which we must recover.' *Le Canadien's* agitation against the
government 'has proved to us just how much the feelings of a large portion of our fellow citizens may be affected by useful or pernicious texts.'[12]
Wilkie insisted on the contrary that 'the methods usually employed to
inflame the minds of a people wholly rude and ignorant ... are neither
pamphlets nor newspapers.' Rumour, gossip, and political insinuations
were the source of political mischief: an educated people knew what to
make of seditious pamphlets or papers, while an ignorant people could
not read them. As did the Tory councillors, Wilkie supported the 1801
School Act, but he had no agenda either of religious or of linguistic assimilation, and his conception of the educated person was of one who
had learned 'to employ his talents, to the greatest advantage for himself,
his family, and his country,' one who could share as well in the great
pleasures and practical benefits to be found in the Republic of Letters.
Those who opposed teaching the people to read selfishly refused them
such things. Rural French Canadians were especially in need of the benefits of instruction: lack of improvement in agriculture was due to their
inability to read. Lives were lost because rural people refused smallpox
vaccination out of ignorance.

Wilkie also intervened in the debate over urban prostitution. Correspondents in various newspapers claimed prostitution was drawing country people to the city, defaming daughters, turning sons into thieves, and
parents against children. 'L'Ami du peuple' had attempted a cost-benefit
analysis of this, 'the most fearful source of depravity, in this land.' Sup-
posing there were 500 prostitutes in the colony, living on 10s. per day, 'for,
in general, those ladies do not live sparingly,' the practice consumed
£91,250cy. yearly: triple the amount of the annual colonial revenue. 'Is it
surprising so many respectable merchants and tradesmen have failed?
Certainly not.'[13] Wilkie argued that education protected women against
seduction and cited Adam Smith's *Wealth of Nations* in support of the argument that it was the most ignorant women who were most likely to become prostitutes.

Finally, Wilkie was one of the first to advocate monitorial pedagogy.
The 1801 School Act provided the means of schooling the countryside,
but the cities needed the 'plan of instruction' of Joseph Lancaster, 'which
possesses every advantage with respect to the labouring classes; which
combines mildness, order, and virtuous tendency, with the highest efficacy in the real business of making scholars.' Wilkie had left Scotland in
1803, so had not seen a Lancasterian school himself (unless he went to
New York), but he was an eager reader of the *Edinburgh Review*.[14]

Wilkie's second notable political intervention was his appearance before the Assembly's Education Committee in 1824. Here he stated that the same desire for education existed in Canada as in Europe, and the country desperately needed a university and a system of parish schools. The university would stimulate learning generally, but would also be able to train teachers. Wilkie said that he frequently had to teach the inferior branches in his school and sometimes many of the advanced branches as well for lack of specialist teachers in the colony. Other serious problems were the absence of an officially sanctioned curriculum which could be used to judge candidates for the learned professions, and a general lack of science instruction and scientific apparatus in the colony. He recommended R.R. Burrage's Royal Grammar School as the best of its sort in the city to the MPPs.[15]

There was no other private teacher of Wilkie's stature in Quebec, although E.C. Collier competed with him for a few years from November 1814. Collier's Academy at the corner of rues St Anne and St Ursule meant to 'prepare young gentlemen for a *College* or *Compting-room*,' all the while uniting '*scientific instruction, with polite and elegant literature.*' Prospective clients were assured that 'respectable pupils only can be admitted.' Collier probably got into trouble with his clientele by teaching Protestant dogma and closed the school in late 1815 or early 1816. When he reopened in April 1816, he announced that henceforth 'the Catechism of the two Churches will be heard in separate apartments; that of the Church of Rome by an Assistant who is a member of it.' A Mr Simpson joined him to run a 'select Quebec Seminary for young Ladies' in separate rooms in Collier's school, where young women would be instructed in both French and English in the three Rs, geography with globes and astronomy for £2 a quarter with an entry fee of 10s.6d.[16]

Collier too held a public examination of his school, in the Assembly rooms of the Union Hotel in late December 1816. The *Mercury* reported that a great many respectable people were in the capacity audience and the Presbyterian Alexander Spark and the Anglicans Satter Mountain and R.R. Burrage took an active part in questioning the students. There were no Catholic luminaries in attendance. *Mercury* noted that 'the most numerous audience we ever recollect to have seen assembled on such an occasion' was present 'when the young gentlemen acquitted themselves with equal spirit and precision, particularly in their recital of the Tragedy of Cato.' By popular demand, the recitations were repeated the following Saturday in the same venue for those who could not get tickets the first time, with the proceeds going to the poor. However, Collier could not survive in the Quebec market, and after a set of moves from the city to the suburbs and back again he took the school to Montreal in the spring of 1818; there was no sign of him in Jacques Viger's 1825 school census.[17]

At the bottom of the Quebec market were an unknown number of petty schools which have left little or no trace. Teachers who advertised rarely offered only elementary instruction.[18] Curé Signäy's 1818 enumeration did not distinguish among the French-speaking teachers in terms of level of instruction, and he identified only three widows as teachers – almost certainly an undercount. Veuve Dupont lived two doors down from the civil secretary, Colonel Ready, in Cap Diamond and so may have aimed at a well-to-do clientele, and another widowed teacher, Magdelene Robitaille (veuve Ponsant) lived in the Upper Town and may have done likewise. The rarity of women identified as teachers is striking in Signäy's enumeration, and no child minders were singled out. One of the French male teachers he named, Joseph Vallerand, lived with the curé in Près de Ville and presumably taught in a vestry school. The best-known French-speaking male elementary schoolteacher in Quebec was Jean-Baptiste Corbin, who taught from 1798 until 1816. Signäy listed no occupation for him in 1818, and Corbin testified before the Assembly's Special Education Committee in 1824 that he had given up teaching because French-speaking parents were so poor that they were willing at most to pay only for two years' worth of elementary lessons.[19] There was a marked ethnic-religious-linguistic disparity in the amount of schooling on offer.

Including Daniel Wilkie's school, nine schools run by men (or husbands and wives), about one-fifth of those advertising, survived for five years or more between 1800 and 1820; four schools run by women survived four years or more. Of course, some schools opened after 1816 and continued in existence for many years – the Royal Grammar School was one and the school of the Misses Aspinall another. The latter, opened in 1820, offered 'every branch of Female Education' and featured dancing instruction by Miss S. Aspinall, who, it was proclaimed when she began, had 'during the last seven years,' been 'constantly under the tuition of Monsieur Vestpis, principal Dancer and Ballet Master at the Opera House, London.' The dance school was still active in 1837.[20]

Schools for Boys and Young Men

Of several of the more durable schools taught by men, little trace survives. One of them was conducted from 1794 to about 1805 and again after 1814 by the deputy Provincial Surveyor Jeremiah McCarthy and offered mathematics and instruction in surveying for the substantial sum of ten guineas. He can have attracted few students and was not likely helped by his alcoholism. A Mr Holden, who advertised first in November 1808 that he would teach geometry, trigonometry, mensuration, and bookkeeping, announced in October 1811 that he was giving up his school after eight years. A third teacher active throughout this period was the government-subsidized schoolmaster James Tanswell, whom we met in an earlier chapter, and a fourth was John Johnston, who advertised his services first in 1808 and was still doing so in 1820. Johnston offered private lessons in mathematics and military subjects, including the study of the weights, dimensions, and trajectories of balls and shells, as well as bookkeeping, at a variety of locations around the city. Johnston did not register as a teacher to curé Signäy, who described him as 'bourgeois,' and it is unlikely that Johnston taught many students, although some of the garrison officers may have patronized him.[21]

Two durable schools were taught by Methodist clergymen, although William Millar was not identified by curé Signäy as such. Millar advertised his evening school at 45 rue Champlain in January 1810, with fees at $4 a quarter. By 1816 the school was at 43 rue St Louis, where Signäy found him in 1818. The suggestion that he was a clergyman, or had some connections with Methodism, comes from his advertisement of 21 December 1811 that he was an agent for the British and Foreign Bible Society; so was George Spratt, whom Signäy identified not as a teacher but as a 'Ministre Methodiste.' Spratt arrived in Quebec early in 1812 and opened an academy for boys and girls on the corner of rues Ste Famille and St Joseph. He taught bookkeeping, Latin, Greek, and geography and by 1814 was advertising for boarders in his house, provided they knew the rudiments already. The school was interrupted briefly in 1815, Spratt said, because he had been ill, but he was better in July and announced that he was taking up permanent residence at 10 rue des Ramparts. His health seems to have responded to marriage, for he now began advertising with a Mrs Spratt, who offered to teach the young ladies needlework and the three Rs. They announced the imminent arrival of a writing master. Signäy claimed Spratt was in the Ste Foye suburb in 1818, but Spratt announced that year he was moving to Hope St (rue Ste Famille), and in 1820 he settled on Quebec's school row at 7 rue Ste Anne.[22]

A schoolmaster named Thom advertised his commercial school at 1 rue Champlain in 1811. He boasted of 'a very extensive Counting-House Practice,' and suggested he would 'qualify his Pupils for becoming uncommonly accurate and expert Men of Business.' In 1816 he moved into Daniel Wilkie's old schoolrooms at 5 rue Carrière and added an evening school for advanced commercial training, stressing his 'eleven years' practice, as a Book-keeper, in two Counting houses of the first eminence.' He announced on another occasion that his students would practise writing commercial letters and drawing up bills of exchange. In 1818, he was at 35 rue Champlain. Perhaps he is the same Mr Thom who taught later as an assistant in the Quebec National School.[23]

The last schoolmaster with a relatively stable presence who advertised in the Quebec press was Thomas Marsden, a man who made a bit of a stir with his troubles with the police in 1820. Marsden first advertised a night school for elementary subjects and bookkeeping in October 1812 and then appeared again in July 1816 to announce his return to the city after an absence. When Thom moved into Wilkie's old schoolrooms in 1816, Marsden took over Thom's old rooms at 1 rue Champlain and stayed there until April 1819. He offered to teach the standard branches of an English education, opened an evening school, and then offered his school and its books on Sundays for three hours for free instruction in reading (of scripture lessons, it appears). He also informed the public that he would be available at other times 'to tune pianos, harpsichords, organs &c.' A few months later he advertised a singing school, with a focus on psalmody, on Saturday evenings for men and on Wednesday afternoons for students of both sexes. At some point in his career, Marsden also acted as a financial agent for teachers seeking government grant money.

His trouble with the law began one summer evening in 1820 when he was roughed up by the night watch and jailed. In Marsden's account of events, he had been innocently standing in the street with his son in front of his house at 3 rue Ste Famille watching a charivari when the watch came by, chasing and beating the participants. He was struck himself. After the crowd moved away, Marsden set out on his usual evening walk but was told by the watch commander that he could not go where he planned. They had words, and the commander told him he was taking him to jail, then relented, saying Marsden could go home on the promise to appear at the police office in the morning. He did so and was called before the sitting magistrate, Mr Caron, who made him read aloud a passage from the Black Act about dressing in disguise. The watch commander testified that he had arrested three men the previous evening, one in disguise and two not, including Marsden. He claimed Marsden had called out to the crowd '"Damn the Canadian Watchman knock him down with a stone,"' and Caron, learning Marsden was a teacher commented, '"hum – I should not like my children to be tutored by such a Schoolmaster."' He committed Marsden to jail, where he spent three days until the solicitor general ordered bail, but he remained charged with a felony. Finally, at the September 1820 Grand Jury sessions, a 'no bill' was returned in the matter. Marsden immediately announced his evening school was open for the winter.[24]

Schools for Girls and Young Women

A number of 'ladies' boarding schools' came and went in the first two decades of the nineteenth century with only a few of them lasting four years or more. Mrs Scott's 'Quebec Boarding School for Young Ladies' was one, open at least in April 1811 and still advertising in August 1818. Joseph Signäy reported a Mr Scott as a schoolteacher that year, but no male Scott advertised in the press. However, in 1811, Mrs Scott offered to teach the basics, English and French grammar, geography, and plain and fancy needlework in her school, which she said was expanding. She charged very high fees: 3 guineas as an entrance fee and then £8.15s. quarterly for board and washing, with £2.10s. extra for tuition. Students were to provide their own sheets and a silver tea and table spoon. In 1818 she offered to teach literature, poetry, and embroidery in the boarding school but did not announce her fees.[25] Mrs Goodman's 'School for Young Ladies' was open in May 1812, its proprietress 'having been for many years in the practice of teaching in London' and by year's end she said it had 'increased beyond her most sanguine expectations.' She had hired a writing master and had written to London 'for a Lady to assist in teaching the Arts and Sciences.' She moved from her initial location near the Chateau to 1 rue St Louis in mid-1813 and the following January announced she had hired a drawing master. In January 1816 she advertised that she had space for two more parlour boarders, but by September of that year another teacher had taken over her rooms and she disappeared from view.[26]

In addition to these two schools, Mrs Abbot's preparatory school advertised once in the *Mercury* on 5 January 1813, and she was listed as a school mistress by Joseph Signäy in 1818. The Misses Dalrymple opened their day and boarding school in rue des Jardins in November 1816, declaring they would only admit twelve boarders and twenty day students, terms to be revealed on application. The school was sufficiently viable for them to move onto school row in May 1818, to 18 rue Ste Anne, across from St Andrews Church. At the rue Ste Anne address, Joseph Signäy reported 'trois delles – maîtresses d'école' in his enumeration later that year. If these were three 'delles' Dalrymple, they were four in 1820 when their sister, Miss E. Dalrymple, joined them to offer private lessons in Japaning, Painting on glass, and Theorem and Transparency painting. One of the sisters probably applied to the Royal Institution for a school only to be told that women could not be RI teachers.[27]

Middle- and upper-class girls and young women were also taught by women who were married to the more stable schoolmasters. Mrs Tanswell offered instruction in French to day students and boarders and Mrs Spratt taught a girls' school, for instance. Other more ephemeral girls' schools opened close to the boys' schools: Mrs Gale taught girls needlework and dressmaking, announcing they could keep the clothing they made, in a house a few doors up rue Ste Famille from Thomas Marsden.[28]

Transience

The large numbers of teachers advertising schools for brief periods under-lines the transient nature of the market. The fact that the same addresses appear again and again in school ads shows the paucity of educational infrastructure in the city. Would-be schoolteachers often started out by working in an established school, then tried to supplement their incomes by teaching a night school, and then branched out on their own, either alone or with some other former assistant. Thus, for instance, T. Green from J. Jones's school and R. Elms from E.C. Collier's academy joined together in May 1816 to open the 'New Commercial School' at which they were willing to accept a few ladies. By May 1818, Green was teaching the school at 13 rue Ste Famille by himself, and by September he had given up his space to two teachers named Briggs and Walsh. They in turn separated in December 1818, with Briggs keeping the schoolrooms, which were now at 1 rue St Georges. Cornelius Doyle and Basil Collyer took over E.C. Collier's school rooms when he moved to the suburbs and taught together for six months. When Collier returned to Quebec, Doyle and Collyer split and started two new schools: Collyer announced 'A Day and Boarding School for Young Gentlemen,' but by mid-1820 he was reduced to teaching the three Rs with geography and to dealing in books in a room in a house in rue St Paul. Doyle opened the 'Classical and Commercial School' at no. 6 rue du Palais, offering to teach geography, English, French, Latin, Greek, and bookkeeping for £2.10 a quarter, with a reduction for begin-ning readers. His school was still open in June 1820.[29]

That even Daniel Wilkie found himself in straitened circumstances by 1820 points to the precariousness of teaching as an occupation for all those who did not have access to government backing or the support of a congregation. Any teaching job with a stable salary attracted a wave of applications. When it was announced in 1816 that the new Quebec Royal Grammar School needed a writing master, five teachers applied at once, including E.C. Collier himself, the Mr Simpson who was teaching girls and young women at Collier's school, Collier's former assistant R. Elms, who had set out on his own, Mr Thom, and the young writing teacher John Burns, who had been teaching with Daniel Wilkie for two months and who claimed to have ten years' experience in London.[30]

In sum, parents who had money and young adults in employment who wanted to improve their knowledge of commercial or military matters could readily find schools for their sons or daughters or themselves. To a person with money, the market offered educational variety: one could learn navigation and the construction of charts from R. Milbourn, but he would also teach German or the flute, clarinet, and fife. One could study English grammar with Thomas Marsden, but he would also teach singing and tune one's piano. The Misses Dalrymple would teach to read and write, but also to decorate glass. What the market did not and could not provide was generally accessible, stable elementary instruction for the population as a whole, including free or cheap instruction for workers, moderately priced advanced instruction within the reach of artisans and petty bourgeois households, and university training for the learned professions. There was no independent body controlling the content or the quality of instruction.

Dunghill Cocks

A debate in the *Quebec Mercury* which ran off and on for over two years from early 1817 shows the considerable dissatisfaction with the schooling on offer. In mid-February 1817 'An Old Subscriber' bemoaned the absence of a good academy offering a complete liberal education in the colony and also complained of 'so many petty schools being set up by persons who are too indolent to work at some decent trade.' Some fugitive debtor from the United States would arrive in Quebec and 'like a dunghill cock on a mount' would set to crowing 'that he is perfectly master of the languages, and of all the arts and sciences' and if he attracted public attention, would then hire some disbanded soldier more ignorant than himself and advertise an '"*Academy for the Instruction of Youth.*"' 'Old Subscriber's' opinions generated a large number of responses, but matters had not improved any by late 1818, despite the opening of the new

Royal Grammar School. It charged £12 a year with extra fees for advanced subjects, and while it did admit a number of students for free, its clientele was composed of the sons of the English colonial elite.[31]

In the late summer of 1818, a correspondent to the *Quebec Mercury* again painted a dismal picture of the state of teaching and the abilities of teachers in the city. His intervention was followed by the formation of a Quebec School Association, which planned to raise funds by subscription to bring a trained English schoolmaster to Quebec and to offer him £200 a year in exchange for teaching sixty students. This proposal generated a very large volume of letters and commentary, with accusations that the association members were attempting to form an oppressive monopoly in order to render independent teachers subservient. Before the association could give effect to its plans, the Church of England organized a monitorial school in the city and another in Montreal. The Anglicans were followed in Quebec by Catholics with their Société d'Éducation. The group involved in the School Association then organized the British and Canadian School Society.[32]

Montreal Inventories and School Statistics

Except for the presence of some institutions subsidized by the Sulpiciens, the supply of schools in Montreal was similar to that in Quebec. So much is evident from the school inventories produced for 1825 and 1835 by the grand voyer and mayor Jacques Viger. They show a transient private market in schooling in Montreal. As Andrée Dufour has pointed out, only six of the twenty-nine private venture schools listed by Viger for 1825 were still in existence in 1835.[33] Indeed, of the forty-seven private venture schools Viger described in 1835, twenty-five had been in existence for less than two years, and almost half these opened in 1835 itself. The inventories also give a measure of the impact of the new monitorial schools organized from 1819 on schooling in the city. In 1825 a large majority of the students Viger counted attended such schools, while by 1835 twice as many students were in more or less permanent schools using monitorial pedagogy than were in private venture schools. Before 1820, schooling in Montreal had been primarily a private enterprise.

Jacques Viger made a rare attempt to combine description and statistical abstraction for urban schooling, and while he was a city official, his was amateur work. Some educational bodies in the city in the 1820s thought it important to know the size of the school-age population, as did some MPPs. Yet before the (re-)incorporation of the cities in 1841, no comprehensive investigation other than Viger's was undertaken. The absence of an administrative agency able to investigate left the field to amateurs. Viger's inventories were political documents in addition to ways to satisfy his pleasure in collecting and arranging facts. That for 1825 was produced in 1828 to aid François Blanchet in framing his school act, while that for 1835 was produced at the request of Viger's cousin Louis-Joseph Papineau as the MPPs were investigating the operations of the Trustees School Act. Viger provided the information he produced in 1836 to his other cousin, Jean-Jacques Lartigue, and later presented it to the Buller Education Commission.[34]

The inventories provided a list of schools in the rural parishes of the county as well as in the city, with a description of what was taught in each and of the fees charged. Viger also produced tabular summaries of his findings and compared those of 1835 with those of 1825. He was dealing with population as a statistical artefact that could be configured in various ways and whose movement over time could be presented as instructive and politically useful. The lack of any discussion by Viger of his observational protocols or of the content or derivation of his reporting categories invites attention to his statistics as performance, since without such information we cannot know how precisely he realized his intentions. Yet he went beyond the rough estimations and guesswork common in debate to take up schooling as a statistical object. A slight reworking of his results can be seen in table 3.1.

While Viger was county census commissioner in 1825 and so had access to enumeration materials for that year, he derived his 1835 numbers by assuming that the average growth rates for the intercensal years 1825–31 held constant to 1835 and, moreover, that they applied uniformly to all categories of population. At the least, that assumption promotes an unusually high mortality rate for six- and seven-year-olds. Viger presented no discussion of what he meant by a 'student,' simply recording after his description of each school a number for them, which sometimes changed from one part of his inventory to the next. Later readers have no way of knowing if he meant those in attendance, those enrolled, those present the day he visited the school, or something else.

Some of his observational practice can be reconstructed by looking at other sources of information and by attending to internal inconsistencies. Viger excluded those five years of age and younger from his count of the school-age population, but his 1835 inventory included students in the Montreal Orphan Asylum, those in the school run by the Montreal Ladies' Benevolent Society, and those in the Montreal Infant School – a

Table 3.1. School-age population and students at school in Montreal county and city, 1825 and 1835

	Aged 6–13	Aged 14–17	Aged 6–17	All students 6–17	As % of 6–17
1825					
County population 37,279	6,550	3,210	9,760	2,911	29.8
City population 22,540	3,586	1,887	5,473	2,550	46.6
1835					
County population 48,810	8,485	4,187	12,762	4,467	35.0
City population 31,193	4,963	2,611	7,574	3,849	50.1

Source: *Enseignement public dans le Comté de Montréal, en 1825. Enseignement public dans le Comté de Montréal, en 1835.* Archives du Séminaire du Québec, Manuscrit 018.[35]

total of about 170 – despite the fact that many of these were younger than six years of age. The Infant School accepted children eighteen months old. A further minor source of exaggeration for 1835 seems to be a willingness on Viger's part to report as 'schools' the child-minding activities of local women, none of which appear in his 1825 inventory. For instance, he reported Anna Holmes as running a school with fifteen students, although she charged only about half the average petty school fee (1s.3d.) and taught only reading, sewing, and knitting. 'The mistress does not know how to write,' he noted.[36]

On the other hand, Viger excluded the city's Protestant Sunday schools from his return and did not report the educational activities of the Protestant clergymen. He was himself relatively devout and was directly interested in Catholic schooling as president of his cousin's École St Jacques. Yet the city's Presbyterians had a Sunday school from at least 1817 whose object was 'to prevent children from trifling on God's holy day, and to turn their attention to the Scriptures, and to explanatory books.' It was claimed in that year 'the School is becoming numerous.' As did the monitorial schools, the Presbyterians gave the scholars 'printed tickets, and prizes in books, &c. And those of them who are poor, require to be supplied gratis with the books also, which are used in School.'[37] In 1824, Montreal Sunday Union School volunteers taught children in groups of six for two to three hours weekly in the British and Canadian School house, presenting elementary instruction in English with the reading of religious lessons and the repetition of passages of scripture. Many of the children wore clothing provided by the Dorcas Society. The Sunday School Union was sponsored by Thaddeus Osgood, who connected it to its sister organizations in London and in York and Kingston and who offered the Unions subsidized books for distribution.[38] A decade later, the Montreal Young Men's Association was running two 'flourishing' Sunday schools, with enrolment reported as 175 and average Sunday attendance as about 100.[39] By 1838, the Wesleyan Methodists had six Montreal Sunday schools, the Presbyterians continued to be active in the field, and there were several other Sunday schools offering free elementary instruction to working-class children and young people, often supplemented with free books and clothing.[40] They offered as much occasion for a young person to learn to read as did Mme Holmes's school, but Viger did not include them in his inventory. In short, Viger probably underestimated the numbers of students in the age categories he used for 1835, but very probably underestimated the numbers of young people in those categories who had some exposure to instruction in reading and writing, in a day school, an evening school, or a Sunday school. The schooling provided by Protestant organizations was under-reported.

Viger also seems to have missed some private institutions. Mrs Blackwood, for instance, was running a boarding school, of which a 'very favorable opinion' had been 'entertained by Lady Aylmer, at an Examination … in the month of June 1831' and for which she was seeking government aid in the summer of 1834. She wanted to train young women in need of earning a living as teachers and she proposed to use monitorial methods. She was still advertising in 1835 but did not appear in Viger's account.[41]

The point is not that Viger's account is not accurate. Rather, what is significant is that already in 1828 – the year in which the Canada Committee problematized colonial government as a whole – Viger attempted to grasp the whole field of schooling. He sought to make his individual descriptions of schools legible in new ways through statistical abstraction. He configured his statistics to present what to him was a pleasing and politically useful analysis that stressed the benign effects of the Catholic institutions. In his second inventory, he made it possible to observe dynamic tendencies in the educational field. This work was proto-social science.

The dominance of the monitorial schools in Montreal was already striking in 1825, and matters were similar in Quebec. In the rest of this chapter, I describe the main institutions in the two cities for the period ending in 1841.

The National Schools – Quebec

After the defeat of the Free School Society, the Church of England organized National Schools in Quebec and Montreal that used Andrew Bell's Madras pedagogy.[42] The schools immediately enrolled a goodly number of pauper children but never gave the Anglicans control over urban education. Their enrolments remained relatively stable over time in absolute terms, but declined relative to the urban population. The schools formed an integral part of the plans of the Board of the Royal Institution for the Advancement of Learning. It was stacked with high church Anglicans and was a ward of zealots in the Quebec Diocesan Committee of the Society for the Promotion of Christian Knowledge (SPCK) formed in 1818.

Archbishop Mountain's son G.J. Mountain was instrumental in organizing the Quebec Diocesan Committee. He had been impressed by British North America's first Madras school when in Halifax in 1817. Having beaten back the Free School Society, hoping that the Royal Institution would soon gain control of the Jesuits' Estates, and perhaps also aware of its parishioners' attempts to form a school association, the Quebec Diocesan Committee announced plans in October 1818 for a National School. It had received a grant of £200 a year for three years from the Society for the Propagation of the Gospel and it described the school project as aiming 'to disseminate a National Education upon the groundwork of a National Religion – and to perpetuate that union of Church and State, which they trust will continue indissoluble to the end of time.'[43] That ambition was never realized.

A year passed before the committee opened a school, in premises offered by the Duke of Richmond in the Hope Gate barracks. These were rooms vacated by the Free School, and the Anglican school managers sometimes slyly called their school 'the Free School' as well. The Diocesan Committee sent for a schoolmaster and mistress from England, who were expected in the spring of 1820, and in the interim hired John Bignell, a Chelsea Royal Hospital pensioner from Matilda in Upper Canada. To cover moving expenses for Bignell and his family, Mills arranged for the civil secretary to pay him the late James Tanswell's £100 salary by a back-dated warrant. However, their English master, William Henry Shadgett, and a school mistress, both trained at the National

Society's London Baldwin's Gardens school, arrived before Bignell and took charge of the new school in November 1819. Shadgett's costs were apparently covered by the back-dated warrant.[44]

A Sunday collection at the cathedral raised over £72 for school support, and the Diocesan Committee described what it expected would take place in the schools in an 1820 pamphlet, *Regulations for the Quebec Central Schools for Boys and Girls.* Similar regulations applied in the Montreal National School. The schools were to adopt Andrew Bell's system, except that Roman Catholics and Presbyterians would attend their own churches on Sundays and the former would, and the latter could, be exempted from studying the Church of England catechism. Nothing was said about Dissenters. Indigent parents had reduced fees of 10s. or 5s. per quarter, and their children would be exempt from cutting firewood or sweeping the schools, while subscribers to the schools could recommend poor children for admission. The female students were to spend much of their time at needlework: the *Regulations* included a very long retail price list for their products, which ranged from women's and boys' Irish shirts at a shilling each down to linsey-woolsey drawers for a penny. The girls could keep half the proceeds from any sale. There was no mention of craft or artisan work for boys.

Despite antipathy on the part of Anglican ideologues in England to Joseph Lancaster's practice of allowing students to accumulate merit tickets to exchange for prizes, the Quebec regulations endorsed and regulated prize giving. Teachers were to track the performance of each student carefully in a 'register of *Individual Proficiency.*' Two female visitors, appointed for a month and drawn from a visitation committee of twenty-four, were to visit the school at least weekly and to note the children's conduct, to inspect the proficiency register and the *'marked books'* of the teachers, and to distribute tickets of merit or demerit to individual students. Both at the public examination of the school and upon students graduating from it, 'those children who shall be found to unite good conduct and due regularity with proficiency in learning, will receive separate prizes on each account – and those who are guilty of misconduct and deficiency of attendance at Church or School, will forfeit title to any prize upon whatever account.' The *Regulations* also specified hours and days of instruction and how the students' attendance at Sunday service was to be supervised. Passing mention was made of treatment for students only attending on Sundays and for those attending an evening school.

The Quebec National School attracted students as soon as it opened, with 89 boys and 40 girls enrolled in 1819 and with 193 boys and 45 girls enrolled by May 1820 – out of a possible catchment of several thousand, however. One hundred twenty-nine boys and 59 girls were present at the first examination of the school that May, which was attended by Sir Peregrine Maitland, the Anglican luminaries, and respectable citizens, with musical entertainment by the band of the 76th Regiment. Another collection in the cathedral yielded more than £80.[45] The fact that girls were expected to sew merchandise for sale while boys learned their letters may explain why relatively few girls attended. W.H. Shadgett proved unable to manage the boys. In August 1821, J.L. Mills informed the executive that 'the conduct of Mr Shadgett, Master of the Free School at Quebec, has been so improper in every respect' that the school's management had replaced him with a Mr Fleming and expected two new teachers from England in 1822. The latter, a married couple named Little, had more success.[46]

The Quebec National School averaged about 200 students throughout the period before 1840, although enrolment and attendance levels fluctuated. Working-class and poor parents sent their children to school when they did not need them to work, and in the absence of any compulsory attendance regulations or enforcement apparatus, students could come and go as they pleased. The National School's committee report for 1840 described the fluctuations in student numbers:

> There is a falling off in the attendance for a short time about the first of May and the first of November, owing to a change of residence [of adults]. Many of the poorer children remain at home during the severe part of the winter from the want of warm clothing – their places are however generally filled up by children who obtain employment during the Spring and Summer months but return during the Winter – The greatest changes take place about the opening of the navigation; when all the boys who are sufficiently advanced are taken from the school as apprentices – The children received about this period are generally small, being from the infant Schools, and such as had never been at School before.[47]

The school's intake was also challenged by the 1820 Papal Bull against Bible schools, by competing institutions in the 1820s, and later by amendments to the School Act of 1829, which qualified suburban trustee schools for government grants.

With its sister institution in Montreal, the Quebec school became increasingly dependent for survival upon financial aid from the Assembly, receiving over £100 annually from 1826 and occasionally much more in aid of its building projects. At least until 1831, both schools also drew £100 annually as Royal Institution schools, and both raised money by subscription and special levies. In Quebec, despite the fact the SPG had offered to subsidize the school only for three years, the Diocesan Committee pressed ahead with plans for the construction of a permanent schoolhouse, which opened in 1824, well over cost, at 10 rue d'Auteuil close to the porte St Jean. Pleas were made for legislative aid and government construction grants amounted to £1,167. There were two elementary schoolrooms on the site, each measuring 46' × 34' × 10', and by the mid-1830s, the site was the Anglican educational complex, with R.R. Burrage's house and the buildings of the Royal Grammar School (by then in decline) at no. 11. The school received £100 stg. from the Special Council for 1838–9 and reported 160 students in attendance in 1840, 92 boys and 68 girls, 89 of them under ten years of age. These numbers were smaller than the school had attracted in 1820, while Quebec's population had increased markedly.[48]

The Montreal National School

In Montreal, application had been made by to the Executive Council by Alexander Neil Bethune (the future rector of Cobourg) to receive the salary of the recently deceased schoolmaster Finlay Fisher in 1819, shortly before the organization of a Montreal Diocesan Committee. Bethune was 'desirous of opening a School in this City, to be taught on the Madrass System. – That his intention, in adopting this System, is to enable him to receive into his Schools, one poor child, to be taught gratis, for every four who shall pay; so that one-fourth of his School shall be taught on *Charity*.' Government aid would be necessary to pay for the charity scholars. At the same time, his brother John Bethune, soon to be rector of Christ Church, was advertising a school in his own house.[49]

The Montreal Diocesan Committee organized its National School some time in the spring or summer of 1819. The £100 salary for a Montreal Royal Institution school went to W.G. Holmes, who was hired with his wife (for £25 or £50) to teach a boys' and a girls' National School. The school, overseen by a management committee of high Tory merchant capitalists and officials, was an immediate success in terms of enrolment, and the committee moved before its Quebec counterpart to build a permanent schoolhouse which opened in rue Bonsecours in 1823. A second storey containing apartments for the male and female teacher was finished by about 1830. The legislature granted £690 over the course of the decade for the schoolhouse, and annual grants to the school were about £110, with further funds coming from the Royal Institution until 1832. After the Assembly gained control over the revenues from the Jesuits' Estates and after the School Act of 1832 sought to absorb the Royal Institution schools into the trustee school structures, the male teacher lost his £100 from the Royal Institution and was paid £72 thereafter. By 1835, the boys' schoolteacher was a W. Green and the girls' a Mrs Howard.[50]

The secretary of the Montreal National School committee and of the Diocesan Committee was Alexander Skakel, master of the Royal Grammar school. As in Quebec, funds were raised for the school through charity sermons in the Anglican cathedral, which showcased the schoolchildren for their benefactors. Nahum Mower of the *Canadian Courant* toured the institution in January 1824 and reported that both the boys' and girls' schools were in a 'high state of order and decorum.' He reported only 90 boys and 30 to 40 girls in attendance, although he did not see the night schools. By contrast, in October, while announcing the upcoming sermon for the benefit of the SPCK, he reported that the school had 349 students in attendance.[51]

The annual report of the Montreal SPCK committee in 1825, delivered by the military chaplain B.B. Stevens, reminded the public that in Montreal as in Quebec the functions of the SPCK were joined with those of the National Society. The committee had established a library and book depot for the distribution of Bibles, prayer books, tracts, and reading sheets, and it had used a donation of £150 from five Montreal gentlemen and a loan of £200 from its English parent to construct its schoolhouse for the accommodation of 400 students, for which it was still in debt. As of April 1825, the school had 202 boys and 96 girls enrolled, although over the course of the year, a total of 443 students had attended the school. Of those then enrolled, only 74 belonged to the Church of England, with 72 Presbyterians, 46 Methodists, 'and no less than 106 are members of the Church of Rome; of which 106 be it specially remarked that 97 are *French Canadians*.' The last fact was particularly agreeable, wrote Stevens, because 'it furnishes a most triumphant reply to the mis-representation of those who publicly and privately represent the measures of the society as "party measures" their system as confined exclusively to the Church of England, and contrast it with, what they term the "conciliatory principles adopted by the British and Foreign School Society," declaring "that no other plan" but their own "can embrace the Roman Catholics."'[52]

Jacques Viger reported in 1835-6 that the Montreal National School had 339 students, 200 boys and 139 girls, all instructed free of charge. The school's committee, by contrast, reported a total of 295 students. According to Viger, the boys were taught the three Rs, grammar, and bookkeeping, while the girls got the three Rs and sewing lessons. No account survives of the sale of their work. While the National School was the city's largest in terms of enrolment according to Viger in 1835 as in 1825, its relative importance had declined. Still, as did its Quebec counterpart, the Montreal school continued to draw an annual parliamentary grant, with interruptions caused by struggles over the Civil List and by the insurrectionary battles of 1837 and 1838, until the end of the period studied here. The National Schools were not funded by the Assembly with the same liberality as were the British and Canadian Schools and the Société d'Éducation de Québec.[53]

The Société d'Éducation de Québec

The Société d'Éducation du District de Québec was formed in response to Lord Dalhousie's reservation of the 1821 School Act. The intellectual Louis Plamondon was one who promoted the society at a large public meeting on 7 May 1821. After lamenting the deplorable state of ignorance in the colony and offering some treacle for the clergy, he argued that it was necessary to form an organization to petition for passage of the 1821 act and, in anticipation of its passage, to form a district board of education to facilitate the establishment of parish schools, the provision of schoolbooks, and the encouragement of teachers. Plamondon said the society would be a subscription society, modelled on the English Society for the Arts.[54]

The Société was remarkable because sixteen of the twenty-one members of the management committee were laymen, including Joseph-François Perrault as president, a notorious liberal in the eyes of conservative churchmen, with the seminary director and science teacher Jérôme Demers and the notary and partisan of *Le Canadien* Joseph Planté as vice-presidents. The MPP Louis Lagueux, a wealthy lawyer and banker, who would support the *patriote* project of a democratic church vestry in the early 1830s, was secretary, with his well-to-do relative Étienne-Claude Lagueux as treasurer. The presence of the curé and future Bishop Joseph Signäy on the society's committee attested to the approval of Bishop Plessis, who also subscribed £15. Religious and political antagonisms over large questions of policy and over matters of educational organization and practice would soon fracture the society, but here was a moment of unity in support of the Catholic education of the poor in Quebec, with the clergy ceding an important measure of control to laymen.

The society set to work at once and published a detailed set of *Resolutions et Règles*. To the number of thirty-one, they proposed a heavily bureaucratic structure in comparison with that of the Anglican bodies and the lay organizations soon to follow. Still, the society aimed to provide a Catholic education, whose absence was described as the main barrier to colonial progress. The society announced it would restrict itself to elementary education and not compete with established Catholic institutions. The management committee of twenty-one members was to be elected by ballot with a third of the members going out of office in turn; seven members were a quorum. There would be quarterly meetings, and all motions or resolutions required advance written notice. No grant for aid or expenditure of more than £10 was to be made without a meeting in which at least fifteen members were present, and two-thirds of those were required to approve it. Other regulations affected accounting matters and empowered the management committee to form specialized subcommittees for such purposes as it saw fit. No teacher would be hired who 'had not been examined as to his way of life and morals, studies and ability by the committee and approved by two-thirds of the members then present.' Presumably in this way the lay elite and the Catholic hierarchy could be secure in what was taught to the poor of Quebec. The society planned to offer much cheaper schooling than was currently available in the district and it raised a public subscription of over £366, almost entirely from French-speaking donors.[55]

The society circulated petitions in favour of the 1821 School Act and tried to raise money for schools by subscription in the district. These distinct objectives confused matters and created scepticism and hostility from the district's *habitants*. The curés were employed to circulate both subscription list and petition, and some curés thought only those who subscribed could sign the petition. Learning such was not the case, they erased subscribers' names from the petition and started to circulate a different list. Juggling with printed documents made peasants suspicious. 'The *habitants* openly refused to put their names to the petition, alleging that Mister so-and-so was not acting in good faith,' because he said he was doing one thing and then another. Worse, the society's committee soon announced it had applied successfully for a grant from the legislature: it seemed to solicit money it did not need, and it was said that some curés, knowing full well the society had the means only for single free school in Quebec, told people that subscriptions would be used to establish free schools in their parishes. Some very poor people contributed in the vain hope of educating their children.[56]

Le Canadien published a mock dialogue between 'un curé' and 'un habitant' in which the former asked the latter if he would not contribute to the Société d'Éducation. The peasant replied that he would not because

> there's a real smart Mister who told me I'd better keep me money for meself. He said that there school warn't but fer de city folk, so the poor *habitants* wuddn't git nothin.' They told us clear that what I gived would be for to build a school in our parish, and are kids and are grandkids would go to that there school. But this Mister told me straight it was for buildin' it inna city. If we'd given me money, we'd'a found ourselves in a fix, us what has such a tough time makin' a livin.'[57]

The *habitant* was astute, for the Société d'Éducation had no impact on rural schooling. It came to be known not as the education society of the district of Quebec, but the education society of the city of Quebec. *Habitant* antagonism to the draining away of rural resources towards urban schools was already evident and would increase over the next two decades.

By the time of the Société's quarterly meeting in November 1821, it had launched a school for boys using Joseph-François Perrault's translation of Joseph Lancaster's system. Perrault's *Cours d'éducation élémentaire à l'usage de l'école gratuite* was a close copy of Lancaster's *Experiment in Education* and stressed the pedagogical principle of energizing and engaging students in learning through constant and varied activity. The apparatus and practices of a typical monitorial school were presented, but Perrault innovated by applying the industrial command structures of monitorial pedagogy to praying and to learning the Quebec catechism. Where Lancaster's boys lined up at their places in front of their benches, responded to the command "Hats off," slung them and hung them on a hook before taking their seats, Perrault's boys heard "Attention! Caps Off! Kneel! Join Your Hands! Cross Yourself! Stand Up! Sit!"[58] Moral cleanliness was sought by questioning students on their catechism at least twice a week and physical cleanliness by daily inspecting their hands, faces, and bare feet.

Perrault reported at the November 1821 meeting that the teacher, the monitors, and the students were progressing rapidly. The proof of the school's worth lay in the fact that beginners had learned as much in five weeks about letters and numbers as they would have in five months under the old method of instruction. The committee had made an expensive purchase of letters and numbers on cut-out and painted tin, which made it possible to give examples to the whole school using the telegraphs which were placed strategically about the schoolroom. Large savings were made by using slates rather than pens, paper, and ink.

While the school was clearly a success, a large number of Quebec children were not in school, and the society petitioned the legislature for aid to expand. Perrault, closely supported by John Neilson, appeared before a legislative committee early in 1822 to answer questions. He revealed that the school had cost about £188 to run in its first year and estimated it would need £158 in its second. Some of the costs involved providing children with winter clothes and shoes. The Société wished to move out of its temporary accommodation in space provided by the Soeurs de la Congrégation into a purpose-built school of its own. It sought a grant of £200 a year and a further £500 for a school, but given the battle over the Civil List, the money bill failed in Council. In 1823 a grant of £200 was made.[59]

J.-J. Jolois has commented that 'the very presence of Mgr. Plessis' at the school's first public examination in May 1822 'conferred considerable importance upon the Société d'éducation.' It was expanding and taking steps to organize a girls' school, but it was challenged in the fall of 1823 by the organization of the Quebec British and Canadian School Society. J.-F. Perrault agreed to preside over the new society, apparently convinced that the Société d'Éducation was not operating as effectively as it might because of its denominational and linguistic orientation and its focus on the catechism. When news of Perrault's involvement in the new society was announced, the secretary of the Société d'Éducation advertised in the Quebec press that his organization 'has nothing in common with the recently formed Society called the "British and Canadian Society,"' stressed that there were completely separate management committees and funds, and announced his organization was opening an English-language school for boys and that henceforth it would offer free teacher training in the Lancasterian system to anyone wishing to attend. Still, there was considerable overlap in the organizational and management committees for the two organizations.[60]

Bishop J.-J. Lartigue responded to Perrault's association with the British and Canadian School with a set of scathing attacks. In a letter to Bishop Plessis, he congratulated himself on having nothing to do with the new school, which was only a front for the Royal Institution. Perrault's school was obviously becoming a Bible school, which for Lartigue meant a Protestant school or a completely impious one. He lamented the fact of Lord Dalhousie's patronage, which would make it difficult to stop the new school. At the time, the press was openly discussing Perrault's efforts to compose a non-denominational Christian catechism for the use of the schools over which he presided. Lartigue's continuing antagonism, perhaps shared by Bishop Plessis as Perrault formulated his 1825 School Bill, forced Perrault to resign as president of the Société sometime after April 1824, to be replaced by a better friend to the clergy in François Romain, whom we have heard described as knowing how to dance to the Catholic bishop's tune.[61]

We know little in detail about the internal operations of the Société's Quebec school after it moved into its new quarters, whose dimensions were 48 feet by 40 feet, two storeys, and built in about 1829 in rue des Glacis. There was little press commentary until the mid-1830s. Like the other urban school societies, the Société was subject to the fallout from ongoing struggles between branches of the legislature – prorogation in 1827 meant it had to wait a year for its grant – but it also received the most generous of the parliamentary subsidies offered to urban schools: £912 in 1830, £880 in 1834, for instance, before the Assembly began to adopt economy measures in its urban education budget, and £250 and £280 under the Special Council in 1838 and 1840.[62]

President François Romain was one of Quebec's 1832 cholera victims. His successor was the Société's secretary, Hector-Simon Huot, the moderate *patriote* MPP for Portneuf, brother-in-law to the Société's first secretary, Louis Lagueux, and the man who followed John Neilson as chair of the Assembly's Permanent Committee on Education after the 1834 elections. Huot was also in the group which relaunched *Le Canadien* newspaper, edited by Étienne Parent, and he supported the 92 Resolutions of 1834. The Société thus continued to have friends in high places, but these were not the friends who had launched it: many of them were champions of lay electoral management of social institutions, including schools and the vestry. The society's existence was threatened by Huot's firing of its teachers in 1834–5, which led to a conflict with the clergy – short-lived, as it turned out – involving the resignation en masse of the lay executive. The surviving public evidence is sufficiently fragmentary that even *Le Canadien* called for someone to clarify matters, but things came to a head at the society's quarterly meeting of 12 February 1835. On 13 February the Quebec papers carried a public notice signed by Huot, the society's secretary, N.-F. Belleau, and its treasurer, Pierre Petitclair, declaring that because of their resignations, they would no longer receive applications from teachers nor offer information; people should refer instead to curé C.-F. Baillargeon, the vice-president. A few days later, the clerics on the executive, Jérôme Demers and Baillargeon, called an extraordinary meeting for 26 February.

Matters were obviously sorted out, for on 11 March 1835, N.-F. Belleau announced that the former executive was again accepting applications and in April gave notice of the society's quarterly meeting in May. There the management committee was expanded from twenty-one to thirty-one members, nine of them clerics, with the sitting executive re-elected and meetings limited to one annually. The new lay membership was drawn almost exclusively from the tight political clique of the Quebec *patriote* party. Immediately after the May 1835 meeting, the society's school hosted the party's Reform Association, organized in the city to counter the agitations of the Quebec Constitutional Association in which John Neilson was heavily implicated. As its spokesman Étienne Parent claimed, the Reform Association was 'a school of Politics for the industrial and working classes, whose constant labour prevents them from acquiring the constitutional knowledge which it is essential for them to possess.' The press could not provide such instruction 'to the working class, which does not read.' The Association provided low-cost entertainment for workers after work and gave them the opportunity to associate with their betters.[63]

Such an evident politicization of the Société d'Éducation lends credence to the claims of the French-language teacher Clément Cazeau that he was fired from his job for partisan political reasons. He was not the only person attacked in this manner in this period of escalating political antagonisms, but his removal and the party realignment of the Société coincided. Cazeau was a client of John Neilson and J.-F. Perrault. He had been assistant teacher in the Quebec Free School Society for eighteen months but lost his job there in April 1817 as the Society ran out of funds. With Perrault's support and that of the seigneur, he was named to the Royal Institution school in St-Roch-des-Aulnaies, where he taught until 1826, when the Société's president urged him to come to Quebec to teach the Lancasterian system. Cazeau hesitated but after a visit to Quebec to meet with Jérôme Demers agreed to take the job on three conditions: that he would keep the post at £120 a year on good conduct, that he would have an annual fifteen-day holiday, and that he would take orders only from one member of the committee. He was told he would be responsible for teaching only reading, writing, and arithmetic, but the management committee refused his requests for a written agreement. He claimed he was told that because he had a letter of appointment and his conditions of work were inscribed in the society's minutes nothing more was necessary.

When the school moved out of the chapel of the Congrégation into its own building in rue des Glacis the number of students increased dramatically and Cazeau petitioned for a salary increase. With the strictest economy, he could support his growing family on £120 but could put nothing aside. The society petitioned the legislature in 1830 for salary increases for its teachers, but in light of the large grant for school construction the increases were refused. Cazeau claimed that secretary Huot told him they would apply again the following year. Instead, in 1832 he learned that the management committee had voted to reduce his salary to £100 and he was invited to give notice if he would not accept the reduction. Cazeau said he produced his correspondence, in which £120 had been guaranteed, to no avail, and without other prospects for employment, he was forced to accept. Then in December 1834 he was informed by letter that both he and the English-language teacher were to be fired effective 1 May 1835, '& that because it was found the children did not progress.'

He agreed that his students did not advance as quickly as did those in the British and Canadian School; but he did not have the means the teachers there enjoyed. He had been to that school himself and had brought back English copies of lessons that had never been provided for the Société's French school. 'These are 120 spelling Cards from words of one syllable up to words of 8 or 9 Syllables 60 word Cards with explanations and the meaning of each word 48 Arithmetic Cards from addition to compound Division 12 Grammar and 60 Geography Cards.' He had asked the management committee repeatedly for such materials in French and had been refused. An examination of his visitor's book would show that he had always done his duty, and the visitors had attributed the students' lack of progress to their irregular attendance. Cazeau's plea was sent to John Neilson in February 1835, just as the lay members of the Société resigned, with the annotation, 'Mr Cazeau wants you to examine his school & report as a defence against the attacks of the patriots,' but Neilson had no political credit with the management committee and so Cazeau was finished.[64]

Étienne Parent went himself to visit the Société's schools in July 1835 to see how the new teachers were making out and reported that they made excellent progress. There were about 300 students in the English and French schools, and Parent commended H.-S. Huot for devoting most of his leisure to school inspection. The annual examination in 1836 was presided over jointly by Lord Gosford and Bishop Signäy, but the previous year's conflict had precluded the annual subscription drive and the schools were quite short of funds. The financial situation worsened in 1837 when parliamentary grants were suspended. However, the Special Council made a grant of £280 in 1838 and enrolment had expanded markedly by 1840, perhaps due to the closing of J.-F. Perrault's schools. H.-S. Huot reported to the government that the Société's schools now had 490 students, 437 of whom were under ten years of age. There were almost twice as many boys as girls in attendance and there were separate schools for boys and girls and for English- and French-speaking students. The boys were now in a two storey stone schoolhouse that measured 88 feet by 36 feet, the English on the ground floor and the French on the floor above, while the adjacent girls' school was much smaller at 36 feet by 30 feet. Behind the boys' school was a two-storey wood teachers' residence. A few students received some more advanced instruction, but the great majority were taught to read the Testament and to write.[65]

La Société d'Éducation des Dames de Québec

In contrast to their competitors in the field of charity schooling, the managers of the Société seem not to have interested themselves much in the schooling of girls until the 1830s. While they attempted to capture both the English- and French-speaking Catholic boys' population, ethnic-denominational instruction took pride of place over gendered instruction. Girls were left to the care of the schools run by women religious, to the private schools, or to the other monitorial schools in the city. However, in 1831, a group of mainly bourgeois French-Canadian women formed a secular association with the approbation of Joseph Signäy, initially called la Société d'Éducation sous la direction des Dames de Québec, whose aim was to provide ragged schooling. In the wake of the 1832 cholera, the women organized an orphanage in a Quebec suburb.[66]

By 1834, the Dames were receiving a small parliamentary subsidy, but their educational efforts were expanding rapidly and they were now under the patronage of Lady Aylmer. Unlike any of the other school societies, they were solvent in the second half of the 1830s, because of their active subscription list, because of the very modest salaries they paid their teachers, but more especially because of their extremely popular bazaars at which they sold donated items. Their school had 139 girls enrolled with 102 in regular attendance early in 1834 and 168 enrolled and 136 in regular attendance by September of that year. They moved to purchase a lot of ground in the Faubourg St-Jean from M. and Mme Charles Trudel and built a new school and orphanage. In 1834 they published a detailed account of income and expenditure for the 1833–4 exercise, a point at which their enterprise was still relatively small. They had £267 in hand at the start, took in about £99, including £50 from the legislature, and spent about £96, most of that on salaries. Their teacher, a Mme Chaffers, was paid £45 for the year, and her assistants, first a Mlle Chevrefils and then a Mlle East, were paid £1.5s. a month. As was the case with the other monitorial schools, they spent very little on school supplies: 7s.6d. for their large record book, another £2.3s.5d. for books, with some small additional expense for paper, crayons, and thread.[67]

In their first report for 1835, the scale of the Dames' operations had grown markedly with their new property and accommodations. They had started the year with a very large debt, but public generosity had enabled them to pay off what they owed for the Trudel property and left them holding over £581, which they intended to use for improvements to their site. They had 176 girls enrolled and an average attendance of 140. Their secretary, Henriette Marett (of whom no trace survives), was replaced in the spring of 1835 by twenty-year-old Flore Buteau, whose merchant father François was an original sponsor of the Société d'Éducation and a member of its recently expanded board. Buteau would act as secretary for the rest of the decade. In July under her name the Dames advertised for a new teacher, specifying that she must 'understand French and English well enough to be able to teach reading, writing and arithmetic.' Candidates were told that 'this school is run under Mr. Lancaster's system.' A new assistant teacher was also sought that summer, someone 'who knew reading, writing, arithmetic, and sewing.'[68]

At year end in 1835, although average daily attendance had fallen somewhat, the school was flourishing and its reserve funds had grown. The Dames were thus able not only to weather the difficult financial times stemming from the battles over the Civil List and the status of the Legislative Council, but also to lend money to the struggling Société d'Éducation. Bishop Signäy was favourably impressed at his 1837 inspection. The school's enrolment almost doubled over the course of the year, from 155 in April to 281 in December, perhaps because J.-F. Perrault's nearby school closed in early September, and perhaps also because of belt tightening in the other charity schools that were more dependent on legislative largesse. Curé Baillairgeon reported in 1838 that the Dames' girls' school's enrolment of 303 was second only to the three schools run by the Ursuline sisters, which together had 308 students, although 100 of those were boarders receiving an advanced education. The French-language boys' school of the Société had an enrolment of 210; the English-language school, 120. Baillairgeon reported that 512 girls were in various kinds of elementary schools in the city: if his numbers were accurate, more than half of them had a monitorial education. At the end of 1839, the Dames reported that 293 girls had passed through their doors in the course of the year, while at year's end they reported a hefty surplus of about £400.[69]

The British and Canadian School Societies

Montreal

Laymen and women responded to the denominational monitorial schools with their own institutions. The Montreal British and Canadian School Society (BCSS) was organized in September 1822 by a group of the city's wealthiest and most prominent merchant and finance capitalists. William Lunn was the prime mover, surrounded by others, like himself, members of the city's Trade Committee (later the Board of Trade) and of the group which founded the Bank of Montreal, supported the General Hospital, and promoted a number of other reform projects. The group was overwhelmingly English-speaking, although some French-speaking merchants and notaries were involved, including F.-A. Larocque, Olivier Berthelot, and N.-B. Doucet. For a time Louis-Joseph Papineau was a vice-president in this organization, which included many of his political arch-enemies. William Lunn served as the school's secretary and managing director for the entire forty-four years of its existence, sometimes with his wife presiding over the Society's girls' school.

At its inaugural meeting in October 1822, the BCSS pointed to the degraded 'state of the Children of the Labouring Classes of the people, and the deficiency of their education,' in the city, both of which 'render[ed] it highly necessary, that some effectual mode be adopted for the improvement of their morals and for affording them a proper education.' The formal title of the organization was 'the British and Canadian School Society for the Education of the Children of the Labouring Class of the People, and the improvement of their morals' and its educational plan was that of the British and Foreign School Society, that is, monitorial schooling on the Lancasterian model. It was a subscription society, aimed at 'the children of all labouring people or Mechanics' in the city or its vicinity, and any member could place one child continuously in the school for each annual contribution of £1. The mention of 'mechanics' points to the Society's intention to engage a broad class spectrum.

The BCSS was managed initially by a fourteen-man committee whose members served gratuitously, with the exceptionally wealthy war profiteer-turned-finance-capitalist Horatio Gates as its first president. The committee was to meet monthly, with a quorum of three, and to report annually to the membership. It was to appoint teachers and to formulate rules and regulations for the management of the school, one of the first of which read that 'no book, pamphlet, or other paper, [shall] be introduced into the School without being first presented to, and approved of by the Committee, and the general reading lessons be confined to the Holy Scriptures, or extracts therefrom, and lessons for spelling and Arithmetic.' Students were to be admitted at age seven or at age eight if the school was full, and an assessment was to be made of each applicant's condition, including parents' names, their residence, the number in the family, the parents' occupation, their 'circumstances (or average of weekly earnings),' and religious denomination. No student would be admitted 'with any infectious disorder,' all were to 'come to School properly washed, and with their hair cut short and combed,' and all were to attend the church of their choice on Sundays. This bourgeois project aimed explicitly at the moral and hygienic discipline of a working class whose taste for reading was to be tied tightly to the Bible and whose respect for worldly authority was to be reinforced by that of the divinity.

Two members of the committee were to take it in turn to serve monthly as inspectors of the schools, to examine the record books, and to be present on Sundays to assemble the students and to send them off to religious service. The teacher was to keep detailed weekly records of student attendance and performance and to report monthly to the committee about the condition of the school. The committee also resolved 'speedily to procure an account of the number of Children, and their ages, who are now in Montreal, and its vicinity having no prospect of education.' No record of such an account has survived, but profiling students in attendance and discovering the number of potential students are both proto-sociological projects.

Secretary Lunn added to the press report of the inaugural meeting that the BCSS was 'formed on the most liberal principles and disclaims all Sectarian or party views.' Its schools were 'open to children of all religious denominations, being established precisely on the system of, and in connection with the British and Foreign School Society in London, and the only School on this System in the Canadas.' The teacher was a

Mr Hutchins, who had 'been trained up in the system, to which he has devoted Eight or Ten Years, and is well recommended to several individuals of rank and character in this Province.'[70]

The BCSS school opened in rooms formerly occupied by the Montreal General Hospital on 14 October 1822, and while it had been planned that Hutchins would teach the boys and girls together, so many students presented themselves that the Society separated the girls from the boys and formed a women's committee to oversee the education of the former. The women's committee hired a local schoolmistress to begin, but sent to England for one trained by the British and Foreign School Society, whose arrival was expected in the summer of 1823. William Lunn informed Governor Dalhousie in June 1823 that the school had 155 boys and 90 girls of all religious denominations in attendance, and over the course of its first eight months of existence, 365 children had passed through it. Many were said to leave the school for work in Upper Canada, on the land, or in domestic service, thereby removing some part of Montreal's vagrant juvenile population. The women's committee was particularly pleased by the girls' needlework, and Lunn added 'it is a very pleasing sight to behold children of all denominations assembled together and instructed in the principles of the Holy Scriptures, which will tend, we trust, to unite all parties.' Lunn sought Dalhousie's patronage and informed him that the BCSS intended to act as a model teacher-training school. After a visit to the school on 22 September 1823, Dalhousie told his diary that he was 'much pleased by the earnest zeal I saw in the individuals who are forcing it under great disadvantages from violent prejudice, & perhaps too many attempts at the same object.' The Lunns were 'very respectable people.'[71]

Nahum Mower of the liberal *Canadian Courant*, by contrast, thought that the colony was finally beginning to move closer to the progressive situation of the United States in educational matters. He agreed that 'of all the garbs with which prejudice was clothed, none appeared more likely to retard the benevolent and wise undertaking' of educating the poor 'than the domino of religion,' but the new city schools showed that it was at last overcome. He visited the BCSS schools in January 1824 and estimated there to be 120 to 130 boys and 50 to 60 girls present. He could see little difference between what went on in the National School and what went on the BCSS schools and approved warmly of both. He thought the joint efforts of all religious denominations would overcome the ignorance characteristic of Lower Canada and suggested that 'the inculcation of useful knowledge, will have a good political as well as a moral tendency.'[72]

By its third anniversary, the Montreal BCSS was solvent and had increased its enrolment again. The girls' school reported ninety-six students in attendance (Jacques Viger claimed there were seventy-four), and the women's committee trumpeted that anyone who had attended the school's public examination 'must be convinced of the unparalleled excellence of an institution, which can thus interweave a code of morality with the common branches of education, unsullied by the slightest shade of Sectarianism.' The curriculum of the girls' school was more elaborate than in other monitorial schools: they were taught to read, write, and to do arithmetic but they also had grammar, geography, and Scripture lessons, in addition to needlework. No one had left the school out of dissatisfaction, reported the committee, and two of the students had been placed in domestic service, but attendance suffered 'from the constant removal of families from the city.' Lord Dalhousie himself subsidized the education and board of two Native children to the tune of £10; the schoolmaster, Mr Hutchins, earned £100 and the London-trained Mrs Chapman, who was to resign for health reasons, earned £43.3s.8d. After paying £40 in house rent, the school showed a surplus of over £32.[73]

The following year, the legislature made the BCSS a grant of £300 for its operating costs and an additional £400 towards the cost of constructing its own school buildings. These were necessary because the existing schoolrooms could not accommodate all the students seeking to attend. There were still 196 boys and 76 girls in attendance in 1826, but President Gates assured the subscribers that relatively stable enrolment meant not the failure of their project, but the necessity of expansion. Tradesmen were continually coming to the school looking for apprentices, and employers treated a boy's attendance at the school as a recommendation. The school committee arranged with James O'Donnell, the New York architect who had designed and was overseeing the construction of Notre Dame Cathedral, to design a new school building, which he did for free. It would be large enough to accommodate 414 boys and 234 girls, with separate living accommodations for the teachers, and its foundation stone was laid on 17 October 1826. The total cost was estimated to be £1,510, of which the Society had raised only half, including its grant, but the four-storey building (which still stands on the corner of what are now rues de la Gauchetière and Côté) opened as scheduled in August 1827.

Not only was the BCSS solidifying its presence on the Montreal educational scene, but it was also pursuing the project of extending monitorial schooling to the countryside, despite the failure of J.-F. Perrault's 1825 bill for urban school boards. In 1826, the BCSS planned a monitorial school at Laprairie for one of its graduates, another had taken a school at Chateauguay, while a third was looking for a place. The Montreal Society had furnished its Quebec relative with a supply of printed lessons and another set had gone to a school at Varennes, paid for by the Catholic Vicar General Deguise.[74]

Nonetheless, like their National School competitors, the BCSS schools had reached an enrolment plateau by about 1830, despite their increased capacity. They were now competing for students with Bishop Lartigue's École St Jacques, within walking distance, which drew 60 students in 1825 and 212 ten years later, with the Montreal Recollet School, and with such other free institutions as the Montreal Union School. The Recollet School was organized by subscription in the late 1820s to offer charity schooling for Irish Catholic children and it grew rapidly as Irish immigration increased. It was granted a parliamentary subsidy in the early 1830s and by 1835 was drawing £300 annually, an amount continued by the Special Council. Under the direction of James Phelan, the elementary school used Lancaster's pedagogy for its eighty boys and eighty girls.[75]

In an appeal to Lord Aylmer for aid in 1830, the management committee of the Montreal BCSS reported that the schools had 157 boys and 82 girls in attendance, and since their organization in 1822, 2,301 students had passed through: 1,379 boys and 922 girls. However, the Society's finances were in poor shape because of the debt it continued to carry for its schoolhouse. In 1829 it cost almost £279 to run the school, which the legislature paid and which enabled the Society to apply its subscriptions to its debt. The school had cost £1,620, of which the legislature had paid £400 and towards which the members had subscribed £400, leaving a debt of £820, rising to £918 at year's end from interest costs. Annual subscriptions had reduced the debt to £704, but the Society petitioned for aid to pay it off. It would be 1832 before the Assembly made a one-time grant to retire the schoolhouse debt, and in the later 1830s, as the rural *patriote* deputies complained more loudly of the funding preference given to the cities, its annual grant was reduced from £300 to £200. It continued to draw that amount until 1841. On the other hand, from 1832 the BCSS in both Montreal and Quebec became eligible for a grant of £5 for each teacher they trained, to a maximum of ten annually, as did the National Schools.

Ludger Duvernay of *La Minerve* explained to a reader who had been surprised to find the Montreal BCSS schools only half-full in April 1833 that the city was 'happily supplied with a large number of good schools,' and there were probably no longer any fathers who neglected 'to provide for their children of both sexes at least the basics of elementary education.' Given the policy of the legislature in funding 'in the cities one principal school tied more or less to each religious persuasion,' parents could choose among several schools, 'which can lead to empty seats in some.'[76] While there certainly was a good deal of choice and variety, Duvernay's suggestion of universal rudimentary education was an exaggeration, even if the existence of choice does offer an explanation for the visible fluctuations in attendance in the BCSS schools.

In this situation, no sect or group could hope actively to dominate the others, but they all argued that their particular version of schooling was the best – the cheapest, the most efficient, the most likely to produce inter-ethnic and interdenominational solidarity, or the least likely to lead to perdition. It was said the excellent Mr Minshall, in charge of the Montreal BCSS's boys' school by 1833, had the French-Canadian students reading English with ease in weeks and paid much more attention to the manipulation of the pen than did most Lancasterian teachers. One-third and in some seasons two-thirds of his students were Catholics. Miss Ross in the girls' school produced students who were remarkably proficient in needlework, reading, writing, arithmetical calculation, and scriptural answers. Still, in an oblique reference to empty benches, the *Montreal Herald* noted in April 1835 that 'the labouring classes of society ought generally to know that pupils are, we may say, thankfully received' in the BCSS schools 'and that there is ample accommodation in the spacious school-room for four hundred boys,' twice as many as had been at the spring examination.[77]

In contrast to the situation in Quebec, judging by the press, interdenominational educational controversy and conflict appeared quite muted in Montreal, at least most of the time. Perhaps that appearance is an artefact of my sources, but it may also be a real result of the state of denominational play in the city. In particular, when the BCSS was organized, Bishop Lartigue was not yet firmly established either in the material or in the political sense, and while he railed at Lancasterian schooling, he railed mainly at his bishop. His authority was openly contested by the Montreal Sulpiciens, and it was they who provided or subsidized most of the petty schooling on offer before 1820. At least until after 1832 when the Soeurs de la Congrégation displaced many of the lay teachers they subsidized, the Sulpiciens supported mixed-sex schools in which male teachers taught girls, practices against which Lartigue railed repeatedly.

The Montreal English press did occasionally attack the Montreal Seminary for offering what was claimed to be an inferior sort of education. *La Minerve* saw an archetypical *bureaucrate* at work when the National Schoolteacher beat up an Irish Catholic boy who sang an obscene song in the street in front of his school.[78] Yet it was after 1828, and especially after 1834, that violent, venomous, and chauvinistic exchanges over the purported ignorance of the *habitants* and the obscurantist policy of the ruling oligarchy became commonplace in the pages of the *Gazette*, the *Herald*, and *La Minerve*. Matters were different in Quebec.

Quebec

The Quebec British and Canadian School Society (BCSS) was organized on 29 September 1823, a year after its Montreal counterpart, on the same model and with the same general management structure. There was likely continuity in membership with the earlier Free School Society and with the group that organized a School Association in 1819. The BCSS was presided over by Joseph-François Perrault, already president of the Société d'Éducation, until he left the new society in 1829. He was followed as president by Daniel Sutherland and the progressive doctor Joseph Parant. Sutherland was postmaster general, a bank director and former fur trader, and also a member of the Board of the Royal Institution. His son-in-law, T.A. Stayner, succeeded him as postmaster general and was also president of the BCSS. The wealthy trader and banker Benjamin Tremain acted as treasurer, and Receiver General Jeffrey Hale acted as secretary throughout the later 1820s and 1830s. Besides Perrault, several other members of the British and Canadian School Society's committee were also members of the committee of the Société d'Éducation: François Romain, Vallières de St Réal, Peter Langlois, and John Neilson, to name four. As a whole, the committee was composed of Quebec merchant and finance capitalists, land dealers, notaries, garrison officers, and politicians and administrators. Most of the women's committee was composed of people related to the men. The group was tightly knit, interconnected by marriage as well as by financial activity, but diverse ethnically, politically, and religiously. At first, political antagonisms did not prevent a common front on schooling the city's working-class and pauper population. For instance, John Charlton Fisher and John Neilson sat together on the committee, despite the fact that Fisher (whose newspaper was printed by another committee member, P.-É Desbarats,) had come to Quebec to displace the Neilsons as King's Printer.

That there was overlap in the membership of the BCSS and the Société d'Éducation underlines the different objectives the two organizations pursued. Unlike the Société, which aimed to provide rudimentary charity schooling for Catholics, the BCSS ran a subsidized pay school that aimed to produce solidarities across denominational, ethnic, and linguistic lines. While its program was unabashedly one of moral and political discipline, it also expressly countenanced social mobility, offering able boys (not girls) training in 'such branches of Geometry as are necessary to [the] Mechanical Trades' and potentially in Latin and other advanced subjects. The Société and the National School offered no such training. The BCSS stressed that it was not running charity schools: while students could be sponsored by a subscriber, others were charged 20s. a year, payable in advance. Clergymen were invited to participate as honorary members without voting powers, and a generic Christianity drawn from the New Testament was presented as the interdenominational grounding for moral conduct. Doctrinal controversy was to be excluded, but of course precisely the liberality of that stance guaranteed opposition from the two Episcopal churches, and the committee members were acutely aware that they were renewing the defeated project of the Quebec Free School Society. Nonetheless, members such as Perrault were convinced both that the Société's schools were not operating efficiently to deliver the rudiments of education and that continued denominational separation could not produce an orderly civil society.

The organizing committee profited from the Montreal Society's experience by forming a 'ladies' committee' at the outset to take charge of a girls' school. The girls were to spend their mornings in needlework and their afternoons in literary instruction, while one day a week was to be devoted by them to the production of clothing for sale, with the older monitors teaching the younger how to cut it out. In both boys' and girls' schools, the last hour of each afternoon was reserved for the most advanced students. It was also resolved 'that the most vigilant attention be given to the cleanliness of the children, by a master who shall examine them daily with particular care,' and if funds permitted, any ragged children were to be provided with clothing. After learning that the schools were to offer instruction in both English and French, Le Canadien came out in support, affirming that 'it is not to be wished that Canada alone shall rest behind, in this universal zeal to spread Education among the people ... we must keep up with other people, if we do not wish them to trample us underfoot.'[79]

As the Free School Society had done, the BCSS challenged the claims of the Episcopal churches to a monopoly over the formation of young people, especially the working class and the poor, rejected their arguments that doctrinal instruction could not be separated from schooling, and attacked their claims to a clerical monopoly over access to the sacred text. If editorials and letters in *Le Canadien* are to be believed, members of the Quebec clergy went from door to door in the city warning people not to send their children to the BCSS schools. The Société d'Éducation made a point of publicizing the fact that it had no connection with the new society and old curé Painchaud, perhaps with the connivance of Bishop Lartigue, was brought out as the Catholic attack dog on Lancasterian schooling in the press. As the BCSS school was set to open on 12 November 1823, *Le Canadien* reported the news that 'a respectable and enlightened class was undertaking great efforts to keep the people away from such a useful and necessary establishment.' Editor Vallerand commented that it had been shown in England that not one of 7,000 boys educated there in a Lancasterian school had ever been convicted of a crime. A BCSS supporter signing 'Un Amis de l'Éducation' argued that more discussion of education was necessary in the colony, where *habitants* were prone to say, '"I never had any learning, and I still lived well ... my children will do just as well, without knowing how to read and write."' Such attitudes could not survive now that farming was becoming so difficult and now that the political age of the Rights of Man was established. Education was essential because Canadians had 'a political existence to preserve,' and because a free people needed education 'if it wishes to compete in the world market with its products, and above all if it wishes to preserve its rights and privileges.' This BCSS partisan argued that Lancaster's system had been shown to be the most effective and efficient possible; that it offered no religious dogmas but based its lessons in morality on New Testament Christianity; and that one of the BCSS members (Perrault) was preparing an interdenominational catechism. The society thus offered the best possible solution to illiteracy and political ignorance, but – who would have believed it! – 'two classes of men (no doubt respectable) who have wrangled with each other for more than 300 years ... today join together, in order to forbid Lancasterian schools, which people wish to establish here, because their dogmas will not be taught in them.' Even J.-F. Perrault had been accused of wishing to destroy all religion, and when he protested by pointing to the reading of the New Testament in the Society's school he was told that he 'stinks like a Methodist.'[80]

'M.C.' [Martin Chinic?] wrote of his surprise at the intensity of Catholic attacks on the new Society. The clergy went so far as to 'visit people's houses, to poison their minds against it,' and they fanned religious prejudices. When a Society member responded by himself going from door to door to counter such attacks, people answered 'but Curé so-and-so forbade us to send our children to that school.' The clergy was condemning people to ignorance, arguing effectively it was better to leave them so if in teaching them to read and write 'they are not taught at the same time, how many holy days there are in the year, and on which days they have to fish for their dinner in the St Lawrence River.' How were children going to learn their catechism in any case if they were left to roam the streets? And why such deep fear of the Bible? If young people read it, they would know better how to conduct themselves, and one could see by looking to the United States that common education would produce morality and interdenominational solidarity.[81]

Another BCSS supporter argued that the advertisement in which the Société d'Éducation dissociated itself from the new Society was itself a hostile and unnecessary act. The BCSS did not want to a start a rivalry; it was not running charity schools, and if its existence caused the Société to open an English boys' school so much the better for everyone. It was common knowledge that the new Society had powerful clerical enemies who were spreading wild fears: they should debate publicly. More generous than their opponents, the BCSS would not attack anyone else's schools because 'the country is still far from having the number of institutions required for educating the population.'[82]

The alarm in clerical circles was increasing with good reason, for the organizers of the BCSS were moving to generalize their project to the colony as a whole. Not only was Perrault producing his interdenominational catechism, but a meeting was called for early December 1823 to consider how best to establish both in town and country 'elementary schools on the basis of a uniform education' to which 'parents of various religious beliefs may be induced with confidence to send their children.' The meeting was an embryonic moment for what would become J.-F. Perrault's abortive 1825 School Bill.

Curé Painchaud, writing as 'l'Homme des bois,' responded to the call with an attack on several fronts. Why did the new society insist on having children read the Bible? Where was the father who would not quake at exposing 'to the modest, virginal eyes of his daughter or son, the nakedness of the scenes and expressions that it contains in so many places?' The Bible of course was an admirable book for whoever could read it 'with profit, but it is certainly not a book to put in just anyone's hands, without comment, and certainly not in those of children.' The Bible needed to be interpreted by those capable of understanding it. If the BCSS claimed that the Bible was used just for the purposes of learning to read, why not choose some other book? And if the society insisted nonetheless in using the Bible, must it not have some other object in view? Anyway, what sort of religion was it that never spoke about religion? Better to have children read their catechism several times a week. Painchaud ended with an attack on 'M.C.' for instructing people not to listen to the advice of their clergy.[83]

Before Flavien Vallerand decided to cease publishing letters when the legislature resumed, a subscriber to the BCSS made a last reponse to Painchaud's sortie. Describing him as 'worthy of certain people who go from door to door in this city in order to raise the alarm' against the new Society because it did not teach the catechism, the subscriber argued that the clergy had no business attempting to impose the work of catechetical instruction on laypeople. Christ had taught that His Kingdom was not of this world, and 'his ministers thus must not concern themselves with current affairs.' The BCSS students only saw the New Testament and there was nothing in it to promote a clerical conspiracy against the Society's schools. Moreover, the Catholic schools were so inferior that no one who went to them could find work when they were finished, and modern society needed people who had learned to be useful. This subscriber solicited public support for the BCSS.[84]

After the parliamentary session, clerical attacks in the press resumed. In May 1824 *Le Canadien* reprinted an editorial and extracts from a letter critical of the BCSS which had first appeared in the *Spectator*. The editorial argued that Lancaster's pedagogy was a great improvement over existing practice and it was controversial only because of its use of the Bible as a reading book. If some other text were substituted for it, the attacks would likely cease. The correspondent quoted was probably Painchaud or one of his brethren for his letter repeated his earlier arguments about the dangers of the Bible, now helpfully pointing his readers to the juicy bits. The Bible wasn't easy to read, so not much use as a school reader, and biblical morality in any case was frequently out of date. The correspondent asked again what father would allow his children or adolescents to read 'chapters 19, 30 and 38 of Genesis, several chapters of Leviticus and Deuteronomy, and of the book of Judges, the Song of Songs, the first chapters of Hosea, several chapters of Ezekiel, &c.?' To this 'L'Ami de l'Éducation' was allowed to reply in defence of the BCSS, pointing out that the Society did not use the Bible but only the New Testament, in which there was nothing objectionable. An efficient school needed to use a common book, and the clarity, simplicity of style, and frequent repetition in the Testament made it perfectly adapted to the purpose.[85]

Antagonistic relations among the denominations did not cease with the end of this published exchange, but unlike the Free School Society, the BCSS survived the attacks and throughout the period under investigation continued to offer a form of cheap instruction that was much more substantial than that of the schools of the Société d'Éducation. On the other hand, the Catholic clergy was correct in its assessment of the threat posed to clerical monopoly over sacred texts by the society. Not only did the BCSS actively encourage lay Bible reading at school, but both branches of the society were sponsors of the British and Foreign School Society's British and Foreign Bible Society. The Bible Societies' secretaries were the BCSS secretaries and both arranged for the import (duty-free) of large numbers of Bibles and Testaments and Protestant religious tracts. Both were also the conduits for books and supplies for the Union Sunday Schools in Quebec, Montreal, and Upper Canada. And it was through these bodies that Protestant interventions into the struggle for the souls of Natives at the missions around Montreal and Quebec were conducted, to the outrage of the Catholic clergy.[86] Reading the sacred text 'without note or comment' was in essence a dissenting Protestant practice and part of a larger attempt to define a 'common Christianity' as the basis for a civil religion. Quebec Protestants organized against the 1838 Durhamite plan for a school system from which the Bible was excluded.

Still, after the noise surrounding its initial organization subsided and despite ongoing attempts on the part of various groups and institutions to undermine any plan modelled on it for urban-based district school boards, the BCSS underwent much the same development as the other urban school societies. It quickly attracted a large number of students, and it also quickly got rid of its first teacher, Julien Saillant, who lasted less than a year before being replaced by a teacher sent from England. Enrolment fluctuated and attendance did as well, but the boys' school generally had over one hundred students present, while the girls' school had half that many. The schism which resulted in the opening of J.-F. Perrault's industrial monitorial school led to a sharp decline in enrolment in 1829, but the school bounced back in 1830 to surpass its earlier numbers. Like its sister societies, the Quebec BCSS went into debt to construct its own schoolhouse and was in a shaky financial situation thereafter. At first the Society took over the old National School space in the guard house and was able to pay its male teacher, William Morris, a meagre £60 a year. Morris tried to make ends meet by publishing an arithmetic book, for which he sought legislative aid, but he moved to the better-paying Quebec National School in the 1830s. The BCSS built its own stone schoolhouse in the faubourg St Roch, large enough to accommodate 300 on the boys' side. Extra funding was still being sought in 1830 to finish the upper storey for the accommodation of the teachers and in 1831 to deal with the £100 borrowed at 6 per cent to purchase the site. The legislature began granting money for the Society's support about 1824. Its annual grant in the 1830s was usually £200, sometimes more, with one-time payments to cover the costs of school construction, although by 1835 the Society was still carrying £500 in debt. The largest part of the operating money went consistently to the boys' school. There is no evidence of a debate surrounding the comparative under-funding of the girls' school.[87]

In its printed report for 1831, the Society claimed the boys' school had 196 students in attendance, of whom 120 were Catholics and 82 of those French-speaking. It was estimated that 1,203 boys passed through the school since its start in November 1823. The girls' school had 80 students in attendance, again with a majority of Catholics (47), 16 of them French-speaking. The boys were taught the three Rs with the addition of French and English grammar, geography, geometry, mensuration, and bookkeeping, while the girls got the three Rs and basic needlework. The cost of running the school was £492.14s., money that came mainly from the public purse, as subscriptions and donations amounted only to about £90.

An important additional source of revenue came from teacher training, which was also an integral part of the plan to spread monitorial schooling to the countryside. Informally in 1830, and formally two years later, the legislature began offering the BCSS a grant to train teachers in the amount of £5 each, up to £50 a year. The Society usually took full advantage of the opportunity, for instance, certifying ten teachers in 1831 and nine more in 1833. Four more studied the Lancasterian system in 1831 but did not remain to be examined in it. Few traces remain of those trained, although Felix O'Neill went to teach at St Sylvestre in 1831 and responded from there to the Buller Commission in 1838. There were two other O'Neills in his cohort, perhaps his brother and sister. A Mrs Purcell trained at the school in 1833 and probably then taught the National girls' school with William Morris as the boys' teacher. One of the teachers examined in 1833 was James Stringer, who had petitioned Lord Aylmer in the summer of 1832 for money to return to Ireland. He described himself as having studied in Trinity College Dublin and as being 'a good Classic Scholar & capable of conducting or assisting in any Seminary of repute.' But he couldn't find any decent classical academies, and 'though in his distress he ha[d] applied for the situation of an Assistant at common & even

elementary Schools' he could get no work. He ended up sick in the Hotel
Dieu before assisting in the Emigrant Hospital during the cholera out-
break. As would be the case later with the Montreal Normal School, the
BCSS's training program was probably partly a refuge for unemployed
teachers attempting to upgrade their credentials.[88]

It is unlikely that many teachers who trained at the urban schools actually managed to use the monitorial system in the countryside, where
the schools would have been too small for it to be practicable, except for
some rudimentary classification of students and for having the older
ones help the younger. Thus, while the BCSS reported that it trained
twelve teachers in 1835, it also commented that 'a greater number of the
country School masters would have availed themselves of the advantages
… if the persons who incur the expense of qualifying themselves, and who
adopt the System as Teachers, became entitled to a moderate encrease in
their Salaries under Legislative enactment.' The teacher-training program did little to spread monitorial pedagogy 'from the inability of the
Teachers, when qualified, to procure the materials which are indispensable to the introduction of the System,' and so the BCSS recommended
the making of small grants from the legislature for this purpose. The monitorial teacher training program ended with the 1836 Normal School Act,
by which time the BCSS had trained forty-one teachers, most of whom it
claimed had found work.[89]

Again, like the other grant-aided schools, the BCSS schools suffered
through the financial stringencies that surrounded the struggles over
the colonial state in the 1830s. They usually got their grant, although it
was often late, and in fall 1837, having had no grant for the year and
desperately short of funds, they convened a public meeting to consider
what to do. The Special Council renewed the society's grants in 1838
and 1839, but in the 1839–40 year they received nothing. The society
petitioned for aid in 1840, claiming that it had 129 boys and 60 girls in
daily attendance, all following the British and Foreign School Society's
course. A Mr Geggie taught the English-language boys for £100 a year, a
Miss Thomson the girls for £60, and French-language instruction was
offered by a M. Langevin. The society claimed to have taught almost
3,000 students in its sixteen years of existence.[90]

J.-F. Perrault and the Industrial Monitorial School

Joseph-François Perrault (1753–1844) was one of the most interesting of
the Lower Canadian school promoters, from his energy and inventiveness,

but also through the contrast between his radical educational projects and his conservative political stances. His experience demonstrates both that educational reform could create solidarities across political, ethnic, and religious divides and that there was no simple correspondence between progressive reform and party loyalty. Perrault was a fixture in cultural life and educational politics in Quebec, from his attempt to block the passage of the School Act of 1801 through to his efforts to be named master of the proposed Quebec Normal School in 1836. He was one of that breed of wealthy, disciplined, and devout intellectuals active in many reform projects of the first decades of the nineteenth century, a man who rose daily at four or five a.m., wrote for three or four hours before showing up at the Quebec courthouse where he was clerk and prothonotary, who left that work at noon to write, visit schools, and socialize, going to bed equally regularly at 9 p.m. There was an elective affinity between the discipline of the monitorial school, which Perrault sought to apply to the working class and the poor, and his own self-discipline. He was an archetypical *bureaucrate*, drawing an income that was often higher than the governor's salary from fees charged on matters passing through the King's Bench, from his position as prothonotary in charge of vital statistics, and from his voluminous writing. His 1803 translation of *Lex Parliamentaire*, for which he received a grant of £200 from the legislature, was the manual of parliamentary procedure used for several decades by his political allies and enemies alike.[91]

How and when Perrault became a convert to the Lancasterian pedagogy remains a mystery. It is entirely possible that he wrote the letters in *Le Vrai Canadien* in 1810 warning of the dangers of an illiterate rural populace susceptible to demagoguery. Perrault was associated in a number of ventures with Daniel Wilkie, the man who first publicized the Lancasterian pedagogy in the colony, who took a similar line but who did not fear the press. In 1814 Perrault declined his election from afar as a member of the Quebec Free School Society, but offered material support and was sufficiently reconciled by 1818 with his erstwhile opponents François Blanchet and John Neilson to join in their project for the Quebec Dispensary as a vice-president. Those two were vigorous Lancasterians. The struggles against the 1822 Union of the Canadas also found him sharing common cause with the seigneurs, petty bourgeois professionals, functionaries, and the Catholic clergy. On the other hand, Perrault's educational politics in the 1820s alienated both the clergy and socially conservative members of the *parti canadien,* and his conduct in the 1827 election earned him some enduring antipathy from what had become the *parti patriote.*

We have seen Bishop Lartigue's vituperative campaign against Lancasterian schooling and Perrault. The latter's 1825 School Bill further alienated the clergy and social conservatives in the *parti canadien* such as Denis-Benjamin Viger for its intent to sideline the parish vestries in educational matters in preference to urban school boards. In 1833, Perrault again enraged both the clergy and the *patriote* party leadership with a Guizot-style school bill that proposed free, tax-supported, and compulsory elementary schooling throughout the colony superintended by central administrative boards. He was denounced as the advocate of a godless police state and as seeking to place even more tyrannical means in the hands of the *bureaucrates*.[92] Although Perrault was in close contact with both opponents and supporters of executive government through the British and Canadian School Society and through such organizations as the Society for the Encouragement of Arts and Sciences in Canada, it was his conduct in Lord Dalhousie's 1827 showdown elections that was responsible for his ouster from the BCSS the following year.

The summer elections followed Dalhousie's desperate prorogation of Parliament when it became clear that his demands around the Civil List would not be met. Convinced that it was the clique surrounding Speaker Louis-Joseph Papineau that was responsible for most colonial unrest, he hoped the election excitement would 'lead people to think upon the folly of disputing & lead the superior classes to spake upon it to those who are ignorant and misled.' Prorogation also meant the failure of an attempt to renew the colony's militia laws and a revival of controversial legislation from 1787–9. Dalhousie expected his candidates to dominate the elections, but to his shock, they were solidly defeated. One was his attorney general, James Stuart, who ran in William Henry (Sorel), and who was beaten when what Dalhousie called 'a great force of the lowest' voted for the radical doctor Wolfred Nelson. Dalhousie believed that ineligible electors had voted for Nelson, and Stuart used his judicial powers to prosecute several Nelson supporters for perjury. Both Stuart and Dalhousie were convinced that the result also showed 'the cunning intrigue of the Catholic clergy,' whose members were angered by Stuart's blocking of an act for the civil establishment of Catholic parishes.

In the midst of all this excitement was a militia muster, and several militia leaders used the occasion to criticize the executive and to abuse Dalhousie, who responded by suspending a number of militia commissions. When Parliament was convened in the autumn, Dalhousie refused to recognize Louis-Joseph Papineau as speaker; the Assembly insisted on him as its choice, Dalhousie again prorogued Parliament, and the disgruntled *parti patriote* organized the monster petition against his policy discussed earlier. Dalhousie was recalled and replaced in September 1828 by Sir James Kempt.[93]

The British and Canadian School Society's secretary Thomas Lee Jr claimed that Perrault had abused his government offices in 1827 by forcing his employees to vote for James Stuart's brother Andrew, who ran in Quebec's Upper Town, who had been a leading Quebec member of the *parti canadien*, but who had moved closer to the executive. Lee was a *patriote* notary who had represented the Lower Town but was defeated in 1816, along with François Blanchet, for speaking in favour of lay control of tax-supported parish schools. Lee, married to John Neilson's sister, had first proposed Louis-Joseph Papineau as speaker in 1815. Lee sat in the Assembly again in the 1820s, and at the moment of the controversy was preparing to run in a Lower Town by-election, which he won. There was competition for the leadership of the Quebec wing of the party. Perrault was accused in the press of using his influence with Lord Dalhousie to have Lee's militia commission revoked, and Lee resigned as secretary of the BCSS. It seems that Perrault served as both president and secretary for 1828, but at the BCSS's annual December elections, with Lee now an MPP, Perrault was unseated as president and left or was forced out of the Society.[94]

Perrault responded by building his own schoolhouses in the faubourg Saint-Louis and by writing and publishing his own set of schoolbooks for their use. A boys' school was built first, at a cost to Perrault of about £400, and opened in late 1829 or early 1830. Fees were charged to a maximum of $4 a year (as at the BCSS), but poor children could pay as little as $1, and nothing was charged for books or school supplies. A nearby girls' school followed in May 1831, large enough to accommodate over 200 students. The press, including the *patriote* press, was now full of praise for Perrault, the benefactor.[95]

An anonymous visitor of 1834 left a detailed account of the internal organization of the schools.[96] The boys' school was in a large stone building with sheds on the grounds to shelter those who arrived before the doors opened. Above the doors, *Ecole élémentaire de M. Perrault* was inscribed in gilt letters; above the windows to the left, *Hautes classes* and to the right, *Basses classes*. Inside on the ground floor were thirty-six benches, each capable of holding seven students, and there were galleries to the side with storage for the agricultural machinery the boys made on winter afternoons. The teacher stood on an elevated platform at the front of the room overlooking the students with the gilt inscription, '*à la gloire de Dieu seul,*' above him. In front of the benches were 'telegraphs bearing lessons and examples to complete, to read, write, and repeat up to eighteen times in the morning, and other lessons and examples just as often in the afternoon.' Every ten minutes at the sound of a clock the students moved from one lesson to the next. The beginners had sand tables in front of them in which they traced out their letters, and there were five other classes, each with a monitor and an assistant. The highest class received direct instruction from the master himself. In summer, the boys worked in the school garden and in winter in the agricultural implement workshop.

In the girls' school, which was in a more modest building, 30 feet square, with an 8-foot-wide corridor down the middle, the students sat on staggered benches, 'three rows wide and three rows high' with a passage at each end and with a similar set of telegraphs. All were equipped with slates and slate pencils. They spent their mornings learning to spell, read, and write and their afternoons learning to spin, knit, weave, and card. Three looms and a carding machine were crammed into the ground floor, paid for by Perrault out of his own pocket at a cost of £1,100, and in an outdoor shed heated by the school chimney was a 'washing machine' and 'a fulling mill,' which were 'crank-driven and which expedite the drudgery with remarkable ease.' In the second storey of the girls' school, the visitor found forty students at work making stockings, gloves, mittens, slippers, rugs, and bolts of cloth for sale, and thought that 'nothing looks more like bees in a hive, than the activity of these little girls.' Perrault hired older or out-of-work craftsmen and women to teach his students their trades and sold their products to help defray the costs of his schools.[97]

Perrault's production of nine schoolbooks in French, including primers, tables of words divided into syllables with demonstrative uses, grammars, and a history of Canada, facilitated the use of the Lancasterian pedagogy for French-speaking students, but also provided a home-grown elementary school curriculum that could have been used in rural schools if legislators had been sympathetic to his larger plans for school boards. His various *Tableaux* were vocabulary builders. His *Premiers Elemens* used a mixed phonic and sight method of instruction for reading, beginning in the vernacular, two innovations at a time when the rural schools still often taught to read first in Latin. Perrault's beginner initially saw a table of words of one syllable, which were to be recited, and then each word was presented in a sample phrase: for 'eu,' 'il les a *eu* au vu et sçu de sa bru' – melodic and playful at once. Perrault used the form of the catechism to instruct about parts of speech, and after the beginner had made it to words with six letters, he or she was presented with a three-page lesson to learn by heart. It began,

'There is only one God, he is the King of kings, the Saint of Saints. God is so good that he cares for me everyday, I owe everything to him, without him I can do nothing, he knows all that I do and all that I say, he sees deep into my heart,' and continued on in the same vein.

Although clergymen such as J.-J. Lartigue were not to be appeased by anything Perrault did, his curriculum was astute politically as well as productive pedagogically. No Catholic or Anglican clergyman could complain that his schools were Bible schools, nor could they claim there was no Christian morality taught in them. At the same time, Perrault was perhaps the only teacher in the colony offering technical training – for girls, well beyond the use of the needle – and also opening mobility channels for boys. His senior class here and earlier at the BCSS contained talented people refused entry to the Séminaire, such as F.-X. Garneau, Napoléon Aubin, and Pierre Petitclair.[98]

Perrault managed to get £100 from the Assembly for his boys' school and £100 for his schoolbooks in 1830, although his initial attempts at securing copyright protection for the latter failed. Nonetheless, now in his late seventies, he was a whirlwind of activity over the next several years. He wrote a practical agricultural manual and attempted to interest the executive in funding practical lessons in gardening for boys on his property on the Plains of Abraham. His nine-page *Plan raisonné d'éducation générale et permenante*, which advocated non-sectarian, tax-supported, compulsory schooling, won the 1830 essay prize competition of the Literary and Historical Society and formed the basis of his 1833 School Bill. He toured Lord and Lady Aylmer around the schools, showing her with great ostentation the girls' school, it 'being a new institution in the country, & which promises to be very useful to persons of this Sex.' When the plans of the Swiss immigrant adventurer Amury Girod for a de Fellenberg-style agricultural college and normal school were refused legislative aid in 1831 (following xenophobic attacks by Louis-Joseph Papineau), Perrault undertook to sponsor the institution himself. Finally, he campaigned vigorously for his pedagogical system to be adopted by the normal schools created by the 1836 Normal School Act.[99]

Perrault's schools and his method were praised repeatedly in the liberal and the *patriote* press and were promoted as the best possible for the colony as a whole. In calling for an investigation into educational conditions in March 1835, the MPP Amable Bertholet argued that the existing 'system of education is too vicious, too old, too oriented to the dead languages, and too little adapted to the social state, and the needs of the Country.' He praised Perrault's new system. *La Minerve* reported on a meeting of concerned citizens in Montreal held in December 1835 to address the problem of children begging in the streets and argued that education offered the best remedy, 'the method of teaching followed in Mr Perrault's schools, we think, is entirely fitted to that object.' 'Jean-Baptiste' writing in *Le Canadien* in the summer of 1837, as mass meetings called for an anti-importation campaign against British textiles, regretted the neglect of manufacturing industry in the colony and called attention to 'Mr. Jos. F. Perrault's establishment, where one can procure at low prices all sorts of linens and woollens, such as table cloths, serviettes, bonnets, belts, druggets, slippers, and a great many other articles, all made by Canadian hands, by little girls aged seven to twelve.'

Yet, despite frequent praise of Perrault's efforts, the legislature was niggardly in its support. He designed a complete machinery for subjectification and vocational training that could have addressed rural ignorance. Yet he managed to alienate many members of the Assembly by the fact of his role in the state bureaucracy, by his support for the extension of administrative power, and by his insistence that urban elites and not the people itself could organize rural schooling. He generally received a grant in aid of the schools, but it was a fraction of that given to the Société d'Éducation and he received little for his buildings. For instance, in 1831 he got a total of £250 for buildings and management expenses for two separate schools; the Société d'Éducation received £850 and the Montreal British and Canadian School £500. His loss in Girod's agricultural school was estimated at between £500 and £600, but the Assembly voted him only a fraction of that and, exceptionally, only after a voice vote in which eighteen MPPs voted against giving anything. Perrault attempted to persuade the Assembly to take over his schools in 1834, but instead the MPPs voted him £150. When Amable Bertholet examined the schools in 1835, he reported that enrolment had declined to sixty to eighty boys and thirty to forty girls because Perrault had been forced for lack of funds to suspend craft training. The Assembly voted him £300 to cover the two years 1835 and 1836, after which he received nothing. He was said to have invested £2,500 of his own money in the schools and to have paid over £500 to run them in 1835. The Quebec Normal School board had no interest in teaching his system, and Perrault finally closed the schools from lack of means in the fall of 1837.[100]

Spin-offs

The interest in and enthusiasm for monitorial schooling in Quebec and Montreal yielded a number of related projects. The Berthier School

Society, which adopted several features of monitorial pedagogy in its program for schools, was taken as a model for the countryside by the *patriote* press, and figures in a later chapter. A Société d'Éducation des Trois Rivières which, despite its name, was modelled on the British and Canadian School Societies, was organized late in 1830. It drew its membership and management committee from across the political and ethnic-linguistic divides, with Vallières de Saint-Réal, the two *patriote* doctor Kimbers, the Jewish merchant Samuel Benjamin Hart, and a member of the Grant family, among others, on its committee. The Société was permitted to take over the town schoolhouse whose construction had been subsidized by the legislature, and it took advantage of the act 10 & 11 Geo. IV c.14, which had offered £100 for a school in the town 'provided that the system of monitorial Instruction be adopted therein, and that children having a Certificate of their poverty from the Trustees be therein admitted Gratis.' By February 1831, the management committee was petitioning the executive for more money. The school, taught by Charles Hubert Lassiseraie and some English-language assistants, had over one hundred students, and the monitorial method required the purchase of new equipment. The £100 legislative grant covered only half of the teacher's £200 salary and another £100 was needed to complete the school buildings, while town subscriptions had raised only £72. The legislature covered some of the expenditure, with a grant that varied between £100 and £150, until 1837. The Special Council granted £100 in 1839. The school claimed sixty-eight English-speaking boys in attendance in 1835, fifty-three of them educated gratis, and an unknown number of French-speaking boys.[101]

Additional attempts were made to extend the monitorial system to some other parts of the colony, at Terrebonne, for instance, where John Lawrence Milton advertised a British and Canadian School in March 1831 and also opened a museum to display mineral specimens. Particularly striking was the adoption of Lancasterian pedagogy in the Collège de L'Assomption organized by the future Superintendent of Education for Canada East, J.-B. Meilleur, in 1833. This institution was meant to offer elementary education and advanced studies of a more practical orientation than did the existing colleges; as Meilleur explained in a letter to *La Minerve*, 'the children will be subjected to that part of Lancaster's plan that involves mutual instruction, and will receive an education fit to enable them to profit easily from a course of study at College, or in all kinds of business, industry, or other things interesting to them.' In parts of Europe at the same time, where the monitorial system was in decline for elementary schooling, it was being adopted in some colleges as a useful way to drill students.[102]

The Infant School Societies

A group of women associated with the Montreal British and Canadian School Society organized the colony's first infant school, an institution initially directed at poor and working-class children too young for the elementary schools. Encouraged by Thaddeus Osgood, who provided them with a set of printed lessons, the women opened a small school in mid-1828 in rue St Dominique in part of the building occupied by the School of Industry. They were sufficiently impressed with the results that they formed the Montreal Infant School Society (MISS) in August 1829, presided over by president Horatio Gates of the BCSS. Louis-Joseph Papineau was a participant. In the winter of 1828–9 they had also boarded a few orphaned or abandoned children, and the MISS decided to formalize the practice by running a joint infant and boarding school. They aimed 'to rescue many children from vice, and to educate them in the principles of piety and virtue, and consequently render them useful and honorable members of Society.' Fees were charged to those able to pay, while clothing from the Dorcas Society was provided to those in need. The MISS committee reported in 1830 that 210 children had passed through the institution in its first year, with 104 in attendance in July. The school took in students aged eighteen months to seven years and was open for public inspection on Tuesdays. It received a warm welcome in the press, which at the time was praising Samuel Wilderspin's infant school experiments as a prophylactic against crime and vice.[103]

The school's 1831 exam was presided over by Lady Aylmer, who was received with due ceremony by Horatio Gates and Major Plenderleath and then escorted to the girls' school, where ninety girls aged between two and five paraded before her singing,

> We'll all go to our places,
> And make no wry faces,
> And say all our lessons distinctly and slow,
> For if we don't do it,
> Our Mistress will know it,
> And then to the corner we quickly shall go.

The press reports stressed the great fun the children had in a system which resembled the Lancasterian, but which modified it by providing illustrated lessons on objects and by having the children sing the alphabet and a table of pence. The school was later visited by a delegation of

MPPs, and the Church of England began sponsoring an infant school in association with the city's Ladies' Benevolent Society.[104]

Women associated with the Quebec BCSS followed suit in 1832, writing to the British and Foreign School Society for two teachers and a set of lessons and opening a school before formally organizing themselves as the Quebec British and Canadian Infant School Society. They too had a male figurehead as president – Chief Justice Jonathan Sewell – but the organizational work of the school was done by its female management committee, composed of such people as Mrs Montizambert, Pemberton, Hale, Stayner, and Kimble. The school had an average attendance of over one hundred in 1834 and cost £110 to run.[105]

Both the Quebec and Montreal societies drew a small amount of income from fees (£15.14s.5d. in 1830 and £50 in 1835 in Montreal; £36 in Quebec in 1835) but made most of their money from annual subscription drives. Both received modest amounts of legislative aid and sought more as they attempted to expand into purpose-built accommodations in the mid-1830s, but no grants were paid in 1834. The Assembly's Permanent Committee on Education claimed to fear a dramatic increase in financial demands if it subsidized the societies, and both were again refused funding in 1835. The Committee cut all aid from institutions deemed incapable of surviving without it and from those deemed of dubious educational value, such as the Montreal Mechanics' Institute, the Quebec Literary and Historical Society, and the infant school societies. There was no attempt to explain why early childhood education was not education – in leading American cities, such as Boston, infant school societies were popular. The Quebec society, which claimed to have 236 children enrolled and an average attendance of about 130, was immediately forced to cease operations and was left with a debt of £100.

The MISS drastically reduced its activities, firing one of its two teachers and reducing the daily attendance from ninety to fifty-four children. It was in better financial shape at the end of 1835, although there was a decline in the participation of men.[106] Still, the institution rebounded, and one of its striking features was the support it drew from across the political spectrum. Men who were prepared to confront one another by force of arms in December 1837 – T.S. Brown and Charles Dewey Day, for instance – sat together to support the MISS and to inspect its boys' school earlier that same year. There was a large amount of pro–infant school publicity in Montreal in 1836 and 1837, especially as Dr Jonathan Barber, soon to be proprietor of the *Morning Courier*, delivered a popular series of lectures on educational questions, with phrenological and patriarchal overspin. Barber publicized Samuel Wilderspin's pedagogy and argued repeatedly that political salvation for the colony lay in non-sectarian public education beginning with infant schooling. In May of 1838, the Special Council restored the MISS's £50 grant.[107]

Despite the fact that the MISS justified itself as a child-saving mission, familiarity with infant schooling encouraged women of the dominant classes to sponsor a 'select' infant school for children of their own social class: an unusual reversal. A press report of October 1833 announced that the success of the infant schools had 'raised a strong desire to furnish to the children of persons in the upper ranks the advantages of which paupers were in the possession,' and a committee of women drawn from those involved in MISS (M.A. Bancroft, Mrs Williams, Holmes, Day, and others) hired one of the infant schoolteachers to take charge of the new school. They had a house near the Methodist chapel and charged 5s. per month per child. In 1837 the city hosted a fee-based model infant school that also attempted to replicate Samuel Wilderspin's methods.[108]

Joseph Lancaster[109]

What, if any, impact the presence in Lower Canada from 1828 to 1833 of its 'inventor,' Joseph Lancaster, had on opinions of monitorial schooling in the colony remains obscure. Since losing control of the Royal Lancasterian Association/British and Foreign School Society in England in 1814, he had travelled from country to country living on his reputation, local tradesmen, and credulous governments. He would arrive at some place – Belfast, New York, Philadelphia, Caracas – declare his fame and his revolutionary new means of instructing young people, attract a following and form some sort of educational association, run up debts, fight with those working with him, and decamp to the next place. En route to England from Latin America in 1828, Lancaster had swung through Montreal and Quebec, giving lectures on his astounding educational inventions and sniffing out the possibilities for making a pound. He stayed for five years. He fled Canada in 1833 to avoid assault charges and was killed by a runaway horse in the streets of New York in 1838. One observer described him as 'a mass of obesity, unwieldy, and of feeble articulation, such as we occasionally see in individuals of objectionable habits, loaded with adipose deposits, "an agglomeration of superabundant redundancies."' But at age fifty in 1828 he was able to exercise a powerful influence over political leaders – at least on short acquaintance.[110]

In an astonishing bit of testimony, Lord Dalhousie told his diary at the end of August 1828 that he had 'had a visit from the well known philanthropist Joseph Lancaster. I found him in my dining room with his broad brim beaver on, which he retained for some time. However when I begged him to sit down he took it off & laid it aside. Imagine a fat square man of about 80, easy and remarkably talkative, his conversation chiefly on Scripture, & bent upon his great pursuit of Education. He is what would be called "a well-spoken man."' Lancaster went on at length about the monster petition the *patriotes* had earlier sent to England, arguing that its profusion of 'X's 'shewed evident proof of the ignorance of the people; not knowing what they signed, it was naturally concluded that they were the tools, perhaps innocent instruments, of malicious & designing men. They could not be considered capable of judging in matters of Government': hence the necessity of his educational system. Lancaster went on about the wild anarchy he had seen in republican Latin America, where 'there is not an honest man nor a chaste woman.' Dalhousie concluded that 'the old man was much affected, very grateful for my reception of him, and in a most pious & patriarchal manner & form, gave me a "father's blessing." He is no doubt an Enthusiast, but I am sure he is a good man, and yet from some fault or other, it is said, the Quakers have put him out of their Society.'[111]

Dalhousie was usually no mean judge of character and was keenly attuned to gesture and bearing in interpersonal politics. That he agreed to accept a father's blessing from this scoundrel who was in fact eight years younger than he is a testament to Lancaster's slickness. It is then not surprising that both Louis-Joseph Papineau and John Neilson took Lancaster under their wings when he returned to Montreal in 1829 to conduct some new 'experiments' in education. He promised both of them that he could teach people how to read and write almost instantly and with support he could adapt his system for a rural peasant population whose national sentiments would thereby be strengthened. Papineau was instrumental in securing him a grant of £200, and, with Neilson chairing the Assembly's education committee, further grants were made in 1830–2, with Lancaster even qualifying for the teacher training allowance. He purported to open and run a school in Montreal, and it seems some children of the merchant elite were sent to him for some time, although they did not learn much. The proposed experiments had to be kept secret, Lancaster insisted, until they were perfected, but when he finally delivered his results after falling out with Papineau in the spring of 1832, they turned out to be the same tired old stuff he had flogged for thirty years.[112]

It was the 1832 Montreal West Ward election riot and the cholera which followed on its heels, both of which transformed Lower Canadian politics, that pushed Lancaster into more erratic behaviour. Lancaster voted for the Tory candidate Stanley Bagg and later claimed the *patriote* party organizers warned him that if he did so he would lose his parliamentary subsidy. Papineau, who was roughed up in the street and who interfered with the subsequent proceedings of the coroner's jury investigating the riot, had to explain to John Neilson that Lancaster's accusations were false. In a deteriorating hand, Lancaster now wrote a long series of hysterical and deluded letters to the governor, Lord Aylmer, warning of the imminent danger of insurrection in the Montreal district. One was entitled 'Review of certain facts and libels which viewed in connection warrant a strong suspicion of a conspiracy for murder, Sedition or Treason' and warned that treasonous libels in the *Vindicator* newspaper were being distributed to the Irish troops, that the editor was forming a political society with the Irish in New York, and that the Catholic clergy had joined together to make martyrs of the election victims.[113]

Lancaster outraged public opinion in the summer of 1832 by setting himself up as an organizer of a subscription campaign for cholera relief funds and by trying to take over the Board of Health. Other activists complained he solicited only the soft touches, but it was his promotion of the charlatan Stephen Ayres – 'the Charcoal Doctor' – that was most offensive. Ayres claimed to cure cholera with a concoction of charcoal, ashes, maple syrup, and hog lard. Lancaster installed him in a house next to his own and acted as his agent. The two invaded the mission at Caughnawaga and claimed to have cured many Native cholera victims, some of whom Lancaster drove around Montreal in his open carriage and liquored up in the taverns. He published a diatribe in the Tory *Montreal Herald* – *La Minerve* refused to print it – against the clergy who objected to his activity. Lancaster fled Montreal sometime in 1833 after publishing a self-serving account of his wonderful contributions to education and the undeservedly harsh treatment he had received from the *patriotes*. When the October Grand Jury reported a true bill against him for two counts of assault and battery and one of simple assault, Lancaster was nowhere to be seen.[114]

The End of the Monitorial Moment

The *patriote* and the moderate reform press castigated Lancaster, the man, after the events of 1832. Nahum Mower of the *Courant* calculated that if Lancaster had in fact told the truth about the number of students he had instructed, he would have made $7,800 in three and a half years from grants and fees, not counting what he still owed tradesmen, all without

producing anything new. *La Minerve* thought the whole Lancasterian affair was a sad case of a person biting the hand which fed him. But neither
went on to tie Lancaster's character or conduct to the worth of monitorial
schooling. There had been a brief discussion in the press of competing
pedagogical systems when Lancaster first began announcing his experiments. A proponent of J.J. Jacotot's method of 'universal instruction' and
its embrace of the concept of the 'ignorant schoolmaster' attracted editorial comment and there was some talk of the relative suitability of the universal and monitorial systems for large schools.[115] As we shall see in more
detail in a later chapter, there was modest diffusion of monitorial or
Lancasterian practices into some village and rural schools, occasionally
with the encouragement of a curé. Yet most village and country schoolteachers had neither the numbers of students nor the complicated apparatus required to put in place a full-blown monitorial pedagogy.

It was the investigations of the abbé Jean Holmes in preparation for the
organization of schools under the 1836 Normal School Act, a parallel investigation conducted by a group of moderate Montreal politicians, and
plans of the reformers around Lord Durham that led to the abandonment
of monitorialism in Lower Canada. Holmes was sent on a tour of the
northern United States and western Europe in 1836 in search of normal
schoolteachers and scientific apparatus for colleges by the Boards of the
Quebec and Montreal Normal Schools. He had seen the monitorial system in operation as a member of the Société d'Éducation de Québec, and
his official instructions – perhaps written by John Neilson, who had likely
visited the BFSS's Borough Road Model School in London in 1835 – enjoined him to determine the 'opinions entertained of Lancasterian and
mutual Instruction Systems.' He reported that such opinions were un-
favourable on the whole: monitorialism was no longer popular in the
northeastern states, Victor Cousin in France was decidedly against it, and
education progressed much more slowly in the Swiss cantons which had
adopted it than in those which had abandoned it.[116]

Yet monitorial schooling changed Lower Canadian society in a variety
of ways, reshaping cityscapes, altering the rhythms of life, organizing and
reproducing new social categories, and reshaping social subjectivities. In
some of its guises it encouraged social mobility but also treated its subjects
as individually responsible for their own fates. It proved unable to produce the deepened interiorities demanded in a developing liberal system
of government, but it underpinned early liberal governmentality.

The following chapter follows attempts to include the peasantry in the
governmental webs that had developed in the cities.

4

Creating a 'Taste for Education' in the Countryside, 1829–1836

This chapter follows the course of rural school legislation in its political context, from the passage of the 1829 School Act to the rejection of the Assembly's 1836 School Bill by the Legislative Council. The next chapter uses state papers, press reports, and official school returns to gauge the effects of the school acts on rural schooling. Huge amounts of public money were spent in the 1830s, in some years a fifth or more of the state budget, but to date the literature contains no serious overview of local conditions.

The generous or 'liberal' 1829 School Act was intended to create a 'taste for education' among the *habitant* population by offering start-up funding for schoolhouse construction and teachers' salaries. It was a didactic undertaking, for its designers believed that once the people had been exposed to schooling, it would want to school itself and would be prepared to pay to do so. The Assembly made some concerted efforts to encourage rural schooling, to improve school legislation in light of experience, and there was some real improvement in local educational conditions. The latter is evident not simply in a greater presence of schools and opportunities for schooling, but also because seven years even of haphazard funding led to an accumulation of resources and to efforts at the systematization and standardization of provision beyond the school district.

However, political struggle prevented systematic and co-ordinated development of colonial schools and made it impossible for schools to be supported through local property taxation. On the one hand, the Councils, colonial Tories, and the imperial government blocked attempts to incorporate trustee boards with taxation powers. On the other hand, the majority in the Assembly refused to create any permanent bodies of non-political educational officials with supervisory or planning powers.

Educational administration was both ad hoc and heavily politicized. The school laws tended to bolster existing relations of power and prestige at the local level while often pandering to an ignorant populism.

The Assembly attempted to specify minimum qualifications for teachers, to influence the range of what was taught, and to encourage some kinds of advanced schooling, including giving support for several academies in the Eastern Townships. It not did create county or regional boards of education or boards of examiners, despite widespread demand on the part of local residents who were displeased with the quality of teachers and schools. *Patriote* party claims of the sovereignty of the people and its minimalist conception of government meant that the school acts accepted as local educational officials anyone whom local property holders might choose. In consequence, a majority of school trustee boards contained at least some people unable to read and write. The connection between schooling and the production of a literate, autonomous citizenry was thereby weakened, especially in French-speaking areas. Uneducated, elected trustees found themselves practically dependent on literate, unelected members of local communities. In most rural parishes the curés were able effectively to limit schooling to child minding, moral training and the study of a few religious books.

The majority in the Assembly were unwilling to contemplate a non-political educational administration: '*bureaucrate*' was a *patriote* epithet not only for the oligarchy that dominated executive government, but also for a function, as the case of Joseph Cary will show. To avoid bureaucratic management, select MPPs were granted extensive administrative powers over local schooling, a conflation of legislation and administration which was contentious and, in some cases, productive of the very 'corruption' it was meant to prevent. Having taken responsibility for school administration, MPPs found their electoral fortunes bound up with the conduct of school matters. Battles for political leadership invaded local educational administration. This situation worked against the efforts of the Assembly's Standing Committee on Education to exert fiscal control over schooling and to use rational planning in educational government, since spending cuts rebounded on the popularity of the MPPs. Opponents of the *patriote* majority were quick to notice that it often acted against the considered opinions of its own Committee in school matters.

Over the period 1829–36, repeated moves and counter-moves were made by the legislative and executive branches to promote the education of the people and the schooling of population. Political battle lines hardened after 1832. A hopeful moment for the resolution of conflict in

1836 was lost to an ill-considered gesture on the part of the lieutenant governor of Upper Canada. The Assembly had elaborated a major, co-ordinated set of educational initiatives, the cornerstone of which was a new rural elementary school act, but the Legislative Council refused to accept it. As colonial politics moved out of parliament, the school act expired and most rural schools closed for a six-year period.

The Trustees School Act of 1829

Early in the winter 1829 session of parliament, as the Episcopal churches and the executive moved to give control over schooling to an expanded Royal Institution, the reform leader John Neilson introduced a set of resolutions in the Assembly calling for a New York–style rural school system. He urged the creation of measures for property assessment and taxation by elected trustees and the creation of a colonial school fund to offer matching grants for local tax revenues.[1] Neilson's resolutions did not make it out of committee, and they may have been a ploy to force the executive to accept the much more modest provisions of François Blanchet's 1829 School Act, commonly known as the Trustees School Act (la Loi des Syndics), which was proclaimed on 14 March. Only as a bare-bones piece of legislation did it squeak through a bitterly divided Legislative Council on the deciding double vote of the speaker.

This modest 'Act to Encourage Elementary Education (9 Geo. IV, c.46),' which was to be in force for three years, simply created five-member trustee boards at the level of township, parish, or seigneury, composed of 'fit and proper persons' elected annually at a meeting convened and presided over by the senior resident militia officer. The election results were to be certified, lodged in the nearest notary's office, and copied to the civil secretary. The act thus immediately implicated two leading members of local elites in school matters, one of them an appointee of the executive. The trustee boards could organize schools and hire and contract with teachers, but not assess or tax property. If they built a schoolhouse, they were eligible for a matching grant of up to £50, although only £2,000 was appropriated for this purpose for the colony as a whole. Any country male or female teacher in a school not under the control of the Royal Institution and with at least twenty students was eligible for a grant of £20 a year for three years, as were the 'proprietors' or teachers of existing private schools. An additional 10s. a year for three years was given for each poor child in attendance to a maximum of 50. The extra money was payable provided that the trustees or the proprietor certified there were not less than twenty poor students in attendance who received free tuition. Rural schools run by religious orders were eligible for the poor student allowance as well. The trustees alone determined all aspects of the internal management of schools. Each school was to conduct an annual public examination, and the trustees were required to report to the three branches of government according to a schedule appended to the act.

The Trustees School Act was silent on most administrative matters. The act said nothing about how many schools would be funded, or about where they could be built; it was silent on how long a school had to be open to qualify for the school grant of £20; no information was offered as to how or to whom the school money would be paid; no time period was specified for trustee elections to be held or for the results to be reported; it did not specify who was to receive school reports. No mechanism was created for resolving disputes resulting from the law. These and many other matters were left to the discretion of executive government, through the agency of the civil secretary, and his office was quickly inundated with correspondence related to the schools, in addition to a wave of correspondence provoked by the 1829 Road Act.[2]

Barely two weeks passed from the proclamation of the school act before the first petitions for funding arrived in the government offices, some of them from curés seeking aid for their own schools. Individual MPPs were also receiving petitions and queries, while the Catholic bishops were refusing demands from churchwardens to elect trustees or to use vestry funds to build schoolhouses so that they could qualify for the government matching grant. Many trustee elections were held quickly. In early April in Boucherville, for example, a meeting convened by the seigneur and Executive Councillor Charles Chaussegros de Léry elected the wealthy peasant Bonaventure Viger, the notary and politician Louis Lacoste, an illiterate Michel Larrivée, and two others as trustees. The group, notorious in *patriote* politics in the 1830s, immediately resolved to petition the bishops for a loan of £50 from the vestry to build a trustee school.[3]

In the absence of procedural information in the 1829 act, the civil secretary, Charles Yorke, conferred with François Blanchet on how to administer it. 'The most liberal construction ought to be put upon it,' wrote Blanchet, for 'the great object is to give the people a taste for education and an interest in the management of it.' Because many curés had their own schoolhouses, Blanchet 'thought [it] prudent not to exclude them from the remuneration' and so any teacher of a school, whether in a trustee school or in a school owned by him or herself or by someone else (other than the Royal Institution) would be eligible for the grant of £20. Provided, Blanchet stressed, that the teacher produced a certificate stating 'that he has 20 Scholars under his tuition,' he or she was also eligible for '10/- for every Scholar above the twenty, being bona fide poor & instructed gratuitously, the number not being less than twenty at the time, nor more than 50.' Churchwardens should be eligible for the matching grant of £50 for schoolhouse construction on the same terms as trustees, but here ended the accommodation Blanchet was prepared to offer to existing schools, 'for, from hence forward every School to be established in the Country parts, must be under the direction of Trustees elected in the manner provided by the act, to entitle it to receive the remuneration.' He also proposed that salaries be paid half-yearly and that no teacher receive a payment unless the school had been open for at least six months. Finally, Blanchet urged 'the propriety of appointing, as a Soothing thing, all the Curates, parsons or rectors of Churches, in the different Parishes or Townships as visitors of the Schools where children of their respective persuasion are instructed.'[4]

With Executive Council approval Yorke then drew up and published a set of administrative regulations. Payments to teachers would be made half-yearly in January and July on condition of the receipt of a report sent to the civil secretary in due form. The report was to include a nominal list of scholars which identified those who did and did not pay fees, with the date of their admission to the school. After the passage of the act, no new school would qualify for funding unless trustee elections were held and a certified copy of the election result was forwarded to the civil secretary. The trustees should certify the school report in a standard form. Yorke also stated that religious communities could qualify for the grant if they submitted attendance lists for their schools and that churchwardens could apply for the schoolhouse grant for vestry schools.

The strikingly 'liberal' – that is, generous – provisions embodied in Yorke's communication were those which stated that schools open for less than six months with at least twenty students would be eligible for a prorated share in the £20 grant, and that it was not necessary for a school to have twenty fee-paying students before claiming the 10s. grant for each poor student. To qualify for the £20 grant, any mix of poor and fee-paying students to the minimum number of twenty was acceptable, but, stated Yorke, no student was to be admitted to a school as a pauper whose parents or guardians were in fact able to pay for its education. Both Blanchet's opinion and a clause in the act held that a school needed forty students as a minimum, twenty of them fee-paying, to be eligible for the extra grant for poor students. Yorke's interpretation eliminated this restriction.[5]

Louis-Joseph Papineau congratulated the executive on these regulations. By mid-May he had already received a large correspondence from 'various Curés and *habitants* in different parts of the country asking me for direction as to the procedures they were to adopt to build schools or to pay their schoolmasters – The detailed and clearly motivated instructions which His Excellency has had published will erase the doubts which were allowed to exist under the law.' Papineau had also interpreted the act to mean that twenty fee-paying students were required before a school could claim the 10s. for poor students, but after considering the matter he concluded that 'His Excellency's interpretation is more just & above all more liberal, and it will be most useful, and satisfactory, for the Legislature, the public, and the school masters.' Papineau's brother and estate manager Denis-Benjamin was urging him at this moment to establish a school at la Petite Nation, both in order to increase property values and to discipline his tenants in habits of industry.[6]

Perhaps it is only in retrospect that this 'liberal' interpretation appears both foolish and highly 'illiberal' – in the sense of a liberalism aimed at the encouragement of the responsible, self-governing community of citizens – for while it certainly worked to give the people 'a taste for schools,' it undermined the principle that this taste would make the people spend its own money on education. No means test applied to parents. People were quick to appreciate that the government might school their offspring for free, and teachers were quick to notice that reporting fifty pauper students might earn them, not £20 and whatever fees they could bully out of parents, but rather £35 from the government.

The Impact of the School Act

The local impact of the 1829 act was often immediate and dramatic, but it varied according to political, economic, ethnic, and religious circumstances. Certainly a large number of schools seeking the grant reported to government, although just how many new schools were created and how many existing schools received government funding is uncertain. Most villages had schools, and the number of villages large enough to support one, two, or sometimes more schools was increasing as manufacturing capital penetrated the river valleys. According to François Blanchet's 1830 Committee Report, in the first six months or so of the act's operation the government subsidized 381 schools: 262 schools managed by trustees, 105 private schools, 12 vestry schools, and 2 schools owned by curés. There were 14,735 students, 7,222 of them paying fees, at a cost of £4,663.0.10, in addition to £1,757.2.5 in matching grants for the construction of 48 schoolhouses. This report was meant to show that the Assembly could produce popular schooling more cheaply than the Royal Institution. The 84 schools of the latter had 3,675 students at a cost of £2,115.10.0: in other words, the schools funded by the Assembly taught each student for 6s.4d., while the RI schools spent 11s.6d.[7]

In such places as Berthier County, where there was a School Society, and in several English-speaking parts of the Eastern Townships where settlers had adopted some version of New England–style schooling on their own, the act offered both a welcome financial stimulus and the opportunity to coordinate educational activities on a larger scale. The Stanstead Township trustees decided not to visit or report any school whose teacher had not passed an examination before them on school management and on teaching spelling, reading, writing, arithmetic, English grammar, geography, ancient and modern history, and natural philosophy. They undertook to visit qualified schools regularly 'to create a spirit of rivalry,' urging parents and guardians to interest themselves in young people's education and to provide books. The strategy worked, and they reported on twenty-three different schools, all but one of them under their direction. However, attendance in the winter of 1829–30 was only 1,064, while in the summer of 1829 and the spring of 1830 it fell below the average threshold of twenty students per school. Still, on their own accord the Stanstead trustees acted as a board of examiners, an agency that was demanded repeatedly by other advocates of public schooling but one that made it into law in 1841 for the cities alone.[8]

Elsewhere the act fed into existing conflicts and created new ones as people scrambled to get government money, to prevent others from getting it, and to contest the trustee elections. From Dundee it was reported that the school act had placed the entire settlement 'in a state of ferment and all determined to have a school as near their own door as possible.' Claims of misconduct in trustee elections were common, and trustees could not resolve local disputes. In the seigneury of Pierre-ville in St François parish, curé Amiot tried three times to get his parishioners to agree on a school site, but farmers and villagers were irreconcilably opposed to one another and to the trustees. From St Mathias a French-speaking correspondent claimed that a wealthy Englishman had convinced the *habitants* that they could not elect trustees without a copy of the statutes in hand. When they dispersed, he and some friends, with the connivance of the curé who was opposed to trustee schools, declared two English-speaking Protestant women to be the teachers.[9]

A particularly striking conflict around trustee elections was that in the political hotspot of St Scholastique and St Eustache, involving the curé F.-J. La Mothe, the English-speaking residents represented by Major James Evans, and the reform MPP Dr Jacques Labrie. La Mothe had been in the parish since 1826, had built at least one school and sponsored some others, including one taught by his nephew Laurent, before the passage of the 1829 act. He decided to place his schools under the management of trustees, but after the trustee election returned a French-speaking board, a group of English-speaking residents led by Evans claimed that the act specified one set of trustees for each school, and since they did not wish to be associated with 'canadians,' they held a second election and sent official notice of the results to the Rector of St Andrew's. Jacques Labrie had not immediately notified the government of the first trustee election, explaining that the trustee school was just getting under way, but when he studied the law and discovered it intended one board of trustees in the parish rather than one for each school, it was clear that a new election was necessary.

Major Evans then claimed that the new election 'was Illegally assembled by the Junior Capt. of Militia ... and in as secret a manner as possible and supposed to be under the influence of Mr La Motte the Resident Priest.' As well, he protested, some of the trustees then elected 'instead of being "fit and proper Persons" according to the Letter of the Act can neither read nor rite, and are therefore incapable of performing the Duties required.' Jacques Labrie insisted that he knew 'with scientific certainty' that this election had been widely and openly publicized, and he rejected claims by Evans that the English-speaking population was almost as large as the French, yet had no trustees. For his part, La Mothe defended himself against the charge of holding a secret election by sending the civil secretary a large number of sworn affidavits from those who had heard it announced. It was true, he agreed, that the election meeting had been heated and controversial in part because of 'the qualifications of the Trustees who, I suppose, ought to know how to read and write; not everyone shared my opinion,' but there was nothing illegal in that matter. The upshot of this controversy, apart from the fact that the schools waited on their funds while it played out and that an extra burden fell on the civil secretary's office, was that La Mothe decided it would be much less trouble not to place his schools under the provisions of the 1829 act. 'So many contrarieties concerning the election of the trustees causing marked damage to the school masters,' it was easier and faster to apply for the grant as a school proprietor.[10]

Trustees often could not agree among themselves, as in St Joachim, where Jean Bolduc and François Lessard protested against their fellow trustees who certified the school taught by Marie Can[e]ur as the parish school. They argued that she should be excluded because 'a number of the children she teaches free, are able to pay, namely the Putin, Bolduc, Racine and other families.' In addition, her school exam had been a farce: the other trustees were content to have her make three students read aloud as a measure of her qualifications. Can[e]ur's school was nothing but a scheme to ensure the school they were themselves building would fail from lack of enrolment. Bolduc and Lessard called for closer scrutiny of school affairs and for more supervision from 'people with standing in the parish and above all from Messire Besserer, curé of this place.' Again, in Sutton, the schools were threatened with the loss of the grant because one trustee refused to sign some of the school reports.[11]

Schooling became a source of competition and conflict among clergy and laity, supporters of vestry schools, Royal Institution schools, and the new trustee schools, as well as between notables and peasants. The Lotbinière trustees were outraged when one of the teachers they supervised received payment from the government on the basis of a certificate signed 'with his usual flightiness' by curé Daveluy, rather than by themselves. This move was meant to 'make the Ignorant Class of the *habitants* believe, that without the Curé's certificate, no master can Receive anything.' It was meant to 'disparage the character of the Trustees.' At Rivière Ouelle, the curé, seigneur, and the leading militia officers opposed the trustees who had installed their teacher, Pierre Boucher, in a school in the village close to the vestry school. The village could not support two schools, they complained, arguing that Boucher should be relocated. Two schools also were too many for Kamouraska. Here curé Narin, Amable Dionne, and J.-B. Taché urged the secretary of the Royal Institution not to support the attempts by some residents to resuscitate the village's RI school. They supported a trustee school, which could only succeed 'if no use at all was made of the Royal Foundation School.' And from Cap Santé old George Allsopp, a sponsor of the Royal Institution school there, wrote in May 1829, 'the people are all astir here about crowding elementary mistresses & masters the £20 gratuity is a strong inducement. It has been remarked in certain quarters,' he continued, 'that the object of the law was power & the watchword is "down with the Institution School."' Allsopp thought the Trustees Act would injure the RI school, 'particularly as there has already been an opposition school to the westward of the church last year which took off a portion of the scholars' and there was 'also a small childs school kept by a young woman on the hill who is aiming at the £20.' Allsopp claimed that 'if our Curé had taken as much interest in encouraging the RI. school it would have been more flourishing.'[12]

In the absence of any robust procedures for local dispute resolution, and given that the school act made no provision for inspection, the executive initially attempted to appoint people to investigate serious complaints of fraud, abuse, or other irregularities. Thus Stephen Sewell, the brother of the chief justice, was dispatched to the area between Chateauguay and St Constant to investigate Abraham Myers's allegations of May 1830 that he had been cheated out of the school money he was due as teacher by Robert Dunn. There had been no trouble in the three years he had kept school, claimed Myers, 'til after the saluary was obtained' under the 1829 act, when Dunn set himself up as the sole proprietor of Myers's school, despite the fact that 'more than twenty people have equal shares in the house.' Dunn kept half of Myers's pay and, when Myers objected, Dunn hired another teacher 'who is in fact nothing of the kind but a chain smith,' set him up in 'a barn,' and 'went around trying to get my scholars and then told the people the smith should have the salury for his wages.' Myers insisted he had forty-four students and that his school had been examined by lawfully elected trustees.

A different report came from J. Mackenzie, a clergyman who visited the area in mid-summer 1830, who portrayed Robert Dunn as a Yorkshire man with a beautiful farm who was remarkable for his 'piety and usefulness' and Myers as 'not a fit person to occupy the important station of a Schoolmaster.' Mackenzie reported 'that the conduct of Mr. Myers in private did not correspond with his public duty; – that he frequented taverns on the Sabbath &c – that a few American families residing there appeared to encourage him in the Course pursued by him to annoy Mr. & Mrs. Dunn.' Mrs Dunn feared for her life. Sewell went to investigate and concluded in August that Myers's trustees had no legal standing and that Dunn's teacher Henry Burrell was entitled to the school money.[13]

It took more than six months for the executive to resolve a dispute in St-Pierre-les-Becquets surrounding the valuation of two schoolhouses, and correspondence on the matter continued for more than a year. The aftertaste of this conflict was still strong nine years later. Petty parish politics provoked intense factional divisions, and interpersonal antagonisms disrupted school and church matters throughout the 1830s, with frequent accusations of fraud levelled against the school trustees. The civil secretary received complaints in October 1829 from some residents, including the justice of the peace Joseph Dionne, that the trustees had managed to get £100 in matching grants for two schoolhouses by over-valuing them. One of the schoolhouses was supposedly occupied as a private residence even after the grant was paid. The trustees claimed that the houses were justly valued and that they had been purchased for less than their claimed value because the vendors had wanted to subsidize schooling. James Brown, who was dispatched from Quebec to investigate, had his every move scrutinized avidly, with the order in which he visited people and with whom he ate cited as evidence of the partiality of his judgment. The trustees denounced their curé for adopting Dionne's position, and one of their allies, Jacques Raimond Baby, was convicted for desecrating the church. Brown eventually ruled that the two schools together were worth about £112 and so the trustees were entitled to about £56, but they were instructed to return the £100 they had received fraudulently before the lower amount would be paid. Brown's investigation cost the government £5.[14] The executive did not have the financial or the administrative means to oversee the operations of the school act by hiring special investigators.

The Revisions of 1830

Calls for revisions to the 1829 act appeared quickly in the press and in government correspondence, as well as in such publications as J.-F. Perrault's 1830 prize-winning essay, *Plan Raisonné d'Education Générale et Permanente.* 'Campagnard' from L'Assomption – probably J.-B. Meilleur – had four long columns in *La Minerve* in August 1829 on the flaws in the law. Particularly weak were the absence of any limits on the numbers of schools and of any obligation on the part of teachers to teach all the students who could not pay. He also criticized the lack of supervision over the private schools funded by the act. The law should be modified so that teachers could easily earn £37 a year, and schools should be established on the basis of parish population as defined by the 1825 census. If schools became crowded in consequence, they could adopt Lancasterian mutual instruction. The schools should also offer practical training and encourage economic improvement in the countryside, something that would involve reforms to the existing agricultural societies whose annual grants of £1,600 simply ended up in the pockets of well-to-do Scottish and English farmers.[15]

Sir James Kempt called for improvements to the 1829 act in his January 1830 throne speech while congratulating the Assembly on the rapid expansion of the schools. Most of his proposed revisions were embodied in the School Act of 1830 (10-11 Geo. IV, c.14), which received royal assent on 24 March. It expressly qualified curés without real property to run in trustee elections and made it clear that no new private venture school was to receive the school grant without coming under the control of elected trustees. Royal Institution schools were subjected to a minimum enrolment condition, a measure that earned Kempt a particularly warm letter of appreciation from L.-J. Papineau, with a promise that the Assembly would work harder to draft better school legislation in future. As well, teachers were to be paid half-yearly, and two public examinations of each school were to be held. Schools built in the suburbs of Montreal, Quebec, and Trois-Rivières were declared eligible for the schoolhouse subsidy, and the act also contained a long list of subsidies for various urban schools, including a £300 grant to train Ronald MacDonald as teacher for a deaf and dumb school in Quebec City. The government began to distribute report forms with detailed instructions as to what was to be reported to whom and with sample powers of attorney for teachers' financial agents.[16]

The number of rural elementary schools and the amount of government expenditure on education increased dramatically in 1830. The inspector general of accounts, Joseph Cary, claimed to audit 1,400 bi-annual school reports, compared to 825 in 1829, and to pay out £18,088.12.7 stg. (over £21,000 cy.) for rural schools, close to a three-fold increase over 1829's £6,439.7.3 stg. His figures did not include £5,250.3.0 stg. for urban institutions in 1829 and £ 5,771.7.3 stg. in 1830. Education was suddenly the largest item of expenditure in a state budget of roughly £120,000.[17]

Some local residents trumpeted the benign effects of the law. The schools in Bolton 'are prosprous and manifest a very marked improvement,' said the trustees, who hoped through education to be 'Enabled to present from among the rising Generation an Enlightened Yeomanry Eager to maintain that Government from which they have Derived such distinguished advantages.' In Ste-Marie-de-Monnoir the trustees noted that apart from two poorly attended Royal Institution schools their parish had had no schools before 1829. By mid-1830, there were eight with over three hundred students attending daily. The change was caused by people acquiring the right to elect their own trustees.[18]

Trustee elections were awkward in some parts of the colony because the 1830 Militia Act removed the resident militia officers who were meant to convene them. The inspector general of accounts, who was responsible for authorizing payment of school monies, was not willing and not empowered to interpret the act so as to pay teachers without the trustee election report.[19] The elections themselves continued to be contentious. In Rivière Ouelle members of the parish elite, disgruntled by the election in

1829 of men opposed to the village's vestry school, agreed in 1830 'on the necessity of selecting Educated Persons in preference to Uneducated Persons to fulfil the Duties of Trustee' and so engineered the election of themselves, over the protests of their opponents. The curé argued that the opposition was entirely due to the fact that the new trustees 'all have the misfortune to know how to Read, write & sign Their names.'[20]

Having one set of trustees for an entire parish or seigneury was unsatisfactory in many places because they could not practically visit the schools or because they could not represent all residents. At la Petite Nation, which contained 104 Catholic and 24 Protestant heads of household, the election of Catholic trustees in 1829 led to a second election by the Protestants for their own trustees on the grounds that the schoolhouse was too distant to be of any use to them. In 1830, a new trustee board chaired by D.-B. Papineau attempted to calm matters by sponsoring a school near the English-speaking residents and by applying for £36 in matching funds and £10 for an English-speaking teacher. Elsewhere trustees exercised their authority to disqualify teachers, or stretched their authority by claiming the right to inspect proprietors' schools or vestry schools.[21]

Many curés adopted an attitude of 'repressive tolerance' towards the schools, serving as trustees to ensure that nothing against Catholic religion (and thus often nothing of substance) was taught in them. The executive found itself drawn into battles between clergy and laity which could not be resolved locally. In one of the most notorious, conflict around schooling got completely out of hand in St-Roch-de-l'Achigan in the Montreal district, and a wave of complaints made it to the civil secretary's office because of curé J.-J. Raizenne's obstruction of the trustees. Raizenne was relocated by his bishop in 1831 after thirty five years as curé. He had been an effective opponent of lay encroachment on schooling as least since 1816 when he blocked a project for a Royal Institution school in the parish.[22] According to Lt-Col. B. Rocher, the parish was bitterly divided, with a small majority, including Jacques Archambault, supporting the curé and opposing those Rocher called the best educated residents, including himself, other militia officers, and the MPP Charles Courteau. Rocher claimed Raizenne blocked the project for a trustee school in 1829 in order to support a private school conducted by his housekeeper's niece and nephew. When Rocher announced the trustee election date for 1830, Raizenne pre-empted him and insisted from the pulpit that schools in the colony were under the control of the bishop, that he was the bishop's representative in the parish, and that he must be named a trustee at once. When his audience did not respond, 'Mr. Raizenne decreed after mass, in the most imperious manner, from the altar rail, before his audience managed to Leave that he was going to the front of the presbytery wanting to Know If people were plotting against him?'

Rocher and the minority party wanted to have a school in the village where English would be taught so that the *habitants* could learn to compete with new settlers by improving their farming techniques. Rocher suspended the trustee election and sought an opinion from the executive on a petition against it signed by his fellow militia officers, among other reasons 'because the party opposed to us claims that it is not at all necessary that the Trustees know how to read in order to fill their duties in their offices, and us, we claim the opposite.' A new trustee election ordered by the executive returned Raizenne, at least one of his supporters, and at least two of his opponents. When the new trustee board arranged for the construction of a stone schoolhouse, Raizenne refused to sign the contract and the executive refused to offer the matching grant in consequence. All of the trustees except Raizenne had signed, and now they appealed directly to John Neilson for relief. It was outrageous, they complained, that they had no trustee school and that children sent to the private school supported by Raizenne were instructed in a miserable little building in which the school mistress had conducted a tavern in 1829 and in which in 1830 she kept 'a Grocery.'[23]

Despite such conflicts, there was widespread support for the 1829 act and the 1830 revisions as a good beginning in rural schooling, even while it was recognized that further modifications were necessary. The *Canadian Courant* thought schooling would not much advance without a university to train teachers. *La Minerve* suggested that in many parts of the colony, the government grant actually discouraged earlier efforts. People abandoned plans to raise money for schoolhouses and salaries by subscription in favour of government money and they appointed unqualified people as teachers in order to create employment for their friends. The attendance rolls were frequently falsified to claim the minimum number of students required by the law, and such activities had dangerous consequences for the morality of impressionable young people. There were many good teachers, *Minerve* agreed, but reforms to the law were necessary to police out abuses.[24]

The Revisions of 1831

After François Blanchet's sudden death in June 1830, parliamentary leadership in education passed to John Neilson. Neilson was the reform party's acknowledged procedural expert and strategist in the hopeful period between the Canada Committee report of summer 1828 and the Montreal election riot of May 1832. In its first session under Lord Aylmer, in addition to a new set of revisions to the school act in 1831, at Neilson's instigation the Assembly established a committee system (against internal opposition) including a Permanent Committee on Education, which Neilson chaired until his defeat in the 1834 elections.[25] At the same time, after wrestling census making away from the clergy in 1825, the Assembly managed to secure a new Census Act, which appointed commissioners to produce extensive information about population and social conditions. The 1831 census was conducted in the same period as the first serious inspections of the rural schools. Together, the results from the two inquiries had an impact on the substance and on the form of colonial political intelligence, encouraging statistical and population thinking on the part of intellectuals and state servants.

The 1831 School Act (1 Will. IV, c.7) was sanctioned on 31 March and dealt with several housekeeping and administrative matters. School monies would still be available until 15 May 1832 but now would be paid only to trustees, or to the private school proprietors funded in 1829. The five county, parish, or seigneury trustees were to collect teachers' reports and forward them to government only when all schools had reported, which they were to do every six months from 15 May 1831. In consequence, it was expected that the civil secretary and inspector general would have fewer and better materials to work with in administering the grant. If trustees used agents to get their money, they were required to send powers of attorney in duplicate along with their returns. An additional £4,000 was appropriated for schoolhouse construction, but only houses closed in and located at a minimum distance from existing schools were eligible, and the trustees had to apply in a manner specified in the law. The most significant change in the 1831 School Act was the nomination of county school visitors – inspectors.[26]

Nineteen visitors were to be appointed, with each typically responsible for the schools in several counties. In what would become an increasingly contentious conflation of legislative and administrative functions, all the school visitors were senior MPPs. Reformers in the Assembly were steadfastly opposed to the creation of any new bureaucracy, and, in January 1831, the Assembly had entertained a first resolution calling for the creation of an elective Legislative Council. As the people's elected representatives, it appeared that MPPs should inspect the people's schools. Those named were meant to undertake a tour of inspection in the summer of 1831, taking along the resident MPP, the curé, senior justice of the peace, and senior militia captain, if any of them were interested. The visitors could examine teachers and disqualify those found to be unfit. More important, the visitors were expected 'to lay out each parish, township, or extra-parochial place, into school districts, suitable for the attendance of children, and assistance from public funds will probably only be allowed in future, to one school in each school district.' Attributing this power to state agents was a significant move away from the practice of allowing property holders to establish schools at their convenience. As such it points to a shift in the educational governmentality of men such as John Neilson, the 1831 act's author, and was an innovation in state administration. Before the school visitors, the colony had few, if any, roaming inspectors. The census would make it possible to apportion the schools to population; inspection would situate the schools on the ground in keeping with local circumstances. Local school visitors had been used by the Royal Institution, but the Assembly extended and systematized the practice.[27] It turned out that few, if any, MPPs besides Neilson specified the limits of school districts.

Naming the visitors fell to the executive, via the civil secretary in consultation with John Neilson, who actually distributed the notices of appointment. Several of those first invited would not serve. For Stanstead and Drummond, the executive named Col. F.G. Heriot, but he refused adamantly, and when the other member, Ebenezer Peck, was invited, he too at first declined 'so extensive a duty,' claiming 'it will require a greater sacrifice of time than I can consistently make.' When convinced to take the position despite his objections, Peck did not visit any of the schools in some townships. The visitors, the great majority of them reformers, were appointed on 16 June 1831, were sent a package of documents with a circular of instructions, and encouraged 'as soon as possible, [to] proceed on the visit of the Schools assigned for [their] inspection, it being very desirable that those visits should take place before the beginning of the vacation, which will probably commence soon.'[28] Most of the visitors set to work in early summer, but it was time-consuming to inspect all the schools. Jacques Labrie, reform politician, medical doctor, historian, and school promoter, was still at it in Two Mountains, Terrebonne, and Lachenaie in October 1831. The pneumonia which killed him that month was contracted during his tour of inspection.[29]

The inspections yielded a key document: John Neilson's *Rapport du Visiteur d'École pour les Comtés de Bellechasse, L'Ilet, Kamouraska et Rimouski*, dated August 1831, presented to the Assembly and then printed as a pamphlet. The work was a practical description of what Neilson saw during his tour of inspection, documentation of 'abuses' under the existing legislation, and an agenda for change in the school acts that was taken up by the Permanent Committee in 1832. It was frequently invoked in debate about the trustee schools after 1832, and, although such was certainly not Neilson's intent, its description of abuses uncovered in the summer of 1831 was used both by the Tory majority in the Legislative Council in 1836 and by those associated with the Buller Commission in 1838–9 as a justification for smashing the trustee school system.[30]

Neilson travelled 200 miles east from Quebec on the south shore of the St Lawrence, beginning at Beaumont on 7 July 1831 and finishing on 3 August at the new parish of Ste Luce, east of Rimouski. He missed some schools and others were closed, but he received correspondence from trustees and local residents about such institutions and he was primed for what he might find elsewhere by friends. Later in the month, he visited schools at Lévis, perhaps in the company of Alexis de Tocqueville and Gustave de Beaumont. He kept rough working notes as he travelled, including a draft list of teachers he planned to disqualify, with a brief reminder of the cause, such as 'irregular,' 'not qualified,' 'too near another School & not qualified,' 'discontinued after 15 Nov 1831 unless he places himself in center of District No.1,' 'Keeps a Tavern.'[31]

His published report translated what he saw into statistical form, with a tabular return of schools, teachers, and students in each parish, distinguishing enrolment from attendance and fee-paying from free students, with a calculation of the average number of students per school. There were about 135 schools under his inspection, with almost 5,000 students enrolled, and on the whole Neilson thought they were well conducted and that the students were making good progress, especially in those schools where *canadien* teachers taught the English language. Despite his generally favourable view of teachers, Neilson disqualified about thirty of them. Neilson was especially positive about women teachers, for they 'seem to have more skill in governing Children of an age appropriate for elementary School attendance, that is from four to eight years.' Of the fifty-five female teachers, twenty-four taught girls' schools, the rest mixed schools.

Neilson's tables helped make local conditions legible to central government, but later critics particularly seized on the section in the report entitled 'Abuses.'[32] Here Neilson denounced the trustees' naming of friends or family members to schools, frequently a husband and wife or brother and sister team, who managed thereby to extract as much as £70 a year of government money, 'with lodging, firewood, &c., which exceeds the income enjoyed by the greatest part of the Farmers in the Countryside.' Such people were not the best teachers, and the abuse was a direct consequence of the failure of the school acts to limit the number of eligible schools. It also resulted from the policy which made it possible for all students to be counted as poor, so that teachers with twenty poor students could get £30 or £35 from government. The result was that many schools able to receive forty students were divided in two, or the attendance roll was faked to present the requisite number for the grant; the teacher, dependent on attendance, lost all disciplinary authority; and even rich parents concluded that teachers were adequately remunerated without their paying any fees. Many of the schools kept no regular hours and followed no consistent plan of instruction. Government aid for schoolhouse construction had not been matched at times by local effort, and Neilson found subsidized schoolhouses that were rented out to private families or that offered no accommodation for teachers. Finally, the responsibility of supervising the schools in a whole parish was beyond the capacity of five trustees. Only the zeal of the curés and of enlightened local residents and the hunger of young people for schooling, claimed Neilson, prevented the complete corruption of the system.

Neilson had remedies for these abuses. On the whole he thought the colony had an adequate supply of teachers, and he noted that if schooling were to become general, it had to be cheap. The best teachers were those familiar with the locality in which they worked, and women were the best at working with young children; he did not explicitly say they could be made to work for less than men, although he must have known it. Neilson divided his counties into school districts 'on the basis of distance and real population distribution.' The districts were large enough to furnish about one hundred students within a catchment area of a couple of miles. With one hundred students, the teachers would acquire experience in school management and their incomes would rise. Neilson urged the classification of students according to achievement and the introduction of mutual or monitorial pedagogy. With respect to the level of instruction, Neilson wrote, 'all the elementary education, in reading, writing, and arithmetic, necessary for the mass of the people, composed of farmers and artisans, can be acquired by children under nine years of age.' Up to nine years of age, young people were not much use at work, and above that age the talented or wealthy ones should move on to a superior school. The numbers of trustees should be increased from five in a parish to three for each individual school to provide closer local supervision.

Well before his counterparts elsewhere in British North America, then, Neilson was proposing elements of the 'common school revolution': rationally distributed schools with defined catchment areas, the feminization of teaching, student classification, and a common pedagogy. And he was thinking of schooling in terms of the relations between population and territory. His vision of the degree of education required by the peasantry was quite modest and he had no interest in challenging the Catholic clergy or the existing regime of sponsored mobility: it is no accident that the clergy claimed Neilson as one of its best political allies as insurrection loomed later in the 1830s.[33] Yet his report was not simply a description; it was also a legislative agenda.

The School Act of 1832

Although educational activists had no way of knowing it, the 1832 School Act (2 Will. IV, c.26), modified somewhat in 1833 and 1834, proved to be the apex of public educational development in Lower Canada. Passed late in February, before May's political explosions, it was based on the recommendations in Neilson's pamphlet. To be in force for two years, the law repealed the Trustees School Act and introduced a large number of changes to school management and administration. It specified the number of school districts in each county for which a school could be subsidized, outside the three urban areas. It limited the maximum annual legislative grant for a teacher's salary to £24 and, in a sop to the Catholic clergy, allowed an additional grant of £20 for a separate girls' school in any Catholic parish with a church or chapel. If the Soeurs de la Congrégation maintained a girls' school, they too could claim the £20, provided their school was open to students of all denominations at the same price. The act created a prize fund of 10s. per school to be awarded by visitors to the best student in each. Visitors were not required to account for this money, and they were also given an expense allowance of 10s. a day while visiting schools. The grant was to be made from 15 May 1832 to any eligible school existing before that date, provided it was under the direction of trustees by the second Monday in August 1832.

School management was decentralized. Three-person trustee boards holding office for two years were to be elected in each school district by qualified parliamentary electors. They were still described as 'fit and proper persons,' but an administrative handbook soon specified that term meant anyone the electors elected. The trustee boards were to continue in existence for the purpose of acquiring and holding school property despite changes in their membership, and when the act came into effect they were to exert their rights over any school built at public expense in their district. They were to account for their financial affairs annually to heads of households, but they could hire and fire teachers and make any arrangement they saw fit for the schoolhouse, except that they needed the written consent of a majority of the school visitors created by the act in order to sell it and they could not sell it at less than its full value.

Teachers' eligibility for the school grant was tightened and clarified. Now they could not be appointed without a certificate of good conduct from two of: the clergyman of the most populous denomination in the school district, the senior militia officer, and a justice of the peace. They were to be certified as able to teach reading, writing, and arithmetic in the language of the majority. They were required to keep their schools open for at least 190 days a year from 9 a.m. to noon and from 1 p.m. to 4 p.m. and to teach at least twenty children between the ages of five and fifteen years. No student was to be charged more than 2s. per month, unless its parent or guardian contracted in writing to pay more. Teachers had to hold a public examination after due notice and were eligible for the grant only if at least three of the school visitors had visited the school at least once and had given their certificate that it was legally conducted, that the teacher was well qualified, and that the students were making good progress and conducting themselves in an exemplary manner. Only those between five and fifteen were to be taught during regular hours; older students could be taught at other times but were not to be charged more than 2s. per month.

Teachers were now also to keep a school journal in a specified form and to have it open for examination by any householder after school hours. The act said nothing about curriculum or schoolbooks, but teachers were required by law to teach their students in classes defined by age and achievement. They were to record the date of students' enrolment, but also to use the school journal to track their progress, noting when they were given which book and when they began to write. With the consent of the trustees, teachers defined school rules, which were to be posted in the schoolroom. Teachers could be removed before the end of their term by the school visitors, on the complaint of three household heads, following a public hearing and decision of the trustees.

Trustees could admit up to ten children of poor parents to be instructed free of charge, provided that for each child admitted free, the parents had enrolled one fee-paying child. In principle it was no longer possible to compose the minimum number of students needed to qualify for the grant only with poor children instructed for free.

The act also modified the provisions regulating school visitation or inspection. Eligible visitors at the county level now included resident members of the Legislative Council and Assembly, the senior justice of the peace, the senior militia officer, and the clergyman of the largest denomination. They were now responsible for hearing and rendering judgments on all school-related disputes and for fixing the limits of school districts. They could order a reduction in the number of districts to increase attendance in a school and they were to report on the best site for a superior school in each county. If they found more than one school in operation in a district, they could choose which to recognize as the trustee school. At least three of them were to visit the schools in their areas in June or July of each year and to give their certificates to the trustees.

In what proved to be a particularly contentious clause, the act specified that the trustees would report on their schools to the resident MPP, or to the one receiving the most votes at the last election. It was this member of parliament who was to draw up the list of schools in his county eligible for funding and to forward it each 15 May to the civil secretary, who would then draw up pay lists for the teachers. Not only did the act thus force the teachers to live on as little as £1 a month for a year or more while they waited to receive their grant, but it placed their fate in the hands of a partisan elected official. All school monies, with the exception of the prize fund, were to be accounted for carefully.[34]

The act thus embodied most of what Neilson's visitors' report had recommended and attempted to eliminate the abuses it identified. It did not place the limits on age of instruction he had sought and it was silent on the matter of mutual instruction and the feminization of teaching. Other members of the Permanent Committee had also apparently considered the possibility that a superior school was necessary in each county to provide more advanced instruction to some students. Still, in its record-keeping provisions, the 1832 act created the potential for much more intensive tracking and administration of rural schooling, down to the level of individual student activity. The central authority could, in principle, if the act worked, draw up an account of the student population as a whole and of individual student conditions in different sections of the colony. In conception, these were the individualizing and totalizing initiatives characteristic of population thinking.

The Administrative Manual

The legislation effectively made senior county MPPs into bureaucrats and boards of education: something unknown in North America or

Great Britain. For their direction, the executive published a *Memorandum. For giving effect to the School Act of 1832*, the first manual of its kind in the colony. The MPPs were to distribute eight different documents to each school district and to keep a store of extra copies for future use. A ninth document was the form for their own annual reports. Each district was to receive a copy of the school act and a copy of the list of school districts created by the visitors in 1831, along with blank minutes of trustee elections and a blank copy of the *acte de dépôt* for the notary. These first three documents were to be sent at once to the senior militia officer or senior justice of the peace in each district. After the trustee election, they were to be certified locally, copied, and returned to the MPP.

The school trustees were to be sent school journals for two years, blank visitors' certificates, which were to be completed in duplicate, with one copy returned to the MPP, along with a completed return from each school, and blank forms granting power of attorney from the trustees so that the receiver general could pay school monies to their agent. The school district was also to receive a list of county MPPs, indicating to which one trustees were to send their reports and returns. In addition to a two-year supply of all these documents, the responsible MPP also received the blank report forms he was to complete using returns from local schools and which he was to send 'to the Civil Secretary, to authorize the issue of Pay-lists,' as soon after 15 May 1833 as possible. Schooling was to be invested in forms.[35]

The MPPs were informed that 'the existing School Masters will lose their allowance after the 15th May [1832], if the election[s] for the Districts in which they act, do not take place on or before the second Monday of August [1832].' No school money was to be paid to any district without a certified return of the trustee election. Legitimate elections were to be held only after public notice given on at least two Sundays preceding the second Monday in August. The election meeting could be held outside the school district, but only heads of household resident in the district were eligible to vote. Any person, resident in the district or not, could be elected as a trustee, and to overcome past conflict around definitions of a 'fit and proper person,' the MPPs were informed that 'the qualification' of a trustee 'is entirely left to the discretion of Families.' The School Act of 1832 thus effectively authorized illiterate men and women to serve as school trustees. Then with a certain insouciance the *Memorandum* suggested that the act itself offered sufficient guidance for the trustees, teachers, and visitors, while warning that its clauses 'must be studied and bona fide complied with, otherwise the payments will be in danger of being suspended.' How those trustees who could not read were to study the act was not explained.

A final section of the *Memorandum* instructed MPPs as to the fate of Royal Institution, vestry, and private venture schools. Now the meeting held to elect trustees could decide to declare one of those schools to be the district school, for a period not to exceed two years. If the meeting did so, the MPP was to recognize it as the district school and to certify it as eligible for the school grant, provided there was compliance with the other requirements of the act. In this way Neilson's Permanent Committee sought not only to eliminate one source of local educational conflict, but also to incorporate other kinds of schools into the trustee system.[36]

Politically speaking, the 1832 School Act left control and manage-ment of country schools in the hands of local electors, supervised and administered by members of local elites and by elected parliamentary representatives. The Permanent Committee of the Assembly could re-flect on the act's operation and could propose alterations to it, but it was not itself an administrative body able to interpret the application of the law in local circumstances. In the absence of a ministry or general board of education, executive government's influence over the schooling of population was limited to financial audit and the verification of compli-ance with specified procedures. There was no planned colony-wide school curriculum, and while the Assembly continued to promote mon-itorial pedagogy, at the local level teachers were free to teach what and how they pleased – with the exception that they were to classify students – provided parents, trustees, and visitors agreed.

Bureaucracy, or 'Remarks became necessary to be made'

In its consecration of the people's right to local self-government – albeit under the supervision of local elites – the 1832 act expressed the grow-ing republicanism of many members of the Assembly. This republican-ism for most was not about colonial liberation, but rather an attack on state bureaucracy, as incarnated in the Legislative and Executive Councils with their 'creatures' in the small state service, and an expression of sup-port for the extension of the elective principle. For the reform moder-ates who dominated the Assembly until 1834, the people could best manage its own educational affairs if empowered to do so. A skeletal central administration would collect information and pay out money to eligible parties. But the school acts overwhelmed the offices of the re-ceiver general, Jeffrey Hale, and of the inspector general of accounts,

Joseph Cary. Both were inundated with applications for school money, and much of the civil secretary's school correspondence was referred to them for report. Both officers made regular pleas for extra clerical assistance to deal with school reports and were unable to deliver the public accounts in a timely manner. The earlier default of Receiver General Sir John Caldwell with a huge amount of public money made members of the Assembly deeply suspicious of late reporting.[37]

Political antagonisms prevented financial 'government by expertise.' In the spirit of the Canada Committee recommendations, the Colonial Office supported the creation of a colonial Board of Audit to regulate all state expenditure. Such a body might have streamlined government finance while subjecting the receiver general and inspector general to greater accountability. School teachers might then have received their salaries more rapidly and without punishing deductions. An audit bill was presented to the legislature by Austin Cuvillier in the same session as the 1832 School Act, passed by the Assembly but amended by the Legislative Council, and allowed to die on the order paper amid wrangling over the composition of an audit board. Cuvillier, who like John Neilson was alarmed by the dramatic increases in parliamentary expenditure after 1829, sought a board composed of 'experts,' while the *patriote* Thomas Lee argued that all appointees should be French-speaking and Catholic. Cuvillier's project had a three-person board composed of T.A. Young, who had Tory connections, but also past experience as auditor general and inspector general, and the *patriote*-friendly Martin Chinic and Jean Langevin, each to receive a salary of £300 stg. Young's presence offended the more radical MPPs and the proposed legislation died.[38]

Joseph Cary's 1832 petition for £150 in compensation for the extra work imposed on him by the school acts provides a rare insight into the cumbersome methods through which some of the money due to a thousand schoolteachers eventually made it into their hands. It also illustrates the politicization of administration.

School reports and certificates were forwarded to Cary from the civil secretary. First he received the copies of minutes of trustee elections, which he examined for form and from which he made a list of trustees for the future payment of monies.[39] These minutes, he claimed, 'are generally lengthy, prepared by Notaries in the French language, and in very many instances were irregular. Remarks became necessary to be made,' he noted, in good bureaucratese, and many of the minutes were returned for correction. At first, since there was no date for elections specified in the school act, the minutes arrived whenever local trustees got around to sending them. Cary then had to deal with the school reports, which involved calculating when attendance at each school had passed the threshold of twenty students, and from that date, prorating the £20 grant to determine the amount due. Despite Kempt's 'liberal interpretation' of the act, Cary tried to follow its letter in restricting the extra allowance for poor students, which involved him in additional calculations and correspondence. Having determined the amount due to trustees, he then compared the signatures of trustees authorizing the school reports with the list of trustees taken from minutes of election, seeking clarification where there was a mismatch.

He next had to send a note to the clerk of the Executive Council inviting him to draw up a warrant for payment of the amount due the trustees. The warrants came back to him, were examined for accuracy, numbered, and entered in a Warrant Book, with a list of warrants issued sent daily to the governor. Then Cary sent the warrants to the receiver general's office, where they were delivered to trustees or their agents, and they came back to him again as vouchers (receipts) on the latter's accounts. Since the vouchers were mainly in favour of agents named by the trustees, he had to ascertain that the agents had powers of attorney. The entire process was repeated for applications for schoolhouse matching funds.

Matters were simplified somewhat after 1831 when Cary's office began to create pay lists rather than having warrants and vouchers circulating from office to office. He seems thereafter to have sent a list of trustees and the names of their agents with the amounts to which they were entitled to the receiver general, who would issue payment, and it fell to the latter to verify that agents had legitimate powers of attorney. Still, Cary claimed that his office had made out about 700 warrants a year before 1829, and over 3,000 in 1831. When the payments were bi-annual, the process was repeated for each school. Clerks made the initial calculations, but Cary stated that he verified their work after office hours at his home, incurring additional costs for stationery. As he noted in his petition,

the sums of money thus paid and divided in very minute proportions, under the sole responsibility of the Inspector of Accounts, are as follows:

In	1829.	£6,439 7 3
	1830,	18,088 12 7
	1831,	17,317 9 0
	1832,	23,324 5 4
	Sterling.	£65,169 14 2
	Currency,	£72,410 15 11.

From 1829 to 15 May 1832, his office had examined a total of 5,241 school reports.[40]

The Assembly's Education Committee echoed Lord Aylmer's recommendation that Cary's petition be granted, but when it came before the Assembly late in the 1832–3 session, it was voted down. In January 1834, despite an acknowledgment of his assiduous past service, the Assembly entertained a *patriote* motion to fire him and to replace him with Martin Chinic, a Quebec party loyalist. The motion was justified by É.-É. Rodier on the grounds that there were too few French Canadians in official positions; it failed by a vote of 24 to 23.[41]

Cary's case is significant as a further demonstration of the interest a considerable portion of the *patriote* party took in politicizing state administration. The 1832 Permanent Committee's first report did hint that Cary had been overzealous in making people adhere to the letter of the school acts and he may have been an officious person. Yet any reading of the civil secretary's correspondence or of the surviving school reports exonerates him from any charge of holding a sinecure. His distinctive hand – usually with red ink – is to be found on the school reports, and he followed carefully the civil secretary's injunction to deliver written reports or written comments on the large amount of school correspondence forwarded to him. In the absence of a central board or of county boards of education, or of a minister of education, and in the absence of financial powers in the hands of local trustees, the inspector general of accounts by default made day-to-day educational policy decisions in Lower Canada. Under the School Act of 1832, the members of the Assembly who acted as county school administrators were frequently displeased to find their work subjected to Cary's (and to a lesser degree Hale's) insistence on form and fiscal rigour, as we shall see in a later chapter. The political attacks on Cary seem to have made him even more legalistic in his interpretation of administrative questions.[42]

Towards the School Act of 1833

As interested parties digested, or choked on, the provisions of the 1832 act, they had a wealth of new of statistical information at their disposal from the publication of 1831 school visitors' reports and the 1831 census results. According to the visitors' reports, there were 1,216 elementary schools in the colony, including the cities, and 1,242 teachers, divided almost evenly between men and women. The visitors had recommended the suspension of 120 teachers. The schools included 66 under the supervision of the

Royal Institution, 37 vestry schools and 230 private venture schools established before 1829. Under the 1831 School Act, 142 schools received no government money, 89 of them in the cities of Quebec and Montreal. At the moment of the 1831 school visits, the schools were said to be attended by 21,613 boys and 20,567 girls for a total of 42,180 students, of whom 23,805 paid fees. The total number of school districts was given as 1,307. In the census summaries, by contrast, there were said to be 1,099 elementary schools in the colony and 38 academies, colleges, and convents. Here the population at school was said to number 25,088 boys and 23,232 girls, or a total of 48,320, out of a colonial population given as 511,917. Although the census results used different gendered age categories, there were perhaps 240,000 'children' in the colony.[43]

The numbers were subject to a variety of interpretations. The reform *Vindicator* in Montreal complained of how badly done the census had been, but was encouraged by the school statistics. 'Thanks to those who have hitherto been at the helm of affairs. – thanks – to our Dalhousies and our Legislative Councillors, the education of the people of this Province has hitherto been most shamefully in arrears. Now however that the people have the management of their own affairs we trust every parent in the province, every member of society, will exert themselves' to extend education. Daniel Tracey concluded, in a position the *Vindicator* was soon to abandon, that it would be 'much better were we all employed in forwarding the Education of the people, than in engaging their attention in visionary dreams of separation and independence.' And it was clear that much work remained, for 'there is one Tavern in the Province for every 128 persons of an age to indulge in Intemperance. There is only one school for every 135 children of an age to receive Instruction.'[44]

In its second report in the 1832–3 session, the Permanent Committee on Education proposed amendments to the 1832 act in response both to petitions against it and to MPPs' observations on its operation. The School Act of 1833 (3 Will. IV, c.4) was sanctioned on 3 April. The Assembly had been moving to allow local trustees to levy a school tax and to hold property in perpetuity, but procedural issues prevented the inclusion of such provisions in the act as passed. The Permanent Committee observed that school matters had been disrupted because of the 1832 cholera epidemic, which prevented many districts from holding trustee elections within the prescribed period, but the 1832 act's attempts to eliminate 'abuses' also generated opposition. The 1833 amendments allowed the visitors to accept schools kept in good faith without trustee elections as eligible for the grant on a prorated basis and allowed them to authorize an additional school in a district if they found one in operation with an enrolment of at least thirty-five. The bi-annual reporting period was restored so that teachers could be paid half-yearly. Principals and professors in academies and colleges and presidents of existing education societies were qualified as school visitors, and the visitors were authorized in some cases to allow students above fifteen and below five years of age to be counted for grant purposes, to increase the number of free students from ten to fifteen, and to waive the rule requiring parents to pay fees for one student to have another instructed free of charge, in schools with at least twenty fee-paying students. Girls' schools were made eligible for the 10s. prize money; teachers able to teach in both languages were to receive an annual bonus of £4; and the grant to the Soeurs de la Congrégation for educating poor girls free of charge was eliminated, since they had refused to accept it. Finally, the allowable number of school districts was altered in many counties and the total number of districts was reduced from 1,321 in 1832 to 1,295 in 1833.[45]

The Permanent Committee was attempting to curb the exploding government expenditure on educational institutions. In dealing with petitions for aid in 1833 it re-asserted a position it had adopted in 1832: new grants would be made only under exceptional circumstances and steps should be taken to reduce expenditure. So far as possible, every town or city was to have one school for each major religious denomination, at which poor students would be taught without charge. Finally, grants to rural schools and teachers would be made only where schools had in fact been kept in good faith. The Committee's first report for 1832–3 lamented that past practice had 'widely spread abroad the idea that the expenses of the Education of youth were to be defrayed out of the public revenues,' but a decline in those revenues was forcing a change in this matter. Support for schooling should be based on the resources of local communities and the Committee could not 'conceive that it will ever be considered as expedient to draw money from the industry of the people by an expensive process, to be returned to them in greatly diminished amount, for objects or which they can at once apply it more certainly, more equitably, and with greater economy, under their own immediate control.'[46] The remark foreshadowed provisions in the Assembly's 1834 School Bill.

The School Act of 1834

The amendments of 1833 did not extend the life of the 1832 School Act; it was to expire on 15 May 1834. Lord Aylmer recommended its speedy renewal in his January throne speech. The political temperature was running high. The 1832 act had passed before the Montreal election riot and the 1832 cholera epidemic ended Aylmer's political honeymoon. Troops had killed three men in the election crowd; the *patriote* leader and speaker, Louis-Joseph Papineau, had been roughed up in the street by Tory goons and had been roundly chastised by Aylmer for interfering with the coroner's jury investigating the deaths. Aylmer had been courted assiduously by the *patriote* party, but he now seemed to ally himself with Tory factions and the military against the Assembly majority. His attempts to have the Assembly make good on its 1828 pledge to grant a Civil List, given that the 1831 Howick Act had accorded it control over the revenue, were seen as a return to the hated policies of Lord Dalhousie. Attempts to push educational reform forward were casualties in the increasingly bitter opposition of legislature and executive.

At the start of the 1834 session, politicians were awaiting the Colonial Office's response to petitions of 1833 from each branch of the legislature. The Assembly had elaborated a set of grievances against the Legislative Council and had called for its transformation into an elective body, if not its outright abolition. The Council in turn had petitioned against constitutional change, denouncing the pretensions of the Assembly to subvert existing structures and to arrogate to itself alone all financial and administrative power. In the pursuit of its objectives, claimed the Council, the Assembly was willing to freeze all activities of government and to prevent the operation of measures aimed at the common interest.

At the opening of the legislative session, Louis Bourdages, the 'doyen' of the *patriote* party, led an attempt in the Assembly to go immediately into committee of the whole to debate the state of the colony without a reply to the throne speech. The success of his motion would have meant that no legislative work would be undertaken. Although the school act would be one casualty, *La Minerve*, the *patriote* party organ, supported the motion, arguing that the act of 1832 was in force until May and new payments would not be due until November, giving the legislature ample time to renew the act after dealing with the pressing political issue of the Council. As Ludger Duvernay put it, 'A nation ought not to focus on minutiae at all when its existence or its liberties are threatened.'[47]

In an amendment to Bourdages's motion John Neilson moved to introduce a revised school act. He argued that if there was no parliamentary session, the governor would be left to do as he pleased. Lord Aylmer was said to be spending public money without legislative authorization, but he had promised to deliver his accounts in the throne speech, and legislators should wait for them before acting. The moderate reformers and *patriotes* supported Neilson: François Duval, for instance, asked, 'Won't we pass a law to remedy the lack of education in the country? The people is moral, and loyal, but it is ignorant.' After heated debate, Neilson's amendment carried by a vote of 35 to 17. A second attempt to move into committee of the whole to draft a response to the throne speech failed by a vote of 42 to 14. However, Neilson's proposal to name a committee to communicate regularly with the Council got virtually no support, and it was at this moment that his opponents narrowly failed to replace Joseph Cary as inspector general with their friend Martin Chinic. In a month, the balance of forces in the Assembly would be completely transformed, but the 'friends of education' had a narrow window of opportunity to revise the 1832 act.[48]

The 1834 session passed four education acts, three of which were reserved by Lord Aylmer for royal sanction. Aylmer proclaimed a new School Monies Act in which the Assembly reduced government subsidies for urban institutions and cut those for the infant schools, the Mechanics' Institutes, and the Quebec Literary and Historical Society, claiming that these were not directly 'educational' institutions or were not directed at the public as whole. Aylmer reserved the Act of Incorporation for the Collège de Ste Anne, 'An Act for the Further and Permanent Encouragement of Education,' and, despite the fact that his solicitor general reported that there were no objections to it, on his own account he reserved 'An Act for the Further Encouragement of Education throughout the Province.'

The 'Act for the Further and Permanent Encouragement of Education' seems to be the one introduced as an amendment to Louis Bourdages's call for a debate on the state of the province. It passed the Assembly within a week and was sent to the Legislative Council, passed there after much debate, but was reserved by Aylmer and then refused by Lord Aberdeen in London on the grounds that it created myriad, unregulated corporations. No copy of the act seems to have survived, but it was Neilson's attempt to remedy the refusal of the Crown to create a school lands fund by allowing school trustee boards, colleges, and academies to hold land in mortmain – in effect, making them into corporate bodies. Neilson hoped that the measure would put an end to the need to subsidize local schoolhouse construction. Acts of incorporation were routinely reserved by Aylmer, as governors were instructed to do with all laws creating corporate bodies. The refusal of this act was denounced by Étienne Parent in *Le Canadien* as part of the wider scheme to drown French-Canadian nationality in a wave of English Protestant immigration by killing off the French colleges. The

Colonial Office found the act to be poorly drafted and objected that the corporations created were subject to no inspection or supervision. Bodies which had not expressed interest in incorporation would have been incorporated nonetheless.[49]

The key piece of educational legislation in the session was what eventually became the School Act of 1834, 'An Act for the Further Encouragement of Education throughout the Province' (4 Will. IV, c.34), passed at the end of the legislative session, approved in London after its reservation by Aylmer, and proclaimed officially on 7 January 1835. The bill was drafted by John Neilson, introduced in January 1834, debated extensively, passed by the Assembly in early February, but returned with unacceptable amendments from the Legislative Council. The act which passed in the last days of the session in March consisted of H.-S. Huot's hastily drafted amendments to the School Act of 1832, extending its life until 1 May 1836. By the time it passed the Assembly, John Neilson's career as an elected politician in Lower Canada was effectively finished.

Students of Lower Canadian political history will appreciate that Neilson's bill was debated and passed on the eve of the introduction of the Assembly's grievance omnibus, the '92 Resolutions.' The large majorities that had been in favour of a legislative session shifted dramatically, and the Resolutions passed in late February by a vote of 52 to 19. Neilson and those who had voted against this rather rambling and repetitive recitation of grievances did not attend the discussion of them. Several resolutions targeted Neilson individually by quoting, and suggesting he had since betrayed, his testimony before the 1828 Canada Committee.

The political shift was caused in the immediate sense by the publication of two dispatches from London. Lord Aylmer certainly had the first and probably had both of them in hand when he made his throne speech. It was alleged that Neilson was privy to their contents and hurried to introduce his education bills before they were published. The first dispatch from Lord Stanley disallowed the Assembly's bill vacating the seat of Dominique Mondelet, earlier a *patriote* champion for his opposition to Lord Dalhousie, but who had become a pariah to the majority for agreeing to replace Pierre Panet as an honorary executive councillor. Indeed Stanley castigated Aylmer for not rejecting the bill out of hand, given that it violated long-established rights of a member of parliament to his seat. The second dispatch, presented to the legislature on 14 January 1834, refused the petition of the Assembly against the Legislative Council, reiterated the recommendations of the 1828 Canada Committee, and pointed to the progress made in fulfilling them, including the cession of control over the revenue to the

Assembly. If it ever became necessary for the imperial government to intervene in colonial constitutional matters, wrote Stanley, it would certainly not
be by 'the introduction of institutions inconsistent with monarchical government,' such as an elected upper house.[50] Notice was given shortly after
the publication of these remarks that the Assembly would go into committee of the whole on 14 February to debate a series of resolutions on the
state of the colony, after which it was likely that no other legislative business
would be conducted.

Neilson's probable stance on the resolutions was the source of much
speculation, fuelled in part by the fact that he and Dominique Mondelet
were named as commissioners to investigate American penitentiaries on
the day the resolutions were introduced. The *patriote* É.-É. Rodier had
moved the appointment of such commissioners, and the party paper
took offence at the fact that not he, but the turncoat Mondelet was
named one of the commissioners. However, it was with Mondelet's
brother Charles and with Neilson that de Tocqueville and de Beaumont
had consulted in 1831. Neilson later declared that as far as he was concerned, the imperial government had acted in good faith to implement
the recommendations of the Canada Committee and that the colonial
constitution was basically sound. The Council's opposition to Assembly
measures was almost always temporary, and the great majority of them
had passed eventually. It was in the nature of the case that a bicameral
legislature would produce friction, but such a legislature was better than
one with only one house.[51]

There had been many calls for changes to the 1832 School Act. Writing
in *La Minerve* in late December 1833, for instance, 'R' had refuted those
who claimed that education was flourishing under the act. It was true that
in many villages, where there were doctors, notaries, and merchants, good
schools had been established, but in the rural districts there was frequently
not one man in twenty who could read. 'R' had heard *habitants* proclaim
repeatedly, 'We've lived really well up to now ... while being ignorant, our
children will do like us. Bah! No need to be educated to plough.' Education
would not become general until the law contained a compulsory attendance clause.[52] In January 1834, Nahum Mower's *Courant* deplored the ignorance of many schoolteachers, claiming he had himself seen 'teachers
being unable to write a small note without palpable breaches in orthography. – Some we have known to travel many miles to procure assistance to
fill up the returns required by Law, being themselves unable to perform
this part of their duty.' Mower called for the creation of normal schools
and the compulsory attendance of teachers at them.[53] Large reform

meetings at Lennoxville and Barnston before the start of the legislative session endorsed a common set of demands and grievances, including calls for an elected Council, an end to sinecurism, a reduction of government expenditure, better mail delivery, and improvements to the school act. The meetings demanded the replacement of the horde of unaccountable school visitors created by the 1832 act by elected township school boards. These boards would make recommendations to the legislature about needed reforms in schooling and would decide the age of attendance for students. A fund to subsidize small schools was also needed.[54]

The most important clause in John Neilson's 1834 School Bill incorporated boards of trustees and granted them powers of taxation, in keeping with the resolutions he had introduced to the Assembly in 1829. Other clauses increased the number of school districts in a few counties, offered a £10 bonus to the best teacher in a parish or township, provided he or she could teach English and French grammar, geometry, and bookkeeping, and provided for an additional subsidy of £50 for any superior school, defined by its curriculum, not already in receipt of a government grant. Some housekeeping work included the payment of matching grants for schoolhouses constructed in 1831–2.

Debating the 1834 Act

The debate over the bill began in late January and turned into a debate over the worth of the Assembly's attempts at rural schooling as a whole. It was explicitly a debate about Neilson's leadership. Speaker Papineau's warm endorsement of Neilson's bill can be read as an effort to overcome the political estrangement between the two which dated at least from Papineau's interference in the 1832 coroner's inquest. At third reading on 4 February, Neilson went on at length with praise for the colony's educational progress in a speech reproduced by most colonial newspapers. 'Nowhere else had education, after it was placed on any thing like a footing, spread more rapidly,' he declared. 'To find a system of education that would satisfy all sides, all beliefs, was an impossibility almost everywhere; – in Ireland this had never been possible. In this country, according to the system followed, no belief, either Protestant or Catholic, had been jealous of each other; all had profited by the law, without the necessity of having recourse to an unnecessary increase of distinct schools; and both were often met together without a distrust or inconvenience having resulted.' Louis-Joseph Papineau announced that he was completely in favour of the bill and praised it loudly.

Yet Andrew Stuart, another erstwhile reform ally, attacked the school system over which he said Neilson had exerted complete and absolute control since its inception. The Assembly majority, claimed Stuart, had done whatever it wished in school affairs for too long and it was time to consider matters critically, especially since the school system 'tends to nothing, rests upon sand, and is rotten from top to bottom.' The colony needed to imitate Europe and spend its money on institutions of higher learning. Stuart attacked Neilson on the manner in which school districts were defined and denounced the tyranny of majority rule in the Assembly, rather than the rule of 'sound reason, good judgement and common sense,' all of which were against the school system. The '£20 schools,' as he called them, were worse than useless, and it would be better 'to have none at all, for reading and writing alone does not form an education, and no more could be expected from 20 pound schoolmasters; donations or endowments, not for the present generations, but those that follow have been entirely overlooked; no benefit can result from a system of education founded upon yearly votes.' Neilson defended all the legislature had done and pointed to the likely benefits of his new bills.[55]

The school bill passed and was sent to the Council on 4 February. The wealthy James Cuthbert, proprietor of several seigneuries, was waiting to attack, ostensibly on political grounds. He objected that 'there was in it no authority to restrain the nomination and appointment of schoolmasters,' and grumbled that 'the instituteurs of many of the schools were natives of France, and have gone backwards and forwards between that country and this Province.' Some of them, he warned, 'had even been dismissed for political offences by the King of the French.' The Councillors debated the bill as the Assembly debated its Resolutions and they also had before them, as did the reading public more generally, the statement that since 1829 £81,685.5.2 had been spent on rural schooling. The Council cut the taxation clauses from Neilson's bill, inserted a clause allowing the executive to name three school visitors to examine teachers and resolve disputes, and sent the amended bill back to the Assembly on 3 March. 'How these fine Councillors are the good people's friends,' commented Jacques Viger, 'how they watch that it is not encumbered with useless taxes!' Étienne Parent added, 'the council is right; every advantage given to the education of the people is a nail in its coffin.'[56]

It fell to H.-S. Huot, soon to be Neilson's successor as chair of the Standing Committee on Education, to draft some sort of replacement bill before the session ended and the 1832 School Act expired. He cut the

Council's school visitors clause, left out the clauses the Council had cut from the Assembly's bill, and the Assembly sent the amended bill back to the Council. There, an attempt by Cuthbert to refuse it without the visitors clause was defeated. Cuthbert again railed against French nationals teaching in the rural schools and claimed that he had seen with his own eyes students reading *La Minerve* and the *Vindicator* in the schools. George Moffatt complained of the Assembly's presumption in expecting Council to pass the bill without the visitors clause simply because it had cut the taxation clause. It was W.B. Felton, soon to be excoriated by the Assembly, who defended the amended bill. The existing provisions for visitation were ones the Council had accepted in the past, he pointed out, and they exempted the executive from the trouble and expense of inspecting the schools. While he did not share the principles of the newspapers mentioned by Cuthbert, parents had a right to decide what their children learned at school, and there was probably nothing harmful in the papers. And teachers from France were at least monarchical subjects, which was better than having Americans. On the whole, Felton argued, the schools were good, and it would be irresponsible to cause them to fail. The bill passed shortly before prorogation, but as we have seen, Aylmer reserved it, and while schools continued in anticipation of its eventual passage, teachers were forced to wait nine months for their pay. In effect, the 1834 School Act continued that of 1832 until 1 May 1836.[57]

The Gosford Commission

Late fall elections in 1834 were effectively a referendum on the 92 Resolutions: their supporters took seventy-seven of eighty-eight seats. The election was a near thing for those such as H.-S. Huot in Portneuf, whose affection for the Resolutions was lukewarm, while candidates opposed to the Resolutions, including John Neilson and Andrew Stuart, lost their seats. A younger, more radical reform and *patriote* party confronted Lord Aylmer's administration for the winter 1835 session of parliament. Speaker Papineau was describing the governor more or less publicly as a thief for having spent money authorized under existing statutes but not explicitly granted by the Assembly, and he had earlier issued his own diktat against attendance at social events in the Chateau for the benefit of those many members of his party, especially those from the Quebec district, prone to bask in the rays of official favour.[58] The parliamentary session lasted from 21 February to 18 March 1835, and only a single bill passed. Business froze as the Assembly refused to reimburse the £31,000 Aylmer had advanced out of the military chest for the expenses of civil government, and it ignored his message presenting estimates for the forthcoming year and seeking reimbursement of arrears. Aylmer in turn refused to grant £18,000 for the contingencies of the Assembly, including the members' per diem and travel expenses, without a detailed accounting and the withdrawal of items he described as unconstitutional, such as the £600 stg. payment to J.A. Roebuck, MP, as the Assembly's agent in London. The majority were outraged by the chartering of the British American Land Company and the sale of a huge amount of public land to it. The demands contained in the 92 Resolutions were rehashed, but MPPs accelerated their usual late winter trickling away from Quebec in the absence of their per diem. The Assembly frequently lost its quorum before prorogation. The 1834 School Act had been approved in London and was proclaimed in January 1835, but the session of parliament ended without the passage of an urban school monies bill, casting urban institutions onto their own resources.[59] Politics had begun its move out of the parliamentary arena, with the opponents of the Resolutions organizing Constitutional Associations to petition the Crown for colonial reform and with their proponents organizing Reform Associations and central and local *patriote* Correspondence Committees.[60]

Faced with repeated and conflicting demands from colonial factions for intervention, the newly elected Whig government in England recalled Lord Aylmer and replaced him with Lord Gosford, an amiable Irish peer known for his progressive estate management. Gosford was named both governor general and chairman of the first Canadian Royal Commission of Inquiry, meant to investigate and to propose (but not to impose) remedies for Lower Canadian grievances. Accompanied by Sir Charles Grey and Sir George Gipps as fellow commissioners and with the old Colonial Office Canada-hand T.F. Elliott as secretary, the commission arrived in the colony in August. Gosford was sworn in on 24 August 1835.[61]

The legislature was convoked for late October. Aylmer's parting gift to his successor was to anger the *patriote* party further by naming a number of his allies to the Executive Council, but Gosford proposed to 'avoid as much as possible consulting them on state matters.' He worked scrupulously to avoid partisan patronage appointments. At a lengthy meeting with Denis-Benjamin Viger and Louis-Joseph Papineau in late September, Gosford declined to reveal his official instructions – which excluded an elected Council in the near term – and met Papineau's repeated insistence that his Commission was useless and that the 1834 elections had shown that nothing less than the introduction of the elective principle would be acceptable, with repeated pleas for 'a little patience & calmness' and with repeated assurances of the 'highly liberal intentions on the part of His Majesty & His Ministers.'[62]

While the *patriote* leadership refused to have any formal communication with the Gosford commissioners, it was wined and dined by them, and Gosford and his colleagues managed to temper the political outrage of many MPPs during the fall of 1835. Already in late October Gosford had dealt with the Assembly's complaints about sinecurism and pluralism by writing formally to officers of executive government who held more than one remunerated office to choose that which they wished to retain. The commissioners' repeated recognition of the justness of many of the other grievances expressed in the 92 Resolutions and their determination to follow a 'liberal' policy earned them the support of the Quebec wing of the reform party. By 30 November even Papineau was writing that his goal of a renovation of the Council on principles as liberal as any in a British colony without a republican constitution was within reach, and in mid-December 1835 he was expecting that the Assembly would both vote the arrears of government expenses and grant a Civil List early in 1836.[63]

Papineau relented on his determination to avoid the Chateau. He partied on the evening of 25 November 1835, writing to his wife that 'Several of the English invited did show up, and there weren't many of them invited in any case. The assembly was *principally Canadian* it was as numerous, as brilliant, & more gay than any other I have ever seen.' Gouty Gosford himself took to the dance floor at 3 a.m. and kept the ladies busy for quite some time. In effect, as Kempt had done with such success seven years earlier, Gosford and his suite launched another 'charm offensive.' 'Such alacrity for and such notice of the Canadians,' wrote Papineau, 'are not with without a purpose and not without effect, [Gosford] has it in mind to make himself agreeable, as a means of making his administration easier.'[64]

The discomfiture of the colonial Tories, manifested in increasingly outrageous, chauvinist political discourse and in an attempt to form a paramilitary organization in defence of 'British liberty,' when added to the favour shown by Gosford and his entourage to the reform party, presaged an opportunity for political reconciliation. As Sir James Kempt had done, Gosford promised openness and impartiality in his speech from the throne, a most sparing use of his power to reserve bills while promising to take special care 'so that any measure aiming at the establishment of colleges or schools for the propagation of Christianity or higher learning shall not henceforth be needlessly delayed.' He announced that the Commission would pay most serious attention to the question of education.[65]

The Assembly expressed scepticism and reiterated the demand for an elected Council, although that was probably a bargaining position. More important for our purposes, in 1836, as in 1829, the Assembly moved to reintroduce educational initiatives refused by the previous administration and to extend and to systematize educational provision. The Gosford commissioners devoted relatively little direct attention to educational matters, in part because the Assembly's Standing Committee on Education and Schools conducted its own investigations and produced a new legislative agenda in 1836.

Two Committees on Schools

While the moderate H.-S. Huot inherited the chairmanship of the Standing Committee as its senior member, a younger and much more radical group now sat with him, including J.-J. Girouard, J.-N. Cardinal, Marcus Child, and Thomas Bouthillier. A semblance of balance was provided by the presence of the moderate J.-B. Meilleur, William Power, who had voted against the Resolutions, and Alexandre Fraser, whose allegiances were mixed. It was a strong committee. The members were themselves well educated and many had practical experience as school visitors and as trustees or promoters of colleges and academies. Still, Huot's leadership and the Committee's control over educational matters were challenged early in the parliamentary session by three reform members from the Eastern Townships: Child, John Grannis from Stanstead, and Ephraim Knight from Missiskoui. At issue were both large considerations of the workings of rural schools and smaller matters of local partisan score settling. In November 1835 Knight called for the appointment of a Special Committee to investigate allegations that his erstwhile rival Ralph Taylor had misappropriated the school prize money while acting as county school visitor. At about the same moment, the Assembly received two petitions from school trustees in Ste Martine laying the same charges against the sitting conservative member for Beauharnois, Charles Archambeault.

Huot and several of his allies attempted to forestall the appointment of a Special Committee, arguing that it would duplicate the business of the Standing Committee, but the motion's sponsors argued that the Special Committee was meant to address only a specific question of fact concerning Ralph Taylor. Yet John Grannis then moved that the Standing Committee be instructed to undertake a general investigation of the working of the school acts. Huot attempted to have all the issues raised referred to the proposed Special Committee on the grounds that the Standing Committee's agenda was already charged. In fact, it had about fifty school petitions to address and the school act to renew or modify. While offering Huot assurances that the Special Committee was not intended to challenge the Standing Committee's authority, the members present (and the press noted that the proceedings were suspended several times for lack of a quorum as members dawdled about in the lobby or smoked in the reading room) voted 22 to 17 in support of the position of Knight and Grannis. A formal instruction to the Standing Committee to investigate the state of rural schooling was made on 20 November 1835, as we shall see shortly.

The cases of Taylor and Archambeault underline once again the politicization of school management stemming from the Assembly's refusal to separate legislative and administrative matters. In fact, all the MPP-school visitors were more or less vulnerable around the the issue of school prize money, as the Standing Committee's general investigation of school conditions soon showed. Taylor, however, was particularly reviled by the *patriote* majority. His seemingly progressive motion to amend the School Act of 1833 to support girls' schools in the Townships on the same conditions as in the parishes had been voted down by 37 to 10. The majority later ordered him imprisoned for a disobliging statement he made in the *Quebec Mercury* about L.-J. Papineau. In February 1836, after some debate, the Assembly resolved that 'the said Ralph Taylor has been guilty of gross malversation and breach of trust; and he has appropriated to his own private use several sums of public money; [and] that he has embarrassed the progress of education in the County of Missisquoi.' It was demanded that he reimburse the sum of £43. Taylor returned some school money but pointed out that he had been condemned without being allowed to defend himself: more partisan score settling.[66]

The petitions against Charles Archambeault were referred to the Standing Committee, which quickly discovered that they had been engineered by a group of *patriotes* in the adjoining county of Laprairie. J.-N. Cardinal did not recuse himself in this matter, despite the fact that it implicated directly his brother-in-law F.-M. Lepailleur and George Baker, who had lost their jobs as inspectors of rafts because of a bill Archambeault had sponsored. Depositions in the matter had been sworn in front of James Perrigo, whom Archambeault had defeated in the 1834 election. The Standing Committee washed its hands of the case by referring it back to the Special Committee, which did not report before the end of the session.[67]

Fewer Schools, Less Expenditure

Before proceeding to its other business, the Standing Committee dealt with a large backlog of funding applications, petitions for the creation of new school districts, and applications for the 1834 School Act's bonus for superior schools. What *Le Canadien* called the committee's 'luminous report' on these matters formed the basis for the School Monies Act of 1836. The report extended principles the Standing Committee had nominally adopted under John Neilson's direction. The committee was swamped with applications for money from existing urban institutions, even though its past expenditure had been intended as start-up funding, not permanent support. It also received many petitions for new school districts, even though the colony already had over 1,200 of them, and for the support of colleges and academies. The financial accounts of the urban institutions were incomplete or contradictory, and to its irritation the committee had to hear testimony in writing on most of the petitions. It resolved that henceforth institutions would have to provide authenticated accounts of their expenditure of government money and of the money they received from other sources before receiving any additional funding. No institution that had not stayed open during 1835, when no grants were made, was to receive any support. In future, only institutions with substantial community support should expect aid, and the committee urged that expenditure be reduced as much as possible.

All petitions for grants for rural schools beyond the numbers authorized in the 1834 School Act were rejected. The number of schools authorized by that act was 'extremely liberal, and in some places more than proportionate to the population,' but many new applications still came from such places. One petition sought a school 'for a place in which there are only three families,' and the committee argued that in future, 'the number of School Districts in each County be regulated by its population.' Attempts by two teachers to claim the £50 bonus contained in the 1834 act for the best county school were rejected, as was a petition in favour of a bonus to F.-X. Valade's school in Terrebonne. Slightly over £18,055 had been demanded in the documents examined by the committee; its grants amounted to slightly over £8,395.

The committee's principles were excellent, commented *Le Canadien*, except for the adoption of the principle of population. New settlements needed more schools than old settlements, because their population was less dense. Yet, gone from rural school administration was encouragement for the people to assemble wherever they chose to establish a school.[68]

The Standing Committee's first report was presented to the Assembly on 11 January 1836 with notice that the School Monies Bill would follow its acceptance, but instead of being warmly endorsed it was vigorously attacked by the seigneur J.-B. Taché from Kamouraska, with support from a number of other MPPs. The attack widened an existing fissure between politicians from the Quebec and Montreal districts and between the more distant rural representatives and those in the two large cities and the towns. This division also reflected growing discontent among the members with Louis-Joseph Papineau's leadership and hardline tactics, given the conciliatory moves of Lord Gosford and his commission.

Taché claimed that the Standing Committee was privileging the cities and towns over rural regions with its grants for schools, colleges, and academies. Schools from his riding had been arbitrarily excluded from funding, and if education in the whole colony were subsidized at the same rate as the cities it would cost £500,000. A heated debate ensued among those members interested in educational questions, with Huot arguing that it cost twice as much to educate a child in the country as it did in the city, while Louis Gugy complained of the committee's refusal of petitions for extra schools in the Eastern Townships. He argued that schooling should be spread over the countryside, not concentrated in the towns, but he also urged the creation of some means of encouraging good teachers and firing those who were incompetent. L.-J. Papineau tried to calm matters, deploring the appearance of sectional jealousy and urging support for the colony's common interest in education. He argued that it did not matter whether schooling happened in the towns or in the parishes, as long as it was well done. Urban schools cost more because they needed bigger buildings and more teachers. Papineau argued that the correct funding principle was 'help those who have helped themselves,' and so some parts of the Eastern Townships that seemed to receive more funding than other places should be congratulated, not condemned for their educational zeal. Several other members spoke for and against the positions articulated, and the Assembly voted on a few items in the report before losing its quorum.

At a second session on 12 January members went through the list of grants in the Standing Committee's reports and approved all of them, except an attempt to reduce the grant to the Charlestown Academy by £50. Yet there was more acrimony. The grant of £300 to J.-B. Meilleur's Collège de L'Assomption was questioned by M.-P. Bardy and L.-H. Lafontaine as excessive when the committee awarded the rural academies only £100. Meilleur defended his institution as a collège like the séminaires in Quebec and Montreal, but the Assembly again lost its quorum before the report could be endorsed. Several days went by before the first report passed by a vote of 32 to 10 and the School Monies Bill was read.[69]

The issue of rural school funding continued to simmer. The late proclamation of the 1834 School Act had led groups in many rural areas to keep schools not authorized under the 1832 act in expectation of the grant. Many of those elected in 1834 and 1835 counted on their influence in the Assembly to promote school petitions, and it rankled – and threatened their standing with their constituents – when these were refused en masse. When the Standing Committee presented its Second Report recommending the £500 purchase of the mouldy collection of stuffed animals that Pierre Chasseur called his 'Natural History Museum' several members were incensed. J.-G. Clapham clashed with M.-P. Bardy over the former's attempt to have the five petitions for schools in Megantic re-examined, and after a heated exchange, H.-S. Huot agreed to have them referred back to the committee. J.-B. Taché declared that the move would not have been necessary if Huot had only acted in good faith at the outset and added, 'There are several honble members from the countryside who dare not speak, who have cause to complain of the report of the committee president; I say it loudly and clearly.'[70]

Closer examination of some of the rejected petitions led the new member for l'Acadie, C.-H.-O. Côté, to discover that two teachers in his riding had been receiving school monies to which they were not entitled. Suspicions were raised when one of them, Jacques Surprenant, tried to claim a pension for his long service. He and another teacher were ordered to make restitution for the money received.[71]

Self-Questioning: The 1835–1836 Committee Investigation

A formal reference to the Standing Committee of the Assembly had been made on 20 November 1835, instructing it to investigate not only the matter of the prize money and the effects of its distribution, but also whether the Assembly's school visitors had in fact visited the schools which they certified; if the other school visitors had been giving certificates to teachers without examining them; if trustees and teachers were falsifying the school attendance register to qualify for the grant; and if teachers who were unable to teach the three Rs were working in any school district.[72]

The committee's third report of 25 January 1836 presented the fruits of its inquiry and made a set of recommendations for legislative change. The report is one of the more striking state documents in this period for those interested in the early practice of social science, 'reflexive government' (where government questions itself), and political theatre because the committee administered a standard questionnaire to forty-three MPPs – almost half the sitting members – including the questions in the formal reference and a number of others about educational 'abuses' and necessary changes. 'This was the most expeditious, and it may be said, the only course' to be adopted, reported the committee, 'more especially as it is well known that the great majority of the Members' were actively involved in school supervision and alone could furnish 'the requisite information.'

In other words, legislators asked administrators about existing conditions, but since they were themselves both legislators and administrators, they questioned themselves. The committee's minutes of evidence offer a glimpse inside this theatre of official knowledge production. One can see the Standing Committee chair leaving the chair to answer as school visitor the questions he helped design as committee chair, and leaving again to answer other questions in his capacity as president of the Société d'Éducation de Québec. There were subtexts both partisan and personal, with an antagonistic exchange between J.-N. Cardinal and Charles Archambeault over school prize money. The conservative member for Megantic, J.G. Clapham, simply read the Anglican missionary J.L. Alexander's detailed plan for school organization, school management, and pedagogy into the official record.[73]

Testimony began with propaganda in favour of normal schools, which were already part of the legislative agenda. The committee questioned Jérôme Demers, teacher and administrator at the Séminaire de Québec, Amury Girod for his experience at de Fellenberg's Höfwyl, and H.-S. Huot in his capacity as secretary of the Société d'Éducation de Québec. While Demers was asked the seemingly simple question, 'Do you think it necessary to establish Normal Schools?' most of his answer was devoted to discussing what should be taught in such schools and how many professors were needed to do so. After Demers, the committee went directly on to logistical matters, asking first the Société d'Éducation and then Amury Girod if and at what expense they could organize a normal school. The Société put the cost at £1,200.

The MPPs revealed the haphazard nature of their own school supervision. Jean Bouffard reported that he had visited all of Dorchester's forty-one schools every year since 1832, yet several of those who had been in office in 1832 reported visiting all the schools in that year, but thereafter had allowed magistrates, militia captains, and the curés to certify teachers and to distribute the school prize money. MPPs' opinions were mixed on the value of the latter, but most reported that students looked forward to it and that it made it possible to get books into the schools. Several of them were at least as vulnerable to charges of malversation as was Archambeault. Taschereau from the Beauce, for instance, was the visiting member for his county but never visited any schools, paying the school grant instead on the recommendation of the other school visitors. He claimed that since they never furnished him with lists of those deserving the prize, 'it was my duty not to part with the said money,' and he 'therefore preferred keeping the money in my hands,' although he was 'ready to account for it when required.'

A few members argued that the existing school arrangements were perfectly fine and that no change was necessary,[74] but the majority painted a sorry picture of a flawed system in need of serious reform. While the schools had done some good work, there were far too many unqualified teachers hired by incompetent and illiterate trustees. The illiterates made board meetings into competitions between ignorance and education, with ignorance typically being more popular. Ignorant trustees favoured ignorant teachers, hired friends or relations, or used the £20 grant as welfare for the aged, widowed, or infirm. As Dr Bardy from Rouville put it, the difficulty likely arose 'from the multiplicity of Trustees who in the greater part of the School Districts are absolutely destitute of education.' Perhaps from fastidiousness Bardy refrained from mentioning that his fellow MPP Pierre Careau, who also visited schools and endorsed authorizations for the grant, could not sign his name.[75]

The proposed solution was to reduce the number of trustee boards and to exclude illiterates. Rocbrune dit Larocque, himself accused of corrupt practices, proposed that the law should 'allow no persons to be Trustees who were not sufficiently educated to judge whether the Teachers performed their duty well or ill,' while Alexandre Fraser argued that the law should 'allow no public employment whatever to be held by any person whomsoever who should not know how to read and write.' To get better teachers, the majority of the members recommended the creation of boards of examiners in some form or other, and the establishment of at least one superior school in each parish with a decent salary attached to it. The boards of examiners could be in each parish, in each district, or in each of the major cities, but the majority of members now rejected the tenet that the people was the best judge of trustees and teachers.

To get better schools and teachers, John Grannis and Marcus Child argued for the creation of county boards of education, more or less on the model of New York State. Child wanted 'inspecting commissioners' at the district level to oversee the work of school visitors, but Grannis was more ambitious. From his own experience of seeing poor local record keeping and falsified attendance registers, and from hearing stories of illiterate teachers, Grannis wanted an elected board of school commissioners or superintendents in each county. The board should meet twice a year, examine and certify teachers, prepare the annual school reports, and keep a record of school district boundaries. The board should have a full-time secretary and, instead of making teachers or trustees appoint agents to get their grants, there should be one agent for the entire province to deliver school money to county board secretaries for payment to teachers. Grannis was alone in suggesting so complete an educational bureaucracy, but many members' suggestions tended in that direction.

The MPPs reported that teachers were underqualified because their pay was so low. The school laws had made matters worse according to C.-H.-O. Côté by offering a £20 grant for teachers: no reputable person would teach for that sum. Or, as Canac dit Marquis asked, 'who can imagine that a person of education will submit to live on £20, with perhaps £10 or £15 received from his pupils in produce, of which he is always made to pay the highest price; while the most ordinary Clerk receives a salary of £35 or £40 and is boarded by his employer, and yet has not too ample means of supporting himself according to his station.' Others claimed the £20 grant multiplied small schools, as neighbours competed to get this little bit of cash money into their communities. The creation of superior schools would provide better opportunities for teachers. Some members suggested a compulsory attendance law to ensure teachers received adequate fees. Finally, a few members argued for taxation for school support, a tax on luxury imports, a tax on assessed property, or in L.-H. La Fontaine's view, a tax on land to be administered by the vestry.

The members were silent on many questions, and some leading activists, such as A.-N. Morin had nothing to say on the matter at all. No member spoke to curriculum or pedagogy, and none addressed gender relations. Two wanted the curés banned from trustee boards and teacher certification, while Dr Bardy argued the curés should preside over boards by right. Charles Courteau thought members should be paid 10s. for each school they visited, provided they visited no more than two in a day. Two others suggested the prize money be used to create school libraries. And foreshadowing later debate in the Assembly, a number of members suggested that more school districts were needed and that the principle of population distribution should guide the distribution of school districts.

Taken as a whole, the Standing Committee investigation showed that a majority of members had moved well away from the populism of the 1829 School Act. They argued that part of what the people had hitherto done for itself, alone or through its deputies, should become the province of more centrally located experts, and minimal levels of expertise were needed in local school government. Joseph-Narcisse Cardinal, a man who went to the gallows for his role in the rising of 1838, and who can scarcely be regarded as a Tory stooge, put it clearly: 'The task of making the General Returns of Schools for the County should be [taken] out of the hands of the Members of this House, to whom it gives too much opportunity of exercising an undue influence, which some of them, I venture to say have had the weakness to abuse.' Legislators should not administer school money.

Such self-reflective criticism identified necessary reforms to the school laws but it also threatened a dramatic increase in expenditure, against the principles of the Standing Committee's First Report. The criticism and the proposed expenditure both provided powerful ammunition for the Legislative Council, and later for the Special Council and the Buller Education Commission, to claim that the Assembly's schools had been a wasteful and useless project.

Recommendations

The Standing Committee concluded that the schools were conducted on the whole in keeping with the law and that students had benefited from them. There were isolated cases of abuse concerning the qualifications of teachers and trustees, but steps had been taken to prevent any recurrence. The committee made only three recommendations. First, the number of school districts should be determined according to population distribution as given in the 1831 census. In older settlements, one school for every 300 'souls' would be allowed, while in the Townships and other new settlements, the ratio would be one school for 200 'souls.' Second, every parish and township with a population of more than 500 should have a 'Superior School' with a fitting salary for the teacher. The report did not mention a figure, but the committee planned to allow £40 plus fees. To avoid additional expense, these schools would be funded out of savings from the abolition of the premiums of £4 for teachers teaching in both languages and £10 for those offering advanced subjects. Finally, the committee announced that its elementary school bill would contain the provision for local school taxation that had been rejected by the Legislative Council in 1834. Distributing schools according to population and date of settlement responded to demands of the Assembly school visitors but undermined the principle of fiscal restraint and the goal of reducing the numbers of schools. Even using the 1831 census's population total of slightly over 511,000 for the colony implied the number of school districts would increase from about 1,200 to over 1,600.

The 1836 Educational Legislation

Encouraged by Lord Gosford's government, the Standing Committee on Education drafted legislation to capture what had been blocked under Lord Aylmer and to adopt new innovations. It embodied its reform agenda in four draft education laws: the urban school monies bill, which became law after the debate we have examined; revised versions of its 1834 colleges and academies bill and 1834 School Bill; and a new bill for normal schools. The last three were introduced to the Assembly on 25 January 1836. There is no evidence of debate in the Assembly over the colleges and academies bill or over the normal school bill. The colleges bill passed the Assembly but was returned from the Council with a modest amendment making incorporation of institutions optional rather than mandatory. The Montreal and Quebec National Schools, under the direction of the Church of England, were forced to incorporate under the Assembly's bill but had no desire to do so. The Assembly did not reply to the amendments before the session ended.[76] The Normal School Act (6 Will. IV, c. 12) was accepted by the Legislative Council at the very end of the 1836 session and immediately proclaimed by Lord Gosford.

The 1836 elementary school bill was based on the recommendations contained in the Standing Committee's Third Report, although it did not take up many of the suggestions from MPPs published in its minutes of evidence. While the bill repealed the 1834 School Act, it left administrative matters in the hands of the MPPs and members of local elites and apparently did not legislate minimum qualifications for school trustees or reduce their numbers. The main changes in the new bill were clauses for the creation of superior schools and for the distribution of school districts in keeping with population and date of settlement. The bill again contained the taxation clause lost in the 1834 School Bill. Superior schools were to be supported by an extra levy of £20 on local residents.

Assembly debate on the Standing Committee's Third Report began on 8 February 1836 with J.-B. Taché's motion that educational money be apportioned on the basis of the 'state of the population' and that the school bill be amended 'in such a manner as to grant to each County a sum proportionate to its population.' Taché argued that allowing a school for 200 residents in the Townships but for 300 elsewhere disadvantaged counties such as Kamouraska and Saguenay and that, since every resident paid the same amount for the schools, all should have the same share in the public money.

Two competing conceptions of equity clashed in the debate: one using population numbers, the other local needs and circumstances. The same clash occurred in the debate that occurred later in the year with respect to political representation. Both conceptions were about schooling population, not simply empowering the people. Huot for the Standing Committee argued that fewer schools were needed in the seigneuries because population density was greater there, whereas the Townships' population was sparse and communications were poor. J.-J. Girouard added that population movement was towards the Townships, so that it made sense to place more schools there. Anyway, the census was defective. Marcus Child agreed that the population principle might disadvantage a few areas, but adopting it would not solve all problems. Some areas would then suddenly have three times as many schools as they did at present, while others would not have enough to meet their needs. The proposed school bill reduced the number of schools in Stanstead from seventy-two to fifty-five; Taché's motion would leave only forty.

Calling for a calm consideration of the justice of the committee's proposal, L.-J. Papineau then gave a typically lyrical and long-winded speech 'on the advantages of statistics and censuses in producing material ease and the physical, moral and political happiness of the people, by enabling it to proportion its numbers to its needs and to the advantages it ought to enjoy.' He pointed to the accomplishments of Washington, Jefferson, and Monroe in using such knowledge to banish ignorance and barbarism from their country as a worthy example. A cranky Taché thanked Papineau for this American travelogue, but pointed out that it did not address the issue. He was not acting out of jealousy or narrow sectional interest, but he abhorred those who embraced 'double standards.' Anyone could see that it was manifestly unfair not to distribute school money equally according to population. His opponents were constantly confusing effects and causes: they claimed the Townships had more schools because more students went to school, but give the seigneuries more schools and they would have more students as well. A large number of other members debated the question, but Taché could not carry a majority.

At third reading of the elementary school bill, there was a further round of debate on the clause requiring residents to raise £20 to support their superior school. J.-B. Meilleur objected, as he said he had done in committee, on the grounds that it would discourage people from establishing such schools. Taché, André Simon, and P.-A. Dorion supported him, while the *patriote* leaders enunciated the conventional liberal argument that the people appreciated at its just value only that for which it was required to pay. L.-J. Papineau suggested it was only the jealousies of local leaders that prevented people from creating institutions. Taché was incensed. 'Every time we seek justice,' he exclaimed, 'according to the honble speaker, it is a result of jealousy. Yes it is jealousy to have equal rights, praiseworthy jealousy it is to have for oneself what is given to others.' Still, Meilleur's motion to remove the £20 local contribution was defeated 44 to 14; the elementary school bill then passed and was sent to the Legislative Council in the third week in February 1836.[77]

The Failure of the 1836 School Bill

Between the introduction and the passage of the Standing Committee's elementary school act, colonial politics were again thrown into an uproar by Lt-Gov. Bond Head's publication in Upper Canada of extracts from the Gosford Commission's official instructions. Sent by William Lyon Mackenzie to the *Vindicator* in Montreal about 1 February 1836, the instructions made it clear that Gosford was not to propose an elective Legislative Council, but rather to improve the composition of the existing body and of the Executive Council. The Upper Canadian Reformers were not alarmed, for in Mackenzie's view, if the instructions resulted in their leaders being called to the Executive Council, the Upper Canadian Assembly would vote the supplies. The chances for political and economic reform would be greatly increased.[78]

In Lower Canada, Gosford and his fellow commissioners believed they were on the verge of winning an Assembly vote to grant the arrears of government expenditure and a Civil List for 1836. Head had not bothered to consult with Gosford and published a garbled text with errors and omissions. Gosford was forced to reveal the complete instructions on 15 February, but the damage was done. The Papineau faction seized on the single issue of the elective Council to denounce Gosford's entire reform agenda. 'From this want of concert' in Head's initiative, Gosford complained, 'impressions have been produced on the Public mind, little to the credit or advantage of government.' It was immediately and generally concluded that his throne speech conflicted with his official instructions, and he was denounced as acting in bad faith. The supply vote was postponed and Gosford wrote that Head's action was likely to cause 'no small embarrassment to my Government, & threatens to be a serious obstacle to my endeavours for a successful arrangement of the financial difficulties of the Province.'[79] When the question came to a vote, the motion to pay the arrears and to grant the Civil List was lost by a vote of 41 to 31. The moderates in the Assembly then voted a Civil List for six months to give Gosford a breathing space, but their bill was rejected in the Legislative Council.

The vote of a six months' list shook L.-J. Papineau's leadership somewhat, Gosford claimed, but 'the High Tory Party here are quite cockawhoop.' His Royal Commission had been sorely compromised and there seemed no chance of any change in the position of the Papineau faction. 'You might as well get the devil to take holy water as to attempt to persuade Mr Papineau to bend one iota,' wrote Gosford to the Colonial Office, ending with the lament, 'Oh that Sir F.H. had been detained one week longer in England'! Two weeks later he elaborated on the events in the legislature, concluding that 'a satisfactory adjustment of the financial difficulties of the Colony appears to be as distant as and more hopeless than ever.'[80]

On 14 March 1836, a headline in Le Canadien read 'EDUCATION! – It pains us to announce that the elementary school bill is destined to be smothered in the Council.' Indeed, a committee of the Legislative Council, many of whose members belonged to the Montreal Constitutional Association, but which also included the once patriote moderate Pierre de Rocheblave, had examined the Assembly's school bill closely and had recommended that it be rejected unless serious amendments were made. The committee reported to Council with a detailed analysis of the bill showing that it extended the politicization of rural schooling. Council, including the francophone members present, with the lone exception of Denis-Benjamin Viger, voted to accept the report. The bill was returned to the Assembly for amendment, but it had no quorum and the legislature was on the eve of prorogation. It is most probable the Council knew that no time remained to make amendments and that the school bill would die.

Tory Radicals

Radical Tory politics played an important role in educational development and in the wider struggles leading to insurrection in 1837, although most historiography has focused instead on the radicalization of the patriote movement. Yet the Gosford commissioners were much more intimidated by Tory than by *patriote* radicalism, especially as the Constitutional Associations of Quebec and Montreal began calling for a constitutional convention in 1836. Even some of its founding members were alarmed at the drift of the Montreal Association and its press mouthpieces the *Herald* and *Gazette* towards a radical republicanism. Indeed, by late April 1836, a large minority in the association were promoting a platform that closely resembled Robert Nelson's *patriote* republican constitution of 1838, with the addition of a large dose of ethnic chauvinism. William Walker, a founding Montreal member, complained to his Quebec counterpart John Neilson: 'We have nothing but babbling about the advantages of a democratic form of Government to be vested solely in the educated, ie the British population, to the exclusion of the Canadian & who are to be deprived of civil rights and their language & institutions exterpated.' Walker claimed that he and other leaders, such as George Moffatt and Peter McGill, were being denounced by the minority for their refusal to embrace measures such as the secularization of the Clergy Reserves and vote by ballot.[81]

For educational politics, what was essential in the association's position was its proposition that the exercise of the franchise, the holding of political office, and participation in public opinion must be restricted to educated men. The widespread ignorance and illiteracy of the *habitants* were grounds for their exclusion from politics and government, and that ignorance was propagated by the Assembly's school system. That system used education as a pretext for the maintenance of the ignorance of the people, its subjection to religious superstition, and its subordination to the petty bourgeois professionals who claimed to represent the people, but who in fact 'impersonated' it. Huge sums of public monies better used for economic improvement had been wasted on this so-called educational system. Several Legislative Councillors belonged to the Montreal Constitutional Association, and while men such as George Moffatt and Peter McGill were not about to support the 'voluntary' principle in religion or vote by ballot, they were being pushed by more radical opinion and they certainly shared the diagnosis of the causes of rural ignorance – if not the remedy of disenfranchisement for *habitants*.

The Legislative Council Report

The Council committee, which *Le Canadien* dubbed the 'EIGHT Vandals,' grounded a clever analysis of the school bill in materials produced by the Assembly's Standing Committee and in John Neilson's 1831 school visitors' report. The system had never been intended to provide permanent government funding for schools, but rather to stimulate local effort. Taking that position as a point of departure, 'the present establishments' had to be seen as 'inadequate as a permanent system of general education,' and the benefits anticipated from them 'have not been at all commensurate with the hopes and expectations' entertained for them. The expenditure on schools had been extremely lavish; now it threatened to consume the entire public revenue. 'The abuses and corruption which uniformly attend the lavish expenditure of public money' were calling education as a whole into disrepute. Echoing John Neilson in 1832, the committee argued it was inefficient to levy general taxes and then to redistribute them to localities. 'The elementary education of the people is,' it continued, 'effected in the cheapest way in common schools. T[hen] it becomes a common concern of the localities, and the common expenses ought, like any other unavoidable expenses, to be provided for in common.' This disingenuous observation neglected to point out that Council itself had repeatedly vetoed any and all attempts to allow local communities to tax themselves for school purposes.

The committee then quoted from successive reports of the Assembly's Standing Committee on Education, where it was stated repeatedly that the expenditure on schools had to be reduced, that the schools were becoming overly dependent on legislative grants, and that those grants were discouraging local efforts. Passages to that effect were cited from the Standing Committee's First Report for 1836, and the Council committee stressed that all these reports had been endorsed by the Assembly as a whole. However, the school bill as submitted, far from reducing an expenditure which had already amounted to £150,000, now proposed to increase even further the number of schools and the size of the annual subsidy. If the bill passed, £40,000 a year at least would be spent annually for years to come. The committee urged Council to encourage education but to follow the principles adopted by the Assembly's Standing Committee and not those in the school bill.

Furthermore, 'the system of management proposed to be continued [is] productive of evil. The direction and superintendence of the sums appropriated by this Bill are entrusted in effect to the County Members of the House of Assembly.' That was an especially important power, and those exercising it could be 'influenced on the one hand by a pure sense of duty, or on the other by the opinion or feeling of party, or by other improper motives.' The committee then recited ten powers over schooling exercised by the County Members: the certificates of the trustees needed to pay teachers and masters of superior schools were sent to them. They made up the pay lists for teachers. They approved all alterations in school districts and in some cases could alter districts themselves. They controlled the school prize fund. They could demand and recover all sums remaining unpaid for prizes. They recorded elections of trustees. They were themselves school visitors. The County Members 'are not required to support by vouchers their account of monies entrusted to them as are other persons.' The bill empowered them to continue to exert their powers in education even if parliament was dissolved.

Taken together, these considerations led the Council committee to recommend 'the propriety of suspending all further appropriations until some general effective system of Education can be judiciously planned and carefully executed ... and the people be influenced to take a more decided interest in the prosperity of institutions for the education of themselves and their children.' The committee also noted that Council had resolved to accept no further money bills from the Assembly until the Civil List had been voted, and it had already accepted votes of £12,000 for educational purposes in the School Monies and the Normal School Acts.

The Legislative Council adopted six of its committee's resolutions on schooling, including the making of future school grants only to impoverished communities, or limiting them to matching grants for sums raised locally. The key resolution was the fifth:

> It is expedient in any future measures which may be adopted by the Legislature for the encouragement of Elementary Schools, that a permanent and efficient system of regulation should be adopted, either by the organization of a Central Board or by Boards in the several districts; or by some other mode of general, uniform and steady superintendence, by which the course of instruction may be more effectually ascertained and directed, and the expenditure of the public money be more usefully applied, and more effectually checked, than by the plan hitherto pursued.[82]

The school bill and the Council's resolutions were returned to the Assembly on or about 15 March 1836, and parliament was prorogued on 21 March. Civil Secretary Walcott published a notice in the colonial papers announcing to teachers and trustees that the school act would expire on 1 May 1836 and that all reports of schools and demands for payment for the period from 15 November 1835 to that date should be made forthwith.[83]

The Legislative Council had killed the Assembly's school bill. But what had it killed? And who tried to inherit the Assembly's legacy? Had the grants worked to create a sustainable 'taste for education?' The following chapter addresses these questions.

5
Schooling the People, 1829–1836

Many of those who have seen a progressive force in the *patriotes* of the 1830s have taken comfort from the belief that the trustees schools constituted a major social advance, one that propelled popular autonomy and self-determination in the face of oligarchic and imperial domination. Such was the *parti patriote*'s portrayal of itself, but in fact because of the Assembly's anti-bureaucratic policies, no one in Lower Canada could have systematic and comprehensive knowledge of the rural schools. I argue that the Assembly's school legislation was indeed precocious in proposing elements of the 'common school revolution' of the 1820s and 1830s, such as educational taxation, graded instruction, a hierarchy of schools, and normal school training. Yet its failure to adopt the administrative structures necessary to put progressive school policy in practice at the local level meant that, in most parts of the colony, the schools bolstered established relations of hegemony and domination.

The Legislative Council's rejection of the 1836 bill was partly based on the claim that the Assembly's politicization of the schools had worked against the education of the people and had wasted huge sums of public money. The Council was silent on its own role in blocking the Assembly's efforts to create local government bodies with taxation powers for schools. Instead, it was repeating a position elaborated some months earlier by the Tory Montreal Constitutional Association, a position taken up by the Gosford Commission after the schools closed. The Commission reported to London that between 1829 and 1836 the Assembly's educational expenditure had been '£172,519. 5. 9 [,] being on an average £24,465.14.3 per annum, or about 1/5th of the total Revenue of the Province.' Despite such lavish funding, proportionately much greater than expenditure in England or Ireland, 'the progress has not been, as far as we can judge, such as might have been expected.'[1] The claim of useless and extravagant expenditure was accepted by the next Royal Commission, led by Lord Durham, which elaborated plans to school the population.

This chapter addresses claims and counterclaims about the trustee schools while exemplifying the texture of schooling. Perhaps at some future date a credible statistical analysis of school conditions may be possible. The best efforts of contemporaries failed to produce such an analysis, and surviving accounts of schools do not constitute a stable series which could be used to do so now. The surviving evidence shows that many villages supported good schools, in an important number of which young people had opportunities for advanced practical instruction. In the Eastern Townships, something resembling the New England school system was being formed, and a network of reasonably well-established elementary schools sent their graduates on to high schools or academies. In the rural parts of the parishes and seigneuries, however, schools restricted *habitant* learning to rudimentary instruction that was tied tightly to doctrinal religious ends.

Tory Critique and Reform Defence

At its general meeting late in November 1835, the executive of the Montreal Constitutional Association presented a lengthy analysis of colonial social and political conditions. The analysis was part justification of the Association's call for a union of all English-speaking residents for purposes of mutual defence and for the convening of a Constitutional Congress, but it was also a warning to the Gosford Commission and to public opinion in England. The Association's executive declared itself in favour of elective institutions, stressing that its membership included many Americans and republicans, but it opposed an elective Legislative Council under the existing conditions. 'The intelligence of a people is the guarantee for the proper use of the elective principle,' argued the executive, but 'when a population is unlettered and unenlightened, to entrust them with the unrestricted use of political power would be in fact to retard the progress of rational freedom.' Any person in private life would contemptuously refuse to have his affairs managed by someone who was ignorant: how then to express the Association's indignation at *patriote* demands that 'such men shall be entrusted the management of our political liberties?' The franchise in the colony was 'almost universal,' and while the Association did not propose to limit it, the general ignorance of the French-Canadian

peasantry demonstrated the necessity of having a check upon its political activities in the shape of an appointed Legislative Council.

The fact of rural ignorance and illiteracy was well known to colonial
residents, the Association claimed. Proof positive of it for outsiders was
shown by 'the facts, that within the last two years, in each of two Grand
Juries of the Court of King's Bench for the district of Montreal, selected
under a Provincial Law, from among the wealthiest inhabitants of the
rural parishes, there was found but one person competent to write his
name; and that trustees of schools are specially permitted, by statute, to
affix their crosses to their school reports.'[2]

That the law explicitly empowered illiterate trustees to govern local
schools was an oft-repeated reason for the English-language press to denounce the Assembly's educational policy. Some commentators went so
far as to imply that the school acts required that trustees be illiterate.
The charge partly justified the refusal of the 1836 School Bill by the
Legislative Councillors, and it was used after 1837 to argue that there
was nothing worth saving in the Assembly's legislation.

The Association's educational analysis was deeply offensive to a broad
spectrum of French-Canadian observers. They found it utterly outrageous to be denounced and insulted as a people on charges of general
ignorance when the Legislative Council and the Colonial Office had
worked together time and time again to block the Assembly's rural
school bills, when the Jesuit college was used as a British military barracks, and the Jesuits' Estates had been pillaged for the private profit of
Legislative Councillors. The Assembly had been tenacious in its fight for
schools, and the progress made under the 1829 act was remarkable, but
as one of Le Canadien's correspondents had put it, 'if the country had got
a bill like that of 1829 in 1793, what a favourable change for us! Men
today aged 25 to 50 who don't know a single letter of the alphabet, would
have been educated and better able to manage our affairs.'

This person conceded the fact of rural ignorance, as did most other
observers, although many made a point of stressing that peasant ignorance was accompanied by hospitality, geniality, marital fidelity, moral up-
rightness, and good common sense. Still, Le Canadien's correspondent
reported that in his parish when the time came to appoint a petty claims
court commissioner there were only two or three qualified French-
speaking candidates out of a population of about 2,200, while among
twenty male English-speaking residents, five or six were qualified. He
acknowledged, quaintly, that much of the habitant population was deeply
prejudiced against schooling. One could hear it proclaimed, '"Ain't I

farmed good without that, ain't I lived good without that; you wanna find a drunk or a scoundrel look for an educated person. Keep your education to yourself and leave us in peace."' However, the remedy for prejudice against schooling was not the adoption of English law, manners, or land tenure, wrote this correspondent. With the last would come primogeniture, the end of mortgages on land, and the reduction of women's property rights; the seigneurs would become sole and absolute owners of lands now held in trust. The education of the people was urgently required, but not through an attack on *canadien* institutions and not under the control of executive government.[3]

However, such a response to English Tory-republican charges did not address the crucial question: if the peasantry was ignorant and prejudiced against schooling, and if executive government was not to organize schooling, how then was it to be organized? It was no remedy for ignorance to allow the ignorant to manage schools, especially if the ignorant thought their excellent material and moral life would be undermined by education. Missing from the *patriote* analysis until the radical wing of the party rose to prominence after 1835 was any systematic attack on the relations of political-economic and cultural subordination imposed on the rural population by the domination of the Catholic Church and the seigneurial system. Neither Church nor seigneur appeared as a grievance among the 92 Resolutions. Before 1837, the moderate party leadership tended to defend seigneurial tenure and the Catholic Church as fundamental elements of national culture, and L.-J. Papineau was eager to extend the reach of the former. Yet both the Church and the seigneurial system reproduced peasant ignorance, if for no other reason than because institutionalized schooling depended upon the availability of surplus product, but Church and seigneury sucked up rural surplus. Reforms to the Legislative Council under Lord Aylmer's reign gave that body a large plurality of conservative French-Canadian Catholics, many seigneurs among them, which made the *patriote* identification of its 'foreignness' as the single most important obstacle to colonial progress rather problematic. The fundamental tension between the creation of an intelligent, literate rural population and the preservation of 'traditional' institutions that produced ignorance and subordination was not resolved in the 1830s.

Educational Statistics

It was impossible for any agency to generate a comprehensive view of the state of the rural schools: debate was speculative. No board, bureau,

Table 5.1. Educational expenditure in Lower Canada, 1829–1836

Source	Period	Amount
Gosford Commission	1829–36	£172,519.5.9 (all forms of educational spending)
Legislative Council	1829–36	£150,000 (urban and rural elementary schools)
Legislative Assembly	1829–33 inclusive	£110,006.1.10 (total expenditure) £81,685.5.2 (rural elementary schools)
Buller Commission	1829	£13,785.16.3 (elementary schools, including the Royal Institution)
Buller Commission	1831	£32,470 (all forms of educational spending)
Legislative Council clerk	1831	£18,000 (rural elementary schools)
Legislative Council clerk	1832	£24,310.9.6 (rural elementary schools)
Inspector general	Nov. 1832–Nov. 1833	£17,140 (rural elementary schools)
Louis-Philippe Audet	1835	£23,229 (rural elementary schools)

office, or department was charged with overall supervision, planning, or policy implementation. The executive specified some administrative procedures and audited school accounts, but made and could make few substantive interventions into school relations. While the Gosford Commission was charged with making a systematic assessment of educational conditions, it did not take up the matter seriously before the end of its mandate in 1836. Only after the Legislative Council caused the failure of the 1836 School Bill were attempts made to take stock of the schools and to devise means to systematize provision. These attempts are examined in a later chapter.

No one in Lower Canada could tell with any precision how many schools or students there were, or how much money was spent on them. Tables 5.1 and 5.2 show some of the claims and reports in circulation, but even the Assembly's accounts of teachers, schools, and students were often internally inconsistent.

While there is no question that the closing of the rural schools in 1836 dramatically reduced the exposure of a large number of rural young people to some forms of book learning, the statistical record cannot tell

Table 5.2. Elementary schools, students, and teachers in Lower Canada, 1831–1836[4]

Source	Date	Schools	Students	Teachers
Census	1831		48,300 (all schools)	
School visitors	1831	1,242	45,322 (all schools)	1,242 or 1,307 (607 men, 635 women, 1,307 'masters')
La Minerve	1831	1,216	43,793 (all schools)	
Buller Commission	1831	1,051	34,590 (rural)	
Buller Commission	1832–3	868	29,377 (rural)	
Inspector General	1832–3	902		
Buller Commission	1835	1,202	38,377 (rural)	
Legislative Assembly	1835	1,202	39,666 (rural, estimate)	
Le Canadien	1835		37,658 (rural)	

us how many people were deprived of what kind and quality of instruction. Most commentators agreed that there was rapid growth in the number of funded schools until 1832, a period of austerity in 1832–3 which led to the closing of 10–15 per cent of the funded schools and a considerable exodus of teachers from the occupation, followed by a return to rapid growth in expenditure, funded schools, and teachers from 1833–4. The Buller Commission claimed that there were usually many more school districts than there were funded schools.[5]

School Placement

The practice of encouraging people to organize their own schools meant that neither law nor administration defined school district boundaries, and they were not surveyed: no one was planning student population catchment and executive government could not locate schools. The MPP visitors had been charged with defining district boundaries in 1831, but the 1832 and 1834 School Acts off-loaded even this element of planning to local visitors. They do not seem to have made any concerted effort to define consistent or comprehensive boundaries. The MPPs' knowledge of boundaries was contextually defined. For instance, Godefroy Beaudet described District 3 in the parish of Soulanges de Vaudreuil in 1831 as extending 'half a league up to Mr. French's, on one side and on the other up to Mr. Felier's'; other descriptions were similar. Catchment areas were defined by accident, convenience, or the status of school promoters, and district boundaries did not correspond to the boundaries of parliamentary ridings. Some parishes existed in civil law, others by canonical decree. Government did not possess detailed maps of its own administrative units. As a result, school trustees could not be certain their schools would be funded.[6]

Before 1831, teachers applied directly to the civil secretary for the school grant when it suited them, and there were no controls on the proliferation of schools. The 1831 act specified the maximum allowable number of funded schools in each county. Some 1831 trustee boards set school locations for entire parishes or townships, but the 1832 act replaced the boards with trustees for each school.[7] From 1832, trustees submitted the school reports to the MPP school visitors and reporting periods were specified. Yet the MPPs remained dependent on the trustees' reports to know how many schools were in operation at what locations in their counties. The reports arrived only at the end of the period for which funding was sought. While MPPs could know the maximum number of eligible schools, they could not know how many would seek funding until the reports arrived. Many trustees and teachers ran schools that were viable only with government grant money and then found that because more schools than the allowable number had applied, theirs would not be funded.

Sometimes schools were excluded by error: school districts were missed or did not report in time for the visitor to include them. Yet trustees and teachers also claimed that the MPPs excluded their schools for political reasons or supported one school in preference to another out of corruption and venality. Other people accused the MPPs of claiming grant money for schools that did not exist. One reason why MPPs continually pushed for increases in the numbers of schools, despite the recommendations of their own Standing Committee, was the trouble and conflict caused by denying funding to schools that had been conducted in good faith. County boards of education would have removed this difficulty, and local school taxation would have limited its impact.

The Battle of Gore

The *patriote* MPP W.H. Scott in the county of Two Mountains was one of those charged with partisan prejudice in school conflicts. One case stemmed from the 1829 division of the colony into new counties, which created an odd triangle of land known as Chatham Gore on the boundaries of the counties of Two Mountains, Ottawa, and Terrebonne. The Gore's English and Irish settlers communicated and did business with their neighbours in the English-speaking villages of Lachute and St Andrews in Two Mountains. Their school was included several times in the Two Mountains report. Gore residents voted in the 1834 Two Mountains election at St Andrews, where Scottish and English settlers used force to keep *patriote* electors away from the poll. When W.H. Scott challenged their votes in person, he was beaten up. His opponents, including F.-E. Globensky, tried the same tactic in Scott's stronghold of St Eustache, where curé Jacques Paquin was a vigorous ally of the executive, but the *patriote* supporters were stronger and Scott was re-elected.

Scott had been squabbling with many members of the old elites in the county for some time. While he was lauded by the *patriote* press as proof positive that the reform movement was not an ethnic-nationalist movement, the established elites regarded him with contempt as a poorly educated, money-grubbing, dissipated radical who lived in sin with his Catholic concubine because curé Paquin refused to marry her to the Presbyterian Scott. The contempt was mutual, and Scott was not a man to be trifled with. He crossed swords with E.-A. Lefebvre de Bellefeuille, co-seigneur of Milles Îles, over allegations that de Bellefeuille had shown partiality on the bench. The latter was mortified when, having protested to the executive that allegations made against him by Scott were not to be believed because Scott was no gentleman, a large group of Scott's supporters swore that de Bellefeuille was a well-known drunkard frequently to be seen staggering about the village and incompetent to sit on the bench.[8]

Complaints and queries about Scott's work as school visitor began soon after he replaced the deceased Jacques Labrie late in 1831. Major Barron of Argenteuil protested in June 1832 that Scott had neglected to return six of the twelve schools authorized for the parish of Two Mountains. He left all of those in the settlements away from his political stronghold in St Eustache off his pay list, despite their having complied fully with the law. Teachers could not live for a year on what they managed to extract from parents in fees, and so the trustees had advanced them money with the expectation of being repaid from the grant.[9] Again, Scott's list of trustees for one authorized school in Terrebonne for 1833 included a man who seemed not to have been elected. The receiver general refused to pay the trustees' agent. An investigation revealed that it was a case of mistaken identity, but a close eye in Quebec was kept on Scott.[10]

That something was seriously amiss in school matters in the Gore came to the attention of government when the Irish schoolmaster in District 1, James Hunter, complained in December 1834 that he had not been paid despite carefully following all procedures. Hunter said that he had taught school faithfully from 15 May 1832 to 15 November 1834, his school had been inspected regularly, his returns had been sent in due course to W.H. Scott, he had given a power of attorney in the authorized form to an agent, Clarke Ross, in Quebec to receive his money, but he had been paid only for one six-month period. When he consulted Ross, Ross would tell him nothing more than that there was some 'irregularity.' Hunter described himself as 'an invalid, having Lost one of [my] Legs,' and as 'entirely dependant on this Occupation' of teaching. He wanted his money. His trustees supported both his story and his claim that 'Mr Scott will not interest himself for this School District owing to the Circumstances attending to the late Election.' In Quebec, Joseph Cary noted that the school had in fact been returned by Scott and the money had been paid to Clarke Ross.[11]

In March 1835, similar allegations were made about Scott by his Tory political rival F.-E. Globensky. Two teachers from St Eustache, Paul Rochon and François Houde, had complained to Globensky that their schools, and a third taught by one Girouard, had been excluded from Scott's official return, despite their having satisfied the conditions of the school act. Thinking there had been a mistake, Rochon, whose school had been open since 1824, asked Scott to submit a supplementary report, only to be told that he, Rochon, had been 'too mixed up in Politics & as a result you won't get Your money until next may Even That will depend upon Your Conduct.' The teachers concluded that Scott wanted to punish them for having 'appeared to take political positions opposed to His.' Teaching was their sole means of subsistence, and they wished to know how to receive the grant.

Scott was called upon to explain himself and responded that these schools were excluded because the teachers did not provide certificates of examination in their reports. Scott told them that he would return their schools in the next reporting period if they produced the necessary documents, but he had been instructed not to make supplementary returns.[12] As to the issue of politics, Scott had merely been replying to 'the complaints (which have been made to me by the Parents of the children attending the school taught by one Hould, as well as the one taught by [Rochon])' that the teachers were 'neglecting their schools to obtain signatures and attend Political meetings.' He reported the complaints to

them 'merely as admonition, shewing the propriety of Teachers not med-
ling in politics as we had already too little [enthusiasm?] amongst the
Inhabitants sending their Children to School without given them any
further protest for so doing.'[13]

After the first pay period in 1835, a large group from Chatham Gore
repeated their earlier complaint, adding that Scott now refused to accept their school as belonging to Two Mountains and told them to apply
for their money in the county of Terrebonne. 'Mr Scott,' they repeated,
'is actuated by political motives in refusing to admit at this period the
Gore of Chatham into the County of Two Mountains.' They knew that
Scott contested their votes 'at the last Election notwithstanding we were
given to understand through the medium of Major Barren [Barron] that
the Gore was actually considered by the Government to be in the County
of Two Mountains.' They asked for an immediate order of £50.

Without any official maps of its own, the office of the civil secretary was
left to consult Joseph Bouchette's *Topographical Description of the Province of
Lower Canada* to see which county contained the Gore. On the residents'
letter of complaint a clerk pencilled the notation, 'By Mr Bouchette's map
this is written the Co of Terrebonne.' Joseph Cary noted that the school in
District 1 had 'regularly been returned by Mr Scott as being within the
County of the Two Mountains up to 15 May 1834 inclusive; it was omitted
in the Return for the 6 months ended 15 November 1834,' after the elec-
tion. Scott's report for the most recent half-year had not been returned.
The money for the period 15 May 1832 to 15 May 1834 had been paid to
Clarke Ross.[14]

Scott was again called upon to explain his administration of the
schools. 'It is quite correct that the school in question was twice included
in my return for the county of Two Mountains,' he replied, 'but when I
did so, it was a favor asked of me by a person with whom I was on terms
of Friendship, latterly I have been requested to include the school in my
return, as by right belonging to the County, which I declined, and referred them to the proper county viz Terrebonne.' That Scott could decide on the basis of requests from friends what to do with the schools
passed without comment. Scott simply said that a glance at the official
division of counties would show 'that I was perfectly justified' in excluding the Gore from the returns. As to the missing money, Scott noted that
'the Receiver General is the proper person to shew to whom the money
has been paid, and that person whether agent or Trustee, I consider to
be the individual of whom the inhabitants of the Gore have the sole right
to complain.'[15]

The reply did not satisfy the trustees. Scott had only told them after the reporting period had passed that he would exclude their school. 'It is evident to the Trustees of the School,' they wrote, 'that Mr Scott is actuated by unfriendly motives towards the people who are benefited by this School in consequence of the Late Election, and that he is wishing to deprive them of the means to obtain the Government allowance.' It was not practical for the trustees to apply to the Terrebonne visitors, for the latter had never visited their school. Scott only wanted them out of Two Mountains so there would never be an English MPP in the county. The trustees asked for a statement from the receiver general of how much money had been paid and how much of it had been paid to Clarke Ross, 'who is the person that we appointed to receive the money for us, And who has declined to answer of late our letter of inquiry addressed to him on that Subject.' Joseph Cary sent them the necessary information. On 2 November 1835 the residents petitioned Lord Gosford to be included in the county of Two Mountains.[16]

No remedy was offered to the school trustees before the failure of the 1836 School Bill. The real villain in this story was Clarke Ross, who defrauded the trustees, and Scott was certainly not guilty of stealing their money. But he made it impossible for their school to be subsidized in Two Mountains after the 1834 election. The case highlighted popular belief in the politicization of the schools and underlined the potential for arbitrary decision making on the part of the MPPs in the absence of an educational bureaucracy. In a report of 1840, the Special Council's district school inspector rehashed all these events and called for a declarative act specifying that the Gore belonged to Terrebonne.[17]

Politics and Venality

Complaints of partisanship were also made about Marcus Child's exclusion of schools from his Stanstead county reports. Yet while the power to exclude was a power of political selection, it was also an administrative obligation that was guaranteed to earn an elected official the antipathy of some of his constituents. The executive refused to fund more schools in a county than the number defined by law. For instance, when Samuel Wood of Shefford tried to include twenty-seven schools in his report for 1834, arguing that although only twenty-five were authorized, the county had claimed fewer than twenty-five in years past, Joseph Cary responded that 'the Number of Schools allowed by Law for this County is 25 The Return contains 27. consequently two must be left out and Mr would should be required to state which two he would consider ought not to be paid.' What was obnoxious to teachers and trustees was that MPPs chose which schools to exclude only after they had been in operation for six months. Again, without advanced planning, there were few practical alternatives. Opposition to bureaucratic power created openings for haphazard or interested management by the MPPs and undermined local efforts at schooling.[18]

It is worth noting that the MPPs often filled more than one administrative function in relation to the elementary schools, beyond those complained of by the Legislative Council. Quite a few served as school trustees – Timothée Masson, Godefroy Beaudet, P.-A. Dorion,[19] and John Neilson among others – for schools that they returned on their pay lists, and several acted as trustees' agents – including Théophile Lemay for Rouville and H.-S. Huot for Portneuf – taking the trustees' power of attorney and getting their money from the receiver general, perhaps for a fee. The MPPs who were notaries likely also authorized and stored the original copies of minutes of trustee elections and issued powers of attorney, both again for a fee. Those who, like François Languedoc in L'Acadie, served as senior militia officers convoked householders and presided over trustee elections. In the conditions of indirect rule that prevailed in the colony, MPPs of all political stripes, even those who denounced pluralism and the cumulation of office in executive government, cumulated functions that might consolidate their own local hegemony. School administration was one such function. Such activities may have been intended entirely as benign accommodations for constituents, but they also exposed the MPPs to charges of venality and corruption.[20]

We have seen the Tory press's contempt for the MPP school visitor Pierre Careau's inability to write his name. Serious charges were also levied against the illiterate Charles Rocbrune, dit Larocque, the farmer, timber trader, storekeeper, and *patriote* elected for Vaudreuil in a by-election of 1833. The senior county magistrate, J.A. Mathison, a well-to-do half-pay naval officer who had constructed a free schoolhouse at his own expense near Hudson in 1829, wrote to the executive in June 1835 for confirmation of a rumour that Larocque had received the half-year grant for a school at Côte St-Charles. No such school existed, Mathison stated, and he included a note from the Anglican minister who confirmed that he had never visited any such school or signed any school report for it. 'The expenditure of the Public Money in like cases is a dangerous application for Political, if not for worse purposes,' Mathison said, and this instance was not the first of Larocque reporting schools that had not been visited. Worse, 'Charles Laroique has this day declared before me, that it is his intention to continue to make Similar returns, and that it is the practice and opinion of the great number of his Colleagues, (Members of the House of Assembly) that he is justified in so doing.'

The issue here was the power of the school visitors authorized by the 1832 act to certify teachers and to approve schools. Mathison received a reply from the executive early in July informing him that Larocque had indeed returned a school at Côte St Charles, naming as trustees John Gusdale, John Hodgson, and Joseph Lancaster, said to be elected on 18 June 1833, with William Bennington Meldrum as teacher. Mathison was outraged: 'This is most notoriously false,' he declared, and the fact that the same school was returned again in 1834, 'the same Trustees named, and the same Teacher paid on the 3d instant, under the authority of a Power of attorney of the same Supposititious Trustees' only confirmed Mathison's complaint. It was 'impossible that Mr Laroique could be acting unadvisedly or under any misapprehension of the unconstitutional assumption' of power whereby 'every individual, differing in opinion with that party to which Mr. Laraique belongs, would be deprived of every shadow of influence or consideration, extending even to that of the local management of a Public Elementary School in the English language.'

To Mathison, the consequences of this abuse of power were obvious. The teacher Meldrum was given credit at Larocque's store. Larocque then used his authority as MPP to get £10 in government school money, kept £8 owing to him from Meldrum, and paid him the remainder 'in the shape of Store goods & Rum with which he, as was usual, did get most perfectly Drunk in company with these said Supposititious Trustees.' When drunk at school, Meldrum had been 'detected in the act of committing himself with one of his own female Scholars, for which he received from her father a sound beating,' yet 'this very father, is one of those Trustees, through whose means, this School Master has obtained the public money in conjunction with Mr. Larocque.' Sex at school was probably 'the worse purposes' to which Mathison had referred earlier. Meldrum was able to have sex with female students 'notwithstanding that the Provincial Statute has wisely provided for the morals of young Children, "by not permitting scholars above the age of fifteen to be taken into the public Schools,"' because Larocque had not allowed the school to be inspected by 'the legitimate Visitors and superintendants of a Public school.' By right these visitors would have included the Anglican minister and Mathison himself, and 'our own local knowledge must have prevented such enormities from taking place.'

The reply to Mathison's second letter has not survived. Joseph Cary noted that the executive should call for a copy of the minute of the trustees' election, but here traces of the case cease in the archival record. Perhaps again it was a matter of class and ethnic conflict, with the established anglophone notables reacting to a perceived threat from an alliance of French- and English-speaking *patriotes*; or perhaps Mathison resented a school competing with the one he had established. On the other hand, male teachers having sexual contact with older female students was not uncommon in frontier Upper Canada at a similar period, and the practice formed one justification for school inspection and for the feminization of teaching. Mathison and the Anglican minister did have the right to visit under the school act and Joseph Cary should have had a copy of the minute of trustee election on file before authorizing the grant. Of course Cary had been refused the extra pay and extra assistance he had sought in 1832 to do his work, and had come close to losing his job out of partisan spite. At least the case likely contributed to the belief that leaving the administration of the schools in the hands of the MPPs led to abuses.[21]

Creating Additional Schools

Perhaps Rocbrune dit Larocque thought he was entitled to establish new schools. The 1833 School Act contained a clause allowing the MPP to form a new school district where he found a school in operation attended by at least thirty-five students.[22] The MPP for Rouville, Théophile Lemay, discovered that the exercise of this power was at least as controversial as that of excluding schools. Notary, magistrate, militia captain, and commissioner in the petty claims court, Lemay initially supported the *patriote* party but voted against the 92 Resolutions. He was despised by his former Rouville *patriote* allies as a turncoat and government toady; was targeted and defeated in the 1834 elections; and was imprisoned by *patriotes* who considered executing him during the 1838 rising. Before the 1834 election, Lemay had complained to the executive that his opponents were trying to overrule him in court. They were all young men, and 'Warm partisans of the new Reform in favour of the Papineau party and Have made it their duty to Censure my conduct in parliament as well as that of others in the minority and even His Excellency.' He later noted that he was having 'lots of trouble with all these schools; For I should like to set up schools in all the places where they are needed. even yesterday I was almost insulted by some of these great *patriotes* who want to stop me from setting up a new school.' He warned that a petition was being got up against his attempt to do so, and indeed soon afterwards one arrived in Quebec from a group of landowners in District 4 of Ste-Marie-de-Monnoir. The group protested against Lemay's decision to create a new district, thereby hiving off many of their neighbours. It was a waste of money, they complained, as an attached map was meant to show, and they requested that the new district, number 12, not receive a grant. The forty-five signatories were led by one of Lemay's *patriote* arch rivals, Dr J.-F. Davignon, and thirty-nine of them made their 'X' on the petition. Joseph Cary annotated it: 'if the School alluded to is established under the Provisions of the Law – and it is included in the Return to be made by the Member for the County it will, in course, be entitled to the allowance provided by the Several Acts.' Lemay was defeated in the 1834 election.[23]

Cary was less encouraging towards a group of residents in Bécancour who petitioned – through their teacher, Pierre Lahaye, since none of their trustees could sign his own name – to have their school included by MPP J.-B. Proulx on his official pay list. They had had forty students in regular attendance for more than six months when they petitioned, but Cary simply told them, 'the Governor has no power to exercise in this case – it rests with the Member and other Visitors of the County.' Their initial petition was sent in August 1834, and they were finally included by Proulx – who was timid when it came to his school responsibilities – in his May 1835 report.[24]

Prize Money

The executive did attempt to intervene in the distribution of the 10s. prize money. The School Act of 1832 allowed that sum for each authorized school district, rather than for each operative school, and did not require the visitors to account for the money. In Portneuf, H.-S. Huot and F.-X. Larue announced to trustees that they would hold examinations and distribute prizes in the county's forty-five school districts during the first week of August 1832, and Huot wrote to Secretary Craig asking for a warrant for £22.10s. Craig referred the matter to Joseph Cary who decided that the money should be based on the number of schools in operation according to the receiver general's pay list. Cary and Receiver General Jeffrey Hale knew that there were more school districts than schools in operation. Huot was told he would soon receive a warrant, but instead, a month later on 25 August 1832, the civil secretary sent him and the other visitors a circular calling for a report of the actual number of schools in operation in their counties. John Neilson replied that he could not report, since he had not yet visited the schools and most others were in the same situation. After Huot advanced between £20 and £25 of his own money to buy prize books and visited the schools with Larue, he was told that the law required payments to be based on the receiver general's school pay list, but that list had not been completed. He and Larue were both incensed. Larue wrote a sharp letter pointing out that the school act specified the number of school districts in Portneuf and stipulated that 10s. would be appropriated for prizes in each of them. Huot complained to Lord Aylmer directly that he had contributed freely to the public service by visiting schools and by advancing his own money, but instead of reimbursement he got a circular asking him how many schools were in operation. Those responsible had not bothered to read the law, and Huot invited Aylmer to introduce some order into the government offices.

Joseph Cary tried to claim that no delay was involved other than that 'absolutely necessary to acquire the requisite information as to the number of Schools actually kept in each County.' But he and Jeffrey Hale misread the law. The MPP visitors were finally sent a second circular in October 1832 informing them that they could draw 10s. for each school district under the act if they accounted for any surplus. Now, ironically, some of the MPPs were worried because they would receive money they could not distribute. J.-B. Proulx preferred the approach Cary and Hale had initially suggested: 'I should like to receive only the Amount owing to the Number of established Schools and nothing more in order to avoid more Responsibility and the trouble of paying it back.' Fifteen pounds for Laprairie's thirty school districts went to J.-M. Raymond, who did promise to account for it carefully 'for not all districts have schools.' Charles Archambeault took all of Beauharnois's prize money for 1832, but had a surplus of £3 in hand in 1833 and so sought less in that year. The largest amount of prize money went to A. Taschereau – £30 for the Beauce's sixty-seven districts. He seems to have distributed none of it. For the 1,295 districts created by the 1833 School Act, together the visitors drew £582.15.0.[25]

Trustees who did not receive prize money for their schools were irate. Those for Ramsay (de Ramezay) in Berthier boasted to the executive that 'there has not been a more general progress made in Learning in any Elementary School of our standing in the Province' than in the one they had opened in 1830. Improved attendance and 'more regular discipline' had been 'effected by the promise made [to students] both by the

Teacher & ourselves of receiving the monies set forth in the Act of Parliament.' They had never received so much as a shilling in prize money and regretted that 'we seem to the Children as Idle Speakers the sad effects of which we see in the Children, for the emulation excited by these promises Seems to be almost extinct.'[26]

Elsewhere, the failure of the Assembly's Standing Committee to act against MPPs who had not distributed the prizes confirmed the assumptions of some that the prize money was a political slush fund. The Val Cartier branch of the Quebec Constitutional Association cited as one of its four grievances the fact that the Assembly had not responded to petitions against MPPs for keeping the prize money. The branch concluded that the Assembly's attitude to petitions was 'we have no time to attend to your complaints we must proceed against the British, we have no time to redress the grievances of the British against our French members.'[27]

Regional Organization

Most of the conflicts discussed thus far can be seen to stem from poor planning and lack of administrative oversight and co-ordination of schooling. Minor administrative reforms, such as having a single colonial school paymaster, could have avoided many of them without creating a substantial bureaucracy or undermining the reform principle that the people could and should educate itself. Most conservatives and some reformers advocated more extensive measures of central or regional regulation of the schools, but in the first years of the Assembly's efforts there were grounds to believe that a systematic organization of schooling was possible without an educational bureaucracy. There were a number of attempts at local self-organization in addition to those discussed in the previous chapter. For instance, under William Chaffers's leadership, in 1830 the trustees for the seigneury of Mondelet sought authority to collect all the school monies and to guarantee teachers a fixed salary. In Farnham Township, the trustees insisted that teachers keep attendance registers and other records before such documentation was mandated by the School Act of 1832. Before the Rebellion, the Eastern Townships produced a growing population of elementary school graduates qualified and eager to receive secondary schooling. Several good academies or high schools were organized in consequence; Shefford or Waterloo Academy was sufficiently reputable to be subsidized by the Special Council in 1839 to train school teachers. The Township schools also fared better than most after the cessation of the legislative school grant

in 1836, and J.I. Little has shown that even in the absence of school legislation, the region developed something resembling a school system
which enabled it quickly to take advantage of the 1841 School Act.[28]

Perhaps the most promising case of local self-organization was the
Berthier School Society (or Education Society). It was formed on 10
April 1827, in the wake of the failure of yet another elementary school
bill, by a group of eighteen notables led by the medical doctor and one-
time MPP Louis-Marie-Raphaël Barbier and the MPP Jacques Deligny.
The eighteen members subscribed funds, and the Society undertook to
establish an academy in Berthierville and attempted to use the 1829
School Act to organize a network of schools, especially in the parishes
and seigneuries fronting the St Lawrence River. The Society first tried to
run the schools as their proprietor. It created a standard curriculum and
a set of rules for school management which were published with some
fanfare and trumpeted in the press in 1831 as a model for adoption by
schools elsewhere in the colony. One free student from each county elementary school was accepted into the Berthier Academy.

Although he did not serve in the Assembly after 1827, L.-M.-R. Barbier
was connected to the moderate wing of the *patriote* party and was early interested in educational questions. He was a sharp critic of the Royal Institution,
which was supported in Berthier by the seigneur and Legislative Councillor
James Cuthbert. At a January 1828 meeting of the Warwick county Constitutional Association Barbier gave a lucid outline of popular grievances
against Lord Dalhousie's administration. The Royal Institution was one of
the worst abuses, and Barbier claimed it showed such a marked preference for Protestants that it refused to hire any Catholic teachers. The administration did accept the 1824 Vestry School Act, he acknowledged, but
the clergy did nothing under it. The creation of the Royal Institution and
the blocking of the Assembly's school bills were abuses 'against which we
most protest most loudly.'[29]

The Berthier Academy began in a rented house in 1827 and taught a
secondary school course resembling that in academies in the Eastern
Townships. It offered secular instruction for boys and girls in English, at
first under the direction of James Murray, MA, a graduate of the University
of Aberdeen. Murray was paid £100 a year with a French-speaking assistant
at £40 (later £50), and the school initially attracted 30 students: 16 boys
and 14 girls, with 19 Catholics, 6 Jews, and 5 Protestants in attendance. By
late 1829, there were 46 students. Murray taught grammar, geography, history, and some Latin, and the academy was cheap by current standards,
charging an entrance fee of 10s. and then £1 a quarter, about one-third of

the going rate in the cities. In 1830 the Society contracted for the construction of a two-storey brick or stone schoolhouse measuring 30' × 40' at a cost of £400, which was subsidized by the Assembly. The following year, L.-M.-R. Barbier informed the legislature that the Society had eliminated boarding fees for students and was seeking to hire additional teachers for Latin and mathematics. The editor of the *Canadian Courant* praised the school as a demonstration that clerical control over education was waning in the colony and people were realizing that the clergy had no business dictating to them the religious beliefs of their children's teachers.[30]

Barbier understood that the Academy's long-term survival depended upon a local supply of students with a good elementary education, and so the Society sought to organize elementary schools. There were four, at least initially, and Barbier was worried that they would not qualify for the school grant because they were not managed by elected trustees. One was meant to begin on 15 October 1829, but it is not clear if the others pre-dated the 1829 act, in which case the absence of trustees would not have been an issue, but Barbier communicated at length with John Neilson on the subject and the schools seem to have been funded. Barbier claimed that the Society succeeded in convincing the *habitants* to tax themselves for the support of schools and argued that such success could easily be repeated elsewhere. Neilson was not the only observer to be attracted by this prospect.

According to Barbier, in the very parts of Berthier parish where it had been most loudly argued that the *habitants* were too poor to support elementary schools the Society's simple plan had worked easily. Wherever thirty students were found whose parents were willing to pay 20s. and half a cord of wood a year for each of their children at school over a period of two years, the Society called a meeting and had the parents elect a 'Patron' or 'Agent.' This person collected two sets of promissory notes from them, one set coming due every month or every quarter over the course of the first year, the second set over the course of the second year. In return, the Patron would provide each subscriber with a written promise that the proceeds would be devoted to establishing and supporting a school entirely under their control.

The Patron would then rent a suitable house or apartment, furnish it with a stove and with tables and benches, for which each parent would contribute a bit of plank, and would hire a teacher able to teach the three Rs and grammar for an annual salary of £25. When enrolment exceeded 30, the teacher would receive extra pay. An association providing the modest sum of £20–25 a year would enable a person to teach full-time and would encourage the peasantry to make additional efforts to school its children. Barbier suggested to Neilson that the Assembly do all in its power to encourage such voluntary associations. If only local leaders undertook to organize *habitant* zeal, schools would be everywhere.[31]

La Minerve reprinted the Society's school regulations in August 1831 and announced that they were producing excellent results in all of the Society's schools. Attendance was regular and the older students helped teach the younger – a suggestion of some attempt at monitorial pedagogy. The Berthier School Society promoted many elements of the nineteenth-century common school movement. Corporal punishment was abolished, and teachers were to work to earn students' esteem and respect. If they could not govern entirely with kindness, they should use moderately escalating punishments, first giving demerit points, then speaking to the student individually, assigning detentions, and ultimately using some kind of public disgrace. Collective instruction and classification were to be adopted, with the taking of places and the weekly distribution of medals to the best students (Lancasterian practices). Reading instruction was by the phonic method, and interrogation was used to teach grammar. When engaged in seat work, students would be equipped with slates, and the teachers were also to sew sheets of paper together to form writing exercise books and to make sure that they lined them themselves, presumably so that young writers would learn to write in the appropriate spaces. The teacher was to go from desk to desk during writing instruction to correct errors and to ensure proper manipulation of the pen. At least a page was to be written every day, and students were to master each lesson thoroughly before continuing on to the next. In the arithmetic class, students would start with the multiplication tables before moving to tables of money conversion, weights and measures, and the four rules, which they should practise on their slates.

Finally, parents were admonished by the Society not to speak ill of the teachers in their children's presence, for doing so would lessen teachers' ability to govern without corporal punishment. On the other hand, teachers were to hold quarterly public examinations of their schools and to listen attentively to parents. All of this material suggests a close acquaintance of Barbier, or of the Academy's schoolmaster, with recent developments in schooling in America and Scotland.[32]

However, what *La Minerve* described as 'all' of the Society's schools seems to have been four. Dr Barbier identified the teachers in three of them but they do not appear in the fragmentary surviving collection of school reports for Berthier. These reports show no signs of the Society's educational program in operation. For instance, only one of the eight schools in the parish of St Barthelémy de Berthier in 1830–1 taught French grammar, although the teacher used no grammar book. Six others reported teaching reading – in the catechism or Catholic religious books – writing, and arithmetic. The eighth taught girls to read and write and to embroider. It seems improbable that a rural elementary school would have had the resources to adopt the Society's program. It would not have been able to claim the school grant for any school established without a trustee election after 1829, and the Society likely had little influence, despite its enthusiastic beginnings.[33]

Dr Barbier admitted as much in a petition for further support for the Berthier Academy in 1835. The academy was successful in its educational mission, if not independently viable. It had abandoned the attempt to have a Latin class and focused instead on the 'useful' branches of learning. It now had fifty-six students, and some of its graduates had gone on to teach, had entered one of the professions, or were successful farmers. Most graduates, however, 'have found work in Commercial houses, where they conduct themselves in a manner satisfying to their Patrons; and all promise to become useful members of Society': the Academy had become a sort of commercial high school. By contrast, the situation in the countryside was lamentable. The well-to-do residents took no interest in and made no contributions to the elementary schools because they sent their children off to one of the colleges. It was the poorest section of the rural population that had most need of the schools but did not support them. Barbier wrote that his experience had shown him that there was no hope for a rural school system even with lavish support from the legislature 'without recourse to direct taxation, assessing all the *habitants* landholders for the support of free Schools in their respective neighbourhoods.'[34]

Just as the promise implicit in the 1824 Vestry Act that the eagerness of the curés would spread schools across the countryside proved false, so too did the promise of local voluntary school organization guided by well-meaning elites. In practice, elementary schooling was left to the care of the elected trustees.

'X,' or Legally Ignorant Trustees and Useless Schools?

The Constitutional Association's charge that trustees were legally entitled to make their marks on school reports was misleading. The School Act of 1829 specified that the trustees should be 'fit and proper persons.' The administrative manual accompanying the 1832 School Act defined as 'fit and proper persons' anyone whom resident householders elected to serve as trustee.[35] Illiterates were thus permitted to serve, and they could and did make their 'X' on the school reports, but their 'X' had to be authenticated by someone who could write. The usual formula for such authentication was similar to that on Eulalie Gagnon's school report for St-Féréol, Montmorency in 1830, which read, 'not able to sign ... each of us has made his usual mark with a cross, in the presence of the under-signed witnesses, after hearing it read.' Some version of that formula was ubiquitous in official reports, communications, and petitions from the 1790s at least. Even the 1835 petition for legislative support for the Collège de L'Assomption employed it, with 13 men writing their names, 402 making an 'X,' and then, after the statement, 'we the Undersigned certify that the Signatures accompanied by a cross Each has been taken by us for the purpose of the petition which precedes them,' the 13 sign-ers signed a second time.[36]

These practices are examples of 'distributed literacy' in which some group, community, or corporate body has to engage in print-cultural work and delegates the physical act of inscription to some of its mem-bers. Although denounced universally in the case of colonial schooling, delegated writing was accepted freely in other instances: lawyers signing for clients, husbands signing for wives, or clerks signing for companies, for instance.[37] Such delegation sometimes enabled those who could not read or write to participate in print-cultural practices, but it also made them dependent on those who could write, and in rural Lower Canada, one such person was the curé. The interesting questions in the present case concern the nature and quality of trustees' dependence, as well as its consequences for local power relations. Behind those questions lies the debate over the relation between local electoral government and colonial political liberty.

How were enfranchised people to make informed and rational deci-sions in political matters? The Constitutional Association and much of the *patriote* party shared the position that political liberty depended upon an educated electorate. For the association, political intelligence was a prerequisite for the government of liberty; delegated writing demon-strated unfitness. Those who could not write could not read, and those who could not read could not know their political interests. For many *patriote* party supporters, by contrast, the exercise of liberty was itself pol-itical training. In educational matters, this stance meant that the people, demonstrably possessed of the common sense needed to make a living and to choose *patriote* MPPs, should select its own teachers and educational officials, subject to the supervision of local elites. For those who could not read and write, such elite members would provide necessary textual legitimacy, while also providing tutelage and supervision. Both positions implied elite domination of the people.

The trend of the Assembly's elementary school legislation was towards the granting of more extensive management powers to more members of local elites and the specification of minimum standards, followed by the creation of a degree of central regulation under the 1836 Normal School Act (which is discussed in the following chapter). While the Legislative Council demanded revisions to the 1836 School Bill to create a central board of education, or boards at the county level, the Assembly's legislation was already tending towards greater regulation of the schools, and public meetings in the Eastern Townships were calling for the creation of school boards, all of which suggests considerable dissatisfaction with the trustee system.

The consequences of trustee management can be assessed by investigating state papers and press accounts of schools and school examinations. The last source is to be treated with caution, since there seems never to have been a press account of a school examination at which teachers and students did not excel. Such 'little red schoolhouse' stories were a staple of the genre of educational writing and were taken up as fact by pre-revisionist historiography. Nonetheless, the sources together point to the existence of many good schools.

Yet the good schools were usually in prosperous villages, and only a few of those funded were originally trustee schools. One with trustees (including curé Besserer) was at St-Joachim in 1830 and was held in a stone schoolhouse able to accommodate 120 students 'in handsome rooms prepared for the lancasterian system,' which the trustees planned to introduce shortly. The students had made prodigious progress in only eighteen months and 'Un Ami de l'Education' claimed there would be more such excellent schools 'if only they weren't impeded by the multiplication of insignificant schools, which prevent the children from attending good ones and keep them ignorant.' Three hundred people were reported in attendance at the 1831 spring examination of S[iméon] Marchesseau[lt]'s trustee school at St-Jean-Baptiste-de-Rouville. The school, which was lauded as one of those using the progressive 'universal method' of J.-J. Jacotot, attracted students from neighbouring parishes. In Chambly village, a college was accompanied by a long-standing proprietor's school run by the desmoiselles Clément which was said to offer excellent instruction. At Pointe-Claire in 1835, a spectator described J.B. Vanasse's vestry school exam as attracting all the local notables, and 'there was even a member of the Clergy to be seen taking interest in the examination.' He continued:

> The Students exhibited in French and Latin Reading and in calculating in a very satisfying manner. They solved the most abstract problems in Boutillier and Bibeau. They answered all questions posed to them on French grammar clearly and precisely. A few exhibited on the first two parts of Latin grammar and translated several chapters of *Epistomae*, correctly naming parts of speech and elements of phrases. The whole mixed with fables in dialogue and talks, ending with an interesting play.

All those present left the event 'completely satisfied.'[38]

The *patriote* matron Marie Victoire Vandandaigue dite Gadbois veuve Davignon's school at St-Mathias-de-Rouville was another proprietor's school funded under the 1829 act whose merits were recognized across party and ethnic lines. In her application for support, Davignon explained that she had been widowed in 1827 and left with eleven children, six of whom still needed to be educated. She had thus converted the top floor of her very large house into a school for girls, with a few little boys in attendance, and had her daughters Victoire, aged twenty, and Rosalie, aged sixteen, teach the three Rs in French, with geography and sacred and profane history. The school was likely to grow, Davignon noted, but she also had her fourteen-year-old Césaire able to help out. While her daughters taught, the school was under her supervision.[39] The fall 1830 school examination drew a large crowd, including the village notables and at least one visitor from Montreal, and lasted about four hours, with the students entertaining the audience by reciting fables and moral tales. Attendance at the school was given as over seventy in the first years of the 1830s, and for some of that period it drew a double grant for a boys' and girls' school. Attendance fell to forty-eight in 1835, and to about forty after the school act expired in 1836. The Special Council's school inspector Robert Armour Jr described the Davignon school late in 1839 as the best female school in the Montreal district. By then, Veuve Davignon's two daughters had been joined by a Miss Freligh, and together they taught the elementary branches in both English and French, music, drawing, and 'the other accomplishments of a polished female.' They took a few boarders, including several girls from the United States. Fees ranged from 1s. to 2s.6d. a month, and the school had been awarded a superior school bonus of £5 by the Assembly.[40]

Perhaps ironically, the school of the Royal Institution in Terrebonne, which had been the object of so much ethnic-religious contestation in the 1810s and 1820s, was recognized by all factions in the 1830s to be one of the best in the Montreal district. Here the teacher was François-Xavier Valade (1803–93), a man trained as a notary but who preferred to teach. He earned £25 from the Royal Institution in 1832, a year in which he also had thirty-five fee-paying students. Valade was active in *patriote* politics, and his 1833 school examination was attended by Louis-Joseph Papineau. He was at the heart of the movement to organize a central correspondence committee in Montreal in the wake of the 92 Resolutions. At the organizational committee meeting of 13 March 1834 Valade was named Terrebonne's representative. In May he was the secretary at a second meeting held at Ste-Thèrese-de-Blainville and he attended the Montreal reform convention in July 1834, where his long speech, 'couched in very eloquent and manly language,' attacking the British American Land Company was loudly applauded. The organizers asked him for a written copy to publish in 'the patriotic newspapers of this province.' Valade continued to be politically active until the summer of 1837, when it became clear that the radical wing of the *patriote* party had embraced armed violence; at that point he broke away. He was not among those subjected to a 'voluntary examination' either in 1837 or 1838.[41]

Between the May and July 1834 political events, Valade held his spring school examination. *La Minerve*'s account was particularly gooey, having half of the 200 spectators weep with joy at 'this most brilliant of examinations.' Still, even curé Porlier was present in the devil's den of the Royal Institution to distribute prizes. *La Minerve* commented: 'It is to be regretted that such a school as this finds itself, with respect to the school grant, on the same footing as the petty schools.' The Standing Committee of the Assembly entertained a petition from Terrebonne to award a bonus to the school but claimed to have no funds and to wish not to establish a precedent by making an exception.[42]

Robert Armour Jr was especially impressed by Valade's school during his inspection of January 1840. Valade had about fifty fee-paying students and was surviving without a legislative subsidy. What Armour appreciated, given his anglicizing agenda, was that 'though the great majority of the pupils are of Canadian origin, not a word of French is permitted during school hours.' Armour could 'speak from personal inspection of the readiness, promptitude, and correctness, with which any portion of their lessons is answered. The system adopted by Mr Valade is somewhat copied from that of Lancaster, combining also many points taken from others.'[43]

The Valade school points to the remarkable confluence of interests made possible by parts of the educational project: Papineau and the parish priest encouraging a Royal Institution school; the Royal Institution paying part of the salary of a *patriote* activist; the promoter of the British and American Land Company praising one of the company's most articulate critics, mistaking second-language training as the smothering of ethnicity – and incidentally not noticing any difference between the Bell monitorial model mandated by the Royal Institution and that of Joseph Lancaster, one of Armour's acquaintances.

One consequence of the Assembly's school acts, then, was to place pre-existing private schools on a more solid financial footing. Yet, despite a considerable number of good village schools, the rural school trustees were generally denounced. They in turn often complained about teachers, and parents and most observers agreed that good teachers were in short supply. *La Minerve* announced in November 1831 that it had received so many letters recounting conflicts between teachers and trustees and criticizing the Assembly's management of rural schooling that it would print none in future which did not suggest positive remedies.

Trustees and School Funding

Trustees under the 1829 act complained that the government grant was paid to teachers and not to them. Trustees contracted with teachers and often advanced them money or credit to teach until the school grant was paid. Most teachers could not live on school fees – if students paid fees – but trustees might find themselves out of pocket if the teacher did not complete the session. In Sabrevois in 1830, they advanced their teacher, a Mr Rabbit, money for board, lodging, and medical care, only to discover that he was a drunkard. They fired him but had to submit a magistrate's affidavit swearing Rabbit owed them money before the receiver general would pay them. The trustees in St-Édouard-de-Gentilly contracted for a year with a husband and wife team to teach two of the parish schools, but at the mid-year examination they fired Jean Pagé, the husband, because he was 'an Immoral man better Able to set a bad example than to train children in good morals.' They could not give him the certificate necessary for him to be paid, but wanted him to get the grant for six months anyway so they would not have to pay him themselves. Joseph Cary approved payment in this case, noting on his report, 'Not to be paid in future.'[44] Such cases led the legislature to provide under the 1832 School Act that trustees, not teachers, would draw the school grant.

Yet trustees could still find themselves personally liable. One issue was the fraudulent activities of some financial agents, as we shall see. Another was that trustees contracted to pay the teachers £20 in school grant money, only later to discover the inspector general had prorated the grant according to an attendance threshold. In a Compton Township school district in 1833, for instance, the trustees complained they had received £13.8s. instead of the £20 they had expected, despite complying with the law. In a Hinchinbrooke district, the trustees contracted with their teacher for the year, but because some residents were 'Situated at a Considerable distance from the School, and the Children being too small to send at such a distance during the Cold Winter Season' attendance fell beneath the threshold needed to qualify for the grant. They were told the government had no discretion in these matters and were left with their debt to the teacher.[45] Matters were exacerbated in the May 1832–May 1833 period when a single report and grant payment were made to save work in the government offices. The school trustees in St Andrews only learned that the pay and examination periods had been changed when they sent their agent, Mr Simpson, to the bank in January 1833 to draw a half-year's salary for their teacher. They urged a return to bi-annual payments in the interest of both teachers and trustees, noting, 'The Teachers are in general very poor calculating on payment to be made in the usual mode having to procure wood for fuel, provisions and other necessaries of life which they obtain on Credit till the funds are obtained and of this there is no avoiding.' A second reason was that 'the Teachers are engaged only for six months, as a check to prove if such are punctual to the hours, temperate, loyal and exemplary. Whereas twelve months engagement would frustrate the salutary Check in a great measure.'[46] A chorus of like complaints produced a return to bi-annual payments after May 1833.

Trustees were sometimes victims of fraud. In St-Michel-de-Yamaska in 1834, two of them, William Maher and Léonard de Tonnancoeur, hired James Duggan to teach their school and, because their neighbours were too poor to pay fees, advanced him living expenses to the amount of £18 with another £2 for clothing. Duggan forged a power of attorney, got the school grant from the receiver general, and absconded with their money. In another case, the agent the trustees employed to get their school money in Quebec refused to pay it to them because one of them was indebted to him. Sometimes one trustee drew the grant money and refused to distribute it, leaving the others vulnerable.[47]

Ignorant trustees could be victims of their ignorance, as could teachers. In District 5 of St-Léon-Legrand, the trustees contracted with Marie

Cité Gelinas to teach from May to November 1834, but 'in the course of the Semester complaints were made from the heads of families' and they fired her after three months. They 'X'd' her school report but, when a warrant for £10 arrived, discovered that her father had made out the report for six months instead of three. They obviously did not and – since someone else wrote to government for them to complain – they probably could not read the school report themselves. They were reluctant to pay Gelinas all the money and feared that they might be sued whether they paid or not. The response of the executive was simply that 'the Member for the County has included this School in his Return for the whole Six Months which has accordingly been paid,' an instance of Joseph Cary's legalism, but also a case of the Assembly subsidizing a teacher who did not teach.[48]

Illiterates

Just how many school trustees and visitors could not write their names cannot be determined with precision because the surviving collection of school reports is incomplete, especially after 15 May 1834. However, a great many people could not sign, especially in the parishes and seigneuries, many more of them with French than with English, Irish, or Scottish surnames, and more of them under the 1832 act, which called for three trustees in each school district, than under the 1829 act, which had five for each parish, seigneury, or township. Government did receive reports of ignorant English-speaking trustees. There was Charles Bradforce from Yamaska Mountain, who complained that his district school had less than the minimum number of students in attendance in 1832 because of the ignorance of his neighbours, including the trustees. Most of them were 'Americans, principally of low origin, and of little Education,' who were 'indifferent about employing Instructors more informed than themselves,' while the visitors and trustees were 'men of no literary attainments and consequently quite inadequate to judge of the requirements of an Instructor.'[49] Such complaints from English-speaking correspondents were comparatively rare.

Of course the MPP school visitors themselves evinced various degrees of comfort with the pen, in addition to men such as Pierre Careau, who could not write at all. Philomen Wright, Joseph Valois, and André Simon, for instance, had trouble signing their names. After 1832, the militia officers could visit and certify the schools, and many of them were also unable to write. Two of the three school visitors certifying the school in District 2 Charlesbourg in April 1834 signed with their 'X.'[50]

Trustee boards usually had at least one person able to sign (there was a handful of female trustees), but there were places in which no trustee could do so. For Julien Saillant's school in St-Joachim-de-Montmorency, for instance, curé Besserer was the sole trustee who signed the report for the period 15 November 1830 to 15 May 1831, while the report for the following six months bore 5 'X's.[51] For Toussaint D'Amour's school in St-Hilaire-de-Rouville four of the five parish trustees made their 'X' on his school reports for the period November 1829 to May 1830. Curé Bélanger was one of the notables present who certified the marks of those who could not sign. In the next round of elections, Bélanger became a trustee, and, at the November 1830 school exam, he signed the school report with two of the four other trustees. In the 1832 exam in the same school, one of three trustees signed. In District 1 in St-Martin parish in Terrebonne, two of three trustees made their marks and all three trustees put an 'X' on Antoine Tanguay's report from St-Pierre in early 1834.[52]

La Minerve published claims and counter-claims about illiterate trustees. One anonymous correspondent objected that subterfuge had been used in his parish to replace literate with illiterate trustees in 1830, men so ignorant the teacher 'had to give them writing lessons, and even had to guide their hands when it came time to sign their reports.' These trustees advised even well-to-do parents not to pay school fees, and the teacher could not live on the grant alone. 'It is effectively ridiculous,' he continued, 'to see men who do not know how to read, invested with absolute power over education, and attending examinations as judges of the scholars' progress and the abilities of the teachers.' The school visitors should intervene. Someone clearly knew who this correspondent was, since 'B' responded that the real issue was an attempt by a small coterie of parish residents to foist an English school on the French-speaking majority. These schemers denounced a perfectly good teacher for the simple reason 'of his refusing them his schoolhouse so that they could preach methodism.' It would be good, 'B' agreed, to have literate trustees, but that was not the issue here.[53]

The School Act of 1832 produced a further round of press criticism from teachers. One from St-Hyacinthe said the act would discourage schooling. 'All the abuses committed in the schools, almost always, come only from the trustees,' he insisted, noting that 'the persons appointed to govern the schools, do not know, often themselves, what a school is.' Under the 1829 act, a teacher was lucky to have one trustee or visitor show up at the school examination to make an 'X' on the school report. The rest stayed home to work and made their own 'Xs' after the fact. The

1832 act even removed the teachers' right to manage their schools and vested it in these ignorant trustees. It was hard enough to find someone willing to teach for the school grant alone, which was all teachers in the poor parishes could get, and now they would be subjected to trustees' whims. The Assembly's education committee failed to understand the pettiness of parish politics, and 'if a master has to deal with mean-spirited people (as happens only too often) even if he should do his duty and be qualified, he will find himself driven out by their gossip.' Under the 1832 act any three household heads could join together to fire the teacher before the end of his term. The law needed to be amended.[54]

John Neilson often received school reports with the trustees' 'X's. In 1833, for instance, in District 1 of St-Ambroise the curé alone signed while two others made their marks. In District 3 of St-Foy, where the settlers were Irish, two of three trustees made their marks; for the vestry school in Beauport the curé alone signed, while the churchwardens made their marks; and in District 1 of Beauport all three trustees made their mark on a note authorizing curé Bégin to draw their school grant.[55] At the fall 1830 exam for Augustin Welling's school in St-Hughes parish in Drummond county, three of the five trustees signed; one of the two who made his mark was the treasurer.[56] Four of five trustees signed the 1829–30 report for David Bousseau's school in St-Étienne-de-Beaumont, as did four of the five trustees for Marie Langlois's school at St-Valier in 1831, although for three of the four in her case the pen was not very cooperative.[57] John Slevin, who would later apply unsuccessfully for a superior school grant, taught with his wife or sister at La Malbaie in Saguenay county. There seem to have been only three trustees active here in 1831 with 'Louis Tramblay' and curé Duguay signing their names, while Jean Maltais made his mark. The school returns for the Slevin schools are both in English and were probably written by the teachers themselves. 'The Trustees change the no. and names of the Poor Children,' reported the female teacher.[58]

As the elementary schooling project developed, school trustees unable to sign their names became less common in some parts of the colony. For instance, four of the five trustees first elected in St-Damase-de-St-Hyacinthe could not sign their names, but all the trustees elected in 1830 led by curé L.-M. Quintal could do so. In the parish of Beauport by late 1833, all three trustees signed the school reports in nine of the twelve boards. The trustee elections in St-Michel-de-Bellechasse in 1834 were hijacked by seven men who met and elected themselves for the four parish schools to ensure literates were in office. Curé N.-C. Fortier presided over all four boards. Very fragmentary evidence also suggests that some of the rough writers among the trustees acquired more polish over time with participation in local school administration.[59]

Where the trustees were illiterate, they were dependent upon someone else to compose the school report and to produce the other necessary correspondence for their teachers to be paid. Of course, they were unable to read the school acts or the 1832 administrative manual. Often the composition of the school report fell to the teacher, and the trustees in such cases were not able to verify its substance: they heard it read but could not, for instance, verify records of attendance or student progress. 'Luce Ponsant épouse de Moïse Houde' wrote the report for her school in District 2 of St-Hughes parish in Drummond County for the six-month period ending 15 May 1833. It bore the 'X's of two of her three trustees and the signatures of one trustee and two witnesses. Ponsant claimed to have fifty-five students on her attendance roll, ranging in age from six to fifteen, although the majority of them had not attended for sixty days. Of the fifty-five, only two were being taught to write; the rest only to read. Ponsant noted 'The Mistress has never been paid by the Trustees who only promised her the Government Grants.' She held a public examination, but 'The Visitors never came after 1831 but that is not the Mistress's nor the Trustees' fault.' She was concerned about her school qualifying for the grant because the trustee election had not been held at the specified time. Worse, she had not been paid for the previous period 'because one did not know how to go about getting paid': 'one' likely meant her trustees.[60]

In St-Jacques in the parish of St-Esprit, the trustees hired the notary Louis Jannot dit Lachapelle to make up their school report for the period ending 15 May 1832 because, as their teacher Joseph Bourguoin dit Bourgugnon put it, 'with the exception of the Curé,' they were 'too ignorant to satisfy the demands of their station.' Bourgugnon complained to the executive that despite having himself to pay Lachapelle's fee of 10s. he received only a fraction of what he was entitled to from the school grant. He thought it was negligence on Lachapelle's part, but in fact Joseph Cary had prorated his grant money. In St-Gervais-de-Bellechasse in 1831, the school reports were submitted in due form, but the trustees did not apply for the teachers' share of the school grant, probably not understanding that the school act required them to do so.[61]

Finally in this regard, there was the issue of the superior school bonus of £10 created by the 1834 School Act. Here the absence of some sort of board of examiners in the colony made itself felt, even as it was shown that the school acts supported some remarkably able teachers. A teacher named C. Hutton was irate because his trustees could not certify that he deserved the bonus for the best school in his parish, and when the matter was referred to his MPP visitors, neither F.-X. Larue nor H.-S. Huot (who had a college education) was capable of examining him in geometry. They suggested that he split the bonus with another good teacher, but Hutton claimed to be the best and wanted it all.[62]

M. le Curé

The school acts had the potential to change local power relations by creating a new category of elected lay officials who were authorized to organize and manage community institutions and to receive government money. The Assembly passed the 1829 School Act in part because of the inactivity of the clergy under the 1824 Vestry Act and because a further sectarian incursion into schooling was imminent. The act was intended to circumvent the powers that blocked the schooling of the people. However, in most parts of the colony the new laws simply reinforced the existing hegemony of petty bourgeois professionals, the curés, and the appointed magistrates and militia officers. There were conflicts over schooling among members of these groups,[63] but they also came into conflict with newly elected trustees.

In the new settlement of District 14 in Frampton, the trustees clashed with the militia captain, Andrew Murphy. Murphy had been appointing schoolteachers to the various districts on his own authority, and in District 14 he appointed a person to whom the trustees 'and the parents of the majority of the children in the district are utterly averse.' Murphy was aware of their opposition but told them he had the power to appoint whom he chose under the school act. When the trustees got a copy of the act and discovered Murphy's lies, they – English Protestants – presented their own teacher to curé John O'Grady to be examined, as did two other trustee boards with their teachers, but O'Grady refused to do so, apparently siding with Murphy. Their MPP visitor P.-E. Taschereau gave the trustees written instructions to present their teachers again, but Murphy called new trustee elections and had other trustees put in their place. The original trustees travelled to Quebec seeking satisfaction, although it is not clear that they found it.[64]

The stance of the curés towards the trustee schools was exceptionally important. They were the masters of the unknown for an often credulous populace and they were men who could read and write in a population most of whose members could do neither. Yet, as Richard Chabot observed, 'the rural curé did not concern himself with ensuring that his parishioners as a whole were taught. Besides, he could not help but realize that an overly educated mob could endanger religion. He was primarily concerned to give religious and moral training to the few peasant boys who attended the schools under his control.'[65] The statement captures well the continuing support of many curés, and of their bishops, for the pastoralist conception of popular schooling and hints at the intense antipathy they expressed towards lay control of education, even if it omits the fact that girls' morality was also an important concern.

However, by highlighting the Catholic clergy's opposition to lay efforts to educate the peasantry, Chabot's analysis tends to underplay the degree of clerical involvement in the trustee schools and, perhaps unintentionally, to sustain the belief that they were progressive *patriote* institutions. In fact, the curés were deeply implicated from the outset. Part of their interest stemmed, as Chabot suggested, from the fact that the government grant relieved them of the necessity of diverting vestry funds away from the splendour of the parish church and the comfort of their presbyteries. In practice as well, some teachers relieved them of their obligation to give catechetical instruction.

The curés ignored their bishops' injunctions not to participate in trustee schools. For the latter, a curé agreeing to a trustee election for the vestry school in order to get government money was beyond the pale, as was using vestry funds to support a new school managed by trustees. Bishop Lartigue warned Bonaventure Alinotte, curé of St Antoine, who sought permission to use vestry funds to help build a trustees school, that the election provisions of the 1829 School Act were so vague that he might find himself stuck with Protestant trustees. If the elected trustees made over all their rights to the vestry and the churchwardens, he could use vestry funds to build a school, but not otherwise. After the passage of the 1832 School Act, and still smarting from the Assembly's attempts to democratize vestry elections, Lartigue told curé Louis Gagné that, whatever the cost, there was absolutely no way he would consider having elected vestry school trustees. Such a practice was against the law, offended morality, and damaged the interests of religion. Bishops Panet and Signäy similarly refused any vestry support for trustee schools. They were not opposed to using government money to build vestry schools; Panet counselled one priest to build a school and to divide the building down the middle so the vestry could try to draw a double construction grant. But the prohibitions were largely ignored and there was a wholesale move to convert vestry schools to trustee schools. In 1828, for instance, there were forty-eight vestry schools in the colony; in 1829 only twelve survived.[66]

Bishop Lartigue was adamantly opposed to co-education, but most trustee schools were co-educational. He instructed curé Laurent Aubry of Sault-au-Recollet to refuse communion to the schoolmaster and to the children attending a mixed-sex school. He wrote to curé Jean-Olivier Chèvrefils of St-Constant, 'I hear that the Schoolmasters in your parish teach girls and even teach them together with boys; inform them, as well as the children's parents, that both [practices] are against all the rules; and absolution cannot be offered to those among them who persist in this serious sin.' Curé Boissonnault of Rivière des Prairies received a somewhat more temperate injunction of the same sort. Joseph Signäy was more tolerant, writing to the curé of Gentilly in 1833 that if he could not get a Catholic teacher, he could temporarily employ a Protestant and that boys and girls could attend the same school provided that they sat apart and did not come and go at the same time. This was not a general permission, for he pointed out to curé Louis-Antoine Montminy that such a practice could be tolerated only under special circumstances.[67]

Yet despite the pronouncements of their bishops, the curés served as trustees or visitors and did so for co-educational schools, which were the great majority in the countryside (*La Minerve* claimed 844 of 1,216 in 1831). Signäy's recommendation of separate seating for boys and girls assumed a rare degree of sophistication in rural school architecture and furnishings and flew in the face of teachers' legal obligation to teach by achievement class. The simple fact was that without co-education, most rural schools could not meet the enrolment threshold to qualify for the school grant.

It was indeed common for boys and girls to be schooled separately where resources permitted. In most large villages there were single-sex schools. For instance, in St-Athanase in 1830, Olivier Pinsonant taught 55 boys and Marie Louise Ménard taught 45 girls. She had 48 students in 1831, while Henry Aubertin had taken over the boys' school and taught 72.[68] In St-Roch-des-Aulnaies in the Quebec district, curé Louis Brodeur and the churchwardens ran a boys' school with about 35 students and a teacher who lodged in the presbytery under Brodeur's critical eye. There were two nearby trustee schools for girls with between 45 and 55 students each. The vestry took over one of them after 1836. While the girls were taught the three Rs, the boys' teacher, 'having been well educated,' taught grammar, history, geography, and Latin. Several boys were said to have gone on to college at Ste-Anne.[69]

The large and flourishing village of L'Assomption had a more extensive educational economy, with schools that predated the 1829 School

Act, including one run by Samuel John Lewis, who taught boys the basics, grammar and geography in both English and French. From 1809 girls could attend the school run by Marie Josephte and Hyppolite Guyon dites Lemoine. Until 1828 the sisters had between twenty-five and forty students, but enrolments reached a high of eighty under the 1829 School Act. They expanded their course of instruction from the three Rs and needlework to include English and French grammar, geography and mythology, and attempted unsuccessfully to split the school, with Hyppolite taking the free students and Marie Josephte those who paid. Splitting the school was meant to double the grant, but also to separate the 'pauper' girls from the rest. Fees were the highest permitted under the school acts – 2s.6d. a month until 1832 and 2s. a month thereafter – and the sisters routinely drew £20 from the legislative school grant. The school continued in operation at least until 1838, but the sisters were then in straitened circumstances.

The village offered a propitious climate for the opening of a college in 1833, a project directed by the future Canada East Education Super- intendent, J.-B. Meilleur. The college was modelled on the American academies. In 1838 it had seventy-seven boys under five professors, and an elementary class was taught by the former private school teacher John Lewis. Girls were not allowed to attend college, but those from well-to-do families, both beginners and the more advanced, could go to Madame Cherrier's select boarding and day school near the church. Boarders who provided their own bedding were accepted for £15 a year. For between 2s.6d. and 5s. per month, Cherrier and her assistants offered to teach reading in English, French, and Latin, arithmetic, grammar in French and Latin, geography and the use of the globe, astronomy, mythology, and history. For an additional 10s. a month, drawing and painting, needle and embroidery work, and artificial flower making could be had. Or, for the same price, a girl could learn vocal and instrumental music on piano and lute. Cherrier also offered at separate prices 'Mezzo Tinting, Poonah Tinting, Drawing and Chinese Lacquering, tracing as well as the art of lace-making.'[70]

Outside the villages, however, co-education was the norm. Given Msgr Lartigue's abhorrence of the practice, it seems odd that it was not a com- mon subject of contention between lay school trustees and local clergy, but state papers, press coverage, and school reports contain virtually no trace of it. If there were conflicts, they were contained locally. There was a single appeal made to John Neilson on the subject, by the trustees in District 3 of Ste-Anne-du-Sud. They asked him to intercede in a conflict with their curé. Pierre Morin wrote to Neilson for the trustees late in 1835, explaining that curé Painchaud did not want little boys and girls to go to the same school and that he had told the trustees that the practice was against school regulations. 'Me, I state that I have travelled around all the parishes below Quebec,' wrote Morin, 'and in almost all the Schools, I saw girls and boys mixed together.' Morin did not believe that government had made some special rule for his parish alone. In any case, without taking boys and girls together, the school would not get the grant, for there were only fourteen boys and eighteen girls on the roll and most were free students, while the others paid only a shilling a month in fees, given how wretched the harvest had been in his parish. The children's fathers were perfectly content to have boys and girls together at school, and Neilson was asked to resolve the matter. His answer does not survive, but more than two-thirds of the schools in his district in 1831 were co-educational.[71]

Unless a curé was particularly heavy handed, or the lay opposition particularly sharp, lay-clerical conflicts rarely spread beyond the parish. É.-É. Parant of Cap-St-Ignace was one of those with heavy hands. He clashed repeatedly with a lay opposition led by the militia captain Abraham Larue. Cap-St-Ignace had a Royal Institution school in the 1820s with a teacher from France named Charles Dolbigny. According to Larue, Parant set out to kill the school by telling his parishioners that, as a foreigner, Dolbigny needed a teaching certificate from his government before he could teach. This claim, wrote Larue, was simply 'the pretext for His opposition, of which the true cause is the Antipathy that he Feels for an Establishment which tends to teach and enlighten the people.' Larue said Parant had actually told him he would have no objection to Dolbigny if the school were not a Royal Institution school. On an earlier occasion, Parant had driven out a teacher by warning his parishioners that the RI schools 'are institutions that contradict religion.' That statement Parant knew to be ridiculous, and the real reason was 'not to beat about the bush, Mr le curé does not want any School, – or at least he wants one only on the condition that he should be the Only patron, the Only Director.'

Charles Dolbigny appealed to the board of the Royal Institution in 1828 for protection but the board delayed a reply, hoping that the bill for two separate Royal Institutions would pass and Dolbigny could be reassigned. Parant, however, quickly got involved with the 1829 School Act, and the trustee schools established under it drew off Dolbigny's students. He moved to Kamouraska to take up another school.[72] Parant was elected a parish trustee in 1830 and tried in May 1831 to have his mandate extended for another year. A group of parish residents was invited to the presbytery, ostensibly to fill a vacancy on the trustee board, but once they were assembled, Parant insisted that they elect all the following year's trustees, but then he refused to accept the result. Only one of the sitting trustees, and not Parant himself, was re-elected: a group headed by captain Larue dominated the new board, but Larue complained to the executive that Parant and the former board refused to hand over any of the school records, including the contract for a new schoolhouse, which was sitting empty and incomplete. Unfortunately for Larue, the executive sided with Parant's board, which claimed that Larue's election was illegal because precocious under the law. The attorney general ruled that unanimous agreement to hold an early election did not affect the matter. This conflict dragged on over the summer of 1831; John Neilson sided with the curé and reduced the number of school districts to eliminate schools supported by Larue.[73]

Parant, then, with Neilson's complicity, succeeded in eliminating any challenge from the school acts to his parishioners' ignorance. Only two of the parish's four districts established schools and they replicated the pastoral project. In 1838, N. Boisseau taught reading and writing in Latin and French to eighteen students (four of them girls) and a Mlle. Silvestre taught six boys and seven girls to read in Latin, with the three Rs in French: the standard eighteenth-century peasant curriculum. The vestry offered no support to the schools, but when questioned Parant told his bishop it might pay the female teacher £6.[74] The outcome in St-Ignace was common in the parishes and seigneuries more generally: the Assembly's school project usually did not challenge clerical hegemony.

Teachers' Incomes

As in pre- or proto-public school systems elsewhere, there was a great deal of variety in the conditions of work, pay, competence, and local standing of Lower Canada's teachers in the 1830s. The 1829 School Act created a wave of new teaching jobs. The large urban monitorial schools and the houses of the Soeurs de la Congrégation offered some teacher training, and the growth of village economies created a demand for clerks, bookkeepers, and shop assistants. Immigration also provided a supply of mainly English-speaking men and women more or less able to teach and willing to do so to earn a bit of cash while looking for something better. Making a living from teaching was far from self-evident, especially in the parishes and seigneuries. The common practice in rural schools in the Townships of having male teachers in winter and female in summer meant that most men and women there could not live from teaching alone. More mundanely, what was considered to be an adequate teacher, and the conditions of teachers' work and pay, were shaped by the peculiarities of local circumstances: the schools did not constitute a 'system.'

The permissiveness of the Assembly's school legislation encouraged variety. Laxity on the part of the school visitor MPPs and the ignorance of trustees and militia officers allowed teachers who could not meet the 1832 School Act's minimum standard to continue in the occupation. While it was becoming more difficult to do so, at the end of the 1830s some teachers could still make a living by child minding without themselves being able to write or perhaps to read. We recall Jacques Viger's listing in 1835 of Anna Holmes as a Montreal schoolteacher who did not know how to write, and Lord Durham, who sent a member of his suite around Quebec City in 1838 to collect the signatures of teachers, discovered Angélique Talion who could not sign her name. The Assembly's '£20 teachers' were denounced in the legislature as proof of the poverty of its educational policy.[75]

The cholera epidemic of 1832 combined with the Permanent Committee's reduction of the maximum allowable school fees and its reduction of the grant for free students put 10–15 per cent of the colony's teachers out of work for at least a year. Despite the committee's intention to improve teachers' lot by driving out the underqualified and increasing average school size, even good teachers found it more difficult to continue to teach, especially since fees were reduced and the grant was paid only once between 15 May 1832 and 15 May 1833. Still, quite a number of illiterate or partly literate teachers were policed out of the occupation in the wake of the 1832 School Act, often to their indignation and to the anger of those who made use of their services. The trustees in some places were redefining schooling as a more substantial form of training – and subjectification – than it was as child minding. Women were most commonly targeted, and, worse, they often learned they would not be paid only after working for several months. Sometimes the school visitors told them they would not be paid in future, and some teachers continued to teach and tried unsuccessfully to claim the grant. At other times, the county MPP simply left their names off his list of authorized teachers. The school visitors in St-Pie in November 1832 refused to authorize Marie Gadoura's school because 'she doesn't know arithmetic, which we would have excused; but she can't write, & can only read French very imperfectly.' Hers was not a case of a lack of kindness or good character, for 'she possesses all the good qualities,' but a matter of teaching as child minding not meeting the new minimum standard in the school act. This teacher's husband was quite shocked, and several parents in the district tried to sign her school report themselves so that she could draw the grant money, but to no avail.[76]

Marie Archange Guy in Ste-Anne-de-la-Pocatière, who met the same fate, expressed her great indignation in a long letter to the Assembly which demonstrated her entirely phonetic command of written French. Among other things, she charged the school visitors with failing to examine her school because of favouritism: 'the Gentlemen Trusteas … set up as a ticher, Robert dupon's little girly 12 years old doin' her sChool in a same house as her dad girls and boy comin' in the same door.' Read at this remove, Guy's letter has aesthetic qualities, but it suggests that in her parish the visitors would not tolerate a semi-literate teacher. Josephte Blondin's appeal of her disqualification by the school visitors in 1834 was also written phonetically. 'Itsa wid allderespek posible,' she addressed Lord Aylmer, 'that I'm askin pertection from yer honoruble Ma gessesty to Munnicate to you me trubbles.' Blondin included a crudely forged version of the trustees' letter of dismissal in which she had changed their remark that her students were 'little forward' to read 'Rilly forward' and their description of her as 'little qualified to teach' to read 'total qualified.' Unfortunately for her, the civil secretary sent this material back to the trustees, who were shocked at her duplicity, and a later petition for the school money in her own hand, but supposedly from five householders, who all made their mark, was curtly rejected. By contrast, in de Ramezay in L'Assomption county, a resident complained that his neighbours and the female school trustees conspired to get the school grant for an ignorant man whom they really wanted as a preacher. 'The parents of the children,' complained John Egerton, 'prefer a person as teacher who will play with their children instead of teach and lessen their expence by preaching – this Preacher teaches his pupils to get Chapter and Hymns by rote while he composes his Sermons … the Parents being all Americans they want no school discipline.'[77]

The new 1832 School Act thus had the consequence in some places of disrupting the function of child minding, often performed by older, needy men and women in the peasant economy, and of eliminating teaching as a means of support for aged or infirm community members. As Charles Décormier put it poignantly in an appeal against his dismissal from a school, 'I am alone with my wife and we're getting up in years.' Teachers often clung desperately to their livelihoods with the support of their students' parents, and violent measures were sometimes taken to remove them. In St-Athanase-de-Rouville in May 1832, the future *patriote* MPP and school visitor Dr P.-M. Bardy, wrote to the civil secretary for government aid in removing 'Mary Louisa Ménard formerly keeping a Girl[s'] school in our Village. This Woman which we have found incapable of governing correctly and properly our said school' nonetheless 'persists in keeping the said school, after having excited in her favour against us several Persons quite ignorant.' Bardy and the trustees had hired another teacher, but could not get Ménard to vacate the house. Bardy's letter was referred to Joseph Cary, who departed from his usual reticence on practical matters to suggest, 'I know no more effectual means than that the Trustees should *smoke* the old Woman out' – a recommendation to block up the school house chimney.[78]

The requirement of a certificate of moral character in the 1832 act was meant to exclude the drunken, violent, or immoral teacher from the occupation, but teachers were quite mobile and did not need to carry reports of past misdemeanours with them to new school districts. There was no way for trustees to track them, and no other agency existed to do so. William Boyce appealed his suspension in 1830 from a school he had taught for two and half years near Maskinongé by claiming to have given perfect satisfaction, only to be turned out of the schoolhouse cruelly in the dead of winter by the Rev. Mr Driscoll – and Boyce with two young children and a wife in childbed! To add to Boyce's injury, the 'new teacher was a boy of about seventeen his parents living on the spot, who required no dwelling house.' The official visitors' report charged that Boyce, by 'blamable severity towards his Scholars and frequent instances of inebriety' had 'so displeased their Parents that they withdrew all their children except nine, from his care.' Boyce would not offer religious instruction, one summer Sunday 'was disgustingly drunk,' beat and swore at his wife in school, and his 'conversation when in company with females was constantly offensive.' He was charged by Driscoll with extorting money from a tavern owner and with keeping a horse in the schoolroom. Boyce got no support from government and so picked up and moved. Two years later he was teaching in District 2 of the Township of Kildare, where he forged the name of one of the trustees on his school report, after the trustee refused to sign on the grounds that Boyce was 'unworthy from Improper Conduct' to receive the school grant.[79]

Another group of trustees warned the executive of James Breckinridge, who had been teaching in their parish before the passage of the 1829 act, but whom they had dismissed 'for grossly immoral conduct.' He continued to teach in a remote part of the parish and submitted his school report for approval on 1 January 1830. The trustees returned the report with a short note informing him that his school was not authorized. Breckinridge cut the trustees' signatures off their letter, pasted them onto his report and submitted it to the government to get the grant. He was exposed and fled to Brockville, Upper Canada.[80]

On the other hand, part of teachers' mobility was due to seasonal employment practices. In St-Georges-de-Rouville in 1829–30, for instance, the parish's ten schools had seventeen different teachers. In eight of the ten schools, women taught from July to November, and men from November to May. In two of the schools, men were employed year-round. In parishes where separate boys' and girls' schools were established, there might be more stable employment for teachers, but same-sex schools were a minority.[81]

Teachers were paid what they could negotiate with the trustees, usually supplemented by the school grant. Almost all country teachers earned less and usually much less than the 5s. a day (about £78 year) that a casual government clerk could earn in Quebec. In St-Georges mentioned above, the teachers charged 2s.6d. a month for each student and received a boarding allowance of 30s. a season. Here the smallest school in 1829–30 had 22 enrolled students and the largest 50. Overall school enrolment increased from 228 before the passage of the 1829 School Act to 436 in 1829–30. Unfortunately for the teachers' incomes, only 121 students paid fees. The maximum allowable fee was reduced under the 1832 act to 2s. a month.

In theory, if all students in the smallest school in St-Georges attended for twelve months and paid all their fees, the teacher would have earned £66 in fees in addition to the £20 legislative grant and the boarding allowance: over £89 for the year. If the proportion of fee-paying students in this school was the average for the parish, fees would have amounted to just over £24, but the grant might have increased from £20 to £27 if all the poor students were subsidized, giving the teacher slightly over £52 for the year. In 1832 the fees would have dropped to £20 and the grant would have done likewise. One could then introduce some more probable conditions: that the students attended for six months on average, for instance, and that the grant for poor students commenced only once the threshold of twenty paying students had been met. The smallest school would then have yielded less than £26, while the largest might have generated twice that sum.

There were six schools in 1829–30 in the parish of St-Benoît, where the trustees included the curé M. Félix and three active *patriotes:* his brother-in-law, J.-B. Dumouchel, Louis Dumouchel, and Jacob Barcelo. All the schools ran year-round, were co-educational, and had a total enrolment of 229, with two teachers in the village school. For the period 15 November 1829 to 15 May 1830 the government grant ranged from a high of £16.8. stg. for Veuve Clairoux in St Étienne, to a low of £6.8 each for Madame Hogue and Ovide Lemaire in the village school. If everyone enrolled attended year-round and if she collected all the fees owed her, Clairoux might have made £50 stg. or £60 cy. in a year; she undoubtedly made less. For the same period in St-Hyacinthe parish, where the seigneur and MPP Jean Dessaulles (married to Rosalie Papineau) was a trustee, François Daigle taught forty-seven students, twenty-one of whom paid fees, and received £14.17 as the government grant. If all his fee-paying students paid the going rate of 2s.6d. per month all year, Daigle too would have grossed about £50 a year. In practice, irregular attendance and irregular payment of fees would have reduced these incomes.[82]

Rector James Reid identified two of the better-paid male teachers of St-Armand in his 1830 school report. 'Daniel Campbell and Alex Young are very capable and successful in their profession,' he wrote, 'and yet such a man as Campbell does not get quite £40 per. annum. Young makes about £70.' He added that 'women Teachers ... answer a better purpose for teaching little children in summer than men, unless we had such as the two I have named, but unfortunately we do not often find men like them.' Young's £70 would have looked very appealing to Thomas Lee. Lee had been 'employed by the inhabitants in the rear of the Township of Grenville on the 1st day of November [1829], for six months at 8 Dollars [£2 cy.] per month for as many Scholars as the inhabitants of the Settlement could possibly send.' When the summer school season started in 1830, residents agreed to pay him only by the head – less than $3 a month. Lee knew he was entitled to something from the government, but did not know how to get the school grant. In fact a warrant for £9.8.0 stg. had been waiting for him in Quebec since 15 June, and Lee was told to get himself an agent. For the winter, Lee would have earned just under £20 stg., but much less than that for the following six months. This may be the same Thomas Lee who moved to the Papineau seigneury at La Petite Nation, where from November 1830 to May 1831 his school grant was a miserable £8.7.0, still better than Lucinda Hayes on the same seigneury who earned £7.12.0. for the period 15 May to 16 October 1830.[83]

Marcelle Guyon was a teacher at Ruisseau-St-Jacques, in Barthélemy Joliette's riding of L'Assomption, who kept a private school in the same parish from 1826. She hired someone to make up her school report so she could get the grant in 1829, but either they didn't do it or didn't send it to government. Then someone told her she wasn't eligible for the grant because her school had changed location, although it was still in the same parish. Thinking she would never be able to draw the grant, and suffering from the competition of the new, subsidized trustee schools, she gave up teaching for a few months. However, curé Paré and several others encouraged her to start again, and when Joliette examined her school in 1831, he told her that she was certainly entitled to some grant money. In her fine, plain round hand, she explained the situation to the civil secretary and managed to draw £13.9 stg. for teaching forty-four students for the period from 15 May to 15 November 1830. For the same period in 1831, she drew £18.1.1 stg. Although she was quite a literate person and taught near the parish church, she likely did not gross £40 a year.[84]

The salary figures reported under the 1829 act thus give the lie to the notion of the '£20' teacher which figured in public debate, although there were some of them, often young women or older widows teaching or minding small children in exchange for the school grant alone. Even under the 1832 act some teachers received little more: the three women teachers in Cap Santé, Nathalie Desroches, Geneviève Matte, and Sophie Richard, 'were paid only the sums they received from the children's parents, an allowance made by the Trustees [,] and the £20-0-0 from the Government & what the parents pay is from 6d to 1/3 per month for each child.' The grant money was prorated. In Rimouski in the Seigneury de Métis, James Paul received no fees, but instead '£25 by Agreement with the Trustees and Firewood and a days Labour Service from Each Household head,' which perhaps enabled him to farm as well as to teach. Two rural Drummond County teachers did better. Nancy Weare in District 1 of Kingsey Township was paid 'Board and Lodging in addition to the Government allowance' for her forty-two students. Her neighbour Lucina Cleveland in District 1 of Tinwick Township was to receive 'allowance seven shillings & six pence per week Exclusive of government money' (a theoretical annual maximum of £39, although she likely taught only for the winter). Other teachers shared Antoine Tanguay's experience. He had to depend entirely on the school grant after discovering that 'the subscription promised by the household heads to support the said school was a simple bagatelle.' Declining attendance late in 1833 pushed the school below the grant threshold and Tanguay had gone into debt not simply to live, but also to furnish the school room with tables and desks. He hoped to get £8.15.6. for a winter's work.[85]

The School Act of 1832 complicated matters for teachers and likely reduced their pay. It forced them in principle to keep detailed records of student attendance and progress, required a certificate of moral character, reduced the maximum fee by 20 per cent, and excluded students under five and over fifteen years of age. The act did offer an annual bonus of £4 for those who could teach in both French and English, but the potential gain for some teachers was more than offset by the move from half-yearly to annual payments of the grant and the tightening of the conditions for free students. One of *La Minerve*'s correspondents said the new conditions would make it even harder to find decent teachers because it was often around age fifteen that young people returned to complete their schooling and now they were excluded. The Lemoine sisters in L'Assomption found that the £4 payment for teaching both languages did not nearly compensate for the reduction in fees, and they were forced to take an additional fifteen free students before they could start to collect the 10s. pauper student grant. The best-paid teacher in Portneuf County in 1832–3 taught the vestry school in Deschambault and earned £43 for the year, £20 from government and the rest from the vestry. His neighbour Benjamin Spillsbury in a trustee school was promised £35 – £15 in fees and the government grant, although the latter was probably prorated.[86]

Some teachers were disgusted by the 1832 School Act. J.L. Milton of the Terrebonne British and Canadian school announced that 'the late Law in relation to Schools appears to my mind so very extraordinary' that he would 'no longer teach under the provisions of Said law.' Augustin Vervais (whom we saw removed from the Terrebonne school in the 1820s) complained from Longueuil that 'the new Bill for Elementary Education is so Complicated, that people trained in Law cannot figure out how to compose the School report.' Worse was the new pay period: 'What! wait a year for £24 – surely it will be necessary to abandon the Teaching profession!' Vervais, now aged forty-three with a wife and small children, objected that he had to go into debt to survive while waiting for the money. The executive sent him a curt note telling him that his trustees had the necessary report forms and he should complete them. Oh, and the grant was £20, not £24. In Rawdon, Thomas W. Carthwright had read the act but could not believe that the pay period was to be annual. 'There are very few StoreKeepers who can afford a years credit,' he noted, 'and if there are any, they will only do it by charging the most exorbitant prices.'[87]

Teachers' Expenses

The bi-annual pay period was restored under the School Act of 1833, but teachers routinely found themselves forced to pay many of the costs of local school management, given the trustees had no funds of their own, and teachers were also forced to deal with obstacles that arose from the trustees' ignorance, incapacity, or neglect. The trustees might not know that they had to appoint an agent to receive the grant or might not trouble themselves to do so, and ignorant trustees could not produce the written contracts for teachers demanded by the 1832 act. In District 4 of St-Mathias, the newly elected trustees continued Dominique Racicot as their teacher from 15 May 1832 but did not bother to give him a written contract; at least two of the three could not write. Racicot knew he now needed a certificate of character to get the school grant, so he went to curé Pierre Consigny to get one, but Cosigny was on his deathbed and could not help him. The new curé did not know Racicot, and the senior militia officer did not know how to read or write. Racicot then went to Remis Seraphim Bourdages, the nearest magistrate, but Bourdages lived just outside Racicot's parish and could not certify him. Thus, at the time of the annual school visit and examination, Racicot had no contract and no certificate, and the MPP visitor and the new curé refused to examine him. They did examine his students and found their progress satisfactory, but they would not give him their report. Finally Racicot got the necessary certificates and had his trustees swear an affidavit concerning his hiring, but it was probably too late for him to be included on the MPP's pay list.[88]

The costs of administering the school acts reduced teachers' already modest incomes. Teachers contributed to furnishing the schools, sometimes providing desks or tables and a stove, as well as a collection of books. The latter were rare in peasant communities. If teachers lived in the schoolhouse, they heated and cleaned it and perhaps had to do so in any case. Teachers had to pay for their certificates of character. The notary who filed the minutes of trustee election and provided a duplicate copy for the trustees to send charged for the service and also charged for drawing up a power of attorney for the trustees' Quebec financial agent. The agent in turn charged for getting the money and for the costs of delivering it to the trustees. The agent's charge was limited in principle to 5 per cent of the value passing through his hands. The grant typically did not arrive for the trustees in the form of cash money, although some money letters were sent – and lost in the mail – but usually as a warrant (credit letter) on government that had to be negotiated by the teachers and was probably discounted in the process. Although no one has been able to document the practice in detail, letters of credit on local merchants were likely the main means of payment by the agents. And of course many teachers lived between grant periods on shopkeepers' credit. They were charged interest as creditors and had no bargaining power in regard to prices. Seasonal male teachers may have been able to live on their land in the spring and summer seasons, and occasional local arrangements allowed teachers a quarter acre for a garden. The whole situation added substance to the remarks by John Neilson that it made no sense to tax the people indirectly for the schools and then to force them to pay costs of collection and administration of their own money when they would better be empowered to tax and pay themselves directly. It strengthened John Grannis's argument before the 1835–6 Education Committee for the creation of county school boards with a permanent treasurer responsible for all money matters. Yet as lawyers, notaries, and merchants, the MPPs themselves often had an active interest in the existing financial arrangements, and teachers were easy pickings.

Seven of the eight teachers in the Township of Rawdon joined together in 1833 to protest the exorbitant fees charged them by a notary for registering the minutes of trustee elections. One teacher had got the duplicate minute from the notary, François-Hyacinthe Prévost of St-Jacques, for 2s.6d. and, seeking to save the other teachers time and trouble, Thomas Griffith, the senior magistrate in the township, invited Prévost to make out the minutes and duplicates for the other teachers, offering to pay him. Prévost sent Griffith a bill for £2.12.6., or 7s.6d. for each minute, and then sued him in small claims court when he refused to pay. The teachers apparently were on the hook for the money. The additional 5s. raised the cost of the minute from under 2 per cent of the maximum school grant to over 5 per cent.[89]

The Agents: Private Public Administration

While trustees and teachers could and did make use of trips by local residents to Quebec to collect the warrant for the school grant, or had their curé perform this task, most employed an agent, usually someone who lived in Quebec City. For a fee, agents took trustees' powers of attorney, used them to get the warrants, and arranged for them to be sent to the school district.[90] In several years it was the MPP school visitors who acted as agents for all or for a great many of the trustee boards in their ridings and sometimes beyond. For instance, for the 1832–3 pay period, twenty-eight of the forty-four warrants for Portneuf county were handled by H.-S. Huot. Over £500 of Portneuf's elementary school money passed through his hands, and he also drew £280 in 1832 as secretary of the

Société d'Éducation de Québec. In 1833 he drew most of the warrants for the county of Verchères and a large portion of them for Two Mountains. P.-A. Dorion, John Neilson, and Théophile Lemay were among the other MPPs who served as trustees' agents. It has not been possible to determine if any of them charged fees for their service, but while Huot was a man activated by a sense of public duty, it is unlikely he acted for the distant counties at his own expense.[91]

The most important of the financial agents was Jean Langevin, who has active from early 1830 until he left the business in the summer of 1833 to become Quebec City clerk. Langevin advertised in *La Minerve* in 1830 that 'in exchange for a modest fee,' he would receive monies as warrants or in some other form at Quebec and forward them on. Printed forms empowering him to act could be had at Fabre et cie. in Montreal, and Langevin repeated the offer in the English-language press. A few days later, 'understanding that the increase of business caused in several of the public offices by the operation of the Acts for the encouragement of Elementary Education is such as to render some farther assistance necessary,' he wrote to Civil Secretary Yorke and offered his services to government as paymaster for all the schools. Langevin proposed to handle 'by warrants of five hundred pounds each, or any other amount, the whole of the monies allowed to School Masters or for School Houses and distribute the same upon Lists to be handed me by the Inspector of accounts or other officer, and account therefor as may be required.' He would do so until some other arrangements might be made and would charge the modest sum of 2s.6d. cy. for each payment.[92]

While Langevin did not receive an official appointment as paymaster, he acted as the agent for a great many teachers and trustees and performed some of the administrative functions made necessary by the absence of an education department or inspector. For instance, residents of the Magdelan Islands could not comply with the school act because there was no resident notary to make an authorized minute of the trustee election. Langevin suggested to the civil secretary that they be allowed to use a magistrate for this purpose and urged the executive to send them a complete set of school laws and regulations. The residents of Blandford township had no resident militia officer to convoke their trustee election; Langevin suggested an alternative. He helped a teacher named Marie Caneur to complete her school report and to get some school grant money, and it was Langevin who later explained to the executive that she had discovered she was not eligible for the money and wished to return it. He delivered the petition and related correspondence of Thomas Ambrose, a schoolteacher from St-Roch-des-Aulnaies whose pay had been suspended at the instigation of curé Brodeur. It was Langevin, and not the executive, who informed teachers and trustees that the reporting period was changed from 15 November to 1 January under the 1831 School Act.

Langevin eventually handled very large amounts of school money: for the first pay period in 1833, for instance, many or most of the payments in the counties of Rouville, Rimouski, Lotbinière, Beauharnois, Orleans, Two Mountains, Nicolet, Richelieu, and Laprairie passed through his hands. He was agent of choice as well for the trustees of the Collège de L'Assomption and for the Soeurs de la Congrégation de Notre Dame. There had been no complaints against him when he left the agency business in August 1833. Langevin's performance, especially in contrast with that of some of his competitors and successors, demonstrated the good sense in John Grannis's later suggestion that all school monies be handled by a permanent official.[93]

In May 1830, curé La Mothe of St Scholastique warned the executive of 'how Schoolmasters are abused by their Agents.' Some of the commission agents cheated trustees and teachers. James H. Kerr, for instance, acted four times for the teacher John Hanamney in St-Georges parish. Hanamney complained to Secretary Craig that while his third pay had been light by £1, his last was short £5.17s.4 1/2d. The full amount had been paid to Kerr. A neighbouring teacher complained he had been charged 17s. for his pay of £23.17s, five times what Langevin charged.[94]

Most notorious was Clarke Ross, who took over a significant part of Langevin's business and defrauded a number of trustee boards and teachers. We saw earlier in the controversy surrounding MPP W.H. Scott that trustees in Chatham Gore employed Ross as their agent but could get no response to queries as to the whereabouts of their money, save that there was 'some sort of difficulty.' The difficulty was in Ross's business, for he had drawn their money but not paid it to them. Before Ross's activities in Two Mountains became known and after Langevin had left the agency business, the trustees of the Collège de L'Assomption had taken Ross as their agent. They had some hesitation, for they urged him, if he got their £200 'to put it in the mail, taking all necessary precautions to ensure it can be recovered should some act of negligence or fraud happen en route.' They were aware that 'several money letters have gone astray this winter,' and they could ill afford a loss.[95] These trustees seem not to have had cause for complaint, but in addition to John Hunter in Chatham Gore, Ross drew but did not pay money owing to at least three other boards of trustees.

The trustees in District 11 of Argenteuil used Ross's services in January and August 1835, but he refused to answer their letters or to send them any money. When they complained to the executive in November, Joseph Cary reported that their money had been placed on the pay list and that Ross had drawn it. Again, a teacher named Caroline S. Cook taught in District 2 in Argenteuil and then in District 2 in Chatham for the two pay periods of November 1834 and May 1835, but never received any grant money, despite following the procedures. When someone finally contacted the executive in April 1836 to inquire after her money – £18 stg. – Joseph Cary noted, 'The payments of these allowances were made to Mr Clarke Ross – the first on 25 March and the second on 25 Augt 1835.' Three days later another complaint arrived from District 12 in Argenteuil, where the trustees stated 'altho' Mr Ross did ... receive the money to the amount of £20 to transmit the same to us, yet he has as yet neglected to do so.' Joseph Cary commented, 'This statement is correct.' How many cases of the sort there were remains to be determined, but in his 1840 report on District 2 of St-Polycarpe in nearby Vaudreuil, Robert Armour Jr wrote that 'the teacher for the District never received his Government allowance, in consequence of the failure of his Quebec Agent, and he is not the single instance, nor one, out of a hundred, that I have found to offer such a complaint.' Ross's fleecing was likely systematic, and the teachers and trustees had no recourse.[96] The matter of the agents was another instance in which minimal bureaucratic organization could have furthered the Assembly's school project.

Curriculum, or How Best to Make Your Day Holy

The dominance of the Catholic pastoral conception of education as moral training in the French-speaking rural Lower Canada of the 1830s is demonstrated in a particularly striking manner by the books and teaching methods used in the schools. Beyond the villages, *'dans les côtes'* or *'dans les rangs,'* French-language books other than works of piety were exceptionally rare, school supplies were lacking, and teachers had little or no exposure to the dramatic changes in pedagogy present in some city schools. There was no classification of students, no collective instruction, and reading was tightly framed by a concern with piety. Only exceptionally was there anything other than a religious book for a student to read, and, although the practice was fading, in some schools beginners still learned to read in Latin. The continuing dominance of ignorance and religious superstition in peasant schooling showed that the reform project depended for its success on a frontal assault on the Catholic Church and on the seigneurial system, which the *patriote* party was unwilling to undertake. Without some secular public sphere, there was no public education. Church and seigneur remained committed to pastoral simplicity. Reading remained subordinate to it.

The surviving collection of 1830s school reports shows that the French-language rural elementary schools continued to use the books and usually the methods of instruction of the vestry schools of fifty or one hundred years earlier.[97] In many villages, as we have seen, a broader course of study was available, although in others the pastoral model reigned. Rural students might stumble upon a qualified teacher, such as Benjamin Joassim in Soulanges, who was teaching while preparing to go to college. A few rural French-language schools reported using a grammar book, for French or Latin.[98]

Parents complained of underqualified teachers, yet old Marie Louise Ménard was 'smoked out' of the St-Athanase village school in 1832 not because of her course of instruction, but because she couldn't manage the students. Every teacher in her parish including the teacher of the village boys' school reported using books similar to Ménard's 'L'A.B.C. le petit Cathéchisme, l'Ancien et nouveau testament.' Emilie Drésy's fifty-nine students were exposed to 'Alphabets Instructions de Jeunesse'; Céleste Derome's brood got 'Le Maître François, le grand et petit Cathéchisme, L'instruction de la Jeunesse'; Marie Leclaire's sixty-one students, 'L'A.B.C. le petit cathéchisme l'ancien et nouveau Testament;' and Henry Aubertin used 'L'A.B.C. le petit cathéchisme, l'ancien et nouveau Testament, l'Instruction de la Jeunesse, Boulilier [Boutillier's Arithmetic?] &c.' for the village's seventy-two schoolboys. The school trustees included the *patriote* Dr P.-M. Bardy and curé Aubry. Bardy was one of those who argued that the curés should by right supervise the schools.[99]

Variations on St-Athanase's list of books appeared in the other rural French-language school districts, at least before 1832; there are hundreds of examples. In 1830 in the girls' mission school on Jean Dessaulles's St-Hyacinthe seigneury, the students had an alphabet, an abridged version of the Testament, and a grammar book. In the same parish, François Daigle's forty-seven students learned from 'Instructions pour les jeunes gens. Ancien et nouveau testament. Syllabaire français.' All the French-language teachers in Two Mountains in 1830 used 'L'A.B.C. instruction de la Jeunesse, nouveau Testament, Grammaire Française, Cathéchisme.' On the Île d'Orléans, Elie Paré used an abcédaire, a Testament, and *La Neuvaine de St François Xavier*. A school run by the Congrégation de Notre

Dame in the same parish reported using a grammar and an arithmetic book. In the boys' vestry school in St-Augustin parish in Portneuf in 1829, 'the books in use are the alphabet, lessons [for the young] , edifying history and the catechism.' Two years later the list was 'l'Alphabet Anglois, François, & Latin, L'éptiomé, l'instruction de la jeunesse, l'Histoire édifiante, la Grammaire Françoise & Latine, le Petit et le Grand Catéchisme.' The girls used 'l'alphabet, l'instruction, l'histoire-édifiante et le catéchisme' late in 1829, and for 1831, 'l'alphabet, l'instruction, le mois de Jesus, l'âme embrasée, et le catéchisme.' In the village girls' school at St-Jacques-de-L'Assomption: 'Le maître François, Histoire abregé de l'ancien Testament, moyen efficace de sanctifier la journée, visites au St Sacrement, Le petit Cathechisme du Diocèse du Quebec.' Louise Létang in St-Étienne-de-Bellechasse varied the typical list by adding Lafontaine's fables, or as she put it, 'Berquin fable de La fontaine.'

Outside the village of St-Denis, where the trustees in 1831 included one of the Nelson brothers, Louise Bousquet used 'l'abécédaire instruction de la jeunesse nouvelle methode pour apprendre lautograph, le Cathechisme et le testament.' Luce Pitt used 'l'abécédaire instruction de la jeunesse abrégé du Testament, Methode françoise, et le Cathéchisme,' while Soeur Ste Gertrude reported that the large boarding and day school run by the Congrégation de Notre Dame, used 'Various books of piety.' By contrast, while the *patriote* activist Siméon Marchesseault's monitorial school in the village used only the 'Ancien & nou: Testament instruction de la jeunesse, abécédaire,' he noted 'French is taught grammatically, Arithmetic and Geography with the use of cards. – Mutual instruction is employed.'[100]

Marchesseault's case suggests that the absence of books in some schools might have been compensated for by the use of spelling and reading cards, or by teachers lining exercise books for student use. The school reports invited teachers to describe their teaching methods, but they usually offered little information. In St-Hyacinthe parish the teachers apparently consulted about this question, for all except one used the same orthography to respond: 'usual Way of Teaching.' The parish's exception was Laurent Bédard, who wrote, 'Lancaster's System is used as much as circumstances permit.' Again at La Malbaie, John Slevin reported that his teaching method was 'Lancastrian as much as possible for the French and the Hamiltonian for English,' while the Irish Foy brother-and-sister team in Sillery Cove also claimed to use the Lancasterian method. Antoine Thomelette in St-Damase wrote in 1829 that his method was 'that of the colleges,' although in 1830 he wrote 'Lancaster's.' The large urban monitorial schools were attempting to train rural schoolteachers and by 1836 collectively had trained about seventy-five. People such as Thaddeus Osgood imported reading cards for distribution. J.-F. Perrault's translation and modification of Lancaster's *Experiment in Education* may have circulated beyond the cities, and in 1833 a teacher named Guillaume Benziger had written a *Guide aux Instituteurs, ou Emploi des tableaux de Lecture et d'Orthographe dans les ecoles d'enseignement mutuel*, so perhaps the real work of rural reading instruction took place using such cards. On the other hand, rural teachers seem to have had a shaky notion of the content of Lancaster's pedagogy and most lacked the resources to use much of it. Hubert Campagna's 1831 report for his school in St-François-Xavier-de-Bellechasse is symptomatic. For the books he used Campagna wrote, 'Joseph L'ancaster's plan, Livres de Prières arithmétique alphabet & & &,' while for his method of instruction he stated, 'The Old System of teaching is used.'[101] While some rural French-language schools then, may have used reading cards, those who reported using some version of Lancaster's pedagogy most likely meant 'mutual instruction' in the sense of having some older students teach some of the younger.

Schoolbooks were rare, and the reluctance of peasant parents to provide school supplies was notorious. As one observer put it to John Neilson, 'the *habitants* wish to have good Scholars, without books or paper.' The respondents to the Buller Commission for Lotbinière noted in 1838: 'In almost all the Schools, most of the children only had mismatched books, and often had none, because of the parents' indifference. They were almost always without paper.'[102] Without paper or slates, likely there was no writing instruction.

In the rural English-language elementary schools, matters were quite different. Of course observers here frequently complained of inadequate supplies of books, of variety in books that made student classification difficult, and English residents sometimes complained of American books. James Reid, the Rector of St Armand, praised the 1829 School Act for its liberality but warned government that with respect to books in use 'too many of our Schools are nearly the same as if we had met with them in the neighbourhood of Boston.' Despite such alarmism, the books used in English-speaking schools were those typically present in common schools in Upper Canada, Nova Scotia, and England itself, with the frequent addition of an American geography book or dictionary. The English standards, Mavor's *Spelling Book* and the international best-selling works by the Quaker Lindley Murray, including his *Grammar* and *English Reader*, were in general use.[103]

The contrast between books used and, by implication, between subjects taught in rural French- and English-language schools is particularly striking where they were located in adjoining school districts. In the mixed-language parish of St-Benoît in 1830, for instance, where all the French-language teachers used 'L'A.B.C. instruction de la Jeunesse, nouveau Testament, Grammaire Française, Cathéchisme,' James Agnew's English-language school used 'Mavors Spelling Books, New Testament, Murrays English Reader, English Grammar, Walkingames Arithmetic.' In St-Georges parish in Rouville, Alexis Cloutier's school used an abécedaire, *Instruction de la Jeunesse*, the Testament, and a grammar book. Twelve English-speaking teachers used a common set of books: Murray's *English Reader* and *Grammar*, the New Testament, Webster's and/or Marshall's spelling book, and Adams's arithmetic. The teacher's country of origin and religion did not make much difference in the list of English books used. The Irish teacher Michael Connolly in the seigneury of St-Jacques, who earned less than £30 in 1830, used Manson's *Primer*, Jenning's *Universals*, Mavor, *The English Reader*, Gough's *Arithmetic*, a bookkeeping text, and a book on mensuration. The Irish Foys in Sillery Cove preferred Fenning's *Spelling Book* to Mavor but used the *English Reader* and *Grammar* and Voster's *Arithmetic* in English, and something they called 'The Novelle Methodes' and a grammar book for their French-language students. English and French both got the Testament. Their neighbour John Kane, probably an Irish Catholic as well, used three of Lindley Murray's reading books and his grammar text, two arithmetic books, the *Universal Spelling Book*, and the *Catholic's Treasure*.[104]

Some rural English-language schools offered the bare rudiments. John Smith on la Grande Ligne in St-Athanase in 1831 had only a spelling book and an arithmetic, and Alexander Cooper in the same place taught the three Rs using only Mavor's *Spelling Book* and the New Testament. Such schools were rare. At the other end of the spectrum were the schools in St-Armand on the American border, where the course of study was very similar, not perhaps to that of Boston, but to that of public schools in the state of New York. For the reporting period ending in January 1832, the 'Jones School House' was typical, using 'Goldsmith's Rome; Murray's English Reader & Grammar; Woodbridge's Geography; Walkingame's Arithmetick; Hutton's Book-keeping; Scott's Lessons; Walker's Dictionary; New Testament; and Marshall's Spellg Book.' Some of the other schools substituted Mavor's spelling book or added Lennie's grammar book to the list, while Lucy Henderson in Frelighsburgh did not have an arithmetic book. The books used, *pace* Rector James Reid, were not radically different from those in English or Scottish schools, with the exception of the geography books and the dictionaries. There was no English geography text that covered North America. The dictionaries were somewhat controversial, since English and Scottish residents often detested the whining, nasal 'Yankee' manner of speech and dictionaries offered lessons in pronunciation.[105]

Harriet M. Townsend from Philipsburgh wrote a detailed report of her village school in her fine hand. She wrote that her twenty-five students used 'The Scriptures Murrays Grammar & English Reader Woodbridge's & Goodrich's Geographies & Atlases Tytler's History – Walker's Dictionary. – Intellectual Grammar Thompson's & Walkingame's – Smiths practical & Mental, Arithmetic's – Lothrop's Philosophy. Elementary Geography for Children with Maps Sequel to easy Lessons—Marshall's Spelling Book Holbrook's Easy Lessons in Geometry with a Chart. Church Catechism. The little Philosopher 5 Numbers. – Various other Elementary Books for small Children.' Given such diversity in texts, it is perhaps not surprising that her description of method began: 'No particular System is followed.' She continued: 'The School is opened & closed with Prayer. The elder Pupils study Grammar, Geography, History, Philosophy, Arithmetic, Orthography & Definition, and are exercised in parsing, Reading, Writing, Composition, & Drawing, according as they are advanced in their Education: The younger ones are instructed according to their years & Capacities, in Reading, Writing; Elementary Geography, Philosophy, Geometry, & Arithmetic; Numerical Letters, Catechism &c. – Attention is paid to the formation of their Manners, and much pains taken to instruct them in the Duties of Religion and Morality.' For the same reporting period for the village of Dorchester in Chambly county – perhaps not so prosperous a place as Philipsburgh – Pierre Caisse's report, also written in a handsome hand, gave his books as 'Grammaire française, Arithmétique, Sphère Géographique, Alphabet Testaments, Instruction de Jeunesse.' He had forty-eight students.[106]

Mavor and Murray

Giving lists of books might seem an invidious manner of making a distinction between English- and French-language schools, for they only show French readers being exposed to more works of piety and to fewer works of grammar, arithmetic, geography, and bookkeeping than were English readers. The school reports cited are also overwhelmingly for the school acts of 1829–31, and the lag in supplies of secular reading materials in French-language schools could conceivably have been overcome under the School Act of 1832. It raised the standards for a minimally acceptable teacher to include the teaching of the subjects more common in the English-language schools. There is no evidence to suggest such was the case.

The more germane issue in terms of the politics of schooling and educational government concerns the framing of reading practices – that is, the purposes for which people were to read, the occasions for reading, and the manner in which they were to read, speak, and write. The key differences between *Moyen de sanctifier la journée* and Mavor's spelling book or between *La Neuvaine de St François-Xavier* and *The English Reader* lie in the fact that the English books had a much greater potential to provide access to a print culture in which reading was directed to ends that were secular and practical, while not thereby simply utilitarian – secular, that is, within a generic New Testament conception of moral conduct. They instructed not simply by precept and they offered encouragement for some kinds of silent reading.

Even Mavor's speller provided simple reading lessons and lessons in geography about a secular universe. It was in its 332nd edition by 1826. The *English Reader* owed its enormous popularity (with the *English Grammar*, it was the first million-seller in English after the Bible) in part to its generic approach to Christian morality, but also to a relatively light-handed treatment of issues of good conduct and to considerable variety in reading material. The *Reader* took readers through pieces meant for recitation, through stories, fables, poetry, and pieces that were wryly amusing as well as morally improving. The level of difficulty and sophistication increased as one went through the book, and Murray later published supplements for younger and older readers, such as *An Introduction to the English Reader* and a *Supplement to the English Reader*. The point is that a student in an English-language or mixed English- and French-language school was likely to be exposed to reading that was not narrowly confined to pious purposes. It is true that there were occasional reports of French-language schools using *La Minerve* as reading material, but such a practice was exceptional, and it would be an unusual reader who could move from an abécedaire or *Moyen de sanctifer la journée* to the newspaper's turgid political analysis.

Augmented by Murray's *Grammar,* or by another grammar book, the *Readers* also had the potential to make language itself into an object of analysis for elementary students. And of course, geography and bookkeeping were thoroughly secular subjects. Again, the analysis speaks to possible reading practices and says nothing about who actually read what. Knowing how to read and write and reading and writing are different things; one may know how to ride a bicycle but always travel on foot. Stephen Randal of the Shefford Academy observed in 1838 that almost all adults in the Eastern Townships could read and write, but for all the reading and writing they actually did they might as well have been ignorant. Nonetheless, the numbers of advanced readers, writers, and counters produced by the Township schools were sufficiently large to sustain at least one academy – high school – in each county where, it was claimed, elementary school teachers were trained.[107]

About writing instruction very little information survives in the archive, although the monitorial method of forming letters was used in the cities. In western Europe and north-eastern America, in any case, until the last decades of the nineteenth century writing instruction did not concern composition, but rather the copying of form letters. Only later in the history of liberal government would the notion that the people had something of its own worth expressing take hold.[108]

Two Cultures of Learning

It was argued by Lower Canadian contemporaries and by later historians that the absence of books and good schools in many parishes and seigneuries was caused by the miserable poverty of the *habitants*. I have argued that the extraction of surplus as tithe and rent played a key role in impeding schooling. Yet the experience of Catholic Ireland in the same period gives the lie to simple economic claims and points to the importance as well of cultural tradition. New France had not had a tradition of popular reading. Ireland was perhaps the poorest country in Europe, with a peasantry subjected to exorbitant rents, taxed for the privilege of being dominated by England, and tithed to support the English Church, while also supporting a Catholic clergy. Many sub-sub-tenant families lived in ditches, subsisting on occasional day labour, potatoes, sour milk, and, if they were lucky, a bit of herring, until they starved in 1846–7. Here, however, there was a vibrant culture of literacy and learning, with 'hedge schools' and itinerant schoolmasters able to prepare young men for classical colleges in Europe. When desultory efforts were made to send military relief to the Gaelic west of Ireland in the famine year of 1847, university-educated English lieutenants could only converse with local people in Latin, which they both knew. The best schoolmasters enjoyed regional and even national renown. Indeed the political-educational problem for colonial rulers in Ireland was not one of removing peasant ignorance, but rather of channelling a well-established popular appetite for print culture towards 'useful knowledge' and away from political works, such as William Godwin's *Caleb Williams*, and scandal sheets, such as the *Life of Lady Lucy, daughter of an Irish Lord, who married a general officer and was by him carried into Flanders, where he became jealous of her and a young nobleman, his kinsman, whom he killed, and afterwards left her wounded and big with child in a forest.*[109] The issue in Lower Canada was one of peasant ignorance, where an alliance of state, seigneur, and Catholic Church fed people *Visites au saint-sacrement* and most professionals either did not interfere or participated in a regime of sponsored mobility.

By the 1830s, the English course of study anchored by works such as those of Mavor and Murray was under attack from two main sources. The proponents of monitorial schooling were losing ground, but they had criticized the typical course of study in rural schools for its inefficiency in teaching beginning students to read individually in books. Earlier attacks on the political dangers of giving books to the 'lower orders' had largely faded. But both Andrew Bell and Joseph Lancaster had trumpeted the advantages to be had from teaching students to read from printed cards mounted on the schoolroom walls. Books, which were fragile and expensive, would not be needed to teach to read. Moreover, readers would not be left to their own devices, but would be occupied constantly in reading under supervision. Both idleness and the dangerous and seditious book would remain unknown.

James L. Alexander, the Anglican clergyman whose educational proposals were presented to the Assembly's Standing Committee in 1835–6, called for government to produce a supply of standard schoolbooks. These should not be bound, however, but pasted onto large cards which could be mounted on the front of students' desks. Reading could then be taught using a simultaneous method. Alexander was certainly not opposed to giving advanced readers books; he urged the creation of school lending libraries for 'diffusing a taste for reading and education among the working population.' Rather, he opposed the inefficiency of individual instruction.[110]

By the 1830s, the critique of the Mavor-Murray model had gone beyond such claims of inefficiency to object that it aimed to produce rhetoricians rather than rational readers. English-speaking critics at least from the middle 1820s rejected monitorialism's simplistic and mechanical methods of instruction on the same grounds. The proponents of monitorial schooling and the popular spelling book authors taught to read by the phonic method, which critics said trained readers to hear words as collections of nonsense syllables. Readers became parrots who only read the expository pieces in Murray's books in order to preen in public. They did not read for meaning or sense, nor did they read silently so as to ponder and analyse what they read. Decorative reading was frivolous and useless; it did not provide students with the 'useful knowledge' necessary to make their way in a changing commercial world. Because readers did not read for sense, they could not understand political speeches: political conflict was a failure in reading instruction, and correct methods of reading were at once correct methods for political subjectification.[111]

The pedagogical criticism of eloquence and rhetoric was an ethnic-cultural criticism in the case of Lower Canada, where resources for French-speaking students were skewed towards secondary and tertiary education, while those for English-speaking students tended to be skewed in the opposite direction. The highest levels of study in the classical colleges, patronized largely, but not exclusively, by the French-speaking petty bourgeoisie, reproduced a classical Greco-Roman culture, including some of its republican political ideals. The best-educated French-speaking Lower Canadians outstripped their English-speaking counterparts in classical learning, often by a considerable margin. One dimension of the ethnic-linguistic divide that played itself out more generally in politics and in educational policy was the training that advanced college students received in rhetoric. Mock parliamentary debates were common, and for the rhetorical field, as Marc André Bernier put it, 'the essence of discourse is defined by its effectiveness at mobilizing and its powers of action over emotions ... the art of oratory consists in leading people's wills by stirring up their passions and senses.'[112]

Louis-Joseph Papineau was a recognized master of rhetorical arts, and his honorific, 'L'Orateur,' meant popularly, 'he best able to Speak.' The pedagogical-cultural divide is evident in this area as well. One of Lord Dalhousie's strongest objections to Papineau was that he abused his parliamentary position as speaker to make speeches, rather than following English parliamentary procedure in which the speaker ensured the decorum of the speech of others. Dalhousie claimed that the Lower Canadian Assembly's rhetorical excesses were worsened by the fact that the members broke for dinner at 4 p.m. and marinated themselves in rum punch before debating political questions.[113] While the French-language press and commentators such as Papineau's cousin Jacques Viger offered him kudos for brilliant, hours-long flights of rhetoric, the English-language press usually heard a repetitive windbag who used exaggeration rather than rational argument, who inflamed passions rather than appealing to reason, who preyed on his auditors' senses and pandered to their ignorance.

There was growing criticism in the 1820s and 1830s of the impracticality and expense of the classical course of study. The newer colleges – St-Hyacinthe with a concern to teach physics, Ste-Anne, with a model farm, and L'Assomption, which aimed at a shorter curriculum including commercial subjects – modified the classical course. Under Jean Holmes's tutelage, the Séminaire de Québec also adopted scientific instruction, mathematics, and geography, and students at the Petit Séminaire revolted against strict discipline in 1830.[114] Yet the ethnic-cultural and religious divides sustained rather different conceptions of the nature and substance of good education in the organization of schooling.

The Impasse

The Legislative Assembly, then, had worked seriously to modify, adapt, and improve its rural schools between 1829 and 1836. On paper, many school provisions were on a par with those in other countries grappling with the challenge of the common school. In practice, French-language rural schooling posed little threat to the local dominance of established elites or to the pastoral vision of peasant life promoted by the Catholic Church. Schooling provided few resources for the production of a literate critical citizenry. A huge expenditure of public money had not created a 'taste for education' for the *habitants* to school themselves or to demand that others school them. Had parliament resumed in 1836 with a determination to pursue a reform agenda while promoting 'improvement,' the Legislative Council's demand for boards of education, supported by reform moderates, might have led to a transformation in local educational power relations and instructional practice. The substance of the political demands of the Montreal Constitutional Association also bore a considerable resemblance to those of the left of the *patriote* party. But the vituperative class, religious, and ethnic hatreds bred especially in the Tory press made the association's version of republicanism an extinction of everything *canadien*. Demands for amendments to the 1836 bill were a cynical move by a body which probably knew that parliament would be prorogued before the Assembly could respond. It is unlikely that any contemporary anticipated that the failure of the bill would lead to a six-year hiatus in rural schooling, but so it turned out. One piece of the Assembly's educational project survived the attacks of the Council and the Association: the legislature passed and Lord Gosford sanctioned a Normal School Act. The fate of this legislation forms the substance of the following chapter.

6

The Normal School

British North America's first 'normal school' for teacher training opened in Montreal in July 1837 under the provisions of the 1836 Normal School Act (6 Will. IV, cap.12). Its operations wound up finally in 1844, after the Canada School Act of 1841 omitted teacher training from its provisions. The operations of the Normal School Act and of the Montreal Normal School have attracted little attention in Lower Canadian historiography, apart from an account offered by L.-P. Audet, and with the exception of the European tour of inspection of the abbé Jean Holmes from the Séminaire de Québec. This chapter provides a detailed history of this project for teacher training and school administration.[1]

The Normal School Act passed on 21 March 1836, shortly after the Legislative Council returned the Assembly's elementary school bill with a demand for fundamental amendments.[2] The twenty-first of March 1836 was also the day that Lord Gosford announced the prorogation of parliament, ending its last serious working session before the Rebellion of 1837, the declaration of martial law in the Montreal district, the suspension of the Lower Canadian constitution, and the institution of political dictatorship by governors and their appointed Special Councils. Both funding and administrative provision for rural elementary schooling ceased on 1 May 1836, and no new legislative provision was made before the reorganization of the colonial state and the passage of the 1841 School Act. The Normal School Act was thus in operation over the course of the six-year period in which there were no publicly supported rural elementary schools in the colony.

Normal schools were to be funded in Quebec and Montreal, but the Quebec school never opened. The Montreal Normal School failed miserably, despite a considerable amount of effort and the expenditure of almost £3,450 of public money. Only one person completed the planned three-year course and only a few of the nineteen male candidate teachers who attended for some period were certified as fit to teach by the school's board of directors. Four female candidate teachers, of the eleven whose tuition was subsidized by the Montreal board in the house of the Soeurs de la Congrégation de Notre Dame, also received teachers' certificates, although none completed the full three-year course envisioned by the law.

The Normal School Act and the school management boards organized under it were both at the centre of a political storm. Three of the ten members of the Montreal board, including its president and secretary, fled the colony in 1837 under charges of high treason. The conduct of the Montreal school was detailed meticulously by its treasurer, and later secretary, the statistician and first mayor of the city, Jacques Viger. A man of rectitude and exactitude, Viger continued to support the school and to agitate for its continued support, even when faced with unmistakable evidence of its futility. Thus the school's history speaks to the end of a particular educational regime in the colony, in which lavish expenditure in the absence of rigorous administration allowed an intellectual elite to dream of enlightening 'the people' without actually risking such an event. The Anglican Church, in control of the Royal Institution for the Advancement of Learning, had dreamt this dream in the period before 1830. French-Canadian moderates such as Viger, with his republican fellow board members, continued to dream it in the decade of the 1830s. Certainly against Whiggish accounts of educational progress, the 1836 Normal School Act is a peculiarity.

Anticipations

There had been repeated calls in Lower Canada in the press and in the Assembly for the creation of normal schools in the 1830s and earlier. Indeed in 1820 *Le Canadien* had run a 'political catechism' by 'Un Vieux Chrétien,' who attributed the lack of parish schools to the ignorance of teachers and called for special institutions to educate them on the level of notaries or professional soldiers. The urban monitorial schools had claimed to train teachers from the outset, and the issue of normal schools was raised in the press at more length as the 1829 School Act came into operation. One of the rare extended newspaper discussions of pedagogy was occasioned by a short-lived debate between Joseph Lancaster and the French immigrant Chevalier N. Lemoult over the relative merits of monitorial schooling and J.-J. Jacotot's 'universal method.' Lemoult briefly taught a school at St-Marc and advertised that his former school in Louvain had been made an official Normal School. He planned to open a normal school in Lower Canada and was advertising with a colleague that he would train teachers in Montreal in 1830–1.[3]

Ludger Duvernay's *La Minerve* called for teacher training in November 1831 and suggested that, if necessary, people able to teach teachers should be recruited abroad. The suggestion was followed in short order by the publication of Amury Girod's plan for a rural model farm and normal school on the Swiss model of de Fellenberg's Höfwyl school, which he had attended. The *Vindicator* was enthusiastic, commenting that 'the benefit of such cannot be to[o] highly appreciated here, when some of the Masters employed under the bounty of the Legislature are not found to be most learned, but such as could be obtained most readily.' We have seen that this attempt at teacher training quickly failed, but about the same time the Assembly began offering bonuses of up to £50 a year to the monitorial school societies to train teachers. Again in 1834, Neilson's *Quebec Gazette* had commented on reports of illiterate teachers at work and emphasized that it was 'high time this evil was remedied, and perhaps one of the most efficient means of doing so would be the establishment of one or two normal schools in the Province, at which all Teachers would be required by law to qualify themselves, and to obtain certificates of this qualification from the directors of the Academy, and from a board of examiners, by law appointed for that purpose.' Neilson reproduced material on the subject from Governor Macy in New York State. The same year, Mrs M. Blackwood sought government support for her Montreal private school so that she could 'afford a solid and ornamental Education to such young females as may be under the necessity of Teaching and who have not the means of acquiring, in any other way, an Education to enable them' to do so.[4]

The academies of the Eastern Townships also claimed to offer teacher training. In seeking legislative aid for Stanstead and Hatley Academies in 1830, Ebenezer Peck told John Neilson that the Stanstead school was 'to prepare males and females to become instructors, to elementary schools, to avoid the necessity of sending to the U.S. for instructors.' Jewell Foster petitioned Lord Aylmer for aid for the Shefford Academy in 1835, reporting that people in the county used to be forced to find teachers in the United States, 'but by means of the Shefford High School ... twenty five youth have been qualified to take charge of our Elementary Schools and fourteen have been successfully engaged in this business.'[5] Finally, several of the MPP school visitors examined by the 1835–6 Standing Committee on Education urged the establishment of normal schools.

The Normal School Act

The Normal School Act appropriated the enormous sum of £5,370cy. each for the establishment and operation over a five-year period of normal schools in Quebec and Montreal. The Quebec Normal School Board was authorized to draw an extra £360 a year to fund tuition for boarders with the Ursulines in Trois-Rivières. The money was to support an international investigation to determine best normal school practice, the acquisition of necessary school apparatus, and the recruitment of normal schoolmasters. It included funds for the masters' salaries, of whom it was intended there be six. In addition, the money was to buy or rent school buildings, for heating and lighting, furniture and school supplies, and household furnishings and lodging for the normal schoolmasters. It was anticipated that each normal school would also organize and run a model elementary school for practice teaching. The allocation included funds to subsidize tuition in the normal schools and board and lodging during the first three years of the act's operation for five male student teachers unable to pay for their own training. A similar subsidy was offered for a number of female students in women religious' houses in Quebec, Montreal, and Trois-Rivières.

The normal schools were to be managed by ten-member boards elected by leading clergymen of various denominations, college teachers, mayors, judges, the Speaker of the Assembly, and Legislative and Executive Councillors for the districts in which they were located. Teacher candidates were to be admitted upon proof of moral character and sufficient basic educational achievement, especially through the recommendation of a Normal School elector. Free tuition in the schools for the planned three-year course of instruction was offered to candidates on condition of a legally binding commitment to teach in an elementary or superior school for at least five years upon graduation. Established teachers wishing to upgrade their qualifications were to be admitted with the requisite certificates of character and morality at their own expense. Normal school graduates could be certified by the board as fit to teach in any elementary or superior school in the colony. They were to have preference in hiring decisions.

The Politics of the Normal School Act

The Normal School Act made sense as a workable legislative initiative only in tandem with the failed 1836 School Bill. Both initiatives resulted from the extensive and sometimes acrimonious investigations of the operation of the Trustees' School Act of 1829, conducted by the Standing Committee on Education in 1835 and early 1836 and examined in an earlier chapter.[6] The 1836 School Bill proposed the creation of a hierarchy of elementary schools and offered locally elected trustees the possibility of raising local school funds through taxation. With the normal school bill and a bill to organize permanent funding for colleges and academies, the elementary school bill was introduced to the Assembly on 25 January 1836, debated, and then engrossed and sent to the Council on 18 February. The normal school bill had been sent up on 16 February.[7] Given that Council refused the school bill, it is surprising that the Normal School Act was passed, received royal sanction, and became law.

Normal schools had been mentioned favourably by several witnesses at the Assembly's special committee proceedings, and the schools figured prominently in elementary educational organization in the New England states, in England, Ireland, Scotland, France, Switzerland, and Prussia. They also had vocal opponents. On the one hand, to anti-statist liberals as well as to some members of the Catholic clergy, their Prussian pedigree made them reek of the police state – the terms in which Joseph-François Perrault's Guizot-inspired draft school legislation was denounced in the press and by the Catholic bishops earlier in the 1830s. In the Lower Canadian setting, they seemed also to threaten to promote sectarian religious and factional political domination.

Catholic Bishop Signäy of Quebec was not alarmed by the provisions of the 1836 Act, probably because two leading members of his clergy, Jean Holmes and Jérôme Demers from the Séminaire de Québec, had a hand in designing it. As well, given the specification of the franchise for the school board election, and the close relations between Signäy and Hector S. Huot, it was possible for the former safely to predict that moderate Catholic electors would control the board.

By contrast, J.-J. Lartigue in Montreal vehemently opposed the legislation, and it seemed at first that the district's Catholic clergy would boycott the normal school board elections because of having to sit with Protestant clergymen. H.-S. Huot wrote to Montreal mayor Jacques Viger that he had been chagrined to learn 'that several individuals in your Clergy do not wish to participate in the Election of the Committee because protestant Ministers are allowed to take part.' By contrast, he wrote, 'Our Quebec Priests do not make such a fuss and all mean to be present,' and in any case it was not necessary for the electors to vote for clergymen: laymen could serve on the boards. Viger initially feared the outcome of the elections would ensure the failure of the Montreal school.[8]

Bishop Lartigue tried valiantly to block the Normal School Act in the legislature. He corresponded at length with a variety of participants in the project in an effort to prevent it or, when it became clear that the project was to go forward, to urge caution in its administration. He tried to convince Bishop Signäy's co-adjutor, P.-F. Turgeon, to resist the scheme, which Turgeon and Signäy seemed to support, by sending him a supposed statistical proof that Catholics would soon be in a minority on the Montreal Normal School Board. Montreal, he complained, was swarming with Protestant ministers of all descriptions and the Scots were poking their noses into his business. One can imagine the alarm of the patriarchal, pastoral, celibate Lartigue at the prospect of those Protestant clergymen training teachers for Catholic parishes. The Normal School Board electors would include not only the Presbyterian Henry Esson, who slept with women (at least one) and who openly supported democratic elections to his presbytery, but also Baptists such as Newton Bosworth. The latter, author of the well-known inventory work *Hochelaga Depicta*, belonged to a sect in which there was little distinction between clergy and laity and in some varieties of which it was expected that both men and women would profess their gifts in church. Bosworth's daughter was running a school in her father's house, where she taught young men and women together in both languages: all extremely alarming for an ultramontane cleric.[9]

Lartigue argued that the bill would grant £2,000 more to Protestants than to Catholics and the Assembly ought first to experiment with two completely separate normal schools, one for each denomination. That tactic would generate a healthy competition in the interests of education, but if joint training of Catholic and Protestants in a normal school proceeded, he warned 'it is likely that soon, as Catholics, we will be obliged warn off our young people from these schools by refusing them the sacraments, at least in Montreal.' After the bill passed the Assembly, he complained that just as the 1829 School Act had taken away control over elementary schooling from the clergy and placed it in lay hands, so the Normal School Act would give away the clergy's influence on teacher training, all in keeping with the schemes of his radical cousin, the Speaker of the Assembly. He urged Signäy to insist when the bill came before the Executive Council that it would never work because Catholics and Protestants would be unable to agree on rules for management of the schools. These protests had little effect on the Quebec bishops, and Lartigue ended up participating in the Montreal board elections.[10]

Still, in keeping with his pastoralist vision, Lartigue claimed to cousin Jacques Viger that an urban normal school would be a breeding ground for moral corruption, especially for children and young people from the countryside. Once corrupted, they would introduce vicious urban habits on their return to the country as teachers. Anyway, most apt candidates for training would be unable pay for urban room and board and so the schools would not be able to recruit students. To forestall both outcomes, the Normal School Board in Montreal should establish a boarding house for Catholic students, supervised by the school's principal and administered by someone named by the bishop. Indeed, urged Lartigue, the board should purchase a house for the purpose on the corner of St Denis and Mignon Streets, which was available for £250, and deed it to the Church.[11] The Montreal board did come to insist that Catholic students be boarders while Protestant students would be day students.

There was also widespread Protestant opposition to the normal school legislation in draft and there was agitation to have it refused sanction once it had passed. The engrossed bill was referred to Attorney General C.R. Ogden for his opinion as to its legality. While offering no strictly legal objections, Ogden urged Lord Gosford to proceed 'with great caution' given that the colony was a 'community composed of very heterogeneous materials, wherein a diversity of religious opinions naturally exist, and wherein every legislative enactment connected with Education' was likely to 'compromise or promote far greater interests' than those simply of instruction. Education was something that must benefit all members of the community, he observed, but the provisions for the normal school elections in the bill meant Catholic control. He put it more delicately, but the thrust was the same: 'It is much to be apprehended that Religious opinions of a distinctive character will inevitably influence the operations and possibly counteract the benefits which may be expected from institutions in themselves unexceptionable.' Ogden called for amendments to ensure equal treatment of Protestants.[12]

Petitions circulated against the bill in Quebec and Montreal. That from Quebec bore the signatures of leading Protestants, mainly English-speaking citizens and politicians from the Constitutional Association, starting with John Neilson and the Legislative Councillor T.A. Young. The bill, they complained was 'vicious in principle … and in practice as virtually conferring undue advantages on the Religious denomination which might happen to have the majority in the said Committees of Management and would tend to spread religious dissentions.' The power of the normal school boards to grant teaching certificates would prevent parents from choosing the teachers, paid out of public funds, who were to educate their children, and it would also discourage many able teachers. The petitioners urged Lord Gosford to reserve the bill.[13]

The Tory press echoed these objections. 'A Citizen' writing in the *Quebec Mercury*, for instance, listed those eligible to vote in the normal school elections, concluding, 'thus the *elective body* of the Committee of Management consists of at least thirty-seven of one denomination (subject to increase), and *eight* of the other.' The consequence, observed the editor of the *Montreal Gazette*, was that the 'schools are placed too much under the control of one class, to the prejudice of the other, and that as the nominees from the Normal School are to enjoy a preference over all other candidates for a Government School, an undue influence will thus be given to that class over the general education of the whole District.' If the role of MPPs as school visitors with extensive powers over teachers' certification was continued, as the school bill had anticipated, the Normal School Act would be a thoroughly political instrument. Religious denomination, for the editor, was a proxy for political opinion.[14] It is strikingly ironic that Tory opinion sought non-denominational schooling in this case against the *patriote* majority and opposed the bill as bureaucratic interference with the liberties of parents.

Given such widespread opposition to the bill among the anglophone Protestant elite, its passage by the Legislative Council is surprising. Why the Council did not simply return it for amendment, as it did with the elementary school bill, remains to be explained. Perhaps the councillors thought that once they had returned the school bill the Normal School Act would be a dead letter. Or perhaps in the flurry of legislation at the end of the session and amid the intensely heated emotions surrounding the attempts to produce support for a Civil List, the normal school bill did not attract much serious study. Perhaps, finally, it was expected that Gosford's Executive Council would make him reserve the bill.

Still, despite vehement and violent denunciations of him by leaders of the *patriote* party for not intervening in parliament to ensure passage of the elementary school bill (which he scarcely could have done), Lord Gosford sanctioned the Normal School Act. In this he demonstrated, not for the first time, that he was following his official instructions not to disturb the autonomy of the colonial legislature except in matters that directly affected the foreign policy of Great Britain, which is precisely what at other times the Papineau clique demanded of him. The bill had passed both houses of the legislature and there were no foreign policy matters at issue. Justifying his support of the act at length to the colonial secretary, Gosford detailed C.R. Ogden's reservations and described the opposition of the Protestants of Quebec, a copy of whose petition he enclosed. Perhaps because religious denomination was used by the act's opponents as a code word for the feared domination of a politically radical, ethnically distinct majority, Gosford was able to treat the issue as one of religious sectarianism. 'Although unfortunately divided by political differences,' he wrote, in contrast to his native Ireland, 'the Inhabitants of this Province are still happily undisturbed by the slightest disagreement of a Religious nature.' Had he reserved the bill, he would have incited sectarian division, while the absence of serious sectarian struggles encouraged him 'to hope that whatever might be the composition of the Committees of Management[,] their conduct would be marked by that spirit of liberality so necessary to ensure success to the important & beneficial object which the Bill is intended to promote.' For Gosford in any case, the colonial population was Catholic by a large majority; by rights the majority should govern its own institutions.[15]

The Normal School Board Elections

There was rapid advance planning for the board elections as the bill was still in the Legislative Council. H.-S. Huot, who was organizing the Quebec elections, was particularly eager for the normal school project to succeed, and well before the bill passed he was urging Mayor Jacques Viger in Montreal to move quickly in concert with his Quebec counterparts to set the schools in motion. The *patriote* MPP J.-J. Girouard similarly wrote to Viger within days of the act's passage, urging him to convene the board electors at once, before the winter roads deteriorated. Girouard promised to attend to ensure that there was a Catholic majority on the board.[16] Again, Jean Holmes, already planning his European and American tour before the school boards which were to appoint him had been formed, argued that the elections would go well for the reform and *patriote* faction 'if we co-ordinate our business ahead of time, and so it must be to prevent the [Protestant] ministers from claiming victory.'[17]

In Quebec on 8 April 1836, after some initial attempts by the Legislative Councillor James Stuart to ridicule the election by calling on the bishops simply to name the board, and over objections to election by ballot from the Constitutionalist MPP J.G. Clapham, the thirty electors chose a relatively conservative, mixed clerical and lay Normal School Board. The Anglican Archdeacon Mountain sat with the Quebec curé Baillargeon and the abbé Jean Holmes. The moderate reformers H.-S. Huot, E.-A. Caron, and George Vanfelson and the more radical L.-T. Besserer were in office alongside the sempiternal civil servant Dominick Daly, the moderate Constitutionalist John Neilson, and his more conservative colleague T.A. Stayner. When the board met to elect its officers, Stayner immediately resigned. By H.-S. Huot's account, the Protestant electors voted only for Protestant candidates, while the Catholic majority did not vote along religious lines. The board chose Mayor Caron as president, with Neilson as vice-president, Huot as secretary, and Daly as treasurer.[18]

The Quebec board then took two serious initiatives. First, it attempted to supply the Ursulines in Quebec with female candidate teachers. It is not clear how many girls or young women actually trained in this way. There were twenty applications in response to a call from the Quebec board in May 1836, of whom five were accepted, but two of those declined to enrol. Another call for applications for a single place in the summer of 1838 ran in the press, apparently unanswered, for several weeks.[19] More important, the Quebec board formally commissioned Jean Holmes to undertake a tour of America and Europe for normal school purposes and it prepared his instructions.

The instructions were drafted by John Neilson and Holmes himself. Holmes was not to spend more than £400, including all his own costs in purchasing supplies. The board wanted him to hire two principal teachers, and, ideally, despite the mention of a chief professor in the act, the two were to be of equal status. If Holmes found that one candidate insisted on being chief instructor, the choice was not to be made on grounds of nationality or religion. The £600 appropriated for salaries should leave enough to hire assistant teachers, but if Holmes could recruit a really eminent teacher the board would leave aside the matter of assistants for the moment. More formally, Holmes was to 'get acquainted with the State of Elementary Instruction, the distribution of School-Houses, Methods of teaching recommended for their practical utility, punishments, and encouragements for pupils and teachers, rules followed by the Managers of superior and common Schools, particularly in places or countries where a diversity of religious creeds prevails, opinions entertained of Lancasterian and mutual Instruction Systems &c.'[20]

The board elections in the Montreal district, the centre of *patriote* agitation, were heavily politicized. Jacques Viger, who was responsible as mayor for convening the electors, in his usual fascination with inventory making, kept a detailed nominal list of candidates, electors, and their choices of candidates (no secret ballot here). In a revealing chart, Viger distinguished a *canadien* and an English electoral slate. Each of the thirty-nine electors had ten votes to divide among the twenty-eight candidates who stood, and nine of the ten men elected were from Viger's *canadien* list, the exception being the French Canadian F.-A. Quesnel on the English ticket. The sixteen *patriote* MPPs and Viger himself voted the straight *canadien* ticket, with the exception of Robert Nelson and John Pickel, who excluded the clerical candidates. Interestingly, Viger placed Bishop Lartigue on the 'English' ticket, although the bishop himself voted the *canadien* line. Viger and the clerical candidates, the Irish priest Patrick Phelan from the Recollet school (who was not present) and the Presbyterian minister Henry Esson, were well ahead of the other candidates: indeed, Viger, who did not vote for himself, received thirty-seven of thirty-eight possible votes, with only the Legislative Councillor Pierre de Rochblave not supporting him. In the first round of balloting, in addition to the three just named, the successful candidates were L.-J. Papineau; James Leslie; the Vicar General P. Viau; Dr O'Callaghan, MPP and editor of the *Vindicator*; and F.-A. Quesnel. There was a four-way tie for the last two places among the MPPs T.S. Brown and Jacob DeWitt, the Anglican Rev. John Bethune, and the Tory Legislative Councillor Peter McGill, chair of the Council committee which had refused the 1836 School Bill. Brown and DeWitt were returned in the second round.[21]

The Montreal Normal School Board was thus overwhelmingly composed of men with reform tendencies, and the *patriote* party leadership, with the support of any one other member, was placed to determine the board's practice. The board assembled at Papineau's house in rue St-Denis on 12 April 1836 and elected its officers: Papineau as president, Quesnel as vice-president, Brown as secretary, and Viger as treasurer.[22] Dominick Daly agreed to act as the board's financial officer in Quebec, a second direct link between the two normal school boards.

The first order of business in Montreal was drafting instructions to Jean Holmes. These resembled those provided to him in Quebec, with a greater degree of urgency. The Montreal board wanted him to provide teachers and books for the school but argued that it was both quicker and more just to find qualified teachers in the colony. If Holmes thought this was not possible, he was to do his best to find an American teacher by visiting Harvard and Yale colleges and other institutions. The board wished to know at once if he found an American candidate, although it agreed that he might wish to examine European normal schools before making a decision. He was to buy good schoolbooks in New York or Boston and to ship them to Secretary Brown as soon as he could. The board took immediate steps to get a warrant for the £650 appropriated by the act for these purposes, although only £400 was actually granted.[23]

Jean Holmes's Educational Tour

English-Canadian educational historiography, including my own past contributions, has tended to see Egerton Ryerson's 1846 *Report on a*

System of Public Elementary Instruction for Upper Canada as the pioneer text for Canadian explorations of international education – excluding Thaddeus Osgood's tour in the 1810s. Jean Holmes anticipated Ryerson by a decade, even to the point of importing a set of Irish National schoolbooks. His letters to his employers, although not collected in the form of a report, were widely publicized in the English- and French-language press and certainly exposed leaders of the *patriote* party to European and American experience and innovation.

Jean Holmes left Quebec on 12 May 1836, visited institutions at Albany, New York, Andover, Boston, Hartford, and New Haven, and then sailed to Europe about 9 June, returning to Canada in the fall of 1837.[24] He travelled in Europe with three young Canadian men, Elzéar-Alexandre Taschereau, David Ross, and Joseph-Octave Fortier, whose parents probably sent them along to be 'finished' with Holmes as chaperon. He was also charged with attempting to resolve some matters concerning the Séminaire de Québec with the English government, and with finding apparatus for the Lower Canadian Catholic colleges.

In the United States, the Andover Academy particularly impressed Holmes, and he shipped a large case of educational documents and reports back to the normal school boards, including a digest of Victor Cousin's report on Prussian schools and a critical pamphlet on the Lancasterian system of instruction. He saw nothing that altered his determination to tour European institutions before hiring masters.[25]

Debarking at Liverpool in July 1836, he visited Manchester and Oxford before presenting his letter of introduction from Lord Gosford to Lord Glenelg in the Colonial Office, as well as a petition from the Séminaire de Québec concerning property lost during the Conquest. Glenelg arranged for Lord Palmerston to provide Holmes with official letters of introduction to European government officials, letters that earned him an immediate interview with Victor Cousin in Paris, official notices of his search for normal schoolmasters in the French government gazette, and immediate access to normal schools at Melun and Versailles.[26] The announcements in the gazette produced a deluge of applications, and so Holmes decided optimistically in mid-October to return to Britain to seek English-speaking masters. He toured Scottish schools and interviewed potential candidates before visiting the schools of the Irish National Commissioners, then returning to winter in Paris and to tour France and Switzerland.

Holmes's report of 21 December 1836 created a great deal of enthusiasm in Lower Canada. The press seemed to believe (as the Gosford

Commission had also just reported) that the mixed Protestant and
Catholic education commission in Ireland was a success, and that the
teaching methods used in Ireland and Scotland went beyond the mutual
or monitorial system. Holmes revealed that he had engaged Andrew
Findlater, a graduate of St Andrews, as normal schoolmaster and hoped
soon to hire a second Scot, A. Shand. He expected no difficulty in finding two French-language masters, and so, commented *Le Canadien*, 'we
can expect the Teachers for our normal schools at the opening of navigation next spring.'[27]

Unacceptable to any Republican

However, writing again to T.S. Brown from Paris on 14 March 1837,
Holmes revealed that only Findlater had in fact signed an employment
agreement, although he expected Shand to do the same, and he was still
waiting on French masters. He had toured a number of normal schools,
including those at Versailles, Melon, and Paris with Findlater in tow.
Holmes was surprised to discover a France rich in colleges, academies,
lycées, and military and medical schools, yet impoverished in elementary
schooling. 'Nothing more simple, nothing more basic,' as he put it, 'than
the country schools; nothing more transient than the so-called schools
d'instruction primaire supérieure.' The problem was that the schoolteachers
were usually transient college or academy graduates who were more interested in stunning visitors and baffling their poor students with big
words than they were in teaching. The countryside was economically
backwards in comparison to England, and the French themselves declared that they set no educational example for others. Holmes wrote,
'they point me to Germany, Switzerland, America.'[28]

Holmes frequently visited and consulted with Victor Cousin in Paris
and reported that Cousin was thoroughly dissatisfied with French schools,
going so far as to insist that it reflected badly on the national character
that Frenchmen were not willing to undertake the arduous duties of the
elementary schoolteacher. For T.S. Brown's consumption as well, Holmes
described Cousin's opposition to monitorial schooling at length:

> According to M. Cousin the lancasterian method is the worst – succeeding
> only when modified to the point of retaining the name only, that is to say,
> only when the monitor has the qualifications of a real teacher – does nothing
> more in comparison to students who, beyond what he calls the *mummery* of
> the circles, receive special lessons from the main teacher ... is not at all suited

to convey principles of religion or morality – finally, for French children above all, comprises a source of insubordination, frivolity and distraction.

The nub was, as Holmes quoted Cousin directly, "'in New England, as in Germany and Holland, this teaching is discredited. *I could not imagine that any republican would endorse it.*"'[29]

The other important piece of news from Holmes was that he had made a preliminary agreement with a French normal schoolmaster, François-Joseph-Victor Regnaud, former director of the Montbrison Normal School, and a man recommended in the warmest terms by local and national educational officials. Although Regnaud seemed exactly what was sought, Holmes proposed to interview him before finalizing his employment contract. In any case, Findlater and Regnaud were intended for Montreal, where they thought they would prefer the climate, and Holmes urged the Montreal board to take initial steps towards the acquisition of a school building.

Writing again on 15 April, Holmes told Brown that it was a good thing he had waited to examine Regnaud personally before contracting with him, because he could not teach some branches of study specified in the Normal School Act. He was competent to teach reading, writing, grammar, and composition in French, history, geography, arithmetic, bookkeeping, geometry, linear drawing and blueprinting, morality, and pedagogy. And he agreed to take charge of the Catholic boarding house. But he was not able to offer the other branches specified in the Normal School Act: mechanics, chemistry, natural history, agriculture and horticulture, public law, or the most important – religious instruction. To satisfy the letter of the law, the board would have to hire an assistant teacher, and Holmes lowered the terms of his offers to both Findlater and Regnaud to allow some funds for that purpose.

Holmes offered Brown a set of recommendations with respect to the organization and management of the Montreal school on the basis of his observation of best practice elsewhere. The board should find a large site in a suburban location which should include a garden and a gymnastics ground. Regnaud was not going to bring his family with him at first, so he would take an apartment in the school. There should be a careful examination of all candidate students by a special commission; none should be taken at the outset who was not clearly fit for elementary teaching, and all must have impeccable references. The money available for subsidized tuition and board should be divided in such a way that candidate teachers would compete for quarter, half, and full bursaries. Protestant students should be day students, but subject to strict supervision, while the Catholic students must be boarders. All students were to attend religious services on Sundays and religious holidays, and school vacations were to be co-ordinated with those in the colony's colleges. Apparently, Holmes expected college graduates to apply to enter the normal school at the end of their course and vacation. The main lessons should be offered simultaneously in both languages. As the school progressed, there should be one or two primary day schools and an adult evening school for practice teaching. Finally, the board should not accept students at age fourteen, as the law allowed, but rather at sixteen or seventeen, 'so that they might be put in charge of elementary schools upon leaving the normal schools, and so that the expenses of which they are the cause might sooner be repaid to the country.'[30]

Brown was invited to pass Holmes's letter on to the Quebec Normal School Board, with the information that he had hired an English teacher for them, Mr Shand, and that he was about to contract with a Monsieur Guertin from the normal school in Laval as their French teacher. In a letter of the following day addressed to Jacques Viger with respect to his engagements with Findlater and Regnaud, Holmes was succinct: 'Here are two teachers: a stout Scot and a stout Frenchman – and thus you may begin the great work.'[31] Holmes was busy at the same time arranging with London book, map, and mathematical instrument dealers for normal school apparatus, including twenty-six copies of the Irish National third, fourth, and fifth readers.[32] He wished to have this material shipped and to have the Montreal masters embark for Lower Canada at the same moment.

The Effects of Papineau's 'Disastrous System of Intimidation'

While matters seemed to be settled for the Montreal school, Holmes proved unable to find anyone willing to come to Quebec. The difficulty was apparent soon after he arrived in England. As he put it to John Neilson's son Samuel, 'Books and apparatus abound every where but the *rare aves* are teachers duly qualified and disposed to take charge of these institutions. As yet I have only met with *one* whom I can recommend, the others I am in search of.'[33] By the end of July 1837, he had abandoned the attempt: 'The refusal of the Assistant Director of the Dijon Normal school is the last that I plan to endure from a European teacher.'[34] The Quebec board would have to find its teachers locally, or take the first successful graduates of the Montreal school.

The news of Holmes's failure to find teachers for Quebec was greeted with anger and bitterness. Étienne Parent's *Le Canadien* blasted Papineau's political agitation for costing Quebec its school: 'The disastrous system of intimidation and semblance of resistance established by Papineau bears its fruit for the institutions likely to contribute the most to our country's future. The venerable messire Holmes, who is in Europe to select teachers for our normal schools, could convince no master to come to Canada for the Quebec district. All refused to come, given the rumours of revolution that have been circulating.'[35]

Still, Holmes considered that he had accumulated an important body of information about educational matters, and his meetings and school visits in the cantons of Geneva and Lausanne had been particularly instructive. In the former, he noted, 'everyone here knows how to read, write, and use numbers,' despite the fact that there was no compulsory attendance law. It was 'the happy necessity of needing at least to read & write in order to accede even to the pettiest respectable job, & even to make a decent living' which did the trick. In Geneva, the monitorial system was the preferred teaching method, but Holmes was struck by how long students stayed in school to learn very little. In Lausanne, by contrast, officials expressed 'a decided opposition to mutual schools.' The director of the Lausanne Normal School, M. Gauthey, agreed that the method might be necessary where one teacher was faced with many students, but in general it was fit only for memory work and not for the development of reason. Gauthey told Holmes, '"We first greeted that method with enthusiasm; today we want no more of it, while our neighbours across the lake sing its praises to the heavens."' Observation showed, however, that Lausanne was the more educationally advanced of the cantons. Monitorial pedagogy would not be adopted in the Canadian normal schools. Holmes ended this, his last long epistle from Europe, with a lengthy argument for the necessity of having separate normal schools for students from different religious denominations. He announced his eager intention to return home, 'despite the dark clouds that cover our political horizon.'[36]

Launching the Montreal Normal School

Hearing from Jean Holmes that two teachers had been hired, the Montreal Normal School Board contracted with Charles Tait, executor of the MacKenzie estate, for the rent of a house. Situated at the corner of St-Antoine and Cemetery Streets, the house was a three-storey stone building with outbuildings and privies standing on large fenced grounds, but it was empty and dilapidated.[37] Andrew Findlater and F.-J.-V. Regnaud arrived in the city early in June 1837. The board's attempt to have their salaries commence from the moment they were engaged in Europe was rejected by the civil secretary and the inspector general, who argued that their pay began when the normal school was in operation. Hence, despite the fact that repairs to the house were underway and that there were no students, the normal school was declared to be open on 8 July 1837.

At least £100cy. was spent to equip the house as a residence for the two masters and potential boarders. Montreal retail merchants enjoyed orders for good-quality bedroom, toilet, and dining room furniture, bedding, linens, cutlery, pots and pans, candles, and brooms and brushes, while Alphonsine Voyez earned £1.2s.10d. for scrubbing out the house and making pillow cases, curtains, and towels. The windows were glazed, locks replaced, and keys furnished, and a local sawyer cut, split, and piled twenty cords of firewood. The construction of a tree-lined promenade on the school grounds was planned.[38]

The Montreal radical press carried a call for applications to the school on 8 July 1837. The school was open for 'the reception and instruction, free of expense, of such young persons above the age of fourteen years, who can read and write, and are acquainted with the elements of Arithmetic, and can produce testimonials of a good moral character, who may be willing to devote themselves to teach either primary or superior Schools, and also of such Schoolmasters as may wish to complete their studies, and to obtain instruction in the best method of teaching and of conducting a School.'[39] A number of applications were received and the school opened formally on 5 September 1837.

Likely in preparation for the reception of students, F.-J.-V. Regnaud produced a rough set of regulations for the examination of candidates for admission, for the day-to-day operations of the school, and for the conduct of both day and boarding students. Candidates were to be at least fourteen years of age and were to present certificates of good conduct from their curé or minister, a magistrate, and a militia officer. Candidates would be examined rigorously to determine their mastery, in their native language, of reading, writing, and the elements of arithmetic, as well as religious knowledge. But the examiners would not limit themselves to matters of technical knowledge, probing also 'the candidates' propensities, their characters, their levels of intelligence and ability.' Aid would be offered for poor students, but no one was to be subsidized who did not give a firm written guarantee to teach for at least five years upon completion of their studies. All were to offer guarantees at the outset that they would repay their boarding money should they quit

before completing their studies. The boarders were to bring their own
bedding and clothing. The course of study was for three years, although
those who demonstrated teaching ability could be certified before the
expiration of that period.[40]

The planned normal school day was to begin at 5 a.m. in summer and
at 5:30 a.m. in winter and to end at 9 p.m. Boarders would rise, wash,
dress, and assemble, with the students taking turns reciting the morning
prayer. They would then study until taking their breakfast at 8:30, and
classes would begin at 9:00. Dinner and a recreation period were from
noon to 2:00, with afternoon classes following until 5:00 p.m. A second
study period from 6:00 to 7:30 was followed by supper and a recreation
period. Students were to be in bed by 9:00 p.m.

The students were to observe principles of decency and to be absolutely silent in the dormitory. They were to rise as soon as the signal was
given, to keep their clothes and persons clean, and not to stand in the
windows in view of the street. Communication among the students in the
schoolroom was forbidden, and they were not to bring in any material
not shown to and approved by their teacher; in particular, no 'bad books'
were to be used. They could enter and leave only with the teacher's permission. Regnaud planned as well to adopt the practices of continuous
evaluation of the students and of competition among them for places:
'The marks which each student has earned for its work and its conduct
are entered each day in a journal which the masters will deliver to the
Director at the end of the day. Similarly on Saturday evening they will
give him their summary marks for the week, to which they will append
their observations.'

In addition to insisting that all students proceed to Sunday religious
service as a group with one of the masters, and that religious and moral
failings could lead to expulsion, Regnaud drafted rules for conduct on
the school grounds during recreation periods and off the school grounds
for those given permission to leave the school on holidays. No behaviour
that might cause damage to property was permitted, and on the school
grounds there was to be no fighting, unruliness, gross language, or card
games. Politeness and good manners were to be observed towards the
masters, and there were to be no visitors without permission. Those allowed off the school grounds were to avoid bars, cafés, and pool halls,
and any conduct calling the institution into disrepute would lead to expulsion. Sleeping outside the institution was grounds for expulsion as
well.[41] None of this material seems to have been printed, which is an
indication of the ephemerality of the normal school project.

The Fiasco Begins

With a well-furnished house and grounds; select European-trained teachers; a large selection of the best available schoolbooks, maps, charts, and mathematical instruments; and a planned course of study, timetable, and internal rules and regulations, operations were poised to begin in the normal school at the end of the summer of 1837. However, the planning, public expense, and work that went into organizing, launching, and running the school proved to be largely useless. There were hardly any students. So rare were applicants for places that the board seems to have decided to accept whom it could get in an effort to make the school viable. Three students were present when operations began on 5 September 1837, and on 10 October enrolment reached its high point over the course of the school's five-year existence – six students. However, one of these – twenty-four-year-old Charles Rolland from Berthier, the only normal school student actually to attend the institution at his own expense – quit after five days, finding the course of instruction too difficult.

Findlater and Regnaud attempted to follow the plan of evaluating students daily; at least for a brief period they kept a few rough sheets on which the students were ranked, but the practice seems to have been abandoned quickly. As they both admitted in 1840 in response to an inquiry from the governor, Poulett Thomson,

> Respecting the Regulations of the Institution, and the Method of Instruction, nothing can be said. The Professors were to be allowed, in the first instance, to endeavour to adapt the most improved methods of instruction to the peculiar circumstances of the pupils; and the Committee proposed, by sanctioning from time to time, such of those plans and modifications as were found to work well, to form by degrees something like a regular system; but as there have never been so many pupils as to form classes, there has been no opportunity of carrying the experiment into execution.[42]

Despite Jean Holmes's insistence on rigorous scrutiny of the fitness of candidates for admission, and despite Regnaud's inclusion of a similar principle in his draft rules, in practice the school accepted students whom Regnaud himself judged to be lazy, stupid, and rebellious. Of the first intake of five (excluding Rolland), one did perform well. Thomas Gerrard, twenty-nine, from Berthier, left the school with a certificate from the board on 5 May 1838 to take charge of the Recollets' Montreal English-language school. Gerrard was probably an established teacher seeking to upgrade his status. Of his two fellows who had entered on 5 September 1837, thirty-eight-year-old Jacques Hubert from St-Denis, said to be irregular in his character and frequently absent, was expelled on 5 February 1838, while twenty-eight-year-old Joseph Marceau from Longueuil, who made 'passable' progress, quit on 5 December 1837 in the midst of the Rebellion. Twenty-one-year-old John Despard O'Keefe, who entered the school in October 1838, also made what his teachers considered 'passable' progress, but fought with Regnaud, attempted and failed to get the board to take action against his teacher, and quit the school on 23 June 1838 when faced with expulsion. The last member of the first intake was John Carpenter, a twenty-year-old from Chambly who entered the school on 10 October 1837 and left on 1 May 1838. Regnaud described him as 'lacking the intelligence required to succeed in his course.'[43]

Pay and Politics

The executive government was slow to pay the normal school teachers. The teachers had contracted verbally with Holmes in Europe, and with the Normal School Board again in Lower Canada, but Viger was sent a chastising note from Secretary Walcott, reminding him of appropriate accounting practices, when he sought salary advances for them.[44] Despite their presence in Montreal from June 1837 and the operation of the school from September, it was only on 27 November that the board's vice-president, F.-A. Quesnel, signed notarized employment contracts with the two men. According to the contracts, Findlater was to work for three years from 8 July 1837, to be paid £250cy for the first year, including all his travel expenses to Canada, and thereafter £200cy, with a £60cy performance bonus at the end of his term. The money was to be paid half-yearly. For his part, Regnaud was hired for five years, and was to receive £305.11s.1d.cy for the first year, including his travel expenses, and then £245.8s.10d.cy each year for the remainder of his term, with a £100cy bonus at the end. Regnaud was also to be paid half-yearly, and both men agreed to devote themselves exclusively to the work of the school.[45]

The date of these agreements is significant. On 22 November, as the British forces were preparing to attack the *patriote* encampments, Viger had submitted detailed accounts of expenditures for the school, explaining that some were signed by the president, Louis-Joseph Papineau, and that others were not. The board had adopted the rule that the president would authorize accounts, although such was not a requirement in the Normal School Act. 'As long as Mr. Papineau was present in the City

and I had only to cross Rue Bonsecours in order to get that authority,'
explained Viger, 'the rule was fine and easy to follow; but from the moment he started running around the Countryside for all these agitation
Meetings, it could not be carried out.'[46] By the 27th, Papineau, the secretary T.S. Brown, and the board member E.B. O'Callaghan were already
fugitives sought on warrants of high treason: it was probably Papineau
who should have contracted with the teachers in the board's name.

More striking, the normal school itself was occupied by Lt Col.
Maitland's volunteers from 26 November to 2 December, and Jacques
Viger feared that, like the Jesuit College, it would be commandeered
permanently as a barracks. The volunteers burned up the candles and
firewood, broke the fire shovel, and left the building filthy. Andrew
Findlater was so traumatized by these events that he insistently ten-
dered his resignation and the student Joseph Marceau left the school
on 5 December, as martial law was declared in the Montreal district. As
Viger put it in a letter of 26 December,

> We have had so much trouble, in this District, for the last month, from the
> insurrection, rebellion, revolution, and war that took place – good lord! every-
> one thought only about their own petty concerns, without much thought for
> those of others, I swear; and as for the Normal School in particular, it was a
> matter – briefly – of suspending its operations and of turning the building
> into a permanent barracks, after it had served that purpose for several days at
> the demand of the authorities. Mr. Findlater even asked to be fired – in black
> and white, and we were on the verge of giving in to him.[47]

Viger had himself advanced some of the money for the support of the
school and the teachers, and the notarized agreements were likely made
in an effort to protect both the teachers' employment and Viger's own
expenditure.

Then, while providing a detailed account of the school's expenditures
in seeking warrants for outstanding debts from the civil secretary, Viger
queried the latter about the Normal School Act. He wanted Secretary
Walcott to confirm that the act established the school for a five-year period, while funding male and female students for three years. Perhaps
naively, Viger also inquired if the board 'would be authorized to hold a
replacement election for Messrs. L.J. Papineau, Dr. O'Callaghan et T.S.
Brown, *absent from the Province* and charged with high treason?' Quite
apart from underlining to the civil secretary that the normal school was
a potential hotbed of revolutionary politics, the legal query meant that

the matters of payment and board elections were referred to the attorney general, C.R. Ogden.[48]

As we have seen, Ogden was no friend to the school, but in any case he had more pressing matters to attend to in dealing with the Rebellion. Viger received no response to his delivery of the notarized teachers' agreements to the government, and no decision as to the issuing of warrants was made until the last day of January 1838. Viger insisted to Secretary Walcott that he was as poor as a 'church rat' and described to Dominick Daly the regular stream of merchants and tradespeople showing up at his door to demand payment of the school's accounts. Andrew Findlater was entirely destitute, sending Viger a pitiful note on 13 January, pleading 'If you have any money belonging to the Normal School in hand, perhaps you could let me have a few pounds today, as I am worse than penniless and, being a stranger, have neither friend nor credit.' Viger advanced him £5 out of his own pocket. Learning later that Gosford, the school's protector, was recalled and that the attorney general himself was in Montreal, Viger wrote to Ogden, pleading the school's case and seeking a personal interview. After he met with him on 26 January, Ogden ruled that warrants should issue to the amount of £300 for salaries, £50 for boarding male students, and £15 for female students. The board's vice-president could hold elections to replace absent members.[49] The release of the money ended the normal school's financial difficulties.

After the Rebellion

While the normal school was able to pay its bills after February 1838, it was not able to fulfil its intended functions. There were few and often no students in attendance, and there is no evidence that Regnaud and Findlater most of the time did anything other than draw their salaries – thereby, of course, respecting their employment agreements. Life must have been cozy after the money began to flow. There was little, if any, teaching to be done, and they could expel any student they found disobedient. Indeed, from 24 June 1838, after John Despard O'Keefe was expelled for questioning his teachers' authority, until 10 August when forty-three-year-old Francis Kelley was admitted, there were no students at all, and Kelley was alone until Régis Pigeon, a twenty-year-old from St-Laurent, entered on 24 September. Presumably despite and not because of having the benefit of full-time instruction from two highly qualified masters, neither student succeeded. Kelley attended irregularly, fought with Findlater about it, and was expelled by the board in June 1839, having managed to live at the public expense for ten months. He appealed his expulsion unsuccessfully. Regnaud described him as 'lacking intelligence and at times seeming to have lost his mind.' For his part, Pigeon made slow progress, but left the school on 1 August 1839 with the offer of a school to teach. There is no evidence that these or indeed any of the students were forced to pay back the money they received for board and lodging. Nor is there any suggestion that the boarding arrangements of men such as Kelley were supervised by the teachers. Regnaud, as master of the school's in-house boarders, himself collared the money paid for their support.[50]

Of the three students admitted in 1839, poverty forced Joseph Monsciau to leave after only eleven days in October. Eighteen-year-old Baptiste Vézina from Rigaud entered on 3 April and stayed in the school until July 1840. Regnaud claimed he made very slight progress, and in any case he was 'little intelligent and with little aptness to teach.' The third student, Béloni Sainte Marie, a seventeen-year-old from Longueuil, came closest to completing the planned three-year course, entering on 14 April 1839 and leaving on 23 February 1842 – the school's last student. Sainte Marie was described as hardworking with an excellent character, and the Normal School Board certified him as a teacher on 21 May 1842.

The school did a bit better in terms of intake in 1840, admitting six students, and adding a final two in 1841. The anticipation of a renewal of the school law after the Act of Union may have produced this minor surge in enrolment. Yet five of these eight students were characterized by Regnaud as slow, juvenile, lacking in seriousness, or unintelligent. Two of the other three, Martin Horan and Pierre Chenneville, received teacher's certificates from the board on 4 May 1841, and the third found a school without a certificate.[51]

In sum, well over £3,000 of public money was spent to instruct nineteen male candidate teachers in the normal school, of whom four were certified by the board of the school as fit to teach, and of whom two more were able to find schools on their own. Five hundred pounds each to produce six teachers was an extravagant expense, far worse than anything for which the Royal Institution could have been called to account.

Female Teachers

The Normal School Board also served as a conduit for money for board and tuition for a number of girls and young women in the house of the Soeurs de la Congrégation de Notre Dame in Montreal, and this proved to be money comparatively well spent. Funding for this purpose was available for three years, and it appears to have ceased in 1840, as the law intended. By contrast, the male teachers continued to receive boarding money until 1842, perhaps hidden in the normal school's contingent funds or provided by some distracted civil secretary.

Eleven girls received subsidized tuition in the Soeurs' establishment, and by the time the money ran out in 1840, four had left with certificates in hand, two had left without certificates, and five were still in attendance. The young women tended to attend for longer periods than their male counterparts, although several interrupted their attendance because of illness. They were also younger, on average, than the men, and there seem to have been among them no old or worn-out teachers looking simply for subsistence. The oldest female candidate was twenty-four-year-old Louise Girouard from Vaudreuil, who entered on 7 March 1837, left for medical reasons on 10 December, returned on 14 March 1838, and left definitively on 14 July 1839 with a teacher's certificate from the mother superior.

Particularly interesting is the case of eighteen-year-old Odile Clairoux from St-Benôit, one of the first students to enter, on 14 May 1836. Odile was one of Scholastique Auger, veuve Clairoux's daughters, and her mother was a long-established teacher, already eking out a living in the first year of operation of the 1829 School Act. All of the trustees' schools in her parish were co-educational, despite the presence of the curé as one of the trustees, and Scholastique Auger taught thirty-four children their ABCs and the catechism at St-Étienne. From the school grant in 1830, she earned £16.8s., and, as we saw earlier, she may have been able to gross £40 a year. In her 1831 school report, Auger pointed to the modesty of her school's efforts: 'Only the first elements of reading, writing, Grammar and arithmetic are taught in it.' It is quite probable that Odile and her sister helped out in their mother's school, and sending Odile to the Soeurs to get her certificate was Scholastique's strategy for providing for her over the long term. Odile had powerful supporters: her certificates of character were signed by Jean-Joseph Girouard, *patriote* MPP and normal school elector, and by the *patriote* lawyer Côme-Séraphin Cherrier.

Odile Clairoux entered the Soeurs' house on 14 May 1836, two weeks after the Elementary School Act expired, and remained there until 14 February 1838, when she left because of illness. She returned on 9 June 1838, but Scholastique Auger apparently believed her return was to be only for a very few weeks, perhaps to receive her teaching certificate. Auger wrote to the Normal School Board member abbé James Phelan in

August, pleading for Odile's return, whom she had sent to the Soeurs in the first place because she had been unable to support her. 'I sent her to you thinking you would send her back to me after a few weeks,' wrote Auger. If she returned, Odile 'will take the school at côte St Pierre,' and, she continued, 'you know one need not be so learned for the backwoods children … Mr Béleau and the *habitants* want her to take the school in côte St Pierre.' If she did, Odile could 'provide for her needs with one of her sisters who will accompany her.' The matter was the more pressing, since both illness and the loss of the school grant made Auger unable to keep up her own school.

Abbé Phelan interceded on Auger's behalf with Jacques Viger, pointing out that the widow was 'quite destitute & is not able to keep up the school committed to her care at St. Hermas.' Given that Odile had bound herself to spend three years in the school Phelan wrote that he 'should be glad to know if Miss Cleroux may retire from the Convent, before the legal Certificate be given her.' Phelan had 'spoken to the Superior of the Nunnery about her & it is her opinion that we ought to allow the girl to go to assist her Mother.' Phelan himself had 'examined her writing & found that she writes a good hand.' She was perfectly able to teach what was required in a country school. Odile Clairoux received her teaching certificate on 9 September 1838.

When Robert Armour Jr made his 1839–40 inventory of the teachers and schools in the county of Two Mountains, he noted that widow Clairoux's school in District 4 at côte St-Étienne had continued for some time after the cessation of the grant in 1836. No schoolhouse had ever been built by the trustees, and Clairoux's school was then closed, although there were about fifty eligible students. In the adjoining District 3, des Éboulis, the school was open and taught by a Miss Clairoux, presumably Odile. There was a schoolhouse measuring 20 × 24 feet with about twenty students in attendance; Armour described the school as 'in good order.' Odile lived in the schoolhouse, receiving $7 a month and her fuel from the parents, money on which it would have been a challenge to support herself, her sister, and widowed mother.[52]

In retrospect, it was infinitely cheaper and more effective to train female Catholic teachers in religious houses than to train male teachers in the normal schools. The Montreal Normal School Board spent £360 to subsidize the eleven female candidates for a three-year period, more than it spent on board for the male students, but a fraction of the total cost of the normal school itself. Neither plan did much to supply the teacher shortage that the Normal School Act was meant to address.

Fall and Closure

Lord Durham's administration continued to fund the normal school in keeping with the act and in response to Jacques Viger's submission of accounts and demands for warrants. Yet the school was the object of attacks in the press, especially as the Buller Education Commission began its work in the summer of 1838. In a sharp exchange with the editor of the conservative Catholic *Ami du Peuple* in July 1838, Étienne Parent defended the Assembly's educational projects, including the normal schools. *Ami* claimed that the *patriote* Assembly had done absolutely nothing to advance the cause of education in the colony because its leaders wished to keep the people ignorant. As he put it, 'The leaders of the revolutionary movement certainly planned to refuse any education to our *habitants* and to keep them in such a condition as to be able to do with them as they wished.' These claims were false, insisted Parent, and the normal schools were the logical extension of a well-thought-out plan of popular education. 'Everyone is familiar with the causes which prevented the Act from coming into full and complete operation up to the present,' he wrote, ' and people know it had nothing to do with the House of Assembly. Political dissent was the only cause.'[53]

The two papers were at it again in August, with *Ami* claiming that there was a general apathy towards education among the rural population, the proof of which was that 'no students could be found for the Normal School established in Montreal.' False again, insisted *Canadien*. The school was having trouble recruiting because candidates had to bind themselves to teach for five years after graduation, and what sensible man would incur such an obligation when the Legislative Council had closed the rural elementary schools? 'Certainly no one can expect a Normal School student to commit himself to taking one of the few schools still open.'[54]

Yet however much friends and opponents of the Montreal school might contest the causes of its failure, its failure was not in doubt. In his June 1839 education report delivered to Arthur Buller, Christopher Dunkin discussed the operations of the school. Although nominally in operation since the summer of 1837, 'I was informed last summer, by parties connected with it,' wrote Dunkin, 'that it had never had a single pupil, who was not a recipient of a share of the fund ... for the support of poor students.' The school could not get five students and in the summer of 1838 actually had none. Dunkin criticized the management committee as politically prejudiced and denounced the discrimination involved in funding only Catholic girls as teachers in nunneries. Of course, he noted, the basic cause of the school's troubles was the failure of the 1836 School Bill.[55]

Christopher Dunkin's education report was followed in early 1840 by a draft school bill intended to serve as the basis of the 1841 Canada School Act. The draft bill contained proposals for the creation of normal and model schools, which were not in fact embodied in the 1841 act, but the plans were authoritative, probably known to people in Montreal, and hence likely cause for some measure of optimism that the Montreal Normal School would find new life after the Union of the Canadas. Dunkin proposed to extend the grant to board students for another two years to 1842 and to allow the governor to fill up the vacancies on the Montreal board. The Special Council had already begun to offer a grant to the Shefford Academy to train teachers. Dunkin proposed that normal schools be placed in Montreal, Quebec, and in or near Sherbrooke, each with a model farm attached. They would prepare teachers for colleges and academies, as well as for elementary schools, and hence would resemble practical universities, but they were clearly to be organs of executive government. Their management boards would be appointed by the governor, not elected by a religious/judicial/political elite, and the governor would also name their professors. The board of education which Dunkin proposed to create would determine the course of study in the schools. Subsidized tuition would continue for women teachers in three Catholic convents, but two Protestant academies would also offer training for women. 'The English language is to be taught to all pupils, not already masters of it.'[56]

It was perhaps in a spirit of optimism about renewed interest in the Montreal school that the board assembled in August 1840 to consider the fate of Andrew Findlater, whose contract had expired 8 July. Viger wrote to Governor Poulett Thomson's secretary Murdoch pointing out that the board had not been spending all the salary allocation provided for it by law, and that it also had not received £333 in the hands of the receiver general for other school purposes. Findlater wanted to have his contract renewed for two years, with a salary increase, and the board had concluded 'that it is highly important that he (Mr. F.) should be retained in the Institution, during the existence of the Act erecting the Normal School.' The board recommended that it be authorized to pay him £220 a year for two years.[57] Viger noted in his letter book that the board never received a reply to this request, although a warrant for money to pay boarding costs did issue. The patent silliness of paying Findlater for another two years to do nothing must have been evident to the executive. Findlater took his £60 bonus and left Canada sometime later.[58]

The normal school lost its grand St Antoine St premises on 1 May 1841. The executor responsible for the house had sold it and had attempted to take possession on 1 November 1840, but Viger insisted on the terms of the lease. He seems to have done little advance planning for relocating the school, since two coachmen billed him in late April 1841 for driving him about to inspect various premises. The board chose to rent a one-storey wooden house at the corner of Craig and St George Sts from P.-E. Leclerc for a year for £50. Perhaps three students moved to the new premises to continue studying under F.-J.-V. Regnaud, but the lease of Leclerc's house was not renewed when it expired at the end of April 1842, and by that time there were no longer any students in attendance. The board was forced to pay Regnaud's salary and the cost of his room and board until his contract expired on 8 July 1842, when he received his £100 bonus. He found work as a government surveyor.

The furnishings of the school were sold at auction on 2 May 1842, earning the sum of just over £36, and Viger moved the school's supply of books and apparatus into the cellar of his own house on the same day. Christopher Dunkin, now employed in the provincial secretary (East)'s office, contacted Viger in August, after the Normal School Act expired, seeking an inventory of apparatus and furniture purchased for the Montreal school at government expense, but it was mid-January 1843 before Viger got around to replying. As he wrote then to Inspector General Francis Hincks, 'the Normal School Act ceased to be in operation (for Montreal) on the 8th of July 1842; our school, lacking *Students* was even closed from the preceding 1st of May.' Viger wanted to be compensated for storing the materials and sought instructions from the governor 'as to removing these objects from my house, or as to selling them. I fear they may be damaged by rust and rats; and as they are not all *insured,* you can easily foresee, that if I had the misfortune to have a house fire, the damage and looting which always so shamefully accompany our fires, would markedly diminish the *items* among the inventory.'[59] Jacques Viger's last action with respect to the Montreal Normal School was the submission of a bill for storage to the government in 1844. The eventual disposition of the apparatus so enthusiastically collected by Jean Holmes in Europe remains unknown. Still, Viger was actively involved with Bishop Bourget's Montreal École St Jacques, later the École Normale St Jacques, at which F.-J.-V. Regnaud returned to teach from 1857 until his death in 1872.[60] Perhaps Holmes's apparatus, too, had a second life.

Conclusion

The Montreal Normal School was a progressive initiative pushed forward by republican and liberal nationalist politicians interested in educating 'the people.' The investigations conducted by Jean Holmes before it was launched were significant in helping to end the colony's 'monitorial moment.' The school's history offers materials for counterfactual argument: for instance, if the 1836 School Bill had passed, the normal school would have attracted a good supply of candidate teachers and the board would have been able to implement interesting teaching methods. If colonial politics had taken a slightly different turn at one of the many junctures that might have led away from armed confrontation in 1837, the colony might have ended up with a public school system. And so on. What remains peculiar in the normal school's history is the failure of the board to open a model school. The money was available and there was a demand for subsidized schooling in Montreal. The running of a model school would have made it possible to recruit promising students, would have given the normal school students a practical apprenticeship, and would have allowed the board to offer some substantial justification for its lavish expenditure on salaries and supplies. Indeed, at its meeting of 4 November 1837, where Jean Holmes delivered a verbal report on his European tour, the board had resolved to organize and to publicize a model school and named a committee composed of Viger, Phelan, Esson, Dewitt, and Brown to do the work. Brown fled Montreal shortly afterwards, and the others seem to have done nothing. Perhaps, as Viger had written, the Rebellion had made the committee members look to their own affairs first.[61]

7

Governmentality and the 'Social Science'

The Lower Canadian legislature did not meet after its March 1836 prorogation until 22 September. The Assembly had sent another address to the Crown with a statement of its grievances, including demands for the elimination of the British and American Land Company and reform of property law. Lord Gosford met the legislature with the response of Lord Glenelg, the colonial secretary, in hand. Glenelg insisted the partial publication of the Gosford Commission's instructions in February had created misapprehensions about imperial policy. Nothing in the instructions or in imperial policy was meant to prevent a completely unfettered investigation of grievances and remedies. Yet he refused to deal with the matter of seigneurial tenure by repealing either the Canada Trade Act or the Canada Tenures Act, arguing that to do so would be to interfere in an internal colonial matter. He also refused to repeal the charter of the British American Land Company unless it could be shown to be unlawful. The Assembly refused to conduct any business until the Legislative Council was made elective. The legislature was prorogued on 4 October and would not meet again until the following summer. Gosford hoped the final report of his commission might advance matters, but politics had now moved effectively out of parliament.[1]

The crisis provoked by the failure of the 1836 School Bill in the larger context of colonial political struggle created a space for conscious consideration of educational futures, for the elaboration of plans to realize such futures, and for attempts to generate systematic empirical knowledge about schools and schoolhouses, teachers and books, and the size and composition of the school-age population. The pursuit of these considerations created some new, if temporary, alliances across the lay / clergy divides and, in the cities at least, across ethnic and political party divides.

Such considerations certainly did not eliminate political divisions, but the alliances point to an interesting space for shared reflection on how to govern the colony through education. Between the two waves of insurrection in 1837 and 1838, imperial liberals and their colonial allies set out to document educational conditions and to replace the Assembly's schools. As the Gosford Commission did, they too attempted to come to grips with colonial politics through the forms of knowledge and analysis associated with population thinking. They thought about school systems as machines for subjectification and as systems of security. They both employed and experimented with the investigative and analytic techniques of the still-new 'social science.' While outlining the course of colonial politics from 1836 to 1839, this chapter attends to the elaboration of a liberal colonial governmentality and to the related practice of the social science in projects to rule by schooling.

The *Patriotes* and the Rural Schools

The educational question was present in rural *patriote* agitation, but usually as a grievance rather than as a plan. There were occasional exceptions, such as the 1835 Union Patriotique et Indépendante in Chateauguay, which announced that it would educate *habitants* by public reading of newspapers and pamphlets, and that it would work to provide schools, books, and schoolhouses to all local children. Louis-Joseph Papineau's public speeches after the failure of the 1836 bill sometimes contained calls for schooling all *habitant* children, but they too were long on grievances and short on remedies.[2]

The failure of the 1836 School Bill and the subsequent closing of the schools were defended in the Tory press but denounced vehemently in reform newspapers and in local political meetings led by the *patriote* MPPs. The *Montreal Gazette* admitted that rural education would suffer somewhat from the loss of the bill, 'but the permanent education of the people' was not the real object of the bill's promoters. Enumerating the powers the school bill gave to the MPPs, the *Gazette* denounced it as a 'cunning attempt to acquire power' and as 'a plan of political aggrandisement and influence throughout the Province' whose true objective was to give a political monopoly to one party. The Assembly had squandered a huge amount of public money supposedly to create 'a taste for education' in the countryside, but in fact it had merely habituated people to government handouts and had undermined their interest in the schools.

This debate raged on for several weeks. The *patriote* and reform press was incensed not simply at Council's amendments to the bill, but by the belief that it had acted quite consciously to kill the schools. Council had the Assembly's bill in hand for a month before it demanded amendments. Had it acted with alacrity, an amended bill would have been possible. The press did not blame the MPPs for trickling away from Quebec before the session ended and speeding prorogation by causing the Assembly to lose its quorum. Rather, if Council had insisted on local property taxation instead of the legislative grants it criticized, the schools would have been placed on a more solid footing. The Council had an obligation to provide an alternative to the Assembly's plan, but instead it killed the schools. The *Montreal Vindicator* argued that the demand for boards of education was simply a Tory move to win back what had been conceded in the wake of the 1828 Canada Committee. What the Councillors were really after was a restoration of the Board of the Royal Institution and exclusive executive power over the people's education. This Irish-Catholic paper claimed that the Councillors were modelling their initiatives on the Kildare Place Society, which pretended to offer Irish children a non-sectarian civil education while really scheming to get them to renounce Catholicism.[3]

Claims and counter-claims about who really wanted to keep the people ignorant flew freely. In a late March election speech, the radical doctor Wolfred Nelson argued that the Legislative Council 'knows perfectly well that it is much easier to master and to abuse an ignorant than an enlightened people. That is the basis of its hostility towards education, which it wishes to restrict to the cities where it lives.' An April meeting at St Benoît passed a series of resolutions denouncing the Council for refusing important legislation, including the school bill, and called for a concerted anti-importation movement to attack the Montreal merchants and the colonial revenue. At Terrebonne in June, a resolution by André-Benjamin Papineau expressing 'the deepest indignation and the most solidly anchored regret' at the Council's opposition to educational progress was endorsed warmly. The Council's actions were repeatedly denounced during the summer banquet season: at Yamaska in July, for instance, where Council was 'the country's greatest political nuisance.' It had caused the loss of many pieces of legislation that were aimed at the happiness of the people 'and especially that of education, which deprives almost 50,000 children of this benefit, and discourages 1,400 educated people [i.e., teachers] in this province.'

By contrast, the *Morning Courier* denied that the Papineau clique had ever articulated any project that envisioned the good of society as a whole.

Education might seem an exception, but 'the system they put in motion was not calculated to diminish the mass of gross ignorance in the land.'[4]

The Closing of the Schools

The failure of the school bill led to wholesale school closures. The trustee boards ceased to exist on 1 May 1836; they held title to the schoolhouses built at public expense, and there was no provision for continuity. Many schools had been in rented accommodation, but the purpose-built schools were abandoned or taken over by whoever acted first. No one had responsible custody of school records or supplies. Teachers lost their jobs. Some kept working and petitioned the executive government for support, only to be informed that there were no funds available. One trustee group thought the news of the failure of the school bill was a false rumour because they had read in the Quebec press that a bill for the encouragement of education had become law, but that was the urban school monies bill and of no use to them. A group of parents in Sherrington township appealed to the Anglican bishop to have their school taken over by the Royal Institution. As we shall see shortly, the Catholic bishops thought they could now use the vestries to seize the trustee schools.[5]

There was some promise that local efforts might keep the schools going. A correspondent from St-Étienne-de-la-Malbaie told *Le Canadien* that a meeting in his parish had named three trustees and planned to raise £53 by subscription for a schoolmaster and mistress 'until it pleases our malignant old council to stop taking revenge on innocent youth.' The day after the meeting, their school had eighty students in attendance, which gave the lie to the Legislative Council's supposition that *canadiens* did not wish to be educated. *Le Canadien* made much of an August 1836 meeting at St-Jean-Port-Joly, which it thought showed that the Assembly schools had succeeded in creating a 'taste for education.' The meeting elected five trustees and promised to raise funds by subscription to support a good school. Fees would be 3s. a month. Étienne Parent proclaimed that 'the people' could not have been interested in education without exposure to it: how could one appreciate something about which one knew nothing? The Assembly had fulfilled its obligation to educate the first generation 'which will undertake to continue this great work, without whose accomplishment a people flatters itself in vain that it might one day enjoy what is called civil liberty.' Parent hoped that if the legislature did not quickly create a new school act people elsewhere would also subscribe for schools. There were reports that some of the Catholic colleges were expanding their elementary classes to take in students from the trustee schools, and towards the end of 1836, the new rural newspaper *Le Glaneur* reprinted a manual for home schooling.[6]

L.-P. Audet later declared that he could not believe that the Catholic clergy would have let the schools fail. He proposed that at least half the trustee schools must have continued in operation through voluntary effort after 1 May 1836, and his belief has been generally accepted. The clergy must have joined with wealthy citizens to keep up the good work; memory of that fact must simply have escaped the historical record. How else could one explain, he wondered, the rapid expansion of schools when a new law was passed in 1841?[7] But then, how could one explain the rapid expansion in the numbers of schools after 1829? Audet could have addressed his question empirically: the results of several ambitious attempts to take stock of the schools show that the great majority were closed by late 1838. Many of those that remained open were privately owned; we recall that about 230 of them had benefited from the government grant under the 1829 act. Most curés did nothing whatsoever to supply schools. Quite emblematic of the situation was a 'Habitant de St-Jean's' November 1836 query to *Le Canadien* about the school project of which the editor had made so much in August. 'What has become of the project formed with such zeal as to earn your praises?' asked this person. 'Talking about things isn't everything, you need to do them.' Would anything be done soon about organizing a school in St-Jean? Nothing was.[8]

A Montreal Think Tank

The mutual exchange of recriminations between supporters of Council and Assembly and feeble attempts at self-help did not exhaust educational activity after the failure of the school bill. As we saw in the previous chapter, abbé Jean Holmes was investigating educational institutions abroad and was shipping reports, books, and apparatus back to the Normal School Board in Montreal. More intriguing – if more elusive – is evidence of a substantial group of citizens meeting in Montreal in mid-1836 to inform themselves of best international educational practice in order to reform Lower Canadian schools. The formation of the group was triggered by a popular August lecture series by the Rev. Mr Kirk from Albany, New York, on J.-J. Jacotot's system of universal education. Kirk was invited to address the new group on 23 August, and it then hosted a public meeting on 5 September to promote education in the colony. A committee of fifteen, composed of Catholic and Protestant clerics, lawyers, businessmen, bankers, and judges was formed to prepare a set of resolutions on the matter. Several of the fifteen were Normal School Board electors, and two members of the Normal School Board were also on the committee – John Phelan and Thomas Storrow Brown. There was one female member, Mrs J.T. Barrett, active in the Female Benevolent Society, whose husband sat on the board of the British and Canadian School Society and belonged to the Montreal Constitutional Association. The conservative judge Charles Dewey Day was a member of the group, and both he and Brown were involved in the Infant School Society. The non-partisan nature of the group is particularly striking: radical *patriotes* T.S. Brown and E. B. O'Callaghan sitting with Montreal Constitutional Association members such as C.D. Day.

In December 1836, the committee, now presided over by Toussaint Peltier fils, with Charles Mondelet and T.S. Brown as secretaries, published the results of its investigations. In an educational parallel to the local *patriote* correspondence committees organized in many parts of the colony, the education group called for the formation of local education committees. A circular meant for distribution in the rural Montreal district said that the colony had fewer schools than neighbouring countries and suffered for it. The uneducated could neither be useful to society nor as successful as they might be, for 'the uneducated man is the educated man's inferior in all the relations of life.' The circular then repeated what was by 1836 the standard liberal line on international educational systems, one propagated especially by Victor Cousin's reports on Prussian and Dutch schools and contained in the Gosford Commission report: Prussia offered a remarkable example of a successful and complete elementary school system, but its success was due in part to a military style of discipline that was unlikely to 'act fruitfully in our social machine.' The concept of a 'social machine' is proto-social scientific.

Lower Canadians should look rather to the common school systems of the United States, which brought instruction within everyone's reach. Any school system in Lower Canada should be supported by a state school fund, by local voluntary contributions in the shape of fees, but more especially by a general property tax. The aim was to instruct all young people, but without taxation the rich would contribute nothing and the poor would not send their children to school unless the school was close by. Compulsory attendance could not be enforced, but a general property tax would cause all to take advantage of the schools.[9] More research is required to uncover additional traces of the work of the Montreal group. It had announced with its circular of December 1836 that it would continue to investigate international educational conditions and that it would publish its findings.

The investigations probably resulted in Charles Mondelet's best-selling *Letters on Elementary and Practical Education* published in 1840–1.

Jonathan Barber's Lectures

Rev. Kirk was certainly not the only person speaking publicly about educational matters. Many of the Protestant clergymen in Montreal and some laymen offered popular lecture series on these questions. Particularly important were lectures given by Dr Jonathan Barber from Boston in the late fall of 1836 and early part of 1837. Barber filled halls in Montreal and Quebec and published his lectures in popular editions. Most of them focused on educational questions more or less directly, and when he spoke to phrenology or health he made frequent reference to the effects of education on the size of the brain or to the necessity of preventing students from injuring themselves by too much study. Barber was a loud proponent of infant schools and spoke at length on Samuel Wilderspin's innovations, calling for support for the Montreal Infant School Society. He favoured women's education but contested Mary Wollstonecraft's argument that women's social inferiority would vanish with educational equality. Women's bodies were more delicate than men's, and phrenology showed that women's brains were smaller and 'less able to contend with obstacles and surmount difficulties.' Thus, Barber presented moderate liberalism's standard line on women's education: as mothers women needed a sound basic education, but they were 'designed by the Creator to be the friend and companion of man' and should strive to fulfil that role. Barber also lectured at length on national education, offering comparative information about international systems, and he echoed most of what the Montreal committee had concluded on the subject.[10]

The important points here are that educational questions were attracting attention, generating public discussion, and encouraging comparative, international investigation. A common line on the nature and the powers of a national or colonial school system had emerged, one that cut across religious and political divides at least in Montreal to an important degree. Conservative and *patriote* activists in Montreal met together to support reform platforms that shared many common planks. Elinor Kyte Senior's analysis of the period points to real possibilities for an alliance across ethnic-linguistic-religious divides on matters of reform that existed until internecine struggle in the autumn of 1837 made compromise impossible.[11] The Montreal educational consensus was made explicit in the final report of the Gosford Commission.

Governing Lower Canada

Schooling figured centrally in attempts by imperial authorities to render Lower Canada governable in the later 1830s. How the colonial state system should be organized and administered was the main focus of the work of the first British North American Royal Commission of Inquiry, the Gosford Commission (or, as it was officially known, the 'Commission for the Investigation of all Grievances affecting His Majesty's Subjects of *Lower Canada*'). The commission, composed of Lord Gosford, who was named governor as well, Sir George Gipps, and Sir Charles Grey, was dispatched as a fact-finding mission by the Whig government in mid-1835 and its final report bore the date 17 November 1836.

The royal commission was a novel instrument and ritual for the production and legitimation of political knowledge at this moment, yet almost every major innovation in the so-called English 'nineteenth century revolution in government' was preceded by a commission of inquiry. The Gosford Commission was one of the first uses of this instrument in a colonial situation, and the conditions under which it was appointed and the impact of its report on English colonial policy have been canvassed elsewhere.[12] The commission called for a series of reforms and improvements to Lower Canadian government but did not agree on any fundamental constitutional transformation. Indeed, the commissioners were divided among themselves, something that may have been planned by the English government. Sir Charles Grey supported the Montreal Constitutional Association's claims of intolerable French domination, while Lord Gosford proposed to place supporters of the 92 Resolutions in the Legislative and Executive Councils. In some ways, Sir George Gipps was the original thinker in the group, a man who grappled intellectually with the abstract problem of designing a system of proportional representation for a minority interspersed among a majority population. Gipps thought about political problems in statistical terms and made an effort to model the relations among population, territory, and security. He discussed the means and ends of government explicitly, distinguishing what he called 'bare empire' – simple imperial sovereignty – from a civilizational project intended to fit Lower Canada for 'British' self-government. In a different way, Grey shared the same interest.

The Gosford Commission's work is thus an instance of 'reflexive government': self-conscious reflection by those who govern on the means and ends of government. From the first decades of the nineteenth century, such reflection was often cast in an abstract political discourse that drew on statistical and cartographic techniques and that employed a stage theory of social development. Given that they had no decision-making powers, the commissioners had a degree of distance from the immediacy of colonial struggles that encouraged such reflection.

'Security' is used here in Michel Foucault's sense of a system of relations operating more or less autonomously to produce a desired end, and not as protection from 'terror' or the safe possession of property (i.e., sécurité, not sûreté). Foucault's example was the Physiocrats' understanding of the operations of a free market in grain which would result in plentiful supply and low prices if left to its own devices.[13] Public education was a system of security in the sense that the manufacture of self-governing political subjects was thought to ensure free and 'cheerful obedience' to a political order whose benefits were supposed to be rationally demonstrable.[14]

Observation of social conditions and reflection on government were at the heart of the developing mode of knowledge called the 'social science.' The condition of schooling in Lower Canada was an important object of social scientific experiment, especially in the colony's second royal commission of 1838–9. The royal commission of inquiry was one way of grappling with practical problems of government in an informed manner. However, most of Lower Canadian historiography's readings of the record have tended to ignore the transformation in epistemological politics involved, especially to attack the agenda of assimilation followed by the second royal commission. The Gosford Commission has usually been dismissed as a simple imperial-Tory delaying tactic of no substantive interest since it did not deliver on most *patriote* demands. Little of what it actually did has been investigated in any detail.[15]

The Neglected Commission

There are at least three reasons for historical sociologists of politics and education to attend to the Gosford Commission's work. First, it signalled a marked shift in the colonial governmentality. Second, the Colonial Office came close to taking up Sir Charles Grey's scheme of solving the problem of rule by dividing the colony into as many as ten parts in a new federation. Third, the commission outlined a project for schooling later taken up by the Durham Commission.

First, even though the Gosford Commission did not officially recommend constitutional change, its members were no longer thinking within the horizon of the colony's mixed constitution. Political equilibrium was not thought by them in terms of stable relations among king, lords, and

commons, but in terms of articulations of broader and more varied social interests. Statistical abstraction made it possible for them to experiment mentally with solutions to the problem of colonial rule through
configuring interests in various ways. Legitimate political interests were
educated interests, rather than the result of descent, alliance, status, or
tradition. The space of rule was reconfigured and the nature of political
subjectivity redefined.

Second, the Gosford Commission's final report of November 1836 and
Gosford's failure to have the colonial Assembly vote a Civil List brought
the Canada question again before the imperial parliament. Against the
'Radical' wing of the Whig party, in March 1837 parliament voted a series
of Resolutions on the colony proposed by Lord John Russell. While con-
ceding nothing substantial to the Assembly's demands – no elective
Council, no ministers responsible to the majority, no repeal of the British
American Land Company Charter, and so on – Russell proposed to authorize Gosford to appropriate the revenues in the hands of the receiver
general, to pay the outstanding arrears of government expenses, and to
fund other projects previously authorized by the Assembly.

The publication of the Resolutions in Lower Canada in mid-April 1837
provoked widespread outrage in the *patriote* party, especially in the Montreal
district. An escalating series of 'anti-coercion' meetings drew large crowds
and violent denunciations of Gosford, the Councils, and the English government. *Patriote* opponents in the countryside were attacked and intimidated, and by the summer of 1837 a parallel system of popular government was in place in the Montreal district. Gosford convoked the legislature
in August, formally presented the Russell Resolutions to it, and made a
final plea – with no expectation of success – for a Civil List. The majority
in the Assembly rejected his plea out of hand, denied the legitimacy or
legality of his commission, and responded that now only force of arms
would maintain the colonial authority in power. Growing political agitation, popular violence, and the project of a constitutional convention in
the midst of a major economic depression issued in an attempted insurrection in December 1837, which was suppressed by bloody force of arms.
These events are documented in a very large literature with more nuance
and detail than is necessary here.[16]

However, the second point of interest in the Gosford Commission's
work has been obscured through the misapprehension by Lower Canadian
historians of the Russell Resolutions as some sort of law or administrative
order. In fact, they were the preliminaries to a new Canada bill which
never made it to the English parliament, and it is that bill which was

potentially explosive. The Resolutions, by contrast, were a bargaining chip
in colonial-imperial relations. It is unlikely in any case that the Commons
would have accepted a bill with a clause removing its Lower Canadian
counterpart's control over public revenue; the Colonial Office was extremely anxious about pursuing the matter and was floating all kinds of
alternative solutions, including giving in on the matter of Council elections. When Gosford met the legislature in August 1837, he had no power
or authority to appropriate the revenues under the control of the
Assembly, and he never did so; he too was bargaining, hoping the threat
contained in the Resolutions would lead the Assembly to accept the position already advocated by Étienne Parent in *Le Canadien*: choose defeat
on the Civil List over civil war and pursue the other reforms promised by
the commission. And he was bargaining from a position of weakness; he
had had no reply from London to his proposed lists of new appointments
to the Legislative and Executive Councils, which would have made half of
the members of the latter men who had voted for the 92 Resolutions, and
did not know that Sir Charles Grey was actively opposing him. He was well
aware that many of the sitting Executive Councillors were 'destitute of
public esteem' and that, despite his vow to remedy the situation, several
still held multiple offices, but he could not accept their resignations in the
absence of new appointments without closing his appeals court. Dithering
in London, he complained, made everyone look bad.[17]

The shifting political situation in England prevented passage of the new
Canada bill that had been drafted with a version of Sir Charles Grey's proposals for a re-division of Lower Canada. It was these proposals that were
especially significant for the colonial governmentality. While Sir George
Gipps speculated about devising a system of proportional representation,
Grey had repeatedly suggested the creation of new colonies or districts in
a new Lower Canadian federation as the means to allow French-Canadian
nationalists to preserve Catholicism and the seigneurial system, while satisfying the demands of the Constitutional Associations, promoting the development of economic infrastructure, and creating zones for systematic
colonization. The principle behind Grey's scheme had strong support in
the Colonial Office. One version of it had a federation of ten new provinces or districts, with English-speaking areas dominating a federal legislature. Grey conceived the project as a practical object lesson that would
produce American levels of prosperity from the elimination of the tithe
and seigneurial relations. This governmental project was explicitly didactic. Grey believed that once in place it would demonstrate, in terms that
the *habitants* left in the French-Canadian province could understand, that

their interest lay in the free conversion of seigneurial into socage tenures and the adoption of 'British improvement.' The death of William IV in June 1837 led to new English elections and prevented any enactment embodying the Russell Resolutions. It also prevented the creation of a new Lower Canadian federation, which surely would have altered the course of the colony's history quite dramatically.[18]

No new Canada bill passed in 1837, but the Gosford Commission's investigations and reports fed directly into the plans and projects of the next royal commission, headed by Lord Durham in 1838. Durham too thought first to organize a Canadian federation, but soon decided to try to eliminate, rather than to cantonize, the French fact. His *Report on the Affairs of British North America* of 1839 fed directly into the reforms proposed by his successor, Poulett Thomson/Lord Sydenham, many of which were included in the Act of Union of 1840 that created the Province of Canada. One thing they all shared were common means of investigating, assessing, knowing, and designing colonial government. That commonality appeared also in the realm of educational government more directly, which is the third, largely neglected, aspect of the Gosford Commission's work.

The Gosford Commission and Colonial Schooling

The commission was formally instructed to devote itself to 'the collection of all such intelligence as may be necessary for framing a general system of provincial education, embracing not the mere rudiments of literature, but all that relates to the culture of the minds and the development of the moral and religious principles of youth in the different ranks of society.' It was not expected that the commission would devise a detailed plan for colonial education, but it was to make a start, and the commissioners were to bear in mind that arrangements in the imperial country might not be well adapted for the colony: permission, in effect, to recommend boards of education and property taxation.[19] The commission's final report presented a detailed description of the existing provisions for rural elementary schooling, with an account of the clauses in the failed 1836 bill and a copy of the resolutions of the Legislative Council committee which refused it. It proposed a scheme for a reformed system of education which was then extended by the Buller Education Commission of 1838–9 and worked up as Christopher Dunkin's first drafts of the 1841 Canada School Act.

The surviving records of the commission do not contain evidence of public hearings devoted to educational questions. Yet, in a novel move, the commissioners were instructed that their investigations were not to be restricted to reading state documents or to canvassing the opinions of established elites. Rather, they were to investigate conditions themselves on the ground, through personal observation and by reading the colonial press, in order to generate a wider knowledge of local sentiment. The instruction to attend to 'civil society' rather than elite opinion points to the growing influence of statisticians and social scientists in the Whig government. There had been lengthy and fairly elaborate discussions about investigative practices in Charles Buller's Records Commission, for instance, with Nassau Senior debating whether local informants or those delegated by a central authority could produce the best information. English intellectuals and statesmen had read Tocqueville, and his style of inquiry was elaborated and improved upon by Harriet Martineau, also a member of Whig intellectual circles. The Gosford commissioners did travel somewhat, and while the *patriote* party leadership refused formally and publicly to recognize the commission or to participate in its work, the commissioners met privately and at social events with leading party members and tested their opinions about necessary reforms, presumably educational reforms among them.[20]

The Constitutional Associations, by contrast, presented briefs and papers on various subjects including calls for a reformed educational system. Lord Gosford received detailed petitions from bodies such as the Royal Grammar School, the Royal Institution, and the trustees of the Quebec St Andrews Church school. In response to a March 1836 demand from the Colonial Office, Gosford sent a circular to the directors, principals, and headmasters of all Lower Canadian colleges, seminaries, and academies, seeking detailed information about their institutions. Most of the responses arrived after the commission's November 1836 report was delivered, but Gosford was thereby enabled to slay one Tory bugaboo – that public money was going to train a horde of Catholic priests in the French-language colleges.

The Gosford Commission's analysis of rural schooling favoured the position of the Legislative Council, the views of John Neilson, and the demands of MPPs from the Eastern Townships, but it also reflected the work of the Montreal education committee discussed above. The account made much of the 'abuses' identified in John Neilson's 1831 school visitor's report and presented in testimony before the Standing Committee in 1835–6, but made no mention of the Assembly's ongoing efforts to address them. It stressed that the 1836 bill multiplied the numbers of school districts despite the Standing Committee's recommendations that they be reduced, but did not delve into the dynamics of local school administration. 'The views entertained' in that committee's reports, wrote the commissioners, 'appear to us generally so judicious, that we can only lament that they have not been more extensively acted on by the House to which they were addressed.'

The commissioners' diagnosis was that the Assembly's schools were defective because there was no central board of education, because teachers were under-qualified, students attended irregularly, parents made no efforts to school their children since they had been habituated to legislative aid, and because there was no local power for educational assessment and taxation, even in areas that had demanded it. Quoting the Assembly's 1835–6 Standing Committee, the commissioners concluded that because of the legislature's excessive liberality the existing system '"had paralyzed [local] efforts instead of stimulating them."'

The prescription for a new school system centred on the creation of boards of education. To forestall the objection that they were after a new Royal Institution, the commissioners argued that the problem with the RI was its membership, not the fact that it was a board of education. They drew attention to recent developments in Ireland where a national board of education had been organized and recommended 'that the fullest information respecting the working of that system should be sent to Lower Canada.' In Catholic Ireland 'abundant proof exists of a willingness to engage in the generous enterprize' of common education. A marginal note to the first draft of their report stressed that Jean Holmes had investigated the Irish system extensively and would soon share information on it. The commissioners also urged Lower Canadians to pay close attention to Victor Cousin's report on Prussian education and to American developments: central boards of education and educational inspectorates were key parts of the school systems found in those countries.

'We do not think that the System of supporting Schools entirely or even principally out of the general Revenue of any Country is a good one,' the commissioners wrote. A reformed system should be funded by a local school assessment and tax, to be matched by a legislative school grant and to be supplemented by student fees. Money raised and expended in the locality would be better and more carefully managed than a general grant. With respect to the Assembly's arrangements for school management and inspection, the commissioners supported locally elected school trustees but opposed the administration of the schools by MPP visitors and local elites. As they put it, 'that it was insufficient to check jobbing and malversation, appears to be admitted in the Reports made to the Assembly, whilst the possible Employment for political purposes of the patronage, which was afforded by it to Members of the

Assembly is objected to, and we conceive not ... without reason, by the Council.' They proposed to subject the local trustee boards to the control and direction of district boards of education. In the Quebec and Montreal districts, the boards of the normal schools should act as district school boards and some similar boards should be established in the two other districts. The commissioners made no comment on the franchise for normal school board elections.

There remained the matter of religious instruction in the schools, and here the commissioners were cautious, claiming not to have enough information to express a firm opinion. Nonetheless, to any informed reader their preference for the Irish solution to this question was obvious. As they put it, 'as it is highly important that such Schools should be as comprehensive as possible, so is it in our opinion desirable that the religious instruction imparted in them, should embrace only such general doctrines as all who are Christians may agree in.' They insisted that they would not presume to prescribe a solution, but given the very low level of acrimony between Protestants and Catholics, they hoped that such a common solution would be adopted and concluded that their own best strategy was to say nothing more about the matter.[21]

The Irish Precedent and the Geopolitics of 1830s Liberalism

The Gosford Commission's recommendation for district boards of education effectively placed schooling in a secular public sphere, for lay preponderance in the Quebec and Montreal normal school boards was well known. The commissioners cannot have been ignorant of the fact that the *patriote* party controlled the Montreal board. Recommending that Lower Canadians read Victor Cousin and hear Jean Holmes's report on Ireland also made the point that school inspectors and visitors would be state rather than church officials. The commissioners were undoubtedly aware that the Catholic bishops and their clergy had effectively killed the Royal Institution; perhaps they knew that the rural Catholic clergy controlled the course of study in most elementary schools. How then to create non-sectarian public schooling? To English Whigs and liberals in the 1830s, the Irish solution of defining a New Testament–style 'common Christianity' to which all denominations could agree as the moral fibre of a secular school system seemed both sensible and workable. Only later in the century did virulent Protestant antipathy in the north of Ireland and de facto Catholic control of the schools elsewhere turn the dream of Christian commonality into a nightmare.[22]

English governments had been funding education societies in Ireland at least since the late eighteenth century, most of them with an agenda of Protestant proselytism. The policy gave rise to organizationally and pedagogically sophisticated organizations, especially the Kildare Place Society (KPS), which sustained schools and pioneered school inspection and curriculum on a national scale. Such organizations met growing Catholic opposition in the 1820s, even as the removal of civil disabilities from Catholics – the project for Catholic Emancipation – came to fruition. Commissioners for Irish Education were appointed to examine into the matter and delivered a first report in 1824. The Catholic bishops insisted that literary and religious instruction could not be separated, but they rejected the practice that the KPS shared with other Lancasterian institutions (including the British and Canadian School Society) of having students read the scriptures 'without note or comment.' As the bishops put it, 'the religious Instruction of Youth in Catholic Schools is always conveyed by means of catechistical Instruction, daily Prayer, and the reading of religious Books, wherein the Gospel Morality is explained and inculcated.' Children reading the scriptures independently without explanation was 'an inadequate Means of imparting to them religious Instruction, as an Usage whereby the Word of God is made liable to Irreverence, Youth exposed to misunderstand its Meaning, and thereby not unfrequently to receive in early Life Impressions which may afterwards prove injurious to their own best Interests, as well as to those of the Society which they are destined to form.'

The Irish Commissioners denounced the proselytism of the education societies, although they exempted the Kildare Place Society. They were enthusiastic about the KPS's pedagogical innovations, which included simultaneous group instruction on a Lancasterian model, tempered with elements of a Pestalozzian-style 'child-centred' approach. If unregulated popular consumption of dangerous reading materials was to be combated effectively, such large-scale collective instruction was necessary. Yet it could work only if Protestant and Catholic students were instructed together. Joint instruction enabled economies of scale, but it was supposed also to create familiarity and solidarity among young people at school which would continue as social solidarity and civil harmony later in life. The common school was seen explicitly as a 'moral engine' or manufactory of good political subjects.

The Irish Commissioners met repeatedly with the Catholic archbishops and discussed and debated possible methods of engineering joint Catholic and Protestant instruction. Their first suggestion, for common literary instruction with separate religious instruction outside school hours, easily met with approval, but the bishops initially denied that common ground on religious issues was possible. After repeated thrashing out of matters – which makes for fascinating reading – Archbishop Murray of Dublin conceded that there was material that Catholics and Protestants could read together: 'no Objection would be made to an Harmony of the Gospels being used in the general Education which the Children should receive in common, nor to a Volume containing Extracts from the Psalms, Proverbs, and Book of Ecclesiasticus, nor to a Volume containing the History of the Creation – of the Deluge – of the Patriarchs – of Joseph – and of the Deliverance of the Israelites, extracted from the Old Testament.' Murray agreed that 'no Difficulties in arranging the Details of such Works would arise on the Part of the Roman Catholic Clergy.'[23]

The appointed National Commissioners of Education, through whom the English government took over the Irish schools from 1832, produced a series of graduated schoolbooks focused closely on what was called 'useful knowledge' that included a book of *Scripture Extracts* selected by a joint committee of Protestants and Catholics. The *Extracts* were the hinge upon which all denominations could be turned towards common secular instruction. In the following decades, the Irish schoolbooks became a major international export and were adopted in many public school systems (including Canada West/Ontario from 1847). If a destitute, peasant Ireland rife with murderous sectarian violence could find common religious ground for the association of schoolchildren, English liberals and Whigs believed the model could be transported to other colonies. They would attempt repeatedly to flog the Irish solution to the Canadian Catholic bishops.

However, Ireland was not Lower Canada, Archbishop Murray was neither J.-J. Lartigue nor Ignace Bourget, and 1825 was not 1836 and much less 1838. On the one hand, in 1836 and more forcefully in 1838, the political position of the Catholic Church in Lower Canada made compromise with the civil authority in educational matters far less pressing that it had been for the Church in Ireland. Canadian Catholics suffered no civil disabilities and the church's right to tithe was intact, while its Anglican rival was weak. The civil authority was indebted to the Catholic bishops for their unwavering support of executive government during the 1837 insurrection, support they repeated in 1838. The teaching order of the Christian Brothers had also come to Montreal, promising a new source of Catholic schoolteachers, and the quantity and quality of postulants (if not their numbers relative to the size of congregations) were improving.[24]

Moreover, the co-operative stance of the Irish bishops in relation to public education was adopted before the Catholic reaction against political liberalism. Rome opposed a world view that assumed inherent human goodness and affirmed human perfectibility through social reform. The Church opposed practical liberal demands, such as freedom of conscience and freedom of the press, and allied itself with authoritarian reaction. Demonic liberalism was seen to have caused the European revolutionary and anti-clerical wave of 1830–1 and liberal doctrine was denounced in the encyclical *Mirari Vos* of 1832. Men such as J.-J. Lartigue, who had been Lamennaisian in some of their political and social views, snapped quickly into line, and some of Lartigue's curés beat the anti-liberal drum loudly. Curé St Germain of St-Laurent, to take one example, portrayed liberalism in 1834 as a plague worse than the cholera. Liberalism was a disease 'which works on the social body, progresses extremely rapidly and whose consequences are even more unfortunate since it attacks morality.' The good simple *habitants,* claimed St Germain, were infected by this malady through the work of agitators from the cities and now were arguing in favour of revolution! The clergy needed to unite to beat back the threat. Of course, some priests were less reactionary, and a few, such as Jean-Charles Prince, the principal of the Collège de St-Hyacinthe where the Papineau boys were schooled, and Étienne Chartier, who had introduced monitorial methods to the new Collège de Sainte-Anne before his incendiary speeches got him into trouble, were committed *patriotes.* Bishop Lartigue had difficulty getting Prince to fall into line and failed with Chartier, but on the whole, the Catholic clergy took a firmly anti-liberal stance.[25]

The liberal promotion of the separation of church and state, which underlay public education, was seen to menace church with good reason, as the victory of liberal forces in the first Carlist War in Spain demonstrated. Here even moderate liberals attacked the power and resources of the Catholic Church, which supported the authoritarian pretender Don Carlos. Mob violence against priests accompanied the suppression of most clerical establishments, the sale of many properties for the state revenue, and, with radicals in power between 1837 and 1840, the abolition of the tithe. Lord Gosford's – and later, Lord Durham's – Whig masters had intervened on the liberal side both by authorizing the recruitment of a British Legion and by using naval force on several occasions against Carlist forces. The Irish Connellites in the imperial parliament supported the government on this issue, and the Lower Canadian *patriotes* frequently compared their cause to that of the Irish, and Papineau to O'Connell. While the Papineau clique and the Quebec moderates in the *patriote* party did not mount a frontal attack on the church or on its feudal properties, the radical factions of the party and the Montreal Constitutional Association were both doing so with increasing intensity from at least 1835.[26]

The Bishops' Attempt to Reassert Control over Schools

The Lower Canadian bishops were even less susceptible to a common Catholic and Protestant public education after the failure of the 1836 School Bill. The Montreal bishops took care to hide their glee from public view, but they gloated in private. J.-J. Lartigue had been arguing for a decade that Catholics should go it alone in elementary schooling, and finally the occasion presented itself to recover the clergy's rights from a liberal laity. Lartigue was enthusiastic about Signäy's circular to the curés giving a blanket authorization to dip into vestry funds to support elementary schools, but he urged his Quebec counterparts to be coy in public about 'our desire for the clergy to seize the education of the people as its right' so as not to stir up lay opposition. Lartigue urged speed in the matter, not only because of the credit it would bring to the Church, but because it was 'the only means of tearing the future generation out of the grip of a detestable education.' He had been reading in the newspaper that 'laymen will renew their bad 1829 law as soon as possible, if we neglect this precious and perhaps unique occasion to take over the education of youth.'[27]

Signäy's circular was dated 2 May 1836, the day after the expiration of the 1834 School Act, and he urged the curés to 'do whatever you can, to procure for your parish at least a part of the advantages it enjoyed under the law which has just expired.' He reminded them that the 1824 Vestry School Act was still in effect, that it allowed them to use up to a quarter of the vestry's funds for school support, and he gave them formal authorization to do so as and when they wished. The curés should act without delay to convince their churchwardens of the benefits of such schools, and, given that the vestry would not have enough money to pay all the costs of schooling, parents should be incited to contribute as well. Lartigue thought it would be legal to use even more vestry money to build and maintain schools.[28]

However, despite the encouragement of the bishops and the reprinting of an edition of *L'Instruction chrétienne pour les jeunes gens*, the curés were not suddenly seized with zeal for an educated peasantry. There were some exceptions. Curé Jean-Romuald Paré of St-Jacques-de-l'Achigan wished to know if he could use vestry funds for schooling and was told by Lartigue that he could spend 3,000 francs (about £10) of vestry money on a school, but not on a school with trustees and not on a co-educational school or one in which a male teacher taught girls. He may have done so, but an investigation of 1838 would show that the great majority of the curés did nothing.

The Half-Dead Royal Institution

In 1835–6, the Tory press presented the Royal Institution, now in its death throes, as one of the few defences against an 'incubus of illiterate paupers' – the *habitant* population – waiting to seize political power and to degrade Lower Canadian civilization.[29] Perhaps it was this sort of reactionary bombast that led the *Vindicator* to suggest that the Gosford Commission had joined with the Legislative Council in a plot to kill the 1836 School Bill in order to restore the Royal Institution as the colonial board of education. In fact, neither Lord Gosford nor his fellow commissioners saw any autonomous future for the RI. They were deaf to pleas from the Institution for support. William Cochrane, president of the RI, and R.R. Burrage and Andrew Skakel, masters respectively of the Royal Grammar Schools established in 1816 in Quebec and Montreal, petitioned pathetically for relief. The teachers had seen their initially rosy prospects decline seriously over the previous two decades. Competition from other urban schools and academies, financial stringency in the RI in the 1820s, and then salary cuts when the Assembly took control of the Jesuits' Estates revenue in 1831 undermined their incomes and forced them to take large numbers of free students. Burrage protested that the Assembly compelled him to take so many that he had to recruit them from the 'lower orders,' which seriously reduced the appeal of his school to rich parents. He had been promised the life of a respectable grammar schoolmaster when he was persuaded to abandon his Cambridge degree to come to Quebec, but now he found himself with a wife, ten children, and a measly £100 a year on which to live in the city. Neither he nor Skakel had been paid anything from the Assembly since 1832.

Alexander Skakel had thirty-seven years' teaching experience, and, while he had earned £200 a year in the late 1810s, he could now barely clear £60 and could save nothing for retirement. When the Gosford Commission's first report revealed that it would not revive the RI, Skakel applied for six months' leave of absence, sending the RI board a doctor's certificate which described him as 'labouring under a derangement of the digestive organs accompanied with general debility and nervous agitation

& mental depression.' The third urban Royal Institution teacher, Selby Burns in Trois-Rivières, had not been paid since 1834.

For his part, William Cochrane petitioned the executive for a permanent endowment for the RI. In an argument later supported by the Legislative Council as well, Cochrane pointed to the unfulfilled promises of the Crown to make an educational land grant in 1801 and to the extensive endowment of grammar schools in Upper Canada and Nova Scotia. While the Royal Institution's schools had no permanent means of support, very large grants of land by gift and endowment had been made to Catholic colleges. These were nominally open to all people in the colony, but English-speaking Protestant parents were unwilling to send their sons to them, with the result that many were educated in the United States. The Royal Grammar Schools could not offer advanced instruction in the classics and mathematics on the pittance awarded by the Assembly, and even that was unpaid.[30]

The Gosford commissioners solicited a memorandum on the state of the Royal Institution schools and found that only thirty-seven survived, scattered about the colony, with twenty-nine male and eight female teachers. Gosford was briefly tempted to consider the matter of a land grant immediately after his failure to get a Civil List, but with the rest of his commission concluded that the RI was finished. 'We cannot help thinking that the Royal Institution should be left to be assisted by the Assembly,' announced the commissioners. The Assembly 'we believe has always shown itself liberal in encouraging the promotion of Education.'[31]

By the end of 1836, then, the imperial government saw the solution to Lower Canada's educational woes not in a revived Royal Institution, but in some version of a state school system, with central boards of education, inspectors, elected trustees, property taxation, normal schools, and curriculum and pedagogy on the Irish model. Political struggle and armed insurrection prevented any new legislation in 1837. Lord Gosford was recalled early in 1838, leaving the Montreal District under martial law. The imperial parliament then suspended the Lower Canadian constitution. Lord Durham's Royal Commission, which arrived in the colony at the end of May 1838, moved to carry the Gosford Commission's recommendations forward. In July 1838, Durham appointed an Education Commission to gather all information about rural schools and schooling, to do the logistical work necessary to put the new school system in place, and to sell the Irish scheme to the Catholic bishops. However, just as Buller's work was gathering momentum, Durham announced his resignation, granted a blanket amnesty to everyone who had participated in the 1837 insurrection, and departed the colony.

A second, better-organized and better-planned, wave of insurrection immediately thereafter was suppressed with extreme violence, including the subjection of much of the French-speaking population in the Montreal district to collective punishment. Arbitrary rule and state-sponsored terror continued in 1839 under the military dictatorship of Sir John Colborne and his Special Council, which was dominated by the Montreal Constitutional Association.[32] A new civilian governor, Poulett Thomson (later Lord Sydenham), arrived later in 1839, charged with organizing the return to civilian rule under a changed constitution.

Teachers and Insurrection

The failure of the 1836 School Bill was an element in the material misery which contributed to insurrection. Material misery was certainly not a main cause of insurrection, for the Quebec district was particularly impoverished, yet there was little or no insurrectionary activity there. Still, the harvest in 1836 and the wheat harvest in 1837 failed in many parts of the colony. People were reportedly eating their dogs and horses in the bitter winter of 1836–7. Snowfall was so heavy that the ice bridge between Quebec and the south shore did not form until very late in the season; the price of firewood and grain and other provisions rose dramatically. The Montreal House of Industry was besieged with impoverished people.

Matters were exacerbated by the international fiscal crisis provoked by American financial speculation. In 1836, the American banks first suspended the circulation of notes under $10 in value and then suspended specie payment. Lower Canada's money was primarily in Spanish and American dollars. The action of the American banks sucked hard cash of all varieties out of Lower Canada very quickly. The extreme scarcity even of small denomination copper coins disrupted everyday exchange. The market was flooded with counterfeit coinage and store tokens, and government attempts to specify legal tender inflicted losses on many people. Excise duties and some land rents were due in coin but could not be paid. The Lower Canadian banks themselves suspended specie payment in late spring and summer of 1837, and there were local bank failures, such as the Banque d'Henry in Laprairie, whose cashier absconded to the United States.[33]

The impact of the failure of the school bill on the economic crisis is impossible to measure precisely, but it must have been considerable. Something in the vicinity of £20,000 found its way into rural districts in 1835 because of the elementary schools, and that sum would have been increased had the 1836 bill succeeded. Perhaps three-quarters of the teachers were thrown out of work entirely, and those who remained had to live on their fees. One might expect some of them to rally to the *patriote* cause in consequence.

It had long been a complaint of colonial Tories that the Assembly's school teachers were indoctrinating the *habitants* by feeding them lessons from the *patriote* press. After the second wave of insurrection, they were described in the Tory press as 'a band of political agitators, expressly chosen for that purpose.' Evidence collected through the 'voluntary' examination of detainees in both 1837 and 1838 identified some teachers who were involved in revolutionary activities, but they were rare in a teaching body that numbered over a thousand. *Patriote* activists did indeed conduct political education sessions for the peasantry, but these seem to have been held in private houses or, less frequently, in the presbytery hall. In St-Eustache, for instance, there were regular meetings for several years before the 1837 insurrection in which the MPPs J.-J. Girouard and W.H. Scott would pepper political discussion with readings from *La Minerve*. In St-Hyacinthe for several weeks in 1837, interested parishioners assembled in the presbytery and heard the MPP Thomas Boutillier and curé É.-J. Crevier debate politics and read from *La Minerve*, the *Vindicator*, and *Le Populaire*.[34]

Siméon Marchesseault and François Nicholas were the two best-known teacher participants in the Rebellion. Marchesseault, whose schools were described earlier and who had attended the Collège de St-Hyacinthe, was active in *patriote* politics, delivering an influential speech against MPP de Bleury's opposition to the 92 Resolutions and his support for the vote of a Civil List in 1836. Marchesseault played a leading role in political agitation and fought in battles at St-Charles and St-Denis in 1837. Arrested when he tried to cross the American border in December 1837, he was among those exiled to Bermuda by Lord Durham in 1838, and he returned to the colony only after the second wave of insurrection was complete.

François Nicholas, who had some college education, was teaching in District 11 of L'Acadie in 1833, earning the miserable sum of the government grant and 1s.6d. in fees from his paying students. He was left off the pay list and got nothing from government for the May-November 1833 period, against which he protested repeatedly. He continued to teach in the parish. Nicholas was seen carrying a red flag and leading an armed group that was helping those fleeing from St-Charles in November 1837. He also led the group which arrested, tried summarily, and executed

Joseph Armand dit Chartrand as a government spy. A sympathetic jury acquitted him of murder in 1838, despite clear evidence of his guilt, but his direct involvement in the second insurrectionary wave led to his execution the following year.[35]

A third activist teacher in L'Acadie was Guillaume Benziger, whose monitorial school manual was mentioned earlier. Benziger was probably Swiss and was born about 1805. The notary L.-M. Decoigne testified to the authorities that Benziger had been conducting military drills for young people at the price of 1s. a month, supposedly preparing them to participate in the procession at the Fête-Dieu. Close to that event, some adults had also drilled with him. Benziger was apparently not questioned in 1837 but the following year was arrested at the American border after the battle of Odelltown. He claimed not to have been involved in the insurrection, but spent almost a year in prison. Military drill was a form of gymnastic exercise favoured by monitorial schools; it is possible Benziger was trying to supplement his fees after the grant ceased.[36]

Here and there in the Rebellion literature there are mentions of the involvement of a few other teachers. Several deponents claimed an unnamed 'schoolmaster' was involved in seizing the manor house at Beauharnois. It was alleged that a teacher in Chambly pushed people to action, and Louis Saint-Martin at Chateauguay was described as eager to do battle. A recent Irish immigrant named Michael Brady was hauled up in the examining magistrates' net in 1838. He'd had the misfortune to arrive in Lower Canada in August 1837, looking for work as a schoolteacher, but after two brief stints as an assistant teacher in Quebec he worked as a shipbuilder's clerk and day labourer. Peter Callaghan, a thirty-six-year-old former artillery corporal who taught at Ste-Marie-de-Monnoir, spent two months in prison for having helped test-fire a *patriote* cannon – made out of wood, with metal bands – and for making a pro-*patriote* speech. He said he'd been drunk. As we saw earlier, the Terrebonne *patriote* teacher F.-X. Valade broke with the party when it moved towards armed struggle.[37]

The great majority of those interrogated in 1837–8 declared themselves to be unable to read and write, but such was typical of the *habitants*.[38] The line taken by Tories and by the Catholic clergy was that the *habitants* were ignorant and thus easily duped by the *patriote* petty bourgeoisie. For imperial observers, colonial Tories, and liberal reformers, the insurrections pointed to an educational failure. Those who could not read and write could not understand politics or know where their own best interests lay. That they did not learn their lesson in 1837 pushed some moderate reformers after 1838 away from a demand for remedial education towards a call for the extinction of French-Canadian law, language, and religion.

Public reading of political newspapers points to efforts at popular political education by the *patriote* petty bourgeoisie, although its members seem rarely to have read competing newspaper accounts. Still, ignorance is not the same as stupidity. Those not able to read received information orally, including having those who could read do so aloud. Yet ignorance also meant learning from hearsay and gossip, rumour mongering, and susceptibility to superstition. Dozens of those interrogated by the magistrates said they were told in 1838 that the Americans were set to invade the colony and that anyone who did not rally to the cause would have his property seized, or worse. One of Louis-Joseph Papineau's auditors at Saint-Scholastique in the summer of 1837 heard him say that the English government wanted to make him an Irish slave, but he could resist because the English had no troops to send to Canada. Cyprine Hurteau from Contrecoeur, a 'snowshoe' (*raquette* or corporal) in the *patriote* secret society the Hunters' Lodge (les Frères Chasseurs), swore that another 'snowshoe' in his company told people that he'd got his curé's magic book, *Le Petit Albert*, which meant the Devil would let him seize and spike English cannon with impunity. Another witness took the secret society oath on *La Vie des saintes*, the commonly used schoolbook.[39] Nonetheless, as Allan Greer has pointed out, it is difficult to claim credibly that a peasantry rallying in 1837–8 behind a standard that included the abolition of feudal rents and the tithe did not understand its interests. As he also shows, the *seigneurs* had abandoned the *patriote* party en masse before the insurrection, and manor house and rent roll were often insurgents' first targets.[40]

The Buller Education Commission

The first wave of insurrection underlined the importance of educating the peasantry to Lord Durham, the governor general and royal commissioner sent by an English Whig ministry to sort out the colony, and to his associates. Before disposing of the *patriotes* languishing in prison at his late May 1838 arrival in Lower Canada, Durham dissolved the sitting Special Council and constituted a new governing body composed of men from his own near entourage, with the colonial bureaucrat Dominick Daly providing continuity. He appointed a number of commissions to investigate policy issues, including one for education. While Durham's mission was preoccupied with practical matters of administration and with larger questions of Anglo-American relations, like the Gosford Commission before it, it too looked at Lower Canada and the rest of British North America as objects of inquiry and objects for political-scientific mastery. The colonies were seen to possess their own internal dynamics, and the governmental problem was one of reorganizing such dynamics in the interests of British 'civilization.' The Durhamites shared a political sociology and were implicated in the projects for systematic colonization that had given rise to the British and American Land Company.

The Education Commission was established by proclamation on 14 July 1838. Arthur Buller, the twenty-nine-year-old commissioner, was formally instructed to inquire into the means available to rural Lower Canadians for the support of educational institutions and to suggest whatever changes to the existing educational system he might think necessary. 'In order better to discover the truth' in such matters, the commissioner was attributed broad and novel powers of inquiry to call such witnesses as he wished and to compel them to deliver any and all documents connected in any way whatsoever with the object of inquiry. Established in the Maison d'Union at Quebec, with the twenty-seven-year-old Christopher Dunkin as secretary, assisted by Georges Futvoye, the commission made preparations for a new Lower Canadian elementary school bill. In fact, with Dunkin doing the great bulk of the work, the commission undertook the most extensive social investigation in the colony's history (with the possible exception of the 1831 census). This investigation failed in its objectives, but success is not the measure of its importance for the study of colonial governmentality and social science. Failed experiments inform successful ones.

Arthur (later Sir Arthur) William Buller remains a little-known figure. He was the youngest son in a wealthy Anglo-Indian family and was tutored with his more famous brother Charles by Thomas Carlyle. At Cambridge, where Charles was a founding member of the radical and libertarian group known as the Cambridge Apostles, Arthur distinguished himself primarily by his homosexual lechery. He published an article in the *London and Westminster Review* in 1836, defending the Radical program of the secret ballot and ran unsuccessfully in the 1837 election. He had some minor involvement in the Charity Schools Commission. He arrived in Canada in May 1838 with the rest of the Durham suite and left in early November, soon after Lord Durham resigned. He ended his working career as a chief justice in Calcutta, probably placed there through the influence of his brother. Conspicuously irreligious, foppish, and perhaps feckless as well, Arthur Buller had no particular expertise in educational matters. The Canadian Catholic bishops saw him as a heretic, but he was tasked with selling them on the Irish school system.[41]

More significant was the Bullers' connection to the English movement of political and administrative reform that propelled the 'nineteenth century revolution in government.' Statistical investigation, mainly in the form of inventory making, was a forceful means of reconfiguring social relations for those interested in reforming the state system. The Bullers were tightly connected to left-Whig and Radical reform circles. Charles especially was an active member of the London Debating Society, whose membership overlapped with that of the Political Economy Club and of the London Statistical Society, founded in 1834. As MP, he was involved in the 1833 Select Committee on Public Documents, the venue for the legitimation of the newly established statistical branch of the Board of Trade, and a site for the discussion of methods of social investigation. He voted against the Russell Resolutions.[42] While Arthur Buller was officially Lower Canadian Education Commissioner, his secretary Christopher Dunkin consulted with Charles Buller in connection with the education inquiry on several occasions, carried it on after Arthur Buller's departure, and drafted a lengthy report on schooling. Dunkin authored a draft of the Canada School Act of 1841. His contributions to colonial schooling are equally little known.

Chances are good that Dunkin and Charles Buller were acquainted at least by sight before they met in Lower Canada. Dunkin, who would go on to a lengthy career in Canadian politics and administration, including service as federal minister of agriculture in 1871 and as the first finance minister of the Province of Quebec, was born in Newington in Surrey, England, in 1812. His earliest education was at a boarding school, and then he attended the Radicals' new University of London in the 1828–30 sessions in the classics course. The institution was quite small and the course in jurisprudence in the same sessions was a roster of Radical activists and intellectuals, including Charles Buller, J.A. Roebuck, Edward Ellis (probably Edward Ellice, Jr, Durham's wife's cousin and his private secretary in Canada), and Edwin Chadwick. John Stuart Mill had been enrolled in the previous session. After the University of London, Dunkin attended Glasgow University from November 1830 to late April 1831, taking the senior class prize in Latin and Greek, before following his newly remarried mother and her husband, Dr Jonathan Barber, to Boston. His stepfather taught elocution at Harvard College, and Dunkin studied and then taught and tutored Greek, provoking an infamous student revolt through his attempts to impose his English manners and discipline on a rowdy undergraduate population. Retained for a face-saving year, he was granted the BA and married his stepfather's daughter in 1835. When the abbé Jean Holmes inspected schools in Albany, New York, where Dunkin was said to be teaching, Dunkin was recommended to him as a possible normal school master, but Holmes was unable to find him. Dunkin's stepfather bought the *Morning Courier* in Montreal in late 1836 or early 1837 and installed Dunkin as editor, where he acted also as a correspondent for the London *Morning Chronicle*. One of the *Chronicle*'s editors, Stewart Derbishire, a member of Radical circles, was Lord Durham's advance man in Lower Canada and, among other things, sussed out possible press mouthpieces for the Durham government. Like Durham himself, Dunkin was a Mason.[43]

The *Courier* was perhaps the most moderate of the loyalist papers and was championed as a foil against the rabidly chauvinistic *Montreal Herald* and the *Montreal Gazette* by Quebec's *Le Canadien*. The Tory *L'Ami du peuple* denounced it as irreligious, chauvinistic, and soft on the rebels. Dunkin's political voice was better modulated than those of his Tory competitors, even if he shared their goal of making Lower Canada thoroughly 'British.' After November 1837 street battles in Montreal between the loyalist Doric Club and the *patriote* Fils de la liberté led to the smashing of the presses of the *Vindicator*, the *Herald* proclaimed that it would have been better to smash the *Courier*'s press, since Dunkin had been printing – in order to criticize – excerpts from *Vindicator* and *La Minerve*. Even in the heat of the excitement of the armed clashes later in the month, Dunkin insisted that the rule of law should prevail and resisted the temptation to rumour monger around the battles of St-Denis and St-Charles. On 4 December he urged support for Gosford's Proclamation of 29 November 1837, calling for a return to peace, and argued that 'the *mass* of those now in arms against the Government in this Province, are precisely the men to whom mercy ought to be extended, if possible. – Their ignorance and credulity have made them the prey of their ambitious leaders.'[44]

It was not the 'peasantry-as-dupes' argument nor its embrace of ethnic chauvinism that distinguished the *Courier*'s analysis, but Dunkin's preference for the constitution, propaganda, and educational discipline over his Tory opponents' calls for a wholesale dispossession of the French-speaking population. On 11 December 1837, he again called for lenience and moderation in treatment of the mass of the insurrectionists, while agreeing that the leaders should be punished severely. There was no doubt that the colony would have to be made British, but not by 'the disenfranchisement and degradation of every man with French blood in his veins ... Education must be made to raise the habitant from his present level. British law, and influence, and enterprise, must have free scope to act, for the improvement of the country and of all ranks and origins among its people.' He continued to follow what was a moderate line in the period of martial law in the Montreal district. He argued against calls for an immediate imperial intervention to eliminate French law and to prohibit the use of the French language in public business. Instead he insisted that the colonial legislature acting under the rule of law should 'introduce registry offices, create new local courts, afford universal facilities for education, make the English language part of that education, enjoin acquaintance with it, after a fixed date, as a qualification for official or professional occupiers, and by these and like means, introduce new life into every portion of the Province.'[45]

In short, like Sir Charles Grey and Sir George Gipps before him and like Lord Durham in 1839, Dunkin was convinced of the inherent superiority of 'British' institutions over arcane and archaic seigneurial property relations and over the ignorance and dependence engendered both by those relations and by the Catholic Church. An intellectual, scholar, and probably a Wesleyan Methodist in religion, Dunkin equated 'Britishness' with rationality. Enlighten the *habitant* population, lay the legal and political infrastructure for commerce, and the enjoyment of 'British liberty' would necessarily result in anglicization and a new national unity.

Finding Facts for Conclusions Known

The Education Commission sought complete school statistics, but statistical inquiry was not a precondition for policy formation. The problem was the unruliness of the people; the solution was the educational discipline of population. Inquiry could produce surprises, but educational policy propelled, rather than issued from, the commission's investigation of conditions. The Durhamites had spent part of their long sea voyage to Canada studying political documents, including the reports of the Gosford Commission, and the Education Commission was intent on giving effect to the recommendation of the Irish school system. In order to do so, the commission had to map the educational condition of the countryside. In contrast to the early conceptions of the Legislative Assembly – that the role of government was to stimulate a 'taste for education,' after which the sovereign people would be left to school itself – from the outset the Education Commission sought to plan a new educational 'engine' or 'machine' for the colony as a whole. To design such a system effectively the relations among population and school-age population, educational infrastructure (schools, teachers, supplies, furniture, etc.) and territory had to be known.

There was also the cultural/political question of whether or not people in the countryside were willing to tax themselves to support schools.

Who Can Tell?

In the absence of local government bodies – given that popular intimidation had unseated many government appointees in the Montreal district, and that the political loyalties of those still in office was uncertain – it was not obvious to Buller and Dunkin where reliable sources of educational intelligence were to be found. Their attempts to identify one or a few reliable informants in every township, parish, or seigneury were inadequate. Other investigative techniques became necessary. As did his fellow commissioners, Buller met with people 'in the know' who happened to pass through Quebec and questioned them about educational matters. For a time as well, he apparently considered acting as a roving educational commissioner himself, going so far as to get a letter of introduction to the parish priests from Msgr Signäy of Quebec which called on them to cooperate with him.[46]

As soon as the commission issued, its office received pleas for funds from colleges and academies as well as offers of assistance from educational activists, some of which Buller entertained. Dr J.-B. Meilleur, MPP, promoter of the Collège de L'Assomption, and future superintendent of education, offered to help, while he made a plea for support for his college and for the inclusion in any new school act of a clause providing retroactive payment to teachers who had kept elementary schools open in good faith. 'The friends of education rejoice' at Buller's appointment and at his plan for an Irish-style school system, wrote Meilleur, and he drew Buller's attention to the clause in the failed 1836 bill, which he claimed to have authored, making provision for county model schools. He promised to have a Quebec friend get a copy of that bill to Buller. Buller responded that the commission would deal with colleges in due course, but in the meantime 'I should feel obliged, could you furnish me with the names of any gentlemen, in your neighbourhood or elsewhere, who in your opinion would be likely to take sufficient interest in the subject to reply to such inquiries with any considerable degree of care & accuracy. It is desired to obtain by this means as complete a view of the Educational Statistics of the whole Country, as possible.'[47] The absence of a well-established central intelligence apparatus is evident in the reply.

Instead of travelling through the rural parts of the colony, Buller announced on 13 September 1838 that, owing to the press of time, he was 'obliged to have recourse' to circular questionnaires as a 'means of obtaining the local information indispensable to my enquiry into the state of Education.' Time pressure increased dramatically with the arrival in Lower Canada on 16 September of the news that parliament had disallowed Lord Durham's ordinance exiling the Rebellion prisoners to Bermuda and with the subsequent announcement of his resignation. Buller collected the handsome sum of £333 for his three and a half months' tenure as commissioner and left the colony early in November 1838.[48]

Creating Local Education Commissions

Shortly before Buller's departure, the commission addressed enormous bundles of questionnaires to people in 269 places in Lower Canada. In all, 1,041 individuals were named on the covers of the packages containing these documents, among them typically some mix of the local curé and/ or minister of religion, the militia captain and senior justice of the peace, the seigneur, the doctor, and one or more of the notaries. In regions where the population was ethnically mixed, both French and English officials were named, and on the margins of settlement the land agent or missionary alone was the recipient. A separate detailed letter of instructions on the completion of the questionnaires was usually sent to someone other than the person who received the bundle. Those named were invited to join together to prepare a response.

The other commissions established by Durham undertook nothing similar. Their commissioners contented themselves with the reigning practices of inquiry: soliciting the verbal opinions of the colonial elite, calling for letters from selected informants, and consulting parliamentary papers. Before Buller and Dunkin's work, only a very few questionnaires had ever been mailed from any central government agency seeking information from distant informants. We have seen that circulars had been used by government on a limited number of occasions to solicit information. The curés were employed several times before 1820 to deliver reports of population and grain supplies, and even the Quebec education committee had contemplated using a circular to drum up support for its university plan in 1789. The secretary of the Royal Institution had sent a questionnaire to teachers in 1820, Lord Dalhousie's interest in land reform encouraged the Assembly to send questionnaires to the curés and to the 'leading inhabitants' of the Townships in 1821, and there were a few other examples in that decade. In the mid-1830s the investigative technique was more common in colonial administration.

The 1835 Penitentiary Commissioners, for instance, administered an eighty-nine-item questionnaire to informants (it was not mailed out) and the Legislative Council in 1836 printed a stack of questionnaires for distribution in the seigneuries to test sentiment about the establishment of registry offices. Information gathering by state agencies had been formalized to some extent as well, for instance, with questions on a standard form administered to arrivals at the Grosse Isle immigration station in the 1830s.[49] Yet systematic, standardized, and colony-wide social investigation was remarkably rare.

Not only did the Education Commission rely on the mails to contact distant and unknown informants, it also incited the formation of local educational commissions for the articulation of the 'interests of education' and for the generation of 'authentic information.' Such a manner of proceeding was in keeping with the spirit of Buller's political liberalism, in which public schooling was one of the infrastructural conditions and supports for liberal-democratic government. Schooling on the Irish model was seen to be 'above politics' and hence something on whose organization members of the dominant classes should be able freely to agree.

The Questionnaires

The six questionnaires distributed by the commission reveal both its ambition to discover everything there was to know about rural schooling and its remarkable faith in the willingness of local notables to cooperate. The questionnaires were folded into a thick bundle whose exterior was the verso of the first schedule, printed on stiff paper. It contained the five other schedules and bore the names of the respondents and the addresses of their townships or parishes on its outside. Those who participated in the inquiry were invited to certify their participation by signing the exterior of this first schedule.

The schedules were enormous. The first was an imposing document, 30" (75 cm) wide when unfolded, with its length determined by the number of schools that were described. Describing four schools yielded a schedule 30 × 12" (75 × 30 cm), and since there could be as many as twenty school districts in a township, some schedules were 2½ feet wide by 5 feet long (75 cm × 1.5 m)! Some examples were hand-sewn together. Seventeen questions were asked on the first schedule, aiming at a general overview of the geopolitical condition and history of each school district. The second schedule, equally imposing physically, contained nineteen questions concerning teachers, subjects of instruction, books

used, teaching methods, and the condition of the schoolhouse. The third
invited the respondents to conduct a census of each school district, giving
a count of the inhabitants by age, sex, national origin, religion, and literary capacity. A further question concerned the number of students being
instructed gratis. The fourth schedule sought a detailed history of the
local educational economy, year by year, from 1828 to 1838, while the
fifth asked for information about regions in the township or parish
whose residents were not served by the school districts established by the
Assembly. Finally, the sixth schedule sought a detailed description of all
other kinds of educational institutions in the locality.

How to Answer a Questionnaire

In addition to the package of questionnaires, recipients were also sent a
printed, four-page explanatory letter outlining the purpose of the inquiry
and instructing them how to complete the questionnaires. The letter is
probably the first instance in Lower Canada of systematic instruction in
social science offered to an important number of amateur observers. It reveals the formative impact of social scientific investigation on its subjects
and objects, an instance of science's 'configuration of the user.'[50] The production of this new form of knowledge demanded the formation of knowing subjects, and, as the method of distribution aimed to organize respondents into groups, so the letter of instructions sought to educate respondents
about how to respond. The information to be entered in each cell of each
schedule was described to them in detail and the author of the explanations knew himself to be dealing with people who had never performed a
similar task, for he described closely how to come at this odd creature, the
questionnaire, and explained its spatial organization. Thus, for example:
'N.B. – The answers on the above subjects are to be given each in its proper
column, as in the former table. Double lines are ruled across the table, to
divide the Returns for the several Schools, from one another.' And further
again, 'the lines ruled across this table, mark off, as in the two former
tables, the space to be taken up with the return for each school District.'
   The author of the letter of instructions also anticipated that the inquiry
might provoke differences of opinion. He told respondents to ensure that
the forms were completed, 'taking care, when any of you differ as to the
correct answer to any particular question, to state the grounds of such difference, and the name of the dissentient.' Where the informants found
themselves unable to answer a question, they were requested to 'state the
fact, and cause, of such inability' – perhaps in anticipation of a follow-up

investigation. The instructions concluded by noting that 'it is of course desirable that all the Returns asked for in the above Tables, should be rendered as nearly *exact* as possible. Where for any reason it is not found possible to make them exact, the word *"about"* should be prefixed to those estimates which are at all conjectural.' If respondents could not agree on their answers, 'it is desirable that the fact should be stated in the column of "Remarks," or in any other more convenient manner.' The producers of the questionnaire sought statistical knowledge in the double sense of the term still current: a descriptive inventory of local conditions, and material that could be abstracted numerically. Yet they had no means practically or conceptually to turn the answer "about," or to turn a local disagreement, into numbers. These were not the worst of their worries.

Not 'Above Politics'

Did Buller and Christopher Dunkin seriously expect that the differences that had again exploded into armed insurrection just as their questionnaires were mailed would vanish when local notables were invited to articulate the interests of education? It is difficult to believe they could be so naive. The press could have alerted them to the contrary, for there the battle lines were drawn clearly. The Tory line was simple: 'the Canadians, of French origin, must forthwith be educated in such a way as will compel them to feel ... that they are in fact British subjects and none other.' To produce such political subjects, 'a truly English education must take the place of that Frenchified and feudal system which has hitherto disgraced and degraded our schools.' *L'Ami du peuple* attacked the Education Commissioners as ridiculously unfit. Could anyone believe that Buller, 'who knows nothing of the country,' with only the help of Dunkin, 'who knows even less than he, who has never had occasion to get to know and to appreciate the population, and who is even unfamiliar with the language of the majority,' could devise a system of education on their own? 'The thing is absurd.' Typically, *Le Canadien* took a cautious line, reprinting the *Mercury*'s praise of Buller's qualifications, but insisting that the work done in the Assembly by John Neilson and H.-S. Huot had already indicated the path to follow in educational matters. Other experiments had been tried and had failed, so the commission should restore the essence of the Assembly's legislation.[51]

Rather than creating a consensus view, in many places the questionnaires revived or refocused local animosities. The inquiry menaced local patterns of social dominance and revealed the class, linguistic, religious, ethnic, and national fissures characteristic of rural social relations. Many Protestant leaders refused to meet with the curé in their localities, many curés refused to have anything to do with the inquiry, and some Protestant clergymen responded with indignation to the suggestion that they could have common interests with Catholic priests, as if light could meet darkness! In several places there were struggles for control over the questionnaires. The commission received competing sets of questionnaires from some places, each claiming to represent educational conditions truly. Moreover, after two years of administrative neglect, the commission was seen as capable of adjudicating all manner of outstanding local school complaints, from the non-payment of teachers' fees to the illegal occupation of schoolhouses built at public expense. A considerable number of potential respondents saw the commission's printed schedules as so much letter paper to be used to convey their grievances.

While some correspondents made valiant efforts to complete the questionnaires, the project was doomed by the opposition of Bishop Lartigue. Dunkin underestimated the strength of this opposition, but Buller, who had both corresponded and met personally with Lartigue and Signäy, was in a position to know what to expect. Indeed, Buller may have decided to distribute questionnaires in an effort to overcome the reluctant cooperation of Signäy and the open hostility of Lartigue and his co-adjutor Ignace Bourget of Montreal to his larger educational plans.

Catholic Opposition to the Education Commission

The Catholic bishops do not seem to have done anything to gauge the effects of their May 1836 encouragement of vestry schools until they got wind of Buller's survey. On 23 July 1838 Lartigue shared with Signäy his fear that the government was going to impose a general system of education on the colony. The danger was not so much from Durham as from his 'acolytes,' among whom there were some obvious heretics, and Lartigue laid out the line that the bishops should take. If Durham was to get their support for any general system, there would have to be independent Catholic and Protestant education offices. The bishops would have to ensure that the Catholic office was clearly under the influence of the clergy, and Durham must be convinced to attribute all the revenues from the Jesuits' Estates to it. If he refused, he should be warned that his system would meet the fate of the Royal Institution.

Lartigue raised the tone of his fears in a letter two days later to Signäy's co-adjutor. Pointing to alarming anti-Catholic material that had appeared in the *Morning Courier*, Lartigue wrote that he had 'already had notices from London, whence people write that preparations are underway to de-catholicize this Province through education, as has lately been tried in Ireland.' His fears were confirmed by reading the proclamation in the official *Gazette* creating the Education Commission. As far as Lartigue was concerned, the commission was nothing but a plan hatched by the Anglican bishop to snoop into Catholic business. Any bill issuing from the commission should be made to fail, and if this was not possible, Lartigue urged intransigent insistence on the formation of separate confessional boards. He was contemptuous of the proposal for Irish-style religious instruction: 'with their general education, they'll also give their students a general religion, the one they'll fabricate in their heads, that is to state an absurdity.'[52]

In August 1838, Lartigue and Signäy belatedly attempted to discover what the curés had done with respect to vestry schools by sending their own questionnaire, asking how many parish schools existed, how many for boys and for girls, what the attendance level was, if anything was taught besides reading and writing, and how much, if anything, was contributed by the vestry for school support. The priests were also to inform the bishop if there were no schools in operation, not to reply by the post if they could avoid it and, to his version of the circular, Lartigue added the remark that the information sought would help him to refute claims from the foreigners now in the colony that there was no schooling in the countryside.[53]

Signäy, at least, received prompt replies from most of the curés – despite repeated claims to government that the bishops had no power to get information from them – but the replies demonstrated precisely what the bishops had hoped not to find. In the great majority of parishes the vestry did nothing; many parishes reported no schools of any sort; and in most the only instruction on offer was rudimentary and not under clerical supervision. In nineteen of the twenty-six parishes in Signäy's diocese for which responses to the circular survive, the vestry offered no funds whatsoever for schooling. Several of the remaining parishes offered support of some sort out of a legacy left by a former curé; a few subsidized the fees of a handful of poor students in a private school. St-Roch-des-Aulnaies was an exception in which the vestry supported a boys' and a girls' school. Elsewhere, curés claimed the vestry was too poor to offer any aid to schools but were encouraged by the bishop's inquiry, since it seemed to presage some systematic attention to the question.

Thomas Cooke, vicar general and curé in the district of Trois-Rivières, wrote that there had been many schools in the district until 1836 but that most were now closed. There was no school at Cap-de-la-Madeleine, none at the Forges de St-Maurice, and none on the Bécancour seigneury. Two schools were still open in the town suburbs, and the town itself had six in operation. In an understatement, Cooke added, 'the stimulus given to education in our rural districts begins to slacken.' At St-François, the schoolhouse built at parish expense with separate accommodation for boys and girls sat empty, but the Soeurs de la Congrégation ran a girls' school. From les Grondines curé L.-O. Désilets complained of the utter disinterest of his flock in schooling and of their cultural backwardness. His parish, he said, 'has never provided Society with a subject: neither priest, nor Doctor, nor Notary, nor Lawyer, nor merchant, not even the meanest Clerk, there is not a single Lord. All there is is a Sort of rambling Christian who goes from door to door and teaches some little boys and girls who learn nothing.' The bishop's permission to use the vestry funds to subsidize a school was 'forcefully rejected[,] everyone was opposed even to giving £1- to encourage a few talented children.' Here the situation was much the same as it had been fifty years earlier. There was no sign of the private or clerical zeal which L.-P. Audet imagined must have existed. Even at St-Jean-Port-Joly, where *Le Canadien* had trumpeted voluntary efforts in 1836, the curé remarked in 1838 that there was no regular school, but it was rumoured that 'a few persons go from house to house as School masters, in different parts of the parish, to teach reading & Writing [the] Only teaching to which the Capacity of the said Schools is Confined.'[54]

Thus the bishops clearly found themselves on defensive ground. They did not have the time, let alone the resources or the logistical capabilities, necessary to organize a religious-based school system as a counter to the Education Commission, and their attempts to revive the 1824 Vestry School Act had failed miserably. They wrote to Archbishop Murray in Dublin for detailed information about the Irish school system and asked him about the strategy adopted by the Irish clergy. They were not comforted by the detailed set of rules and regulations established by the Irish National Commissioners, and they learned that Rome had not pronounced on the Irish scheme, despite the Irish bishops' inquiries. Still, most of the Irish bishops encouraged the organization of national schools.[55]

The Canadian bishops knew, then, before Buller's inquiry was launched that there was no credible way they could claim that the Church was fulfilling its touted role as guardian of the education of the people, if education was defined as substantial schooling. Having failed to organize their own schools, they still had at least two options. As did the Irish bishops, they could have accepted the model of non-denominational civil

instruction with a generic Christian morality, augmented by separate religious instruction before or after school hours. Instead they chose to do
their utmost to obstruct plans for secular public education and to demand denominational school boards and schools. They were encouraged by Lord Durham's departure and the doubt it cast on the status of
his Education Commission.

Lartigue refused to give the commission any access to his questionnaires; Signäy provided only a summary. Arthur Buller met on several
occasions with Lartigue, Signäy, and Thomas Cooke and wrote to them
at length, urging support for the generic non-denominational Christian
model and elaborating the by-now standard arguments in its favour. He
defined the overriding goal of education in civil terms: 'I think you will
agree with me,' he wrote to Signäy, 'that, in a country, where the distinctions of religion and race prevail to the extent that they do in Lower
Canada, it is highly important that every one of its institutions should be
framed with a view of uniting and nationalizing its entire population.'
There followed not an account of plans to extirpate the French fact, but
rather a lengthy description of the Irish *Scripture Extracts*, assurances that
Buller's schools would remove no powers of religious instruction from
the clergy, and a plea for reasonableness. The demands of the Catholic
clergy to name schoolmasters and to specify books were not acceptable:
an interdenominational board of examiners would do the former and
the curriculum would be centred on secular subjects. Buller copied them
draft school legislation, but it was all to no avail.[56]

Lartigue told Buller that he saw no possible grounds of agreement and
repeated his insistent calls for separate denominational school boards.
To Buller's plea for cooperation on the eve of his departure for England,
Signäy replied, in politely insulting language, that the plan in its entirety
was unacceptable and demonstrated an ignorance of conditions in the
colony which a longer residence might have remedied. Lartigue told his
clergy that they were under no obligation to respond to the commission's questionnaires and to reply to demands for information that educational matters were the purview of their bishop. Buller's attempt to
have Jacques Viger act as intermediary to the curés for the commission
yielded only a copy of Viger's 1835 Montreal school inventory. The bishops drafted a petition insisting that government involvement in schooling be limited to the funding of Catholic denominational schools under
clerical control.[57]

In January 1839, when the progress of the commission's investigation
was stalled both by the aftermath of the second wave of Rebellion and by

the refusal of most curés in the Montreal district to respond, secretary Georges Futvoye wrote to J.-J. Lartigue seeking the results of Lartigue's earlier investigation and the cooperation of his clergy. Lartigue replied that his questionnaire had posed a very few simple questions about schools in his diocese for his own use and he had yet to receive all the answers. By contrast, the commission's questionnaire asked so many complicated questions that he, Lartigue, would not know himself how to reply to it. As to the means of getting his clergy to cooperate, Lartigue declared that he knew of none. First, he said, 'because I have no official or certain knowledge of the present existence of the Commission of Education, nor of its Commissioners'; second – stretching everyone's credulity – because he had no right to tell the clergy to cooperate; and third because they would not be able to answer in any case. Futvoye would be better off reading the reports of the Assembly to inform himself about the schools.[58]

The Catholic hierarchy was not alone in its opposition to the Irish model of civil religion and non-denominational instruction, for a meeting of Protestant clergy held in Quebec on 30 October 1838 resolved to oppose any educational plan that excluded the study of the Bible from the schools, a resolution certain to alienate Catholics. But the Catholic hierarchy occupied a hegemonic position in spiritual politics; without its cooperation in the wake of the Rebellion, the chances of a complete inquiry conducted at a distance into rural educational conditions were nil.[59]

Added to the obstruction of the Catholic Church was confusion about the status of the commission after Lord Durham's departure on 1 November 1838. Notices appeared briefly in the colonial press informing correspondents not to communicate with the commission for the present time. One person wrote to Le Canadien asking if the commission still existed, because its inquiries were so detailed and time-consuming it would not be worth responding otherwise. The commission retracted its earlier notice on 8 November and confirmed that an officer was in Quebec waiting to receive completed questionnaires and wished to have them without delay. It had been discovered that many of the clergymen named in the questionnaires had moved; respondents were encouraged to join with whomever had replaced them.[60]

The Encounter with the Questionnaires

Despite many obstacles, a goodly number of respondents tried seriously to complete the unwieldy schedules. If this had been a sample survey, and even if the amount of time required to complete the questionnaires had been modest, the response rate of around 33 per cent would overjoy a modern polling company. The inquiry was something unheard of at the time, and the commission had no effective sanctions to apply to anyone who did not reply. The participation rate suggests a fairly broad-based interest in furthering the work of educational reform, or at least an interest in taking advantage of the attention of the government. Since the work asked of respondents was enormous and unusual, the reactions of those who tried to answer are doubly interesting: for the fact that they tried and for the manner in which they did so.

There were two poles of reaction. Some groups simply ignored the task of filling in the tables and responded to the commission in prose. Others went beyond what was required of them, filling in the forms completely, annotating them, and writing essays on educational policy. In some places, the notables assembled with ceremony to deal with the forms; elsewhere some minor clerk was assigned the task. In between was a variety of reactions, but none resulted in stable statistical knowledge – knowledge whose categories were established sufficiently firmly to allow for variations only of quantity.

The questionnaires for St-Foy were addressed to a group that included John Neilson, Louis Massue, the curé Huot, and two others but were returned blank. Huot said it was too much work for a person like himself to respond and suggested the commission enlist 'some of the Official Gentlemen Sinecurists, whose highly paid Situations, leave them so much leisure time.' Those solicited in Kamouraska also avoided completing the questionnaires. These were literate men of political substance, among them two members of the colonial Special Council: the lieutenant colonel of militia, judge, and seigneur J.-B. Taché, who would also sit on the Legislative Council until 1849, and the equally illustrious Amable Dionne. They were joined by the English-speaking doctor Thomas Horsman and by curé Varin. No one in the group answered the commission for some months, earning them a letter in the spring of 1839 seeking the forms.

They returned the blank schedules, saying it was impossible to fill them in satisfactorily, but replied in prose in the order of the tables as it was preferable to 'use this method rather than have recourse to your columns, which we would be forced to leave almost entirely blank.' There were four school districts in Kamouraska parish, but there had been no school open continuously since 1828. At the moment of writing, the parish boasted two schools, although one of the schoolhouses had fallen into serious disrepair. As to the title of the four houses built with government money, a notary since deceased had them, and the group knew nothing about them.

With respect to the second questionnaire, these gentlemen briefly described the teachers of the two open schools and added a few remarks about the branches of study. They did not complete the third questionnaire because the 1831 census had not used school districts as enumeration districts, so to find out how many people were literate would require 'a house-by-house survey and an examination of each individual,' which was beyond their resources. To reconstruct the history of the schools of Kamouraska since 1828, as the fourth questionnaire demanded, the commissioners would be better off consulting the inspector general, Mr Cary, at Quebec. There were no areas of the parish not covered by a school district, and the group gave a few details about three small private schools. They could not say more, but they sincerely hoped that their answer would aid the government in taking measures 'as prompt as efficient to bring to an end the deplorable situation in which Education in our parish has been cast since the Expiration of the Statute.'[61]

Seven men who assembled to consider the questionnaires in Ste-Marie-de-Beauce decided that it was 'impossible to fill in these blanks without suffering a great loss of time & much expense.' Instead, they proceeded to write general comments on the forms. On the first questionnaire, they simply noted that all the schools had ceased in May 1836, with the exception of a small private school, and to have more complete information, the commissioners could consult the reports of the former school visitors, a portion of one of which was pasted on to the end of their last page. On the second questionnaire, they merely noted and that all the schools had been French-language schools, while on the third, fourth, and fifth, the commissioners were again referred to Joseph Cary's office. The sixth form contained a description of the girls' school run by the Congrégation de Notre Dame. Although they refused to do the work of taking a literacy census of the parish, the correspondents from Ste-Marie, with no sense of incongruity, added 'In the parish there are a large number of people who can read, especially among persons of the sex – this instruction is passed down from father to son, in families.'[62]

The census demanded by the third schedule brought many willing correspondents to a halt. From la Petite Nation, for example, Denis-Benjamin Papineau and two other men answered the commission by filling in the first two questionnaires, remarking on the third that they did not have the information necessary to answer it, and leaving the others blank. The same reaction came from curé Parant of Cap St Ignace in L'Islet. Other respondents saw nothing but blank paper in the carefully ruled and headed forms sent to them. In St-Laurent-d'Orléans, for instance, the response to the commission consisted of a very few phrases scrawled in a very shaky hand across the first two questionnaires.[63]

Elsewhere, on the margins of settlement, or where an educational economy had never flourished, no attempt was made to fill in the questionnaires. From Hunterstown township in St Maurice, for instance, Truman Kimpton wrote that the township had not been inhabited before 1828, that at the moment only the village of Kimpton's Mills was established, and there had never been a school. From Halifax township, in Megantic, John Lambly and Thomas McKie wrote on their first schedule that there had once been a school in the only school district in the township. It opened 'between the years 1831 & 32 and continued for six months, the Master went to Quebec and died of the Cholera The School has never since been [recommenced?] There are at present no records of the School to be found.' They completed the third schedule (the census) but none of the others. On the Isle d'Orléans, in St-François parish, 'there has never been a district or an elementary School section. thus no answer to be made' to the first questionnaire. In this case, where the reply was prepared by the curé, the doctor, the militia captain, and one of the church-wardens, the group did conduct a census of the parish's 689 residents, finding 156 of school age, with 30 attending school. They indicated on the fourth form that there were private schools in the parish but did not describe them as requested to do on the sixth form. Here, where no Assembly school districts had ever been defined, many of the questions asked by the commission did not apply to the local situation, and such was the case elsewhere.[64]

Local Conditions

Many correspondents used the questionnaires to communicate with the government about their educational concerns. For that reason they were potentially a rich source of intelligence for Christopher Dunkin as they are for later researchers. P.M. Benson, from Brandon in Berthier county, used the forms to justify his work as a teacher and to promote his Royal Institution school. His was the only school in the parish and he was himself educated 'at the Santry institution, within three miles of Dublin.' He had 'fitted many young men for Counters' [i.e., clerical work] since the school bill failed in 1836. Yet his income, from a high of £42 in 1828, was a miserable £26 ten years later. He used the sixth schedule to describe his course of studies in detail. Others used their answers as a pretext to get information from the government. From Clarendon township in Ottawa county, the first three schedules were completed, but the respondents were far more interested in learning if the government was planning to compensate those teachers who continued to teach after 1836.[65]

In addition to describing local conditions, the commission's correspondents called for government action to establish better schools. From l'Isle aux Coudres in Saguenay county came a long description of the schools, the strategies used to keep them open, the obstacles to a successful system, and a call for reform, all carefully drawn up by the curé, two militia officers, and two men who had been school trustees. Here were three schools in operation, one of which opened in 1837 after Bishop Signäy's authorization to use vestry funds for school support. The group managed to keep their schools going because as a safeguard they had banked the matching funds for schoolhouse construction received earlier. Yet promoting rural schooling in current conditions was exceptionally difficult. The lack of government aid and the refusal of most residents to pay for schooling were obstacles for the commission to overcome. The teachers received almost nothing in school fees – 18 pence a month and even less in one of their three districts – and the fees were levied only on the condition that they would be waived if a child was absent for fifteen days in a month. A great many students thus attended less than half-time, and no fees were paid during planting and harvest seasons.

Under such circumstances it was impossible to get good teachers. The group called for the elimination of school trustee elections and an end to the practice in the parish of electing school visitors and of voting on teacher hirings. Nothing was more obnoxious. It was degrading for any educated person trying to encourage schooling 'to find his plans stopped in an instant because Mr. N, for whom the thing is Hebrew, doesn't find them appropriate; or to be examined by people who ought first to receive some instruction &c &C.' The group thought it would be better to have local educational leadership in the hands of 'a moderate aristocracy' than in those of 'a short-sighted, disreputable, and some times brutal radicalism. The axiom[,] as many ideas as minds, is really poisonous for furthering the business of a corporation or of a community.' Everyone knew, they concluded, that rural *canadiens* liked to meddle everywhere and that they saw stubbornness as a virtue.[66]

Curé J.-H. Sirois refused to help Antoine Déhays St Cyr fill in the schedules in St-Stanislas in Champlain county. St Cyr thought the commission might be surprised at the lack of progress in schooling in his parish but it was easily explained. Friends of education were excluded from the management of the schools by people who did not understand their own best interests. Then there was the problem of the teachers, 'of whom a goodly number would not shine brightly on the benches of an elementary school kept and managed the way it ought to be.' Finally, there was 'the election of trustees, who for the most part unlettered, were nonetheless the persons appointed to examine into and to report on the Students' progress.' The four school districts allowed by the Assembly had only ever had one school in operation, and it closed in 1836.[67]

In St-Pierre-les-Becquets, the fight over the false valuation of the schoolhouse in 1829 continued nine years later and initially prevented a response to the commission. The questionnaires were addressed to the leading protagonists in the earlier fight, but the magistrate J.-P. Dionne, who had exposed the fraud, and the curé refused to join with Jacques Raimond Baby to answer them. Dionne and the curé denounced Baby and his brother François for the fraud and said that Baby was too stupid to be able to answer the questions anyway. Plus he was accused of the capital crime of destroying their church. Georges Futvoye addressed a second set of questionnaires to the parish, omitting the Babys. Dionne, the curé, and another magistrate then filled them out, adding a long recitation on the 1829 fight and a request to be informed if the money fraudulently paid had ever been recovered. They revealed that the two schoolhouses paid for with public money were now in private hands. The parish had nine school districts and eight operating schools in 1836 for a school-age population of 583. In that year 253 young people were at school. In late 1838, all eight schools were closed and there were no students.[68]

In the neighbouring parish of Gentilly, the notary Thomas Fortier reported that eight of the nine parish schools were closed. There was one spacious and well-maintained schoolhouse, and Fortier commented that it would be good to be able to offer a liberal education to the parish. However, he noted that 'all Systems of Education, which are not accepted by the Catholic Clergy will be firmly rejected by the *habitants*; the moreso since the Educated are the Gentlemen Clergy who oppose any innovation that might in any manner direct or indirect give the least offense to the dogmas of the Religion that they profess.' He called for inter-denominational instruction.[69]

Two sets of questionnaires were eventually sent to Rawdon township after a struggle over the first set pitted English and Irish [Catholic?] residents against American Protestant settlers. At issue was the question of who could speak the truth about conditions, and again the commission's attempt to create a local consensus view of schooling failed. There was a school in the township supported in part by the Young Ladies' Society of

Andover, Massachusetts, and taught by a Miss Foster. The Church of England clergyman R.H. Bourne led a group which subscribed funds to keep the school running in 1838 but claimed before the inquiry began that two Catholic priests had attempted to seize the school and to evict its occupiers.[70]

The commission's explanatory circular was sent to Bourne calling on him to meet with the crown lands agent, named McGie, to whom the questionnaires had been mailed, and with the others named to complete the forms. Bourne wrote that when he went to see McGie, the latter told him he had no forms and when they went to the post office, they were told there was nothing there for them. However, 'there was something ambiguous in the manner in which Mr McGie was received at the Post Office' by Colonel Thomas Griffith, the postmaster, justice of the peace, and senior parish militia officer. Griffith claimed that the questionnaires were addressed to him, not to McGie, and Bourne wrote to the commission for clarification. The answer was that the questionnaires were intended for McGie, but Griffith refused to give them up, and swore at McGie when he tried to collect them. Bourne in turn went to see Griffith and was cursed out by Griffith's quartermaster, a former schoolteacher named William Holtby. Bourne then learned that Griffith had mustered his militia company in order to answer the inquiry without McGie and Bourne. Griffith was planning to report that the school Bourne was involved with was closed, and Bourne was afraid of losing future legislative aid. Georges Futvoye sent Bourne a second set of returns on 21 December 1838 and wrote to Griffith asking him why he had not replied to the inquiry.

Griffith responded at once, pointing out that he had been the senior school visitor under the 1834 School Act. He had called on the others named by the commission to meet with him but got no response and then was preoccupied by the organization of a 'Corps of Loyal Volunteers' to defend the parish. 'The Rev'd Mr Bourne is an American by Birth and Education,' warned Griffith, 'and has an invenerable dislike to any institution let it be ever so good that is of British Origin and ... this Mr McGie is a personage of little or no education, and not fit to transmit any business without an amanuences.' Bourne was busy trying to have McGie 'appointed the Chairman of the meeting Knowing that he would have but little Trouble in Subverting our institutions and replacing them with others of the American Sistym.' Griffith's group returned the completed questionnaires in January 1839, reporting that all ten of the parish schools open in 1836 were now closed.[71]

Incomplete Statistics

In a statement to Arthur Buller in May 1839, Dunkin reported that of the 269 bundles of questionnaires, addressed to 1,041 individuals throughout the colony, 88, bearing the signatures of 286 of the 359 persons addressed in them, had been returned. A few more would trickle in during the summer of 1839, but the project for producing complete colonial educational statistics announced at the outset of the investigation had failed.

Dunkin delivered a post-mortem. 'In some cases,' he wrote, 'a difference of religious or political opinion has prevented the persons nominated from associating together,' while 'in the French Counties' the names of addressees who did not sign the returns were 'generally those of English gentlemen.' By contrast, in the Eastern Townships, many people who were not addressed on the bundle of questionnaires joined in completing them. Dunkin added that in remote parishes where people did not read the public press, delayed responses were due to the fact that Durham's departure was assumed to eliminate his Education Commission. Where people had seen the Commission's announcement of 8 November 1838 that it was still in operation, the insurrection, the absence of relevant documents, and the high costs associated with the investigation made them unable to answer. 'In a few cases,' he added, 'the Catholic clergy have refused to give any information, stating that they acknowledge no other superintendent of Education than the Bishop.'

The quality of information generated by the investigation was 'very imperfect, and in many cases contradictory. In one [county] the subdivisions of the gross population amount to nearly three times the whole population. Not one has been received in which all the questions are answered, or reasons assigned for leaving them blank.' Only the Eastern Townships and the counties of Beauce and Ottawa returned nearly complete sets of questionnaires. In the Montreal district counties, 'which were the principal in which unfortunately open rebellion existed in the winter, no attention whatever has been given to the Returns ... 55 parishes &c were supplied with the forms,' but none replied. The same lack of response obtained in the counties of Montmorency and Quebec. Dunkin noted: 'No Returns made from these 2 Counties; the one from St Foy being in blank.' He added: 'I purpose collecting them in by personal visit,' although it is unlikely that he did so.[72]

A further attempt at an overview of the commission's work was contained in a document sent to Buller by Dunkin on 6 July 1839, after Buller's official report had been made. The responses received from various counties were discussed and the high quality of returns from the county of Ottawa was noted. Dunkin added: 'Ottawa is the only County from which all the Returns received are fully & fairly made out. The whole of the Township returns would have been received, thus making Ottawa the only C[ount]y from which all have been forwarded; but that in the two Tps left blank, Hull & Petite Nation, it was supposed Visitors were about to gather in the Returns.' This supposition was due to the recent proclamation of 'the 43d ordinance of the Sp[ecial].C[ouncil]. Sec 2 item 21 appropriating £200 for that purpose, being considered as intended to follow up the measures adopted by the Com[missio]n of Ed[ucatio]n. This, it is to be feared, is the case in many other parts of the Country.' In effect, Dunkin was informing Buller that Sir John Colborne's ruling Special Council was taking its own steps to reconstruct colonial schooling. One step was the appointment of a school inspector who was sent to collect information on and to make assessments of the surviving schools in the Montreal district. Any further effort by the commission to gain information through the distribution of questionnaires was thus useless.[73]

Despite Christopher Dunkin's discontent with the results of the commission inquiry, its failure to produce complete and coherent educational statistics is not a measure of its interest for an investigation of projects of colonial governmentality. On the one hand, it made a difference in colonial politics and social relations and not just by exercising the Catholic bishops. It yielded information about local school conditions. It focused attention in some areas on policy reform. Moreover, it made Christopher Dunkin think systematically about educational government, both in a workaday (but nonetheless revealing) manner and as part of a much broader exercise to connect what he came to see as the flawed course of colonial history to the possibilities of an improved 'British' future through the schooling and anglicization of the colonial population. Much earlier historiography has halted at this point to denounce the anglicization project and, satisfied with denunciation, to ignore the practical workings of politics and administration in the Durham mission.[74]

However, with respect to local school conditions, the commission investigation exemplified the fact that the majority of rural schools had ceased to exist. This matter was significant in the debate over educational reform, especially since papers such as *Le Canadien* were arguing that the foundation laid by the Assembly should be preserved and improved upon, while conservatives claimed that nothing of substance had been accomplished by the Assembly and that the schools were so little rooted in the countryside that they vanished without government handouts. The commission returns spoke to these matters, and its findings were supplemented, as we see in the following chapter, by an investigation of conditions in the Montreal district by a special inspector.

The commission's returns offer examples: Dunkin could not produce a tabular summary. Nor can I, but the examples tell a common story: the great majority of the schools had ceased to exist. In the parish d'Écureuils in Portneuf, the trustee school of 1836 was open as a private school in 1838. Of 120 people of school age, 37 had attended school in 1836; 16 did so in 1838. In Rivière-du-Loup, where there were eight school districts, four schools were open, one of them a Royal Institution school. In St-Vallier-de-Bellechasse, in the 1829–31 boom years of school grants, there had been 224 students in ten schools. Ten teachers together received £208 in grant money and £181 in fees. By 1835, six schools were left, with 140 students and school revenues amounting to £128 in grant money and £120 in fees. At the end of 1838, one school with 50 students remained and the teacher earned about £30 in fees. In la Malbaie parish, the school-age population was given as 944; 251 young people had been at school in 1836; 124 were attending in 1838.[75]

All ten schools open in Rawdon township in 1836 were closed in 1838, as were all seventeen in Frampton township; in fact of Beauce county's thirty-seven school districts, only one had a functioning school in 1838. Six of seven schools in Gentilly parish were closed, seven of eight in Ste-Croix-de Lotbinière, five of six in Leeds township, four of six in St-Léon-de-St-Maurice, and all four schools in St-Jean-Deschaillons. All four schools open in 1836 at la Pointe du Lac were closed in 1838; the two school-houses built with government aid were rented to private residents. In St-Thomas-de-l'Islet, 214 young people attended school in 1836 out of a school-age population returned as 944. In 1838, 119 were at school. Of the five districts allowed under the 1832 School Act, two never had a school, and two of the other three districts had schools that closed in 1838. In the district centred on the village, there had been three schools, a trustee school, a vestry school, and a Royal Institution school. It seems the vestry school remained open and one of the other teachers kept a small school in his or her house. Four of the six schools open in Kingsey township in 1836 were closed in late 1838. One closed in April 1836, one in the spring and two in the fall of 1837. One of the two remaining schools was not held in a schoolhouse. The best-surviving school belonged to the vestry. It had opened in 1833 in a house valued at £75 with a good cast iron stove and pipes and an acre of ground. In Bécancour in the years of large grants, there were eight schools in six school districts. Only the vestry school in the village remained open in 1838. In the parish of Pointe de Levi, six schools were open in 1836 and three remained in 1838 in private houses. The schoolhouse built at public expense was now occupied 'as a home for beggars.' Three of four schools in Pointe aux Trembles were closed and the schoolhouses rented out as private residences. Here there were 534 residents of school age; 157 had been at school in 1836; in 1838, 33, all boys, remained.[76]

There were efforts like those described earlier for l'Isle aux Coudres to keep schools open. In parts of the Eastern Townships, where schooling was seasonal, the schools were not much affected by the cessation of the school grant. From Dudswell township, Amos Bishop reported that one of four township schools was closed permanently, while two of the remaining three were open seasonally and one continuously. There were two good schoolhouses subsidized by the legislature, especially one '26 feet square, with 9 windows & 1 Door 3 rows of Galery Seats on each side with writing Desks to each seat.' It was valued at over £75. Bishop had no school registers and so could not report attendance, but the teachers were good and had been educated locally. As elsewhere in the Townships, the teachers 'boarded 'round': 'the Teachers generally Receive the Money drew & Board at the families who send their Children in proportion to the number of Children sent Also the Teacher Receives firewood and Candles & what they need; and no Receipts are passed – these things are gratuitous – we are not particular; Some poor people are free from geting wood and freed from boarding Teacher.' The loss of the school grant had cost the schools about £20 each. Again, in Shipton township, all thirteen township schools were closed in December, but only one was closed permanently.[77]

While the returns were exemplary rather than comprehensive, there was nothing in them to contradict the conviction that Dunkin had already expressed in his report to Arthur Buller and in the draft school act he had prepared: the trustee school system was a failure, but that meant to him that the field was wide open for a new educational scheme. In the Eastern Townships, where the schools fared better, there had been repeated demands for many of the changes Dunkin would propose.

Colonial Governmentality

It is clear from the surviving rough compilations of commission materials and from the scratch sheets on which Dunkin worked while drafting a school ordinance in 1839–40 that, like the Gosford commissioners, he too was thinking in terms of population, territory, and security. The compilations failed – but nonetheless attempted – to construct an image of the Assembly schools as a dynamic system. Returned questionnaires were filed according to county of origin, and, where it was sufficiently ample, the information was summarized. Dunkin attempted to calculate the number of literate adults in each county and the proportion of those of school age who attended school before and after the cessation of the grant.[78] He attempted to chart the growth in numbers of school districts and to identify the years when there were most schools. He sought to determine the numbers of people not contained in organized school districts. In some counties, the expenditure on schoolhouse construction was totalled up and the numbers of surviving schoolhouses indicated.

Dunkin then attempted to give a synthetic overview in tabular form of the condition of popular education throughout Lower Canada. For instance, he drafted tables giving the population per district in 1831 and 1838, with the number of people knowing how to read only and the number knowing how to read and write, by sex in two age categories. The number of teachers was calculated for 1836 and 1838, classed according to their qualifications ('good,' 'bad,' 'indifferent'). In another table, Dunkin attempted to reconstruct the historical development of the educational economy, with the number of schools, the size of the grant, and the number in attendance annually by county from 1832 to 1836. The table also compared the number of schools and students in 1835 and 1838 in an effort to evaluate the consequences of the cessation of the government grant. This table was meant to address the question of whether or not the Assembly's schools could be self-sustaining. It also sought to distinguish Protestant from Catholic schools. Because of imperfect or missing information, none of the draft tables could be completed, but the attempt was made to identify the dynamics of a system, to create statistical abstractions, and to reconfigure statistical returns into meaningful or revealing combinations – to totalize, to differentiate, to re-totalize: the essence of population thinking.[79]

Dunkin's surviving papers contain several working drafts of an educational law and a variety of related material, ranging from formal memoranda to rough scratchings and calculations. Here too he was thinking of the self-replicating dynamics of an educational machine. Thus, for instance, in one document he reflected that there needed to be a hierarchy of schools and that it would be the task of school inspectors to divide the colony into convenient school districts. The physical size of districts was more important than their population; they should be neither too small to support a teacher nor so large that young people could not walk to school. Wherever possible, inspectors should define 'first class districts,' which would have 1,000 inhabitants within 1.5 miles or 1,400 within 2 miles of some central point.

Dunkin thought through mechanisms to make competition among teachers into an engine for their mutual improvement. Teachers had to be presented with the prospect of earning a comfortable living, but for the prospect to work, grants had to be unevenly distributed. The hope of gaining a superior school and the higher salary that went with it would stimulate competition, and the school grant had to be distributed in keeping with this possibility. 'Many districts must pay poor,' Dunkin noted, 'some must be made to pay well. The very worst possible distribution of a limited fund, is that which divides it into equal portions, every one of them inadequate to its intended object.'

Again, we can see Dunkin calculating the costs of running the machine, assuming the existence of certain parameters: there were 1,202 elementary schools in Lower Canada in November 1835 and together they had cost £14,305.7.9 over the preceding six months, or, say, £23.15.6 each a year. The number of schools in the exemplary school system of New York State showed there really should be more than 1,200 in Lower Canada, but say one settled on 1,200 to start. Teachers should be guaranteed an average of at least £30 annually, but half of it should come from local taxation, so the grant would have to be £18,000 plus a discretionary fund of £2,500, plus £2,000 for school buildings, so £20,500 for rural schools, plus say £2,000 for city schools and £5,000 for all institutions of higher education, for a total of £29,500. The 1841 School Act would allocate £30,000 to Lower Canada.

We can see Dunkin sketching out a scenario in which the machine would be built in successive annual stages, and calculating expenditures on that basis. So, given the size of the colonial population and the physical area of the colonial territory, one could start modestly, but still have a complete system up and working at the end of four years. In 1840–1, one could take the money left over from the past schooling appropriations and use it to fund urban elementary and secondary schools, to support teacher training and the McGill medical school, to appoint a superintendent of education, and to provide him with a contingencies fund: cost £6,702. One could start funding rural schools and school construction again in 1841–2, add a provincial school inspector, and create a supervisory provincial school board: £16,250. In 1842–3 one could add another inspector and expand the numbers of schools: £25,500. And in

1843–4, to complete the system, one could add a third inspector and increase the level of expenditure in all categories, except for the medical school: £34,000.[80]

Whatever one might wish to conclude about the relative political and literary merits of the *patriote* Assembly's attempts to lead the sovereign people to educate itself, the Catholic clergy's demands for sole control over schooling to preserve the people in pastoral simplicity, and the liberal chauvinist state of tutelage proposed by imperial officials from Gosford onwards, Christopher Dunkin's manner of casting and solving the question of the education of society was distinctively different from earlier conceptions. It was prospective, rather than simply reactive. Gone from it was any notion of a stable political equilibrium among king, lords, and commons, as imagined in Lower Canada's original constitution. Gone too was the patriarchal notion of the fathers of families allied with the Catholic clergy to reproduce an organic community. Gone were other notions of the delegation of government to the 'natural rulers' of a pre-industrial society. In their place was the concept of a fundamentally undifferentiated population to be governed by being sectioned and inserted in a hierarchy and segmented and subjected to discipline and training in new state institutions. This population could be known in its elements through the techniques of the social science. The following chapter examines the social and political substance, and the miserable failure, of attempts to put the new school system in place.

8

Governing through Education

The discipline of population through schooling seemed more palatable to some of its earlier opponents after the forceful suppression of insurrection in the colony. However, pillage, terror, random violence, and collective punishment were the first lessons offered to *habitants* and to the village and urban French-speaking petty bourgeoisie. Lower Canada was subjected to military and political dictatorship until the Act of Union of 1840 came into effect in 1841. Martial law was in effect in the Montreal district, and the imperial parliament suspended the Lower Canadian constitution on 10 February 1838, authorizing the governor to rule through the proclamations of his appointed Special Council. Armed bodies of 'loyal volunteers' held sway in the countryside and roamed the streets of Montreal, extracting revenge for the *patriote* campaign of intimidation in the summer and fall of 1837 and for the second insurrection of November 1838.[1] *Le Canadien* in Quebec and the Montreal and Quebec Grand Juries denounced the arbitrary use of police power and the harassment to which respectable citizens were subjected in the streets.

Stewart Derbishire, the point man for Lord Durham who would arrive as governor general at the end of May 1838, found the Legislative Councillor Denis-Benjamin Viger so frightened of the volunteers roaming Montreal's streets that he had pulled down his name plate and had not left his house for several months. He would be arrested in November and spend almost two years in prison without charge. Viger warned Derbishire of the hatred and desire for revenge generated by the volunteers, who murdered people in the countryside and burned their properties as they pleased. The burning of St-Benôit two days after the *patriotes* had surrendered their arms was outrageous. Derbishire interviewed Marie-Félix Dumouchel, whose husband and two of her sons were in prison. The volunteers had burned seven houses belonging to the family, seized all their possessions, and threatened her repeatedly with drawn swords. Derbishire overheard volunteers bragging of these exploits. None of his French-speaking informants spoke of the earlier *patriote* campaign of intimidation.[2]

'About St Charles, the people seem heartbroken,' wrote the Queen's Printer J.C. Fisher in October 1838. 'The village is ruined. At St Denis great unnecessary pillage was committed by the troops, and there is a strong feeling of injustice in consequence. The innocent, as usual, suffered for the guilty,' he continued, suggesting that 'more hangings and less burning would have been better for the peace of the country.'[3]

During the second wave of insurrection some rural and village properties were pillaged by les Frères Chasseurs, but far more were torched by troops and volunteers. Jane Ellice, who was married to Durham's private secretary, had been held captive by *patriotes* for a week late in 1838 at Beauharnois before being freed by the Upper Canadian Glengarry Highland militia. She thought the Glengarries were the most fearsome men she had ever seen. Those who rowed her across the St Lawrence, on a November night brightly lit by the buildings they had torched in Beauharnois and neighbouring villages, boasted that they had burned everything they saw in a six-mile-wide swath on their march to Beauharnois. They proposed to burn anything they had missed on their return. Six hundred men who had set out as infantry returned as cavalry. Edward and Jane Ellice and her sister Tina were quite safe, wrote Charles Buller to Durham on 12 November 1838. The second wave of insurrection had been defeated easily. 'The chiefs behaved as usual like cowards,' he commented, '& the poor deluded peasantry are paying the penalty by having their country ravaged with fire & sword.'[4]

A series of public executions was substituted for Durham's earlier policy of selective transportation and general amnesty. The rural population in the Montreal district was subjected to collective punishment. Sir John Colborne, the military governor, was warned, uselessly since he did not listen, to be extremely circumspect in arming volunteers by a colonial secretary worried both about increasing political antagonism in the colony and about burdening the Exchequer with military expenditure. 'Politically,' Lord Glenelg cautioned, 'the encrease of existing animosities by arming one part of the population against another, and the fostering in one class [of] a taste for the excitement of a military life, are evils of the gravest kind,' and 'the heavy expense which must be thrown upon this Country is also a most serious inconvenience.' Perhaps the cautions about sparing the Exchequer encouraged the forces in their pillage of

the countryside. Armed groups went from village to village after the insurrection had been suppressed terrorizing local residents and shipping
suspects off to prison in Montreal.[5]

Dr Thomas Boutillier, on the *patriote* side in 1837 but opposed to the
1838 uprising, described the arrival of a volunteer force of fifty or sixty
Dragoons at St Hyacinthe on 25 November, on the heels of a larger
guards regiment. It was announced that the troops had orders to billet
themselves in the village, and officers and men moved into people's
houses. One village widow had thirty-eight soldiers in hers. The officers
demanded only the best and threatened people when they didn't get it.
'Several soldiers with an officer were sent into designated houses,' wrote
Boutillier, and 'there they seized beef, cows, fat pigs and fowl ... Nor was
firewood spared and grain and hay, especially the last two articles, were
removed by the Dragoons everywhere they found them.' Among those
targeted was Boutillier's sister-in-law, Louis-Joseph Papineau's sister,
Rosalie Dessaulles, whose loss was as much as £75. Colonel Cathcart, the
commanding officer, presided over an inquiry into the village's participation in the insurrection and shipped eight men off to prison. Having
emptied the village of its supplies, the troops left as winter descended.[6]

French-speaking urban residents other than Denis-Benjamin Viger were
subjected to random violence, or were afraid they would be. There were
nighttime arrests in Montreal – of Louis-Michel Viger, for instance, the director of la Banque du Peuple, who was in prison from mid-November 1837
to late August 1838, only to be re-arrested in October while his Tory enemies engineered a run on his bank. *Le Canadien*'s criticism of the contempt
shown by the police for the law and the courts, and the paper's attacks on
Sir John Colborne's Special Council late in 1838 for reaffirming its suspension of the right of habeas corpus, led to the arrest and imprisonment of
both editor and publisher on charges of high treason. The paper's editorial
offices were ransacked more than once, and the publisher, J.-B. Frechette,
spent a month in jail before posting bond. Editor Étienne Parent was in for
five months and demanded that Colborne establish a state censorship
board if trial by jury was not to be re-established. Given the paranoid fanta-
sies of the political authorities, the few newspapers not 'dedicated heart and
soul to the dominant party, are at any moment liable to seizure, and their
Editors and proprietors to imprisonment,' even for reporting what were
everyday topics of political conversation in England. The Quebec Grand
Jury delivered an indictment against the chief of police and one of his officers for the assault and false imprisonment of the Education Commission's
managing clerk, Georges Futvoye, who had been roughed up in the street.[7]

The Durham Analysis

In this new 'war between sword and tongue,' educational reform seemed a soft option by comparison to the Prussian-style police state that many colonists saw being established. The arrival of Lord Durham as governor general at the end of May 1838 was greeted with great enthusiasm at Quebec. Durham's reputation as 'Radical Jack,' a liberal reformer and champion of the oppressed, when combined with his studied distance from the old Legislative and Executive Councils and his amnesty for the Rebellion prisoners, encouraged French-speaking moderates such as L.-H. Lafontaine, Étienne Parent, R.-É Caron, and H.-S. Huot to hope for progressive constitutional reform. Parent in particular looked forward to a new representative government in which French Canadians would be able to play interest group politics, at least in the domains of language, culture, and religion, even within the confines of a new British North American federation.[8]

Their hopes were quickly dashed. Durham took up the substance of the Montreal Constitutional Association's portrayal of political struggles as entirely based on mutual hatred of the 'races.' Perhaps the first public confirmation of this alarming stance was Durham's appointment of the rabid francophobe Adam Thom to his municipal commission in mid-August. *Le Canadien* was still hoping this was a sign of a balanced approach: Christopher Dunkin, the moderate constitutionalist to the Education Commission, the Tory Thom to the Municipal Commission, and then surely next some leading French Canadian to another important office. But already in a dispatch to the Colonial Office on 9 August Durham's determination to eliminate the French fact was perfectly clear, and the light finally dawned on *Le Canadien* in October with Durham's resignation speech.[9]

In the August dispatch, Durham told the colonial secretary that while he had expected to find a struggle pitting popular opinion against oligarchic power, what he saw instead was 'the existence of a most bitter animosity between the Canadians and the British, not as two parties holding different opinions and seeking different objects in respect to Government, but as different races engaged in a national contest.' Durham presented this observation as a new discovery, but in fact it was in his baggage when he arrived. He had met frequently in England in the winter of 1837–8 to discuss Canadian questions with his wife's uncle Edward Ellice, owner of the Beauharnois seigneury and an influential voice in Whig politics and in Durham's own thinking. Ellice had been a prime mover in the failed attempt to reunite the Canadas in 1822 and had inserted a clause in the 1822 Trade Act for the commutation of seigneurial tenure under which all the commons would become the seigneur's personal property, a colonial counterpart to his own Highland Clearances. Ellice was very influential on the Canadian question in Whig circles despite both his naked self-interest and the loathing with which he and his estate manager, L.S. Brown, were regarded at Beauharnois for their extortionate rents.[10]

Ellice had corresponded with Lord Gosford about Canadian political strategy and spent the late spring and summer of 1836 at Beauharnois, as he said, 'to put my House in order for the storm which I see gathering, & which there is neither wisdom nor energy [in London] to avert.' As far as Ellice was concerned, there was no exit from the political crisis around the Legislative Council and the Civil List without imperial legislative intervention. 'You might as well attempt to govern Canada as Ireland' – then under a Coercion Act, as Gosford well knew – 'in the spirit of British Institutions.' The Papineau faction would accept nothing less than an elective Council. Ellice told his nephew, Lord Howick, Papineau 'is stupidly – if a clever man can be stupidly – obstinate on the point – He will consent to no supplies without an Elective Council. English People will never, especially if supported from Upper Canada, and after the heat that has existed, submit to one.' The alternatives were imperial intervention or civil war.[11]

Ellice was the conduit between Durham and the moderate *patriote* L.-H. Lafontaine in early 1838. Lafontaine rigorously opposed the plan Ellice had already articulated to govern Canada by excluding French Canadians from politics. 'Let the local administration cease, in all its administrative and social relations making and maintaining race distinctions,' wrote Lafontaine, 'and also put a stop to its favoritism towards privileged classes, and, let it direct its steps towards a liberal but firm policy, you will see harmony restored much sooner than one might imagine.' Lafontaine's reports of his meetings with Ellice encouraged the Quebec moderates to see Durham as a Radical who would undo their Tory opponents, but Ellice was deceiving them.[12]

He had long been promoting the view of a 'war between the races' that had no grounding in social conditions other than the ignorance of the *habitants* and the defects of French national character. He urged Gosford to 'remember you are dealing with french, not with english people, – Nothing appears fairer on principle, nothing more delusive in practice, than classing them together as men to be dealt with on the same rules – at least in their present state of information and education.' The French Canadians were not able to handle representative institutions, while the English 'altho' the numerical minority' were 'the majority in intelligence

& with the largest portion of the active capital.' 'Race' and national character grounded a justification for excluding the majority from politics while claiming to respect liberal political principles.

'On my Seigniory where we have the best and richest Farmers of both Classes,' Ellice told his nephew Lord Howick, 'the French without an exception vote on one side – the Scotch and English on the other. The English and Scotch are as intelligent and as independent as your Northern Farmers – the French as good and kind hearted and well meaning a people as it is possible to conceive – much the most amiable of the two – but not one in a hundred can write his name. I had an Address from a whole Parish the other day in which the Notary was obliged to attest "the mark" of every subscriber. They are told it is essential to the security of their Religion and Institutions to send people to the Assembly to assist M. Papineau in protecting them from being turned out of their Lands by the English – they believe it and vote.' But none of them had any idea about the substance of politics, he continued. They couldn't read the *patriote* newspapers, and L.-J. Papineau's political meetings at Beauharnois were a joke, 'attended by the Notary and half a dozen stirring spirits – the people not being disposed to leave their fields and rafts to hear speeches which they cannot comprehend.' They would be happy with political despotism – a line Durham would repeat.[13]

Stewart Derbishire painted the same picture more vividly for Durham. Without repeating his version of the then-current sociology of national character and civilization, the point was that there were no reason for the insurrection except the ignorance of the *habitants* and their susceptibility to propaganda. 'The habitans up to the period of their revolt laboured under no practical grievances.' It was striking that 'their condition, social and political was an enviable one, as compared with that of all other people upon the face of the globe.' He described an undifferentiated, amiable, and comfortable colonial peasantry whose main defect was that 'their minds have been exercised within a very confined circle, and they are ignorant. As a purely agricultural people they have but little occasion for the arts of reading or writing as ancillary to their occupations and they have not the stimulus which in Protestant Countries is supplied by a reverential desire to puruse the Scriptures. Hence they have not the aid which reading furnishes to the power of independent thought.' No sign of seigneurial rent or tithes here.[14]

Discourses such as these were very common on both sides of the Atlantic. They provided a means for English imperialism to penetrate what was unintelligible to it – if not to understand much of the dynamics of colonial social relations. A deeper, more focused, and less prejudiced mind than Durham's was needed to think in other terms, but such discourses offered a variety of means for someone who professed liberal principles to justify illiberal policies.

The War between the Races

Durham wrote in his August 1838 dispatch that the separation of the 'races' was a common fact of everyday colonial social intercourse. 'Grown-up persons of a different origin seldom or never meet in private society; and even the children, when they quarrel, divide themselves into French and English like their parents. In the schools and the streets of Montreal, the real capital of the province, this is commonly the case.' Durham stressed that the struggle was by no means a class struggle, for 'the station in life ... of an individual of either race seems to have no influence on his real disposition towards the other race; high and low, rich and poor, on both sides ... exhibit the very same feeling of national jealousy and hatred.' All the other pretended issues were simply manifestations of this fundamental and irreconcilable antagonism, Durham claimed. The concept 'race' did the work of breaking the unity of 'the people' and of making it possible to recodify unruliness as unfitness to rule.

Despite the colony's apparent calm, warned Durham, it was only his presence and dictatorial powers that kept the simmering hatreds in check. 'The exercise of the very extensive powers placed in my hands seems to have operated as a sort of charm, like oil poured upon troubled waters. At this moment all is still,' and people were starting to look with hope to a better future. Yet, well aware of the attacks on his mission in England, Durham warned that a firm and unshrinking determination to eliminate the 'barbarous institutions' of French Canada was the only path to successful retention of British North America: 'there can be no permanent safety for people of British descent, except by rendering the colony thoroughly British.' Parliament would have to 'sanction such measures as will effectually provide for the abstraction of all legislation on British interests from the control of a French majority.'

In keeping with a liberal colonial governmentality, Durham claimed that 'this great object can be legitimately effected without violence to Canadian rights, and in strict accordance with the soundest principles of constitutional government.' The extinction of French Canada was initially envisaged through the creation of a British North American federation, a political declension of Sir Charles Grey's proposal to subdivide Lower

Canada into federated provinces. Majority rule would still prevail, but under new conditions of security the majority would be English-speaking. The colony was in a state of exception that justified this violation of the rights of French Canadians. As Durham put it, 'not Government merely, but society itself seems to be almost dissolved; the vessel of the State is not in great danger only ... but looks like a complete wreck.' Exceptional steps had to be taken 'to meet the emergency.' In his *Report on the Affairs of British North America* Durham would add that British immigration to the Eastern Townships and to the west of Canada would surely suffocate French Canada in the long run: better to do so quickly and with less pain in the present than to prolong the patient's sufferings. Finally, he flattered himself that French-speaking Lower Canadians were 'charmed at being relieved from self-government, & being for the time under a pure despotism.' Despite their leaders' republican simulacra, the people preferred less rather than more democracy.[15]

In keeping with this logic, Durham pursued the idea of federation and invited the Maritime governors to Quebec for discussions. However, his chief secretary, Charles Buller, warned that federation would ensure French-Canadian survival. 'The great argument against a federal Union,' wrote Buller 'is that it does nothing to attain the main end which we ought to have in view. That end is the keeping Lower Canada quiet now, & making it English as speedily as possible. This a representative English government would do most effectually.' On the other hand, 'a federal system would keep up French Canadianism. It would recognize its existence, & maintain its peculiarities; & it would most assuredly do nothing to efface it. I look upon federation as having no single argument in its favour except with those who want to keep the Canadians French, which is precisely what you do not want.'[16] Durham would urge the Union of Upper and Lower Canada, with representation by population to ensure an eventual English voting majority in the legislature. However, 'race' turned out not to be the main line of division in the new colony, and reformers from both sections in 1841 united across the supposed barriers of language, religion, and national origin to dominate the agenda.

Schooling in the Durham Project

Most people are familiar with Durham's aims, if not with the logic of his justifications or the nature of his sociology, but the role of schooling and educational administration in the anglicizing governmental project has received almost no attention. Schooling was an indispensable means of government: new state forms were dependent upon new and congenial forms of subjectivity, and schooling and school administration jointly would produce them. Plans, projects, and schemes for both proliferated before and after the publication of Durham's 1839 *Report on the Affairs of British North America*. The great majority of English-speaking proponents of new school systems urged these as a sure means of anglicization, with tactics that varied only with respect to the violence and rapidity used to achieve it. The second wave of insurrection in November 1838 pushed many to take a hard line. The Montreal Constitutional Association's francophobic rhetoric came to dominate public discourse in English, as its membership practically dominated Sir John Colborne's Special Councils and as its mouthpieces gained a privileged position after the elimination of the *patriote* press.

The smashing of the radical press and the cowing of moderate *patriote* or reform supporters limited the visibility of opposition to educational reform as anglicization. Nonetheless, the surviving papers publicized the proposals of Jean-Baptiste Meilleur for a reform based on the Assembly's past efforts, and Étienne Parent's *Le Canadien* consistently called for a revival and improvement of the Assembly's schools. The Catholic clergy and its conservative allies worked behind the scenes to prevent the recreation of any secular public school system. The establishment of the ultramontane paper *Mélanges Religieux* late in 1840 gave Bishop Bourget of Montreal his own press tribune from which to attack reform proposals.

Lord Durham's educational commissioner, Arthur Buller, in cooperation with his secretary Dunkin, had sketched out a new school system and had drafted a preliminary version of a new school act by October 1838. The educational inquiry underway at that time was meant to provide the detailed knowledge of rural population and school conditions necessary to administer such an act. Christopher Dunkin was at work on a history of colonial schooling and on ways to use the Jesuits' Estates as a school fund. A few days before his departure from Quebec, Buller outlined the draft act to Bishop Signäy and sought his support for it, which, as we have seen, was not forthcoming. Nonetheless, the draft of October 1838 sketched much of what Buller would recommend in his own November report on education, which appeared as an appendix in the later versions of Lord Durham's *Report*. Dunkin would extend and polish it into a draft educational ordinance in 1840.

To the bishops, Buller harped on the theme of interdenominational Christian solidarity, but his draft legislation proposed a hierarchically organized, state-administered system removed from party politics. He grappled with organizational devices that would implicate the bishops without giving them real power. His draft plan was a cumbersome hybrid of arrangements in Ireland, New York, Connecticut, and Massachusetts, with some echoes of the Royal Institution Bill of 1829. At the top of the hierarchy was a salaried, full-time superintendent of public instruction appointed by the governor and holding office on good behaviour. There was no mention of any parliamentary education committee. It was the superintendent who would manage the lower levels of the system, aided by a Central Board of Education. He would report annually to the legislature. The Central Board was to be composed of six government-appointed school inspectors, three Protestants and three Catholics, each with an assistant. The assistant inspectors were named by an 'inspectorship board,' again with six members, half Protestant and half Catholic. The Catholic and Anglican bishops or their designates would be permanent members of this body, which was described as a board of advice.

The bishops were to be empowered to instruct the assistant inspectors in matters of religious education, and the Central Board was to be divided into two denominational committees. These would deal with any and all religious questions. Neither was to encroach on any religious rights of the other. They would decide on the schoolbooks to be used or prohibited in the schools and to frame school rules and regulations in keeping with the school law – which implied that the superintendent or the legislature would specify a list of acceptable books from which the Board could select. An assistant inspector would accompany each school inspector on his rounds, and the members of the Central Board would also inspect every institution of higher education at least annually.

Buller offered the Catholic bishop direct control over the substance of the schooling of his flock in exclusively Catholic settlements. In such areas, local trustees and clergy would decide on religious instruction, provided no one objected. Where there were objections, or where the denominations were mixed, Buller commented 'it becomes necessary to provide by law for the separation of religious from other teaching.' In such cases, religious instruction was to be set apart from secular instruction and students objecting to the former would be excused. 'General morality' was to be taught in all such schools: 'a series of Extracts from the Bible (the Irish book of extracts with such modifications as may be agreed upon by both parties) to be authorized as a reading or lesson book.' The series would be published in both languages, and no teacher was to offer any opinions on the lessons or to refuse to teach them. Denominational instruction could be given in the schoolhouse after hours. Buller wrote that 'any infringement of religious rights, whether by teacher or other officer, to be treated as – "misconduct," and, on proof to cause his dismissal from his office.'

Such provisions might seem to work against a secular public school system by enshrining the practice of education as moral training and pious reading which sustained peasant ignorance in Catholic areas. But Buller was looking forward to anglicizing social and legal reforms and to massive immigration from the British Isles. These changes would either cantonize the French-speaking population, create mixed populations, or empower lay opinion, and thus remove religious teaching from the schoolroom during regular hours. 'General morality' would command a new public sphere: Lartigue and Signäy had no desire to be his subordinates.

Buller said nothing about urban schools and nothing about school finance. He proposed to divide the colony into three inspectorships and to divide these in turn into five school divisions. Each inspectorship was to have a normal school and each district was to have a model school for teacher training. Rural municipalities would elect a three-member Board of School Commissioners using the municipal franchise. The members would sit for three years, one going out of office annually. They would be joined by up to six municipal residents, either legally recognized clergymen or others, to form a Municipal Board of School Visitors. The commissioners would divide the municipality into convenient school districts, and, if approved by the district inspector and the chief superintendent, the district boundaries were to be binding. The commissioners managed school finance and reported annually on school matters to their inspector, via their visitors' board. The visitors were to be required to visit the schools annually at least four times 'at irregular intervals and giving no previous notice of their intention to visit on a particular day,' another Irish practice.

Buller preserved elected school trustees in each school district to manage the finances of individual schools, to hire teachers, and to report on school matters to their commissioners. They could not confirm their teachers' employment until the latter had been examined and approved by the school visitors. Teachers were to be required to attend their division model school for a specified period each year until they were examined and granted a '"full qualification" for teaching in an Elementary school.' Normal school graduates were exempted from this requirement, and the inspectors were empowered to certify other qualified candidate teachers.[17]

Buller apologized to Signäy for sending what he described as this 'hasty exposé' of his school plans, which he intended to complete after the leaving the colony, but supposed nonetheless that 'there can surely be no objection to [Signäy's] expressing his opinion on the points raised' in the draft. He hoped that the bishop would be able to comment at least on the main points, adding that if he did not, 'I am afraid I shall be deprived the advantage of having his opinion at all.' Faced with this threat of unilateral action, Signäy responded to the draft act in much the same terms as he had to Buller's plea for support for interdenominational schooling. While he needed more time to consider the details, the simple fact of there being a single superintendent of education who was not guaranteed to be a Catholic made the scheme completely unacceptable.[18]

The Buller Report

Despite the fact that the Education Commission's questionnaires had only just been circulated, Buller's report to Durham on the commission's work was dated 15 November 1838.[19] In it he added spice to the Assembly's Standing Committee reports in order to endorse the Legislative Council's refusal of the 1836 School Bill. The Assembly seemed to have laboured hard in the cause of popular education, he wrote, but 'the moment they found that their educational provisions could be turned to political account, from that moment those provisions were framed with a view to promote party rather than education.' The Assembly never had the courage to impose educational property taxation, and the schoolmasters, thus dependent upon political favour, were among the worst opponents of government. Buller had been 'assured by many witnesses that the "Minerve," an exciting and seditious paper, was in frequent use in the schools as a class-book.' Teachers needed to be removed from politics, and Buller proposed both that they be prevented from voting at elections or attending political meetings, and that other sources of employment be opened to them as a reward – clerkships in registry offices, for instance.

Yet Buller's educational sphere 'above politics' was structured by the anglicizing political project. His report did three kinds of ideological work in its support. First, and again despite the fact that his school survey was just underway, he declared repeatedly that the field of education in the countryside was *terra nullius*. 'Go where you will,' he wrote, 'you will scarcely find a trace of education among the peasantry.' All that remained of the schoolhouses was litigation over whose property they would become. But the 'complete destruction of past systems, and the utter absence of any at the present time, are matters of great good fortune and congratulation, for now a clear field lies open for the future.' There were 'no individuals to compensate,' there was 'no old machinery forced upon our use,' and so the ruins of the Assembly's schools furnished 'unencumbered room for the erection of a new and durable edifice.'

As well, for an English audience Buller analysed the educational field using the rudimentary sociology of civilization and national character common to the Durham mission. The French in Canada were 'a people eminently qualified to reap advantage from education; they are shrewd and intelligent, very moral, most amiable in their domestic relations, and most graceful in their manners,' wrote Buller. However, 'they lack all enterprise; they have no notion of improvement, and no desire for it. Their wants are few and easily satisfied. They have not advanced one step in civilization beyond the old Bretons who first set foot on the banks of the St Lawrence, and they are quite content to be stationary.' The 'barbarous institutions' of feudal property relations and French law prevented the *habitants* from scaling the heights of British civilization. Worse, added Buller in an attack on colonial masculinities, that description applied only to the men. The difference in the character of the two sexes was remarkable. 'The women are really the men of Lower Canada. They are the active, bustling, business portion of the habitans; and this results from the much better education which they get, gratuitously, or at a very cheap rate, at the nunneries which are dispersed over the province.' We recall that the attack on dower and women's property rights was an essential part of the Durham plans to make men out of the peasants.[20]

Buller aped Durham's 'war between the races' to argue that 'until Canada is nationalized and Anglified, it is idle for England to be devising schemes for her improvement.' There was no hope for the current generation which had been habituated to a life of civil war. Instead, 'the children of these antagonistic races should be brought together' as 'the first and most important step towards the regeneration of Canada.' Thus in the 'great work of nationalization, education is at once the most convenient and powerful instrument.' Assemble all colonial children in a secular, depoliticized school system, train them in the English language and in the tenets of British civilization, and social peace and civic harmony would ensue.

Buller admitted freely that this project would be deeply unpopular. His third contribution was an attempt to reconcile the liberal notions of equitable political representation and majority rule with the necessity of destroying French-Canadian resistance to cultural extinction. The case was exceptional, and 'under other circumstances' Buller would not have presented suggestions to Durham that 'would be repugnant' to his 'generous disposition and liberal principles.' But in Lower Canada 'original blunders and continuous mismanagement have produced such desparate diseases as to leave none but desparate remedies.' The original blunder was the Quebec Act of 1774; the subsequent mismanagement was a vacillating imperial policy that preserved both the French fact and a corrupt and negligent official oligarchy. As Buller summed up the necessary strategy, 'the colony will not be worth our keeping unless it is Anglified. The French majority detest and will resist such an attempt. If made, it must be made at once, and vigorously, – openly avowed and steadily pursued. Every new institution given to the country must be subservient to this end, which, the sooner accomplished, the shorter the struggle, and the earlier the recompense; but, in the painful interval, popularity must not be hoped for, conciliation not attempted.' In the state of political exception, ends trumped means; violence was necessary to produce security.

Dunkin's Memorandum

After Buller's return to England in late November 1838, Christopher Dunkin examined the school systems in operation in the northeastern United States more closely. On 10 June 1839 he sent Buller a 250-page memorandum on Lower Canadian educational history, the bulk of which was a demonstration of the 'utterly useless and misguided nature of the Assembly's school legislation and administration.' Dunkin based the legitimacy of imperial domination in schooling on a demonstration of the unfitness of rule in the past. The Assembly's schools inevitably reproduced the war between the races.[21]

For Dunkin again it was the 1774 Quebec Act, guaranteeing the existence of feudal property relations and of the Catholic Church as a state church, that had produced not only the colony's current difficulties, but also the American War of Independence. Attempting to graft English institutions onto those of the ancien régime allowed an alien country to exist in Quebec. After the Constitutional Act of 1791, the executive began a misguided policy of making annual grants at its own discretion to individual schools, and it compounded its errors by establishing the Royal Institution, which Dunkin argued was bound to fail because of the composition of its board and its proselytizing initiatives. The Assembly's 1814 School Act 'may be looked upon as the decided express[ion] of the popular sentiment within the Province (so far as any popular sentiment was at that time formed)' both with respect to the Royal Institution and as to 'the best means of promoting Public Education.' The executive's consistent opposition to all measures for granting popular control over local schooling (including the power to tax) and its support for the Royal Institution blocked any kind of progress in rural schooling.[22]

The period between the attempted 1814 School Act and that of 1829 'had certainly done nothing to add to the intellectual fitness of the Country population' for the management of local schools. Instead the period 'had done much, by the introduction or excitement of national and party feeling, to disqualify them morally from discharging' such responsibility, unless they had been placed 'under a system of restriction more carefully devised than might have been necessary fourteen years before.' Rather than greater supervision, however, suddenly the School Act of 1829 allowed the country population 'by a Suffrage in effect universal' to elect trustees who had complete and unsupervised control over local schooling. Only the clergy was capable of exerting some measure of responsible supervision, and its members were prevented from sitting as trustees.

Dunkin then offered his own gender and class analysis of rural social relations. The mass of the peasantry was not fit to judge in educational matters, and its sons, who had become doctors, notaries, and lawyers, had an interest in preserving rural ignorance to bolster their own power and to set themselves up as parish notables. They kept the ignorant masses in a state of political agitation, against which the central government's only ally was the clergy. Priests were generally moderate in their political views 'and the especially strong hold they have on the minds of the female sex and consequently on the movements of the younger part of the Community' meant that 'for success in school reform it was necessary to enlist their aid if possible.' His analysis of rural social relations made no mention of the seigneurs and did not consider the effects of seigneurial rents or the tithe and other religious obligations on the availability of funds for school support.

Dunkin then attributed the greatest defect in the rural schools – that trustees were not a corporation able to hold property in mortmain – to the political interests of the *patriote* Assembly. 'The power of their House as the one great popular Corporation of the Province, was in full course of development and extension' in 1829, he wrote, and it refused to allow the creation of any rival institution. 'The School-boards are to be made the dependent creatures of the House and their constant subserviency secured by their having to look to its votes, continually renewed for short periods, as their only source of revenue.' He added in a note that such was characteristic of the Assembly's treatment of most other institutions. There was a half-hearted suggestion that the Assembly might not bear the entire responsibility for the absence of trustees' corporate powers, but there was no sign in Dunkin's account of the Legislative Council and Colonial Office's repeated rejection of acts of incorporation, of the Assembly's attempts to attribute taxation powers to trustees, or of the refusal of governor and council to account for state expenditures or to eliminate plural office holding in the struggles over the Civil List. Every attempt at improvement of the schools by the Assembly was rejected out of hand or described as not going far enough. Dunkin cited the 1831 visitors' reports, especially that by John Neilson, as descriptions of abuses in the system, which the Assembly's subsequent attempts only made worse.

He was on more solid ground in his description of the operations of the 1832 School Act. Its address to the unregulated proliferation of schools under the earlier act was to limit their numbers and to empower school visitors to determine their locations. The result was that there were no definitive district boundaries and the nineteen visitors on their own could decide which schools to fund. Dunkin marshalled 1831 census returns and the Assembly's school reports to show the resulting incoherence in the distribution of schools. The average number of people per school district in the colony was 345; in Terrebonne county it was 831, while in Sherbrooke it was 95!

The 1832 act needlessly multiplied the numbers of trustees and failed to impose any literary qualifications upon them. Ste-Marie-de-Beauce, for instance, ended up with thirty-three three-man trustee boards, and school visitors meant to supervise trustees were themselves not subject to any literary qualification. Dunkin told Buller that he had in front of him a visitors' certificate from l'Ancienne Lorette where two of five men made their marks, a third spelled his name wrong, and a fourth could barely write. He supplemented the Legislative Council's denunciation of the powers accorded to the MPPs under the 1832 act with a long excursus on the psychology of a peasantry habitually subservient to the MPPs as political authority incarnate. Popular parties elsewhere in North America attempted to rule by such manipulation, but it was especially obnoxious with an ignorant peasantry.

Before he moved on to justify the Council's rejection of the 1836 School Bill, Dunkin concluded that the Assembly's efforts to that point had always violated the basic principle of educational improvement: 'Steady, permanent encouragement to private effort in behalf of education can be given only by a judicious course of permanent prospective legislation.' The Assembly instead set conditions for funding schools but then often did not fund those which met them. It encouraged fraud. 'An irresponsible committee pronounced yearly, according to any rule it might please for the time to adopt, for or against their several applications – and where, there-fore, was the inducement to expend their own money on such a chance?'[23]

The potentially progressive dimensions of the 1836 School Bill were discounted out of hand. The reforms it suggested were 'partial & insuffi-cient,' while other provisions, such as the multiplication of school dis-tricts, made the existing system worse. Dunkin saw only a sham in the Assembly's proposal to empower trustees to levy a school tax. Local taxa-tion was a true principle of sound schooling, and Dunkin was convinced that H.-S. Huot appreciated this fact in drafting the relevant clause. 'But here as in other points the temper of the House was to be deferred to, & on no other point was the French Canadian prejudice of constituent & representative alike, stronger than on this direct taxation. To draw from the public chest for their local uses, was the object of all others to be desired; to limit these drafts by direct local taxation, the last object to be thought of. Hence arose the deficiencies which characterised the Bill in this respect': namely, that the tax was levied at local option only.

Equity and Population

Dunkin defined political and administrative equity and justice by con-necting population, territory, and security. The 1836 School Bill might seem progressive in its attempt to make population distribution the guid-ing principle for the distribution of school districts, but in fact it merely institutionalized existing inequities. Dunkin accepted that earlier bills had taken into account that new settlements required more schools than older settlements, but that fact did not blunt his criticism. The 1836 bill based its distribution on population as given by the 1831 census, but that census was already outdated in 1836 and was to remain the basis of cal-culations for another five years. It did not take into account the more rapid growth in population from immigration in the new (mainly English) settlements compared to the natural increase in the old (mainly French) settlements.[24] Dunkin presented a comparative tabular sum-mary of projected population growth in the Eastern Townships counties with the adjacent, mainly French-speaking, counties to bolster his claim. The nub was that 'the grants under the new bill to the English Counties, and perhaps, to the new settlements everywhere, were very nearly as large as before. A great & most unnecessary increase was made in favor of the older settlements, where the bulk of the voters (the partisans of the assembly more especially) were, to share in it.' For example, the number of schools in seven English-speaking counties was reduced from

250 in 1834 to 234 in 1836. In fourteen 'stagnant' French-speaking counties, it increased from 455 in 1832, 82 of which received a double grant for single-sex schools, to 655 in 1836, again with 82 receiving a double grant.

Thus, in a manner parallel to the justification of the domination of English over French on the grounds that the former were an intellectual, if not a numerical, majority, the distribution of schools was to be based not on actual population but on expectations about the future peopling of sparsely settled regions with immigrants from the British Isles. However interested and ideological his claims, Dunkin was grounding them in statistics of population and perceived demographic tendencies.

The Normal School Act was easy prey for Dunkin, and he ended his memorandum with criticism of the ways in which corporations for institutions of higher education were endowed. As Buller had done in his report to Lord Durham, but with greater detail and authority, Dunkin sought to bolster the claim that there was absolutely nothing of value to be preserved in the Assembly's schools. They were simply patronage institutions meant to buy off ignorant *habitants*, while anchoring the power and authority of the Assembly and while discriminating against the progressive, English-speaking portion of the colonial population.

J.-B. Meilleur's Alternative Proposals

Buller and Dunkin engaged in such extensive ideological contortions not simply because their support of a majoritarian liberalism made it challenging to justify the cultural elimination of the majority, but also because there were articulate alternative schemes for reforming schooling on the basis of the Assembly's past efforts. These came not from *patriotes* in exile, but from that group of Lower Canadian politicians and intellectuals who, in Durham's words, had 'learned to estimate the practical abuses of Government which affect all classes, and to wish for many reforms without reference to Canadian nationality.'[25] One of the most influential was Jean-Baptiste Meilleur, MPP, medical doctor, census commissioner, promoter of the Collège de L'Assomption, scientific textbook author, and school promoter. Meilleur was a moderate *patriote* and a voluble commentator in the press on educational policy and practice. As were most of his compatriots, he was outraged at the actions of the troops in the 1832 Montreal election and organized one of the public meetings in L'Assomption to express support for L.-J. Papineau's controversial interventions at the subsequent coroner's inquest. Meilleur supported the 92 Resolutions and was named to the *patriote* correspondence committee – the party executive – in his parish in May 1834. With É.-É. Rodier, he was elected to the Assembly in the fall elections.

Yet he had more affinity with the Quebec moderates than with the Papineau faction in the Montreal district. He voted with the minority in 1835 in support of Lord Aylmer's request for a vote to pay the arrears of government expenses and justified himself to his constituents on the grounds that not to do so threatened the parliamentary session. If the Assembly did not sit, the many pressing public improvements would receive no attention, and especially 'liberal education in several places' would be 'held back from its advance, and several educational institutions would have been inconvenienced, perhaps even stopped.' As we saw, there was no money vote for schools in 1835, and many institutions indeed suffered. Meilleur supported bilingual education and addressed the lack of suitable textbooks in the colony by producing both an English grammar for French-speaking students, and a French grammar for English speakers, in addition to a chemistry text.

He sat on the Assembly's Standing Committee on Education in the 1835–6 session and had a hand in drafting the 1836 School Bill, although his fellow MPPs rejected many of his suggestions. In committee and in the house he opposed unsuccessfully the clause in the bill imposing the cost of model schools on local residents, on the grounds that the towns were not taxed for schools. As well, most *habitants* were not interested in schooling, while those who cared often were too poor to pay such a tax. In fact, Meilleur consistently opposed a compulsory school property tax, and it may have been he who made taxation optional in the 1836 bill. His preferred solution for creating local involvement in schooling was a compulsory attendance clause. Meilleur voted in favour of a six months' Civil List in 1836, and while he was an organizer of one of the anti-coercion meetings at L'Assomption and showed up for the 1837 parliamentary session dressed in homespun, he broke with the radical wing of the *patriote* party after calls for civil disobedience changed to demands for armed struggle at the Six Counties meetings in October. He publicized Bishop Lartigue's *mandement* of 24 October against resistance to authority in his parish.

At the college level, as we saw in an earlier chapter, Meilleur was critical of the classical curriculum offered in most of the colony's colleges, and for L'Assomption he promoted more practical instruction and a shorter, cheaper course in which the classics were taught only at the end. He supported some elements of monitorial instruction and was critical of Catholic churchwardens for draining away money best spent on good elementary schools towards 'things useless to God and man.' Bishop Lartigue refused to sponsor his college.[26]

J.-B. Meilleur published a detailed plan for school reform in the moderate *Le Populaire* as advice to the Buller Commission in the summer of 1838.[27] He accepted that it might be necessary to have a central board of education – although he did not propose one – but essentially described a program drawn from testimony before the Assembly's Standing Committee in 1835–6. Meilleur also took advantage of exceptional circumstances to push for coercive reform, but his main conclusion was diametrically opposed to that to come from Buller and Dunkin: leave local management of the schools in the hands of trustees and parents with the supervision of the clergy, train better teachers, and create stable school funding: 'in a word, let us follow the route traced out by the act of 1835–36. We doubt we could do better.'

Perhaps because of rumours circulating about new taxes, Meilleur began by rejecting the notion that schools could be supported by property taxation alone. The Assembly had been right to give local residents the option to tax to support their schools, but their efforts needed to be encouraged by a matching legislative school grant. The *habitants'* fear of taxation was manipulated by the wealthy, who did not want to contribute to school support, and by those who sought to prejudice the people against education 'so as to be able, themselves alone, better to monopolise its incalculable advantages as it might suit them.' Meilleur pointed to the difficulties he had had as census commissioner in 1831 over fears of taxation.

Nonetheless, many people had come to appreciate schooling under the Assembly's legislation, and the proof was in the fact that many schools had continued for some time after the grant ran out. The field was not empty. Although he did not proclaim his responsibility for the model school clause in the 1836 bill, Meilleur described it as the best. The creation of well-paid model school teaching positions would encourage teachers to compete to improve themselves. The Normal School Act was also a wise piece of legislation, although flawed in practice because of the school boards' belief that only Europeans could be normal school teachers.

According to Meilleur, the colony had four branches of education: colleges, academies, and primary and elementary schools. They provided different sorts of education, and there was a fifth form which Meilleur called 'Social Education.' By that term he meant learning about other peoples and about the natural world, and learning the pleasures

and graces of body and mind. These two kinds of learning, with the aid
of the emotions, would produce virtuous citizens able to appreciate
beauty and to pursue benevolence, charity, modesty, decency, hospitality,
and so on. In Meilleur's thinking, in contrast to the utilitarian political
socialization proposed by Buller, education was fundamentally humanis-
tic, even with its practical dimensions.

Meilleur described each of the colony's colleges, all of which he found
to be excellent. They should all be incorporated under the direction of
the clergy, funded out of the Jesuits' Estates, and left alone. The academies, then concentrated in the Eastern Townships, should enable students
with a good foundation to receive the BA degree in four years. They
should concentrate on training for business and commerce or for further study in the classics, and the legislature should fund one of them in
every two or three counties throughout the colony. Meilleur noted how
impressed he had been with those in the United States while he was at
medical school. He called the normal and model schools 'primary
schools.' He wanted one model school in each parish teaching an advanced elementary course to fit students to be teachers. The normal
schools were well conceived but needed to be staffed by Canadians. Most
of his attention was addressed to the elementary schools.

Improving on the 1836 Bill

Meilleur was not opposed to the 1836 School Bill's general principles,
but it was in need of improvement. There had been too many schools
before it was drafted and it increased the number further. A revised bill
should provide better qualified teachers and administrators, closer
supervision in school administration, and better pay and more respect
for teachers. Meilleur made no mention of a central board of education,
nor of centrally appointed inspectors, but many of the elements of his
system were coercive and disciplinary.

Meilleur proposed to create boards of examiners – at Montreal,
Quebec, Sherbrooke, and New Carlisle. Teachers would have to present
themselves with a certificate of moral character from a clergyman and
undergo an examination to prove they could meet specified qualifications before being allowed to teach. The boards would meet quarterly. A
school visitor from each board would visit every school at least twice a
year to examine records and to verify the results of the public examination. He would maintain and publish a list of places in need of teachers.
Teachers were to be paid £25 annually with additional fees of 2s. a month

in elementary schools and 3s. in model schools or academies. Elementary school teachers would teach poor students identified by the local trustees free of charge. Meilleur thought his scheme would produce £50 a year for model school teachers and £75 for teachers in academies. Model school teachers could also claim a bonus of £4 or £5 for each student teacher who succeeded before the board of examiners.

Trustees would be subjected to a minimum literacy and morality qualification, would reside in the school districts, and would manage the local schools. They would hire and supervise certified teachers and determine which parents to exempt from the payment of fees. As they had done in the past, the trustees were to report on the schools to the visitors. The latter were now to make available a set of school supplies, through the medium of the curé, to each parish school. Government aid should be available to ensure that schoolhouses were acceptable, and each school should contain a clear set of written rules that were actually enforced.

Meilleur saw the school trustees as truant officers, empowered to compel all children between the ages of six and twelve to attend school on pain of a fine of between 5s. and 20s. to be charged against their parents on summary conviction. Parents were to send their children to school as soon as one opened in their district, and their liability for fees began at the same time. Meilleur conceded that compulsory attendance was 'a rigorous measure,' but it was past time that parents appreciated the benefits of education and those who did not needed to be taught 'by the importance and the severity which ought to be placed in all compulsory measures to that effect.' The best way to make the *habitants* understand that they should send their children to school was to impose a statutory obligation that ten years hence no person would be admitted to any public office however minor – down to fence viewer and beadle – who did not have at least an elementary education. Six years hence, no child or young person was to be accepted anywhere as an apprentice who did not have a similar education. Christopher Dunkin had proposed a literary qualification for public office in the *Morning Courier* earlier in 1838, and it was a reasonably common element in contemporary English liberal political theory. Jean Holmes had noted its positive effects in Switzerland, but French-Canadian advocates of the position were rare.

There were many silences in Meilleur's account: on curriculum, pedagogy, modes of appointment of visitors, and so on. He had nothing to say about co-education, the language of instruction, or the creation of ethnic solidarity at school. Nonetheless, on the platform of the Assembly's past legislation, he reasserted lay control of the schools and sought to undermine the pastoral ignorance and simplicity promoted by Church and seigneury. Such centralization as the plan proposed remained at the county and district level, and no new, unified state bureaucracy was envisaged. His plan did not lend itself to the ethnic assault demanded by the Durhamites, but Meilleur was prepared to go much further towards schooling as coercive social discipline than the legislature would be in 1841.

The Montreal District Inspector

While the exact form that the colonial state would take after the Durham mission and the second wave of insurrection was unclear, it was at least evident that a major reform of the schools was on the agenda. Sir John Colborne's second Special Council included the long-standing educational activist John Neilson from Quebec, but it was dominated by the Montreal Constitutional Association. Quite apart from the potential offered by schooling to the anglicizing ambitions of the association, good schools were an attraction for immigrants and some association members were directly implicated in the British American Land Company's efforts at the settlement of the Eastern Townships. Yet the insurrection and the intransigence of Bishop Lartigue had prevented the Education Commission from generating any useful information about schools and schooling in the Montreal district. Arthur Buller had proposed that the colony be divided into three inspectorships for school purposes. In its winter session of 1839, the Council appropriated £200 to pay the salary and expenses of Robert Armour Jr as a roving school inspector (see Appendix B). Between July 1839 and April 1840, Armour produced fifteen county reports on school conditions.

Armour was officially appointed in the first week of July 1839. Civil Secretary Gouldie sent him with a letter of explanation to confer with John Neilson at Quebec about educational issues and to collect any relevant documents he could find in preparation for drafting his official instructions. Armour had been appointed for the entire colony except the Gaspé, but Gouldie knew he would not be able to do so much and wanted to know where he should concentrate his efforts. Council planned to adopt at least two other dimensions of Buller's recommendations for school reform. It was sitting on a large pot of money and wanted to fund schoolhouses in the places Armour would find most appropriate. The schools were to be of 'a neat style of architecture so as to show they belonged to the Government and sufficiently large to accommodate the Master or Mistress in the building.' At least one board of examiners for teachers was to be established, and teachers' salaries were to be 'about £30 per annum, to be included in the yearly estimates ... I understand,' Gouldie wrote to Neilson, 'that in the disaffected parts of this district the habitans are very anxious for the establishment of Parochial Schools and attribute in a great measure their late troubles to a want of education.'[28]

At the earliest, Armour can have set to work only in the second week of July 1839, but by the end of the month he claimed to have visited sixteen parishes in the counties of Chambly, Richelieu, and Verchères, in which there had been 82 school districts under the 1832 School Act and in which the failed 1836 bill would have created 133 districts. He had 'entered into minute e[n]quiries as to the qualifications of the teachers, the system of instruction they have adopted, the branches of education, which they assume to impart to their pupils – the means of support upon which they may depend – the works which they place in the hands of the children – the character they bear for morality, and sobriety, and their feelings towards the Government.' His aim was to detail the current state of schooling, compare it to conditions under the 1832 School Act and 'to draw the conclusion whether the mode in which that aid was granted has stimulated or deadened the exertions of the inhabitants.' He informed the civil secretary that he planned to deliver individual reports for counties, detailing school conditions, and to follow them with a set of thematic reports covering teachers, curriculum, pedagogy, and superior schools, with an examination of 'the cumbrous and inefficient system which has been hitherto adopted and the remedies which have been suggested to me by various competent individuals.' He had already answered the question his tour was meant to address.

It is unlikely that Armour wrote the thematic reports; if he did they have not survived. Four months before he delivered his final county report on Sherbrooke, Governor Thomson invited Christopher Dunkin to draft an elementary school ordinance and Armour's efforts were sidelined, although the 1841 parliamentary committee on schools would call for copies of his reports. His report on Sherbrooke was a paean to the British American Land Company and a denunciation of the Assembly's 1836 plans to decrease Sherbrooke's allotment of school districts.

In any case, it was clear from the outset that Armour's 'minute enquiries' actually consisted of going from village to village and taking from 'the Curé and other respectable inhabitants such information as they might have it in their power to communicate, as to the present state of education, comparing it with its condition while the legislative aid was granted.' Armour reported that his informants in most parishes did not know or could not remember how many school districts there had been nor what their boundaries were. Armour likely took some of this information from the documents he collected in Quebec. Often no one knew how schoolhouses had been built and Armour could find no records from the schools that were not in operation – not even from those in subsidized schoolhouses. The trustees forgot everything or had moved or were dead, and the curés were often recent arrivals. 'In short,' Armour put it, 'a total apathy appears to have prevailed ever since 1836.'[29]

Despite such warnings of how little he could learn, and despite some silences – about schoolbooks, for instance – Armour produced detailed information about the surviving educational infrastructure. In most parishes and seigneuries, he described each school district individually, and it is probable he visited many or most districts where there were schools under the 1834 act. So much is suggested by his exculpatory comment on his report for Beauharnois, 'as the roads at the time of my passing through the County were in a very rough condition, I did not personally visit these School districts.' Again, in Ottawa county he stopped his visits at Aylmer. 'From the extreme length of the territory occupied by these townships the thinness of the present pop[ulation], the limited number of schools, and also the state of the weather and the road, I did not deem it advisable to lose time in going beyond Aylmer village.' Here he sent written questions about the schools to some local residents. For the history of colonial social science, Armour's investigation merits more attention than can be offered here, but the reports provided much of the information that the Education Commission had sought unsuccessfully for the Montreal district.

It would be challenging (I tried twice) for a later researcher to work up Armour's materials into the sort of before-and-after-1836 statistical summary which his general reports were meant to contain because of his inconsistent treatment of schools. From the category 'school' he excluded most, but not all, rural dame or petty schools. As he put it in his report for Longueuil, 'in this parish as in many others that I have visited there are occasionally kept Small Schools by young Women on their own account, but they are only made use of by a few of the younger children of the neighbours, and the education imparted Scarcely beyond the alphabet. To these I scarcely conceive it to be necessary to allude more particularly as they do so little to advance the education of the people.' Given that child minding had not been the aim of the school acts, such an exclusion could make sense. Yet Armour was inconsistent. When such petty schools were the only ones to survive in organized school districts, he described them. In District 3 in St-Cuthbert in Berthier county, for instance, he noted that no Assembly school had ever been organized but described a petty school with about twelve students partly subsidized by the curé. In addition to petty schools held in private houses, Armour sometimes identified men who taught in schools before 1836 and who afterwards made a living as itinerants – 'maîtres ambulants.' He was attempting an inventory, but his investigative categories were haphazard. From the perspective of a later social science, this 'travel modality' of knowledge production was a transitional one, lying between the gentleman's personal knowledge (on which it depended) and impersonal statistical investigation.[30]

Armour sought to discover how many of the 1832 districts had been used to organize schools, how many had school buildings, whether these were paid for in part by government, their current condition, and how many were in use in 1839–40. He compared local schooling practices with the numbers of districts proposed for 1836 and sought to identify where new schools were needed and where a superior school could be located. While he estimated how many districts were necessary for each parish or township, usually he could not say where the schools should be placed. As he put it, 'the propriety of the limits designated for the schools would require to be tested by one of more local knowledge than a stranger may be supposed to possess.'

Districts

Still, his inquiries demonstrated the incoherence of the Assembly's distribution of schools, from the point of view of a centrally planned system meant to capture population. Armour found many authorized school districts in which schools had never been organized. And he found many parishes and townships in which schools were kept in areas not included in the districts recognized by the school visitors. Some authorized districts had more than one funded school. Given that the Assembly's school reports usually gave the number of schools in operation as very close to the number authorized, Armour's investigation gives rise to a troublesome anomaly. What was the source of the mismatch between numbers of districts authorized, schools conducted, and schools subsidized? Did the MPP school visitors put on their pay lists as many schools as were authorized, without regard to where they were located? Were schools subsidized that did not exist? Was their systematic fraud? These are questions for future research, but they trouble the Assembly's accounts of its schools and caution scholars against taking its reports at face value. Perhaps they underline as well one cost of not having a colonial Audit Office.

For the Papineau seigneury of la Petite Nation, D.-B. Papineau had authorized five school districts. One of the five never had a school and three of the remaining four had schools that were closed when Armour visited. As we saw earlier, there had been conflict between French- and English-speaking residents over trustee boards in 1829. The government eventually subsidized a school for each group. When Armour visited, only the English-speaking residents' school was open. In Richelieu county, Armour reported that 'but few of the Districts originally recommended by Mr St Ours,' the school visitor, 'have been adopted by the inhabitants of the several parishes, and that the increased number of districts proposed by the Bill of 1836, which from 33 was augmented to 52 was uncalled for by the state of the Country or the desire of the inhabitants themselves.' Again, in St-Elizabeth-de-Berthier, the 1831 school visitor recommended eight school districts, and the 1836 School Bill increased that number to fourteen. Three of the original eight districts never had schools, but government money was drawn to subsidize schoolhouse construction in the remaining five. Of those, only one was in operation in 1839, with fourteen students in attendance. The schoolhouse in another district, number 3, had been built in 1835 with a matching grant of £50 but sat empty when Armour visited, despite the fact that the district was described as wealthy and able to provide fifty students. The other houses were in more or less deteriorating condition, except for that in District 6, which had been destroyed.

In other parts of the Montreal district – especially the new and often English settlements – Armour found that the school visitors had allowed fewer districts than there were schools, and the 1836 bill sometimes proposed to reduce the number still further. The finding vindicated an opposition complaint. In Beauharnois county, for instance, Godmanchester's eighteen districts were to be reduced to thirteen. At the time of Armour's visit, there were only eight schools in operation, but he claimed that under a new school law the township would immediately support twenty. Schoolhouses existed in sixteen of the eighteen original districts, and a seventeenth school had only recently burned. Township residents had built schools in three other places. Many of these schools were sufficiently anchored in their communities to be named – the Huntley School, the Limerick School, the Tyrone School, and so on. In nearby Hinchinbrooke Township, both the 1836 bill and the 1832 School Act allowed eight districts, and Armour found eight schools in operation despite the cessation of the government grant. In District 7 in the 'Irish settlement,' for instance, Armour reported that the schoolhouse built in 1833 with about £11 of government aid had burned in 1836, but the inhabitants had built another at their own expense. The teacher, a man named McGiven, had between twenty-five and thirty students and received a regular salary of £4.5s. a month. On the seigneury of Argenteuil, where the settlers were mainly English and Scottish, the 1836 bill preserved the twelve school districts authorized in 1832. Armour found fourteen operating schools.

Town and Country

Armour discovered a good deal of variation in the 'taste for education' in different parts of the Montreal district. Most of the large villages supported schools, and those with a parish church by 1840 almost always had a boys' and a girls' school, usually in purpose-built buildings and subsidized to a greater or lesser degree by the vestry. He noted several places where the boys' school was taught by a college graduate and found a few others where the vestry had taken advantage of the failure of the 1836 bill to take over a trustees' school.

Verchères county, for instance, with a primarily French-speaking population, had nineteen school districts in 1832 – although the school visitor had granted none to the parish of St-Marc, which had a thousand residents – and the county was to have thirty-seven districts after 1836. Here was an extreme case of a pattern that Armour found elsewhere. Each of the county's five parishes had a boys' and a girls' school in separate rooms in a common building in the village near the parish church, and four of them were open when Armour visited. In Contrecoeur, the village had a stone school with separate rooms for boys and girls built with £50 of government money in 1832. It closed in 1836 when the school grant ceased, but the curé had paid to open it again in May 1839. About thirty boys were taught by a student from the Collège de St-Hyacinthe, and a smaller number of girls were taught their ABCs by a young woman. The schools in St-Marc were closed, but people planned to open them again soon. The imposing 36-by-60-foot schoolhouse in St-Antoine had been subsidized by £50 of government money. The vestry paid nothing for schools in this parish, but after the schools had been closed for two years, the villagers supported a teacher who had been to the Séminaire de Québec for the boys and 'a young woman of rather humble acquirements' for the girls. Again at Beloeil, the boys had a classically educated teacher offering the advanced branches in both languages, while his sister taught the girls in French. Here the vestry contributed £25 a year, on condition that eight boys and eight girls be taught for free. Matters were similar in the villages of Verchères and Varennes.

Apart from these substantial village institutions, Armour found only two small schools anywhere in the rural parts of the county. The 1831 census had reported a county population of 12,695, and Armour put school attendance in 1839–40 at less than 400. In effect, the eighteenth-century model of classical training for a few select boys and elementary instruction for middle-class girls remained in place. There was no sign of the Assembly's efforts, apart from a few schoolhouses. The clergy had taken back schooling. 'It is to be exceedingly regretted,' Armour concluded, 'that a county so populous in comparison with its territory and represented [in Joseph Bouchette's *Topographical Description*] as being the second county in the province for its agricultural production should be so deficient in schools or so relax in exertions to supply them, as that of Vercheres appears to be.'

Elsewhere, Armour also found flourishing village educational economies surrounded by a countryside bereft of schools. The village of Laprairie had never had an Assembly school but supported five other institutions: an elementary school for boys and girls run by a Mr Black; an academy run by the Church of Scotland minister; a large girls' school managed by the women religious of Notre Dame; and two small petty schools. Armour could find no schools in the rural parts of the parish and commented, 'the inhabitants are but little disposed to do anything of themselves for the schools, relying here as in many other parishes upon the aid of government or the fabrique funds which cannot always be obtained.' In the wake of the 1837 burning and pillage in St-Denis and St-Charles, there were no schools in the rural districts. St-Denis village had six school districts under the 1832 act and two remained in operation, while there was a single school at St-Charles.

Incidentally, Armour did other kinds of inspector's work, such as attempting to resolve local disputes over schoolhouse locations and alerting the executive to matters requiring more immediate action. He described the situation in District 6 in St-Elizabeth-de-Berthier, where the trustees owed money for the schoolhouse and lot to Louis Voltigny. Voltigny tore down the school fence, destroyed the house, and retook possession of the lot in 1836. Near Sorel village, Armour found the schoolhouse in combined districts 6 and 7 'in the forcible and illegal possession of a man named Joseph Jacques and family, persons of doubtful reputation.' Jacques 'broke open the door of the house, turned a part of it into a stable and maintain[s] possession in opposition to the wishes of the Trustees and the Magistrates.' Armour reported the case to the civil secretary. This school had thirty or forty students under the 1832 act, although Armour said there were one hundred within two and half miles. 'The British inhabitants in the neighbourhood are anxious to see it reestablished and would willingly pay 2/ per month for each child,' he commented, 'but among the Canadians too much dependance is placed upon the aid of Government or the Fabrique funds, to exert themselves individually.' As well, Armour detailed the frauds committed in Beauharnois by the school visitor and MPP Charles Archambeault.

Robert Armour Jr seems to have believed the stories the curés told him about a French-speaking peasantry so indifferent to the advantages of education that it would not even take up offers of free schooling. He made no comment on the effective re-establishment of a pastoral educational logic. Yet, he was transparently sceptical of most claims that poverty prevented rural school support, noting on several occasions that residents chose to spend money on church and presbytery rather than on schools. He did find one parish were people were utterly destitute and commented that while the Assembly had seen fit to offer them free grain it had not attempted to educate their children. Yet it was to culture and national character that Armour attributed the paucity of schools in French-speaking areas. We know of his ethnic prejudices, but they were muted in his reports. He made no sectarian religious comments and did not present any explicit analysis of national character. In any case, by the end of 1839 the Montreal Constitutional Association was no longer active and even the *Montreal Gazette* was beginning to appreciate that the Union of the Canadas would lead to a new era of coalition politics in which French-speaking reformers would be players to be managed and cultivated. Slagging French-Canadian ignorance began to fall out of fashion, as the possibilities of an east-west reform alliance loomed.

Many Assembly schools in English-speaking districts closed when the school grants ceased, but many more than in the rural French-speaking districts stayed open with local support. There were clear cultural differences in rural school promotion. Eleven of twelve schools in Argenteuil, for instance, were open, and Armour was full of praise for the Irish settlers in the nearby parish of St Columban. 'The circumstances of the inhabitants of this parish are far from being flourishing,' he reported. 'They are for the most part new settlers who have hardly yet passed through the severe inconveniencies to which those in their situation are exposed[,] but the exertion they have made for the support of school-masters and the erection of suitable buildings when their means were so prescribed reflect infinite credit upon these hardy and industrious back-woods men.' Again and again Armour attributed an interest in schooling in mainly French-speaking areas to the presence of a 'British' popula-tion. To take only one example, in Boucherville parish in Chambly, the rural French-speaking people had no schools, but 'a different feeling is manifested among the inhabitants of the town where many of British origin are resident and where a superior academy would meet with gen-eral support.' He was careful to point out areas in which English-speaking residents did not have access to English-language schooling and to rec-ommend aid for their schools. It may be Armour's documentation of the absence of schools for the minority that led to a clause for the creation of separate schools in the 1841 School Act.

Boosting Sherbrooke County

Armour was full of praise in his final report on his adopted county of Sherbrooke. It 'was one of the most important and at the same time most extensive within that portion of the province commonly known as the "eastern townships,"' and its history was one of ill-treatment by the Assembly. Deprived of political representation until 1829 and still in wil-derness in many areas, the settled parts were 'teeming with an active, industrious enterprising and intelligent population.' The British and American Land Company had generously constructed a number of ex-cellent schools.

Ebenezer Peck, the 1831 school visitor, reported fifty schools in oper-ation for a population of just over 7,100 and recommended the author-ization of seventy-five districts. But the 1833 School Act reduced the number to fifty-one, and the 1836 bill had proposed only forty. The number was far below that of the schools actually in operation, even if it respected the principle of population. For Sherbrooke alone Armour produced a tabular summary of school conditions under the various it-erations of the 1829 School Act and claimed that there were sixty-five districts established by county residents, sixty of which had continuously operative schools. He compared the numbers of schools allowed for Sherbrooke with those in each of the other fourteen counties he had visited, as they were in 1832 and as they were to be after 1836. Together, the other counties were allowed 433 schools in 1832–3, and this number was increased to 824 for 1836. In Sherbrooke, by contrast, operating schools had their funding cut. The inequity was palpable. The county was growing and improving so rapidly that it should be allowed 100 schools, not 40.

Armour's work was finished by April 1840. Christopher Dunkin made no comment on Armour's reports in drafting his own school ordinance, and there was no department, minister, or board of education to take them up. Indeed, the reports painted a more nuanced picture than those of Dunkin and Arthur Buller: the large and wealthy villages in the Montreal district had many functioning schools, some of which were described as excellent, and there were many purpose-built schoolhouses in existence. In English-speaking and mixed-population areas in the countryside, a large number of local, voluntary elementary schools survived and new ones were being opened by recent settlers. While it might have been fair to describe the field of schooling as empty and unencumbered for most of *habitants* and hence perfectly susceptible to central planning, elsewhere, central planning would confront local self-organization. In the Catholic villages, it would confront the re-established, pastoral power of the Catholic clergy. The legislative committee considering school reform in 1841 called for Armour's reports, and the minimalist legislation contained in the 1841 School Act may have been influenced by his findings.

The Thomson Administration

When Poulett Thomson, a Radical MP who had been president of the Board of Trade, assumed the Canadian governorship in the fall of 1839, his official instructions urged him to pay 'earnest attention' to 'the promotion of Education among all classes of the people.' He was told he would find all necessary information on the subject in reports produced by the Gosford Commission and by Lord Durham, and he was assured that it would 'afford Her Majesty's Government the most sincere satisfaction to cooperate with you in any measures which you may adopt for the furtherance of this important object.'[31] Thomson had been tutored at length in Lower Canadian affairs by Lord Durham and Edward Ellice. He took on the work of sorting out colonial government on the ground after the two waves of insurrection and of carrying forward the anglicizing project.

As was the case with the Durhamites before him, Thomson wanted a new state system that enshrined local, representative self-government while insulating central state authority from popular struggle and giving it reliable channels of communication into local affairs. He also understood that to make new forms of political rule it was necessary to make the ruled apt and able to support them. Successful political subjection and political subjectification were inseparable. As I have shown else-where, for the liberals among whom Thomson moved, representative local government was an educational project in and of itself – the 'great Normal School' for training the people, as J.S. Mill put it. Schools would discipline the rising generation; responsible local school management and finance would school the present one. The manipulation of rela-tions of population and territory – especially the division of the colony into new municipal units – and educational discipline were prime mech-anisms for ruling the people.[32]

Thomson moved quickly on the schooling front, enlisting Christopher Dunkin to prepare an ordinance on the subject in November 1839. He did not involve John Neilson, even though Neilson sat on the Special Council until 1840, or Robert Armour Jr. Neilson was strenuously op-posed to the Union of the Canadas. Armour was passed by for unknown reasons – he was still delivering his school reports in the winter of 1840 and so should have been visible as an expert, and he was soon pestering Thomson's administration for employment. Perhaps Dunkin was recom-mended to Thomson in England by Durham or in Canada by Gibbon Wakefield or Stewart Derbishire, both of whom would stand for the new legislature as Thomsonites. In any case, Dunkin's politics were much closer to Thomson's than were Armour's. Some proposals for reform left over from Durham's administration were referred to Dunkin for com-ment (see Appendix C).

Dunkin travelled to Quebec late in 1839, gathered up the materials he could find from the Education Commission, and set to work. He had with him 'a complete collection of the School-laws, reports, &.c. of the three States of New York, Massachusetts & Connecticut, [which] shows [its] system of schools is among the best in the United States.'[33] In February 1840, he delivered a draft ordinance for a rural and urban school system clearly influenced by them. Its spine was sketched in Arthur Buller's re-port of the Education Commission, but Dunkin added flesh and bones to a document he may have written in any case. Designing a public school system that would embrace the different realities of town and country, implicate antagonistic religious denominations, provide secure funding – in part through hitherto unknown property taxation – specify curricu-lum, create graded schools, incorporate existing private school societies, train and license teachers, prevent fraud and misappropriation, and in-stall a central regulatory bureaucracy with authority over the whole was no mean feat, but Dunkin pulled it off.

As detailed in Appendix D, Dunkin's plan created a chief superintendent of education with broad powers. It divided the colony into inspection districts under the direction of travelling inspectors and created an interdenominational provincial board of education. Urban education was organized by municipal education boards, which were to be elected directly in Montreal and Quebec. There were to be urban high schools and two classes of rural elementary schools. Teachers would be trained in normal schools and at rural model schools. The Irish curriculum was to be adopted. Local school commissioners appointed by the executive would manage schools following executive direction and were to impose a school tax. The chief superintendent would design school districts to ensure comprehensive catchment of the school-age population and could intervene in most areas of local management on the advice of his inspectors.

As a program of educational government, Dunkin's ordinance was brilliant, strikingly radical for Lower Canada, and quite authoritarian. It provided an internally consistent set of solutions to all of the criticisms levelled at the Assembly's school legislation and practice. It re-articulated the Assembly's piecemeal address to colleges, academies, urban school societies, and rural schools into a coherent system. It removed the opportunities for the idiosyncratic exercise of political influence, fraud, and venality, as well as the fiscal inefficiency that plagued the Assembly's schools. It provided the means to have technically competent teachers in schools built to a minimum standard and furnished with books and supplies, and removed earlier opportunities for local officials to get government school money without providing substantial schooling in return. It resolved the central dilemma created by the Assembly's more or less enthusiastic belief in the self-educating powers of 'the people,' if shown the light by its petty-bourgeois representatives. The population as a whole was to be organized, disciplined, and trained by a central state authority.

The mix of liberty and coercion characteristic of nineteenth-century political liberalism was evident in the plan. Minima were enforced, but educational activists were free to pursue maxima.[34] The system might function automatically once set in motion to generate an educated populace; coercive checks were present to ensure that it did in fact operate. In addition to authoritarian aspects, there were elements of enticement: the teacher who consented to discipline, scrutiny, and training could find reward in advancement, promotion, better pay, and perhaps – although Dunkin never used the word – a career. A student might excel at district school and find a subsidized place in a normal school, embarking on the

teacher's path. In principle, he or she would not need an elite patron to
do so. With the wisdom of hindsight, one can see that most of what Dunkin
proposed came to be the reality of public education – but not in the Lower
Canada / Canada East / Quebec that he was targeting.

Dunkin's draft ordinance still had to put into legal language, and his
plan depended on the success of Thomson's state-forming agenda. It
presumed the creation of rural and urban municipal corporations managed by elected councils, as well as property registration, assessment, and
tax collection. The success of the schooling project demanded the displacement of rural community regulation from the vestry and the petty
claims court to the elected municipal council. Yet Poulett Thomson's
administration did not proclaim a school ordinance before the return to
constitutional government that followed the passage of the Act of Union
in July 1840, and the latter did not contain a local government clause.
C.F.J. Whebell has argued that the municipal legislation was effectively
opposed in parliament by Edward Ellice, at a moment when the Whig
ministry was quite weak. Ellice resisted the imposition of taxation on his
Lower Canadian estates, which he was attempting to unload.[35]

Opposition to State Schooling

'Very meddling, very determined to have his own way, & very ill-
tempered & waspish if he is not allowed to have it': so Charles Buller on
Poulett Thomson, by then Lord Sydenham. Thomson felt stung by the
Catholic bishops for their enthusiastic promotion of a petition against
the proposed Act of Union. In the Montreal district, every Catholic
clergyman signed it, and the Church made common cause with some
remnants of the *patriote* movement. Now Lord Gosford, detested and excoriated by the Papineau and Nelson factions in 1836–8, was rehabili-
tated as the champion of the anti-Union cause in the House of Lords.
The petitioners complained the Union was unfair because it gave equal
representation to Upper Canada's much smaller population and imposed that colony's huge public debt on the new united provinces. The
Rebellion was merely a pretext for this outrageous project. As one petition sponsor – probably L.-H. Lafontaine – put it to Gosford, the
Rebellion was too minor an affair to result in so unjust a measure. 'The
Districts of Quebec and Trois Rivières were entirely exempt. It can be
said truthfully that out of a population of 750,000 not more than 1000
to 1200 people took part in that rebellion which was stirred up and led
by Strangers.' In the Lords, Gosford warned that the 1822 attempt to

unite the two colonies had spawned L.-J. Papineau. The new attempt was equally unjust and deeply unpopular.[36]

The wave of anti-Union opposition arrived just after Christopher Dunkin had completed the details of the education ordinance. Thomson summoned Bishop Ignace Bourget, soon to succeed the dying Lartigue, to explain the activities of his clergy, and Bourget claimed to have told Thomson to his face that the petition was a necessary act of self-defence, since the British 'have on every occasion shown strong opposition to everything Canadian.' The Church was actively presenting itself as the embodiment of the nation and the champion of French language and culture. It would carry this position successfully in the following decade in alliance with some other anti-Unionist factions and in the midst of a major Catholic revival sponsored by Bourget. Bourget and the Sulpiciens had also come to an agreement to install the Frères de la Doctrine Chrétienne in a large establishment with a school as part of an educational counter-offensive. Indeed, the *Montreal Herald* remarked with a mixture of scorn and alarm on the 'daily troops of school boys proceeding from the school-house of "Les Frères Chrétiens" to the different suburbs.' The bishops were actively seeking more information in London and Dublin about the Irish clergy's educational strategy.[37]

Christopher Dunkin had insisted on the need to secure the cooperation of the Catholic clergy, but Thomson was so incensed by the bishops' overt political interventions that he wanted nothing to do with any of them. He planned to go around them by enlisting the support of the Sulpicien Joseph Quiblier in Montreal and of the Vicar General Thomas Cooke of Trois-Rivières. Cooke was summoned for an audience on 2 April 1840 and went expecting to receive a blast on the anti-Union agitation, but instead the meeting was about education. Thomson gave Cooke an outline of the proposed non-denominational school system, which Cooke immediately reported to Signäy in Quebec. 'Mr Duncan, known under Lord Durham is the great editor of the school project,' revealed Cooke, who had been dismissed by Thomson, told to consult on the project with Quiblier, and to return the following day with his opinion. Cooke promised Signäy he would try to delay matters as much as possible, but reported that the Thomsonites 'are fearful of the opposition to this mode [of education] on the part of the Quebec Clergy, and they will satisfy themselves by starting here by establishing the board before their plans have gone further.'[38] It seemed to Cooke, and to some other observers, that the Special Council would proclaim a school ordinance.

Cooke was shaken by a long second interview with Thomson the following day. Thomson outlined in detail his educational project and then
listened calmly while Cooke tried to convince him that as a simple priest
he could not make any decisions. Thomson would have to deal with the
Quebec and Montreal bishops. Cooke lauded the zeal and loyalty of
Signäy to a seemingly receptive governor, but Thomson then declared '"I
have not the least desire to communicate with the Bishop of Quebec."
He has shown himself too openly hostile to a ministerial measure; several
members of his clergy have followed his counsel too closely, even to the
point of exciting the people by representing the union as a measure
bound to destroy the catholic religion.' Cooke pleaded that the bishops'
opposition to the Union Bill was proof of their loyalty. They argued
against it because it would serve as a new pretext for the Rebels. The
clergy signed the petition against the Union because all members of
their flock had done so; if a few had said it was an anti-clerical measure,
that was an imprudence on their part. After the Union bill passed, no
more enthusiastic supporter of it would be found than Bishop Signäy.

Cooke then played the old tune of clerical enthusiasm for education, as
evident in the creation of the Collège de Nicolet and in Signäy's plans for
an English-language school. Thomson was mollified only to the point of
telling Cooke to send Signäy an overview of his school plan and stating
that he anticipated with pleasure Signäy's approval of it. Cooke commented that the plan was one which 'we will be obliged to accept in the
end for fear of something worse.' Thomson had underlined to him the
Church's precarious position because of its insistence on preserving the
right to tithe granted under the Act of Capitulation. Catholics had a
powerful incentive to convert to Methodism to escape the tithe, and the
Church would be much wiser to exchange the tithe for a share in the
Clergy Reserves. That argument was unlikely to endear the bishops to a
plan for public education based on a generic Christianity – as near
Methodism in their eyes as made no difference.[39]

These events helped take Signäy out of the game; he did not support
the 1841 School Act, but he did nothing during the summer of that year
to prevent its passage. Bourget was made of sterner stuff. He had learned
from Lartigue that the best way for the clergy to deal with the English
government was to chart its own course and later to present whatever it
wanted as a fait accompli for approval. After learning of Cooke's inter-
views, Bourget wrote to Signäy that since the governor had not consulted
them on the education plan they were perfectly free to reject it. Care was
necessary because Christopher Dunkin was back in Montreal from the

United States and was again active in educational matters. But Bourget's Irish informants told him there was no formal agreement between the Irish church and the government on education and the Holy See had not pronounced on the matter, so the Bishops could chart their own course. In fact, the official line from Rome, which arrived in Canada in January 1841 and which made no objection to interdenominational civic education provided there was separate religious instruction, had no impact on Bourget. As the education bill sped its way through the new Canadian parliament in the summer of 1841, he was in Europe on a recruiting drive aimed at bringing a range of religious orders to the colony.[40]

Shifting Alliances under the Union

The Union of the Canadas led to new political alliances that determined the fate of the public education project. The anti-Union camp itself was divided. There was a reactionary and pro-clerical faction, led by John Neilson and Denis-Benjamin Viger, which advocated a return to the Constitution of 1791 and which supported a confessional school system opposed to the Dunkin plan. There were some committed anti-Unionists, such as A.-N. Morin, who did not share in the first group's pro-clerical stance, but who made common cause with the clergy on occasion. A second faction included younger, anti-clerical former *patriotes*, such as L.-H. Lafontaine and Thomas Boutillier, who opposed the Union Act's clauses concerning public debt, sectional representation, and the hegemony of the English language, but who saw the Union as an opportunity for a majority reform alliance. Such an alliance would preserve French language and civil law in the eastern section while abolishing the seigneurial system and promoting responsible government and social and economic improvement. This group supported interdenominational common schooling, but not the authoritarian dimensions of the Dunkin plan. The faction was strengthened after 1842 by the return of many *patriote* exiles and their re-entry into politics. Finally, there remained pro-Union and more or less rabid Tory factions eager to conclude the 'war between the races' by the extinction of Lower Canadian culture and the French language. Republican and pseudo-republican political discourse had largely disappeared.[41]

While the Act of Union stipulated that English would be the sole written language of parliament – a clause inserted at the insistence of Upper Canadian Tories and quickly overturned – it did not contain either a linguistic or a literacy qualification for the exercise of the franchise or for holding public office. The only thing vaguely representing an attempt to keep ignorance out of politics was the imposition of a £500 property qualification on MPPs. There was reasonably broad support for a literacy qualification, but not as a means of excluding French-speaking electors, and thus at least not for a generation after the organization of a general school system. Such a position was effectively that of Christopher Dunkin, but gradualism in the project of assimilation alarmed the Tory press before the Union elections. It was already clear to the *Montreal Herald* in the spring of 1840 that an east-west reform coalition was in the cards. The paper warned that a reform alliance would block what *Herald* considered to be progressive change in Lower Canada, including a school system. The peasantry, 'it is an acknowledged fact,' claimed the editor, 'will believe anything told them by those in whom they place confidence, almost against the evidence of their own senses.' After the elections created a reform majority, the *Herald* gestured towards the French-speaking members by inviting them to lead their fellow citizens to assimilation. Assimilation was inevitable but should not be so sudden 'as to snap the cords that have held the habitant to the peculiar customs of his forefathers. We would rather wear them out by attrition.'[42]

Perhaps Lord Sydenham, as Thomson was from August 1840, did not proclaim a Lower Canadian school ordinance because he expected that Dunkin's school reforms would easily win majority support in the new legislature. Reformers in Upper Canada had long been agitating for a popularly controlled public school system. They had successfully dismantled the Anglican General Board of Education in 1833 – the western version of the Royal Institution. Before it was defeated in the 1836 elections, the Reform majority had commissioned the radical doctor Charles Duncombe to investigate and to report on American school systems. Duncombe's draft school bill bore some resemblance to Christopher Dunkin's plan, but it accorded few powers to the central authority. In the Duncombe scheme, there was an appointed superintendent of common schools, but its functions were largely distributional, informational, and co-ordinating, although it did serve as a final court of appeal in local disputes. Duncombe too had school commissioners and inspectors, but they enjoyed much more autonomy than in Dunkin's plan. Duncombe's officials were elected at the township level – three commissioners and three inspectors – and they formed a school corporation empowered to hold property. They established school district boundaries and apportioned the provincial matching grant, acted as the township board of examiners to license or disqualify teachers, and determined curriculum. Duncombe also had elected trustees for each school, but in his plan they called school meetings when they pleased, chose the site for their school, contracted with teachers, and levied and arranged for the collection of the school tax, with the power to distrain. Finally, Duncombe proposed normal schools for men and women. His plan aimed more to create local self-government than to discipline population.

Tory opinion in the upper province also called for a general system of elementary schools in the report of an 1839 Education Commission. The commission's system was centrally planned and regulated and did not require the creation of representative local government. The plan lacked detail, but called for an appointed inspector general of education and a provincial board of commissioners to have direction of schooling. The inspector would chair the board and together they would frame rules and regulations, decide on a common curriculum, publish a set of school books, and specify where schools were to be organized. Means would be found to improve teachers' salaries, and teachers would be trained in township model schools and in a provincial normal school. At the county or district level (i.e., two counties) there would be an appointed board of trustees responsible for supervising and inspecting individual schools. The latter would be managed by those voluntarily paying for school support, and they could be – but need not be – elected by ratepayers. Additional school funds would be raised by a tax of three farthings in the pound on local property to be levied by the Quarter Sessions.[43]

Propaganda efforts in favour of a new school system and cultural assimilation were underway in Lower Canada in the fall and winter of 1840–1 in anticipation of the spring parliamentary elections. Charles Dewey Day, who would serve as solicitor general in the first parliament and who would introduce the 1841 School Act, was campaigning already in late summer 1840 with school reform as one in a three-plank platform. The *Herald* trumpeted his efforts: 'the very first efforts of the Assembly ... ought to be directed to the education of the people. The mass of ignorance, which weighs upon the Province, must be broken up, piece by piece, until it be finally removed. The Legislature must devise measures for affording every one the means of education.' An earlier Grand Jury Presentment in Montreal had deplored the lack of rural schools and demanded the creation of a board of examiners for teachers.[44]

The Mondelet Letters

Particularly striking in the pre-election atmosphere was the series of letters by Charles Mondelet published in the fall of 1840 in the new *Canada*

Times, an ephemeral paper perhaps sponsored by Sydenham for propaganda purposes. The letters were reprinted early in 1841 as a fifty-page pamphlet, *Letters on Elementary and Practical Education*, with a French translation included. It was a colonial best-seller, with a print run of about 1,700 copies. The *Letters* were also reproduced or summarized by many other colonial newspapers.

Mondelet had been active in 1837 in the Montreal Correspondence Committee, and it was he who defended the *patriote* F.-P. Jalbert against murder charges in 1838. Imprisoned later that year with L.-H. Lafontaine and D.-B. Viger, he refused to recognize the authority of the investigating magistrates. His support for the school project seemed like a sharp volte-face to many, but he had already gone from the Reform to the Constitutionalist camps and back again earlier in the 1830s. With C.D. Day, Mondelet had been part of the Montreal educational think tank formed in the late summer of 1836 to study best international school practices. He and brother Dominique were slagged repeatedly as rebels in the *Herald*, but when the *Letters* appeared the paper summarized them and commented, 'we are glad to perceive the energies of a cultivated mind directed to such an important subject.'[45]

Buller's Education Commission report had received little public attention in Lower Canada, and Dunkin's draft ordinance was largely unknown. Mondelet gave the first clear and comprehensive exposition and defence of what should appear in a new school bill and urged readers to demand that election candidates explain their stance on the issue. Common schools were an absolute necessity for the new colony. 'No community is safe without them; no Government is secure if it neglects or proscribes them. An enlightened people will, in most cases, guard against the corrupting influence of bad rulers. It will equally be free from the snares of ignorant, or of intriguing and unprincipled demagogues. In either case, the governed will escape the tyranny of one, that of a few, or the tyranny of the many. The cause of education is, therefore, the cause of liberty.' Good schools would produce a people that was moral and religious; they would encourage prosperity and social happiness, which depended on 'the degree of intelligence, and practical knowledge prevailing in a community.' Everyone in the colony must surely agree that 'the state of anarchy we have lived in for some time past, is destructive to our happiness': schooling was the means to eliminate that state. In a jab at the Episcopal clergy and the old colonial councils, Mondelet urged voters to take care that a new government was not 'a servile imitation of the Governments of the feudal ages, always bent upon patronizing academies, colleges and universities, for the education of the few; and in their selfish and inhuman career, leaving the bulk of the people in ignorance and degradation.'

Mondelet called for each new elementary school to contain an English- and French-language class in the same building. This arrangement would produce the kind of friendly association between children of different 'races' needed to produce social harmony. He wrote that English was bound to be the dominant language on the North American continent, but it need not be the only one. What the new Canadian colony needed was a common language and an end to distinctions of national origin. 'However paradoxical or absurd it might at first appear,' he wrote, 'the more you encourage the French language, the sooner the English language will be learnt, and the sooner it will become in general use.' That alone, Mondelet continued, was all that was needed 'to make of us all, one people, and to make us forget our origin. The moment the masses are enabled to convey their thoughts, meanings and wishes, by one and the same language, the end will be attained, and the sooner it is attained the better.' Tories and those in favour of cultural assimilation could read an end to the French language in those statements; French-Canadian reformers could read a strengthening of the French language and second-language learning for French speakers.

Teachers required training and needed to be able to offer instruction beyond the three Rs, including moral education. They must be excluded from politics. On religious issues, Mondelet laid out the Buller-Dunkin version of the Irish model with its book of Scripture Extracts. He followed it with an explanation of the necessity of direct taxation for school support, accompanied by an exposition cribbed from Buller showing that the cost of schooling the entire countryside could be much less than the Assembly had spent and that the tax burden would be insignificant when spread across the entire population. As in Dunkin's draft ordinance, property taxes would be matched by grants from a state school fund, but Mondelet called for the creation of an extra school libraries' fund and quoted the New York State School Superintendent on the necessity of cultivating a popular taste for reading.

There were some modifications of the Dunkin draft, while Mondelet reproduced its substance. A specially appointed commission rather than a superintendent of schools would divide the colony into school districts. Mondelet assumed that the schools would operate within the framework of the new District Councils proclaimed in Lower Canada. The district treasurer would handle school monies. Ratepayers would elect school assessors and name a collector, but Mondelet had no elected school trustees. 'Wardens' would manage individual schools, and they would consist of local clergymen with two people named by the school inspector and two named by the municipal council. The colony would be divided into inspection districts – five to Dunkin's three – and there would be a chief superintendent of education. Mondelet did not mention any board of education, but he reproduced the standard recommendations for normal and model schools.

Mondelet went beyond his predecessors in calling attention to the work of Horace Mann of Massachusetts on school management, school architecture, and curriculum. He was alive to the educative tendencies of the physical space of schooling, and copied Mann on the nature of the school site, its outbuildings, pump, and well. He was precocious in recommending blackboards for the schools. Curriculum should include history and geography – Mondelet mentioned in passing that he was translating Peter Parley's geography text into French to that end. Teachers needed to learn to govern the schoolroom gently and to be trained to do so at normal and model schools. School design should enable teachers always to see all of their students, and they needed to study character types to understand how to manage different kinds of students. Mondelet proposed the division of the students into comportment classes and the keeping of careful records of merit and demerit, to be read out regularly and to serve as the basis for rewards at the time of the school examination. A short, concise list of school rules should be posted and enforced intelligently rather than slavishly. Corporal punishment was outlawed, but Mondelet proposed the organization of school juries for the trial of offences. He spoke approvingly of the education of girls as the future moral leaders of society but did not discuss co-education.

In sum, Mondelet reproduced and justified for a popular audience the Buller-Dunkin educational project, but his governmentality went beyond their fascination with the educational administration of population in territory to articulate a practical technology of subjectification. Governing in the schoolroom was homologous with governing the representative state as a whole. His description of the peer jury trial at school is symptomatic: 'the effects of such a system' for students 'must inevitably be; a diligent search for the truth, a practical and businesslike habit of viewing matters submitted to their consideration, a safe training to form correct judgments, and an impartial, just and fearless discharge of a duty alike important and honorable.' No need to worry that adult jurors trained in Mondelet's schools would let the guilty go free, as Montreal jurors had done.[46]

Mondelet's work is also significant for marking a definitive break with the colony's 'monitorial moment.' There were some devices in his plan that had been in the monitorial school, such as merit and demerit books, the raised platform for the teacher, and the school jury, but the serial manufacture of political subjects under conditions of quasi-military discipline was gone. The teacher was not a military commander or factory foreman, but rather one with intelligence and tactical wisdom, able to use its subjects' own capacities as means of government. The pedagogical model was no longer from Joseph Lancaster, but from Horace Mann and Victor Cousin, a model that aimed to create self-disciplining and autonomous political subjects who had acquired 'a taste for reading' and who found pleasure in rational truth and civic virtue. No need any longer to keep books out of their hands and no need to fill their heads with religious dogma.

The School Act of 1841

On 12 July 1841, a month after the new Canadian parliament opened its first session in Kingston, Canada West, Solicitor General Charles Dewey Day gave notice of motion to present a school bill. As with other matters, the stakes in public schooling had changed with the union of the two colonies. A new school act did not have to undo any Lower Canadian legislation since the 1834 School Act had expired. Instead it had to repeal legislation in force in what had been Upper Canada. Day tried to create a parallel to the Jesuits' Estates in the western section to support the schools – although he failed to do so. For his school legislation to work, he needed a District Councils Act for Canada West. Its passage was a near thing, and in fact its provisions came into effect only after those of the school act, which depended on it.

As many observers had anticipated, reformers from Canada East and West joined together to make common cause, initially in support of 'responsible government': that is, that ministers in the newly created government departments should hold office only so long as they could command a parliamentary majority. Reformers demonstrated a spirit of inter-ethnic solidarity on these questions, while respecting a notion of sectional autonomy in matters of culture and language. The anglicizing project was stillborn and there was a clear interest in respecting sectional differences. The literature of political history has made much of the progressive nature of the Reform alliance in the first united parliament. It cast aside ethnic-linguistic divisions and pushed for the substance of

representative government and responsible administration. Yet it was a
disaster for public education in Canada East. The legislation it eventually
passed represented a major retreat even from the 1836 School Bill and
squandered the opportunity for the province to participate in the 'common school revolution.' The plans of Meilleur and Mondelet had attracted favourable responses from urban laypeople, and they both wrested
control over schooling from the clergy. Mondelet's plan especially would
have deepened the substance of school education. None of the substance
of these plans made it into legislation.

Reported debate on first reading of Day's school bill on 20 July 1841 is
almost all that survives in the record. Day argued that it was clear that the
Upper Canadian district (grammar) schools had failed to provide education for more than one in eighteen potential students and that had it not
been for the Catholic clergy, 'a class of men to whom he could not pay too
high a tribute of praise,' in Lower Canada 'no means for public instruction existed.'[47] Everyone would thus agree on the necessity of his bill,
which he said owed its substance to Charles Duncombe's 1836 bill and to
the work done by Christopher Dunkin and Charles Mondelet. He praised
Mondelet's pamphlet at length. Day also stressed that his bill was a first
step in a larger process of educational reform. Additional provisions, especially for normal schools (or 'Norman schools,' as MPP Captain Steele
called them), would necessarily follow.

At this point, the members were staking out the positions they would
adopt through the legislative process. John Neilson and Denis-Benjamin
Viger both contested the claim that there were no schools in Lower
Canada, but Neilson declared his support for an attempt to systematize
schooling, provided the bill encouraged local effort and did not interfere with people's religious opinions. Viger argued against the Irish
model of 'general morality,' presenting it as an obnoxious government
monopoly. The dangerous effects on society of such monopolies had
been demonstrated clearly in France and Germany; thus, he insisted in
the colony's schools, 'all classes should be equal in the eye of the law as
regards ... religious liberty.' The surviving records do not allow us to see
if Viger explicitly advocated denominational school boards as the means
to religious freedom, but he favoured them.

The religious question was the most visible issue in the parliamentary
debate. Parliament received a torrent of petitions demanding that the
school act legislate the use of the Bible as a schoolbook. Already at first
reading the issue was present and created strange bedfellows. The Montreal
Tory member Benjamin Holmes opposed the proposition, arguing that

'every man is answerable for his religious belief to his own conscience and his God, and every man should be at liberty to instruct his children in that faith which his conscience dictates.' Étienne Parent was more pithy: 'the Bible was a very improper book to be put into the hands of children at schools, and he, as a Catholic, could not sanction it.'

After second reading, Sydenham's ministers and their Tory allies attempted to strike a select committee to examine the petitions in favour of using the Bible. As Colonel Prince put it, if the motion for a select committee failed, 'we virtually repudiate the admission into our schools of that sacred volume upon which all our hopes in a future state depend.' The vote on the motion followed party lines quite closely, with 28 in the ministerial party in favour and 34 – including all French-speaking members – opposed. The house then voted 40 to 12 to have one of the petitions referred to committee of the whole, but it was not subsequently debated. The majority thus voted against Protestant domination of the schools, although how strongly committed members were to public as opposed to separate denominational schooling was not made explicit.

Unfortunately no more record of debate survives. The school bill was sent to committee on 3 August 1841, and the school committee called for a copy of Robert Armour's reports on 24 August. An amended version of Day's bill was reported on 6 September and passed quickly on 14 September. The Legislative Council made no amendments, and the act was proclaimed on 18 September 1841 by the dying Lord Sydenham.[48]

The Catholic Clergy and the School Act

The Montreal Catholic clergy claimed to have had no inkling of the bill until it had passed second reading. It is both odd and striking that it could have been so completely out of the political loop, given the presence of Bishop Rémi Gaulin in Kingston – although he was in ill health. At the time, Bishop Bourget was in Europe on the recruitment campaign that would bring a wave of religious orders to the colony over the following five years, and the Catholic clergy was riding high on the energy of a major religious revival provoked by the evangelical preaching of C.-A.-M.-J. de Forbin-Janson, the Bishop of Nancy. Bourget had started his own propaganda organ in 1840, *Les Mélanges Religieux*, with J.-C. Prince, formerly of the Collège de St-Hyacinthe, as editor. Prince assailed Charles Mondelet's *Letters* as the debate over schooling unfolded in Kingston, but the attack had few teeth – generic Irish Christianity meant the end of all morality – and was unlikely to impress the reform majority in parliament.[49]

Signäy in Quebec had been taken out of the game, by his lack of sympathy for his Montreal counterpart's ultramontane politics, by Sydenham's threats, perhaps by the Vatican's acceptance of the Irish school system, and by John Neilson's support of reform. His co-adjutor, P.-F. Turgeon, was more active. Turgeon learned of the substance of the bill through an unnamed intermediary before his Montreal counterparts did and made his objections known. He attempted to enlist John Neilson's aid to block the bill in Council or to have it reserved. Bishop Bourget's Vicar General Hyacinthe Hudon explained to Signäy's secretary on 12 August 1841 that the Montreal clergy had acted on its own to oppose the school bill because they had learned of it only at second reading and had needed to move quickly. It would have been better if the clergy had concerted its efforts. Hudon forwarded a copy of their proposed petition against the bill, commenting that if it did not block the legislation, at least they would be on record has having opposed it. The petition simply repeated most of what the bishops had said since Arthur Buller first floated his education plan.[50]

The Quebec Tory MPP Henry Black had earlier sent a copy of the draft bill to the Catholic lawyer and secretary of the Quebec Société d'Éducation Jacques Crémazie. Crémazie probably shared his copy with Bishop Turgeon before expressing Catholic opinion on it. Crémazie insisted that 'the Bill meets with my entire approval, save for a few details,' but the details were serious. He opposed the governor's appointment of the five-member boards of examiners, two of whom were to be clergymen. They would divide on the use of the Bible in the schools and would have to compromise by excluding religious instruction altogether, which would be disastrous, 'for without religion of any kind, education is nothing but a horrible plague.' Separate denominational schools would be needed to address this matter, and Crémazie warned that the Catholic clergy and its flock were deeply concerned, especially given the petitions arriving at the legislature in favour of the use of the Bible in the schools. The use of the Bible would certainly alienate Catholics, and the schools would fail, just as they had in France.

But Crémazie was in favour of coercive measures. He noted the bill's taxation provisions but thought they lacked detail. His experience as secretary of the Société had demonstrated clearly that without forcing the *habitants* to pay and to send their children to school, they would not attend. 'I know our *habitants*; put a free school at their door step, they won't send their children to it.' Only coercion would work. In a marginal note, he suggested the imposition of a literacy test for public office: 'For example after ___ years anyone not knowing how to read, write, and count, will be ineligible to be a churchwarden, militia officer, road inspector, or district councillor, innkeeper &c.' Perhaps some would object 'that it tramples on the liberty of the subject,' but Crémazie didn't believe it; it would be worth it in any case to have an educated populace, and other countries did the same. Apart from the suggestion of separate schools – which had been in Dunkin's draft ordinance – none of this influenced the bill.[51]

There was a move to have Turgeon travel to Kingston to second the efforts of an ailing Rémi Gaulin, and Thomas Cooke in Trois-Rivières was encouraged by Rémi de Vallières's opinion that no government would pass a measure so hostile to Catholics. Turgeon wrote to John Neilson that the bill 'cannot, in effect, but lead to evil, because, if its result is not to lead to the forgetting of all moral principles, it will certainly exasperate those who respect religion and wish their children to be brought up in its principles.' What could incense a people more than forcing it to pay for schools to which in good conscience it could not send its children? It was all too late: the school act (4 & 5 Vic., cap. XVIII) had been passed and sanctioned before a coordinated petition against it arrived in Kingston.[52]

The Gutted School Law

Given the necessity of winning approval from a reform majority for a school law that would apply to both sections of the colony, Charles Dewey Day presented a draft bill that was hugely anti-climactic after the noise about systematic compulsory schooling and anglicization that had dominated debate in the east since 1837. Day retreated from most of the bureaucratic, anglicizing ambitions of the Buller-Dunkin-Armour triad. Almost all of the coercive elements suggested by that group and by J.-B. Meilleur and Charles Mondelet were scaled back by Day in his draft, only to be rejected in committee. The legislature passed a weak version of Charles Duncombe's 1836 School Bill.

Day's draft bill deferred the normal and model schools to some future legislation. It retained the office of a centrally appointed superintendent of education with broad powers to frame rules and regulations for educational administration. Day wanted him to distribute school monies and collect information about the operations of the schools. In place of the colony-wide board of education containing denominational committees charged with defining rules for school management and curriculum, Day proposed that the superintendent would name five-member boards of examiners in each of the newly created rural municipal districts. These boards would each include two clergymen. They would specify curriculum and rules and regulations for school management in district schools. They would examine and certify teachers, and some members would act as paid school inspectors. They reported directly to the chief superintendent.

In the draft, the new District Councils were to be district boards of education, empowered to tax property for school purposes, both to match a government school grant and to build and furnish schools. They would divide the municipality into school districts according to population. They too reported directly to the superintendent. Trustees for individual schools were replaced by five-member boards of school commissioners elected in each township. The commissioners were responsible to the appointed district boards and were to hold school property and to manage the various schools in keeping with the boards' regulations. They could contract with licensed teachers. Finally, in the cities, Day had the city council as a board of education, and the board of examiners was appointed directly by the governor.

The Assembly gutted the bill in keeping with its interest in extending local elective institutions. It retained the office of chief superintendent of education but removed its powers to frame rules and regulations. This officer was to apportion the monies from a provincial school fund to consist of £50,000, divided between the two sections, with £30,000 going to Canada East. In each section, the school money was to be distributed according to population. The superintendent could collect information and seek out and publicize innovations in school management and teaching, but he had no enforcement powers. The inspections with which Day had charged district officials now devolved on the superintendent – eliminating any effective, centrally directed inspection – and on elected township commissioners. Day's rural district boards of examiners were excised. The municipal councils were still district boards of education but their powers of taxation were limited to £60 in each school district for buildings and supplies. They taxed in addition to match their share of the government school grant.

Christopher Dunkin's carefully conceived mapping of the colonial territory into continuous catchment areas of a minimum size was abandoned. The 1841 School Act allowed the boards to define school districts that were so small as to contain only fifteen students, fewer even than under the Upper Canada School Act of 1816. The threshold for a school to receive a share in the government fund was set at an attendance of fifteen students for nine months of the year – convenient to parents, but a barrier to classification in the schoolroom. The school act retained the elected township school commissioners proposed by Day and charged them with all the work of regulating the schools. They specified rules and regulations at the township level, certified rural teachers, and decided upon curriculum; their members inspected the schools. They reported to the district board, which reported to the superintendent. The rural boards gained the important power to tax property, provided that their District Councils agreed to appoint assessors and tax collectors in order for them to do so. In the cities, the act retained boards of examiners appointed by the superintendent. And there was a 'dissentient' school clause that made it possible for those who objected to the management of the schools by the school commissioners to pay to organize their own schools.[53]

The provisions of the law were congenial to reformers in Upper Canada/Canada West and in the Eastern Townships, where there was support for representative local government in the form of the District Councils. The act embodied Reform support for electoral local self-government by landholders and removed most of the proposed control by executive government and appointed officials. It empowered the people to educate itself. But, in effect, the 1841 act returned matters in most of Lower Canada/ Canada East close to what they had been under the School Act of 1832, but without school administration being a responsibility of MPPs. The changes from the situation under the 1832 law were significant: there could now be corporations for school purposes, able to hold property in perpetuity and to tax property to support schooling. And day-to-day school administration reverted to officials in townships, within the new municipal districts. Yet no authority appointed by the executive could influence local school management beyond the very limited conditions attached to the distribution of the government school grant.

The 1841 act was a retreat in important respects from the system of public education planned by the *patriote* Assembly in 1836 and from demands made before the Assembly's Permanent Committee in 1835–6. There were no normal or model schools and no provisions for advanced schools in a parish. Rural schoolteachers were not examined in keeping with any general standard of competence. Instead of addressing repeated complaints from 'friends of education' that the Assembly's acts had encouraged schools that were too small to be viable, the 1841 act proposed to fund even smaller schools. There was no compulsory attendance clause. There was an attempt to apportion schools to population distribution, but it was guided by the local convenience of the people, not by any administrative or pedagogical plan.

In sum, in the name of the civil and religious liberties of electors and parents, the Reform majority in the united parliament re-embraced the notion of the self-educating people, the very notion which had sustained clerical control and peasant ignorance in rural French Canada. In some parts of the Eastern Townships in Canada East and in the majority of districts in Canada West, property owners quickly took advantage of the act to organize township school commissions and to revive and extend local common schools. In many parishes and seigneuries, there was systematic and successful opposition to the election of District Councils. Where councils did come into existence, those elected often refused to serve or to levy the taxes necessary for the schools to function. The grand project of ruling Quebec by schooling it in the elements of British civilization had failed. The field was left open to the Catholic Church and to local elites.

Conclusion

The Reform majority in the new parliament of Canada did not deal with either of the two main obstacles to schooling the peasantry in what was now Canada East. The status of the Catholic Church was not altered before the end of the 1840s, and in the interim, the Church was strengthened by the immigration of European religious orders and by the creation of new colonial orders. The discrediting of *patriote* republicanism, the violent suppression of the Rebellions, chauvinistic Tory demands for the exclusion of French Canadians from politics, and Durhamite schemes for cultural assimilation created a fertile ground for self-affirmation through religious enthusiasm.

No solution to the issue of seigneurial property appeared before 1854. Given that economic surplus in the French-speaking countryside continued to be drained away from secular community projects through tithe and seigneurial rents, and given the intense anti-Union campaign, the new District Councils on which the School Act of 1841 depended were seen to be nothing other than foreign taxation machines. While all twenty-two District Councils in Canada West set to work soon after their legal existence began on 1 January 1842 – and in some cases before that date – only seventeen of the twenty-two in Canada East did anything, and the vast majority passed no bylaws after the first few months of the year. There were persistent refusals on the part of electors to elect council members, on the part of those elected to serve, and on the part of those who did serve to impose property taxation. At first, no penalties existed in law for such refusals, but even when they were introduced they had little effect. By 1845, all except the Sherbrooke Council were completely inactive. The people played truant from J.S. Mill's Great Normal School of representative government.[1]

Repeated attempts were made in the 1840s to rejig the municipal legislation into some workable form and to transform the 1841 School Act into something that would actually operate in the French-speaking countryside. The plan to have a single Superintendent of Education for the colony to perform administrative work was abandoned at once and J.-B. Meilleur was appointed Assistant Superintendent East. But the distribution of government matching grants according to population was inoperative because the District Councils did not conduct a census. Meilleur had to obtain permission to distribute school monies according to his own judgment. In Canada West, the permissive character of school legislation was limited through a new School Act of 1843 that created an administrative corps of county and township school superintendents, but it was 1846 before something similar was attempted for Canada East.

The eastern District Councils Act was followed by a new municipal act in 1845 which attempted to replace the councils with elected parish and township officers and to compel them to act. But the School Act of 1845, passed in the same legislative session, continued to use the municipal divisions of 1841, just abolished. A more coercive School Act followed in 1846, but it ceded entire control over curriculum not to elected school officials, as in Canada West, but to the curés, allowing the pastoral educational model to continue. It was followed in turn by a new municipal act of 1847 which attempted to overcome local refusals to tax for improvements by replacing parish and township by county councils and by raising the property qualification for councillors. An effort was made to tax seigneurial property. This municipal act eliminated the officials meant to conduct the 1847 census, which was abandoned. It would be 1855 before a more or less stable rural municipal act was finally in place.

This struggle to 'force government downwards' in Canada East occurred despite earlier *patriote* party demands for elective local government. Opposition was due to the anti-Unionist agitation which equated all legislation under the Union with the Durhamite plan for French-Canadian assimilation and which allowed elites at the local level to preserve their privileges and resources. Schools were especially targeted in this agitation, and in the middle 1840s what came to be called *la guerre des éteignoirs* [the candle snuffers' war] involved the burning of schools and tax rolls in parts of the Montreal district. Outside the Eastern Townships, the secular schooling of the countryside was unworkable.[2]

It is beyond the scope of my interests to follow the fate of schooling in French Canada East on to the establishment of the Council of Public Instruction, its subsequent dismantling, the installation of denominational schooling in 1875, and the absence, until the 1960s, of any ministry or department of education.[3] Yet the experience of the 1840s underlines the speciousness of republican beliefs of a decade earlier in the capacities of 'the people' to educate itself if only the executive would empower it to do so. Various attempts were made to compel or to permit 'the people' to educate itself; in the French-speaking countryside it did not and would not do so. The dynamics of political struggle equally prevented projects by central authorities to rule the colony through schooling, leaving the field to the Catholic and Protestant churches.

Schooling and Political Insurrection

From the 1990s, the Rebellions of 1837–8 have (again) provided master themes for Quebec political history.[4] Most of the popular and some of the scholarly outpouring of writing on the subject appears in a heroic mode that both defines political struggle in sharply antagonistic terms and champions the final Reform or *patriote* position of 1838, often treating its call for a Lower Canadian republic as if it had been the underlying aim of the party from the outset. Very little attention, comparatively, has been paid to the Tory or Constitutionalist positions or to divisions and shifting alliances within the Reform position. A good deal of misinformation circulates. Given loud claims of the worthlessness in principle of any historical work not taking the struggle for Quebec national self-affirmation as foundational, Jocelyn Létourneau has pointed to a process of memory 'sacralization' surrounding the Rebellions.[5]

Educational history figures marginally in the Rebellion literature, but somehow the claim that the *patriote* Assembly followed a progressive – even a social democratic – policy through its Trustees School Act has become a commonplace. The refusal of the 1836 School Bill figures as a further example of the perfidy of the colonial oligarchy, while the *patriote* leader L.-J. Papineau is presented as a 'friend to education.' Collections of his speeches certainly show him celebrating the Assembly's effort to spread monitorial schools. Yet it is clear that he supported schooling as labour discipline, with sponsored mobility for select boys and clerical control of collegiate education.[6] Support for education is not the same as support for universal common schooling, democracy, or social mobility. Heroic history writing seems to have offered a dispensation to those championing *patriote* republicanism from critical examination of the causes and consequences of peasant ignorance. Ethnic nationalist movements shared with the Catholic clergy a desire to preserve a pure and simple peasant base. Without coercive social policy and institutional reform, peasant ignorance and subordination were bound to flourish. Varieties of republican theory that took up Thomas Paine's minimalist conception of government and his credence in the self-educating capacities of the people could not come to grips with the phenomenon.

I have shown that colonial schooling was an odd mixture, especially in the mid-1830s, of the most progressive elements of the international 'common school' movement, and of intransigent opposition to the major administrative institutions and practices which made that movement work elsewhere. While executive government refused the reforms that allowed schools to flourish in the northeastern United States, the majority in the Assembly refused the administrative structures necessary for the development of a secular public school system.

The politicization of schooling by conflating legislation and administration, making the certification and funding of individual schools a prerogative of MPPs, reinforced the local hegemony of the professional petty bourgeoisie which dominated the Assembly. That the *patriote* Assembly frittered away such a gigantic sum of public money on rural elementary schools – some of it embezzled by the MPPs – to so little effect does not reflect well on the acuity of its policy. It was prepared to spend £500 on a *patriote* widow's pension and £500 on a mouldy menagerie, but not £100 to support early childhood education. School politics was not simply a battle between a progressive Assembly and a reactionary Tory Legislative Council.

This stance is not to champion executive government. The obtuse opposition of the imperial government to William Smith's university plan and the subsequent half-hearted attempt to establish the Church of England both blocked real possibilities for a secular school system at the end of the eighteenth century. The project of the Royal Institution for the Advancement of Learning was at once stupidly sectarian in design and then half-heartedly pursued in execution. It had the main effect of blocking efforts at schooling the colony. Councils, governor, and the Episcopal churches joined together to kill a promising plan for non-sectarian urban elementary schooling in 1815–16. The governor and the Colonial Office combined to block legislation in 1821 that might have made it possible to have a rural parish school system. Serious imperial attention to the colony was sporadic at best; careful analysis of colonial government was rare before the 1830s.

Quebec and Lower Canada's educational past is marked by a great deal of contingency: many different educational futures were possible. Yet initiatives by the executive allowed a popular culture of peasant ignorance to reproduce itself and strengthened the rural Catholic clergy and the seigneurs in their encouragement of pastoral subordination. The refusal of the imperial government to give effect to colonial demands for a school lands fund, its occupation of the Jesuit College as a barracks, and the pillage of the Jesuits' Estates for the private profit of Legislative Councillors deprived the colony of important educational resources. The persistence of Reformers in the Assembly, especially François Blanchet and John Neilson, and of activists such as J.-F. Perrault, in the face of repeated failures at school legislation is remarkable.

However, the consistent parasitism and venality of many Legislative Councillors and the Council's persistent opposition to the extension of local electoral democracy should not lead one to conclude that none of its political analyses or positions had other than a dogmatically reactionary content. After all, many Councillors had been promoted from the Assembly, and they were often divided among themselves on key questions, sometimes in surprising ways. Toryism already contained libertarian and authoritarian elements. All the French-speaking members, with the exception of D.-B. Viger, endorsed Council's committee report that criticized the Assembly's 1836 School Bill, but Viger was no partisan of a democratic, secular school system. And even the dictatorial Special Council has been seen as putting in place long-overdue economic and administrative reforms that had been delayed by earlier struggles.[7]

The *patriote* Assembly's persistent antagonism towards expert administration and its conflation of the functions of legislation and administration helped block the emergence of a sphere of education 'beyond politics.' Its conflation of 'bureaucrate' as political faction with 'bureaucrate' as administrative function allowed its own particularistic preferences to reign. It prevented simple reforms that would have benefited those involved in rural schooling, such as having a dedicated government paymaster for school monies. The local hegemony of *patriote* MPPs was usually based on a cumulation of functions in their localities. Those who represented ridings with seigneurial tenure lived more or less directly from the peasant agrarian economy. Because of the absence of non-political educational administration, many were placed to take advantage of the school money making its way into their communities and of the financial dependence of teachers. Many were public-spirited, but the MPPs themselves accused one another of venality and corruption in school government.

In the northeastern United States, a particular cultural heritage of learning combined with small-property-holder electoral democracy to create universal literacy at a relatively early date. In industrializing England

and in some other European countries, working-class communities or craft guilds undertook self-education campaigns, providing people with real alternatives to educational initiatives by church or state. In peasant Ireland, a long-standing tradition of community self-education, developed as an anti-colonial strategy, also produced remarkably high levels of learning. Lower Canada's parishes and seigneuries often had strong community organization, but no autonomous tradition of book learning able to yield self-education projects.

Governmentality, Schooling, Social Science

State formation is inherently a practice of subject formation. Particular techniques of rule and modes of government depend upon the existence of subjects apt and able to be ruled and governed accordingly. Lower Canada was a site for experiments in liberal government and its associated techniques and forms of knowledge and analysis. The production of liberal political subjects involved work on the unruly mass of the people through the conceptual and administrative instrument of population, through the theoretical framework and developing techniques of the social science, and through attempts to organize new institutions. Already in the 1820s amateur observers, legislators, and administrators were thinking Lower Canada not as an organic community with fixed features, but rather as an entity with dynamic tendencies that could be grasped in statistical terms and acted upon. The liberal reformers of the 1830s analysed Lower Canada as a combination of population, territory, and institutions, and they schemed to articulate these elements in ways that would produce a self-replicating system of government, a system of security.

Unlike much early governmentality work, which attended to the formal relations between mentalities and technologies of government and was not enthusiastic about empirical or historical investigation, I have stressed the importance of the gritty and contradictory practices of government and administration and the power of institutions. The institution of monitorial schooling played an important role in the shift towards liberal conceptions of the means and ends of rule. The monitorial school was thought of as a machine, or engine, that could work on the raw material of juvenile subjectivity to produce an orderly, literate, and disciplined people. That notion presumed human perfectibility and in itself was a blow to conceptions of a fixed social order, but monitorial schooling was directly a form of population government. It segmented the people, sorting out that portion in need of discipline, and then segregated students periodically from the rest of the social body. It grouped and classed, individuated and total-ized population in new forms. It altered urban space and the rhythms of urban life, at the same as it created a new epistemological space and novel techniques of knowledge.

Attempts to know and to administer school population in Quebec can anchor a genealogy of Canadian social science in more varied and prac-tical lineages than is commonly the case. The term 'social science' was in use in France at least in the 1820s and in the correspondence of J.S. Mill in England by the end of that decade. By the second half of the 1830s, it had reasonably broad currency. Several scholars have argued that sociol-ogy's English origins can be traced to the work done by administrative agencies of state, in collaboration with amateur investigations and the activities of private associations.[8] The modestly sized literature on the history of Canadian social science and sociology, by contrast, has tended to locate their origins in the late nineteenth and early twentieth centur-ies. Here sociology's roots especially are unearthed in the engagements of the social gospel movement and social Catholicism with industrial capitalism. The lines of intellectual descent owe more to LePlay than to Quetelet – more to speculation than to measurement and calculation – as an early moralizing engagement with poverty, misery, and 'social prob-lems,' including drunkenness and prostitution, laid hold of techniques of social observation. Paired with more or less reformist social theories, the story goes, observation and moral concern were institutionalized in the universities in the twentieth century and made more rigorous.

The literature does identify some nineteenth-century antecedents. Yvan Lamonde pointed to important LePlaysian influences on social thought in Quebec in the late 1880s. In J.-C. Falardeau's account of Quebec sociology, Étienne Parent, the editor of Le Canadien newspaper, is treated as a nineteenth-century proto-sociologist because he thought 'society.' Yet it is ironic that Falardeau counts Errol Bouchette as an early twentieth-century sociologist, because he read LePlay, but consid-ers neither Errol's father, the patriote politician R.S.M. Bouchette, nor his grandfather, Joseph Bouchette, to be in this lineage. Joseph was already thinking about population as a dynamic object with its own tendencies in the late 1820s, was attempting to measure those tendencies, and used them to configure possible futures.[9] The literature has also ignored the remarkable social scientific work of Joseph-Charles Taché. In the 1840s, Taché was attempting to measure population movement and to under-stand its structural causes. His efforts at census making in the mid-1860s involved technical innovations, such as field-testing census schedules and the mapping of territory, and he analysed population trends as part of a wider vision of the possibilities for social development. His work can be seen to be continuous with that of his guardian, the seigneur, MPP, and Executive Councillor J.-B. Taché, who was arguing in the educational debates of the mid-1830s that political equity lay in apportioning resources to population distribution. In educational debate in the same period, international comparison, which is one of sociology's laboratories, was commonplace. Christopher Dunkin worked in one of the others: historical investigation.[10]

The Royal Commissions of 1835–6 and 1838–9 were especially important in changing the terms in and through which politics and government were understood. The displacement of the 'mixed monarchy' theory of government by an analytic that invoked population in territory as an object to be configured in congenial ways marks a key moment in colonial governmentality. The two commissions both involved attempts to make sense of the colony through still-novel social scientific techniques and practices.

Lord Gosford, the first royal commissioner, suffers mainly from benign neglect in the existing literature, and his mission is usually waved away as a roadblock on the path to colonial independence. A thorough study of all dimensions of the Gosford Commission's work remains to be undertaken, but Gosford was a modernizer in Ireland, sponsoring an original social scientific investigation of conditions on his own estates. His fellow commissioner, Sir Charles Grey, proposed to cut up Lower Canada into as many as ten districts or provinces, arguing that grouping different population segments together and subjecting them to different institutional arrangements would produce a self-civilizing system of rule. For his part, Sir George Gipps wrote about colonial government as preparation for political independence and outlined a system of proportional representation.

For colonial education, the Gosford Commission was significant for proposing the Irish 'education experiment' as a solution to political conflict, even if changed geopolitical conditions meant it was unacceptable to the Canadian Catholic bishops. Still, had there been slightly more discretion on the part of Gosford's Upper Canadian lieutenant in the winter of 1836, there would likely not have been a Lower Canadian insurrection and the Assembly and Council would likely have modified the 1836 School Bill to address the issue of administrative school boards – at the expense of clerical control of curriculum. Gosford's proposed 1837 Executive Council had a majority of francophone members, many of them supporters of the 92 Resolutions.

The second royal commissioner, Lord Durham, remains perhaps the most reviled figure in Quebec's nationalist memory, loathed for the analysis of 'national character' he promoted, for his project of replacing French law and property relations with representative self-governmental institutions, and for seeking to marginalize the French language, all in order to create a new Canadian nation. Whatever he may have to answer for to the historical record, it is unfortunate that more attention is not paid to the substance and to the execution of the political science and sociology of his mission. While I have examined his Education Commission, the other investigations undertaken by his mission are objects of neglect, even though they directly implicated people and projects involved in liberal reform in England.[11]

Durham's Buller Education Commission inquiry of 1838–9 gave clear expression to a social scientific ambition to know everything there was to know about colonial education in statistical form and it pioneered investigative techniques. Its social science was not first and foremost a discovery science, yet it encountered unexpected problems of inquiry, to which it attempted to adapt, and it involved colonial state servants in new ways of thinking. It points to an early move towards government by expertise.

Yet most of Durham's social and political analysis was thoroughly conventional. It simply applied to colonial social relations the premises and propositions of social theory rooted in the Scottish Enlightenment and reworked as policy prescriptions by precursors of liberalism, such as Jeremy Bentham and James Mill. Durham's infamous characterization of the *habitants* as a people without literature and history made perfect sense within that analytic framework. For the Scots, the history of civil society – and thus of 'civil-ization' – dawned with freehold property, manufacturing industry, the division of labour, specialization, and global commodity exchange. It was held that such developments refined manners; broadened people's horizons; developed their taste and intelligence; stimulated literature, poetry and theatre; and increased people's ability to conduct themselves freely. Many of the Scots had taken up David Hume's proposition that there was a universal human nature and that observed differences in conditions, character, and conduct were due to such forces as climate, social institutions, and material life. Thus, for instance, it was a commonplace that different occupations had different consequences for manners, morals, and intelligence. We saw Durham's Canadian point man, Stewart Derbishire, describing the effects of peasant farming on political consciousness. At a higher level of generality, forces of nature and society produced hierarchies of 'race' and of national character.[12]

At the same time, the Scottish social analysis bequeathed to liberals the conviction that changed circumstances and changed institutions would lead to changed characters, changed subjectivities, and hence changed modes of being. Lord Durham had direct personal experience of such matters in the late 1810s and 1820s in dealing with the Durham county mining proletariat on whose labour power much of his gigantic wealth was based. He had undertaken campaigns aimed at the moralization of ignorant miners in an effort to combat the appeal of utopian socialism, which was thought to be encouraged by radical Methodist preachers. The campaigns involved attempts to improve material conditions of life in re- lation to sanitation and housing, company unions, and savings plans. They were also moralizing and didactic, based on the premise that ignor- ance, not working conditions or wages, caused dissipation, intemperance, and misery. It was in the Durham social campaigns that Harriet Martineau, the influential author of improving tracts on political economy for work- ers, got her start, and it was Durham who encouraged her to undertake the observational tour that led to *Society in America* and to her sociological classic *How to Observe Morals and Manners*. A second figure who gained practical experience in social engineering through these campaigns was Edward Gibbon Wakefield, author of the theory of systematic coloniza- tion; a third was Stewart Derbishire.[13]

Durham's largely conventional analysis of the colonial *habitants* was based on social engineering and on the propositions of Scottish sociology, with a hefty dose of ethnic chauvinism. He believed that there was no 'spirit of improvement' on the part of the peasantry and that it was 'con- tent to be stationary' – had no interest in actively engaging in a manufac- turing commodity economy. His uncle by marriage had convinced him that no one could read and write. Indeed, it would have been hard for any observer to uncover a hotbed of peasant literature, poetry, or theatre in the 1830s in Lower Canada – the colony's first novel only appeared at the end of the decade, and neither Quebec nor Montreal supported a French- language theatre. The clergy opposed the theatre as much as it opposed lending money at interest – and almost everybody agreed that the *habi- tants* did not read. Feudal social relations were commonly understood in Enlightenment theory to be stupefying forms of subordination; history began when they ended. Catholicism was held to substitute mystification and mummery for a rational appreciation of religion.

Most of Durham's diagnosis was thus unremarkable for a liberal Whig. Even his attack on the French language was consistent with his sociology. Language use was understood to form the face and body, as well as the character. English did so best. So common was such analysis that even the Montreal Natural History Society solicited essays 'On the Connection between the Language and the Character of a People,' late in 1836.[14] I am not suggesting that Durham's diagnosis was correct, simply that it was conventional and that vilification of the man prevents examination of the science. After all, many of the practical remedies proposed to 'civilize' Lower Canada, such as the establishment of property registration, the elimination of the seigneurial system, and the establishment of public education, had been called for in the French-language press and were also contained in the Constitution of the Republic of Lower Canada drafted by *patriote* radicals.[15] Durham's several commissions of investigation applied social science to colonial conditions, proposing reforms recently adopted in England – such as elected local government – while experimenting with and extending techniques of investigation and analysis.

Perhaps Durham's use of 'race' and 'race war' was unusual. The concepts worked to break the unity of the people organized around social and political grievances that crossed ethnic lines. They were used to refashion political solidarities into national characters. They provided the grounding for a conception of a new nationality and for an attack on the French language. Education was an important element in this sociology. It made it possible for those in favour of rule by an elected majority to argue with a measure of consistency that the majority should be disenfranchised. Free self-government was possible only by those schooled to the use of a reason which recognized the value of free self-government. Under liberal conditions of freedom, once again, 'the people' was to be free to educate itself, provided it did so freely. Ignorance was unfreedom and 'the people' was not to be free to be ignorant. Ignorance in practice corresponded to *habitant* national character, while much of the educated petty bourgeoisie was seen to be more interested in rhetoric and display than in reasoning about the common good. Lord Durham could claim to be liberal and also argue consistently that freedom demanded the forcible refashioning of the political subjectivity of the *habitants*. The significance of the moment was heightened by the fact that it was explicitly understood as a moment of 'emergency,' one in which 'Society' had virtually ceased to operate, and thus could legitimately be redesigned by a dictatorship.[16]

A final dimension of the Durham mission's intellectual and political work that calls for more attention is its implication in the project for systematic colonization. Systematic colonization was at once a plan for primitive capitalist accumulation, a project to deal with pauperism in Britain, and a theory of civilization and character formation. The author of one version, Edward Gibbon Wakefield, was meant to be Durham's Crown Lands Commissioner, although scandal blocked his appointment. Durham, Wakefield, J.S. Mill, and Charles Buller were already involved in New Zealand colonization projects.[17] As director of a later colonization society, Wakefield bought the Beauharnois seigneury from Edward Ellice, was elected to the new parliament of Canada, and hoped under Lord Sydenham to develop his schemes.

Politically, the mission's involvement with this plan is significant because it demanded the elimination of French law and called for the division of the colony, but it also divided the Radical faction in England. For those drawing their thinking about colonies from the elder Mill and Bentham, it was possible either to oppose colonialism as an unacceptable interference with political liberty, or to promote colonialism as a necessary element in the promotion of liberty and civilization. The inability of the Radicals to agree on a stance towards colonialism divided them on the line to follow in relation to the Rebellions. English champions of colonial autonomy, such as Roebuck and Thompson, were marginalized after the 1837 elections; the pro-colonialism wing was strengthened.

In terms of governmentality and the development of colonial social science, systematic colonization was significant for its conception of capitalist social relations as elements in a self-replicating and civilizing system, which could be engineered practically. Already in 1831, the Colonial Secretary Lord Goderich expressed his support for some version of systematic colonization to Governor Aylmer, in opposition to demands of the colonial Assembly for an easy land grant policy, because 'without some division of labour, without a class of persons willing to work for wages, how can society be prevented from falling into a state of almost primitive rudeness, and how are the comforts and refinements of civilized life to be preserved?'[18]

In Wakefield's version, young married couples would receive passage money to colonies where the state or a private company monopolized land, offered for sale at upset prices. On their arrival, they would work for wages to pay off their passage money, especially on the construction of transportation infrastructure. Such wage labour was seen itself to be educative in a technical and moral sense. Couples would learn to save to purchase land and then would raise families, produce agricultural surplus (which might sustain English workers), create demand for commodities and promote the division of labour, and in the next generation, reproduce the cycle. The sale of land would provide the state or the land company with the necessary resources to pay passage money and wages. The value of its land would increase as settlement proceeded.

Systematic colonization survived in the study of sociological theory largely thanks to Marx's devotion of a final chapter of his first volume of *Capital* to its fundamentally flawed premise: that new immigrants to colonies would wait around to work for wages in infrastructure projects when they could squat on unoccupied land or work at something else. Yet its presence at the core of the Durham mission helped to reinforce Durham's stance towards the elimination of existing colonial institutions.[19]

Self and Others

Systematic colonization points to concerns in liberal governmentality with engineering class structure, and with domesticity and the life course, matters that receive little attention in most governmentality work. I have been constrained to focus on geopolitics, political discourses, administration, and empirical conditions in order to come to grips with the dynamics of governing through ignorance and ruling by schooling. Yet the domestic domain and networks and practices of sociability, as well as the homologous relations that obtain between government of the self and the government of others, call for more attention. The extent to which the colonial Rebellions were political-economic as opposed to ethnic-national-religious struggles continues to be debated. More concrete investigation of the contours of colonial networks of association and practices of sociability needs to be undertaken to assess where and when these crossed ethnic-national boundaries. At least it is clear that colonial politicians did not only come into contact with one another punctually to trade doctrine or gunfire. Colonial society was small, colonial Society smaller still, and only some times did political divisions undermine mutual participation in common projects or attendance at social events. While political work was visible in parliament, in the press and pamphlet literature, and at formally organized political meetings, it also took place in dining and drawing rooms, at balls and banquets, in parades and exhibitions.

While men most commonly wrote and spoke publicly about grand politics, men and women both acted politically in the domestic domain; the two fields were inseparably connected. For instance, it was through a breakfast given by Bishop Lartigue that Lady Aylmer was connected to the Mesdames Viger and Papineau, and through them that the invitation was delivered to a *soirée dansante* at the Papineau house, where all the cakes and jellies were decorated with Lord Aylmer's coat of arms.

Papineau, thought Lady Aylmer, showed he 'aimed to please.' These women and men implicated in the government of the state were also pre-occupied with the government of their own and other people's house-holds, and with the education of their own children as well as the educa-tion of society. The *patriote* doctor Wolfred Nelson, for instance, co-operated with Bishop Lartigue in the sexual regulation of marriage. From his prison cell in Montreal in 1838, where, for all he knew, he faced execu-tion, Nelson's words of wisdom to his daughter Sophie were that she should practise her handwriting because writing well 'is taken as proof of a young girl's modest and upright character.' If she loved her father, she would practise her English too and only speak English when alone with her brothers. For her part, as the political horizon darkened, Julie Papineau continued to be preoccupied with the apparent laziness of her sons at college.[20]

Saying politics worked through networks of sociability is not to say eve-ryone was friendly. Just how vituperative political relations became in the Rebellion decade can indeed be seen in the partial breakdown of net-works of sociability, within as well as across ethnic-linguistic divides. Louis-Joseph Papineau's diktat against socializing with Lord Aylmer after 1834 is a case in point, as is the refusal of Papineau and other *patriotes* to attend the 1835 funeral of Jean Dessaulles – seigneur of St-Hyacinthe, Papineau's brother-in-law and a favourite of his children – because he had accepted a Legislative Council appointment. On the other hand, even late in the 1830s, members of different political factions and ethnic groups could be found socializing and cooperating together on such projects as infant schooling and teacher training. A well-developed net-work of commercial relations between Scots and French Canadians was relatively immune to political strife. Joseph Masson, the extremely wealthy merchant, seigneur of Terrebonne, a co-founder of the Bank of Montreal, who had begun as a minor clerk in a Scottish mercantile house, sent beginning Scottish clerks to live in the countryside to learn French – sometimes with the *patriote* J.-J. Girouard. Despite his close con-nections to Tory finance capital, in the 1820s at least, Masson was close to the Papineaus. The only mention of Rebellion-related events in Masson's personal diary is a note that he lent the Bank of Montreal, of which he was a director, £5,000 during the 1837 fiscal crisis.[21] Everyone knows that politicians have domestic lives; reflexive historical sociology, at least in its game-theoretic variants, encourages a view of politics in which interpersonal connections and strategies and tactics of sociability are taken seriously.

Statistical modes of knowing and estimating a changing social world came increasingly to frame social policy across the period studied here, but they also made broad cultural inroads and influenced individual subjectivities and self-understanding. While there may not have been a Lower Canadian counterpart to Cline Cohen's American doctor, who kept a meticulous record of all substances of whatever description he imbibed and excreted over a long period, there were people like Jacques Viger and Joseph Bouchette, taking pleasure in making inventories of passing events, charting, mapping, and laying out social conditions in tabular form in order to discover their inherent meaning.[22] Such techniques of knowledge objectivized the social, but were at once techniques of self-formation. Ruling by schooling is inextricably bound up with both.

Appendices

APPENDIX A

Legislation for Rural Elementary Schooling in Lower Canada

The following list does not usually include the acts voted for the support of elementary schools and other educational institutions in the cities unless they also affected rural schooling.

1793 Elementary School Bill, 'An Act for the instruction of youth in useful learning by the establishing of schools in the different parishes of this province, and to enable the children of the poor and necessitous to share the common benefits arising therefrom,' proposed to create a parish school system on the model elaborated by William Smith. Did not make second reading in the Assembly.

1801 'An Act for the Establishment of Free Schools and the Advancement of Learning in this Province' (41 Geo. III, cap. 17). Made provision for the incorporation of a Royal Institution for the Advancement of Learning to organize schools and to subsidize schoolmasters at local instigation. The Board of the Royal Institution was not incorporated until 1819.

1814 Elementary School Bill, promoted by François Blanchet and J.-T. Taschereau, aimed to grant funds annually to the support of rural schools. Lost in the Assembly.

1816 'Bill for encouraging and facilitating the establishment of Schools throughout the Province.' Envisioned a parish school system by incorporating the churchwardens and allowing them to assess property. Died on the order paper.

1818 Elementary School Act. Reproduced the substance of the 1816 bill and passed both houses of the Legislature. Reserved by the governor for royal sanction and then rejected in London on the grounds that it created large numbers of independent and unregulated corporations and that it did not give the executive control over teachers.

1819 Elementary School Act. A close copy of the 1818 act, rejected by the governor following instructions that no colonial bills substantially the same as those refused royal sanction were to be approved.

1821 Elementary School Act. Another version of the 1819 act, but local school corporations were to be composed of the curé, the seigneur, the senior militia officers, and one churchwarden. All nominations of teachers subject to executive approval. Passed in the legislature, reserved for royal assent, which was refused until the resolution of the Civil List question. Never enacted.

1822–3 'Bill for establishing free schools and more effectually to encourage the advancement of learning in this province than heretofore.' Proposed to create a Catholic Royal Institution. Rejected in London before being submitted to the legislature.

1824 Vestry School Act of 1824 (or La loi des fabriques, 4 Geo. IV, cap.31, 'Acte pour faciliter l'établissement et la dotation d'Écoles élémentaires dans les paroisses de cette Province'). Authorized the Catholic churchwardens to accept limited donations and to hold modest amounts of property to support vestry schools. Up to a quarter of the vestry's funds could be diverted to school support. The act remained in force until the end of the period studied here, but few vestry schools were organized.

1825 School Bill. Written by J.-F. Perrault, the bill proposed to create district boards of education, located in the cities, with the power to establish and to manage schools in town and country. The boards would be incorporated and would support schools through a mixture of government grants and local taxation. The *parti canadien* leadership opposed the bill, and it did not make second reading.

1826 A declarative Act, 7 Geo. IV c.20, increased the amount of property the vestries could hold for school purposes.

1827 Rural Elementary School Bill. Sponsored by François Blanchet, the bill proposed to allow rural householders in the Quebec District to organize and to manage schools at their own discretion. A government grant of £10,000 would provide support as well as match funds for schoolhouse construction. Passed in the Assembly, but parliament was prorogued while it was still in the Council.

1829 'An Act to authorize the formation of two separate and distinct boards of trustees in the Royal Institution for the Promotion of Learning.' Passed in the Council, sent to the Assembly, passed second reading, was printed, then deferred. Never enacted.

1829 'An Act for the encouragement of elementary education,' 9 Geo.IV cap. 46. Known as the Trustees School Act or Loi des Syndics. Provided for the election of parish and township school trustee boards to organize and manage rural elementary schools. Teachers' salaries and schoolhouse construction subsidized by government.

1830 Elementary School Act, 10-11 Geo. IV, cap.14. Revised the Trustees act and funded urban schools; qualified the curés to stand for trustee elections; no new schools to be funded without a trustee election; minimum enrolment threshold imposed on Royal Institution schools; specified half-yearly payment for teachers and bi-annual school examinations.

1831 Elementary School Act, 1 Will. IV, cap. 7. Revised the Trustees act to specify pay periods, to whom money will be paid, and had the five trustees collect all school reports and forward them to government at the same moment. Additional matching funds for schoolhouses were appropriated. The act created nineteen county school visitors, all of them MPPs, with powers to define school district limits, and to examine teachers.

1832 Elementary School Act, 2 Will. IV, cap. 26. Repealed the Trustees School Act. Three school trustees to be elected in each district. The maximum number of funded schools in each county was specified. Offered

salary increases to teachers and allowed the funding of a second school
for girls in each parish with a Catholic church. Created a prize of 10s
for the best student in each school. Specified school hours and the school
year and minimum qualifications for teachers. Limited the age of instruction and limited eligibility for pauper students. School reports and applications for funding to be made to the resident or highest-polling MPP;
this official to submit a list of eligible schools to government. The MPPs
were now to perform other administrative functions in addition to visiting the schools.

1833 Elementary School Act, 3 Will. IV, cap.4. Amended the 1832 act to
restore the bi-annual pay period for the school grant. Allowed schools
kept in good faith during the cholera epidemic without trustee elections
a prorated share in the grant. Added new categories of school visitors.
Altered slightly the numbers of county school districts, modified the pauper student funding scheme, allowed a bonus for bilingual schools. The
visitors could authorize new schools if they were in continuous operation
with at least thirty-five students. Other minor housekeeping provisions.

1834 'An Act for the Further and Permanent Encouragement of
Education.' Incorporated colleges and academies and permitted them
to acquire and hold property in perpetuity for the support of education.
Reserved for royal sanction and refused in London.

1834 'An Act for the Further Encouragement of Education throughout
the Province,' 4 Will. IV, cap.34, or Elementary School Act, extended
the life of the 1832 School Act to 1 May 1836. The Assembly's version
of this act incorporated trustee boards and gave them powers of taxation.
Amended in the Legislative Council to remove taxation powers and to replace them with extensive executive control over schooling. The Council's
amendments rejected in the Assembly, and the act as passed simply extended the life of the 1832 act. Reserved for royal sanction. Proclaimed
7 January 1835.

1836 School Monies Act. Renewed funding for urban educational institutions. Enacted and proclaimed early in 1836.

1836 Colleges and Academies Bill. A close copy of the disallowed act
of 1834. Passed in the Assembly, amended by the Council to make

incorporation optional rather than compulsory, and returned to the Assembly. The amendments were not voted on.

1836 Elementary School Bill. Repealed the act of 1834 and attributed taxation powers to locally elected trustee boards. Redistributed funded schools in keeping with population and made provision for superior schools in each county. Passed by the Assembly and returned by the Council with demands for major amendments, including the creation of a colony-wide board or county-wide boards of education. Returned on the eve of prorogation. Led to the expiration of the School Act of 1834.

1836 Normal School Act 6 Will. IV, cap. 12. Created and funded normal schools for male teachers in Montreal and Quebec with additional subsidies for women teachers in Catholic religious houses. Passed by both houses and proclaimed by Lord Gosford over belated objections from his Executive Council and from conservative opponents.

1841 Common School Act, 4 & 5 Vic., cap. 18. Created a Superintendent of Education for the Province of Canada and a legislative school grant of £50,000, £30,000 of which was to be distributed in Canada East on the basis of population. The Superintendent's powers were largely distributive. The act made new District Councils and Municipal Councils into school boards, charged with creating school districts and with levying a tax on property for school support to a maximum of £50 for schoolhouse construction and an additional £10 annually for books and supplies. The District's share in the school fund was conditional upon the levying of an equivalent school tax. Three elected Township School Commissions managed all aspects of local schooling and served as school inspectors. They determined school fees. In urban municipalities, executive government appointed Boards of Examiners for teachers.

APPENDIX B

Robert Armour Jr (1806–1845)

There is no stand-alone entry for Armour in the *Dictionary of Canadian Biography*, although he does receive brief mention in the entry for Armour Sr. There has been a tendency to confuse the two in some of the Rebellion historiography. Robert Armour Jr (1806–45) was thirty-three years old when he was named school inspector. He had attended the University of Edinburgh and studied law under Samuel Gale, one of the justices especially targeted (unsuccessfully) for removal from office by the *patriote* majority in 1835–6. Armour received his legal commission in 1829, although he was already handling petitions as an eighteen-year-old. Robert Armour Sr, the King's Printer and proprietor of the *Gazette*, was a core member of the Montreal arch-Tory circle, active in the city's merchant banking, insurance, and gas lighting companies. Although Junior was capable in his own right, as he showed by compiling and publishing the *Montreal Almanac* for several years and also by editing the *Gazette* for much of the early 1830s, his father's influence was an important stepping stone. Before the 1832 West Ward election entrenched political antipathies, the Armours could be found associating publicly with leading *patriotes* in Montreal's philanthropic and educational institutions: on the committee of the Montreal Mechanics' Institute in 1829, for instance, the following year on the management committee of the British and Canadian School Society, and in 1831 with a group that included Bishop Lartigue in support of the Emigrant Society. Robert Jr acted as secretary and archivist for the Montreal Natural History Society and was active in the Montreal Board of Sanitation in the wake of the 1832 cholera.[1]

Armour apparently had little interest in practising law, but was consistently on the lookout for respectable money-making opportunities through his Tory patronage networks. He acted as receiver for the Fire

Assurance Society and sold shares in the Quebec Bank. Hearing in 1832 that the Assembly might fund the production of a digest of the colonial statutes, he petitioned the civil secretary for the job, including a prospectus endorsed by the Montreal justices. The new 1832 Montreal Trinity Board, formed to manage the harbour, of which his father was a member, appointed Armour as acting registrar, a position that was soon converted to permanent clerk and registrar with £75 and flexible working hours. He held that position until early 1836 and at times worked as an extra Legislative Council clerk.[2]

Armour was active in Montreal politics from his teens. In its early anti-Semitic mode, *La Minerve* commented in 1827 that a Montreal political meeting from which Tory speakers were excluded had no need to hear from 'le petit juif Hart,' nor from 'Mr Robert Armour fils du propriétaire de la Gazette,' who attended and wished to speak. His petition of 1832 demanding an inquiry into the management of the Post Office Department pushed the Assembly into demanding colonial control of it. His father was one of the dissident Presbyterians arrested in 1831 for occupying Henry Esson's church after Esson accepted that Elders should be elected by parishioners. Armour Jr may not have accepted this stance, but he was an early member of the St Andrew's Society, one of the four ethnic societies which provided the organizational basis for the Montreal Constitutional Association and which furnished volunteer militiamen in 1837–8.[3]

In the 1832 Montreal election Armour attended and spoke at candidates' meetings in both wards and helped organize the Tory campaigns. In the East Ward he supported the wealthy merchant A.-O. Berthelet as a needed spokesman for merchant capital. Berthelet's handy defeat of C.-C. de Sabrevois Bleury encouraged the Tories to believe they could take the West Ward as well. Armour signed the election address of the Tory candidate Stanley Bagg, and as the outcome teetered between Bagg and the *patriote* Daniel Tracey amid pitched battles for control of the polling place, Armour was busy rounding up Tory voters and escorting them to vote – Joseph Lancaster among them. He testified in defence of the troops at the coroner's inquiry that followed the election riot, and he interrupted and tried to stop L.-J. Papineau, who had no official standing, from questioning witnesses. Papineau had earlier been roughed up in the street, and these events signalled a dramatic increase in colonial political – and personal – antagonisms. For instance, Jacques Viger noted two years later that as the *Gazette*'s parliamentary correspondent, Armour would report nothing that Papineau said in debate. *La Minerve* slammed Armour as a Tory spy in the legislature, always skulking about in the lobby, waiting to sneak into the chamber and pilfer bits of notepaper from someone's desk.[4]

Armour was also an active promoter of the British and American Land Company and one of the founding members of the Montreal Constitutional Association in 1835. He was reported by Solicitor General O'Sullivan (wrongly, it seems) to be the lone government employee to join the paramilitary 'British Rifle Corps' later that year, and it may have been Lord Gosford's message that such conduct was unbecoming in a public officer that led him to resign his position as clerk of the Trinity Board in the winter of 1836. Believing that the future development of the English-speaking population of the colony would be centred on the Eastern Townships and the Land Company, Armour moved to Sherbrooke and purchased the *Sherbrooke Gazette and Township Advertiser* in 1837. Only two numbers of the paper survive, but Armour turned it into a Tory rag, reprinting the Constitutional Association's platform and calling for the Union of the Canadas. It has not been possible to trace his involvement in the volunteer forces in 1837–8 with any precision, but it is probable that he attended the 'Grand Loyal Meeting' held in Montreal the same week in October 1837 as the *patriotes'* 'Réunion des six comtés' at St Charles. The Montreal meeting was followed by a ward-by-ward muster of mounted volunteers.[5]

Finally, Robert Armour Jr was in the group that responded to the Buller Commission for Ascot and Orford townships in December 1838. The group estimated the townships' population at 3,500 with 1,150 of school age and 240 at school. Most of the Assembly schools were closed and the Sherbrooke Academy was occupied by troops. Much of the report was praise for the efforts of the Land Company, whose Ascot school was 'about to be occupied by Mr King a teacher under the Newfoundland & North American School Society in London.' More kudos were offered for the Company's generous contributions to schooling in Bury and Lingwick townships. The group noted that 'the French children are taught English.'[6]

His reports are quite useful as descriptors of schools, and also as examples of the 'travel modality' and of early inspection activity in the generation of state knowledge. The reports seem not to have been taken up by Poulett Thomson, perhaps because of the antipathy between the liberal Christopher Dunkin and the Tory Armour.

APPENDIX C

Stephen Randal's 1838 Educational Proposals

There were a great many more or less well-articulated plans, schemes, and proposals in circulation for ruling and schooling Lower Canada in the wake of the failure of the 1836 School Bill and the insurrections. One of the more striking proposals was made by Stephen Randal (1804–41), which Governor Poulett Thomson found among the unanswered correspondence in the civil secretary's office. He thought the proposal sufficiently important to refer it to Christopher Dunkin for his consideration and report, but if Dunkin did report in writing, his opinion has been lost. The proposal contained draconian measures that Dunkin would not have supported; that Thomson referred it to him suggests that the new governor thought there might be merit in an immediate, full-blown frontal assault on French-Canadian culture and institutions.

Randal's biographer describes him as "'a very odd but gifted young man.'" Educated by the Anglican establishment in St Armand and Montreal, Randal had fallen on hard times after attempts to make a living earlier in the 1830s in Hamilton, Upper Canada. There he had served as town clerk and edited the *Free Press* before wandering about the colony, failing at various other activities, such as publishing *Randal's Magazine* and, after shipping his wife and family back to relatives in Lower Canada, lecturing on politics and teaching school. The Rebellion in the upper province encouraged him to return to Lower Canada, and he agreed to teach the Frost Academy for the miserable sum of £40.[7]

Randal's education proposals were part of a larger plan for responsible government and reform of the state system. He suggested – something Thomson was about to do in any case – the creation of government departments with responsible ministers, among them a department of education. Randal offered three 'Preliminary Measures for Imperial or local Enactment' to remedy the colony's ills. They included a general education system to take the English language into French-language settlements, the imposition of an educational qualification for the franchise, and a 'complete system of Census and Registration, which should furnish the government annually with the following information in detail – 1. Names of all heads of families. – 2. Amount of unincumbered landed property – 3. Country of their birth or whence emigrated – 4. Period of their settlement in this Province. – 5. Religious Persuasion – 6. Whether they could speak, read, write and keep accounts in the English language.' The 'last qualification by the majority should determine the time of returning to popular election' for any municipal district or riding. The use of the census as a direct monitoring device was an innovation in relation to the many other demands for English literacy as a condition of exercising the franchise.

Randal followed these recommendations with 'Observations preparatory to a General Plan of Education for Lower Canada,' a critique of past policy and of the existing educational condition of the people. The Assembly's policy had multiplied schools in the French-speaking countryside without offering them means of support. 'Learning being thus rendered dog-cheap, was of course little better than dog's learning.' In the Eastern Townships, people imitated the American system, but in the absence of adequate funding it produced bad teachers, bad schoolhouses, and bad books. Almost everyone in the Townships could read and write, but no one did. Adults were in need of instruction too, and Randal argued that every schoolhouse should have its own library stocked with periodicals – 'the rail-roads of modern literature.' A cynic might suppose he wanted *Randal's Magazine* to be the mainline.

Randal stated that the education of the French-speaking population 'must be put down at zero.' What it needed were manual labour schools for instruction in agricultural technique. If people would not send their children to such schools, Randal suggested that the government draft English-speaking immigrant children to work in them. The latter would learn to farm and would improve the French through their example. In language that Arthur Buller might have cribbed, Randal insisted, 'at whatever risk – at whatever sacrifice, the principle must be adopted and acted upon – boldly and resolutely, without subterfuge or disguise that the English language shall in all cases be the language of the subject before his admission to the free institutions of the English government.'

To achieve the goal of anglicization 'what is wanted is an active and efficient system of public instruction under the entire control and direction of the government.' But the system should not be extended past the point where teachers could earn a respectable living. Government should provide schools and books, determine fees and other charges, and name teachers; and if resources did not permit the education of all, some at least should receive a good education. Randal then proposed that there be a provincial normal school, superior schools in each county, and common schools in each district of five square miles, all subject to inspection by the central authority. The Bible and the Church of England catechism were to be used in all Protestant schools. He offered some suggestions as to funding, but the bulk of his plan was short on specifics.[8]

APPENDIX D

Christopher Dunkin's Draft School Ordinance of 1840[9]

The Central Bureaucracy

The main administrators in Dunkin's system were a financial officer, a chief superintendent of education, three school inspectors, and a twenty-seven-member board of education. The financial officer was the treasurer of a state school fund created through the investment of the accumulated revenue of the Jesuits' Estates (£25,000) and through an annual appropriation estimated at £25,000. He was paid a percentage of the monies passing through his hands and acted as paymaster for school monies.

The chief superintendent presided over the education 'department,' but he was not a government minister. He and the inspectors were debarred from participating in politics. The superintendent apportioned money and supervised its disbursement; ensured compliance with the school law; advised the Executive on patronage appointments; collected and examined annual returns; and reported on them to the Governor. He was visitor-in-chief of all educational institutions, he was the court of appeal in non-judicial matters, and he chaired the board of education and the normal schools. He was the source of circular instructions issued to lower-level officials. Appointed on good behaviour, the superintendent had two clerks to assist him and was paid £800 annually, with extra for his expenses and a pension fund – a novelty.

District inspectors were appointed for Montreal, Quebec, and Sherbrooke, each with a salary of £500, in addition to expenses and a pension fund. One of the three was to serve as secretary to the board of education. These travelling officers ensured that local school officials complied with the school law and followed procedures for assessing and taxing property, maintaining the schoolhouse, hiring and paying teachers, and so on. Local disputes over school matters were decided in the first instance by them.

The board of education was modelled on Buller's 1838 proposals. It included the five senior administrative officers with six clergymen sitting ex officio: the Anglican bishop, the moderator of the Kirk, the chairman of the Methodist Conference, and the three highest 'Dignitaries of the Catholic Church.' The remaining sixteen members were to be half Protestant and half Catholic but always with a lay majority. The board contained two standing denominational committees. The whole board could appoint committees to deal with particular matters of concern and make rules for their guidance, subject to the governor's approval. It could censure any lower-level official provided that that person be removed immediately from office. It could reverse the superintendent's decisions, subject to the governor's approval, with such reversals not to be considered censure. The board made rules and regulations for the schools, named visitors to the normal and model schools, and recommended and prohibited books. The denominational committees were restricted to a single annual meeting at a fixed date, although extraordinary meetings could be called with the governor's consent. They were the system's religious police. They could censure and remove any lower-level officer for violating the school law with respect to religious teaching, and they suggested visitors for their own schools. They had a veto over schoolbooks that dealt with religious matters and enjoyed the right 'to have all questions of a religious character referred to them, before action of the Bd. thereon.'

The draft legislation embodied the Irish solution to religious instruction. Local trustees could regulate religious teaching as they pleased provided no one objected. If any one did object, formal religious teaching was to be offered after school hours. The board of education would prepare a book of "Scripture Extracts" for interdenominational instruction, and it was to be used in the schools unless a majority of ratepayers objected to it.

City Schools

City councils were required to organize a minimum number of schools in each city ward in keeping with population distribution. Such schools offered all urban children 'the opportunity of receiving a good elementary education free of charge, during a certain term in every year, under qualified Teachers, & according to a course of study to be to some extent prescribed by law.' Council chose school sites. The schools had separate departments or classes for students over and under ten years of age. No mention was made of separation of the sexes. The school year was ten calendar months, and instruction was to be given five days a week for five hours a day. If a school had only a single teacher, that person must hold a certificate of 'full qualification' from a normal or model school and be able to speak English. Assistant teachers were exempt from those qualifications.

Except in Quebec and Montreal, city council was to create a school council to manage the schools composed of a councillor from each ward with the mayor as chairman. In the two main cities, school council members were elected directly by ratepayers. The school council would contract with head teachers, subject to the approval of the superintendent. Assistants could be appointed and removed by school council, but the superintendent's permission was required to fire a head teacher. School council determined curriculum, again subject to the approval of the superintendent and the board of education and in keeping with the provisions regarding religious instruction. School inspection was by a group composed of the ward councillor, as many other people as he chose to name, with a like group named by the superintendent.

For elementary schooling, the most radical provisions in Dunkin's scheme were for urban and rural property taxation. In the cities, the school tax was to be at least double the amount granted from the provincial education fund and was entirely for teachers' salaries. City councils could raise an additional tax for building, maintaining and furnishing schools up to a maximum mill rate. A city's share in the provincial fund was determined by its population, but within city limits, the money was distributed to schools according to attendance. The ordinance empowered the superintendent to withhold some or all of a city's grant money if it did not establish enough schools or violated some other provision of the law. The money in question would go to the general provincial fund. Cities could acquire and hold other properties or endowments for school purposes, but the minimum tax revenue was to be spent first.

Dunkin allowed the existing urban school societies to participate in the new arrangements. They first had to be incorporated, and their management committees would act in place of the city school council, subject to the same conditions of curriculum and hours of instruction. In order to share in the education fund, the societies had to accept free of charge all children wishing to attend up to a third of their total enrolments. Their teachers were not to be paid more per student than were other city teachers.

High Schools or Academies

Having dramatically expanded urban elementary school provision and access, Dunkin made arrangements for publicly supported secondary schooling in both town and country. In the cities, the municipal council could vote to tax for the support of a '1st class' school or academy for either or both sexes. To qualify for public support, the school in question had to be incorporated and had to possess some property on a permanent basis. Its school buildings qualified as property, and it could also be endowed with other resources. Incorporation followed an application in a standard form to the superintendent, and continuation of the corporate charter depended upon the delivery of annual reports in a prescribed form to the superintendent as well. City council would be the management corporation. The first-class school could not offer denominational religious instruction (if anyone objected) and was to follow a prescribed course of studies. 'Among these studies must be the English language. For girls' schools, the Classical languages may not be required.' In the countryside, the school would be managed by trustees elected by ratepayers, subject to inspection by commissioners appointed by the executive. Dunkin created a separate secondary school fund, initially to consist of £1,500 to £2,000 annually, which was distributed to the schools according to attendance levels.

Rural Schools

Christopher Dunkin's ordinance sought completely to transform the organization of rural elementary schooling by subjecting it to central planning and administration through the offices of the chief superintendent and newly appointed school commissioners at the level of parish, township, or seigneury. There were school trustees elected locally for a two-year period who were to meet at least annually for administrative purposes and to manage individual schools, but the trustees were tightly confined to a set of prescribed activities. What sort of person they could hire to teach, the minimum amount they could pay, what kind of schoolhouse they could build and where, what the boundaries of their districts were, what could be taught in their schools, what records and papers they were to keep, and other matters were all specified by law.

Using the criteria of territory and population and respecting existing boundaries where possible, the chief superintendent would specify the limits of school districts so 'that each may have within it a school-site accessible to all its inhabitants.' He could define or redefine districts that crossed municipal boundaries. In keeping with Dunkin's earlier calculations, wherever possible these districts would contain 1,000 people within a radius of 1.5 miles or 1,400 or more within two miles. The more populous districts were to be considered '1st class' districts. Dunkin distinguished 'preparatory' schools for students under ten years of age from 'district' schools for older students. He set the school leaving age at fifteen. The superintendent could require any first-class district without an academy to maintain one district and two preparatory schools. Trustees could organize more schools, if they could fund them, and they could organize same-sex schools if they could prove to the superintendent that they had the necessary funds. A vestry school or a convent school could be declared a district school for the trustees' two-year term of office, provided it came under the provisions of the school act.

Only schools on sites and in premises approved by the superintendent were eligible for the school grant. The school day and year varied according to the kind of school in question and the amount of its government grant, although if the district supported only one preparatory school, it was to be open at least nine months of the year. All children aged from five to ten years of age were to attend the preparatory schools free of charge. District schools could charge specified fees to students over ten years of age.

The three township, parish, or seigneury school commissioners appointed by the executive were the channel of communication between the central authority and the school trustees at the district level. With local clergy, they were a board of examiners for candidate teachers and acted as school visitors, examining records and journals and reporting annually to the chief superintendent. Where a district had two or more schools, school property was vested in the commissioners, who could buy or sell property under conditions specified in the law. School monies reached the trustees via the commissioners, and both groups were to account publicly for such money and were personally liable for misspent or misdirected funds even after leaving office. The school records and papers were not to disappear again as they had in 1836, for 'all books, papers &.c. belonging to bd. are to be recoverable by summary process, of ex-members, by their successors in office, – if their delivery be refused or delayed.'

The ordinance required the trustees to levy a school tax, although it imposed no penalties if they refused or neglected to do so. The minimum tax was to equal the amount of the government school grant and was to pay teachers' salaries, with an adequate additional amount for school maintenance and supplies. Annually, before the trustees' meeting, the commissioners would inform them of their share of the government grant. At their meeting, the trustees were to vote at least an equivalent amount in tax and to report to the commissioners the amount voted and the name of their teacher(s). The commissioners would inform the superintendent of the proposed tax – or if the trustees did not report, they could define the necessary amount – with any remarks as to its adequacy. It then fell to the superintendent to approve the amount. Dunkin stressed that he 'must always have power to direct the levying of a sufficient sum' for the maintenance of acceptable schools. The superintendent would then 'return his tax-warrant in the proper form to the collecting officers without delay,' and the school tax would be collected in the same manner as other taxes under governor Thomson's planned municipal legislation. Costs of collection were not to exceed 5 per cent, and Dunkin suggested that tax collection would take place in November and December. The school grant would only be paid after the trustees and commissioners had certified that the money raised by taxation had been spent. The superintendent could choose to withhold some or all of the grant money if trustees had not complied with the law or with school regulations.

Dunkin fixed the annual rural grant at £10,000, to be distributed according to population distribution. An additional 'poor schools' fund of £2,000 would subsidize teachers' salaries in the amount of £10 per school, and an annual school construction fund of £2,000 would subsidize schoolhouses to a maximum of £30, providing ratepayers doubled the amount. Any unexpended monies in the schoolhouse fund would be available to support rural school libraries.

Dunkin was not explicit on the matter, but it seems he intended that the education department's financial officer would be the single paymaster and government money would come to the trustees via the appointed school commissioners. The latter were unsalaried, although they could claim for their time and travelling expenses from the school fund. School visitors were to serve at their own expense, as were trustees. Trustees would effectively be the immediate objects of the ire of ratepayers.

Teachers

The directly political nature of this school system 'above politics' was already clear in the powers granted to the chief superintendent over local schooling, but it became more explicit in the regulation and training of teachers. The superintendent and the board of education were to specify the forms to be used in hiring teachers. Trustees would follow them in nominating their teachers for the approval of the school commissioners. The latter would join with all resident clergymen to examine those nominated, and 'Moral Character & loyalty' as well as technical teaching abilities were to be investigated closely according to a specified standard. Candidate teachers who had a certificate 'signed by a Normal School Professor or other authorised party, declaring them "fully qualified"' were only examined on their moral character and political opinions. If the examining board had doubts on these last two scores, the district inspector would have to approve the teacher's appointment. Any teacher without a certificate of qualification would be hired only on condition of six weeks' attendance at a model school, 'acquaintance with English language, to be always a condition of such certificate.' Both the superintendent and the district inspector could intervene to remove teachers and to close schools, for instance, if attendance fell below a specified threshold or if the trustees attempted to pay the teacher less than a minimum salary. Getting loyal, moral, technically competent English-speaking teachers into all rural schools was furthered by Dunkin's proposed normal and model schools.

The Normal and Model Schools

In keeping with Amury Girod's 1832 experiment and Jean Holmes's 1836 recommendations, the normal schools were to be rural institutions equipped with a farm and were to train both secondary and rural elementary school teachers. If the municipal council subsidized it, a normal school could join an academy to its operations. The Montreal Normal School was still nominally open; Dunkin proposed to have the governor fill the vacancies on its management board caused by the flight of the political refugees and to give it another £100 to subsidize poor students for two years until his school act came into effect. The clause in the 1836 Normal School Act creating a Normal School at Quebec was to be repealed. Unlike the 1836 act, under Dunkin's ordinance the governor named the schools' teachers and management boards, with the chief superintendent and the district school inspector ex-officio members of the latter. The course of study was to be specified in general terms by law, to be non-denominational, and to be detailed by the superintendent or the board of education. 'The English language is to be taught to all pupils, not already masters of it.' For women teachers, there were to be normal school departments in religious houses in Quebec, Montreal, and Trois-Rivières, and in two Protestant academies chosen by the governor. These institutions were accepted on condition of teaching the prescribed curriculum, not interfering with religious loyalties, and teaching the English language. All these institutions would be open nine or ten months of the year and would charge fees for instruction and board, with a specified number of students receiving free tuition. The normal school professors could grant certificates of "full qualification" to candidate teachers.

In keeping with Dunkin's ambition to cause competition among teachers, only those with a certificate of "full qualification" already working in a district school were eligible to teach in his summer model schools. For six or seven weeks' work during summer vacation, the model school teacher would earn the handsome sum of £30, with an additional £7.10s. for his expenses (and perhaps for her expenses, since the model schools were same-sex institutions). The chief superintendent was to name one school in each county as a model, subject to the approval of the trustees, and it was to be open for seven weeks a year during regular school vacation. Instruction was free to all current or former teachers, provided they came equipped with a certificate of moral character. Anyone not able to speak English was to be taught it. At the end of the model school sessions, student teachers would be examined by the superintendent or by one of the inspectors; those who passed were 'fully qualified' and no longer required to attend.

A final minor clause in Dunkin's ordinance had major unintended consequences for Canadian educational and political history – not, it turned out, in the Canada East/Quebec at which it was aimed, but rather in Canada West/Ontario. The clause allowed a group of at least 25 per cent of the ratepayers in any school district to apply to the commissioners and the inspector before the annual trustees' meeting for permission to manage a 'special school.' If they paid their share of the general school tax and raised an amount at least 25 per cent greater, sufficient to cover all expenses, they could conduct their own school for a renewable two-year term. The clause was meant to allow the Protestant minority in predominantly Catholic areas of Lower Canada to manage its own schools and to use the Bible as a schoolbook. Under the Canada School Act of 1841, and its successors in Canada West/Ontario, Catholics used the clause to establish separate religious schools.[10]

Notes

Introduction

1 New France was conquered by British force of arms in 1759–60 and ceded to the English Crown by the 1763 Treaty of Paris. The conquered territory was called Quebec. In 1791, it was divided on a south-east/north-west axis, roughly along the line of the Ottawa River. The division created the colonies of Upper and Lower Canada, equipped with elected representative Assemblies and appointed Executive and Legislative Councils. The two were joined again by the Act of Union of 1840, which created the Province of Canada, with two parts now called Canada West and Canada East.

2 Pierre Bourdieu, *The Science of Science and Reflexivity* (Chicago: University of Chicago Press, 2004). Pierre Bourdieu and Loïc Wacquant, *An Invitation to Reflexive Sociology* (Chicago: University of Chicago Press, 1992). Arpad Szakolczai, 'Reflexive Historical Sociology,' *European Journal of Philosophy* 1 (1998): 209–27.

3 Norbert Elias, *The Civilizing Process* (New York: Routledge, 1994); Elias, *The Court Society* (New York: Pantheon, 1983); Elias, 'The Retreat of Sociologists into the Present,' in *Modern German Sociology*, ed. V. Meyer and et al. (New York: Columbia University Press, 1987), 150–72. Arpad Szakolczai, 'Norbert Elias and Franz Borkenau. Intertwined Life-Works,' *Theory Culture Society* 17 (2000): 45–69.

4 Even if I can't offer enough information for game-theoretic accounts, I provide leads for those who may go further in investigating the relations of biography and history. In this regard, Yves Gingras, 'Pour une biographie sociologique,' *Revue d'histoire de l'Amérique française* 54 (2000): 123–31. For a game-theoretic analysis of Lord Durham's Canadian adventure, Bruce Curtis, 'The "Most Splendid Pageant Ever Seen": Grandeur, the Domestic,

and Condescension in Lord Durham's Political Theatre,' *Canadian Historical Review* 89 (2008): 55–88.

5 Alain Desrosières, 'Histoire de formes: statistiques et sciences sociales avant 1940,' *Revue française de sociologie* 26 (1985): 277–310; Desrosières, 'How to Make Things Which Hold Together: Social Science, Statistics and the State,' in *Discourses on Society. The Shaping of the Social Science Disciplines,* ed. P. Wagner, B. Wittrock, and R. Whitley (Dordrecht, 1991), 195–218.

6 Appendix A contains an overview of school legislation. With a research team mainly of graduate students from Carleton, Laval, UQAM, and Toronto, I explored state papers in colony and imperium; the contemporary press in both English and French; Catholic and Anglican Church records and archives; the diaries and private correspondence of some colonial governors, administrators, intellectuals, and politicians on both sides of the Atlantic; records of the Royal Institution for the Promotion of Learning; contemporary colonial pamphlets and the English periodical literature; biographical material; school records; and a variety of secondary sources.

7 François Melançon, 'Émergence d'une tradition catholique de lecture au Canada,' *Cahiers de la recherche en éducation* 3 (1996): 343–63.

8 Allan Greer, 'The Pattern of Literacy in Quebec, 1745–1899,' *Histoire sociale/Social History* 11 (1978): 295–335. Michel Verrette, *L'alphabétisation au Québec 1660–1900. En marche vers la modernité culturelle* (Quebec: Septentrion, 2002); Verrette, 'The Spread of Literacy,' in *History of the Book in Canada,* ed. Patricia Lockhart Fleming, Gilles Gallichan, and Yvan Lamonde (Toronto: University of Toronto Press, 2004), 165–72. For the U.S., William J. Gilmore, *Reading Becomes a Necessity of Life: Material and Cultural Life in Rural New England, 1780–1835* (Knoxville: University of Tennessee Press, 1998).

9 See especially, Michel Ducharme, *Le concept de liberté au Canada à l'époque des révolutions atlantiques. 1776–1838* (Montreal and Kingston: McGill-Queen's University Press, 2010). Louis-Georges Harvey, *Le printemps de l'Amérique française. Américanité, anticolonialisme et républicanisme dans le discours politique québécois, 1805–1837.* (Montreal: Boréal, 2004). J.G.A. Pocock, 'Civic Humanism and Its Role in Anglo-American Thought,' in *Politics, Language and Time. Essays on Political Thought and History* (New York: Atheneum, 1971), 80–103; Pocock, *The Machiavellian Moment. Florentine Political Thought and the Atlantic Republican Tradition* (Princeton: Princeton University Press, 1975); Pocock, 'Political Thought in the English-Speaking Atlantic, 1760–1790, Part 2: Empire, Revolution and the End of Early Modernity,' in *The Varieties of English Political Thought, 1500–1800,* ed. J.G.A. Pocock,

Gordon J. Schochet and Lois G. Schwoerer (Cambridge: Cambridge University press, 1993), 283–317; Pocock, 'Political Thought in the English-Speaking Atlantic, 1760–1790: (i) The Imperial Crisis,' in *The Varieties of English Political Thought, 1500–1800*, ed. J.G.A. Pocock, Gordon J. Schochet, and Lois G. Schwoerer (Cambridge: Cambridge University Press, 1993), 246–82. Quentin Skinner, *Liberty before Liberalism* (Cambridge: Cambridge University Press, 1998). Jean-Pierre Wallot, *Un Québec qui bougeait. Trame socio-politique du Québec au tournant du XIXᵉ siècle* (Montreal: Boréal, 1973).

10 In a large and growing literature, Tim Allender, 'Learning Abroad: The Colonial Educational Experiment in India, 1813–1919,' *Paedagogica Historica* 45 (2009): 727–42. Marcelo Caruso, 'The Persistence of Educational Semantics: Patterns of Variation in Monitorial Schooling in Columbia (1821–1844),' *Paedagogica Historica* 41 (2005): 721–44. Marcelo Caruso and Eugenia Roldan Vera Vera, 'Pluralizing Meanings: The Monitorial System of Education in Latin America in the Early Nineteenth Century' *Paedagogica Historica* 41 (2005): 645–54. S. Seth, *Subject Lessons: The Western Education of Colonial India* (Durham: Duke University Press, 2007). Michel Foucault, *Discipline and Punish: The Birth of the Prison* (New York: Pantheon, 1979). David Hogan, 'The Market Revolution and Disciplinary Power: Joseph Lancaster and the Psychology of the Early Classroom System,' *History of Education Quarterly* 29 (1989): 389–417. Carl F. Kaestle, ed., *Joseph Lancaster and the Monitorial School Movement. A Documentary History*. Classics in Education 47 (New York: Teachers College Press, 1973). Phillip McCann, ed., *Popular Education and Socialization in the Nineteenth Century* (London: Methuen, 1977). George W. Spragge, 'Joseph Lancaster in Montreal,' *Canadian Historical Review* 22 (1941): 35–41; Spragge, 'Monitorial Schools in the Canadas, 1810–1845' (D. Paed., Toronto, 1935). Jana Tschurenev, 'Diffusing Useful Knowledge: The Monitorial System of Education in Madras, London and Bengal, 1789–1840,' *Paedagogica Historica* 44 (2008): 245–64.

11 Pocock, *Machiavellian Moment*. I go beyond two of my earlier contributions, Bruce Curtis, 'Joseph Lancaster in Montreal (bis): Monitorial Schooling and Politics,' *Historical Studies in Education/ Revue d'histoire de l'éducation* 17 (2005): 1–27, and 'Monitorial Schooling, "Common Christianity" and Politics: A Trans-Atlantic Controversy,' in *Transatlantic Subjects: Ideas, Institutions, and Social Experience in Post-Revolutionary British North America*, ed. Nancy Christie (Montreal and Kingston: McGill-Queen's University Press, 2008), 251–79, after more research.

12 L.-P. Audet, *Le système scolaire de la province de Québec*, 6 vols. (Quebec: Éditions de l'Érable, 1950–6).

13 Réal Boulianne, 'The Correspondence of the Royal Institution for the
Advancement of Learning in the McGill University Archives,' *Fontanus* 5
(1972): 55–72; Boulianne, 'The French Canadians and the Schools of the
Royal Institution for the Advancement of Learning, 1820–1829,' *Histoire
sociale/Social History* 5 (1972): 144–64; Boulianne, 'The Royal Institution
for the Advancement of Learning: The Correspondence, 1820–1829, A
Historical and Analytical Study' (PhD, History, McGill University, 1970).
Richard Chabot, *Le curé de campagne et la contestation locale au Québec de 1791
aux troubles de 1837–1838.* (Montreal: Hurtubise HMH, 1975). Helen
Kominek, 'The Royal Institution for the Advancement of Learning: An
Examination of Its Educational Agenda in Lower Canada, 1818–1833'
(PhD, Educational Research, Calgary, 2008). Marcel Lajeunesse,
'L'Évêque Bourget et l'instruction publique au Bas-Canada, 1840–1846,'
Revue d'histoire de l'Amérique française 23 (1969): 35–52. Fernand Ouellet,
'L'enseignement primaire: responsabilité des Églises ou de l'État (1801–
1836),' *Recherches sociographiques* 2 (1961): 171–87.
14 Andrée Dufour has engaged with a number of issues concerning the trustees'
schools; for instance, 'Diversité institutionelle et fréquentation scolaire dans l'île
de Montréal de 1825 à 1835,' *Revue d'histoire de l'Amérique française* 41 (1988):
507–535; Dufour, 'Financement des écoles et scolarisation au Bas-Canada:
Une interaction État-communautés locales (1826–1859),' *Historical Studies in
Education/Revue d'histoire de l'éducation* 6 (1994): 219–52; Dufour, 'Les institutrices rurales du Bas-Canada: incompétentes et inexperimentées?' *Revue d'histoire
de l'Amérique française* 51 (1998): 521–48; Dufour, *Tous à l'école: État, communautés
rurales et scolarisation au Québec de 1826 à 1859.* (Ville La Salle: Éditions
Hurtubise HMH, 1996). Ollivier Hubert, 'De la diversité des parcours et des
formations dans les collèges du Bas Canada: le cas de Montréal (1789–1860),'
Historical Studies in Education/Revue d'histoire de l'éducation 21 (2009): 41–65. Yvan
Lamonde, 'Classes sociales, classes scolaires: une polémique sur l'éducation en
1819–1820,' Rapport de la Sociéte canadienne d'histoire de l'Église catholique
(1974): 43–59. Roderick MacLeod and Mary Anne Poutanen, *A Meeting of the
People. School Boards and Protestant Communities in Quebec, 1801–1998* (Montreal
and Kingston: McGill-Queen's University Press, 2004); MacLeod and Poutanen,
'"Proper Objects of This Institution": Working Families, Children, and the
British and Canadian School in Nineteenth-Century Montreal,' *Historical Studies
in Education/Revue d'histoire de l'éducation* 20 (2008): 22–54.
15 Bernard Bailyn, *Education in the Forming of American Society* (New York:
Norton, 1960). Later versions of revisionism include Michael Katz, *The Irony
of Early School Reform* (Boston: Beacon Press, 1968). Samuel Bowles and
Herbert Gintis, *Schooling in Capitalist America* (New York: Basic Books,

1976). This was particularly a North American development; European
literatures contained long-standing socialist and social democratic accounts.

16 Chabot, *Le curé de campagne*. Nadia Fahmy-Eid, 'Éducation et classes sociales:
    analyse de l'idéologie conservatrice-cléricale et petite-bourgeoise au
    Québec au milieu du 19ᵉ siècle,' *Revue d'histoire de l'Amérique française* 32
    (1978): 159–79; Fahmy-Eid, *Le clergé et le pouvoir politique au Québec: une
    analyse de l'idéologie ultramontaine au milieu du XIXᵉ siècle* (LaSalle: Hurtubise
    HMH, 1978). Jean-Jacques Jolois, *Joseph-François Perrault (1753–1844) et les
    origines de l'enseignement laïque au Bas-Canada* (Montreal: Les Presses de
    l'Université de Montréal, 1969). André Labarrère-Paulé, *Les instituteurs
    laïques au Canada-Français 1836–1900* (Quebec: Les Presses de l'Université
    Laval, 1965).

17 The rehabilitation of women's religious vocations began especially with
    Micheline Dumont-Johnson, 'Les communautés religieuses et la condition
    féminine,' *Recherches sociographiques* 19 (1978): 79–102. Also, Micheline
    Dumont and Nadia Fahmy-Eid, eds., *Les Couventines: L'éducation des filles au
    Québec dans les congrégations religieuses enseignantes, 1840–1960* (Montreal:
    Boréal, 1986). Nadia Fahmy-Eid and Micheline Dumont, eds., *Maîtresses de
    maison, maîtresses d'écoles. Femmes, familles et éducation dans l'histoire du Québec*
    (Montreal: Boréal, 1983). Neither Ducharme, *Le concept de liberté*, nor Harvey,
    Le printemps de l'Amérique française, engages with the issue of the state church.
    Church history has little to say about the social politics of the period.

18 For an elaboration of this description, Bruce Curtis, 'Beyond Signature
    Literacy: New Research Directions. Introduction,' *Historical Studies in
    Education/Revue d'histoire de l'éducation* 19 (2007): 1–11. Also Curtis, 'On
    Distributed Literacy. Textually Mediated Social Relations in a Colonial
    Context,' *Paedagogica Historica* 44 (2008): 231–42.

19 Yvan Lamonde, 'Conscience coloniale et conscience internationale dans
    les écrits publics de Louis-Joseph Papineau (1815–1839),' *Revue d'histoire
    de l'Amérique française* 51 (1997): 3–37; Lamonde, *Histoire sociale des idées
    au Québec*, vol. 1 (Montreal: Fides, 2000); Lamonde, 'La Librairie Hector
    Bossange de Montréal (1815–1819) et le Commerce International du
    Livre,' in *Livre et lecture au Québec, 1800–1850*, ed. Claude Galarneau and
    Maurice Lemire (Quebec: Institut québécois de recherche sur la culture,
    1988), 59–86. Yvan Lamonde and Gilles Gallichan, eds., *L'histoire de la
    culture et de l'imprimé. Hommages à Claude Galarneau* (Quebec: Les Presses de
    l'Université Laval, 1996). Yvan Lamonde and Frédéric Hardel, 'Lectures
    domestiques, d'exil et de retraite de Louis-Joseph Papineau (1823–1871),'
    in *Lire au Québec au XIXᵉ siècle*, ed. Yvan Lamonde and Sophie Montreuil
    (Montreal: Éditions Fides, 2003), 19–67; Lamonde and Hardel, 'Pour une

histoire des pratiques de lecture: éléments de méthode et pacte fondateur,'
in *Lire au Québec*, 7–17.

20 See Brian Street, 'Literacy Events and Literacy Practices,' in *Multilingual Literacies: Comparative Perspectives on Research and Practice*, ed. M. Martin-Jones and Karen Jones (Amsterdam: John Benjamin, 2000), 17–29; Street, 'What's "New" in New Literacy Studies? Critical Approaches to Literacy in Theory and Practice,' *Current Issues in Comparative Education* 5 (2003): 1–14.

21 Bruce Curtis, 'The Speller Expelled: Disciplining the Common Reader in Canada West,' *Canadian Review of Sociology and Anthropology* 22 (1985): 346–68. David Vincent, *Literacy and Popular Culture. England 1750–1914* (Cambridge: Cambridge University Press, 1989).

22 Inês Signorini, 'Literacy and Legitimacy: Unschooled Councilmen in Legislative Sessions,' *Journal of Pragmatics* 29 (1998): 373–91.

23 Maurice Lemire, 'Le discours post-révolutionnaire sur la place du peuple dans la société,' in *La Révolution Française au Canada Français*, ed. Sylvain Simard (Ottawa: Les Presses de l'Université d'Ottawa, 1991), 171.

24 Bruce Curtis, 'Foucault on Governmentality and Population: The Impossible Discovery,' *Canadian Journal of Sociology* 27 (2002): 505–33. Jacques Rancière, *Disagreement. Politics and Philosophy* (Minneapolis: University of Minnesota Press, 1999).

25 The point is elaborated in the introduction to Bruce Curtis, *The Politics of Population: Statistics, State Formation, and the Census of Canada, 1840–1875* (Toronto: University of Toronto Press, 2001).

26 Jean-Pierre Beaud and Jean-Guy Prévost, 'Back to Quételet,' *Recherches sociologiques* (1998): 83–100; Beaud and Prévost, 'La Forme est le Fond: La Structuration des Appareils Statistiques Nationaux (1800–1945),' *Revue de synthèse* 4th series (1997): 419–456; Beaud and Prévost, 'La structuration de l'appareil statistique canadien, 1912–21,' *Canadian Historical Review* 74 (1993): 395–413; Beaud and Prévost, 'Statistics as the Science of Government: The Stillborn British Empire Statistical Bureau, 1918–20,' *The Journal of Imperial and Commonwealth History* 33 (2005): 369–91. J.-G. Prévost, 'Espace public, action collective et savoir social : Robert Gourlay et le Statistical Account of Upper Canada,' *Histoire sociale/Social History* 35 (2002): 109–39. See also the masterful account of statistics and politics, Jean-Guy Prévost, *A Total Science. Statistics in Liberal and Fascist Italy* (Montreal and Kingston: McGill-Queen's University Press, 2009).

27 As Beaud put it, a consequence of this conceptual instrument is to 'mettre à distance les choses que l'on mesure, ce qui permet de travailler sur elles sans égard à ce qu'elles sont et de créer de nouvelles choses dont la réalité n'est pas cernable physiquement mais qui évoluent dans le temps ou dans

l'espace.' Such new things are artefacts of observational practice, but they may become actionable objects as well. Jean-Pierre Beaud, 'Émergence, migrations et routinisation du pourcentage dans les sciences du politique (XVIIᵉ–XIXᵉ siècles),' *Revue de synthèse* 130 (2009): 646. Joseph Bouchette, *A Topographical Description of the Province of Lower Canada, with Remarks upon Upper Canada and on the Relative Connexion of both Provinces with the United States of America* (London: W. Faden, 1815). Joseph Bouchette, *The British Dominions in North America* (London: Henry Colburn and Richard Bentley, 1831).

28 Roland Barthes had employed the concept 'governmentality' in the 1960s to refer to the mainstream press's fascination with the activities of the government. Roland Barthes, 'Myth Today,' in *Mythologies* (New York: Hill and Wang, 1972), 109–59; at 130: 'a barbarous but unavoidable neologism: governmentality, the Government presented by the national press as the Essence of efficacy.' Curtis, 'Foucault on Governmentality and Population.' Michel Foucault, *Security, Territory, Population. Lectures at the Collège de France, 1977–78* (New York: Palgrave Macmillan, 2007).

29 Bruce Curtis, 'Surveying the Social: Techniques, Practices, Power,' *Histoire sociale/Social History* 35 (2002): 83–108.

30 M. Ducharme, and J.-F. Constant, eds., *The Liberal Order Framework for Canadian History* (Toronto: University of Toronto Press, 2008). Michel Foucault, *Naissance de la biopolitique. Cours au Collège de France, 1978–1979* (Paris: Hautes Études/Seuil/Gallimard, 2004). For a different view, Jean-Marie Fecteau, *La liberté du pauvre. Sur la régulation du crime de de la pauvreté au XIXᵉ siècle québecois* (Montreal: vlb éditeur, 2004).

31 Michel Foucault, 'Technologies of the Self,' in *Technologies of the Self: A Seminar with Michel Foucault*, ed. Luther H. Martin et al. (Amherst: University of Massachusetts Press, 1988), 18.

32 Michel Stephen J. Collier, 'Topologies of Power: Foucault's Analysis of Political Government beyond "Governmentality,"' *Theory, Culture and Society* 26 (2009): 78–108. See also Mark Bevir, 'Rethinking Governmentality: Towards Genealogies of Governance,' *European Journal of Social Theory* 13 (2010): 423–41. Mike Gane, 'Foucault on Governmentality and Liberalism,' *Theory, Culture and Society* 25 (2008): 353–63. Thomas Lemke, 'From State Biology to the Government of Life: Historical Dimensions and Contemporary Perspectives of "Biopolitics,"' *Journal of Classical Sociology* 10 (2010): 421–38. Nancy Meyer-Emerick, 'Public Administration and the Life Sciences. Revisiting Biopolitics,' *Administration and Society* 38 (2007): 689–708. Mariana Valverde, 'Genealogies of European States: Foucauldian Reflections,' *Economy and Society* 36 (2007): 159–78. Rueben S. Rose-Redwood, 'Governmentality, Geography, and the Geo-Coded World,'

Progress in Human Geography 30 (2006): 469–86. R. Walter, 'Governmentality Accounts of the Economy: A Liberal Bias?' *Economy and Society* 37 (2008): 94–114. Roshan de Silva Wijeyeratne, 'Colonialism, Caste and Custom in Indian History: Revisiting Governmentality' *South Asia Research* 27 (2007): 355–61.

33 Type 'governing through' in the subject line of Google Scholar for a list. To take a leading example, the criminalization of poverty and mental illness from the 1970s and the creation in some jurisdictions of massive, permanent prison populations led to the analysis of 'governing through crime.' Other work has taken up varieties of governing through risk and the 'responsibilization' of citizens, of governing through conceptions of community, through accounting, and, of course, through (in)security.

34 Sir C.P Lucas, ed., *Lord Durham's Report on the Affairs of British North America*, 3 vols. (Oxford: Clarendon Press, 1912).

35 Uday S. Mehta, 'Liberal Strategies of Exclusion,' in *Tensions of Empire: Colonial Cultures in a Bourgeois World*, ed. Frederick Cooper and Anna Laura Stoler (Berkeley: University of California Press, 1997), 59–86.

36 Bernard Mandeville, 'An Essay on Charity, and Charity-Schools,' in *The Fable of the Bees*, ed. Philip Harth (Harmondsworth: Penguin Books, 1970 [1723]), 261–325. John H. Middendorf, 'Dr. Johnson and Mercantilism,' *Journal of the History of Ideas* 21 (1960): 66–83, quote at 69–70.

37 Jean-Jacques Rousseau, 'A Discourse on the Moral Effects of the Arts and Sciences,' in *The Social Contract and Discourses* (New York: Dutton 1973 [1750]), 12, 19–21.

38 Reprinted in the *Quebec Herald*, 18 March 1790.

39 Since a French-language reviewer once claimed my usage of *habitant* stank of the English-Canadian cultural imperialism that ridiculed French Canadians as 'pea-soupers,' I notice here J.-P. Wallot's description of peasant tenant farmers: 'ceux-ci récusent d'ailleurs le terme de "censitaires," symbole de servilité. Ils réussissent éventuellement à se faire identifier dans les documents officiels comme des "habitants."' I use the term *habitant* interchangeably with 'peasant' and 'peasantry.' See Wallot, *Un Québec qui bougeait*, 230.

40 Jean-Jacques Rousseau, 'A Discourse on Political Economy,' in *The Social Contract and Discourses* (New York: Dutton 1973 [1755]), quotations at 123–36.

41 Jeremy Bentham, *Chrestomathia* (London: Payne and Foss, 1816). John D. Brewer, 'Adam Ferguson and the Theme of Exploitation,' *British Journal of Sociology* 37 (1986): 461–78. Ronald Hamowy, 'Adam Smith, Adam Ferguson and the Division of Labour,' *Economica* 35 (1968): 244–59.

Lisa Hill, 'Adam Smith, Adam Ferguson and Karl Marx on the Division of Labour,' *Journal of Classical Sociology* 7 (2007): 339–66. Elissa Itzkin, 'Bentham's *Chrestomathia*: Utilitarian Legacy to English Education,' *Journal of the History of Ideas* 39 (1978): 303–16. James Mill, 'On Education,' in *Political Writings*, ed. Terrence Ball (Cambridge: Cambridge University Press, 1992), 137–94.

1. The Battle between the Sword and the Mouth

1 Ordinances and Proclamations, 23 November 1759, *Report of the Public Archives of Canada* (Ottawa: King's Printer, 1918), 3–4. As the card money, estimated at 1 million livres, continued to be acquired in large quantities by English and American speculators, Governor Murray attempted unsuccessfully to protect its owners by registering individual notes; A.G. Bradley, *Sir Guy Carleton (Lord Dorchester)* (Toronto: University of Toronto Press, 1966 [1927]), 23.

2 Marcel Trudel, *L'église canadienne sous le régime militaire 1759–64*, 2 vols. (Montreal: L'Institut d'histoire de l'Amérique française, 1956), 1: 89–91. Also, 'Au XVIIIᵉ siècle, le vent des "Lumières" souffle aussi de l'Angleterre,' in *Mythes et réalités dans l'histoire du Québec* (Montreal: Hurtubise, 2001), 1: 159–73.

3 Serge Gagnon, *Quand le Québec manquait de prêtres. La charge pastorale au Bas-Canada* (Quebec: Les Presses de l'Université Laval, 2006), 3. Yvan Lamonde, *Histoire sociale des idées au Québec* (Montreal: Fides, 2000), 1: 58.

4 Pierre Tousignant, 'The Integration of the Province of Quebec into the British Empire, 1763–91, Part 1: From the Royal Proclamation to the Quebec Act,' in *Dictionary of Canadian Biography* (Toronto: University of Toronto Press, 1979).

5 Louis Phillipe Audet, *Le système scolaire de la Province de Québec* (Quebec: Éditions de l'Érable, 1950), 2: 8–9; Tousignant, ' Integration of the Province of Quebec.' Louise Dêchene, *Habitants et marchands de Montréal au XVIIᵉ Siècle* (Paris: Plon, 1974), 468. Michel Verrette, *L'alphabétisation au Québec 1660–1900. En marche vers la modernité culturelle* (Quebec: Septentrion, 2002), 92. J-Edmond Roy, *Histoire de la Seigneurie de Lauzon* (Lévis: L'Auteur, 1900), 3: 342. Allan Greer, 'The Pattern of Literacy in Quebec, 1745–1899,' *Histoire sociale/Social History* 11 (1978): 295–335.

6 The Society for the Propagation of the Gospel in Foreign Parts was the offspring of an earlier English Society for the Propagation of Christian Knowledge and was formed in 1701 to combat Catholicism internationally. It was the main source of Church of England missionaries in British America.

7 *Rapport de l'Archiviste de la Province de Québec. Pour l'année 1948–1949.*
[Hereafter, RAPQ, + year] 'Church and State Papers for the Years 1789–
1786 ... ,' 10 April 1767, Archbishop of York to H.M. Government;
3 January 1775, George III to Guy Carleton.

8 G.P. Browne, 'Murray, James,' in *Dictionary of Canadian Biography* (Toronto
University of Toronto Press, 1979), 569–78. The contrast between the
terms of the Proclamation of 1763 and those of the Quebec Act of 1774
has stimulated recent scholarly interest. See Philip Lawson, 'A Perspective
on British History and the Treatment of the Conquest of Quebec,' *Journal
of Historical Sociology* 3 (1990): 253–71. David Milobar, 'The Origins of
British-Quebec Merchant Ideology: New France, the British Atlantic and
the Constitutional Periphery, 1720–70,' *The Journal of Imperial and Commonwealth History* 24, no. 3 (1996): 364–90. Karen Stanbridge, 'Quebec
and the Irish Catholic Relief Act of 1778: An Institutional Approach,'
Journal of Historical Sociology 16 (2003): 375–404; Standridge, *Toleration
and State Institutions: British Policy Towards Catholics in Eighteenth Century
Ireland and Quebec* (Lanham, MD: Lexington Books, 2003).

9 RAPQ, 1929–30, Inventaire de la correspondance de Mgr Jean-Olivier
Briand, Évêque de Québec. 1741–1794, n.d. January 1761; n.d. 1762.

10 RAPQ, 1929–30, n.d., 1763.

11 Sir Henry Cavendish, *Government of Canada. Debates of the House of Commons
in the Year 1774, on the Bill for Making More Effectual Provision for the
Government of the Province of Canada* (London: Ridgway, 1839 [1774]).
Michel Chartier de Lotbinière spoke in favour of an assembly, supervised by
a council dominated by *la noblesse.* Among the more eloquent opponents of
the Quebec Act were Edmund Burke and Charles Fox, Burke especially
calling for an English constitution for Quebec.

12 G.P. Browne, 'Carleton, Guy, 1st Baron Dorchester,' in *Dictionary of
Canadian Biography* (Toronto: University of Toronto Press, 1983), 141–55.
Bradley, *Carleton.*

13 J.G.A. Pocock, 'Political Thought in the English-Speaking Atlantic, 1760–
1790: (I) the Imperial Crisis,' in *The Varieties of English Political Thought,
1500–1800,* ed. J.G.A. Pocock, Gordon J. Schochet, and Lois G. Schowerer
(Cambridge: Cambridge University Press, 1993), 246–82.

14 RAPQ, 1929–30, Inventaire de la correspondance de Mgr Jean-Olivier
Briand, Évêque de Québec. 1741–1794, for instance, 22 May 1775; Roy,
Seigneurie de Lauzon, 3: 46ff.; Honorius Provost, 'Taschereau, Gabriel-Elzéar,'
in *Dictionary of Canadian Biography* (Toronto: University of Toronto Press,
1983), 793–5.

15 Bradley, *Carleton,* 82.

16 Jean-Paul de Lagrave, *Fleury Mesplet, 1734–1794: Diffuseur des lumières au Québec* (Montreal: Patenaude Éditeur Inc., 1985); Jean-Paul de Lagrave and Jacques G. Ruelland, *Valentin Jautard, 1736–1787. Premier journaliste de langue française au Canada* (Sainte-Foy: Le Griffon d'argile, 1989); Yvan Lamonde, *Histoire sociale des idées au Québec*, vol. 1 (Montreal: Fides, 2000). Stephen Manning, *Quebec: The Story of Three Sieges* (Montreal and Kingston: McGill-Queen's University Press, 2009).

17 RAPQ, 1927–8, 'Journal. par messrs Frans. Baby, Gab. Taschereau et Jenkin Williams dans la Tournée qu'ils ont fait dans le District de Québec par ordre du Général Carleton tant pour l'Établissement des Milices dans chaques Paroisse que pour l'Éxamen des Personnes qui ont assisté ou aider les Rebels dont nous avons pris Notes. 1776,' passim.

18 Le Spectateur tranquille, *Gazette du Commerce et Litteraire, Pour la Ville & District de Montreal*, 10 June 1778.

19 Lui Seul, *Gazette du Commerce et Litteraire, Pour la Ville & District de Montreal*, 17 June 1778.

20 Various contributors, *Gazette du Commerce et Litteraire, Pour la Ville & District de Montreal*, 1, 8, and 29 July; 5 August; 2 and 6 September; 7 October 1778. For governmentality readers, I notice both the upwards and downwards continuity in power and this particular version of pastoral power–quite different than Foucault's preoccupation with the good shepherd.

21 Nova Doyon, 'L'Académie de Montréal (1778): fiction littéraire ou projet utopique' *Mens* 1, no. 2 (2001): 115–40. Doyon, 'Valentin Jautard, un critique littéraire à la *Gazette de Montréal* (1778–1779).' *Portrait des arts, des lettres et de l'éloquence au Québec (1760–1840)*, ed. Bernard Andrès and Marc André Bernier (Quebec: Les presses de l'Université Laval, 2002), 101–8.

22 *Gazette du Commerce et Litteraire, Pour la Ville & District de Montreal*, 11 November 1778.

23 Andrew Porter, 'Religion and Empire: British Expansion in the Long Nineteenth Century, 1780–1914,' *The Journal of Imperial and Commonwealth History* 202 (1992): 370–90.

24 William Smith, *Report of a Committee of the Council on the Subject of Promoting the Means of Education/Rapport du Commité du Conseil Sur l'Objet D'Augmenter les Moiens d'Education* (Quebec: Samuel Neilson, 1790), 1–2.

25 Smith to Ryland, 14 August 1787, in L.F.S. Upton, ed., *The Diary and Selected Papers of Chief Justice William Smith 1784–1793*, The Publications of the Champlain Society 62 (Toronto: The Champlain Society, 1965), 2: 222–5. Ryland was the father of Herman Wistus Ryland, whom Smith managed to place as Dorchester's Civil Secretary in 1792. Upton argues that the

younger Ryland pursued Smith's plan after the latter's death, but with an
emphasis on the Church of England alien to Smith's conception.

26 De la Grave, *Fleury Mesplet*, 248.

27 In English in the *Quebec Herald* (postscript), 29 January 1789; in French in
Montreal Gazette / Gazette de Montréal, 5 March 1789.

28 Library and Archives Canada (hereafter LAC) RG4 A1 45, Petition from
Laprairie, 16 March 1790 [misfiled as 6 March].

29 'Catholicus' in the *Quebec Herald*, 1 March 1790.

30 LAC RG4 A1 42, Grant to Delery, 12 March 1789.

31 *Montreal Gazette / Gazette de Montréal/Gazette de Montréal*, n.d., 1 January (?) 1785.

32 *Quebec Herald*, 26 April 1789. On Sunday schools and the effect of learning
in rendering the poor miserable and lazy, 5 and 19 April 1790.

33 LAC Q Series 35 no. 48, Dorchester to Sydney, 10 December 1787. The
petition is reproduced as a facsimile in RAPQ, 1944–5, and includes the
signatures of the Quebec elite, both English and French. One signatory is
Jean-Baptiste Corbin, but it is unclear if this is the Quebec schoolmaster
enumerated by J.-O. Plessis or the curé of the same name.

34 The justice dispatch is LAC Q Series, no. 50, Dorchester to Sydney,
10 December 1787.

35 Louis Phillipe Audet, *Le système scolaire de la Province De Québec*, vol. 1: *Aperçu
général* (Quebec: Éditions de l'Érable, 1950), 171–90, gives a good account
of Inglis's papers, but misses the divisions among Protestants over the lay /
clerical divide.

36 Judith Fingard, 'Inglis, Charles,' in *Dictionary of Canadian Biography*
(Toronto: University of Toronto Press, 1983), 444–8.

37 Ibid.; L.F.S. Upton, *The Loyal Whig: William Smith of New York and Quebec*
(Toronto: University of Toronto Press, 1969); Upton, 'Smith, William,' in
Dictionary of Canadian Biography (Toronto: University of Toronto Press,
1979), 714–18.

38 William Smith, *Report of a Committee of the Council on the Subject of Promoting
the Means of Education/Rapport Du Commité Du Conseil Sur L'objet D'augmenter
Les Moiens D'education* (Quebec: Samuel Neilson, 1790 [1789]).

39 Ibid., 9–19.

40 Ibid., quotations 2off.

41 Bernier, Marc André, 'Portrait de l'éloquence au Québec (1760–1840),'
Portrait des arts, des lettres et de l'éloquence au Québec (1760–1840), ed. Bernard
Andrès and Marc André Bernier (Quebec: Les Presses de l'Université Laval,
2002), 410–23.

42 Quoted in Audet, *Système scolaire*, 1: 165, and de la Grave, *Fleury Mesplet*,
329–30.

43 RAPQ, 1929–30, 'Inventaire de la Correspondance de Mgr Jean-Olivier Briand, Évêque de Québec, 1741–1794,' Briand to Dorchester, 2 May 1790.

44 *Réflexions sur les établissements à faire pour des Ecoles dans les Campagnes & des Collèges dans les villes tels qu'ils sont proposé par un Comité du Conseil tenu le 26 Novembre 1789 & publiés en 1790*, in the *Montreal Gazette / Gazette de Montréal*, 18 March 1790.

45 Audet, *Système scolaire*, 1: 166–70.

46 *Montreal Gazette / Gazette de Montréal*, 25 November 1790; *Quebec Herald*, 1 November 1790.

47 *Montreal Gazette / Gazette de Montréal*, 27 May, 3 June, 15 July 1790.

48 The largely indecipherable original is LAC RG4 A1, 48, 3 October 1790; its dispatch to London and some additional information are given in 48, 1 November 1790; Motz to Williams, 3 October, 9 November 1790; Williams to Motz, 4 October 1790, assembling a dossier of education papers for dispatch; Schedule of dispatches, 10 and 11 November 1790. A legible copy with the list of those signing was printed in the *Quebec Herald*, 8 November 1790.

49 *Montreal Gazette / Gazette de Montréal*, 21 October 1790.

50 Un Citoyen, *Montreal Gazette / Gazette de Montréal*, 4 November 1790.

51 Civis, *Montreal Gazette / Gazette de Montréal*, 18 November 1790.

52 L'Homme Mûr, *Montreal Gazette / Gazette de Montréal*, 18 November 1790.

53 Un Citoyen, *Montreal Gazette / Gazette de Montréal*, 23 December 1790.

54 *Montreal Gazette / Gazette de Montréal*, 15 March 1792. The April meeting asked if the difference between men and women's intelligence was merely due to educational influences. *Quebec Magazine*, 1 August 1792.

55 Smith to Dalhousie (draft) 7 November 1788; 'Draft letter on education,' August 1793 in Upton, *Diary and Selected Papers*; Province of Lower Canada, Legislative Council, *Journals*, 1 and 17 April, 1793; LAC CO 42/63-2, Clarke to Dundas, 3 July 1793; Dundas to Dorchester, 6 July 1793, cited in Upton, *Diary*, 312–14. *The Quebec Magazine/Le Magazin de Québec*, vol. 2, 1793, *Montreal Gazette / Gazette de Montréal*, 4, 18, and 25 April 1793.

56 Nancy Beadie, 'Education, Social Capital and State Formation in Comparative Historical Perspective: Preliminary Investigations,' *Paedagogica Historica* 46 (2010): 15–32. For Council papers related to the admission of ex-patriot French priests, LAC RG4 A1 55, 7 and 12 March, 16 April 1793.

57 'Un de vos souscripteurs' in *Montreal Gazette / Gazette de Montréal*, 15 March 1792. The visit was said to have taken place on 27 February.

58 For instance, *Quebec Herald*, 6 May 1790.

59 *Montreal Gazette / Gazette de Montréal*, emphasis in the original; 8 and 15 March, 19 July, 6 December 1792; 14 February, 9 May, 7 November 1793; *The Times/Le Temps*, 19 January 1795. See also Serge Gagnon,

'Labadie, Louis,' in *Dictionary of Canadian Biography* (Toronto: University of Toronto Press, 1987), 379–81. Gagnon remarks that the conflict must have been about something more than instructing poor students; I suggest that Bible reading was probably as important.

60 LAC RG4 A1 55, 21 January 1793.

61 RAPQ, 1948–9, 'L'Association Loyale de Montréal.' Joseph Papineau seems to have attended only the first meeting on 5 July 1794.

62 LAC RG4 A1 58, 4 June 1794.

63 LAC RG4 A1 58, Holt to government, 9 July 1794; Allsopp to Dunn, 12 and 13 July 1794; Sauralt and Fraser to Dunn, 14 July 1794; Panet to Dunn, 24 July 1794; Bélangé to Dunn, 20 July 1794; Corbin to Dunn, 21 July 1794; Canet to Dunn, 25 July 1794; Leinster is 4 June 1794.

64 François Baby, *Le Canadien et sa femme* (n.d., n.p., probably 1794) http://canadiana.org/record/51142. See also John Hare, 'Comment évaluer l'influence de la Révolution française au Bas-Canada: Le témoignage des mots,' in *La Révolution Française au Canada Français*, ed. Sylvain Simard (Ottawa: Les Presses de l'Université d'Ottawa, 1991), 147–62.

65 LAC RG4 A1 64, 6 October, 30 October 1796.

66 LAC RG4 A1 65, Sewell to Prescott, 12 May 1797.

67 Denis-Benjamin Viger, *Avis au Canada, à l'occasion de la crise important actuelle contenant une relation fidèle d'un nombre de cruautés inouies, commises depuis la Révolution françoises, par des personnes qui exercent actuellement les pouvoirs du gouvernement en France et par leurs adhérents* (Quebec: La Nouvelle Imprimerie / CIHM no.20839, 1798), III.

68 Audet, *Système scolaire*, 2: 8–9.

69 Cited in Yvan Lamonde, *Histoire sociale des idées au Québec* (Montreal: Fides, 2000), 1: 79; but 33,000 would have been double the urban population.

70 *Montreal Gazette / Gazette de Montréal*, 7 November 1793.

71 RAPQ, 1948–9, 'Les dénombrements de Québec faits en 1792, 1795, 1798 et 1805 par le curé Joseph-Octave Plessis.'

72 James H. Lambert, 'Spark, Alexander,' in *Dictionary of Canadian Biography* (Toronto: University of Toronto Press, 1983), 768–71; RAPQ, 1948–9, 'Les Dénombrements de Québec faits en 1792, 1795, 1798 et 1805 par le curé Joseph-Octave Plessis.'

73 *Montreal Gazette / Gazette de Montréal*, 6 May 1799; *Montreal Herald*, 23 November 1840; Stanley Brice Frost, 'Skakel, Alexander,' in *Dictionary of Canadian Biography* (Toronto University of Toronto Press 1988), 809–10.

74 The English class was advertised from 1789 and Roger Bergin taught it in the summer of 1791; *Montreal Gazette / Gazette de Montréal*, 22 October 1789; 23 September 1790; 7 July 1791.

75 John Pullman, Montreal, to Haldimand, n.d. 1782, RAPQ, 1949, 'Church and State Papers for the Years 1789–1786.'
76 *Montreal Gazette/Gazette de Montréal*, 15 June 1786.
77 *Montreal Gazette/Gazette de Montréal*, 24 February 1791; Jules Bazin, 'Dulongpré, Louis,' in *Dictionary of Canadian Biography* (Toronto: University of Toronto Press, 1988), 254–7.
78 Mary Jane Edwards, 'Tanswell, James,' in *Dictionary of Canadian Biography* (Toronto: University of Toronto Press 1983), 789–91; J. Keith Jobling, 'Fisher, Finlay,' in *Dictionary of Canadian Biography* (Toronto: University of Toronto Press, 1983), 321. For early announcements by Fisher in the press, *Montreal Gazette/Gazette de Montréal*, 11 December 1788; 3 December 1789, 26 May 1790, and 2 January 1794 for accounts of his school exams; Mrs Allen is in 7 January 1790; Chief Justice Smith noted that Fisher had 49 students in 1786 and received £50 from government – see Upton, *Diary and Selected Papers of Chief Justice William Smith*, vol. 2, entry for 28 November 1786. Smith also noted in the same entry that Tanswell's school had two teachers, 25 day students and 15 to 20 evening students. He also received £50, and his early advertisements are in *Quebec Herald*, 24 November 1788; 9 September and 1 November 1790. He particularly sought the children of those in government service.
79 RAPQ, 1948–9, 'Les dénombrements de Québec faits en 1792, 1795, 1798 et 1805 par le curé Joseph-Octave Plessis'; *Canadian Courant*, 12 November 1810; *Montreal Herald*, 23 December 1815; *Vindicator*, 20 July 1830.
80 *Quebec Herald*, 9 November 1789; 22 May 1790; *Montreal Gazette / Gazette de Montréal*, 6 February 1794; 19 October, 28 December 1795; 1 February 1796; 7 January 1799. Notice that Alexander takes over the house in which Sketchley taught in the spring of 1799.
81 *Montreal Gazette/Gazette de Montréal*, 1 and 8 February 1796; 10 November 1812; *Montreal Herald*, 19 April 1817.
82 *Montreal Gazette/Gazette de Montréal*, for Rivière, 12 January 1786; for Watts, 18 June 1789.
83 *The Times / Le Cours du Temps*, 8 December 1794. Also, Quebec *Mercury*, 28 October 1805, where McCarthy described himself as 'Senior Deputy Provincial Surveyor.' No one has systematically investigated incomes or standards of living for Quebec or Lower Canada. The fees were almost certainly beyond the reach of artisans – although young people may have attended school only briefly.
84 *Montreal Gazette/Gazette de Montréal*, 15 March, 6 December 1792; 7 November 1793.

2. The Eunuch in the Harem: School Politics, 1793–1829

1 The later official reworking of the 1831 census gave Protestant denominational strength as: Church of England 34,620; Church of Scotland 15,069; Presbyterians 7,810; Methodists 7,018; and Baptists 2,461. There were about 446,000 Catholics. For a detailed account of the conditions and development of Protestantism in the Eastern Townships, J.I. Little, *Borderland Religion: The Emergence of an English-Canadian Identity, 1792–1852* (Toronto: University of Toronto Press 2004).

2 T.R. Millman, *Jacob Mountain, First Lord Bishop of Quebec* (Toronto, 1947).

3 H.W. Ryland, 1804, quoted in Robert Christie, *A History of the Late Province of Lower Canada. Parliamentary and Political. From the Commencement to the Close of Its Existence as a Separate Province*, 6 vols. (Montreal: Richard Worthington, 1866), 6: 73.

4 Indeed, in Mountain to Portland, 25 April 1794, he complained that without the ability to sit on the Executive Council he could not get Lord Dorchester to do anything with respect to schools; see A.R. Kelley, *Jacob Mountain First Lord Bishop of Quebec: A Summary of his Correspondence and of Papers Related thereto for the Years 1793 to 1799 Compiled from Various Sources.* (Quebec: Archives de la Province de Québec, 1943).

5 Mountain to Dorchester, 15 and 17 July 1795, quoted in Kelley, *Jacob Mountain*, 171; see also Millman, *Jacob Mountain*; Jean-Pierre Wallot, *Un Québec qui bougeait. Trame socio-politique du Québec au tournant du XIXᵉ siècle* (Montreal: Boréal, 1973).

6 LAC RG4 A1 62, Church wardens, William Henry, to Bishop of Quebec, 17 April 1795; Sewell to Dorchester, 10 June 1795; 63, same to same 1 October 1795.

7 LAC RG4 A1 69, Mountain to Milnes,19 October 1799.

8 LAC RG4 A1, 69, Osgoode to Milnes, 22 October 1799.

9 There was a retrospective account using the Assembly's journals published in *Le Canadien*, 30 May 1821; see also Jean-Jacques Jolois, *Joseph-François Perrault (1753–1844) et les origines de l'enseignement laïque au Bas-Canada* (Montreal: Les Presses de l'Université de Montréal, 1969), 92; L.-P. Audet, *Le système scolaire de la Province de Québec*, vol. 3: *L'institution Royale. Les débuts: 1810–1825* (Quebec: Les Presses Universitaires Laval, 1952), 43ff.

10 LAC RG4 A1, 156, Plessis to Sherbrooke, 19 October 1816.

11 LAC RG4 A1, 80, Mountain to Milnes, 6 June 1803; 111, to Prevost, 30 November 1811; 156, to Sherbrooke 22 October 1816; also to Drummond, 2 February 1816.

12 LAC RG4 A1, 128, Mountain to Prevost, 26 April 1813.

13 LAC RG4 A1, 149, documents from the Mountains, 19 and 28 December 1815.

14 For the translation request, RAPQ, 1932–3, Prevost to Plessis, 22 March 1815. For the rest, RAPQ, 1932–3, Circular of 22 March 1810 on the *Canadien* and loyalty of the clergy; Prevost to Plessis, 22 October 1812, on prayers for Wellington; LAC RG4 A1, 126, n.d. 1813 on the census; 151, Plessis to Drummond, 15 February 1816, with the results of the first agricultural census in response to the famine.

15 LAC RG4 A1, 120, Plessis to Prevost, 'Memoire touchant l'Eglise Catholique au Canada,' 15 May 1812; for the title as councillor, 162, Bathurst to Plessis, 30 April 1817.

16 Neither of the most thorough histories of the Royal Institution attempts to unravel the causes of the failure to incorporate in 1802, and the literature more generally gives the question even less attention than I am able to. See Réal Boulianne, 'The French Canadians and the Schools of the Royal Institution for the Advancement of Learning, 1820–1829,' *Histoire sociale/ Social History* 5 (1972): 144–64. Helen Kominek, 'The Royal Institution for the Advancement of Learning: An Examination of Its Educational Agenda in Lower Canada, 1818–1833' (PhD dissertation, University of Calgary, 2008). RAPQ, 1932–3, Dalhousie to Panet, 28 October 1825, quoting Bathurst to Dalhousie, 15 December 1824, inter alia, 'I should not have approved of such an act even for the general object proposed.' He did not elaborate.

17 LAC RG4 A1, 93, Sewell to Ryland, 8 May 1807.

18 Parliament of Canada, *Sessional Papers*, no. 80, 1900, 'Report on Canadian Archives.'

19 RAPQ, 1927–8, 'Inventaire de la Correspondance de Mgr Joseph-Octave Plessis, Archevêque de Québec, 1797 à 1925[*sic*],' Plessis to Jean-Baptiste-Antoine Marcheteau, 14 July 1810.

20 J.-Edmond Roy, *Histoire de la seigneurie de Lauzon* (Lévis: L'Auteur, 1900), 3: 345–54. The seigneur Caldwell was named one of the commissioners and Malherbe received government funds as a schoolmaster until 1820, when the Royal Institution removed him for incompetence.

21 Réal Boulianne, 'Schools of the Royal Institution,' 150–1.

22 LAC RG4 A1, 75, P. Panet to Ryland, 22 November 1801. It is unclear if this is Pierre or the younger Pierre-Louis Panet. Volumes 74 and 75 of the correspondence are full of material discussing fears of invasion, seditious pamphlets, and conspiracies.

23 LAC RG4 A1,109, 21 June 1810, Roderick Mackenzie to Ryland with Ogden to Commissioners, n.d.; 156, Cochran to Chief Justice, 24 October

1816. Successive governors simply disregarded the law in order to pay the schoolmasters out of general revenues, until retrenchment in the Colonial Office after 1815 led to questions about the source of the funds in question.

24 LAC RG4 A1, 108, a collection of depositions before the Terrebonne magistrates, and Laforce's examination before Council, 23–9 March 1810. A very free translation of the song. Reading aloud gave illiterates access to the *Canadiens'* message; the song made it replicable.

25 LAC RG4 A1, 111, Mackenzie and Porteous to government, 14 November 1810; Mackenzie to Louis Foy, 18 November 1810; their warrant should be included with 14 November but instead is in vol. 115 p. 36374, which has the description of Bouc's disguise.

26 LAC RG4 A1 109, Mackenzie to Ryland, 21 June 1810; 117, Mackenzie to Brenton, 6 January 1812; Brenton to Taylor 10 January 1812; *Montreal Gazette/ Gazette de Montréal*, 19 August, 1811; *Montreal Herald*, 31 December 1819.

27 RAPQ, 1928–9, 'Inventaire de la correspondance de Mgr Joseph-Octave Plessis, Archevêque de Québec, 1797 à 1925 [sic],' Plessis to Varin, 6 January 1811; 13 April 1812.

28 LAC RG4 A1, 135, 26 April 1814, a package of documents related to the second school, including a petition from the original commissioners; a petition from area residents for a second school; character reference for Vervais from Varin; certificate from Mr Roque of Vervais's education at the Petit Séminaire; Mackenzie to Noab Freer; 136, Oldham and Turgeon to Brenton, 30 May 1814; 139, Turgeon and Oldham to Prevost, 10 November 1814; 140, Ross to Taylor, 31 December 1814; 155, Vervais to Sherbrooke, 22 August 1816; *Montreal Herald*, 28 January 1815.

29 LAC RG4 A1, 207, Mills to Cochran 8 March 1822 for Walker's initial appointment; 217, same to same, 10 March 1823, to move Vervais; 219, Walker to Dalhousie, 4 June 1823, his orthography, for the quotation and comments on the act of 1801. In French in the original.

30 LAC RG4 A1, 241, Mills to Cochran, 17 April 1826, with notation 'Approved D[alhousie]'; 242, Vervais to Dalhousie, 15 June 1826, with notation of 29 June, 'I am quite confident that all justice will be done this individual by the Royal Institution for the Superintendence of Schools in this Province. D.'; 263, same to same, 20 April 1828, explaining his school in St Jacques failed, his wife died, and Lartigue refused to accept him into the seminary, pleading for a government post; 393, Vervais to Secretary Craig, 20 June 1829, from Longueuil applying for school money, includes class list; Vervais to Yorke, 5 August 1829; 299, Vervais to Yorke, 7 October 1829; 323, May to Yorke, 17 May 1830, Vervais received £11.7.6 cy. More

correspondence later in the collection would make it possible to do biographical work on Vervais.

31 Herman W. Ryland 1793–1813; Edward B. Breton 1813–15; Robert R. Loring 1815–16; Andrew W. Cochran 1816–18; John Ready 1818–22.

32 LAC RG4 A1, 152, Residents, parish of St Roch, 13 April 1816; 153, J.-B. L'Hereux, 26 May 1816; 154, 24 June 1816, several documents including L'Hereux and Besse; 156, Jean Baptiste Grenier, sindic, to Sherbrooke, 26 October 1816, claiming L'Hereux is still in office and still negligent; on cover, 'Dismissed from 1st_ Nov_r 1816'; 111 J.Bte L'hereux, he had petitioned to be appointed as master, first on 20 November 1819.

33 On Chambers, LAC RG4 A1, 112, Foy to Taylor, 3 January 1811; 156, commissioners Eaton Twp. to Sherbrooke, 25 September 1816; 194, Mills to Ready, 14 June 1820. On Green, RG4 A1, 151, Loring to Taylor, 14 February 1816; 170, Green to Sherbrooke, 9 November 1817; 171, Heriot to Cochran, 10 December 1817 and 14 February 1818; 236, Mills to Cochran, 31 October 1825 applying for a back salary for Green, who had spent seven years living with the Shakers, came back utterly destitute to Drummondville and needed passage money to England, which was granted. On Shea, RG4 A1, 139, petition by MacRea and Johnston, 17 October 1814, with Shea's deposition that they had come to the schoolhouse, broken the lock and carried it away; 139, residents, Douglastown, 22 October 1814. RG4 A1, 109, Jacques Plamondon to Colonel Baby, L'Ancienne Lorette, 31 May 1810. On petitions for more pay, for instance, RG4 A1, 158, Antoine Côte to Sherbrooke, 17 December 1816; Côte (as he signed himself) reported he had been teaching the elements of Latin and French in St Thomas since 1803, but could no longer live on the salary. On the priest as teacher, RG4 A1 154, residents St Roch de l'Achigan 29 July 1816; 155, Tremaine to Cochran, 12 August 1816; they were refused on the grounds that they had not built a house.

34 LAC RG4 A1, 165, Hutchins to Sherbrooke, 23 June 1817, with a number of documents including an indenture whereby John Ely agreed to teach for a year under Hutchins's direction; and a petition for the appointment of a replacement for Ely. 174, 19 February 1818, a certificate in favour of the proposed replacement signed by 'a committee of arrangements'; Cochran to Taylor, 24 February 1818, appointing Woods as Ely's replacement.

35 Lack of space prevents a more detailed examination of Costin's case, which is interesting because it involved the Great in the parish opposing the wishes of a very large number of ordinary parishioners. For the quotation and the demand for trustees, re Costin, LAC RG4 A1, 169, Taché and Roy to Sherbrooke, 31 October 1817; 183, n.d. 1818; for the three teachers'

complaint, 174, Cochran to Taylor, 24 February 1818; 185, Reid et al. to government, 3 May 1819; 186 commissioners, St Armand, 3 June 1819; 187, Bingham to Ready, 23 June 1819; G. Mountain to Montizambert, 9 July 1819; 190, replacement of Bingham, 15 November 1819.

36 *Quebec Herald, Miscellany & Advertiser*, 5 April 1790; *Quebec Mercury*, 5 December 1808, reproduced in *Le Canadien*, 17 December 1808; I am not inclined to accept that this was P.-S. Bédard's conviction, as is suggested in Louis-Georges Harvey, *Le printemps de l'Amérique française*, 74. The letter was more likely a striking piece of copy for the readers. On the other hand, the French-Canadian members, including Bédard and Blanchet, did vote in the same period repeatedly to expel Ezekiel Hart from the Assembly because he was a Jew; *Canadian Courant*, 29 February 1808. On Osgood himself, *Montreal Gazette / Gazette de Montréal*, 28 November 1808. LAC RG4 A1, 105, Osgood to Ryland, 16 and 17 October 1809; 106, Osgood to Craig, 21 December 1809.

37 LAC MG24 B1 [Neilson papers] 2, Osgood to Neilson, 2 November, 21 December and n.d. 1809; to Neilson and Spark (book society) 18 November 1811; to Neilson, 13 December 1811; *Quebec Mercury*, 23 October 1809; 20 August 1810; 30 September 1811; 3 November 1812; *Montreal Gazette / Gazette de Montréal*, 21 October 1811.

38 LAC MG24 B 2, Osgood to Neilson, 10 May 1814; RG4 A1, 138, Fox to Prevost, 3 September 1814; 144, Mure to Loring, 5 May 1815; Bruce Curtis, 'Monitorial Schooling, "Common Christianity," and Politics: A Transatlantic Controversy,' in *Transatlantic Subjects: Ideas, Institutions, and Social Experience in Post-Revolutionary British North America*, ed. Nancy Christie (Montreal and Kingston: McGill-Queen's University Press, 2008), 251–79.

39 LAC RG4 A1,144, Mure to Loring, 5 May 1815; MG24 B1, 2, Michel Dostier to Neilson, 18 May 1815; *Montreal Herald*, 8 October 1814; *Montreal Gazette / Gazette de Montréal*, 11 October 1814; also, *Gazette de Québec*, 13 October 1814, quoted in Jean-Jacques Jolois, *Joseph-François Perrault*, 97n24.

40 LAC RG4 A1, 144, Mure to Loring, 5 May 1815; 145, Council Minutes, 5 June 1815; 155, Coltman to Cochran, 15 August 1816, with a complete account of the Committee's proceedings; *Quebec Mercury*, 22 and 29 November, 12 December 1814; 21 and 28 February 1815; 11 April 1815; *Montreal Herald*, 21 April 1815, has a proposal for opening a Montreal Free School by subscription.

41 *Montreal Herald*, 3 February 1817; *Quebec Mercury*, 2 May 1817; LAC RG4 A1, 162, Cazeau to Sherbrooke, 29 April 1817; by this time, the president was J.-F. Perrault; Cazeau sought to replace L'Heureux at St Roch and had the

support of the seigneur; on Johnston, MG24 B1, 3, Robert Stanton to
Neilson, 22 April 1818; George W. Spragge, 'Monitorial Schools in the
Canadas, 1810–1845' (unpublished D.Paed., Toronto, 1935); also *Quebec
Mercury*, 17 September 1816, where Johnston advertises a night school at
his residence, 10 rue St Louis.

42 *Montreal Gazette/Gazette de Montréal*, 8 March 1814 for Edwards (but dated
17 January); for the tickets, 10 November 1814; similar material in *Montreal
Herald*, 19 February, 17 December 1814; the prospectus is *Montreal Herald*,
21 January 1815.

43 LAC RG4 A1, 140, Mountain to Prevost, 27 December 1814. W.P.J. Millar,
'Osgood, Thaddeus,' in *Dictionary of Canadian Biography* (Toronto:
University of Toronto Press, 1985), 665–7.

44 RAPQ, 1927–8, Inventaire de la Correspondance de Mgr Joseph-Octave Plessis,
Archevêque de Québec, 1797 à 1925 [*sic*], Plessis to Vasnier, 24 November
1814; notice also RAPQ, 1933–4, Panet to Plessis, 21 November 1814,
suggesting they act 'pour prévenir le mal qui pourrait résulter de cet
établissement' and Boucher to Plessis, 14 December 1814, cited in Spragge
'Monitorial Schools,' 'Le dit Osgood est un fanatique qui d'abord s'annon-
coit comme voulant procurer des écoles dans les Townships, in the back
settlements, et qui maintenant élève dans les villes de Montreal et de
Québec, des écoles où l'on parlera pas de religion!'

45 For Burrage, *Quebec Mercury*, 31 December 1816; 8 August 1817; he started
at 2 rue Ste Anne and then moved to 18 Hope Street; LAC RG4 A1, 157,
John Burns to Burrage, with Daniel Wilkie to Burrage, seeking the assistant's job, 2 December 1816; 159, Burrage to Cochran, 29 January 1817,
reveals he got £110 for school rent in 1816; 166, Burrage to Montizambert,
9 July 1817, request of permission for absence to study in Halifax, shows
this is considered to be a government school. For Skakel, *Canadian Courant*,
9 January 1819; on his career and the important social function of grammar schools, LAC RG4 A1, 462, Skakel to Gosford, 24 October 1835.

46 LAC RG4 A1, 169, Plessis to Sherbrooke, 17 October 1817.

47 *Quebec Mercury*, 20 February 1816, proceedings of the Assembly; 30 April
1816 (for Lee); *Montreal Herald*, 2 March 1816, proceedings of the
Assembly. *Le Canadien*, 17 February 1819 for provisions of the 1816 bill.

48 *Montreal Gazette / Gazette de Montréal*, 4 March 1816, debates of the Assembly
from 16 and 17 February. In Upper Canada in 1816, by contrast, parliament passed a permissive elementary school act, empowering any group
able to promote a school to assemble, to elect trustees, and to be eligible
for a grant of £25. The government provided money for the printing of
schoolbooks; see LAC MG24 B1,3, John Strachan to Neilson, 16 April

1816, with a request for an estimate for printing books; Mavor's Spelling Book and Lindley Murray's First Book were high on the list.

49 *Montreal Gazette / Gazette de Montréal,* 'Gracchus,' 22 April 1818;

50 *Le Canadien,* 22 and 29 November 1817, reporting a speech by Blanchet of 17 February with commentary.

51 *Le Canadien,* 22 and 29 November, 2 December 1817.

52 LAC RG4 A1, 175, Pyke to Cochran, 17 March 1818; the decision to reserve appears in vol. 172.

53 For an analysis of elite opposition to corporations, Jean-Marie Fecteau, 'État et associationnisme au XIXe siècle québecois: éléments pour une problématique des rapports État / société dans la transition au capitalisme,' in *Colonial Leviathan: State Formation in Mid-Nineteenth Century Canada,* ed. Allan Greer and Ian Radforth (Toronto: University of Toronto Press, 1992), 134–62.

54 LAC RG4 A1, 185, Uniacke to Ready, 17 April 1819. Province of Lower Canada, *Journals of the Legislative Council,* 29 and 30 March, 2 and 13 April 1819.

55 J. I. Cooper, 'McGill, James,' in *Dictionary of Canadian Biography* (Toronto: University of Toronto Press, 1983), 527–30. Stanley Brice Frost, *James McGill of Montreal* (Montreal and Kingston: McGill-Queen's University Press, 1985).

56 LAC RG4 A1, 134, Brenton to Chief Justice, 4 February 1814; 135, Report of Executive Council, 23 March 1814; 141, Richardson and Reid to Loring, 13 May 1816.

57 LAC RG4 A1, 190, several draft letters patent constituting the Royal Institution, naming its board and specifying its powers, 13 December 1819. [misfiled in vol. 187.]

58 Mountain had long been agitating for direct control over the Reserves, even if their revenues were still inadequate for his projects. In LAC RG4 A1, 128, 12 April 1813, Executive Council proposed to do so; 151, Loring to Ryland, 10 February 1816, the draft instrument is presented to Council and 153, 16 May 1816, was approved. 156, 23 October 1816, for a second draft and 160, n.d. March 1817, the letters patent are read into the Council record.

59 For a copy of the questionnaire, LAC RG4 A1, 192, Mills to Monk, 8 February 1820; Kominek, 'Royal Institution,' provides a close analysis of the responses, and of the board's rules, also reproduced in L.-P. Audet, *Système scolaire,* 3: 193–8. On funding conditions, LAC RG4 A1, 193, Mills to Civil Secretary, 10 and 22 April 1820; for dismissals, same to same, 28 April 1820, at the instigation of John Caldwell, member of the board and seigneur of Lauzon, the board recommended the dismissal of François Malherbe, teaching in the seigneury, and his replacement by Pierre

Romain; 194, same to same 14 June 1820, dismissal of Robert Chambers. Three petitions, including the Dalrymple application are in 194, same to same, 20 March 1821. For the Campbell case, 203, residents, St John's to governor, 17 October 1821; 206, Mills to Ready, 14 January 1822; or not, since Campbell was subsequently dismissed, as we learn in 213, Adam Miller to Dalhousie, 5 October 1822.

60 LAC RG4 A1, 204 [* mislabeled 174], Mills to Ready, 2 November 1821, marginal notation, 'Approved Dalhousie Gov' in his hand.

61 Kominek, 'Royal Institution,' chapter 3.

62 RAPQ, 1928–9, 'Inventaire de la correspondance de Mgr Joseph-Octave Plessis, Archevêque de Québec, 1816 à 1825,' Plessis to Jean-Henri Roux, 29 March 1819 (mixed schools); Plessis to Charles-Joseph Ducharme, 10 October 1820 (against Anglican visitors); Plessis to Jean-Baptiste Saint-Germain, 12 April 1821 (subordination to Mountain); same to same, 16 February 1822 (what he will give as reasons for his refusal); Plessis to Jean-Baptiste Kelly, 16 February 1822, and to Charles Denis Dénéchaud (return the RI's questionnaire unanswered). RAPQ, 1941–2, 'Inventaire de la Correspondence de Mgr. J.-J. Lartigue,' Lartigue to François-Xavier Deguise, 14 April 1821 (organize a school); Lartigue to Clément-Amable Boucher de la Broquerie, 22 February and 2 March 1822 (prevent parents from sending to Protestant schools).

63 The Bull is described in *Quebec Mercury*, 10 June 1817; *Le Canadien*, 17 May 1820 and *Quebec Mercury*, 20 May 1820, with a circular from Rome on Bible societies; RAPQ, 1941–2, 'Inventaire de la correspondence de Mgr. J.-J. Lartigue,' Cardinal Fontana to Lartigue, 20 May 1820; Gilles Chaussé, *Jean-Jacques Lartigue, premier évêque de Montréal* (Montreal: Fides, 1980), 59ff. For the priest buying the lot of ground, Vincent-Charles Fournier, curé du Baie du Febvre, à Mme Loynes de Morett, 20 July 1817, cited in Jolois, *J.-F. Perrault*, 54n44; this letter is quoted widely in the historical literature.

64 This debate also involved 'A.B.C.' as d'Estimauville's critic; d'Estimauville was a member of the preliminary organizing committee of the Société d'Éducation de Québec, and was busy on the social scene, organizing a 'Société Harmonique' and events of the recreational Quebec Assembly, as well as acting as secretary to the Emigrant Society. See *Quebec Mercury*, 26 December 1808; 1 September 1818; 19 January, 9 March, 27 July 1819; *Montreal Herald*, 12 May 1821; *Le Canadien*, 16 May 1821. D'Estimauville's name was used as shorthand later in the period for archaic educational views.

65 In 'Classes sociales, classes scolaires: une polémique sur l'éducation en 1819–1820,' *Rapport de la Société canadienne d'histoire de l'Église catholique*

(1974), 43-59, Yvan Lamonde shows that the debate involved nine different newspapers; many of them reprinted de Calonne's original sortie, which was in *La Gazette des Trois Rivières*, and I quote a reprint with commentary from *Le Canadien*, 24 November 1819. Lamonde tends to conflate Lancasterian and Madras pedagogies and misses the reverberations of the Quebec Free School Society affair. Notice that Calonne and the poet laureate Robert Southey shared the same fetish of the schoolbook.

66 *Montreal Gazette / Gazette de Montréal*, 29 January 1819, reprinting and commenting on material from *La Gazette des Trois Rivières*.

67 Painchaud's application of medical slurs to A.B.C., and the latter's replies in kind suggest he was addressing the doctor Réné-Joseph Kimber or perhaps François Blanchet. For instance, 'Comment! encore une évacuation de sept colonnes et demie!!! Je n'en reviens point, vous êtes serieusement malade,' in *Le Canadien*, 9 February 1820. Or again, *Le Canadien*, 16 January 1820, A.B.C. was said to have a bilious constitution and to give off morbid and pestilential exhalations; A.B.C. replied that Painchaud was infected with poison and needed an antidote. The period was also one in which Quebec reformers, including Blanchet and Neilson, were organizing a free Dispensary.

68 *Le Canadien*, 24 November 1819; *Montreal Gazette / Gazette de Montréal*, 29 January 1820. Notice that some of the items in *Le Canadien* appear twice at short intervals, marking the shift of editorship from Laurent Bédard to Flavien Vallerand.

69 *Le Canadien*, 26 January, 9 and 16 February, 8 March 1820. See also the defence of the Royal Institution in the *Quebec Gazette*; the manuscript version is LAC MG24 B1, 3, Vindex to editor, 16 and 20 June 1821.

70 *Le Canadien*, 8 March 1820, 9 May 1821.

71 Reproduced in *Montreal Gazette / Gazette de Montréal*, 9 January 1820; I am speculating somewhat, but Duvernay was the editor; notice he was said to be taught by Louis Labadie.

72 *Le Canadien*, 26 January 1820; Richard Chabot, *Le curé de campagne et la contestation locale au Québec de 1791 aux troubles de 1837–1838.* (Montreal: Hurtubise, 1975), 242.

73 RAPQ, 1941–2, 'Inventaire de la correspondence de Mgr. J.-J. Lartigue,' Lartigue to Cardinal della Somaglia sous préfet de la Propagande, 22 February 1821; to Antoine Girouard, 23 January 1822; to Plessis, 13 February 1822; to della Somaglia, 27 October 1822.

74 *Montreal Gazette / Gazette de Montréal*, 5 January 1820; *Le Canadien*, 2 February 1820.

75 *Montreal* Herald, 13, 20, and 21 January 1821; Le *Canadien*, 20 January, 7 March 1821; Province of Lower Canada, Legislative Council *Journals*, 23 January, 2 and 26 February, 4 March 1821.

76 RAPQ, 1928–9, Plessis to Bathurst, 28 April 1821; Plessis to Macdonnell, 3 December 1821; RAPQ, 1932–3, Bathurst to Plessis, 10 September 1821; LAC CO 42 Q, Papineau to Wilmot Horton, 14 July 1822.

77 Lord Dalhousie, *The Dalhousie Journals*, ed. Marjory Whitelaw (Ottawa: Oberon Press, 1981), 2: 61–5. Despite his belief that 'the Executive Council is badly composed, & does not possess the respect, much less the confidence of the public,' that 'the public offices are converted into sinecures' and that 'the contingent expences and exorbitant salaries' led to 'just dissatisfaction of the public,' Dalhousie wanted a permanent Civil List. But he also noted that his Councils were themselves divided and that the level of personal animosity between individuals such as the Speaker of the Assembly Louis-Joseph Papineau and his own chief justice were so intense as to make collaborative political work next to impossible. Dalhousie invited members of both groups to dine indiscriminately but noted how unpleasant it was 'to find them side by side, without exchanging words; stiff & erect like dogs snarling at each other.'

78 *Montreal Gazette / Gazette de Montréal, Le Canadien,* 11 April 1820. See also *Le Canadien*, 28 August 1822, where the Association is said to support twenty students at the College; St Ours gave the students access to his library. For Varennes, RAPQ, 1928–9, 'Inventaire de la correspondance de Mgr Joseph-Octave Plessis, Archevêque de Québec. 1816 à 1825 [*sic*],' Plessis to Macdonnell, 3 December 1821.

79 LAC C.O. 42, Dalhousie to Bathurst, 10 June 1821; Province of Lower Canada, Legislative Assembly, *Journals*, 29 November 1823.

80 L. Lagueux, *Rapport du Comité Spéciale de la Chambre d'Assemblée du Bas-Canada, Nommer pour S'enquerir de l'état actuel de L'Éducation dans la Province du Bas-Canada* (Quebec: Imprimeur du Roi, 1824). Perrault briefly presided over both the Société d'Éducation du District de Québec and over the British and Canadian School Society, the latter an attempt to revive the Quebec Free School. He was soon forced out of the former, and Lagueux took over as president. See Jolois, *Joseph-François Perrault*, 106–10.

81 For Viger's speech on introducing the bill, *Canadian Courant*, 23 December 1823; also, *Le Canadien*, 31 December 1823

82 *Le Canadien*, 9 June 1824. The Neilson papers allow one to trace the early history of the Val Cartier settlement. There is an especially handsome advertisement for settlers in LAC MG24 B1, 191, 12 January 1816; the ongoing difficulties Neilson and Andrew Stuart had in getting the settlers

to subscribe for a schoolmaster start with Mcartney et al. to Stuart and Neilson, 6 December 1819.

83 Louis-Phillipe Audet, *Le système scolaire de la Province de Québec*, vol. 5: *Les écoles élémentaires dans le Bas-Canada, 1800–1836* (Quebec: Les Éditions de l'Érable, 1955). Audet squirms away from admitting that the curés and vestries did little.

84 *Le Canadien*, 4 February 1824; for some reason, this legislation seems to have escaped the notice of both recent biographers of Perrault: Claude Galarneau, 'Perrault, Joseph-François,' in *Dictionary of Canadian Biography* (Toronto University of Toronto Press, 1988), 687–90; Jolois, *Joseph-François Perrault*. Jolois does discuss Perrault's 1833 bill, for which he was roundly attacked, and which was close to the 1825 bill. However, perhaps 'Ami' was F. Blanchet, given the figure of a £10,000 school fund, which is discussed below, but it smells like Perrault.

85 *Le Canadien* 24 December 1824, reproducing *Le Spectateur*.

86 *Le Canadien*, 19 January 1825; Province of Lower Canada, Legislative Assembly, *Journals*, 11 and 15 January, 1825.

87 LAC RG4 A1, 232, Mills to Coltman, 28 February 1825; but note the marginalia: 'Rec'd from Mr Edwd Hale June 23 1826,' which would suggest the letter did not make it to the Civil Secretary's office for more than a year. Actually, Mills said there was one teacher appointed before the act of 1801 at work in Quebec, but I think he must have been mistaken; James Tanswell had died.

88 LAC, CO42 Q, 166, Dalhousie to Bathurst, 13 and 16 June 1823, the latter enclosed Chaboillez's pamphlet; Dalhousie to Horton, 19 December 1823; 167, Opinion of Counsel on a draft bill to amend the Act of 1801, 11 December 1823; 168, Dalhousie to Bathurst, 1 November 1824; same to same, 19 November 1824 (reassertion of authority); RG4 A1, 180, Bathurst to Richmond, 4 September 1818 (Bibles); Augustin Chaboillez, *Questions sur le gouvernement ecclésiastique du district de Montréal* (Montreal: T.A. Turner, 1823); Chaboillez, *Réponse de Messire Chaboillez, curé de Longueuil, à la lettre de P.-. Bédard, suivie de quelques remarques sur les Observations imprimées aux Trois Rivières* (Montreal: T.A. Turner, 1824). Gilles Chaussé, *Jean-Jacques Lartigue*, chap. 4. Dalhousie, *Dalhousie Journals*, 2: 126.

89 *Canadian Courant*, 9 October 1824; LAC MG24 B1, 17 Osgood to Neilson, 21 November 1825; CO 42 / 174, Osgood to Bathurst, 17 June, 1 and 18 July 1825; to Wilmot Horton, 4 August 1825, Horton makes a substantial donation; several others to Bathurst follow. For the dispute around Caughnawaga, *Canadian Courant*, 14 October 1826; RG4 A1, 248, McCulloch and Fisher to Dalhousie, 1 February 1827, enclosing copies

of their correspondence with Lartigue. Notice especially RAPQ, 1941–2, 'Inventaire de la correspondence de Mgr. J.-J. Lartigue,' Lartigue to Panet, 23 October 1826: 'Une clique de ministres et de maîtres d'école d'Angleterre est venue fondre sur mon district; et deux d'entre eux, sans en prévenir le missionaire, se sont déjà établis parmi les Sauvages du Sault-St-Louis, où ils ne manqueront pas de faire beaucoup de mal aux Sauvages, sous prétexte de les éduquer.'

90 *Canadian Courant*, 19 January 1825; *Le Canadien*, 19 January 1825.

91 *Le Canadien*, 26 January 1825; also reproduced in Chabot, *Curé de campagne*, 148–52.

92 RAPQ, 1941–2, 'Inventaire de la correspondence de Mgr. J.-J. Lartigue,' Lartigue to Plessis, 25 January, 10 February 1825; Lartigue to Panet, 25 November 1826. RAPQ, 1928–9, 'Inventaire de la correspondance de Mgr Joseph-Octave Plessis, Archevêque de Québec, 1816,' Plessis to Lartigue, 14 February 1825. While Perrault's bill was under discussion, Papineau dined with Plessis, for pleasure, but also because he was seeking a resident curé for his seigneury of La Petite Nation; he was not quoted in the debate on the bill; RAPQ, 1953–4 and 1954–5, 'Correspondence de Louis-Joseph Papineau (1820-1839),' Papineau to Julie Bruneau, 5 February 1825.

93 LAC CO42 Q 157-1, Dalhousie to Bathurst, 10 June 1821. I think it is significant that Taschereau's appointment to the RI board was made *after* he had contacted Plessis about a Catholic RI. His appointment was LAC RG4 A1, 209, 14 May 1822; his letter to Plessis, RAPQ, 1932–3, 23 January 1822.

94 LAC CO42 Q, 166-1-2-3, Dalhousie to Bathurst, 13 June 1823; 167-1-2, Opinion of Counsel, 11 December 1823; 168-2, Dalhousie to Bathurst, 1 November 1824, with memoranda from Sir James Stephen and James Stuart; Dalhousie to Bathurst, 19 December 1824; RAPQ, 1932–3, Dalhousie to Plessis, 28 October 1825, enclosing Bathurst to Dalhousie, 15 December 1824.

95 LAC CO42 Q, 171, Burton to Bathurst, 29 March 1825 (the petition).

96 RAPQ, 1932–3, Dalhousie to Panet, 18 March 1826; Panet to Lartigue, 20 March 1826; Panet to Dalhousie, 21 March 1826; Panet to Lartigue 4 April 1826; Dalhousie to Panet, 9 June 1826 (includes Mills to Cochrane, 2 May 1826).

97 LAC RG4 A1, 242, Panet to Dalhousie, 13 June 1826; 244, Panet to Dalhousie, 4 November 1826.

98 RAPQ, 1932–3, Panet to Lartigue, 30 November 1826; same to same 11 November 1826.

99 *Canadian Courant* reproducing 'Education of the Roman Catholic Youth, under the Royal Institution' from the *Quebec Gazette*, 13 December 1826.

100 LAC RG4 A1, 248, Panet to Dalhousie, 9 February 1827; also in RAPQ, 1933–4.

101 *La Minerve*, 19 February 1827; Christie, *History*, 3: 128–9n.

102 Apart, that is, from an abortive attempt to prod Lord Dalhousie into establishing a university and medical school, see LAC RG4 A1, 237, Blanchet to Cochrane, 27 December 1825.

103 *La Minerve*, 1, 6, and 26 March 1827. The act is also mentioned in 29 November 1827, in a discussion of Dalhousie's inappropriate conduct in the elections, published just before Duvernay's arrest.

104 RAPQ, 1933–4, Cochrane to Panet, 10 April 1827; LAC RG4 A1, 252, Opinion of Chief Justice, 9 June 1827; 258, Mills to Cochrane, 15 December 1827.

105 RAPQ, 1933–4, Panet to Lartigue, 30 December 1827; Dalhousie to Catholic Bishop of Quebec, 25 March 1828; 1942-3, 'Correspondence de Mgr. J.-J. Lartigue de 1827 à 1833,' Lartigue to Plessis, n.d. February 1825; Lartigue to Panet, 29 March 1826, in Jolois, *Perrault*, 123n1; also in Chabot, *Curé de campagne*, 157–8; in Audet, *Système scolaire*, 4: 28–9.

106 RAPQ, 1942–3, 'Correspondence de Mgr. J.-J. Lartigue de 1827 à 1833,' Lartigue to Panet, 10 June and 1 August 1826, 1 March 1827, 14 January 1828, in Audet, *Système scolaire*, 4: 33–5, 57–8, 71.

107 RAPQ, 1942–3, Lartigue to Plessis, 11 October 1827. LAC CO42 Q, 179-1-2, Dalhousie to Huskisson, 27 November 1827; *Dalhousie Journals*, 1: 5 December 1825, 28 October, 4 November 1827.

108 RAPQ, 1953–4 and 1954–5, 'Correspondence de Louis-Joseph Papineau (1820–1839),' a repeated refrain of Papineau, which appears as early as his letter to Julie Bruneau of 12 March 1825. See also Fernand Ouellet, 'Papineau et la rivalité Québec-Montréal (1820–1840),' *Revue d'histoire de l'Amérique française* 13 (1960): 311–17.

109 LAC RG4 A1, 264, Panet to Dalhousie, 3 May 1828; RAPQ, 1933–4, Vallières to Panet, 3 May 1828.

110 LAC RG4 A1, 266, the response of the board is dated 10 June 1828; the cover letter, 30 June 1828.

111 LAC RG4 A1, 273, Mills to Yorke, 24 November and 3 December 1828.

112 RAPQ, 1933–4, Taschereau to Demers, 3 December 1828; Panet to Taschereau, 3 December 1828; Panet to Kempt, 13 December 1828.

113 Audet, *Système scolaire*, 4: 91–7.

114 The Canada Committee report and the Assembly Resolutions are abstracted in W.P.M. Kennedy, ed., *Documents of the Canadian Constitution, 1759–1915* (Toronto: Oxford University Press, 1918), 345–54.

115 Peter Burroughs, *The Canadian Crisis and British Colonial Policy, 1828–1841* (London: Macmillan, 1972), 41.

116 *La Minerve*, 12 and 16 February, 1829. If Township residents claimed they were disenfranchised because they were too far from polling places, it was their own fault for not following the French system of settlement 'de proche en proche.'

117 LAC RG4 A1, 287, Papineau to Kempt, 19 May 1829; on the 'charm offensive,' RAPQ, 1953–4 and 1954–5, 'Correspondence de Louis-Joseph Papineau (1820–1839),' Papineau to Julie Bruneau, 8 January, 1829, where Kempt to a degree managed 'à empêcher le scandale de les voir journellement se quereller dans le parloir en présence du public.'; 7 February, 9 and 23 March 1829, the last on bitter divisions in the Council, 'Ces imbéciles, tirés du néant par le Gouvernment pour le servir.' Also, *La Minerve*, 12 January 1829. For Armour, LAC RG4 A1 282, Armour to Yorke, 25 March 1829.

118 McGill University Archives, Royal Institution, Glackemeyer to Mills with blank questionnaire, 17 December 1828; the Assembly was to discuss the return from Mills in February, see *La Minerve*, 2 February 1829; LAC RG4 A1, 274, Fortier to Glackemeyer, 16 December 1828. Demers of the Séminaire de Québec responded at length, 276, Demers to ?, 5 January 1829.

119 RAPQ, 1942–3, 'Correspondence de Mgr. J.-J. Lartigue de 1827 à 1833,' Lartigue to Viger, 28 January 1829.

120 LAC RG4 A1, 275, n.d. [December 1828?], Richard Pope to 'The Honorable, the Committee of the House of Assembly on Education.'

121 LAC RG4 A1, 277, James Harkness and H. Esson to Kempt, 23 January 1829.

122 *La Minerve*, 16 February 1829.

3. The Colonial 'Monitorial Moment'

1 These figures are rough. Jacques Viger's recapitulation of the Montreal census of 1825, for which he was an enumerator, gave the county population as 37,279 and the city's population as 26,154. For his 1835 school census, when he was mayor, Viger put the county population at 48,810 and the city at 36,194. Statistics Canada's official site does not separate the city and county populations for either city in 1831. http://estat.statcan.gc/cgi-win/cnsmcgi.pgm (accessed 14 September 2009). My other figures are drawn from contemporary newspaper reports, except for Quebec in 1818, which is from Honoré Prévost's adjustment of curé Joseph Signäy's enumeration of that year. At least we can see quite rapid population growth, and a shift from large town to small city over the period in both cases.

2 Lancaster reprinted and adapted his *Improvements* repeatedly. Some of his
   main versions are: Joseph Lancaster, *Improvements in Education, as it respects
   the industrious classes* (London: Darton and Harvey, 1805); *An Account of the
   Progress of Joseph Lancaster's Plan for the Education of Poor Children, and the
   Training of Masters for Country Schools.* (London: Royal Free Press, 1810);
   *Report of J. Lancaster's Progress from the Year 1798, with the Report of the Finance
   Committee for the Year 1810; To which is prefixed, an Address of the Committee for
   Promoting the Royal Lancasterian System for the Education of the Poor* (London:
   Royal Free Press, 1811); *The British System of Education; being the complete
   epitome of the improvements and inventions practised by Joseph Lancaster; to which
   is added a report of the trustees of the Lancasterian School at Georgetown, D.C.*
   (Georgetown, 1812); *The Lancasterian System of Education with improvements by
   its founder.* (Baltimore, MD: Lancaster Institute/Wm. Odgen Niles, 1821).
   Ralph H. Turner, 'Sponsored and Contest Mobility and the School System,'
   American Sociological Review 25 (1960): 855–67.
3 Elizabeth Hamilton was one Scottish commentator who thought there was
   value in monitorial pedagogy but that it needed to be supplemented by a
   'child-centered' approach adopted from Johan Pestalozzi; see Elizabeth
   Hamilton, *Hints Addressed to the Patrons and Directors of Schools; Principally
   Intended to Shew, that the Benefits Derived from the New Modes of Teaching May
   Be Increased by a Partial Adoption of the Plan of Pestalozzi* (London: Longman,
   Hurst, Rees, Orme, and Brown, 1815).
4 Sarah Trimmer, *A Comparative View of the New Plan of Education promulgated by
   Mr. Joseph Lancaster, in his tracts concerning the instruction of the children of the
   labouring parts of the community; and of The System of Christian Education
   founded by our pious forefathers for The Initiation of the Young Members of the
   Established Church in the principles of the Reformed Religion* (London: R.C.
   and J. Rivington and J. Hachard, 1805).
5 Henry Lord Brougham, 'Education of the Poor,' *Edinburgh Review* 17
   (1810): 58–88.
6 Brian Simon, *The Two Nations and the Educational Structure, 1780–1870,*
   vol. 1 (London: Lawrence and Wishart, 1974). David Vincent, *Literacy and
   Popular Culture: England 1750–1914* (Cambridge: Cambridge University
   Press, 1989), 361. R.K. Webb, *Harriet Martineau: A Radical Victorian* (New
   York: Columbia University Press, 1960).
7 His population count excluded members of the seminary, the religious
   orders, the members of executive government, and the garrison, perhaps
   another 2,100 people. Honoré Provost, *Recensement de la Ville de Québec en
   1818, par le curé Joseph Signäy,* Cahiers d'Histoire 29 (Quebec: La Société
   Historique de Québec, 1976). I am not suggesting that no French-speaking

residents went to schools with English-speaking teachers. Adding the seminaries and the three schools run by women religious might halve the number of Catholics per teacher, but counting the teachers Signäy omitted would likely restore the disparity in number per teacher.

8 I chose the *Mercury* rather than the *Gazette* because of its polemics with *Le Canadien*. A canvass of all Quebec papers would likely reveal a few more teachers but would not affect the argument I make. The French-speaking teacher was J.-P. Salen, whose ad for a night school in William Millar's schoolroom ran once on 21 December 1816.

9 Socinianism generally rejected Christian beliefs in the Trinity and in the essential divinity of Christ. In its more Unitarian versions, common to English and Scottish liberal dissent, it was loosely deist.

10 James H. Lambert, 'Wilkie, Daniel,' in *Dictionary of Canadian Biography* (Toronto: University of Toronto Press, 1985), 936–9.

11 *Quebec Mercury*, 11 August 1809; 30 December 1811; 29 December 1812; *Montreal Gazette*, 21 August 1809; 12 July 1820; LAC RG4 A1 119, Mountain to Prevost, 11 May 1812; 185, Wilkie to Richmond, 29 April 1819 with the refusal in a marginal note. Wilkie probably taught St Andrew's church school in the 1830s; see LAC RG4 A1 464, petition to Gosford, 9 November 1835.

12 *Le Vrai Canadien*, 6 June 1810. Wilkie was bilingual, and this argument appeared as or just before his pamphlet was written; he did not name de Bonne directly.

13 *Quebec Mercury*, 26 December 1808. A debate raged on the subject until February 1809 but quickly turned into a discussion of which correspondent used the best language: boring rather than titillating and so dropped by the editor. It was taken up again in *Le Vrai Canadien*, 29 August, 26 September, 3 October 1810.

14 Daniel Wilkie, A.M., *A Letter, most respectfully addressed to the Roman Catholic Clergy and the Seigniors of Lower Canada, recommending the Establishment of Schools* (Quebec: John Neilson 1810). All quotations above are from this source.

15 L. Lagueux, president, *Rapport du Comité Spécial de la Chambre d'Assemblée du Bas-Canada, Nommer pour s'enquerir de l'état actuel de L'Éducation dans la Province du Bas-Canada* (Quebec: Imprimeur du Roi, 1824).

16 *Quebec Mercury*, 8 November 1814; 2 April, 7 May, 30 July, 13 September, 8 October, 19 November 1816.

17 *Quebec Mercury*, 31 December 1816; 3 June, 23 September, 7 October 1817; 7 and 14 April 1818; 2 June, 1 August 1820; *Montreal Herald*, 30 May 1818.

18 Three teachers did advertise elementary schools (once each) between 1800 and 1820, but there was probably not enough money in such teaching to make advertising worthwhile. Beginners were taught in Mrs Abbot's

preparatory day and boarding school, which accepted four-year-old boys and girls, and in Miss Martin's school which accepted boys aged three to seven and older girls, and these two schools survived for some years. Mrs Abbot advertised first in 1813, Miss Martin in 1815, and both were still working in 1818, Miss Martin with at least one assistant teacher. *Quebec Mercury*, O'Keefe, 2 October 1809; Cook, 17 June 1816; Brand, 2 May 1820; Abbot, 5 January 1813; Martin, 10 January 1815; the two last are both in *Recensement de la Ville.*

19 *Rapport du Comité Spécial; Recensement de la Ville.*

20 *Quebec Mercury,* 26 May, 14 November 1820; *Le Canadien,* 24 October 1836 and 8 October 1837, where Miss Aspinall had just returned from England with all the latest dances; private lessons for older students gladly offered. RAPQ, 1934–5, L.A. Aylmer, 'Recollections of Canada, 1831,' shows Lady Aylmer watching the girls dance and being very impressed.

21 *Quebec Mercury,* McCarthy, 8 December 1794 and 28 October 1810. McCarthy did train a young Jérôme Demers at some point and, debilitated by alcoholism, spent his last days in Louis-Joseph Papineau's sister Rosalie's house; Holden, 7 November 1808 and 28 October 1811; Tanswell, repeatedly, e.g., 28 October 1807 and 25 March 1811; Johnston, 28 November 1808; 3 October 1815; 2 September 1817; 27 November 1818; 15 October 1819; 13 January 1820; *Recensement de la Ville;* in fact he may not have been dependent on teaching.

22 *Quebec Mercury,* 23 June 1812, 17 August 1813, 5 April 1814, 18 October 1814, 24 July 1815, 31 October 1815, 21 June 1817, 12 August 1817, 28 April 1818, 16 June 1820.

23 *Quebec Mercury,* 30 September 1811, 20 December 1813, 1 January 1816, 11 October 1816, 7 November 1817; *Recensement de la Ville; Montreal Vindicator* (copying the *Mercury*), 21 December 1820.

24 *Quebec Mercury,* 20 October 1812, 6(?) July 1816, 11 September 1816, 12 November 1816, 28 January 1817, 23 April 1819, 29 August 1820 (Marsden's account of events in a full-page ad), 26 September 1820. It is not clear if the magistrate was Aléxis Caron, or the future mayor, Éduoard Caron.

25 *Quebec Mercury,* 22 April 1811, 11 August 1818.

26 *Quebec Mercury,* 18 May 1812, 29 December 1812, 15 June 1813, 4 January 1814, 2 January 1816, 9 September 1816.

27 *Quebec Mercury,* 22 November 1816, 26 May 1818, 3 October 1820.

28 *Quebec Mercury,* 11 May 1819, 20 November 1820.

29 *Quebec Mercury,* 7 May, 10 September, 29 November 1816; 3 June, 23 September, 7 October 1817; 7 and 14 April, 8 September, 11 and

22 December 1818; 2 June, 1 August 1820. Doyle appears in curé Signäy's 1818 enumeration of the city as in rented space at no. 6 rue des Pauvres; he is said to be twenty-seven years old and to have an assistant named Murphy (p. 254).

30 LAC RG4 A1, 158, R.R. Burrage to Chief Justice, 8 December 1816; 157, Burns to Burrage, 1 December 1816, followed by Wilkie to Burrage, 2 December 1816, 'He not only writes an exceedingly fair hand, but practises with facility every Species of ornamental Writing, Specimens of which and of the Progress of the young Gentlemen under his care, may be seen.' He also taught arithmetic, algebra, and geometry. Joseph Signäy, *Recensement de la Ville*, returned Jean Burns, aged thirty and married to seventeen-year old Hélène Keating, as a schoolmaster. He first marked the couple down as Protestants, but changed his entry to Catholics, noting 'mariés par Mr Spark.'

31 The School was open in late 1816 and by August 1817 was at 18 rue des Jardins. It offered 'a Classical and Mathematical Education, according to the system used in the Free Grammar Schools and Universities in England,' as well as accepting some beginners. *Quebec Mercury*, 31 December 1816; 8 August 1817. Burrage said before the 1824 Assembly committee that his school had about fifty students, eighteen of them 'on the foundation' in 1824. See L. Lagueux, *Rapport du Comité Spéciale de la Chambre d'Assemblée du Bas-Canada, Nommer pour s'enquérir de l'état actuel de L'Éducation dans la Province du Bas-Canada* (Quebec: Imprimeur du Roi, 1824).

32 I deal with these fascinating debates in '"My brothers were learnt out and my sons soon would be": Public Debate over the Provision of Schooling in Quebec, 1814–23,' *History of Education* 40 (2011): 615–34.

33 Andrée Dufour, 'Diversité institutionelle et fréquentation scolaire dans l'île de Montréal de 1825 à 1835,' *Revue d'histoire de l'Amérique française* 41 (1988): 507–35; see also her 'Les institutrices rurales du Bas-Canada: incompétentes et inexperimentées?' *Revue d'histoire de l'Amérique française* 51 (1998): 521–48. Dufour offers a different account of Viger's numbers than mine.

34 On his pleasures as collector, see Léo Beaudoin and Renée Blanchet, *Jacques Viger: Une Biographie* (Quebec: vlb éditeur, 2009); Nathalie Hamel, 'Collectioner les <monuments> du passé. La pratique antiquaire de Jacques Viger,' *Revue d'histoire de l'Amérique française* 55 (2005); 73–94. Notice that Viger's attempt to show the relative shares of Protestants and Catholics in the permanent schools invoked different numbers than those given elsewhere in the same document; for instance, in the account of schools by religious affiliation, the National School is said to have 233 students; in its descriptive entry, 339. This part of his account resembles an attempt to bolster the importance of the Catholic Church in school provision.

35 In each case I have excluded the rural part of the parish of Montreal in calculating the population of the city and suburbs. For the number of students returned in 1835, I have included the forty-six Viger listed as an addendum to his main return. In both 1825 and 1835 I have excluded from the county totals those students returned as living outside the county and from the city totals both those living outside the county and outside the city. I have also indulged in an anachronism, because Viger did not use or think in terms of percentages. My thanks to J.-C. Robert for the original reports. The current official tabulation of the censuses of 1825 and 1831 is at http://estat.statcan.gc.ca/cgi-win/cnsmcgi.pgm (accessed March 2011) and gives quite a different and larger set of numbers of young people. We see that Viger used age categories not in the 1831 census.

36 *Enseignement public dans le Comté de Montréal, en 1835.* Archives du Séminaire du Québec, Manuscrit 018, p. 27.

37 *Montreal Herald,* 6 December 1817. Rev. J. Bethune was advertising the school later; for instance, *Montreal Herald,* 12 October 1818. Viger applied for the school grant for the École St Jacques in his capacity as president; see LAC RG4 A1,322, Viger to Yorke, 12 May 1830. Later, he challenged the right of executive government to any information about the school, beyond a description of its buildings; LAC RG4 B30 11, Viger to Craig, 12 March 1832.

38 *Canadian Courant,* 21 January 1824; 19 February 1825.

39 *Montreal Herald,* 1 January 1834.

40 *Morning Courier,* 1 January 1838.

41 LAC RG4 A1 435, Blackwood to Aylmer, 10 July 1834; *Montreal Herald,* 5 January 1835.

42 For two contemporary comparisons of Bell and Lancaster, see Anon., 'A comparative View of the Plans of Education, as detailed in the Publications of Dr. Bell and Mr. Lancaster. By Joseph Fox. [London] Darton and Harvey,' *Monthly Review Enlarged* 56 (1808): 445–6. R.G. Bowyer, *A Comparative View of the Two New Systems of Education for the Infant Poor, in a Charge Delivered to the Clergy of the Officiality of the Dean and Chapter of Durham, at Berwick-upon-Tweed, May 12, 1811.* By the Rev. R.G. Bowyer, L.L.B. Prebendary of Durham (London: Rivington, 1811).

43 *Quebec Mercury,* 13 October 1818. George W. Spragge, 'Monitorial Schools in the Canadas, 1810–1845' (D.Paed., Toronto, 1935), quotation at 53.

44 LAC RG4 A1 189, Mills to Ready, 4 October 1819; Mountain, not addressed, 8 October recommending Bignell. For the back-dated warrant, 189, 1 October 1819 – issued and inserted in the archive after he arrived in November. 189, Mills to Ready, 15 November 1819; 191, same to same, 8 December 1819. No trace of Bignell remains.

45 Anon., *Regulations for the Quebec Central Schools for Boys and Girls. Conducted upon the Madras System.* CHIM 56340 (Quebec: National and British Printing Office, 1820). Helen Kominek, 'The Royal Institution for the Advancement of Learning: An Examination of Its Educational Agenda in Lower Canada, 1818–1833,' (PhD dissertation, University of Calgary, 2008), 73, identifies the visitors. On the exam, *Quebec Mercury*, 26 May 1820; on the collections, *Quebec Mercury*, 14 December 1819, 31 October 1820. Spragge, 'Monitorial Schools,' gives the initial numbers, but says maximum attendance at any moment was 143 – less than the numbers reported at the 1820 examination. T.R. Millman, *Jacob Mountain, First Lord Bishop of Quebec* (Toronto, 1947), 179–81.

46 Notice that Mills has even stolen the Free School's name! LAC RG4 A1 202, Mills to Ready, 24 August 1821; Spragge, 'Monitorial Schools,' says Shadgett was replaced by a Mr Truro, not as Mills said by a Mr Fleming. What exactly was improper about Shadgett is unknown. He remained in Canada, for he answered the government's questionnaire about conditions in the townships in 1821 and the following year sought government support for a Quebec City directory and census which would remove the 'inconvenience experienced, in the want of regular Nos being affixed to every House in the City and Suburbs.' In 1830, he petitioned Sir James Kempt and the Assembly, and in 1831 Lord Aylmer from Beauport, for support for a proposed agricultural college and model farm, which he would direct. LAC RG4 A1 199, 7 May 1821; 206, 11 January 1822; 309, Shadgett to Kempt, 26 January 1830; 350, 24 January 1831. *La Minerve*, 6 February 1830; François Blanchet presented the petition.

47 Quoted in Spragge, 'Monitorial Schools,' 172.

48 Spragge, 'Monitorial Schools,' 55; LAC RG4 A1 425; a description of the site is in the Council Reports of March 1834. Also, 425, Burrage to Daly, 28 February 1834; 428, Burrage to Craig, 31 March and 11 April 1834; 432, 12 June 1833 [reference from Crown Lands, misfiled in 1834 or misdated], around efforts to overcome the omission of a legal patent for the lands in the 1820s. 425, Bethune to Smith, 24 March 1834 on a patent for the National School house in Montreal; B30, 13, Mackie to Murdoch, 27 June 1840.

49 One free for four paying was a fifth of the students. LAC RG4 A1 184, 25 February 1819, is a draft warrant appointing Alexander Bethune government schoolmaster at a salary of £50; accompanied by the petition. It was not renewed and perhaps not paid, as W.G. Holmes was hired. John Bethune advertised his school in his house, *Montreal Herald*, 19 December 1818, and was advertising a free Sunday school the following October. These are the moments in which the parish of Montreal was being established

legally, so J. Bethune may not yet be rector; the patents issued 7 June 1820; see LAC RG4 A1 194.

50   LAC RG4 A1 189, Ross to Ready with Ross to Montizambert, 7 October 1819; Viger, *Enseignement publique ... en 1825*; *Enseignement publique ... en 1835*; Spragge, 'Monitorial Schools,' 254. A Mrs Holmes had advertised to teach grammar, geography, plain and fancy needlework, tambouring, embroidery, painting and drawing in her private school, *Canadian Courant*, 14 June 1820, and was apparently hired to teach in the National School in 1822.

51   *Canadian Courant*, 21 January, 9 October 1824.

52   *Canadian Courant*, 23 April 1825.

53   Viger, *Recensements*; Musée de Québec, Archives du Séminaire, fonds Verreau-Viger, P32/022/052. *Montreal* Gazette, 2 January 1836; *Le Canadien*, 7 May 1838, published the lists of school subsidies; LAC RG4 B30 11, 2 March 1835, is the directors' account of enrolment.

54   *Montreal Herald*, 12 May 1821; *Le Canadien*, 16 May 1821.

55   Anon., *Resolutions et Règles de la Société D'Éducation du District de Québec*, CIHM 56461 (Quebec: J. Neilson, 1821). *Le Canadien*, 10 June 1821; in 4 July 1821, notice that the patronage of Lord Dalhousie was granted. Jean-Jacques Jolois, *Joseph-François Perrault (1753–1844) et les origines de l'enseigne-ment laïque au Bas-Canada* (Montreal: Les Presses de l'Université de Montréal, 1969), 99–105.

56   'Triptoleme' in *Le Canadien*, 11 and 22 September 1818. See also RAPQ, 1928–9, 'Inventaire de la Correspondance de Mgr Joseph-Octave Plessis, Archevêque de Québec, 1816 à 1825,' Plessis to Macdonnell, 3 December 1821, in which the success in getting the petitions signed is mentioned, but Plessis has learned from Dalhousie that the Colonial Office refused to sanction the school act until after the matter of the Civil List was resolved.

57   *Le Canadien*, 20 March 1822. 'Mister' is my compromise for 'Messieu'; I don't know if he meant a priest or a gentleman.

58   Joseph-François Perrault, *Cours d'éducation élémentaire à l'usage de l'école gratuite, établie dans la cité de Québec en 1821* (Quebec: La Nouvelle Imprimerie, 1822), 9.

59   *Le Canadien*, 14 November 1821; 13 February 1822; Jolois, *Perrault*; Perrault, *Cours d'éducation*. LAC RG4 A1 216, n.d. [1823] is the petition for aid; 217, reference of Uniacke, 4 March 1823; 224, 9 February 1824 Uniacke's favourable report. That Council thought it necessary to refer the question of a grant to the attorney general is suggestive of opposition. Already Perrault was providing basic elementary education to some boys who would go on to the Séminaire and would make their mark in the life of the colony; see for instance Daniel Perron, 'Pierre Petitclair et son alliance

avec Le Télégraphe (1837),' in *Portrait des arts, des lettres et de l'éloquence au Québec (1760–1840)*, ed. Bernard Andrès and Marc André Bernier (Quebec: Les Presses de l'Université Laval, 2002), 313–23.

60 Jolois, *Perrault*, 104; *Le Canadien*, 8 October, 19 November 1823.

61 RAPQ 1941–2, 'Inventaire de la Correspondence de Mgr. J.J. Lartigue,' Lartigue to Plessis, 21 October, 3 November 1823; Gilles Chaussé, *Jean-Jacques Lartigue*, 157; Jolois, *Perrault*, 107–10; *Le Canadien*, 29 October 1823; 16 January 1825.

62 LAC RG4 A1 295, petition for schoolhouse property, 1 August 1829; 318, Huot to Yorke, 19 April 1830; *La Minerve*, 26 and 27 May 1834; *Le Canadien*, 7 May 1838; 3 April 1840.

63 *Le Canadien*, 2, 11, 13, 18 February, 11 March, 29 April, 13, 20 May 1835; on the Reform Association, 22, 25, 27 (the quotation), 29 May 1835, and more through the month of June, including the platform, 10 June 1835.

64 LAC MG24 B1 8, Cazeau to Société d'Éducation, 11 February 1835; an earlier concern about his job is 29 January 1834. For Cazeau's earlier career, RG4 A1 162, Cazeau to Sherbrooke, 29 April 1817; 163, Cochran to Taylor, 1 May 1817. He taught a private school after losing his job, at 49 rue St Eustache, *Le Canadien*, 26 September 1834 (a night school first); 29 April 1835 in côte de Lévis; 16 September 1836 (with boarders); 6 October 1837. Archives de l'Archechêché de Québec (AAQ) 60 C N, Gouvernement du Canada, vol. A: 209, the response of curé Bailliargeon to Arthur Buller's questionnaire has Cazeau in a boys' school with thirty students in the Upper Town.

65 LAC RG4 B30 13, Huot to Murdoch, 27 June 1840; *Le Canadien*, 25 July 1835; 20 May 1836; 6, 29 September 1837; 3 April 1840.

66 *La Minerve*, 19 May 1831.

67 Further research may clarify my reading of the scanty evidence in the press and state papers, but it seems the Société's girls' school was effectively the school run by the Société des Dames at least in the 1830s. LAC RG4 A1 434, Huot to Civil Secretary, 1 July 1834; *Le Canadien*, 7 March 1834; *La Minerve*, 27 May(?) 1834; *Le Canadien*, 17 September 1834.

68 For the advertisement, *Le Canadien*, 25 February, 10 April, 13 and 27 July, 30 December 1835. Flore's father François was a member of the Fire Assurance Company founded in 1816 in which many other committee members were associated. We know nothing about Flore's education. Perhaps a measure of her independence is that she married only at age twenty-seven in 1842, to Joseph-Édouard Turcotte, lawyer and MPP. They had nine children.

69 *Le Canadien*, 2 November 1836; 11 December 1837; 23 March 1838; 2 December 1839; AAQ, 60 CN, Gouvernement du Canada, vol. A: 209, n.d. 1838; the teacher was described as 'Delle. Malherbe.'

70 *Montreal Herald*, 5 October 1822; on the school, especially in the later period, Roderick MacLeod, and Mary Anne Poutanen, '"Proper Objects of This Institution": Working Families, Children, and the British and Canadian School in Nineteenth-Century Montreal,' *Historical Studies in Education / Revue d'histoire de l'éducation* 20 (2008), 22–54.

71 LAC RG4 A1 219, Lunn to Dalhousie, 12 June 1823; Lord Dalhousie, *The Dalhousie Journals*, ed. Marjory Whitelaw (Ottawa: Oberon Press, 1981), 2: 161.

72 *Canadian Courant*, 21 January, 9 October 1824.

73 *Canadian Courant*, 9 November 1825.

74 *Canadian Courant*, 28 October 1826. President Gates regretted the loss of Mrs Chapman, the trained schoolmistress, who had been replaced temporarily while the Society sought a replacement for her and for Mr Hutchings, who was resigning for health reasons, from London. The teacher in Laprairie, Thomas Smart, later claimed he had taught in the village from 1817, when a committee invited him to begin a school on the BCSS plan in the summer of 1826. He said he taught for free for six months and sought compensation long after the fact under the 1829 School Act. See LAC RG4 A 1 286, 1 May 1829. While the BCSS dispatched teachers and supplies, Thaddeus Osgood was urging John Neilson to promote legislation allowing any place that opened a school in association with the BCSS to elect trustees and to receive £10 from the Assembly. See LAC MG24 B1 6, 26 Osgood to Neilson, December 1827 [misfiled in 1828].

75 On the Recollet School, 'Lower Canada, Journals of the Legislative Assembly, *Sessional Papers* 6 Will. IV, Appendix O.O. 'First Report of the Standing Committee on Education.' *Montreal Vindicator*, 25 March, 15 September 1831; *Canadian Courant*, 3 November 1832; *Montreal Gazette*, 2 January 1836; LAC RG4 A1 478, Lindsay to Walcott, 6 May 1836; RG4 B30 13, 31 August 1840.

76 *La Minerve*, 15 April 1833.

77 *Montreal Herald*, 10 and 19 February 1834; *Montreal Herald Abstract*, 27 April 1835.

78 Flavien Vallerand of *Le Canadien* was also highly critical of the college courses, 19 January 1823; *La Minerve*, 16 July 1832; the boy was said to be eight or nine years old and was beaten with the teacher's rod; 'des personnes présentes ayant fait quelques observations au Cinglant bureaucrate, il s'emporta en imprécations et juremens,' the editor commented, showing the equation between National School and governing clique.

79 *Le Canadien*, 1 and 8 October 1823. Biographical information is from various volumes of the *Dictionary of Canadian Biography* and the press, as well as from the *Recensement de la ville de Québec*.

80 *Le Canadien*, 12 November 1823.

81 *Le Canadien*, 19 November 1823.

82 *Le Canadien*, 26 November 1823.

83 *Le Canadien*, 3 and 10 December 1823.

84 *Le Canadien*, 17 December 1823; 7 January 1824.

85 *Le Canadien*, 12 May 1824.

86 LAC RG4 A1 336, Lunn to Yorke, 25 September 1830; 381, Hale to Craig, 26 April 1832. On the Natives, 393, Forest to Napier, 1 October 1832; and a long series between Signäy and governors and Lartigue, in RAPQ, 1937–8, 'Inventaire de la Correspondence de Monseigneur Joseph Signäy, Archevêque de Québec (1835–1836),' starting 19 August 1835.

87 On William Morris, LAC RG4 A1 405, Morris to Craig, 18 March 1833. The Assembly had voted £50 to aid publication of the book but no Quebec printer would produce it for so little; a New York printer would do 1,000 copies for £60, but Morris needed to have the import duties waived. In 415, Dunbar Jameson to Craig, 21 September 1833, 1,000 copies of the *Accountant's Guide* were in print. MG24 B1 9, Morris to Neilson, 4 December 1837. On Purcell, RG4 A1 407 Stayner to government, 25 April 1833; RG4 B30 Report of the Quebec National School, 27 June 1840. On the debt, RG4 A1 446, n.d. January(?) 1835.

88 Anonymous, *Report of the Quebec British and Canadian School, for the Year 1831* (Quebec: Thomas Cary and Co., 1832). LAC RG4 A1 407, certified list of teachers trained, 25 April 1833; 548, petition of Felix O'Neill, ?September 1838; RG4 B30, report of the Quebec National School, 27 June 1840 (Purcell); 386, James Stringer to Aylmer, 17 July 1832.

89 LAC RG4 A1 436, Petition of British and Canadian School Quebec, 4 November 1835; also 475, Hale to Walcott, 2 April 1836; 482, Simpson to Walcott, 1 June 1836; 490, Stayner to Walcott, 26 August 1836. One teacher using monitorial methods was John Sleven of les Eboulements; LAC RG4 B30 50, 15 May 1831.

90 *Le Canadien*, 6 November 1837; also, 7 May, 20 July 1838; 18 March, 27 December 1839; LAC RG4 B30 13, report of Quebec British and Canadian School, 29 June 1840; notice in the same folder, Stayner to Murdoch.

91 LAC RG4 A1 81, Panet to Ryland, 4 July 1803 for the grant. Perrault reminds me somewhat of his Upper Canadian near contemporary, Dexter D'Everardo, whom I discuss in *True Government by Choice Men? Inspection, Education and State Formation in Canada West* (Toronto: University of Toronto Press, 1992).

92 RAPQ 1943–4, 'Correspondence de Mgr. Jean-Jacques Lartigue de 1833 à 1836,' Lartigue to Signäy, 5 October 1833.

93 Dalhousie, *Journals*, 3: 94–109; Robert Christie, *A History of the Late Province of Lower Canada. Parliamentary and Political. From the Commencement to the Close of Its Existence as a Separate Province*, 6 vols. (Montreal: Richard Worthington, 1866), 3: 132–203. On the importance of militia commissions to their holders, see Allan Greer, *The Patriots and the People: The Rebellion of 1837 in Lower Canada* (Toronto: University of Toronto Press, 1993).

94 Jolois, *Perrault*, 118–19.

95 *La Minerve*, 29 October, 16 November 1829; 16 May 1831.

96 Anon., *Rapport d'un Québecois sur quelques Écoles Élémentaires du District de Quebec*, CIHM #21452 (n.p.: n.p., 1834). Perrault gave his own account of the schools in 'À M. le rédacteur de la Gazette de Québec,' 21 October 1835, CIHM# 53953.

97 Ibid. £1,100 must be an exaggeration or misprint.

98 Joseph-François Perrault, *Manuel pratique de l'école élémentaire françoise* (Quebec: n.p., 1829); Perrault, *Premiers Elemens Pour montrer à lire en François aux Enfans de l'âge le plus tendre* (Quebec: C. Le François, 1830); Perrault, *Tableaux de mots de deux syllabes à l'usage des écoles élémentaires du Bas-Canada* (Quebec: C. LeFrançois, 1830).

99 Jolois, *Perrault*, for the prize essay; LAC RG4 A1 307, petition of J.-F. Perrault, 15 January 1830 (with a note dated 3 May 1831 quoting a price for printing his history book); 321, 12 May 1830 opinion of Crown law officer; 356, Perrault to Glegg, 7 April 1831 (money for boys' school; the history book now in print); 379, Perrault to Craig, 2 April 1832 (Aylmer visit; unfortunately Lady Aylmer's diary ends shortly before the visit); Joseph-François Perrault, *Traité d'agriculture: adapté au climat du Bas-Canada; pour l'usage des établissemens d'éducation dans les campagnes* (Quebec: Fréchette, 1831); on the Normal School plan, Musée de l'Amérique française, Dépot du Séminaire de Québec, Fonds Viger-Verreau P32/61/40.5 and /40.6, Perrault to Caron, 8 April, 3 May 1836; P32/48/027 is n.d. sample instructions for normal-school students. On Girod and Papineau, *Montreal Vindicator*, 23 December 1831, provides a lengthy transcription of the debates around Girod's petition for aid. The debates offer a useful corrective for the tendency of Girod's most recent biographer to attribute the school's organization and failure to Perrault's meddling. Bernard's work offers valuable insight into *patriote* party organization but seeks to rehabilitate Girod as a *patriote* hero and so tends to gloss over his adventurism and even, on the basis of no evidence, to deny his suicide. The debates show a Papineau contemptuous of Girod as a newcomer, but also that he perceived the project as a potential threat to the British and Canadian School Societies, which were still his model of good

pedagogy. Agriculture was best learned '*de proche en proche*.' See Philippe Bernard, *Amury Girod: Un Suisse chez les Patriotes du Bas-Canada* (Sillery: Septentrion, 2001). Interesting as well is Girod's fawning declaration of loyalty to Aylmer and his wish to show his gratitude to the colony by donating to the executive his remarkable invention for restoring lost polarity to compasses, LAC RG4 A1 367, Girod to Aylmer, 25 October 1831.

100 Jolois, *Perrault; Montreal Vindicator*, 12 March 1833; *La Minerve*, 14 March 1833; *Le Canadien*, 6 March, 23 November, 11 December 1835 (reprinting *La Minerve*); 7 July and 6 September 1837. Lower Canada, Journals of the Legislative Assembly, *Sessional Papers*, 6 Will. IV, Appendix O.O. 'First Report of the Standing Committee on Education.'

101 *La Minerve*, 8 November 1830; 27 May (?) 1834; *Le Canadien*, 15 April 1839; LAC RG4 A1 334, Kimber to Yorke, 20 August 1830. This letter is a bit confusing because there is a marginal notation, probably from Yorke, reading 'is the whole L500 for the School House at 3 Rivers paid' followed by 'Appr of 1829 all paid JC,' presumably Joseph Cary. In the following communication, 345, St Réal and Kimber to Glegg, 14 December 1830, the managers apply for their money; Cary notes on their letter the act and £100 mentioned in the text and adds, 'the above sum is not yet paid and is now required. J.C.' 368, petition of the Société for funds, 7 February 1831; 379, St Réal to Craig, 9 April 1832; 428, Bell to Craig, 5 April 1834; 463, petition of the Société for funds, 5 November 1835.

102 On Milton, *Canadian Courant*, 12 March 1831, 14 July 1832; LAC RG4 A1 383, Milton to Craig, 12 June 1832; here Milton expresses his disgust at the provisions of the 1832 School Act. On Meilleur, LAC RG4 B30 111, Trustees, L'Assomption, to Craig, 17 December 1832; *La Minerve*, 26 September and 3 October 1833.

103 Anonymous, *First Report of the Montreal Infant School Society, for 1830*, CIHM #35991 (Montreal: Workman and Bowman, 1831). *La Minerve*, 20 April 1829; *Canadian Courant*, 5 August, 7 October 1829; *La Minerve*, 26 April 1830; *Canadian Courant*, 1 May 1830.

104 *Canadian Courant*, 15 June, 19 November 1831; 10 October 1832. *La Minerve*, 10 May 1834.

105 *Montreal Herald*, 2 October 1834. LAC RG4 B30, 11, n.d. 1835, Petition for aid for Quebec British and Canadian Infant School.

106 LAC RG4 A1393, Bancroft to Craig, 8 October 1832; 477, Clapham to Wolcott, 30 April 1836; *Montreal Gazette*, 14 November 1835, 2 January 1836; *Le Canadien*, 30 November 1835; Lower Canada, Journals of the Legislative Assembly, *Sessional Papers*, 4 Will. IV, 1834, Appendix D.d. 'Second Report of the Standing Committee of Education and Schools.'

4 Will. IV, 1835–6, Appendix O.O., 'First Report of the Standing Committee on Education and Schools.'

107 Barber's lectures were copiously reported in the *Morning Courier*, beginning 1 December 1836; his address at the anniversary of the MISS in 1837 was reported in full, as well as the motions made by Brown and Handyside, with Day in attendance in *Morning Courier*, 2 and 7 January 1837.

108 *Canadian Courant*, 5 October 1833; *Le Canadien*, 3 May 1837 (copying *La Minerve*) reported that a new infant school based on Wilderspin's plan was opening in Montreal in Mme Côté's house; and the *Morning Courier* of 18 May 1837 contained the prospectus for the 'Montreal Model Infant School,' a pay school not intended to interfere with the charity MISS.

109 For more detailed discussion of Lancaster see Bruce Curtis, 'Joseph Lancaster in Montreal (bis): Monitorial Schooling and Politics,' *Historical Studies in Education / Revue d'histoire de l'éducation* 17 (2005): 1–27; and 'Monitorial Schooling, "Common Christianity," and Politics: a Trans-Atlantic Controversy,' in *Transatlantic Subjects: Ideas, Institutions, and Social Experience in Post-Revolutionary British North America*, ed. Nancy Christie (Montreal and Kingston: McGill-Queen's University Press, 2008), 251–79. Since writing those two pieces in 2004, I found more material on Lancaster, which is included here.

110 John Franklin Reigart, *The Lancasterian System of Instruction in the Schools of New York City*, Contributions to Education 81 (New York: Teachers College, Columbia University, 1916), 18–19, quoting an earlier work. There are several Lancaster letters in the Public Record Office of Northern Ireland, Belfast, which show him at work; for instance, D/530/22/7 Lancaster to Thompson, 13 May 1815, where he has spent all his money and needs help to get his clothes and his box back from a hotelier. 'They run my bill up there very much though I dine [lightly?] & was very moderate.'

111 Dalhousie, *Journals*, 3: 166–7.

112 As Robert Christie had it in *A History of the Late Province of Lower Canada*, 3: 286, the money was '"towards enabling him," it was said, "to make experiments in the method of instruction invented by him," but in reality a gratuity to the worthy itinerant quaker.'

113 LAC RG4 A1 384, Lancaster to Aylmer, 20 June 1832. This file contains the series of letters, which start 4 June and which follow 383, Lancaster to Craig, 28 May 1832, where we learn Lancaster is in Quebec, has seen Aylmer, and wants to arrange with Craig to get the £50 grant for training teachers.

114 Joseph Lancaster, *Report of the singular results of Joseph Lancaster's new discoveries in Education made at Montreal, from the commencement in 1829 to complete*

development of systematic principle in 1833, CIHM #89895 (Montreal: n.p. 1833). *La Minerve* 31 October 1833; *Canadian Courant,* 19 March 1834.

115 Jacques Rancière, *Le maître ignorant: Cinq leçons sur l'émancipation intellectuelle* (Paris: Fayard, 1987).

116 LAC RG4 B30 12, 11 and 16 April 1836 for the instructions; Neilson's letter is MG24 B1 8, 15 April 1835. More on the Normal Schools in a later chapter.

4. Creating a 'Taste for Education' in the Countryside, 1829–1836

1 *La Minerve,* 23 February 1829.

2 Anyone reading the civil secretary's incoming correspondence, LAC RG4 A1, can see the dramatic increase in its volume from the late spring of 1829.

3 LAC RG4 A1 283, 1 April 1829, curé Robitaille from St Charles de Chambly petitioned for aid for his school; Boucherville is A1 284, 19 April 1829, and also in *La Minerve,* 11 May 1829; this group was also active in the Chambly vigilance committee in 1832; LAC MG24 B1 6, petition from Vincent Ferrier, schoolmaster at Jeune Lorette, for aid to John Neilson, 15 April 1829; RAPQ, 1934–5, four letters from Panet to various curés attempting to take advantage of the act: to Marc Chauvin, 11 April 1829, forbidding the vestry to sell some of its lands for a trustee schoolhouse, they should build their own vestry school; to Dénéchaud, 18 May 1829; to Ducharme, 30 May 1829; to Chauvin, 1 June 1829. Lartigue in Montreal took the same line; for instance, RAPQ, 1942–3, to Alinotte, 30 September 1829. The press followed trustee elections closely. For instance, *La Minerve,* 30 April 1829; in 4 May, the paper carried a notice from Joseph Paradis of La Présentation, announcing the trustee elections had been held on 13 April and calling for applications from teachers. On Bonaventure Viger, later leader of the 1837 Longueuil attack, see Allan Greer, *The Patriots and the People: The Rebellion of 1837 in Lower Canada* (Toronto: University of Toronto Press, 1993), 238.

4 LAC RG4 A1 284, Blanchet to Yorke, 23 April 1829.

5 LAC RG4 A1 283, Executive Council Report, 30 April 1829, Attorney General Stuart had first argued that the government could make no regulations with respect to some of the schools; but with the regulations in hand, 291, Executive Council Report, 9 May 1829, inter alia, 'the subject seems to have been so well considered that the Committee do not think it necessary to suggest any additional Regulations.' The Anglican bishop was present at this meeting. In 288, Kelly to Yorke, 9 June 1829 submits a set of queries and in 291, Kelly to Yorke, 2 July 1829, thanks for sending a

copy of the regulations. Other correspondents were copied the regulations: the executive did not intervene more directly. *La Minerve*, 18 May 1829, printed the regulations. In *La Minerve* of 7 May 1829, 'Un Campagnard' claimed that debates around the numbers of students were commonplace in the countryside and 'les personnes les plus instruites, différent d'opinions extraordinairement, et donnent à cet acte différens sens que les jettent dans le plus grand embarras.' He showed clearly the kinds of calculations people were making in order to extract the greatest amount of government money possible. On 14 May, Duvernay regretted there was not more clarity in the act.

6 LAC RG4 A1 287, Papineau to Yorke, 19 May 1829: orthography as in the original. D.-B. Papineau to L.-J. Papineau, 20 April 1829, in Richard Chabot, *Le curé de campagne et la contestation locale au Québec de 1791 aux troubles de 1837–1838* (Montreal: Hurtubise HMH Ltée., 1975), 154–6.

7 Lower Canada, Journals of the Legislative Assembly, Sessional Papers, 11 Geo. IV, 1830, Appendix R., *Report of the Special Committee on Education*, March 1830. The committee also declared Kempt's administrative regulations to be 'judicious, and hope they will be adhered to during the continuance of the said Act.' The numbers reported are suspicious: they would suppose about thirty-eight students per school, while the manuscript school reports themselves (LAC RG4 B30) rarely show a rural school to be so large.

8 *Canadian Courant*, 16 June 1829; they were John Parker, James C. Peasley, Elisha Gustin, John Brown, and David Wallingford.

9 LAC RG4 A1 300, Residents, Ireland to Yorke, 26 October; 293, Hoyle to Yorke, 21 July 1829; 301, McLean to Yorke, 13 November; 304 McLean to Yorke, 17 December 1829; 323, Bellefeuille to Yorke, 14 May 1830. Bellefeuille wrote again, 308, 17 January 1830, to inquire if a building divided by a stone wall with the boys schooled on one side and the girls on the other was one school or two. On St François, 306, Amiot to Yorke, 12 January 1830; for Dundee, 293, Davidson to Yorke, 21 July 1829. On St Mathias, *La Minerve*, 9 July 1829.

10 The relevant documents are in LAC RG4 A1, 288, notice of trustee election, 8 June 1829; 289, 'de la Mothe' to Yorke, 15 June 1829; 295, Evans to Yorke, 15 August 1829; 297, Labrie to Yorke, 14 September 1829; 298, 'La Mothe' to Yorke, 20 September 1829; 299, same to same, 26 October 1829, including the affidavits; 301, same to same, 15 November 1829; 324, same to same, 26 May 1830, cover letter with his returns of six schools, which he did not visit because the roads were bad; also a warning about the abusive treatment of teachers by their agents in money matters.

In 286, before the debate began, Laurent Lamothe, 1 May 1829, applied for the grant for his school himself.

11 LAC RG4 A1 306, Bolduc and Lessard, Syndics, St-Joachim to Yorke, 1 January n.d. [probably 1830]; in RG4 B30 59, Langevin to Yorke, 3 March 1830, there is an enclosure from Marie Caneur in which she returns the government money, stating that she read the act after she received the money and concluded she was not eligible. This person writes a reasonably clear hand. Marie Caneur was later denounced by curé Besserer for a fraudulent attempt at the school monies, but the denunciation was made after she had returned them; RG4 A1 328, Besserer to Yorke, 27 June 1830. For Sutton, RG4 A1 314, Trustees, Sutton, to Yorke, 15 March 1830.

12 LAC RG4 A1 304, trustees Lotbinière, 26 December 1829; 306, Daveluy to Yorke, 8 January 1830; 292, notables, Rivière Ouelle, 11 July 1829; McGill University Archives (MUA), Royal Institution for the Advancement of Learning (RI) Accession #447 Folder #9663 196 RG 4, C.49, Narin et al to Mills, 8 May 1829; Accession #447 Folder #9667 200 RG 4, C.49, Allsopp to Mills, 29 May 1829.

13 LAC RG4 A1 323, Myers to Yorke, 18 May 1830; Mackenzie to Sewell, 26 July 1830; Sewell to Yorke, 25 August 1830.

14 Quite a voluminous correspondence begins LAC RG4 A1 299, Malhiot to Yorke, 16 October 1829. Brown's formal report is 306, 8 January 1830. The payment to him is mentioned in *La Minerve* 16 March 1830.

15 *La Minerve*, 10 August 1829: all of this is straight Meilleur and duplicates what he proposed for the Collège de L'Assomption; François Blanchet took up the matter of agricultural societies in the education committee in February 1830; *La Minerve*, 6 February 1830.

16 *La Minerve*, 28 March, 20 May 1830; *Canadian Courant*, 28 April 1830; Louis-Phillipe Audet, *Le système scolaire de la Province de Québec: Les écoles élémentaires dans le Bas-Canada, 1800–1836* (Quebec: Les Éditions de l'Érable, 1955), 5: 115–20. The fiasco of the Deaf and Dumb school awaits its historian; the building still stands in rue d'Auteuil in Quebec. LAC RG4 A1 317, Papineau to Kempt, 18 April 1830. A good copy of the report form is RG4 B30 58, n.d., 1830, St Jean Baptiste de Rouville.

17 Lower Canada, Journals of the Legislative Assembly, *Sessional Papers*, 3 Will. IV, Appendix I.i. 1833, 'First Report of the Standing Committee of Education and Schools,' no. 11; *La Minerve*, 17 July 1831, gave a different set of figures, but Cary's were reproduced in *Canadian Courant*, 15 February 1834; *Montreal Herald*, 17 February 1834, although in a later polemic the *Montreal Gazette*, 23 July 1835, put it at more than £27,000.

18 LAC RG4 A1 309, trustees, Bolton, to Kempt, 25 January 1830; *La Minerve,*
    26 July 1830; the press had begun printing the ritualistically celebratory
    accounts of local school exams, which were soon a fixture of the educa-
    tional literature.

19 See, for instance, LAC RG4 B30 49, Poirier to Kempt, 23 December 1830;
    trustees, St Denis, to Kempt, 24 December 1830, with Cary's notations; also
    A1 351, Dufresne to Glegg, 14 February 1831.

20 LAC RG4 A1 327, Viau et al to Yorke, 21 June 1830; 330, Wyss to Yorke,
    15 July 1830; Boucher to Yorke, Garon to Yorke, 30 July 1830.

21 LAC RG4 A1 324, Trustees, la Petite Nation, to Yorke, 29 May 1830; 309,
    Trustees, St Mathias (including Eustache Soupras) to Yorke, 24 January
    1830; 329, Béchard to Yorke, 5 July 1830; 342, Trustees, Maskinongé, to
    Glegg, 12 November 1830, with long comment from Cary on this propri-
    etor's school.

22 LAC RG4 A1 154, petition, St Roch, 29 July 1816; 155, Tremain to Cochran,
    12 August 1816. Original orthography.

23 LAC RG4 A1 324, Rocher to Yorke, 29 May 1830; 325, Rocher to Cochran,
    12 June 1830; 344, Trustees, St Roch, to Glegg, 1 December 1830. MG24
    B1 7, Trustees and militia officers to Neilson, 21 February 1831. Rocher's
    brother was the MPP. It is not clear that they got the grant, although the
    Attorney General ruled on a similar case somewhat later that four of five
    signatures sufficed for the school grant: RG4 A1 358, Trustees,
    Godmanchester, to Aylmer, 21 May 1831; 362, Opinion of Crown Law
    Officer, 11 July 1831. For more on St Roch, Jean-René Thuot, 'Elites locales
    et institutions à l'époque des Rébellions: Jacques Archambault et l'episode
    du presbytère de Saint-Roch-de-l'Achigan,' *Histoire sociale/Social History* 38
    (2005): 339–65; Thuot, 'Elites locales, institutions et fonctions publiques
    dans la paroisse de Saint-Roch-de-l'Achigan, de 1810 à 1840,' *Revue
    d'histoire de l'Amérique française* 57 (2003): 173–208.

24 *Canadian Courant,* 20 January 1830; *La Minerve,* 30 September 1830.

25 *La Minerve,* 3 February 1831; *Montreal Vindicator,* 4 February 1831; both
    give the members of the committee.

26 *La Minerve,* 28 April 1831; *Canadian Courant,* 18 June 1831.

27 *Montreal Vindicator,* 24 June 1831; *La Minerve,* 27 June 1831, for the
    provisions of the act; Louis Bourdages's resolution for an elective council is
    discussed in *La Minerve* 12 and 23 January 1831. It was defeated by a vote of
    37 to 15, with Neilson, Huot, and W.H. Scott in the majority and with
    Papineau, D. Mondelet, and Morin in the minority. Notice the article of
    16 January where the council is referred to as 'Les Éteignoirs du Bas-
    Canada.' It may be noted that a similar attempt to locate schools and

specify districts took place in Upper Canada only in the mid-1840s; see Bruce Curtis, 'Mapping the Social: Jacob Keefer's Educational Tour, 1845,' *Journal of Canadian Studies* 28 (1993): 51–68.

28 LAC RG4 A1 410, Glegg to [?not named and this is misfiled in a later folder; it is clearly spring 1831, since Glegg is also discussing census appointments], inter alia, 'I am sadly at a loss to know what is to be done respecting the arrangement of School Visitors'; MG24 B1 7, Gugy to Neilson, 13 June 1831, enclosing Peck to Gugy, 10 June 1831; RG4 B30 86, School Report, Stanstead, 1 June 1833, with notation by Peck. A1 360, 11 June 1831, lists of proposed nominations; 361, 16 June, draft instrument of appointment; 22 June, cover letter with relevant documents and forms. MG24 B1 7, Montizambert to Neilson, 20 June 1831. In A1 361 Lukin to Glegg, 22 June 1831, the Montreal census commissioner solicited the visitor's appointment for Laprairie and Lacadie, marginal note 'Too late Done.'

29 The necessity of appointing a replacement so the school monies could be paid was pressing; LAC RG4 A1 369, Courteau and Rochon to Craig, 29 November 1831; 370, Opinion of Crown Law Officer, 5 December 1831; Ogden to Craig, 8 December 1831, appointment of Scott.

30 Unless otherwise noted the citations which follow are from Jean Holmes's copy, Musée de la Civilisation, Fonds du Seminaire de Québec, Polygraphie 42, no. 20 H.

31 LAC MG24 B1 17 for the list, n.d. 1831; and Miville de Chêne to Neilson, 25 July 1831 about a mutual acquaintance's son teaching at Rivière du Loup, where 'les habitants voudroient avoir de bons Ecoliers, sans livres ni papiers.' At least the French visitors went to the country with him on 28 August. Gérard Bergeron, 'L'interlude canadien pendant le voyage d'Amérique (1831) d'Alexis de Tocqueville et de Gustave de Beaumont,' *The Tocqueville Review* 12 (1990–1): 127–40. Bruce Curtis, 'Tocqueville and Lower Canadian Educational Networks,' *Encounters in Education* 7 (2006): 113–29. Jean-Michel Leclercq, 'Alexis de Tocqueville au Canada (du 24 août au 2 septembre 1831),' *Revue d'histoire de l'Amérique française* 22 (1968): 353–65. G.W. Pierson, *Tocqueville and Beaumont in America* (New York, 1938). Jacques Vallée, ed., *Tocqueville au Bas-Canada* (Montreal: Éditions du Jour, 1973).

32 On legibility, see the first two chapters in James C. Scott, *Seeing Like a State: How Certain Schemes to Improve the Human Condition Have Failed* (New Haven, CT: Yale University Press, 1998).

33 See, for instance, LAC MG24 B1 8, Joly to Neilson, 21 March 1834; Raby to Neilson, 24 March 1834, two curés offering to do all in their power to find

him a safe seat in the impending elections; Turgeon to Neilson, 13 October
1835, with more proof that Neilson was 'l'ami de votre pays et du clergé
catholique canadien.'

34 Audet, *Système scolaire*, vol. 5, reprints the text of the act; it was summarized
in *La Minerve*, 26 April 1832. There is a good copy of the French-language
printed MPP's county report form in LAC RG4 B30 58.

35 Compare Bruce Curtis, 'Social Investment in Medical Forms: The 1866
Cholera Scare and Beyond,' *Canadian Historical Review* 81, no. 3 (2000):
347–79.

36 *Memorandum for Giving Effect to the School Act of 1832* (n.p., n.d.), CIHM
#46030. LAC RG4 A1 378, Smith to Craig, discusses plans for printing
2,000 copies of the forms.

37 LAC RG4 A1 307, Cary to Yorke,11 January 1830; Hale to Yorke, 13 January
1830: 'in the Six Months ending 10 October last I paid 599 Warrants; while
in the corresponding period of the preceding year, 364 only were paid.'
341, Hale to Glegg, 4 November 1830: 'the number of Warrants payable to
Schoolmasters, (above 600).' 342, Cary to Glegg 11 and 15 November
1830; 353, Hale to Glegg, 8 March 1831: 'The Establishment of Schools
has caused to [*sic*] great an increase of Business in my office, where the
greatest degree of responsibility is incurred, that I venture to recall the
Subject to the attention of the Governor … the number of Warrants issued
to this 8 day of March in the year 1829 was 601. and that I have now paid
within the same space of time 2572.' After 1832, it fell to Hale rather than
to Cary, to match pay lists to powers of attorney claimed by trustees' agents.

38 LAC RG4 A1 339, Yorke to Kerr, 7 October 1830; *La Minerve*, 10 December
1832; Helen Taft Manning, *The Revolt of French Canada 1800–1835*
(London: Macmillan, 1962), 324–5.

39 Christian Dessureault, 'Les syndics scolaires du district de Montréal (1829–
1836): une sociographie des élus,' *Revue d'histoire de l'Amérique française* 63
(2009): 33–81, has made use of Cary's trustee book in an effort to identify
Montreal district trustees under the 1829 act.

40 Lower Canada, Journals of the Legislative Assembly, *Sessional Papers*, 3 Will.
IV, Appendix I.i. 1833, 'Third Report of the Standing Committee of
Education and Schools.'

41 Lower Canada, Legislative Assembly *Journals*, 6 February 1832 [Aylmer];
La Minerve, 30 January 1834.

42 One could trace out Cary's legalism through the case of Benoît Hoffaÿ, a
teacher in St Michel de Yamaska, who tried to get back pay: LAC RG4 A1,
381, Hoffaÿ to Craig, 26 April and 22 October 1832; 416, same to same,
30 October 1833; 420, same to same, 12 December 1833; 435, same to same,

21 July 1834. Each of these has Cary's comments and sometimes Craig's note as to what to respond to Hoffaÿ. Also, RG4 B30 89, no. 42, School Return County of Yamaska, 25 January 1834. Other instances in which Cary's notations reveal that no discretion was to be exercised in applying the law include RG4 A1 437, Trustees no. 3 Hinchinbrooke to Aylmer, 28 August 1834; and the last in another long series, 456, Lahaye to Craig, 24 June 1835.

43 Most of the colonial press reprinted these tables in some form or other; *La Minerve* printed abstracts of them in February 1832. The information cited here is from *Canadian Courant*, 'Statistical and Population Returns of Lower Canada,' 28 March; and 'General Table of Education,' 4 April 1832. For the later tabulation: http://estat.statcan.gc.ca/cgi-win/CNSMCGI.EXE (accessed March 2011).

44 *Montreal Vindicator*, 27 March 1832.

45 Audet, *Système scolaire*, 5: 220–8; *La Minerve*, 11 March 1833; *Canadian Courant*, 8 May 1833.

46 Lower Canada, Journals of the Legislative Assembly, *Sessional Papers*, 3 Will. IV, Appendix I.i. 1833, 'First Report of the Standing Committee of Education and Schools.'

47 *La Minerve*, 6 January 1834, before the throne speech.

48 The debates were reported in full in most papers. *Quebec Mercury*, 9 January 1834, and *La Minerve*, 9 January 1834, give complete accounts. Duval is quoted in *La Minerve* of 13 January.

49 C.R. Ogden's recommendations on the four acts are all in LAC RG4 A1 426, 'Opinions of Crown Law Officers,' 7 and 12 March 1834. See also, *Montreal Herald*, 25 January 1834. Lower Canada, Journals of the Legislative Assembly, *Sessional Papers*, 4 Will. IV, 1834, Appendix D.d. 'Second Report of the Standing Committee of Education and Schools,' 14 February 1834. *Montreal Herald Abstract*, 4 June 1835. LAC CO42/269 et seq., n.d. [November 1836] General Report of the Commissioners for the Investigation of all Grievances affecting His Majesty's Subjects of Lower Canada, Appendix to General Report: Education, 'Extract from a Despatch from the Earl of Aberdeen, dated 1st Jany 1835, so far as it relates to the Reserved Bill "for the further and permanent management of Education."' The despatch was reprinted in translation, followed by Parent's denunciation in *Le Canadien*, 11 March 1835. In *La Minerve*'s 25 June 1835 report of the formation of the Montreal Reform Association, the despatch is treated as an instance of imperial religious hatred.

50 Aylmer to the Assembly, 14 January 1834, in W.P.M. Kennedy, ed., *Documents of the Canadian Constitution, 1759–1915* (Toronto: Oxford University Press, 1918), 364–5.

51 *La Minerve*, 10 February, 14 April, and 30 June 1834. Aylmer named them, said the editor, knowing they had 'abandonné la cause du pays, pendant que le patriotisme de M. Rodier lui était trop bien connu.' Neilson's lengthy statement of his political position was reported in *La Minerve*, 6 March 1834.

52 *La Minerve*, 19 December 1833; the same page has a long account of education in Pennsylvania, quoting the governor's education-as-prophylactic-against-crime speech.

53 *Canadian Courant*, 15 January 1834.

54 *La Minerve*, 3 February 1834, translating reports from the *British Colonist*. The Lennoxville meeting was 26 December 1833; the Barnston, 7 January 1834.

55 *Le Canadien*, 5 February 1834; *Canadian Courant*, 8 February 1834. *La Minerve*, 10 February 1834; *Montreal Herald*, 5, 8, and 10 February 1834; *Montreal Gazette*, 13 February 1834.

56 *Montreal Herald*, 15 and 17 February 1834. Musée de la Civilisation, Dépôt du Seminaire de Québec, Fonds Verreau, o-147, 3 March 1834. *Le Canadien*, 3 March 1834; *La Minerve*, 6 March 1834.

57 *Le Canadien*, 3 March 1834; *Montreal Herald*, 10 and 22 March 1834; *La Minerve*, 13 and 21 March 1834. Audet, *Système scolaire*, 5: 249–53.

58 RAPQ, 1954 and 1954–5, 'Correspondence de Louis-Joseph Papineau (1820–1839),' Papineau to Julie Bruneau, 12 January 1834.

59 Robert Christie, *A History of the Late Province of Lower Canada. Parliamentary and Political. From the Commencement to the Close of Its Existence as a Separate Province* (Montreal: Richard Worthington, 1866), 4: 43-70.

60 Philippe Bernard, *Amury Girod: Un Suisse chez les Patriotes du Bas-Canada* (Sillery: Septentrion, 2001), 77–90, describes the corresponding committees as like modern political party executives.

61 Bruce Curtis, 'Le rédecoupage du Bas-Canada dans les années 1830: un essai sur la "gouvernementalité" coloniale,' *Revue d'histoire de l'Amérique française* 58 (2004): 27–66. The argument there in part is that this first Royal Commission has been almost completely ignored as such, compared to the attention paid to the second headed by Lord Durham.

62 PRONI D/2259/1/3A, Gosford to Glenelg (private), 18 September 1835; D2259/8/13, 28 September 1835, Gosford's fascinating memorandum to himself on his meeting with Papineau and Viger. The PRONI collection also contains Gosford's responses to the wave of requests for patronage appointments that greeted his nomination; he uniformly declined to make any. See D/2259/9/1/ to 9/30/.

63 [Archives Nationales de Québec] ANQ R2 3 A 019 01-07-003A-01, Gosford to Smith, Gosford to Cochrane, 22 October 1835; RAPQ, 1953–4 and

1954–5, 'Correspondence de Louis-Joseph Papineau (1820–1839),' Papineau to Julie Bruneau, 30 November, 3, 9, 17 and 23 December 1835.

64 RAPQ, 1953–4 and 1954–5, 'Correspondence de Louis-Joseph Papineau (1820–1839),' Papineau to Julie Bruneau, 30 November 1835.

65 The full text of the throne speech was in *Le Canadien*, 28 October 1835. LAC CO42/266, 17 July 1835, shows the education instruction as no. 82 of about 100.

66 *Montreal Vindicator*, 8 March 1833; *La Minerve* justified his imprisonment, 25 March 1833; *Le Canadien*, 13 April 1835, for a list of prize money for MPPs; *Montreal Gazette*, 4 February 1836, for the resolution; LAC RG4 A1 469, Taylor to Walcott, 11 February 1836; 482, Opinion of Crown Law Officer, 6 June 1836.

67 The Archambeault case would be revived after the Rebellion by the Special Council and used as ammunition for further denunciations of the Assembly's schools. The petitions are in Lower Canada, *Journals of the Legislative Assembly*, 6 Will. IV., 30 December 1835. The Standing Committee's actions on them are *Sessional Papers* 6 Will. IV, Appendix O.O. 'Fourth Report of the Standing Committee on Education,' 16 February 1836. For their roles in the 1838 insurrection, Cardinal was executed in December 1838; Lepailleur was transported; Baker, whose farm was the site of an armed battle, apparently fled to the United States; Perrigo was interrogated but not detained for long. See Georges Aubin, ed., *Insurrection: Examens volontaires*, vol. 2: *1838–1839* (Montreal: Lux Éditeur, 2007).

68 *Le Canadien*, 30 December 1835, gives the entire text of the report followed by Parent's comments; *Montreal Gazette*, 31 December 1835, 2 January 1836; Lower Canada, Journals of the Legislative Assembly, *Sessional Papers* 6 Will. IV, Appendix O.O. 'First Report of the Standing Committee on Education.' At the same moment, a similar argument was being made before the Gosford Commission with respect to the distribution of political representation. Curtis, 'Le rédecoupage.'

69 *Le Canadien*, 13 and 18 January 1836; *Montreal Gazette*, 14 January 1836.

70 *Le Canadien*, 22 January 1836. Chasseur was a *patriote* party stalwart; J.-B. Meilleur was charged with making an inventory and valuation of the collection, which L.-J. Papineau thought was wonderful and that visiting it was a healthy form of recreation; see RAPQ, 1953–4 and 1954–5, Papineau to Julie Bruneau, 13 March 1826.

71 Their petitions appeared in the 'First Report.' Also, LAC RG4 A1 415, Surprenant to Civil Secretary, 14 September 1833; 470, Surprenant to Gosford, 23 February 1836; *Le Canadien*, 10 February, 11 and 12 March, 1 April 1836.

72 Lower Canada, Journals of the Legislative Assembly, 6 Will. IV, 20
    November, 1835; *Montreal Gazette*, 24 and 28 November 1835; *Le Canadien*,
    25 November 1835.

73 Unless otherwise indicated, all citations in this section of the chapter are
    from Lower Canada, Journals of the Legislative Assembly, *Sessional Papers* 6
    Will. IV, Appendix O.O. 'Third Report of the Standing Committee on
    Education.'

74 Beaudoin for Dorchester, Toomy for Drummond, Amiot for Verchères, and
    Le Boutillier for the Gaspé, for instance.

75 Careau's 'X' is on LAC RG4 B30 12, School Returns, Rouville, 8 June 1836.
    The Tory press was outraged at him; for instance, the *Montreal Herald*,
    12 January 1835:

    Interesting to Blockheads.

    Pierre Carreau, who like some dozen other tools of Citizen L.J. Papineau,
    in the Assembly, can not write his name, but as a substitute appends his
    cross to the reports made for him, is one of the members returned for the
    populous county of Rouville. To this honorable gentleman is confided the
    task of framing our laws – he is also charged with the surveillance of
    education within that county, where he decides upon the fitness and
    capacity of the various teachers under the Elementary School Acts.

    His

    X

    Mark.

    The title is a play on 'tête carrée' and Careau.

76 *Montreal Gazette*, 19 March 1836. Audet, *Système scolaire*, 5: 274–5.

77 *Le Canadien*, 15 and 24 February 1836; *Montreal Gazette*, 13 February 1836.

78 LAC MG24 B1 9, 1 February 1836, Mackenzie to Neilson. After Head
    did appoint Reformers to Council, Mackenzie wrote, 22 February 1836,
    'there is no doubt but that we will now vote supplies and give Sir F. Head
    a comfortable reception. Education will thus be encouraged, the people
    made to feel more kindly and good natured towards each other.' He
    regretted the political estrangement between Papineau and Neilson. After
    the Reformers were roundly defeated in the 1836 elections, the prospect of
    a Reform Executive Council vanished.

79 PRONI D/2259/1/2B, Gosford to Glenelg, draft Civil Government no. 18,
    19 February 1836. In Gosford's memorandum to himself after meeting
    Viger and Papineau on 28 September 1835, D2259/8/13, it sounds as if
    Papineau believed Gosford had the power to change the constitution and
    Gosford seems to have implied to him that after a supply vote, careful
    consideration would be given to an elective Council.

80 PRONI D2259/8/17, Gosford to Bentinick, 29 February 1836; D/2259/1/2B, Gosford to Glenelg, 12 March 1836.
81 LAC MG24 B1 9; the quoted passage is in Walker to Neilson, 17 March 1836. For more discussion of the Montreal association's moves, see same to same, 2 March, 5 and 23 April, 25 May 1836. The *Morning Courier*, 21 December 1836, gave the association's executive: Peter McGill, George Moffatt, Stanley Bagg, Dr Robertson, John Molson, Henry Dyer, James Gibb, Dr Stephenson, Adam Thom, J. Guthrie Scott, Thomas Phillips, Henry Corse, T.B. Anderson, William Walker, Alexander Miller, Henry Griffin, Thomas Cringan, J.T. Barrett, C.D. Day, William Badgley, William Stephens, P.E. Leclere, Robert Armour Jr, James Holmes, John M Tobin. On the commission's view, Curtis, 'Le redécoupage.'
82 The report was dated 15 March 1836 and was reproduced in its entirety in the press, for instance, *Montreal Gazette*, 24 March 1836.
83 *Montreal Gazette*, 14 April 1836; *Le Canadien*, 18 April 1836; *Montreal Herald*, 3 May 1836.

5. Schooling the People, 1829–1836

1 LAC CO42/269, 'General Report of the Commissioners for the Investigation of all Grievances affecting His Majesty's Subjects of Lower Canada' [manuscript], n.d. November 1836.
2 *Montreal Gazette*, 8 December 1835; the claim was repeated in *Montreal Herald Abstract*, 11 July 1835, and reappeared in later debate.
3 *Le Canadien*, 'Un Ennemi déclaré du Statu Quo,' 30 May 1834; also 'Lancette,' 4 June 1834. They are responding to a correspondent in the *Quebec Gazette* who apparently wrote against the 92 Resolutions and in favour of the status quo in the colony. The arguments, however, are typical of the moderate *patriote* position.
4 The figures in the two tables are extracted from LAC CO42/269, 'General Report of the Commissioners for the Investigation of all Grievances affecting His Majesty's Subjects of Lower Canada' [manuscript], n.d. November 1835. The census returns and a table from the visitors' reports are in *Canadian Courant*, 28 March and 4 April 1832. For a completely different version of the same figures, *La Minerve*, 13 February 1832. *Montreal Herald*, 17 February 1834; *La Minerve*, 13 February 1834. LAC MG24 B1 17, Robert Armour Jr, to John Neilson, n.d. May 1833. LAC RG4 A1 428, Memorandum on expenditure by Joseph Cary, 15 April 1834. L.-P. Audet, *Le système scolaire de la Province de Québec. La situation scolaire à la veille de l'Union 1836–1840* (Quebec: Les Éditions de l'Érable, 1956), 6: 7–13,

65–9. Sir C.P Lucas, ed., *Lord Durham's Report on the Affairs of British North America* (Oxford: Clarendon Press, 1912), III, Appendix D, 'Report of the Commissioner of Inquiry into the State of Education in Lower Canada.' *Le Canadien*, 6 April 1836. A printed table, whose provenance is unclear, in Musée de la Civilisation, Dépôt du Seminaire de Québec, Fonds Verreau, P32/59/111, meant to calculate whether the townships or the seigneuries were getting relatively more or less government money for roads and schools, put educational expenditure for 1833–4–5 at over £68,700.

5 I don't share the position proposed by Andrée Dufour, 'Financement des écoles et scolarisation au Bas-Canada: Une interaction État-communautés locales (1826–1859),' *Historical Studies in Education/Revue d'histoire de l'éducation* 6 (1994), 219–52, at 229, that 'on peut avancer que la majorité des enfants bas-canadiens fréquentaient l'école pendant trois ou quatre ans en 1831.' As far as I can see, the claim is based on the 40,000 attendance figure and the 1831 census' report of the number of people aged six to thirteen, about 93,000. There is nothing cited about frequency or duration of attendance, and the numbers said to be at school declined dramatically, according to Dufour's own account, in 1832–3. There are not four years left after that before the school act fails.

6 Musée de la Civilisation, Dépôt du Seminaire de Québec, Fonds Verreau, 32/63.010, not dated, a printed form headed 'Comté de Vaudreuil,' with descriptions of the schools in four parishes. Many – five of seven in Rigaud – are marked 'A établir.' The provenance of this form is unknown, but perhaps the school visitors in 1831 delivered descriptions of the school districts which were printed for the use of the executive. For examples of the difficulty caused by canonical erection of parishes, LAC RG4 A1 299, Reid et al. to Yorke, 3 October 1829. Two parishes for religious purposes were in St Armand, but were not recognized for civil purposes; thus there were too many trustees elected here and Reid had trouble getting the school money. He and his fellows then decided to apply as trustees for the seigneury. Again, 306, Trustees, Abbotsford, 1 January 1830; 311, Caron and Wyss to government, 10 February 1830. In 351, Dufresne, St Nicholas, to Glegg, 14 February 1831, St Nicholas and St Sylvestre parishes cut across county boundaries, and the new militia act had eliminated the militia officers who could have called trustee elections. In B30 11, 3 January 1832, it looks as if a group from Lansdowne, Upper Canada managed to claim the school grant.

7 John Neilson had the support of some of the parish trustees for school placement. For instance, A. Turgeon from St Gervais wrote to him that his trustee board had reduced the number of schools 'quelques-unes parce que

l'instituteur n'avois été nommé que pour enseigner les premieres regles de l'Education; d'autres (Comme le nommé Jean Deaucher) par manque de caractêre, dautres enfin parce quelles étoient trops près les unes des autres.' LAC MG24 B1 17, Turgeon to Neilson, 11 July 1831.

8 The de Bellefeuille-Scott dispute is detailed in Bruce Curtis, 'On Distributed Literacy: Textually Mediated Social Relations in a Colonial Context,' *Paedagogica Historica* 44 (2008): 231–42. Scott was a leading radical *patriote* in his parish, but Rebellion history has not been kind to him because he refused to take up arms in 1837.

9 LAC RG4 B30 11, Barron to Craig, 16 June 1832.

10 LAC RG4 B30 33, Turgeon to Craig, 3 December 1833. The trustee signed as Moyse Félix, as he was popularly known – his father was Félix Granger – not as Moyse Granger, as he was called on the certificate of election, and a magistrate has to swear the two men were one and the same. A similar case is in B30 83, Proulx to Gagnon, 13 June 1833. They show a remarkable degree of follow-up in Joseph Cary's office.

11 LAC RG4 A1 444, Hunter to Craig, 12 December 1834.

12 Indeed, the executive had sent a circular to that effect to the visitors. A copy is in LAC MG24 B1 8,19 October 1833.

13 LAC RG4 A1 450, Globensky to Daly, 7 March 1835; 451, Scott to Craig, 25 March 1835; 453, Scott to Craig, 18 April 1835. Earlier for Rochon, 291, petition of 22 June 1829 for funding; 299 Labrie to Yorke, 12 October 1829, complaining that Rochon only got £3.5 when entitled to the £20 grant. And in B30 11, 28 May 1833, it was Rochon who applied on behalf of curé Paquin for the government grant of £100 for the latter's schoolhouse; Paquin and Scott were enemies.

14 LAC RG4 A1 456, Trustees and residents, Chatham Gore, 29 June 1835, with notations and Cary's comment.

15 LAC RG4 B30 11, Scott to Craig, 14 July 1835.

16 LAC RG4 A1 457, Trustees, Chatham Gore to Craig, [?August] 1835; 458, Hale to Craig to Trustees, [?August] 1835; 462, Petition, residents of Chatham Gore, to Gosford, 2 November 1835.

17 LAC RG4 B30 14, 4 February 1840.

18 For Child, LAC RG4 A1 438, Child to Craig, 3 September 1834, where he writes to have a school he included on his pay list removed after the fact; and 441, trustees, Potton Twp. to Craig, 21 November 1834: 'we do not wish to censure any one unjustly but we believe that if we had been of the same political opinions as the resident member of this County we should have received our money.' Cary's notation on the same, 'The allowance for this School was not paid as more Schools than were allowed by Law were

returned by the Member of the County – and this School with others were in consequence left out by direction of the Member (Mr Child).' Again, in 455, Trustees no. 9 Barnston to Craig, 15 May 1835, for another of Child's exclusions. In 444, Clapham to Craig, 12 December 1834, Clapham decided to remove two schools already included in his pay list and in 447, Fairburn to Craig, 16 January 1835, Fairburn went to Quebec to get his wife's school grant only to learn her school had been left off the Megantic list. In 451, Filiatrault to Craig, 31 March 1835, a school in Terrebonne followed the regulations but was left off the pay list by the MPP; in 455, Trustees no. 5 Brome to Craig, 21 May 1835, and in 475, Bourassa to Walcott, 6 April 1836, for several schools removed from the pay list by the MPP after the fact.

19 In fact, Dorion was a trustee in five different schools in Ste Anne de la Pérade, LAC RG4 B30 11, n.d. 1835.

20 LAC RG4 A1 400, 1 January 1833; François Languedoc was assailed in a petition purported to be from householders in Babyville on the grounds that he kept an incompetent teacher in place, 'as his wife delights in receiving presents from the Schoolmasters wives. And Mr Languedoc being fond of Rum, prefers the Schoolmaster who gives him most rum to drink : & he will sign the Certificate& School returns for such.' Languedoc got a doctor to state he was too ill to attend the Assembly, when in fact he was drunk, and the trustees kept the teacher because he let their kids attend free. Henry Craig's marginalia: 'As the Signatures and the petition are all written in the same hand, no notice has been taken of it – but it may be taken up whenever the complaint is renewed in a more formal manner H.C.'

21 LAC RG4 A1 294, Mathison to Yorke, 28 July 1829, for support of the school he built; B30 11, Mathison to Craig, 27 June and 27 July 1835, the second with Cary's notation. We don't know if Larocque was called upon to explain himself. It is just within the realm of possibility that the Joseph Lancaster mentioned as a trustee was the monitorial school reformer. He was still in the colony in late summer 1833, but not in 1834. Mathison thought the school was not established according to law, but the three men mentioned existed, and if they did in 1834, the monitorial Lancaster wasn't one of them. On sex at school in Canada West/Ontario, Bruce Curtis, '"Illicit" Sexuality and Public Education in Ontario, 1840–1907,' *Historical Studies in Education/ Revue d'histoire de l'éducation* 1, no. 1 (1989): 73–94.

22 Perhaps even if there weren't vacant districts; see LAC RG4 A1 408, Ogden to Craig, 25 May 1833.

23 LAC RG4 B30 89, 17 January 1834; A1 427, Lemay to Craig, 25 March 1834; 428, same to same, 11 April 1834; 429, Trustees, Ste Marie de

Monnoir, petition, 12 April 1834; 431, Lemay to Craig, 15 May 1834; 437, same to same, 26 August 1834. On the players here, Gilles Laporte, *Patriotes et Loyaux: Leadership régional et mobilisation politique en 1837 et 1838* (Quebec: Les éditions du Septentrion, 2004). Julien S. Mackay, *Notaires et patriotes. 1837–1838* (Sillery: Septentrion, 2006). Marcel J. Rheault and Georges Aubin, *Médecins et patriotes, 1837–1838* (Sillery: Septentrion, 2006). The exchange of fire between the Montreal Cavalry troop which had arrested Davignon and a group led by Bonaventure Viger was the opening salvo in the 1837 insurrection.

24 LAC RG4 A1 436, petition, residents of Bécancour, to Aylmer, 9 August 1834; 444, Lahaye to Craig, 18 December 1834; 456, Lahaye to Craig, 24 June 1835. In the last, Lahaye cannot understand how he is to be paid the grant.

25 LAC RG4 A1 386, Huot to Craig, 30 July 1832; 389, Huot to Aylmer, 24 August 1832, with notation from Cary; 387, Larue to Craig, 6 [August, misdated September] 1832; John Neilson's copy of the circular is MG24 B1 7, 25 August 1832; his reply, RG4 A1 392, Neilson to Craig, 6 October 1832; 391, Buffard to Craig, 26 September 1832, seeking the prize money; 393, Raymond to Craig, 13 October 1832; 393, Proulx to Craig, 20 October 1832; RG4 B30 11, Dorion to Craig, 10 June 1833, seeking the prize money; RG4 A1 411, Archambeault to Craig, 13 June 1833; RG4 B30 85, 24 June 1833 and 90, 25 May 1834 are manuscript pay lists for the MPP visitors, giving the various amounts paid over to them under the school acts.

26 LAC RG4 A1 425, Trustees, Ramsay, to Glegg, 24 February 1834.

27 LAC MG24 B1 191, Wolff, Val Cartier, to S. Neilson, n.d. [winter 1836].

28 For Chaffers, LAC RG4 424, Chaffers to Yorke, 21 May 1830. There is no trace of a reply. Notice in passing Chaffers's arrest of G. Côté of the third batallion of the St Hyacinthe militia for having ripped down Lord Gosford's anti-demonstration proclamation in 1837. As *La Minerve* had it, 1 September 1837, after a political meeting 'quelqu'un du peuple, ayant ôte le chiffon en question du mur où il était placardé' before Chaffers intervened. *Minerve* called Côté 'cette nouvelle victime.' For Farnham, 315, Wood to Yorke, 18 March 1830. For the Shefford Academy, *Le Canadien*, 15 April 1839. J.I. Little, *State and Society in Transition: The Politics of Institutional Reform in the Eastern Townships 1838–1852* (Montreal and Kingston: McGill-Queen's University Press, 1997), 171ff.

29 *La Minerve*, 13 January 1828.

30 *Canadian Courant*, 29 July 1829; *La Minerve*, 8 April 1830. LAC RG4 A1 351, Barbier petition for aid, 3 February 1831. Barbier had two English wives, and his second wife was the daughter of Cuthbert's seigneury

A

manager. For all his attack on the Royal Institution in 1828, Barbier joined with Cuthbert, Thomas Barron, and others to support the petition of the Royal Institution schoolmaster (1810–23) Augustus Wolff for the restoration of his pension, which had been cut off in 1831 on the grounds that the Institution lacked funds. See 461, Wolff to Gosford, 21 October 1835.

31 LAC MG24 B1 6, Barbier to Neilson, 10 October 1829.

32 *La Minerve*, 22 August 1831: reprinting the *Gazette de Québec* with additional commentary.

33 Pierre Piché was one of the three, and there was a person of that name teaching in Boucherville in 1834. See *La Minerve*, 20 May 1834. Joseph Marceau was another, and a person of that name, aged twenty-eight, briefly attended the Montreal Normal School. See Musée de l'Amérique française, Dépot du Séminaire de Québec, Fonds Viger-Verreau, P32/98/77, 26 April 1842. I've found no trace of the third, Isaac Benoit.

34 LAC RG4 B30 11, Barbier to Craig, 5 November 1835. Notice quite a different account in the 1835 petition to the Assembly, Lower Canada, Journals of the Legislative Assembly, *Sessional Papers*, 3 Will. IV, Appendix I.i. 1833, 'Third Report of the Standing Committee of Education and Schools,' no. 5. Here there were thirty-three students in attendance, seventeen paying £4 a year, two paying £2 a year, and the rest attending free of charge. One student from each county school was accepted free.

35 For an occupational profile of a sample of Montreal district trustees, Christian Dessureault, 'Les syndics scolaires du district de Montréal (1829–1836): une sociographie des élus,' *Revue d'histoire de l'Amérique française* 63 (2009): 33–81.

36 LAC RG4 B30, 51, 17 May 1830; 11, 27 October 1835. The formula is in use already in 1790, A1 45, petition for a court of small causes at Laprairie, 16 March 1790; another example is the petition for the construction of a canal to feed the banal mill in Terrebonne, 83, 31 March 1804.

37 Curtis, 'On Distributed Literacy'.

38 *La Minerve*, 29 May 1830; 1 April 1831; 4 August 1834; 11 July 1835. Another Vanasse examination is described in the issue of 15 December 1834, where he is said to have thirty-two students. One of his school reports is LAC RG4 B30 89, 3 March 1834. The school was built by curé Rivard, so the reporter's crack about a clergyman's presence at the 1835 exam speaks to *La Minerve*'s increasing anti-clericalism. We see below that Marchesseault, Wolfred Nelson's right-hand man in 1837, was reported to be in St Denis at this time, or shortly afterwards.

39 LAC RG4 A1 284, petition of Veuve Davignon for support for her school, 20 April 1829. She was asked to submit a report which has not survived, but

the cover letter 288, notables, Rouville to Yorke, 8 June 1829, has the remark, 'cette Ecole est tenue sur un Excellent Pied & est d'une grande avantage pour cette Partie ici de la Paroisse.' Veuve Davignon's sons included three medical doctors, among them the *patriote* activists Joseph-François and Pierre-Alexis-Hubert, both implicated directly in the events of 1837–8. Relations of marriage knit the Davignons closely to other activists in the village and county; Eustache Soupras's daughter Euphémie-Cordélie, for instance, married Pierre-Alexis-Hubert in 1833. Timothée Franchère was one of the patrons. For more on the Davignon sons, Rheault and Aubin, *Médecins et patriotes* and Laporte, *Patriotes et Loyaux.*

40 *La Minerve,* 21 November 1830; another examination story in 20 May 1834. LAC RG4 A1 436, Davignon to Craig 1 August 1834. This is the plea to accept her late report; the letter was sent to Lemay, who comments on it that he will indeed approve it. B30 14, 6th Report, Parish of St Mathias, n.d. October 1839.

41 For Valade generally, Mackay, *Notaires et patriotes.* Lower Canada, Journals of the Legislative Assembly, *Sessional Papers,* Appendix Ii no. 11, 3 Will. IV, 1833. *La Minerve,* 29 August 1833 (Papineau at the exam); 6 and 13 March, 14 April, 3 July 1834.

42 *La Minerve,* 9 May 1834.

43 LAC RG4 B30 14, Tenth Report, Terrebonne, 22 January 1840.

44 LAC RG4 A1 312, Hill to Civil Secretary, 25 February 1830, and 315, 23 March 1830; RG4 B30 50, Trustees, St Édouard to Aylmer, 30 November 1830.

45 LAC RG4 B30 11, Trustees, district 1, Compton Township to Craig, 23 September 1833; A1 437, Trustees, district 3, Hinchinbrooke Township to Aylmer, 28 August 1834.

46 LAC RG4 A1 400, Trustees, St Andrews to Aylmer, 10 January 1833. This Mr Simpson was probably J.A. Roebuck's father or stepfather.

47 LAC MG24 B1 26, Petition, William Maher, 21 January 1834; RG4 B30 11, Clancy et al. to Craig, 18 June 1833.

48 LAC RG4 B30 11, Louis Guillet to Craig, 14 December 1834.

49 LAC RG4 A1 400, Bradforce to Craig, postmarked 13 January 1833.

50 LAC MG24 B1 17, 28 April 1834. RG4 B30 86, 6 March 1834, is a thick bundle of school visitors' receipts where one can see the signing abilities of the county visitors.

51 LAC RG4 B30 59, various school reports for Montmorency.

52 LAC RG4 B30 56, several reports; for St Martin, 86, 6 March 1834. MG24 B1 16, Tanguay to Neilson, 6 January 1834.

53 *La Minerve,* 6[?] and 21 November 1831.

54 *La Minerve,* 17 May 1832. This is the first such letter the paper printed after its declaration in November 1831 that it would print no more of them.

55 LAC MG24 B1 17, various school reports for 1833.

56 LAC RG4 B30 57, 15 November 1830.

57 LAC RG4 B30 50, 15 November 1830; 53, 7 February 1831.

58 LAC RG4 B30 50, 15 May 1831. The claim wasn't followed up; if it was truthful, the curé must have been one of those implicated, since presumably if Maltais could not write he could not change names.

59 LAC RG4 B30 49, various school reports for St Damase; A1 432, minutes of trustee election, 9 June 1834. In B30 53, there are several iterations of the signature of a trustee which seems to become more polished over time. His first signature in November 1830 appears as 'fran soi le sieur sains dic' and rather shaky. By October 1831 he seemed to have a better hold on the pen.

60 LAC RG4 B30 86, 19 July 1833, signed and dated at Drummondville by Edward Toomy MPP, 12 August 1833. It is not clear if she was paid.

61 LAC RG4 A1 386, Joseph Bourguoin dit Bourgugnon to Craig, 23 July 1832; 391, same to Aylmer, 30 September 1832; 387, Augustin Dessin and Joseph Jolivet to Aylmer, 2 August 1831. Could the 1834 hijacking of the St Gervais election be related?

62 LAC MG24 B1 9, Hutton 'To the editor of the Quebec Gazette,' 25 August 1836.

63 In Rouville the *patriote* notary É.-G. Coursolles offered to build a school for the poor children in his neighbourhood at his own expense if the trustees would then take it over. The latter, led by Coursolles's political ally Eustache Soupras, agreed; but when Coursolles applied for the school grant to pay his teacher, Gabriel Salière, they refused to accept him. Soupras explained to the executive that 'au meilleur de notre connaissance le maître qu'il auroit engagé pour enseigner n'est pas Suffisamment instruit, quoiqu'il Soit un homme de Moeurs irréprochables.' They would pay only if ordered to do so. LAC RG4 A1 306, Coursolles to Yorke, 7 January 1830; 309, Trustees, St Mathias to same, 24 January 1830; two of the five could not sign, but Soupras did.

64 LAC RG4 A1 441, Kenneth Sutherland and John Fortune to Craig, 15 November 1834.

65 Richard Chabot, *Le curé de campagne et la contestation locale au Québec de 1791 aux troubles de 1837–1838* (Montreal: Hurtubise HMH Ltée., 1975), 64–5. The work remains highly readable thirty-five years after its publication, despite Chabot's somewhat simplistic economic-functionalist arguments about the logic of educational development. Chabot tends to see

anglophone capitalist interest in peasant schooling in economic terms, to the exclusion of the political, moral, and religious.

66 RAPQ, 1942–3, 'Correspondence de Mgr. J.-J. Lartigue de 1827 à 1833,' Lartigue to Alinotte, 30 September 1829; to Gagné, 6 September 1831. 1836-1837, 'Inventaire de la correspondance de Monseigneur Joseph Signäy, Archêveque de Québec – 1825–1835,' Signäy to Dénéchaud, 17 September 1834. RAPQ, 1934–5, Panet to Chauvin, 11 April and 1 June 1829; to Dénéchaud, 18 May 1829; to Ducharme, 30 May 1829. Dufour, 'Financement,' 226n.

67 RAPQ, 1942–3, 'Correspondence de Mgr. J.-J. Lartigue de 1827 à 1833,' Lartigue to Aubry, 30 October 1829; to Chèvrefils, 13 May 1830; to Boissonnault, 8 July 1833. 1936–7, 'Inventaire de la correspondance de Monseigneur Joseph Signäy, Archêveque de Québec – 1825–1835,' Signäy to Carrier, 4 March 1833; to Montminy, 16 March 1833.

68 LAC RG4 B30 45, 17 May 1830; 17 May and 13 December 1831; 14, Sixth Report. Armour noted that in one of the back concessions of St Athanase there was a school taught by Veuve Morin which had been reduced from forty-five students to fifteen, because 'she was to take girls only as the clergy disapprove of the Association of boys and girls in the same School.'

69 LAC RG4 A1 295, Brodeur to Yorke, 2 August 1829, 296, same to same 29 August 1829; 317, Brodeur fired his first teacher and worked to block him from setting up a trustee school with John Neilson's connivance. He also convinced Neilson to exclude a parish girls' school. Ambrose to Yorke, 3 April 1830; B30 11, Dupont to Cary, 26 March 1832, with enclosures; Brodeur to Cary, 9 November 1832, covers the dispute with the first teacher, Thomas Ambrose, and Brodeur's blocking of schools run by the Dupont brother and sisters team. Three of the five trustees refused to sign their school reports, saying they were not in the right district. Robert Dupont finally managed to get some grant money for them when he discovered the 1829 act did not actually mention districts, 456, Dupont to Craig, 8 June 1835. For the schools in St Roch, Archives du Archédiocèse de Québec, 60 CN, Gouvernement du Canada, vol. A: 179, Louis Brodeur, 27 August 1838. LAC RG4 B30 109, Brodeur et al., 5 November 1838.

70 LAC RG4 A1 306, Lewis to Kempt, n.d. [1830?], Samuel Lewis taught a boys' school in French before the organization of the College. He had begun his career at St Antoine de Chambly but could not earn a living there, and in October 1827, with curé Gaulie's support, he set up in the presbytery hall. He applied for support under the 1829 act in the letter cited above and reports of his school examinations appeared until after 1830. See La Minerve, 4 October 1827, 18 October 1828, 24 August 1829,

13 May 1830, 13 and 31 May, and 14 June 1830. Perhaps the college did him in. LAC RG4 B30 109, Meilleur to Buller, 24 July 1838, with a description of the College. But the Cherrier school was first co-educational and may have cost Lewis students. The former is described in *La Minerve*, 27 May, 22 November 1830, and 11 June 1835. The Lemoine sisters' school in *La Minerve*, 21 November 1830; LAC RG4 344, Lemoine to Glegg, 1 December 1830; B30 109, Meilleur to Buller, 28 July 1838, enclosing a letter from the Lemoine sisters to himself; 14, Robert Armour Jr, 12th Report, 4 February 1840.

71 LAC MG24 B116, Morin to Neilson, 2 November 1835. Struggles over co-education would have been localized and are unlikely to have made it past the visitors, so it may be that my sources are not capturing them.

72 McGill University Archives (MUA), Royal Institution for the Advancement of Learning (RI) Accession #447 Folder #9654 187 RG 4, C.48, Larue to secretary, 2 February 1829. LAC RG4 A1 275, Mills to Yorke, 22 December 1828; 306, Dolbigny to Yorke, 9 January 1830.

73 LAC RG4 A1 358, Larue to Glegg, 20 May 1831 with enclosures; 362, Opinion of Crown Law Officer, 11 July 1831; 363, Larue to Glegg 23 July 1831, tries to argue it was a replacement election and so not premature; rejected in 364, Opinion of Crown Law Officer, 31 August 1831; MG24 B1 17, Larue to Neilson, 16 August 1831. B1 7, Trustees to Neilson, 27 February 1832, states they have changed teachers, but it is not clear who changed what.

74 AAQ, 60 CN, Gouvernement du Canada, vol. A: 194, E.E. Parant curé à Cap St Ignace, 29 August 1838; LAC RG4 B30 109, Commission Return, Cap St Ignace, 29 November 1838.

75 For instance LAC MG24 B1 17, certificate of school examination for district 2, Charlesbourg, 28 April 1834. The Quebec teachers' signatures are in MG24 A27 27, n.d. 1838.

76 For Gadoura, LAC RG4 A1 396, Antoine Sénéchal to Craig, 26 November 1832. In B30 11, 16 April 1832, Rosalie Endeverque from L'Assomption learned she would not be paid for four months' work when 'Messieurs les visiteurs d'école pour ce Comté, avaient recommandé que le salaire que je recevais pour mon Ecole fût discontinué par faute de qualification de ma part.'

77 For Guy, LAC MG24 B1 8, Guy to 'tous les Messieurs de la législature et a tous les Membres de la Chambre d'aSemblées,' 17 December 1834; for Blondin, RG4 A1 440, Blondin to governor, 19 October 1834; 442, Dion to Craig, 24 November 1834; 444, Blondin to governor, 19 December 1834; ANQ R2 3 A 019 01-07-003A-01, Civil Secretary to Blondin, 26 May 1838.

For Egerton, LAC RG4 B30 11, 10 and 12 May 1835; he got an answer but it has not survived.

78 LAC MG24 B1 17, Charles Décormier to Neilson, 30 March 1833, the disqualification was imposed 'par la mauvaise intention' of the militia captain. RG4 A1 381, Bardy to Craig, 15 May 1832, with Cary's marginalia.

79 LAC RG4 A1 321, Boyce to government, with a package of other documents, 5 May 1830; B30 11, Goss to Craig, 29 January 1833.

80 LAC RG4 B30 53, M. Townsend to Civil Secretary, 1 June 1830.

81 LAC RG4 B30 50, School Report, St George de Rouville, 1830.

82 LAC RG4 A1 324, Daly to Yorke, 24 May 1830, for the clerks' pay; B30 53, School Report, St George de Rouville, 15 November 1830; 46, School Report, St Benôit, 24 May 1830; 57, School Report, St Hyacinthe, 2 January 1830.

83 LAC RG4 A1 324, Reid to Yorke, 24 May 1830; 335, Lee to Yorke, 11 September 1830; B30 36 for La Petite Nation.

84 LAC RG4 B30 58, Guyon to Glegg, 16 August 1831.

85 LAC RG4 B30 87, School Report, Drummond County, 15 November 1833; 84, School Report, Portneuf, 27 May 1833; 89, School Report, Rimouski, 20 December 1833; MG24 B1 16, Tanguay to Neilson, 6 January 1834. His three trustees each made their 'X' on his petition.

86 LAC RG4 B30 109, Meilleur to Buller, 28 July 1838, encloses Lemoine to Meilleur; 84, School Report, Portneuf, 27 May 1833. *La Minerve*, 16 April 1832.

87 LAC RG4 A1 383, Milton to Craig, 12 June 1832; 393, Vervais to Craig with marginal notations for the response, 20 October 1832; 395, Carthwright to Craig, 9 November 1832; he was supporting a wife in Ireland and had been sending her money half-yearly.

88 LAC MG24 B1 7, Racicot to Neilson, 29 October 1832, with a bundle of related documents.

89 LAC RG4 A1 402, Teachers, Rawdon, to Aylmer, 7 February 1833.

90 LAC RG4 A1 603, Report on Education, 20 February 1840. There is a sample of the standard warrant in RG1 E15A 73, Schools, Societies and Institutions, 1831, St Hyacinthe. The entire matter of the technicalities of state finance in the period before 1841 has been almost completely neglected in the literature, and reconstructing it is a hermeneutic exercise of some complexity.

91 For Huot, LAC RG4 B30 84, 15 June 1833; B30 84, 10 June 1833.

92 *La Minerve*, 22 February 1830; LAC RG4 A1 322, Langevin to Yorke, 6 May 1830.

93 Langevin was a member of a committee with John Neilson and H.-S. Huot in Quebec in 1828 preparing the statement that accompanied the monster

petition of that year. He was appointed a justice of the peace in 1830, sat on
the Quebec Board of Health in 1833, from which he resigned to become city
clerk, but did write a report on drainage. He was proposed as one of the
three members of the colonial Board of Audit, and his wife was a member of
the Société d'Éducation des Dames de Québec. Langevin also participated in
the non-partisan movement to eliminate begging in the city and with Huot,
James Sewell, and one of the Cary brothers was a director of the House of
Industry. For his first advertisement, *La Minerve*, 22 February 1830; again
28 March 1831. For changed reporting dates, *La Minerve*, 28 November 1831,
and his announcement that he was quitting business, 1 August 1833. LAC
RG4 B30 59, Langevin to Yorke, 3 March 1830 (Caneur); A1 322, Langevin
to Yorke, 6 May 1830 (the offer to distribute all the money); 336, same to
same, 22 September 1830 (Magdelan Islands); 342, Langevin to Glegg,
11 November 1830 (Blandford); B30 45, 7 December 1830 (les Soeurs
de la Congrégation); A1 410, Langevin to Craig, 23 May 1833 (Collège de
L'Assomption). In B30 84, 8 June 1833, we see Langevin paid £450 of the
£850 due to schools in Berthier, Shefford, and Megantic; 10 June 1833 has
the list of monies he paid to the other counties mentioned.

94 LAC RG4 A1 324, La Mothe to Yorke, 26 May 1839; 378, Hanamney to
Craig, 26 March 1832; 387, Quin to Craig, 6 August 1832. Kerr advertised
in *La Minerve* first on 28 March 1831. His father was probably Judge Kerr.
LAC RG4 A1 317 [misfiled here for 1830], Kerr to Glegg, 11 April 1831.
He seems to have started the agency business after preparing the 1830
Blue Book in duplicate, a monumental task which he complained 'has only
yielded me 4/7 a day, a rate at which a common scrivener can hardly be
obtained.' He informed teachers in the *Canadian Courant*, 17 April 1833
of the £4 for teaching in French and English, ending 'Agency, be it of the
most complicated nature, transacted. Fair claims on the Government
brought forward.'

95 LAC RG4 A1 429, Ross to Craig, 21 April 1834, enclosing Trustees to Ross,
15 April 1834.

96 One of Ross's agency advertisements is *La Minerve*, 12 May 1834. LAC RG4
A1 464, Trustees, district 1, Upper Chute, Argenteuil to government,
11 November 1835; 477, Clarke to Walcott, 26 April 1836; Trustees,
no. 12 Argenteuil to Walcott, 29 April 1836; B30 14, Armour, 8th Report,
Vaudreuil, 1July [?] 1839. The money was small potatoes compared with
the tens of thousands of pounds for which John Caldwell defaulted, and
he was knighted.

97 John and Samuel Neilson's book business lets us see a good bit of what was
ordered earlier for schools. For instance, LAC MG24 B1 2, Deguise, curé de

Varennes, to Neilson, 15 November 1811, ordered '6 Douzaines de
Neuvaines, 6 Douz de petits Cathéchismes historique de Fleury. 6 Douz.
d'alphabet Latin 1 Douz de petites heures de vie,' thus beginning instruc-
tion in Latin and books of piety. By contrast, B1 3, Strachan to Neilson,
16 April 1816 for the Upper Canadian common schools, Archdeacon
Strachan sought a quote for a large quantity of: '1. Tickets with the
Alphabet of three different sizes 2. Pelham's Primer or Murray's First book
3. Mavor's Spelling book or Blairs reading lessons 4. Enfield's Speaker 5.
Walker's Lessons 6. Burrens [?] Questions on the New Testament 7. A
System of Arithmetic usual size.' The collection also lets us see what was
sold over the counter in some years; for instance, MG24 B1120, Brown
and Gilmore Cash Book, 1831-3, has a list of titles and prices.

98 LAC RG4 A1 294, School Petition, 23 July 1829.
99 LAC RG4 B30 45, is a relatively complete collection for St Athanase,
    1829–31.
100 Material from the preceding two paragraphs is drawn from the school
    reports in LAC RG4 B30 45, 46, 49, 50, 51, 57, and 58. I went through
    most of the collection but found it too tedious to replicate every list of
    books; the ubiquity of the pattern can easily be verified. Earlier, we saw
    Marchesseault, called 'Marchesseau,' described as using Jacotot's method
    in the nearby village of St-Jean-Baptiste-de-Rouville in the same year.
101 LAC RG4 B30 49, 50, 51, 52, 57; I have no idea what the 'Hamiltonian'
    method was. Benziger's autograph manuscript is 16, n.d., 1833. It may not
    have made it into print.
102 LAC MG24 B1 17, H. Miville de Chêne to Neilson, 25 July 1831; RG4 B30
    110, 5 December 1838.
103 LAC RG4 A1 311, Reid to Kempt, 5 February 1830.
104 LAC RG4 B30 45, 46, 51, 53, and 58.
105 LAC RG4 B30 44, 1 January 1832. On the similar controversy over
    American books in Upper Canada, Bruce Curtis, 'Schoolbooks and the
    Myth of Curricular Republicanism: The State and the Curriculum in
    Canada West, 1820–1850,' *Histoire sociale/ Social History* 6 (1983): 305-329.
106 LAC RG4 B30 44 (Townsend) 15 May 1831; 59 (Caisse) 4 May 1831.
107 LAC MG24 A27 26, Stephen Randal, 'Preliminary Measures for Imperial
    or local Enactment,' n.d. 1838; RG4 A1 447, Foster et al. to Aylmer,
    15 January 1835.
108 David Vincent, *Literacy and Popular Culture: England 1750–1914* (Cambridge:
    Cambridge University Press, 1989).
109 One already wonders, what happened to her? PRONI, *Appendix to the First
    Report of the Commissioners on Education in Ireland*, Appendix No. 221 'A List

of Books used in the various Schools situated in the following four
Counties in Ireland ...' gives almost 400 different titles. More generally,
Antonia McManus, *The Irish Hedge School and Its Books, 1695–1831*
(Dublin: Four Courts Press, 2002).

110 Lower Canada, Journals of the Legislative Assembly, *Sessional Papers*, 6 Will.
IV, Appendix O.O. 'Third Report of the Standing Committee on Education.'
Minutes of Evidence, 1835–6.

111 For an elaboration of this argument, Bruce Curtis, 'The Speller Expelled:
Disciplining the Common Reader in Canada West,' *Canadian Review of
Sociology and Anthropology* 22 (1985): 346–68.

112 Marc André Bernier, 'Portrait de l'éloquence au Québec (1760–1840),'
in *Portrait des arts, des lettres et de l'éloquence au Québec (1760–1840)*, ed.
Bernard Andrès and Marc André Bernier (Quebec: Les Presses de
l'Université Laval, 2002), 411.

113 Lord Dalhousie, *The Dalhousie Journals*, ed. Marjory Whitelaw (Ottawa:
Oberon Press, 1982), 3: 47ff.

114 For instance, *Montreal Vindicator*, 16 and 19 November 1830; very patronizing of the students. The course of study was denounced as inadequate
for North America in the *Canadian Courant*, 1831, reproducing Mackenzie's
Colonial Advocate.

6. The Normal School

1 L.-P. Audet, *Le système scolaire de la Province de Québec: La situation scolaire à la
veille de l'Union 1836–1840* (Quebec: Les Éditions de l'Érable, 1956), 6:
126–65. For some reason, Audet claimed the Montreal school had
between thirty and forty students, which is not what his sources showed.

2 *Le Canadien*, 21 March 1836.

3 *Le Canadien*, 31 May 1820; *La Minerve*, 30 July, 13 August, 16 November
1829; 7 January, 25 February, 6 and 22 March, 27 August, 7 and 8 September, ? March 1831. For more of the debate, Bruce Curtis, 'Joseph
Lancaster in Montreal (bis): Monitorial Schooling and Politics,' *Historical
Studies in Education/ Revue d'histoire de l'éducation* 17 (2005): 1–27.

4 *La Minerve*, 28 November 1831, 6 February 1832; *Le Canadien*, 3 December
1831; *Montreal Vindicator*, 23 December 1831, 17 February 1832; *Canadian
Courant*, 3 March 1832, and quoting *Quebec Gazette*, 15 January 1834; LAC RG4
A1 435, Blackwood to Aylmer, 10 July 1834. Blackwood claimed to have fifteen
girls in attendance and proposed a genteel version of monitorial instruction.

5 LAC MG 24 B1 7, Peck to Neilson, 14 March 1830; RG4 A1 447, Foster to
Aylmer, 15 January 1835.

6 LABC, *Sessional Papers*, 6 Will. IV, 1836, Appendix (O.O.), Third Report of the Standing Committee of Education and Schools.
7 *Le Canadien*, 29 January, 3, 5, 15, 17, and 19 February 1836.
8 Musée de l'Amérique Française, Dépôt du Seminaire de Québec, Fonds Verreau-Viger (hereafter MAFDSQ, Verreau-Viger), P32/60/44.2, Huot to Viger, 3 March 1836.
9 For the material here on Lartigue, see the following note. On Newton Bosworth, later a school inspector in Canada West, Bruce Curtis, *True Government by Choice Men? Inspection, Education and State Formation in Canada West* (Toronto: University of Toronto Press, 1992). Miss Bosworth's school is advertised in the *Morning Courier*, 1 December 1836.
10 RAPQ, 1944–5, 'Correspondance de Mgr Lartigue 1836–1837,' Lartigue to Turgeon, 1, 2, 4, 5, 10, and 20 February, 10 and 28 March, 13 April 1836.
11 MAFDSQ, Verreau-Viger, P32/98/1-135 (62.11.1), document 1b, Lartigue to Jacques Viger, n.d, 1836.
12 LAC RG4 A1, 471, Ogden to Walcott, 15 March 1836.
13 LAC RG4 A1, 472, Inhabitants of Quebec, 9 March 1836.
14 The first quotation is reproduced in the *Montreal Gazette*, 26 March 1836; the second appears in the same paper, but as an editorial comment on the act.
15 Public Record Office of Northern Ireland, Gosford Papers, [PRONI] D/2259/1/2C, Gosford to Glenelg, 9 July 1836. Étienne Parent closed a discussion of the politics of schooling in *Le Canadien*, 23 March 1836, by observing: 'Nous ne devons pas, en justice, laisser ce sujet, sans reconnaître la fermeté que lord Gosford a montrée en sanctionnant le bill des écoles normales, dont l'objet est d'instruire les maîtres. Son Excellence avait reçu une pétition nombreusement signée contre ce bill, pétition dictée par l'esprit d'ascendance et de bigotisme. Son Excellence a été sourde à la voix des sirènes, et elle a écouté celle du peuple, qui demandait depuis long-temps des maîtres pour ses écoles. La sanction de cette mesure, malgré les remontrances des hommes qui ont ordinairement les sympathies des gouverneurs, est un acte qui mérite à lord Gosford la reconnaissance du pays entier … Malheureusement le système est tellement vicié, corrompu, qu'il faudrait une force plus qu'humaine pour résister à son influence: c'est l'étable d'Augias, on l'a dit cent fois, il faudrait un demi-dieu pour la nettoyer.'
16 MAFDSQ, Verreau-Viger, P32/60/035.5, Girouard to Viger, 26 March 1836.
17 MAFDSQ, Viger-Verreau, P32/98/14, Holmes to Viger, 28 March 1836.

18 *Le Canadien,* 23 March, 6, 8, and 22 April 1836; MAFDSQ, Verreau-Viger, P32/60/44.3, 44.4, 44.5, Huot to Viger, 9, 12, and 18 April 1836.

19 The notice, with the conditions of entry, appeared in *Le Canadien,* 25 May 1836; the decline of two of those accepted in *Le Canadien,* 5 and 19 September 1836; in *Le Canadien,* 28 September 1838, a call for an application with an expiry date of the previous 15 July was still running. The Ursulines in Trois-Rivières were eager to get a share of the training funds; see MAFDSQ, Viger-Verreau, P32/98/24, Sr. Sainte Marie to Huot, 12 July 1836.

20 MAFDSQ, Viger-Verreau, Extraits du Régistre de l'Ecole Normale du District de Québec, 16 April 1836.

21 The Tory press (e.g., *Montreal Gazette,* 26 March 1836) understood that the board elections were politicized but misread the role of religious denomination in the mix. Five of the seven men on Viger's 'Anglais' ticket were Catholics. Four of ten on the *canadien* ticket were Protestants. The *patriote* / 'Constitutionalist' divide was the operative one. For Viger's electoral table and his official account of the results of the election, MAFDSQ, Viger-Verreau P/32/98/4, /5, /6, /7, 12 April 1836.

22 MAFDSQ, Viger-Verreau, P32/98/ 342 'Livre de Correspondance du Trésorier de l'Ecole Normale du District de Montréal,' Viger to Daly, 17 April 1836.

23 MAFDSQ, Viger-Verreau P32/98/9, draft memorandum of instructions (in Papineau's hand), 16 April 1836. It is not clear if Holmes received £400 for each board or simply £400.

24 There is a good overview of the tour, with information on the fate of the normal schools in Audet, *Système scolaire,* 6: 126–63. Audet draws heavily on A. Gosselin, 'L'abbé Holmes et l'instruction publique,' in *Memoires de la Société royale du Canada* (1908), 142–69.

25 MAFDSQ, Viger-Verreau, P32/98/26, Holmes to Huot, 30 July 1836; anyway in P32/98/10, Holmes to Papineau, 19 April 1836, it seemed likely he would go on to Europe in any case. Holmes thought it might be best to hire American teachers, since he said they were less pretentious and more likely to be able to adapt to Canadian conditions, but he did not want to be carried away by his first observations.

26 LAC, CO42/266, Holmes to Glenelg, 16 July, 2 November 1836; draft of Glenelg to J. Backhouse, 21 July 1836.

27 *Le Canadien,* 10 February 1837; in the version in the *Morning Courier* of 16 February (reproducing the *Montreal Gazette*) the claim was that the two Scottish teachers had been signed up. LAC, CO42/269, for the manuscript version of the Gosford Commission report dealing with education.

28 MAFDSQ, Viger-Verreau, P32/98/31, Holmes to Secretary (Brown), Montreal Normal School, dated 14 February 1837. The letter is almost certainly misdated; Holmes says it has been two and a half months since he last wrote (on 21 December) and in an April letter refers to this one as from last month.

29 MAFDSQ, Viger-Verreau, P32/98/31, Holmes to Secretary (Brown), Montreal Normal School, dated 14 February 1837, original emphasis.

30 MAFDSQ, Viger-Verreau, P32/98/33, Holmes to Secretary, Montreal Normal School, 15 April 1836.

31 MAFDSQ, Viger-Verreau, P32/98/102, Holmes to Viger, 16 April 1837.

32 MAFDSQ, Viger-Verreau, P32/98/123, 3 May 1837; and the following items in the series, with /126 giving a list of all that was shipped.

33 LAC MG24 B1 9, Holmes to Samuel Neilson, 7 September 1836.

34 MAFDSQ, Viger-Verreau, P32/98/45, Holmes to Secretary, Montreal Normal School, 31 July and 2 August 1837.

35 *Le Canadien*, 22 September 1837.

36 MAFDSQ, Viger-Verreau, P32/98/45, Holmes to Secretary, Montreal Normal School, 31 July and 2 August 1837. For more on monitorial schooling in Switzerland, see Christian Alain Muller, 'L'enseignement mutuel à Genève ou l'histoire de l' "échec" d'une innovation pédagogique en contexte: l'école de Saint-Gervais, 1815–1850,' *Paedagogica Historica* 41 (2005): 95–117.

37 MAFDSQ, Viger-Verreau, P32/98/193, 1 May 1838. This is a renewal of the lease of the house for the year 1838–9.

38 MAFDSQ, Viger-Verreau, P32/98/107-119, various itemized accounts. /41 is Brown's inquiry about trees. /160 is a bill from William Tate for work, started 8 July 1837, which included glazing most of the windows, for more than £20. The house must have been empty and dilapidated.

39 *Vindicator*, 8 July 1837.

40 MAFDSQ, Viger-Verreau, P32/98/66, n.d., autograph 'Conditions d'admission à l'école Normale de Montréal.'

41 MAFDSQ, Viger-Verreau, P32/98/67, n.d., autograph rules and regulations.

42 MAFDSQ, Viger-Verreau, P32/98/65; n.d. [probably August 1840]; this is the English version in Findlater's hand; the same text appears in French in Regnaud's hand.

43 MAFDSQ, Viger-Verreau, P32/98/77, 26 April 1842; certified list of those attending the Montreal Normal School during its years of operation. There are nineteen students. A slightly different list is /82. It is clear that L.-P. Audet was overly enthusiastic in his claim that there were thirty or forty

students in attendance over the life of the school: Audet, *Système scolaire*,
6: 161. He claims to have used the same sources on which I draw.

44 MAFDSQ, Viger-Verreau, P32/98/128, Walcott to Viger, 28 July 1837.

45 MAFDSQ, Viger-Verreau, P32/98/133 &/134, 27 November 1837.

46 MAFDSQ, Viger-Verreau, P32/98/ 342 'Livre de Correspondance du
Trésorier de l'Ecole Normale du District de Montréal,' Viger to Joseph
Cary, 22 November 1837.

47 MAFDSQ, Viger-Verreau, P32/98/ 342 'Livre de Correspondance du
Trésorier de l'Ecole Normale du District de Montréal,' Viger to Holmes,
26 December 1837. P32/98/162, 19 February 1838, is the bill sent by
Regnaud to Maitland and the school's insurance company. In /167, 3 April
1838, the company demanded an extra premium in consequence of the
occupation.

48 MAFDSQ, Viger-Verreau, P32/98/ 342 'Livre de Correspondance du
Trésorier de l'Ecole Normale du District de Montréal,' Viger to Walcott, 26,
18 and 31 December 1837; Daly to Viger, 6 January 1838; Walcott to Viger,
8 January 1838.

49 MAFDSQ, Viger-Verreau, P32/98/ 342 'Livre de Correspondance du
Trésorier de l'Ecole Normale du District de Montréal,' Viger to Daly,
16 January 1838, has Findlater's note; Viger to Ogden, 25 January 1838;
Walcott to Viger, 31 January 1838.

50 Unfortunately, his domestic economy is very challenging to reconstruct,
with only his claims for expenditures on behalf of the school for such things
as firewood and candles surviving. The external students seem to have
received warrants directly and thus presumably may have arranged expenditure to their own advantage.

51 MAFDSQ, Viger-Verreau, P32/98/77, certified list of students having
attended the Normal School, 26 April 1842; /82 offers a slightly different
list, mentioning three others who were examined in 1840. The latter may
never have attended. On Kell(e)y, P32/98/50 and 51. Copies of certificates
for Sainte Marie, Chenneville, and Horan are P32/98/78-80.

52 The letters from her mother and the official list of students refer to 'Odile
Clairoux'; the certificates of good character to 'Marie-Adèle.' I assume
Odile and Marie-Adèle are the same person. The relevant material on the
Clairoux is located as follows: LAC, RG4 B30, 46, 7 January and 24 May,
1830, 31 December 1831; RG4 B30, 14, 14 January 1840 (9th Report);
MAFDSQ, Viger-Verreau, P32/98/16, Girouard to Brown, 16 May, 1838;
/18, Cherrier to Dumouchel, 23 May 1836; /28, 2 August 1836; /198,
Phelan to Viger, 24 August 1838 (includes Auger to Phelan); /52, 'Filles
placées au Couvent des Soeurs de la Congrégation N.D. de Montréal par le

Comité de Régie de l'Ecole Normale du District de Montréal ... et dont
le Comité paye la pension et l'Instruction ... pendant trois ans, à compter
du jour d'entrée de chacune des dites Filles ou Elèves.' 6 April 1840.
Notice that one of the other women certified to teach was Louise Girouard
from Vaudreuil; in RG4 B30 14, Armour reported two Girouard women
teaching in St Eustache parish: Sophie and Angélique. There is no trace of
Rosalie Barbarie of St Benôit, who attended for the full three years and was
certified to teach.

53 *Le Canadien*, 25 July 1838.

54 *Le Canadien*, 22 August 1838, reproducing parts of *L'Ami du peuple*.

55 There are two versions: a copy in LAC RG4 B30 vol. 15, and the autograph
version RG4 A1 586, 10 June 1839.

56 LAC RG4 A1, 603, n.d. February 1840, manuscript of draft school law with
emendations.

57 MAFDSQ, Viger-Verreau, P32/98/ 342 'Livre de Correspondance du
Trésorier de l'Ecole Normale du District de Montréal,' Viger to Murdoch,
14 August 1840.

58 MAFDSQ, Viger-Verreau, P32/98/263 14 July 1840, Findlater's receipt for
his last salary instalment, and /266 14 August 1840, for his bonus.

59 MAFDSQ, Viger-Verreau, P32/98/ 342 'Livre de Correspondance du
Trésorier de l'Ecole Normale du District de Montréal,' Viger to Hincks,
14 January 1843.

60 Audet, *Système scolaire*, 6: 162. Regnaud was enumerator for the St-Laurent
ward in Montreal for the 1852 census; see Bruce Curtis, *The Politics of
Population: Statistics, State Formation, and the Census of Canada, 1840–1875*
(Toronto: University of Toronto Press, 2001), 129.

61 MAFDSQ, Viger-Verreau, P32/98/46, Board Meeting Minutes. There is,
however, one intriguing element in the Normal School's accounts:
P32/98/175, a very heavy consumption of pens, pencils, and ink. In April
1838 the board received a bill for 100 pens, 100 pencils, and 6 packets of
ink power. That seems like a lot for four student teachers, but perhaps it
was just an economy move to buy in bulk. There is no mention anywhere
else of a model school.

7. Governmentality and the 'Social Science'

1 LAC CO 42/266, Gosford, Throne Speech, 22 September 1836; PRONI
[Public Record Office of Northern Ireland] D/2259/1/2D, Gosford to
Glenelg, 1 October 1836; W.P.M. Kennedy, ed., *Documents of the Canadian
Constitution, 1759–1915* (Toronto: Oxford University Press, 1918), Glenelg

to Gosford, 7 June 1836; see also 'Resolutions of House of Lower Canada'
and 'Address to the Inhabitants of British North America, 1836,' which
precede Glenelg. Robert Christie, *A History of the Late Province of Lower
Canada. Parliamentary and Political. From the Commencement to the Close of Its
Existence as a Separate Province* (Montreal: Richard Worthington, 1866), 4:
320–44.

2 *La Minerve*, 13 July 1835. Most of Papineau's relevant speeches are collected in Yvan Lamonde and Claude Larin, eds., *Louis-Joseph Papineau. Un
demi-siècle de combats. Interventions publiques* (Montreal: Fides, 1998); for
instance, 456–70 for the speech at L'Assomption, 29 July 1837. Gilles
Laporte, *Patriotes et Loyaux: Leadership régional et mobilisation politique en 1837
et 1838* (Quebec: Les éditions du Septentrion, 2004), 34, has resolutions in
favour of education in six of fourteen 1837 *patriote* rallies.

3 *Montreal Gazette*, 31 March and 5 April 1836; *Le Canadien* (which includes
the material from the *Vindicator* in translation), 26 March, 6 and 20 April,
6, 16, 18, and 23 May, 17 June 1836. O'Callaghan was out of date; the
Kildare Place Society had been replaced by the Irish National
Commissioners for Education in 1832.

4 Georges Aubin, ed., *Wolfred Nelson: Écrits d'un patriote* (Montreal: Comeau et
Nadeau, Éditeurs, 1998), 37. *Le Canadien*, 18 April, 20 June, 13 July 1836;
Morning Courier, 3 December 1836; the last article could be by Christopher
Dunkin but is probably just before his time as editor.

5 LAC RG4 A1 475, residents, Sherrington, to Bishop of Quebec, 7 April
1836; 477, Bartell to Gosford, 25 April 1836 (the money bill); Archives
Nationales de Québec, R2 3 A 019 01-07-003A-01, Civil Secretary to
Mrs Mary O'Sullivan, 4 May 1836 (no funds).

6 *Le Canadien*, 23 May, 13 June, 24 August 1836; *Le Glaneur*, 16(?) December
1836, inter alia, 'Si dans nos campagnes du Canada un nombre de personnes instruites, suivant ce noble example,' of home schooling in France, and
'consacrait ainsi une partie de ses loisirs à l'émancipation intellectuelle de
quelques-uns de ses semblables, nous pourrions espérer de voir bientôt les
bienfaits de l'éducation pénêtrer jusque dans les plus humbles chaumières.'

7 L.-P. Audet, *Le système scolaire de la Province de Québec: La situation scolaire à la
veille de l'Union 1836–1840* (Quebec: Les Éditions de l'Érable, 1956), 6:
13–18: 'il nous semble inadmissible.'

8 *Le Canadien*, 9 November 1836.

9 *Le Canadien*, 31 August, 23 December 1836; *Le Glaneur*, 16(?) January 1837.

10 More than 2,200 tickets sold for Barber's eleven Montreal lectures in the
autumn of 1836 generated the comfortable sum of £128.7.3, leaving him
£75 after expenses and after a donation of £15 to the Montreal House of

Industry. So much information on Barber has survived because he purchased Montreal's *Morning Courier* newspaper and installed his stepson-son-in-law Christopher Dunkin as editor. Lord Gosford particularly appreciated the moderate political tone of the paper. *Montreal Herald*, 16 November 1836; *Le Canadien*, 21 November 1836, and most numbers of the *Morning Courier* (of which only a broken collection survives) starting 1 December 1836. The account of his income is 22 December 1836. For Gosford's view, LAC MG24 A27 26, Gosford to Durham, 30 June 1838.

11 Elinor Senior, *Redcoats and Patriotes: The Rebellions in Lower Canada, 1837–38* (Ottawa: Canada's Wings, 1985), 38.

12 I follow Peter Burroughs, *The Canadian Crisis and British Colonial Policy, 1828–1841* (London: Macmillan, 1972), but have extended his work in Bruce Curtis, 'Le rédecoupage du Bas-Canada dans les années 1830: un essai sur la "gouvernementalité" coloniale,' *Revue d'histoire de l'Amérique française* 58 (2004): 27–66.

13 Michel Foucault, *Security, Territory, Population: Lectures at the Collège de France, 1977–8* (New York: Palgrave Macmillan 2007). The early twenty-first-century fixation with 'security' is perhaps an instance of security in Foucault's sense, but only in that it operates autonomously to generate the insecurity which is its basis. It is the infatuation with the notion of a self-regulating and self-regulated system of liberty that seems to draw Foucault on to neoliberalism in *Naissance de la biopolitique: Cours au Collège de France, 1978–1979* (Paris: Hautes Études/Seuil/Gallimard, 2004).

14 Mitchell Dean, 'Risk and Reflexive Government,' in *Governmentality: Power and Rule in Modern Society* (London: Sage, 1999), 176–97. For more on the subject, Bruce Curtis, 'Reflexive Government and Colonial Governmentality: A Case Study,' paper presented to the American Educational Research Association (Montreal, 2006).

15 Gosford was responsible for an early social survey when he commissioned the Scottish road surveyor and social commentator William Greig to detail conditions on his recently expanded estates with a view to increasing his rents. The results were published as William Greig, *General Report on the Gosford Estates in Co. Armagh, 1821* (Belfast: Her Majesty's Stationery Office, 1976 [1821]). I am not suggesting that this developing science was benign, rather that it involved new ways of thinking about and intervening in the domain of 'the social' – which it also configured.

16 The best accounts remain Allan Greer, *The Patriots and the People: The Rebellion of 1837 in Lower Canada* (Toronto: University of Toronto Press, 1993); Senior, *Redcoats and Patriotes*.

17 PRONI D/2259/1/2D, Gosford to Glenelg, 5 September 1836. His delay
    in recalling the legislature allowed the opposition agitation to gather steam
    and also meant that there was no response to the Council's calls for
    amendments to the school bill. *Le Canadien*, 14 and 17 April 1837.

18 For more on Grey's schemes and their reception in London, see Curtis,
    'Le redécoupage.'

19 LAC CO42/266, official instructions dated 17 July 1835. Education is
    number 82 in the list.

20 Alexis de Tocqueville, *Voyages en Angleterre, Irlande, Suisse et Algérie. Vol. V,
    Oeuvres complètes* (Paris: Gallimard, 1958); de Tocqueville, *Voyages en Sicilie et
    aux États-Unis, Vol. V pt. 1, Oeuvres complètes* (Paris: Gallimard, 1957). Harriet
    Martineau, *Society in America*, 3 vols (New York: AMS Press, 1966 [1837]).
    On Buller, David A. Haury, *The Origins of the Liberal Party and Liberal
    Imperialism: The Career of Charles Buller, 1806–1848* (New York: Garland
    Publishing, 1987). On the links between government and the statistical
    societies, Philip Abrams, *The Origins of British Sociology: 1834–1914* (
    Chicago: University of Chicago Press, 1968). RAPQ, 1953–4 and 1954–5,
    'Correspondence de Louis-Joseph Papineau (1820–1839),' Papineau to
    Bruneau, 9, 16, 19, and 23 November 1835, for political dinners and
    meetings with the commissioners T.F. Elliott and Secretary Walcott.

21 LAC CO42/269, 'General Report of the Commissioners for the Inves-
    tigation of all Grievances affecting His Majesty's Subjects of Lower Canada,'
    mss., n.d. [November 1836].

22 On the various colonial attempts to present Lower Canada as Ireland, Mary
    Haslam, 'Ireland and Quebec 1822–1839: Rapprochement and Ambiguity,'
    The Canadian Journal of Irish Studies 33 (2007): 75–81.

23 Quotations in the preceding paragraphs are from PRONI ED/10/26/1,
    'First Report of the Commissioners of Irish Education Enquiry. Presented
    by His Majesty's Command to both Houses of Parliament,' and Appendix
    no. 257, 'Examination of the Most Reverend Dr Murray, Roman Catholic
    Archbishop of Dublin; of the Most Reverend Dr Kelly, Roman Catholic
    Archbishop of Tuam; and of the Right Reverend Dr Doyle, Roman Catholic
    Bishop of Kildare and Leighlin, on Oath; Thursday, 14th April 1825.' On
    the Irish school system, D.H. Akenson, *The Irish Education Experiment*
    (Toronto: University of Toronto Press, 1970). Bruce Curtis, *True Government
    by Choice Men? Inspection, Education and State Formation in Canada West*
    (Toronto: University of Toronto Press, 1992).

24 RAPQ 1938–9, 'Inventaire de la correspondence de Monseigneur Joseph
    Signäy, Archevêque de Québec 1837–1840,' Signäy to Bonenfant, 4 June
    1839; the assistant director of the Séminaire is told that there are now so

many applicants for holy orders that none is to be accepted who does not
have a perfect command of English.

25 St Germain to Lartigue, 11 November 1834, quoted in Richard Chabot, *Le curé de campagne et la contestation locale au Québec de 1791 aux troubles de 1837–1838* (Montreal: Hurtubise HMH Ltée, 1975), 189–91. Gilles Chaussé, *Jean-Jacques Lartigue, premier évêque de Montréal* (Montreal: Fides, 1980). T. Matheson, 'La Mennais et l'éducation au Bas-Canada,' *Revue d'histoire de l'Amérique française* 13 (1960): 476–91. RAPQ 1943–4, 'Correspondence de Mgr. Jean-Jacques Lartigue de 1833 à 1836,' Lartigue to Prince, 30 August 1834. For Prince's report on his college in response to Gosford's circular, see LAC RG4 A1 485, 9 July 1836. Signäy's co-adjutor Pierre-Flavien Turgeon had to expurgate phrases from the clergy's proposed petition to the Crown for reform in late 1837, since they made it seem that all the clergy supported the *patriotes*; RAPQ 1938–9, 'Inventaire de la Correspondence de Monseigneur Joseph Signäy, Archevêque de Québec 1837–1840,' Turgeon to Lartigue, 18 November 1837. In 1838, Prince refused to read aloud Colborne's circular giving prayers of thanksgiving for the defeat of the Rebellion and at the annual examination that year had the students recite an incendiary passage on Napoleon. RAPQ 1945–6, Lartigue to Prince, 5 June 1838.

26 Roger Bullen, 'Party Politics and Foreign Policy: Whigs, Tories and Iberian Affairs, 1830–6,' *Historical Research* 51 (1978): 37–59. Philip E. Mosely, 'Intervention and Nonintervention in Spain, 1838–39,' *The Journal of Modern History* 13 (1941): 195–217. Maurice R. O'Connell, 'O'Connell and the Spanish Civil War, 1834–39,' in *O'Connell: Education, Church and State. Proceedings of the Second Annual Daniel O'Connell Workshop*, ed. Maurice R. O'Connell (Dublin: Irish Pub. Ad., 1992), 35–9. Stanley G. Payne, 'Spanish Conservatism 1834–1923,' *Journal of Contemporary History* 13 (1978): 765–89. Nancy A. Rosenblatt, 'The Spanish "Moderados" and the Church, 1834–1835,' *Catholic Historical Review* 57 (1971): 401–20. Nicholas Tromans, 'J.F. Lewis's Carlist War Subjects,' *The Burlington Magazine* 139 (1997), 760–5.

27 RAPQ 1944–5, 'Correspondance de Mgr Lartigue 1836-1837,' Lartigue to Turgeon, 28 March 1836; to Signäy, 1 May 1836.

28 Québec, Archidiocèse, *Mandements, Lettres Pastorales et Circulaires des Evêques de Québec* (Quebec: Imprimerie Générale A. Coté et Cie., 1888), 3: 341–2; RAPQ 1944–5, 'Correspondance de Mgr Lartigue 1836–1837,' Lartigue to Turgeon, 13 April 1836. There seems to have been some disagreement about how to proceed or how much to spend, given Lartigue to Signäy, 14 July 1836, 'Je m'en tirerai comme je l'entendrai pour l'application des revenus de fabrique aux écoles.'

29 *Montreal Gazette*, 20 February 1836; see also the *Montreal Herald Abstract*, 12 August 1835.

30 Material for the three last paragraphs is taken from LAC RG4 A1 459, Burrage to Walcott, 8 September 1835; 462, Skakel to Gosford, 24 October 1835; 464, Burrage to Walcott, 12 November 1835; 466, Cochran(e) to Commissioners, 24 December 1835 [also included as Appendix no. 10 in the commissioners' first report, CO42/267, 30 January 1836]; 468, Skakel to Burrage, 30 January 1836 (with medical certificate); 477, Burrage to Walcott, 26 April 1836; 480, same to same, 24 May 1836; 487, Burrage to Gosford, 11 August 1836, with a large amount of enclosed correspondence [there is an odd filing problem here, compare 477 with 488, which looks like the same material again?].

31 LAC RG4 B30 12, unsigned 'Return of the Number of Schools &c. under the Superintendence of the Board of Royal Institution for the advancement of Learning, Established by Act 41 Geo 3rd Cap 17,' 23 February 1836; PRONI D/2259/1/2B, Gosford to Glenelg, 22 March 1836; LAC CO42/269, November 1836, Final Commission Report, and 'Appendix to General Report. Education.'

32 Steven Watt, 'Authoritarianism, Constitutionalism and the Special Council of Lower Canada, 1838–1840' (MA thesis, McGill University, 1997).

33 The colonial banks did quite well out of the fiscal crisis and out of the Rebellion. They were permitted by the Special Council to continue their suspension of specie payments after these had resumed in the United States. When the Council and the banks arranged for the importation of coin and Council began to pay the arrears of government expenses in 1838, the banks handled and discounted the payments. The manipulation of exchange rates enabled them to profit handsomely from the influx of British silver that came with the arrival of large numbers of troops in 1838 and 1839. PRONI D/2259/1/2E, Gosford to Glenelg, 21 December 1836. The crisis can be traced through the press; for the failure of the Banque d'Henry, *Le Canadien*, 11 December 1837; generally, Fernand Ouellet, *Economic and Social History of Quebec, 1760–1850* (Ottawa: Carleton University Press, 1980).

34 Georges Aubin and Nicole Martin-Verenka, eds., *Insurrection: Examens volontaires*, vol. 1: *1837–1838* (n.p.: Lux Éditeur, 2004), 170–1, 195–6. Also, Georges Aubin and Nicole Martin-Verenka, eds., *Insurrection: Examens volontaires*, vol. 2: *1838–1839* (Montreal: Lux Éditeur, 2007). *Le Canadien* 21 June 1839 (translating the *Mercury*).

35 Michel De Lorimier, 'Marchesseault, Siméon,' in *Dictionary of Canadian Biography* (Toronto: University of Toronto Press, 1985), 615–17. The

speech was reported in *L'Echo du Pays*, 27 March 1836 [my thanks to J.-P. Proulx for this reference]. For Nicholas, see Aubin and Martin-Verenka, *Insurrection*, 1: 170, 215; 2: 108–9; Laporte, *Patriotes et Loyaux*, 217. LAC RG4 A1 425, Nicholas to Craig, 14 February 1834; 426, Nicholas to 'Dominique Dealy,' 8 March 1834. For his scaffold speech, *Le Canadien*, 18 February 1839.

36 Aubin and Martin-Verenka, *Insurrection*, 1: 68; 2: 43, 260–1. LAC RG4 B30 16, n.d. 1833.

37 Ibid., 1: 44–5; 2: 78–9, 90–1, 162–6, 237–9, 431–2; the cannon Callaghan fired was made of wood with iron bands holding it together – a ridiculous, desperate, or simply unrealistic device with which to face British arms.

38 The two volumes of Aubin and Martin-Verenka, *Insurrection*, show that those interrogated were asked if they could read and write; the vast majority could not. The executive was told repeatedly it was bearing the fruit of an educational failure. For instance, LAC RG4 A1 301, 'Major Denny's Evidence as to Montreal District' [misfiled and misdated in the collection], 1 November 1839: 'of 200 Prisoners only 3 could write – few read.'

39 Aubin and Martin-Verenka, *Insurrections*, 2: 195–6, 228–9, 306.

40 Greer, *Patriots and the People*, 258–93.

41 Arthur Buller, 'Bribery and Intimidation at Elections,' *London and Westminster Review* 3 (1836): 485–513. P. Allen, *The Cambridge Apostles* (Cambridge: Cambridge University Press, 1978). Bruce Curtis, 'The "Most Splendid Pageant Ever Seen": Grandeur, the Domestic, and Condescension in Lord Durham's Political Theatre,' *Canadian Historical Review* 89 (2008): 55–88. Patricia Godsell, ed., *The Diary of Jane Ellice* (n.p.: Oberon Press, 1975). Haury, *Origins of the Liberal Party*. It is difficult to agree with Jacques Monet, *The Last Cannon Shot: A Study of French-Canadian Nationalism 1837–1850* (Toronto: University of Toronto Press., 1969), 53, in describing him as Charles Buller's 'brilliant younger brother'; there is little evidence in the record of brilliance.

42 Abrams, *Origins of British Sociology*; 'Buller, Charles,' *Dictionary of National Biography* 3: 246–8; S.E. Finer, *The Life and Times of Sir Edwin Chadwick* (New York: Barnes and Noble, [1952] 1970). V.L. Hilts, '*Aliis exterendum*, or, the Origins of the Statistical Society of London,' *Isis* (1978): 21–43; Anon., 'Statistical Information Department of Government,' *Westminster Review* 20 (1834): 87–100.

43 Glasgow University Archives, Matriculation Register; McGill University Rare Books Library [MURB], Protestant Education in the Province of Quebec, MSS BD214; University of London Archives, *Register of Students, Sessions 1828–1829*. Heather Lysons, 'Christopher Dunkin's Contribution to

Education in Lower Canada, 1838–1841' (MA thesis, University of Toronto, 1972). I think Elinor Senior is clearly mistaken in associating the *Courier* with the Montreal Constitutional Association, as what follows suggests; Senior, *Redcoats and Patriotes*, 12–14. André Beaulieu and Jean Hamelin, *La presse Québécoise: Des origines à nos jours*, vol. 1: *1764–1859* (Quebec: Les Presses de l'Université Laval, 1973), have no entry for the *Courier* and mention neither Dunkin, Barber, nor Derbishire.

44 *Morning Courier*, 10 and 27 November, 4 December 1837.

45 *Morning Courier*, 11 December 1837, 29 January 1838. Like some of the other papers in the colony even in this period of political crisis, the *Courier* was not all serious analysis and stern admonition. Dunkin marvelled at the novelty of the arrival of the first gaslights in Montreal. He was sufficiently well-connected to English sources to reprint Charles Dickens's hilarious send-up of the London Statistical Society, 'Full Report of the First Meeting of the Mudfog Association for the Advancement of Everything,' and he also serialized Dickens's *Pickwick Papers*.

46 LAC RG4 A1 548, handwritten letter of introduction, 1 September 1838; see also Buller to Noel Bouchard in St-Paschal-de-Kamouraska, 3 August 1838, with marginal notation, suggesting Buller would be travelling to that parish. 7 September 1838, 'List of Townships in Lower Canada and of one or two respectable resident inhabitants in each Township.' They only managed about seventy names, nine with French surnames, including the only two women named. In R.L. Rusher to Dunkin, 8 September 1838, the names and stations of eighteen Wesleyan Methodist missionaries are given.

47 LAC RG4 B30 109, Meilleur to Buller (with enclosures), 24 July 1838; same to same, 28 July 1838; Buller to Meilleur, 1 August 1838.

48 LAC RG4 B30 108 (French version), 114 (English version) cover letter with questionnaires, dated 13 September 1838. RG1 E15A, warrant number 442, 31 October 1838; Dunkin drew the same amount in warrant number 443.

49 LAC RG4 A1 192, Mills to Monk, 8 February 1820; 197, printed circular in French addressed to curés, 27 January 1821; 198, 'Form of a Circular Letter addressed to the leading Inhabitants of the Townships,' 1 April 1821; 408, Grosse Isle questionnaire, 1 May 1833; 448, Penitentiary Commission Report, 22 January 1835; 468, Special Council questionnaire blanks, 19 January 1836; also 494, Mignault to Civil Secretary with answers to the imperial government's circular on colleges, 20 October 1836.
J.I. Little, '"The fostering care of Government": Lord Dalhousie's 1821 Survey of the Eastern Townships,' *Histoire sociale/ Social History* 43 (2010), 193–212.

50 Steve Woolgar, 'Configuring the User: The Case of Usability Trials,' in *A Sociology of Monsters: Essays on Power, Technology and Domination*, ed. John Law (London: Routledge, 1991), 58–99.

51 *Kingston Chronicle and Gazette* (reprinting the *Montreal Gazette*), 23 July 1838; *Le Canadien*, 13 July 1838; *L'Ami du peuple*, 27 August 1838.

52 RAPQ, 1945–6, 'Correspondance de Mgr Lartigue 1838–1840,' Lartigue to Signäy, 23 July; to Turgeon, 6 and 13 August 1838.

53 Archives de l'Archevêché de Québec, AAQ, 60 CN, Gouvernement du Canada Vol. A:131, 13 August 1838, also in RAPQ, 1938–9.

54 AAQ, 60 CN, Gouvernement du Canada, vol. A: 141, T. Cooke, 21 August 1838; 156, A. Gosselin, 24 August 1838; 167, J.-E. Cecil, 25 August 1838; 173, L.-O. Desilets, 26 August 1838. Desilets is to be taken with a grain of salt, since he whined repeatedly at being stuck in les Grondines where the tithe was small; he was soon reassigned to a more lucrative parish.

55 AAQ, 60 CN, Gouvernement du Canada, vol. A: 193, Bissonault, 29 August 1838; RAPQ 1944-5, 'Correspondance de Mgr Lartigue 1838-1840,' Lartigue to McReavy, 1 September 1838; AAQ, 60 CN, Gouvernement du Canada, vol. A: 231, Murray to Lartigue, 18 August 1838: 'There has not been any arrangement formally agreed on between our Bishops and the Government (as your Ldsp seems to suppose) but the Government gives partial aid to all Schools conducted according to the accompanying Regulations, and the Majority of our Bishops encourage the establishment of such Schools.' This question preoccupied the Canadian bishops, and they repeatedly sought more information about Ireland.

56 AAQ, 60CN, Gouvernement du Canada, vol. A: 225, Buller to Signäy 23 October 1838 [dated by the archivist]; 228, Buller to Signäy, 'Projet d'éducation soumis à l'Évêque le 29 Octobre 1838 par Mr Arthur Buller,' 29 October 1838.

57 RAPQ 1945–6, 'Correspondance de Mgr Lartigue 1838–1840,' Lartigue to Buller, 6 October 1838; to Bourget, 20 October 1838 (no need to answer questionnaires); 1938–9, 'Inventaire de la Correspondence de Monseigneur Joseph Signäy, Archevêque de Québec 1837–1840,' Signäy to Buller, 30 October 1838. For an English translation of the last, with commentary, Bruce Curtis, 'Irish Schools for Canada: Arthur Buller to the Bishop of Quebec,' *Historical Studies in Education/ Revue d'histoire de l'éducation* 13 (2001): 49–58. The blooper in the text of this piece (grrr!) is the editor's work, not mine. For Viger, Musée de la Civilisation, Dépôt du Seminaire de Québec, Fonds Verreau, P32/59/111, Buller to Viger, 13 September 1838; the reply is n.d. P/32/022/052. The bishops' petition is in RAPQ 1938–9, 28 October 1838. In LAC RG4 A1 548, Gagnon to Buller, 27 October, the

curé tells Buller he answered his bishop's questionnaire and that is all he will do.

58 LAC RG4 B30 110, Lartigue to Futvoye, 7 January 1839.

59 McGill University Rare Books Library [MURBL] MSS BD214, Protestant Education in the Province of Quebec, folder c.1/19, 30 October 1838.

60 *Le Canadien,* 14 and 16 November 1838.

61 LAC RG4 B30 112, Commission return, St-Foy, 14 November 1838; 109, Commission return, Kamouraska, 31 May 1839.

62 LAC RG4 B30 108, Commission return, Ste-Marie-de-Monnoir, 9 November 1838.

63 LAC RG4 B30 111, Commission returns, La Petite Nation, 4 July 1839; 109, Cap St Ignace, 20 November 1838; 111, St Jean d'Orléans, 7 November 1838.

64 LAC RG4 B30 113, Commission returns, Hunterstown Twp., 24 October 1838; 110, Township of Halifax, 27 October 1838;111, St François d'Orléans, 19 December 1838.

65 LAC RG4 B30 108, Commission return Brandon Twp., 23 November 1838; 111, Clarendon Twp., 21 November 1838.

66 LAC RG4 B30 113, Commission return, l'Isle aux Coudres, 28 October 1838.

67 LAC RG4 B30 108, Commission return, St-Stanlislas, 12 November 1838.

68 LAC RG4 B30 111, Dionne et al to Buller, 20 October 1838; Commission return, St-Pierre-les-Becquets, 28 November 1838.

69 LAC RG4 B30 111, Commission return, Gentilly, 11 January 1839.

70 J.I. Little, *Borderland Religion: The Emergence of an English-Canadian Identity, 1792–1852* (Toronto: University of Toronto Press, 2004), 300n39, identifies a Bourn as a Methodist Episcopal clergyman who might be the same person.

71 Bundled together in LAC RG4 B30 109, Bourne to Buller, school petition, 24 October, 1838; same to same, 2 and 16 November 1838; Bourne to Futvoye, 7 and 28 December 1838, 3 January 1839; Griffith to Buller, 22 December 1838, 11 January 1839; Commission return, Township of Rawdon, 10 January 1839. Also, Commission return, Township of Kilkenny: Bourne did the returns for the township, where John Lawler, trained by the Kildare Place Society, had taught for two years for £30 and board and washing. That school was closed. We saw Griffith earlier trying to arrange with a notary for minutes of trustee elections for the whole township at a reduced rate.

72 LAC RG4 A1 548, 'Return of Answers to the Circulars of Enquiry addressed by the Edn Comn in L.C. in 1838; so far as the same had been

received in Quebec, up to May 16/39. Received from Mr Futvoye, May 23/39 Christr Dunkin.'

73 LAC RG4 B30 13, n.d. comments on a fragmentary table for Ottawa, Two Mountains, Terrebonne, Lachenaie, and L'Assomption. A marginal note reads 'Recd June 28 forwarded by L'pool July 6 C.D.' There was a return later from la Petite Nation, 111, 4 July 1839.

74 Curtis, '"The Most Splendid Pageant."'

75 LAC RG4 B30 112, Commission return, parish d'Écureueils, 10 December 1838; 113, Commission return, Rivière-du-Loup, 19 December 1838; 108, Commission return, St-Vallier-de-Bellechasse, 31 December 1838; 113 Commission return, Malbaie parish, 4 December 1838; 108, summary return for Beauce, 12 November 1838.

76 LAC RG4 B30 Commission returns, 108, Frampton twp., 29 November 1838; 109, Rawdon twp., 10 January 1839; 111, Gentilly, 11 January 1839; 110, Leeds twp., 13 November 1838; 110, Ste-Croix, 1 December 1838; 113, St-Léon, 30 November 1838; 110, St-Jean-Deschaillons, 1 December 1838; 113, Pointe-du-Lac, 24 November 1838; 109, Kingsey twp., 15 January 1839; St-Thomas-de-l'Islet, 12 January 1839; 111, Bécancour, 26 January 1839; 109, Pointe de Levis, 9 February 1839; 112, Pointe aux Trembles, 28 October 1838.

77 LAC RG4 B30 114, Commission return, Dudswell township, 10 February 1839; Commission return, Shipton twp., 11 December 1838. The last cited is in too fragile a condition to open all of its parts.

78 See Allan Greer, 'The Pattern of Literacy in Quebec, 1745–1899,' *Histoire sociale/ Social History* 11 (1978): 295–335, for an early attempt to estimate literacy rates from the questionnaires.

79 These materials are scattered through the LAC RG4 B30 collection; e.g. 112, n.d. and a large table recounting existing statistics from the Assembly reports 13, n.d. 1839; another 13, 12 November 1838, population by district. There is a large, incomplete chart in RG4 A1 548, 23 May 1839.

80 MURBL MSS BD214, Protestant Education in the Province of Quebec, c.1/4. 'Memorandum on Grants for Education ca 1838.'

8. Governing through Education

1 The best account of the Special Council is Steven Watt, 'Authoritarianism, Constitutionalism and the Special Council of Lower Canada, 1838–1840' (MA thesis, McGill University, 1997). Accounts of the volunteers' violence are in Allan Greer, *The Patriots and the People: The Rebellion of 1837 in Lower Canada* (Toronto: University of Toronto Press, 1993). Elinor Senior, *Redcoats*

and Patriotes: The Rebellions in Lower Canada, 1837–38 (Ottawa: Canada's
Wings, 1985). Brian Young, 'The Volunteer Militia in Lower Canada,
1837–50,' in *Power Place and Identity: Historical Studies of Social and Legal
Regulation in Quebec*, ed. Tamara Myers, Kate Boyer, Mary Anne Poutanen,
and Steven Watt (Montreal: Montreal History Group 1998), 37–54.

2 LAC MG24 A27 37, Derbishire to Durham, 24 May 1838.

3 LAC MG24 B1 9, Fisher to Neilson, 8 October 1838.

4 Actually at this moment Edward Ellice Jr had been replaced by Frederick
Villieres, since Ellice wouldn't do the necessary work, as Durham's private
secretary. Ellice's father, Durham's uncle by marriage, had sent his son
along with Durham mainly so he could look after the Beauharnois seigneury, which Ellice senior wished to sell. Edward Gibbon Wakefield would
be the purchaser. LAC MG24 A27 [Durham papers], 27, Buller to Durham,
12 November 1838; Patricia Godsell, ed., *The Diary of Jane Ellice* (n.p.:
Oberon Press, 1975), entries for 10–12 November 1838, 'the water was
lighted up by the reflection of the villages, burning in all directions.' The
original is at LAC R2823-0-1-E Edward Ellice and Family Papers. That claim
was not simply the victor gloating, for the *patriote* radical Robert Nelson also
commented to William Lyon Mackenzie that 'the whole unlettered part of
Lower Canada is courageous, determined to lose no opportunity to upset
British authority, while the Catholic-College-educated part ... are ...
disposed to accept of any arrangement for their return that will not expose
their cowardly skins.' Nelson quoted in Senior, *Redcoats and Rebels*, 149. See
also PRONI [Public Record Office of Northern Ireland] D2259/8/56,
Wetherall to Gosford, 21 December 1837: 'This unnatural rebellion has I
trust been put down. The poor Canadians have more [excessive?] courage,
than any people, excepting the natives of India, I ever saw – at St Eustache,
they held the Church & adjoining houses most obstinately.'

5 LAC MG24 A27 27[?], Glenelg to Colborne, 24 November 1838.

6 LAC MG24 B1 9, T. Bouthillier [sometimes he signs Boutillier] to John
Neilson, 20 December 1838.

7 *Le Canadien*, 29 August and 10 October 1838 for L.-M. Viger; 26 December
1838 and successive issues until March 1839; for Futvoye, 11 January
1839; for the Montreal Grand Jury, 26 July 1839; for the quotation,
15 March 1839.

8 On Huot especially, Musée de la Civilisation, Dépôt du Seminaire de
Québec, Fonds Verreau, P32/60/44.3, Huot to Viger, 22 April 1838.

9 *Le Canadien*, 17 August 1838, 'Déjà le parti Constitutionnel modéré se
trouve représenté par M. Dunkin, et le parti ultra-tory va l'être par
M.Thom ... '; 10 October 1838 for the disenchantment with Durham.

10 Petitions against his rent increases are LAC RG4 A1 402, Executive Council Reports, 4 February 1833. Durham's diary shows at least weekly dinners with Ellice late in 1837 and early in 1838. Other members of his mission were sometimes present; see MG24 A27 41, for instance, 13 February 1838, where Ellice, Easthope, Stanley, and Charles Buller dined with Durham.

11 PRONI D2259/8/18, Ellice, Paris, to Gosford, [7 or 11?] April 1836; /21, same to same 15 May 1836; Musée de la Civilisation, Fonds du Seminaire de Québec, Polygraphie 3, no. 71, Ellice to Howick, 24 July 1836 [a copy not in Ellice's hand and not signed, but seems to be him].

12 Musée de la Civilisation, Fonds du Seminaire de Québec, Polygraphie 31, no. 31, Lafontaine to Ellice, 15 March, 17 April 1838. In the last: 'You shall never succeed in establishing an aristocracy where none could exist, and let your government do what it may, it cannot prevent the influence of the institutions of our neighbours to react on ours.'

13 Musée de la Civilisation, Fonds du Seminaire de Québec, Polygraphie 3. n.71, Ellice to Howick, 24 July 1836; notice that Howick was also Durham's brother-in-law.

14 LAC MG24 A27 37, Derbishire to Durham, 24 May 1838.

15 Durham to Glenelg, 9 August 1838, in W.P.M. Kennedy, ed., *Documents of the Canadian Constitution, 1759–1915* (Toronto: Oxford University Press, 1918), 455–66, where it is followed by Durham to Glenelg, 16 and 20 October 1838, pointing to the organization of the Hunters' Lodges and the preparations for a second rising. Also, ibid., 'Address of the Constitutional Association of the City of Montreal to the Inhabitants of the Sister Colonies,' 13 December 1837. On Lower Canadians' preference for despotism, LAC MG24 A27 46, Durham to Melbourne, 30 June 1838.

16 LAC MG24 A27 28, n.d. 'Notes on advantages of Legislative over Federal Union of N.A. Provinces' (in pencil) 'By Mr. Charles Buller.'

17 Archives de l'Archevêché de Québec [AAQ], AA, 60CN, Govt. du Canada, vol. A:228, 'Projet d'éducation soumis à l'Evêque le 29 Octobre 1838 par Mr Arthur Buller,' 29 October 1838.

18 AAQ, AA, 60CN, Govt. du Canada, vol. A: 229, Buller to Cazeau, 29 October 1838; RAPQ, 1938–9, 'Inventaire de la Correspondence de Monseigneur Joseph Signäy, Archêveque de Québec 1837–1840,' Signäy to Buller, 30 October, 5 November 1838.

19 Quotations in this section are taken from Arthur Buller, 'Report of the Education Commission,' in *Lord Durham's Report on the Affairs of British North America*, ed. Sir C.P. Lucas (Oxford Clarendon Press, 1912 [1839]), vol. 3. The report apparently was not published until the later edition of Durham's *Report* in 1839. It was probably written in New York, where the Durham

suite lingered for much of November. The somewhat prissy Jane Ellice, who thought Arthur was twice as handsome but not half as nice as his brother Charles, was irritated by the former's flippant irreligion. As she told her diary on 25 November, 'Charles Bullar & brother arrived – Asked the latter in the morng if he was going to Church – "Alas! I've no hat." Met him in the afternoon wth a hat – "Well are you going to church now[?"] – "Alas! my boots pinch me!" Godsell, *Diary*.

20 See Bettina Bradbury, 'Debating Dower: Patriarchy, Capitalism and Widows' Rights in Lower Canada,' in *Power, Place and Identity: Historical Studies of Social and Legal Regulation in Quebec*, ed. Tamara Meyers and et al. (Montreal: Montreal History Group, 1998), 55–78. The *patriotes* had already removed women's rights to vote.

21 The work is an example of Bernard Cohn's 'historiographic modality'; see *Colonialism and Its Forms of Knowledge: The British in India* (Princeton: Princeton University Press, 1996), 1–17. Dunkin's memorandum did such work for education; his 'British American Politics,' *The North American Review* 39 (1839): 373–431, did the same work on colonial policy as a whole.

22 There are two surviving versions of this memorandum or report: LAC RG4 B30 15, 10 June 1839, with a cover letter headed 'Hartford, Connecticut,' is 349 pages long. The second is the autograph version, A1 586, same date and 242 pages long. The material cited above is in Dunkin's chapter one, and further citations in this chapter are from the first version, unless otherwise noted.

23 LAC RG4 A1 586, 170; the remaining quotations in this section and the next are from B30 15.

24 He did not cite his sources but apparently extrapolated the rate of increase between 1825 and 1831 forwards, taking immigration statistics from reports of the Emigrant Office.

25 Durham to Glenelg, 9 August 1838, in Kennedy, *Documents*. Not that Meilleur supported anglicization, but rather did not tie French-Canadian cultural survival to linguistic solitude nor to the seigneurial system. His medical degree was from Vermont and he was fluently bilingual.

26 Meilleur was probably 'Le Médiateur,' in *La Minerve*, 9 March 1829; 'Un Compatriot de L'Assomption,' in *La Minerve*, 10 August 1829; 'C.D.' in *Le Canadien*, 14 May 1834; there are thanks to Papineau, a call for an investigation into the riot, and a critique of the 1832 School Act, in *La Minerve*, 16 July, 8 November 1832; for descriptions of the College course and support for Lancaster, *La Minerve*, 3 and 26 October 1833; the correspondence committee is *La Minerve*, 27 March 1834; his defence of the 1835 vote, *Le Canadien*, 1 April 1835; book notices in *L'Echo du pays*, 11 June

1835; against the model school tax, *Le Canadien*, 24 February 1836; on the classical course, *Le Canadien*, 6 September 1837; the comment on the churchwardens quoted in Richard Chabot, *Le curé de campagne et la contestation locale au Québec de 1791 aux troubles de 1837–1838.* (Montreal: Hurtubise HMH, 1975), 71. There is a good deal of information about Meilleur's controversial work as census commissioner in LAC RG4 A1, beginning with 349, Meilleur and Roy to Glegg, 21 January 1831. For Lartigue, RAPQ 1943–4, 'Correspondence de Mgr. Jean-Jacques Lartigue de 1833 à 1836,' Lartigue to Meilleur et al., 4 August 1834. É-É Rodier worried about Meilleur siding with the moderates in 1835; as he put it, 'Je crains aussi que Meilleur ne les suive, mais je le suis de près, et il me redoute.' RAPQ, 1926–7, Papiers Duvernay, no. 231, 'Le citoyen Rodier' to Duvernay, 28 February 1835.

27 All quotations in this and the following section are taken from *Le Canadien*'s reprint of the version in *Le Populaire*, in successive numbers beginning 22 August and ending 12 September 1838.

28 LAC MG24 B1 9, Gouldie to Neilson, 6 July 1839.

29 LAC RG4 B30 14, Armour to Goldie, cover letter with first report, 1 October 1839. The fifteen autograph school reports are in this file, and all citations and quotations in the sections which follow are taken from them. The reports are: 1. Chambly. 2. Verchères. 3. Richelieu. 4. Laprairie. 5. L'Acadie, part 1 (there is no part 2 in the file). 6. Rouville, part 1 (there is no part 2 in the file). 7. Beauharnois. 8. Vaudreuil. 9. Deux Montagnes. 10. Terrebonne. 11. Lachesnaye. 12. L'Assomption. 13. Berthier. 14. Ottawa. 15. Sherbrooke. The last might seem to be an outlier, since the county did report to Buller, but Armour was advertising.

30 Cohn, *Colonialism*, Introduction.

31 LAC RG7 G1, vol. 43, Russell to Thomson, 7 September 1839.

32 Bruce Curtis, *True Government by Choice Men? Inspection, Education and State Formation in Canada West* (Toronto: University of Toronto Press, 1992), chapter 1.

33 LAC RG4 A1 603, Dunkin to Murdoch, 4 January 1840.

34 Two concepts themselves the creation of Jeremy Bentham; see Bruce Curtis, 'From the Moral Thermometer to Money: Metrological Reform in Pre-Confederation Canada,' *Social Studies in Science* 28 (1998): 547–70.

35 C.F.J. Whebell, 'The Upper Canada District Councils Act of 1841 and British Colonial Policy,' *The Journal of Imperial and Commonwealth History* 17 (1989): 185–209.

36 LAC MG24 A27 29, Buller to Lady Durham, 2 January 1841; RAPQ 1945–6, 'Correspondance de Mgr Lartigue 1838–1840,' petition against the Union bill, 25 February 1840; ANQ R2 3 A 019 01-07-003A-01, Gosford to Davidson,

12 December 1839: 'an attempt to disenfranchise will lay the seed for much future commotion & strife. it is lamentable to reflect on the ignorance that prevails here as to the real state of Canada.' PRONI D/2259/8/81, printed petition against the Union in both languages, with /82, cover letter probably in Lafontaine's hand in support; /80 Gosford's draft speech against the Union bill.

37 RAPQ 1945–6, 'Correspondance de Mgr. Ignace Bourget Coadjuteur de Montréal Du 19 mai 1837 au 25 avril 1840,' Bourget to Signäy, 21 February 1840; *Le Canadien*, 22 November 1839, *Montreal Herald*, 7 September 1840. Ollivier Hubert, 'Petites écoles et collèges sulpiciens,' in *Les Sulpiciens de Montréal: Une histoire de pouvoir et de discrétion. 1657–2007*, ed. Dominique Deslandres, John A. Dickinson, and Ollivier Hubert (Montreal: Éditions Fides, 2007), 395–444. More generally, Marcel Lajeunesse, 'L'Évêque Bourget et l'instruction publique au Bas-Canada, 1840–1846,' *Revue d'histoire de l'Amérique française* 23 (1969): 35–52.

38 AAQ 1 CB Vicaires Généraux XI:12, Cooke to Signäy, 2 April 1840.

39 AAQ 1 CB Vicaires Généraux XI:12, Cooke to Signäy, 3 April 1840.

40 RAPQ 1945–6, 'Correspondance de Mgr. Ignace Bourget Coadjuteur de Montréal Du 19 mai 1837 au 25 avril 1840,' Bourget to Signäy, n.d. [circa 5 April 1840 in the series]; AAQ 90 CM Angleterre, vol. 4 37, 16 January 1841 [my thanks to Jacques Chevalier and colleague for help with the Church Latin]. See also Lucia Ferretti, *Brève histoire de l'Église catholique au Québec* (Montreal: Boréal, 1999), 56–60; René Hardy, *Contrôle social et Mutation de la culture religieuse au Québec, 1830–1930* (Montreal: Boréal, 1999). I find Ferretti's treatment of the Buller plan, which she describes as 'whimsical,' and of the 'guerre des éteignoirs,' 77–80, which she suggests allowed local residents to get some government funding for the schools, to be odd.

41 For political factions, Jacques Monet, *The Last Cannon Shot: A Study of French-Canadian Nationalism 1837–1850* (Toronto: University of Toronto Press., 1969). Robert Rumilly, *Papineau et son temps*, vol. 2: *1838–1871* (Montreal: Fides, 1977).

42 The Act of Union was 3&4 Vic., c.35 and the property qualification, sec. XXVIII. *Le Canadien* supported assimilation of the 'races' but understood that to mean the abolition of the seigneurial system and the introduction of representative institutions, e.g., 4 November 1839. For the paper's support of a literacy qualification, 20 November 1839. *Montreal Herald*, 25 May and 28 August 1840.

43 For more detail, Bruce Curtis, *Building the Educational State: Canada West, 1836–1871* (London, ON, and Sussex, England: Althouse Press and Falmer Press, 1988), chapter 1.

44 *Montreal Herald,* 17 March, 24 August 1840.

45 *Montreal Herald,* 12 November 1840.

46 All quotations in the preceding section are from Charles Mondelet, *Letters on Elementary and Practical Education. To which is added a French translation.* (Montreal: John James Williams, 1841). For a more detailed examination of the homologous relations between the government of state and school, Philip Corrigan, Bruce Curtis, and Bob Lanning, 'The Political Space of Schooling,' in *The Political Economy of Canadian Education,* ed. T. Wotherspoon (Toronto: Methuen, 1987), 21–43.

47 All quotations in this section are from *Debates of the Legislative Assembly of the Province of Canada,* the so-called 'newspaper Hansard' edited by Elizabeth Nish. Why Day spoke of the district schools – which were grammar, not common schools – is unclear. Perhaps it was because the former had been a central issue in the struggle against elite control of schooling in the 1820s and 1830s.

48 He had fallen from his horse on his way from the legislature to his house in the suburbs and broken his leg, which became infected and killed him, at least sparing him life in Kingston, described by Charles Dickens soon thereafter as one of the dirtiest, muddiest, and most tedious places on the continent.

49 Ferretti, *Bref histoire;* Lucien Lemieux, *L'établissement de la première province ecclésiastique au Canada, 1783–1844.* (Montreal: Fides, 1967), 457ff. *Les mélanges religieux,* 23 July 1841, e.g., 'Partout où le clergé catholique instruit et dirige, il y a loyauté, moralité, progrès, paix, et bonheur,' quoted in Monet, *Last Cannon Shot,* 87.

50 AAQ, 26 CP Diocèse de Montréal H: 117, Hudon to Cazeau, 12 August 1841. He said the petition was enclosed, but it no longer is. A summary is in RAPQ 1946–7, 'Correspondance de Mgr. Ignace Bourget 1840–1841,' n.d., but placed in the series at 11 August 1841.

51 Musée de la Civilisation, Dépôt du Seminaire de Québec, Fonds Verreau, P32/42/16, Crémazie to Black, 12 August 1841.

52 AAQ, 26 CP Diocèse de Montréal H: 118, Hudon to Cazeau, 13 August 1841; 1 CB Vicaires Généraux XI: 55, Cooke to Turgeon, 20 August 1841; LAC MG24 B1 10, Turgeon to Neilson, 17 August 1841; RAPQ 1946–7, 'Correspondance de Mgr. Ignace Bourget 1840-1841,' Hopkirk to Gaulin, 29 September 1841.

53 The Common School Act of 1841, 4 & 5 Vic. Cap. XVIII. See also Roderick MacLeod and Mary Anne Poutanen, *A Meeting of the People: School Boards and Protestant Communities in Quebec, 1801–1998* (Montreal and Kingston: McGill-Queen's University Press, 2004), 55ff.

Conclusion

1 C.F.J. Whebell, 'The Upper Canada District Councils Act of 1841 and
   British Colonial Policy,' *The Journal of Imperial and Commonwealth History* 17,
   no. 2 (1989): 185–209.

2 Lower Canada, 1835–51,' *History of Education Quarterly* 37 (1997): 25–43;
   Wendie Nelson, '"Rage against the Dying of the Light": Interpreting the
   Guerre des Éteignoirs,' *Canadian Historical Review* 81 (2000): 551–81.

3 See Jean-Pierre Charland, *L'entreprise éducative au Québec, 1840–1900*
   (Quebec: Les Presses de l'Université Laval, 2000). Andrée Dufour, *Tous à
   l'école: État, communautés rurales et scolarisation au Québec de 1826 à 1859*
   (Ville La Salle: Éditions Hurtubise HMH, 1996).

4 Simply by way of example, Georges Aubin, ed., *Wolfred Nelson: Écrits d'un
   patriote* (Montreal: Comeau et Nadeau, Éditeurs, 1998). Georges Aubin and
   Nicole Martin-Verenka, eds., *Insurrection. Examens volontaires*, vol. 1: *1837–
   1838* (n.p.: Lux Éditeur, 2004), and vol. 2: *1838–1839* (Montreal: Lux
   Éditeur, 2007). Philippe Bernard, *Amury Girod: Un Suisse chez les Patriotes du
   Bas-Canada* (Sillery: Septentrion, 2001). Gilles Laporte, *Patriotes et Loyaux:
   Leadership régional et mobilisation politique en 1837 et 1838* (Quebec: Les
   Éditions du Septentrion, 2004). Julien S. Mackay, *Notaires et patriotes,
   1837–1838* (Sillery: Septentrion, 2006). Julie Papineau, *Une femme patriote:
   Correspondance, 1823–1862* (Quebec: Septentrion, 1997).

5 Marcel Bellevance, 'La rébellion de 1837 et les modèles théoriques de
   l'émergence de la nation et du nationalisme,' *Revue d'histoire de l'Amérique
   française* 53 (2000): 367–400. Jocelyn Létourneau, 'Pour un autre récit de
   l'aventure historique québécoise,' in *Les idées en mouvement: perspectives en
   histoire intellectuelle et culturelle du Canada*, ed. Damien-Claude Bélanger,
   Sophie Coupal, and Michel Ducharme (Quebec: Les presses de l'Université
   Laval 2004), 53–75. More generally, Barbara A Misztal, 'The Sacralization
   of Memory,' *European Journal of Social Theory* 7 (2004): 67–84.

6 Yvan Lamonde and Claude Larin, eds., *Louis-Joseph Papineau: Un demi-siècle
   de combats. Interventions publiques* (Montreal: Fides, 1998), 188–94 for the
   speech 'Santé à l'éducation' of 5 May 1831. The full transcription is in *La
   Minerve*, 9 May 1831. See also the speech at 'l'Assemblée des comtés de
   L'Assomption et de Lachenaie' of 29 July 1837, reproduced at pp. 456–70.
   Yvan Lamonde, 'Conscience coloniale et conscience internationale dans les
   écrits publics de Louis-Joseph Papineau (1815–1839),' *Revue d'histoire de
   l'Amérique française* 51 (1997): 3-37.

7 Steven Watt, 'Authoritarianism, Constitutionalism and the Special Council
   of Lower Canada, 1838–1840' (MA thesis, McGill University, 1997). Brian

Young, 'Positive Law, Positive State: Class Realignment and the
Transformation of Lower Canada, 1815–1866,' in *Colonial Leviathhan: State
Formation in Mid-Nineteenth-Century Canada*, ed. Allan Greer and Ian
Radforth (Toronto: University of Toronto Press, 1992), 50–63.

8 For instance, Philip Abrams, *The Origins of British Sociology: 1834–1914*
(Chicago: University of Chicago Press, 1968). J.H. Burns, 'J.S. Mill and the
Term "Social Science,"' *Journal of the History of Ideas* 20 (1959): 431–2.
Sanford Elwitt and Lawrence Goldman, 'Debate: Social Science, Social
Reform and Sociology,' *Past and Present* 121 (1988): 209–19. Lawrence
Goldman, 'The Social Science Association and the Absence of Sociology in
Nineteenth Century Britain,' *Past and Present* 114 (1987): 154–61.

9 Yvan Lamonde, *Histoire sociale des idées au Québec* (Montreal: Fides, 2000),
1: 457–8; Jean-Charles Falardeau, 'Antécédents, débuts et croissance de
la sociologie au Québec,' *Recherches sociographiques* 15 (1974): 135–65.
Marlene Shore, *The Science of Social Redemption* (Toronto: University of
Toronto Press, 1988). J.-P. Warren, *L'engagement sociologique: la tradition
sociologique du Québec francophone* (Montreal: Boréal, 2003); Warren,
'Sciences sociales et religions chrétiennes au Canada (1890–1960),' *Revue
d'histoire de l'Amérique française* 54 (2004): 407–24.

10 Taché figures centrally in Bruce Curtis, *The Politics of Population: Statistics,
State Formation, and the Census of Canada, 1840–1875* (Toronto: University of
Toronto Press, 2001). For Dunkin, his 'British American Politics,' *The North
American Review* 39 (1839): 373–431.

11 The literature seeks to present Durham as either a key liberal theorist or a
man of no intellectual significance. The sociology of national character gets
short shrift. See Janet Ajzenstat, *The Political Thought of Lord Durham*
(Montreal and Kingston: McGill-Queen's University Press, 1988). Ged
Martin, *The Durham Report and British Policy* (Cambridge: Cambridge
University Press, 1972); Martin, 'Le Rapport Durham et les origines du
gouvernement responsable au Canada,' *Bulletin d'histoire politique* 6 (1998):
33–51; Martin, *Past Futures: The Impossible Necessity of History* (Toronto:
University of Toronto Press, 2004). But no one does the gritty work to
detail what was done by whom, how, on the basis of what evidence, through
what techniques, etc., in relation to land reform, municipal reform, and
so on.

12 This sort of argument is already well-developed, down to the level of the
effects of different occupations on different forms of character, by the
1760s. For instance, Adam Ferguson, *An Essay on the History of Civil Society*
(New Brunswick, NJ: Transaction Books, 1980 [1767]). Adam Smith, *The
Theory of Moral Sentiments* (Indianapolis: Liberty Classics, 1982 [1759–90]).

13 L. Cooper, *Radical Jack: The Life of John George Lambton, 1st Earl of Durham, Viscount Lambton, and Baron Durham* (London: Cresset Press, 1959). Stewart Derbishire, 'Stewart Derbishire's Report to Lord Durham on Lower Canada, 1838,' ed. Norah Story, *Canadian Historical Review* 18 (1937): 48–62. Mark Francis, *Governors and Settlers: Images of Authority in the British Colonies, 1820–1860* (London: Macmillan, 1992). Patricia Godsell, ed., *Letters and Diaries of Lady Durham* (n.p.: Oberon Press, 1979). Harriet Martineau, *Society in America*, 3 vols. (New York: AMS Press Inc., 1966 [1837]). Chester New, *Lord Durham: A Biography of John George Lambton First Earl of Durham* (Oxford: Clarendon Press, 1929). Stuart J. Read, *Life and Letters of the First Earl of Durham, 1792–1840*, 2 vols. (London: Longmans Green, 1906). William Thomas, *The Philosophic Radicals: Nine Studies in Theory and Practice, 1817–41* (Oxford, 1979). R.K. Webb, *Harriet Martineau: A Radical Victorian* (New York: Columbia University Press, 1960).

14 *Morning Courier*, 16 December 1836.

15 *Morning Courier*, 13 January 1838, reproducing *Le Populaire*.

16 As Michel Ducharme, *Le concept de liberté au Canada à l'époque des révolutions atlantiques: 1776–1838* (Montreal and Kingston: McGill-Queen's University Press, 2010), 231–3, points out. See also, Jean-Marie Fecteau, '"This Ultimate Resource": Martial Law and State Repression in Lower Canada, 1837–8,' in *Canadian State Trials*, ed. Murray Greenwood and Barry Wright (Toronto: University of Toronto Press, 2002), 207–41.

17 Edward Gibbon Wakefield, *England and America Compared* (New York: Harper and Brothers, 1833), has a list of members for the National Colonization Society as of 1832. Durham is not yet present, but Mill and Buller are, and there is a least one of Durham's relatives.

18 Goderich to Aylmer, 21 November 1831, in Robert Christie, *A History of the Late Province of Lower Canada* (Montreal: Richard Worthington, 1866), 3: 374–80n.

19 Ibid., vol. 5. Albert Faucher, 'La condition nord-américaine des provinces britanniques et l'impérialisme économique du régime Durham-Sydenham, 1839–1841,' *Recherches sociographiques* 8 (1967): 177–209. R.N. Gosh, 'Malthus on Emigration and Colonization: Letters to Wilmot-Horton,' *Economica* (February 1963): 45–62. David A. Haury, *The Origins of the Liberal Party and Liberal Imperialism: The Career of Charles Buller, 1806–1848* (New York: Garland Publishing, 1987). William Ormsby, ed., *Crisis in the Canadas: 1838–1839: The Grey Journals and Letters* (London: Macmillan, 1964). Thomas, *The Philosophic Radicals*. Michael J. Turner, 'Radical Agitation and the Canada Question in British Politics, 1837–41,' *Historical Research* 79 (2006): 90–114.

20 Such matters are central to recent stands in social history and historical sociology; see Michael J. Braddick, 'Introduction: The Politics of Gesture,' *Past and Present* Supplement 4 (2009): 9–35. L.A. Aylmer, 'Recollections of Canada, 1831,' in *Rapport de l'archiviste de la Province de Québec pour 1934–1935* (Quebec: Imprimeur de Sa Majesté le Roi, 1935 [1831]). Aubin, ed., *Wolfred Nelson.* Papineau, *Une femme patriote.*

21 Henri Masson, *Joseph Masson: Dernier seigneur de Terrebonne* (Montreal: by the author, 1972). On Dessaulles, *La Minerve,* 30 June 1835.

22 Patricia Cline Cohen, *A Calculating People: The Spread of Numeracy in Early America* (Chicago: University of Chicago Press, 1982).

Appendices

1 George Parker's entry, 'Armour, Robert,' in *Dictionary of Canadian Biography* (Toronto: University of Toronto Press, 1985), 21–3, on Robert Sr has a couple of paragraphs on Robert Jr. For the preceding in addition to Parker, *La Minerve,* 29 December 1828; 25 June 1829; 20 and 30 May 1833. In the last, Armour informs the Board of Sanitation that the Trinity Board won't pay for privies on the docks for the use of immigrants. LAC RG4 A1 276, 9 January 1829; 306, n.d. 1831; 348, n.d. [January?] 1831. The Natural History Society became a public venue for Tory propaganda, as revealed by its 1836 prize essay competition, 'On the Connection between the Language and the Character of a People,' meant to show the debilitating moral influence of speaking the French language.

2 *La Minerve,* 8 April 1830; *Canadian Courant,* 1 June 1831; LAC RG4 A1 373, Armour to Craig, 30 January 1832, and 402, same to same, 8 February 1833, both on producing a digest of the statutes; on the Trinity Board, 380, Turner to Craig, 21 April and 11 May 1832; 393, Turner to Craig, 13 October 1832; as clerk, MG24 B1 17, Armour to Neilson, 6 May 1833.

3 *La Minerve,* 18 July 1827; 10 March 1831; 20 February 1832; *Montreal Gazette,* 18 August 1835.

4 *La Minerve,* 5, 12, 16, and 23 April, 24 December 1832; 11 March 1833; 28 October 1834; *Montreal Vindicator,* 25 December 1832; all on the West Ward election. *La Minerve,* 18 April 1833, for spying. Joseph Lancaster, *Report of the singular results of Joseph Lancaster's new discoveries in Education made at Montreal, from the commencement in 1829 to complete developement of systematic principle in 1833* (Montreal: np CIHM #89895, 1833), for Lancaster's account of his vote. Musée de la Civilisation, Dépôt du Seminaire de Québec, Fonds Verreau, o-147, Viger to his wife, 19 February 1834.

5   LAC RG4 A1 16 December 1835, 'British Rifle Corps,' membership list,
    with O'Sullivan to Walcott; 467, Walcott to O'Sullivan, 9 January 1836;
    476, Armour to Walcott, 16 April 1836; *Morning Courier*, 12, 13, and
    14 December 1836; *Sherbrooke Gazette and Township Advertiser*,
    23 September 1837; *Morning Courier*, 17, 18, and 21 October 1837.
6   LAC RG4 B30 114, Commission returns, Ascot township, Sherbrooke
    county, 8 December 1838.
7   Katharine Greenfield, 'Randal, Stephen,' in *Dictionary of Canadian Biography*
    (Toronto: University of Toronto Press, 1988), 7: 733–4.
8   LAC MG24 A27 26, n.d. 1838.
9   LAC RG4 601, n.d. February 1840. The draft ordinance contains a number
    of repetitions and several inconsistencies. The original has been amended
    in several places in a hand other than Dunkin's. The ordinance also
    embodies Dunkin's calculations about schooling and population.
10 As I write, supporters of non-denominational public education and
    proponents of sectarian education in Ontario endure the ridiculous
    situation of full public funding for Catholic denominational schools, which
    impose religious and moral tests on teachers in clear violation of civil rights,
    with the approval of all political parties. A 'separatist' government in
    Quebec, by contrast, appealed to the federal government in 1997 to amend
    the Canadian Constitution to end its guarantee of the existence of de-
    nominational school boards in that province. Vagaries of history, indeed!

Index